UNDERSTANDING AMERICAN SPORTS

Since the nineteenth century the USA has served as an international model for business, lifestyle and sporting success. Yet whilst the language of sport seems to be universal, American sports culture remains highly distinctive. Why is this so? How should we understand American sport? What can we learn about America by analyzing its sports culture?

Understanding American Sports offers discussion and critical analysis of the everyday sporting and leisure activities of "ordinary" Americans as well as the "big three" (football, baseball, basketball), and sports heroes. Throughout the book, the development of American sport is linked to political, social, gender and economic issues, as well as the orientations and cultures of the multilayered American society with its manifold regional, ethnic, social, and gendered diversities.

Topics covered include:

- American College Sports
- The influence of immigrant populations
- The unique status of American football
- The emergence of women's sport in the USA

With co-authors from either side of the Atlantic, *Understanding American Sports* uses both the outsider's perspective and that of the insider to explain American sports culture. With its extensive use of examples and illustrations, this is an engrossing and informative resource for all students of sports studies and American culture.

Gerald R. Gems is Professor of Health and Physical Education, North Central College, Naperville, Illinois, USA. He is past president of the North American Society for Sport History.

Gertrud Pfister is Professor of Sport and Social Sciences at the Institute for Exercise and Sport Sciences, University of Copenhagen, Denmark. She was president of the International Society for the History of Physical Education and Sport (1984–2000) and President of the International Sport Sociology Association (2004–2008).

UNDERSTANDING AMERICAN SPORTS

GERALD R. GEMS AND GERTRUD PFISTER

Routledge
Taylor & Francis Group

LONDON AND NEW YORK

First published 2009
by Routledge
2 Park Square, Milton Park, Abingdon, Oxon, OX14 4RN

Simultaneously published in the USA and Canada
by Routledge
270 Madison Avenue, New York, NY 10016

Routledge is an imprint of the Taylor & Francis Group, an informa business

Typeset in Zapf Humanist and Eras by
Keystroke, Tettenhall, Wolverhampton
Printed and bound in Great Britain by
TJ International Ltd, Padstow, Cornwall

British Library Cataloguing in Publication Data
A catalogue record for this book is available from the British Library

Library of Congress Cataloging in Publication Data
Gems, Gerald R.
    Understanding American sports / Gerald R. Gems and Gertrud Pfister.
        p. cm.
    1. Sports—Social aspects—United States. I. Pfister, Gertrud, 1945– II. Title.
    GV706.5.G45 2009
    306.4'83—dc22   2008047461

ISBN10: 0–415–44364–4 (hbk)
ISBN10: 0–415–44365–2 (pbk)
ISBN10: 0–203–88617–8 (ebk)

ISBN13: 978–0–415–44364–7 (hbk)
ISBN13: 978–0–415–44365–4 (pbk)
ISBN13: 978–0–203–88617–5 (ebk)

CONTENTS

ILLUSTRATIONS

FIGURES

IX

illustrations

illustrations

INTRODUCTION

OR – WHY DO WE NEED A BOOK LIKE THIS AND WHAT IS IT ALL ABOUT?

If you can answer all of the following questions, you do not have to read this book.

- What is interscholastic sport?
- Why do colleges and universities offer athletic scholarships?
- Why do some coaches at American universities earn more money than the president?
- What are owners and salary caps?
- Why are football competitions accompanied by pep rallies, cheerleaders, and tailgaiting?
- What is Title IX – and was it an advantage for women?
- Who administers and provides "sport for all"?
- Why is the obesity rate increasing in the United States?
- Is race still an issue in American sport?
- Why do Americans spend billions of dollars and numerous nights and weekends on sport consumption?
- Why are Americans so fascinated with statistical performances in sport?
- What is a home run and what is a touchdown?

AIMS

Sport is a global player in Westernization, and often specifically Americanization processes which are driven by, among other things, unlimited flows of information and communication, media without frontiers, global heroes and stars, transnational audiences and fans, and sporting mega-events like the Olympic Games.

The principles of modern sport and its orientation towards international competition and world records have led to a worldwide unification of rules, techniques, strategies, and practices. Closely linked to sport, business, sponsors, and media transmissions operate throughout the world. The language of sport seems to be universal, and the attraction of sports, teams, and athletes is no longer restricted by borders. Sport seems to be a universal phenomenon shared by the global community. Yet, there is resistance to the flow of global sport, and numerous and various culturally specific types of sport and movement cultures flourish. Each culture has developed specific sport practices and meanings, and sport is an excellent example of "glocalization," the integration of local agents in the discourses of sport and the embedding of ideologies and practices in local communities and cultures. Despite its common rules, sport does not have the same meaning everywhere; on the contrary, we can only understand sport in its cultural context and we can only gain a comprehensive insight into cultures and societies if we take bodies and embodiment, physical cultures and leisure activities, sport and sport consumption into consideration.

Since the nineteenth century, America has played a central but ambivalent role in the ideologies and politics of other countries. America was the "promised land" with seemingly unlimited opportunities, where immigrants have sought material sustenance, freedom and/or democracy. The USA has served as a model for business, lifestyle, and sporting success. But the United States has also been regarded as a country that exemplifies a quest for unlimited profit and materialism; a place without high standards of culture. America is a world power with aggressive politics and a sense of manifest destiny, admired and feared, loved and hated. Admiration or repudiation – America was always, and still remains today, a center of interest and attention in the world. This is also true of American sport.

However, in spite of the worldwide interest in America and American sport, there is still little knowledge about the distinctive American sport culture outside the USA. Few non-American authors are experts on American sport, and for sport students in Europe, South America or the Far East understanding American sport is a challenge. There are some European studies available on sport and physical activities in the USA, such as the comparison between American and "European" sports like soccer and baseball (Szymanski and Zimbalist 2005) or about soccer in the USA (Markovits and Hellermann 2004b). Other studies concentrate on the role of physical activities in immigrant cultures in the US (Hofmann 2001). Details of American sport history may be found in Christensen *et al.* (2001) and Levinson and Christensen (2005). Nevertheless, there remains a gap in the literature for a broader, general guide to understanding American sport.

Within the USA the majority of publications about sport focus on the "big three sports": football, baseball, and basketball, and on famous athletes. Higher level studies aimed at students and researchers take a basic understanding of US sport culture for granted. However, we must also ask whether within such a unique and "self-contained" sporting culture there may be a need for further objective insight – from outside the USA – to gain a truly in-depth understanding of American sport in the context of world sport.

This book is written from European and American perspectives, and will discuss and critically analyze not only the national sports, elite sport performances and the well-known heroes but also the everyday sporting and leisure activities of "ordinary" Americans.

CONTENTS

Arising in particular historical situations (sport) cultures[1] are dependent on the prevailing social conditions and develop in conformity with political, social and economic influences. Of particular significance here are the origins and the initial phases of developments.

Following Bourdieu's concept of the social field (see p. 9), developments in sport have always taken place in a specific field which determines the position of a sport in society. Here, the time of the establishment of a sport is important because "latecomers" have difficulty displacing already popular activities. In the USA, the "hegemonic sport culture" was shaped in the nineteenth and the first part of the twentieth century. This might explain why soccer, the world's most popular sport, has been unable to dislodge football, baseball, and basketball in the USA. Although our focus is thus on this period, we will also cover developments before and after.

We give a general introduction to American history and the evolution of American sport as a background for all chapters. In addition, we address the various groups of immigrants which had an impact on American culture and became ingredients in the American "melting-pot." American sport cannot be understood without insight into the emergence, development, and meanings of baseball and football. While Chapter 4 on the relevance of baseball also provides an insight into the evolution of professional sport, the history of American football (Chapter 2) explains the interrelations between sport and schools. In both chapters, white men are the focus of attention. Women's sport has a specific history in the USA. It has always differed decisively from men's sport, and also from women's sport developments in other countries. Thus, a separate chapter (Chapter 11) is devoted to women's long struggle for equality in sport. A distinctive feature of the USA is the segregation and, later, the integration of the different ethnicities and races. As illustrated in this book, sport has played an important role in the integration and acceptance of African-Americans. In addition, the wide diversity and complexity of activities, organizations, discourses, and practices from elite sport to fitness programs will be described and analyzed. The second part of the book contains information about the sports participation of Americans (numbers, age, gender, race, social class) and their lifestyles, as well as the structures and organizations of professional sport, school sport as well as "sport for all" in communities and commercial institutions. Today, American sport is closely intertwined with the media and markets. The media and their influence, audiences and their activities and tastes, and sport markets are important issues for understanding American sports. Information about media and markets, and their role in the lives of Americans, are presented in Chapters 13 and 14. But the best way to gain insight into the significance of sport in the USA is the analysis of sporting heroes (Chapter 12). Heroes represent and embody the values, (self-) image, and dreams of the American population. The whole book, especially the chapter on sporting heroes, reveals the close interrelations between American sport and American culture.

DEFINITIONS

Games and dances, physical activities, performances and "movement cultures" have always existed and continue to exist in all societies. On closer scrutiny we detect that the multi-faceted world of sports and games has different culture-specific patterns. On the one hand the body and physical activities are governed by the laws of physiology; on the other they are also subjected to the prevailing social norms. The forms and aims of physical activities as well as the motives, feelings, and associations connected with them depend on the social context. Quite different forms of movement, for example, may have the same object (the worship of gods, say) while the same movements may be associated with different objectives or intentions. Running, for instance, may be aimed at imitating the cosmic cycle or at breaking the 100m record. Consequently, the analysis and interpretation of physical activities must always pay heed to their context, with emphasis upon the fact that physical culture "embodies" (i.e. adopts, presents, and reinforces) the values and norms of a society.

In the early modern era many traditional sports and games were played all over Europe which were more often than not connected with religious festivals and which, being restricted to certain social groups and/or certain regions, did not aim at being universally propagated. Among sport historians there is general consensus that "modern sport" developed in England (Guttmann 1978; Mangan 1981; Mason 1982). Modern sport is characterized by the (theoretical) equality of opportunity, orientation towards performance and competition, and the principle of setting and breaking records, which is connected with an "abstract" form of performance. In this context "abstract" means that the performance relates neither to the achievement itself, nor to the athlete nor to an opponent; it is merely expressed in an abstract figure. In this way, performances in running, for example, can be compared with each other even though they take place at different times and in different places, without the runners ever having met each other. Activities which cannot be measured quantitatively, like gymnastics or figure skating, are evaluated, and these evaluations are transferred into quantitative figures with the help of a *code de pointage*. Games are organized in a complex and hierarchical system of tournaments and leagues which make it possible to identify the best teams of a city, a region, a nation, or worldwide.

A further characteristic of modern sport is that the movements and actions in a given sport are not determined by an objective but by rules. Soccer, for example, is not defined by getting a ball into the goal but by the rule that only kicking the ball is allowed. Sport is therefore a ritual based on social arrangements which adapt to the prevailing conditions. In the course of the nineteenth century numerous physical activities were "sportified." The concept of "sportification," meaning the transformation of a physical activity into a modern sport, has often been interpreted as rationalization and "civilization" following Elias' deliberations on the civilization process (Elias 1971). As Guttmann (1994), among others, has emphasized, the principle of competition and the pursuit of records had numerous consequences, including rationalization, the quantification of performance, standardization of apparatus and facilities, bureaucratization, specialization, and professionalization.

Sport has always been a contested term and its meaning has changed in the course of time. In colonial America, sport meant amusement. Therefore, cockfights could be termed sport, and later in the taverns of the "Wild West" female prostitutes could be called "soiled doves," "painted ladies" or "sporting women." And large numbers, perhaps even the majority, of "sportsmen" in the sports bars of the nineteenth century engaged in drinking, gambling, and watching sports without getting involved in any physical activity. Even today many sports fans would identify themselves as active sports participants.

Most people would agree that sport has to do with physical skills and movement, and that sedentary activities are not sport. But a closer look reveals that this distinction is blurred, not least because especially games like chess and poker claim to be sports. It seems normal and natural to define football, rowing, sailing, ski jumping, or running the 100m as sports; however, defining something as normal also means concealing the social arrangements. All sports are social constructions which have developed in a certain situation and change continually following new demands from participants, audiences, and the media. Sport aims at physical performance, but the range of physical activities involved and the "nature" of performance is open to discussion. Here, one must also consider that amazing achievements do not necessarily have to be quantifiable and measurable.

The American definition of sport emphasizes performance, competition, and record orientation. This notion of sports fits nicely in the above-mentioned framework developed by Allen Guttmann (1978). In Europe, sport has a much broader meaning, including the concept of "sport for all," which was developed in the 1960s. In the USA, "sport for all" is not a common term; it can be translated into recreational physical activities.

In this book, we have chosen a broad approach to sport. We focus on sports (in the narrow sense), but we also include recreational physical activities, not least because the large majority of the physically active population engages in "sport for all." In addition, we include information about sport consumption, i.e. the broad range of activities in which sport is used as a service or product. A special focus in this context will be on sport audiences. Sport consumption is a very important part of American culture; however, it should not be confused with active sports participation.

THEORETICAL APPROACHES

It is a common saying that sociology without history is empty and that history without sociology is blind. However, many (sport-)historical studies are rather descriptive, and the authors seem to be content with reconstructing historical developments inductively by interpretations of various sources. On the other hand, there are numerous sociological analyses whose approaches and findings are not rooted in the past and thus lack explanatory value.

Our book has an interdisciplinary approach: it combines sport history and social sciences and provides insight into the emergence of the most important physical activities and sports as well as into current sporting structures and practices. This allows us to show how historical developments have influenced or, better, shaped American sport. History helps to explain the way sport is played, perceived, understood, structured, organized, and sold in the USA. Explanations require theoretical approaches which provide questions and hypotheses, as well as guidelines for analysis and a framework for interpretation.

The topics covered in this book are diverse and include a broad range of issues from race to gender, from physical education to the mass media. Therefore, we propose various theoretical concepts and perspectives.

As a whole the book is based on the ideas of Cultural Studies, developed since the 1950s in England. Cultural Studies combine various disciplines from political economy to media studies, sociology and history. They focus on gender, race and class issues, and deal with ethnicities, nationalities and ideologies. Culture is seen as the "whole way of life". (Symbolic) interaction, discourses, power, representation and contextualization are key terms in this approach (Andrew and Sedgwick 2005).

We explore the historical development of sport using Elias' ideas about the civilization process. We interpret sport and sporting heroes as important parts of the collective memory, the political myths, and the popular history of the USA. We have based our approaches to gender, race, and ethnicity on constructivist concepts as proposed by Judith Lorber or R. Connell, and we interpret sport as a field and playing sport as a means of social distinction in Pierre Bourdieu's sense of the terms.

PLACES OF MEMORY AND NATIONAL IDENTITY

Since the publication of Pierre Nora's monumental seven-volume *Les Lieux de Mémoire*, research into "remembered places" is being carried out throughout the world with growing enthusiasm.[2] In the USA, a young nation and a nation of immigrants, collective memories, and the construction of American identity was, and still is, of central importance.

The study of cultures of "remembering" makes use of various research approaches and strategies. It starts out from a hypothesis attributed to the French sociologist Maurice Halbwachs that, namely, "historical interpretations and patterns of perception result from a dual interplay of, firstly, personal reminiscences and the common 'collective' memory and, secondly, the perception of the past and the expectation of the future" (Francois and Schulze 2001; see also Assmann and Harth 1991; Francois 1996). In communicative processes cultures reconstruct their pasts and incorporate those events into their collective memory, which they require for their current circumstances. From this point of view, remembering means the "ongoing production of sense in connection with a currently perceived necessity to act" (Reichel 1996, 107). The reminiscences of individuals and collective memory are the result of – and are also partly produced consciously and intentionally by – stories, histories and myths, rituals and symbols, monuments and memorial celebrations as well as the evocation of outstanding personalities and important events. However, collective reminiscences are by no means confined to products of "high culture" but are also anchored in everyday culture, in the trivial as well as in the sublime. Baseball, for example, plays an equally important role in the American cultural memory as Theodore Roosevelt; and, as far as their effect of creating identity is concerned, Oprah Winfrey may be of just as much significance as the Capitol, burgers, or Marilyn Monroe.

For Pierre Nora all the immaterial and material "anchorages for the memory" are places, entries in the collective memory, which he imagines as a spatial arrangement, i.e. a storage room or a museum, in keeping with the Greco-Roman tradition of rhetorical mnemonics (Assmann 1996, 19).

Whereas history studies used to treat the formation of nations formerly from a political and social perspective, a central focus of today's research is on the question of how national awareness is culturally molded. If nations are cultural constructs, it follows that national identity, too, is nothing that one acquires "by nature," but something that has to be permanently produced and staged. For this purpose, societies develop a "cultural memory" which furthers group formation and ties because "it enables the emotional bonding of personal recollections with the memories of the other individual members of the community" (Francois and Schulze 1999, 1). A sense of nationhood is based on a diffuse mixture of "cognitive and emotional as well as collective and individual elements" (Francois et al. 1995, 15). This form of internalized affinity through common memories, notions, and visions is expressed by the term "imagined community", coined by Anderson (1987). Nations, too, are "imagined communities," and the collective memories are of major significance in their origin and development.

The creation of a feeling of belonging – even among people who have never met and will never interact concretely with each other – is a subject discussed not only in Nora's reflections on remembered places but also in various other theoretical concepts, for instance, in the British historian Hobsbawm's approach of the "invention of tradition" (cf. Hobsbawm 1938). Further, the notion of the "invention of ethnicity" was derived from this approach and applied to the construction of ethnic identity (Sollors 1989).

Various groups of a society, among them historians, are involved in the invention of tradi-tions and constructions of memory. They produce, whether consciously or subconsciously, "remembered places" by writing myths, stories, and histories which are bound to the interpretations of their own national projects and which endow historical events with a meaning that is teleologically oriented towards the contemporary situation. National myths are by no means mere propaganda, i.e. a conscious manipulation "from above"; they involve a great number of social groups, including the recipients, who select, interpret, evaluate, and, perhaps, internalize these messages. In order to be effective, certain rules apply: national myths must be personified in individuals and/or events in order to trigger identification processes; further, they must contain contemporary references and positive messages, and they must be associated with emotionally appealing values. In the USA, public history, meaning the public productions of knowledge about the past, is booming.[3] According to Michael Gordon (http://www.uwm.edu/Course/448-700/syllbus.html), "public history involves the presentation of the past for public citizens . . . in ways that are especially important in shaping collective memory."

As many chapters of this book will show, sporting events and athletes play an outstanding role in the construction of American identity and public history. Memorials and halls of fame, baseball statistics and football books celebrate the past, ascertain common values, and legitimize America's claim of superiority.

POLITICAL MYTHS

American sport was accompanied by, and is still embedded in, various myths, among others the myths of the frontier and the manifest destiny of the Americans. Myths are a particular form of collective memory composed of narratives offering a selective and condensed account of events from the distant past. They appeal to the emotions, confer legitimacy on social organizations and structures, rationalize ideologies and norms, and lend meaning to a community's quest for self-reassurance. In modern societies myths are anchored in collective and individual memory as "fragmentary references, indirect allusions, watchwords, slogans, visual symbols, echoes in literature, film, songs, public ceremonies, and other forms of everyday situations, often highly condensed and emotionally charged" (Flood 1996, 84). Such fragments are frequently found as elements of political ideologies, whose messages are expressed by symbols such as a country's flag, and are experienced through rituals and symbolic actions such as singing the national anthem.

> Political myths, as fixed and stereotypical images of the past, place emphasis on things in the collective memory which a particular society or culture deems vital for its existence. They are ultimately an explanation and interpretation of historical events and a declaration of the fundamental values, ideas and behavior of a group.[4]

Like places of memory generally, political myths are of great significance for the present since they make developments appear "natural," thus legitimizing and stabilizing the prevailing conditions. They strengthen the power of those who have control over the choice and interpretation of "things remembered." Myths of origin allude to persons, events, and/or places who or which play a key role in the development of a community. They often combine with myths of persons, which focus on someone whose historical achievements are augmented, embellished, and construed as being superhuman. This is especially true of American sports events and sporting heroes.

SPORT AND THE PROCESS OF CIVILIZATION – NORBERT ELIAS

In several contributions Elias has applied the fundamental ideas of his civilization theory to sport (Elias 1971; cf. also Elias and Dunning 1986). In an article on the "genesis of sport" the point of departure is a comparison between modern sport and Greek agonistics, which is presented as an example of physical culture typical of pre-industrial societies. Using many examples, the author shows that the same forms of movement may be linked to different intentions and meanings. In this way, for example, the brutal boxing contests of antiquity, which not infrequently ended in death, are compared with today's boxing matches governed by rules.

Elias attributes the differences in the norms and standards of physical culture to the different stages reached in the civilization process, which is marked by a growing trend towards interdependence, monopolization and control of power as well as internalization of pressures. The author notes that "state formation and conscience formation, the level of socially permitted physical violence and the threshold of repugnance against using or witnessing it, will differ in specific ways at different stages in the development of societies" (1971, 95). The body and physical strength also play different roles in different historical eras, the civilization process being accompanied by a "civilizing" not only of minds, but also of bodies. Elias emphasizes the interrelations between power, behavior, emotions and knowledge and bridges thus the macro–micro divide, the divide between structure and agency, individual and society.

According to Elias, sport – as a regulated and rationalized form of physical confrontation – is a practice of physical culture typical of industrial nation-states with industrial production, state-controlled power, and a high degree of internalized discipline. In these societies sport is "one of the great social inventions" which helps to reduce tensions and channel aggressions. The development of sport in the USA may be described as "sportification" and a civilization process in the sense given to it by Norbert Elias.

SPORT AS CULTURAL CAPITAL – PIERRE BOURDIEU

Like Elias, Bourdieu (1986) links the macro with the micro perspective and connects social structures and individual behavior. In contrast to traditional theories of class, Bourdieu stresses that social stratification is determined by both vertical and horizontal diffe-rentiations. Members of each social group take up a position in a hierarchically and vertically structured social field according to their social, cultural, and economic capital. They are characterized by a set of behavior patterns and self-presentations which are condensed to specific lifestyles. The positions of the various class factions are not totally fixed; instead there is a continuous process of social distinction, i.e. marking oneself off from the group below, and striving towards the acquisition of status symbols, tastes as well as the general "habitus" of the social strata situated higher on the vertical scale. The social reproduction of power and its legitimization takes place in the form of the struggle not only for economic resources but also for legitimacy.

For Bourdieu the hinge between the individual and society is formed by the habitus, whose development depends on social conditions and which consists of the totality of human dispositions; in determining thoughts, perceptions, and actions the habitus produces specific cultural practices in each social group. Habitus and the tastes related to it thus characterize social classes and groups. A central role in this is played by the body, which assumes an important symbolic function, expressing values which are specific to an individual, group, or class, and thus becoming the bearer of social distinction and cultural capital. It is the body habitus, i.e. the socially structured system of bodily dispositions, which determines not only individual attitudes to the body and its management but also the choice and patterns of physical activities and sporting habits (see, for example, Bourdieu 1982).

Bourdieu turns his attention to sport as a significant field of daily culture and practice, which serves to produce and present the legitimate body and the "right" taste. Sport may be considered a relatively autonomous field which has its own dynamics and is an object of struggles between the various groups in the field. On the one hand, sports participation depends on resources and the amount and form of capital; on the other hand, sporting activities can provide social and cultural capital and serve as social distinction. The distinctive value of a sport depends on its image, the costs, and also the environment. Golf in an expensive club enables the players to accumulate much more cultural capital than golf played on a public course. In addition, sport has specific meanings, attractions, and (imagined) effects on health and appearance – for instance the development of muscles – which attracts some groups and deters others.

> Part and parcel, then, of an understanding of sports participation is the conscious and unconscious orientations of different groups toward engaging in distinctive (as conceived by their social group), potentially rewarding (economically, culturally, and socially), and reinforcing (especially their positions in their local community) practices.
>
> (Washington and Karen 2001, 210)

Not only sports participants but also sports providers are in constant competition:

> The field of sporting practices is an arena of combat, in which the object is, among other things, the monopolistic domination of a legitimate sporting practice . . . And these specific struggles are further embedded in a more extensive field of struggle for the definition of the legitimate body and the legitimate use and management of the body.
>
> (Bourdieu 1988, 9)

The evolution of American sport as well as current sport practices are permeated by class struggles and distinction processes. Using Bourdieu's perspective allows us to understand, among other things, the soccer craze in rich suburbs or the fitness boom in American society.

GENDER AND RACE AS SOCIAL CONSTRUCTIONS

Using a constructivist approach to gender, we can define gender as "a process of social construction, a system of social stratification, and an institution that structures every aspect of our lives because of its embeddedness in the family, the workplace and the state as well as in sexuality, language and culture" and – we would like to add – in sport (Lorber 1994, 5). Gender always has an institutional, an individual, and an interactional perspective, which means that the gender order of a society is appropriated by individuals who develop gendered identities and present gendered images. At present there is general agreement among scholars of gender studies that gender has different dimensions and must be interpreted as a lifelong process with ambivalences and contradictions.

Connell (2002) emphasizes the role of bodies and of "social embodiment" in gendering processes. "Bodies are both objects of social practice and agents in social practice . . . The practices in which bodies are involved form social structures and personal trajectories which in turn provide the conditions of new practices in which bodies are addressed and involved" (Connell 2002, 47). Social processes always include bodily activities from childbirth to sport, and bodily activities, in turn, are connected with social norms and interpretations.

How then does the gender order become embedded in people's bodies and minds, and how do men and women continually construct and reconstruct gender as an institution? People are categorized as belonging to social groups and also to one or other of the sexes by means of outward features such as dress, hairstyle, the way they move, or their body language – and as a rule this happens unconsciously. Gender, therefore, is not something we are or have but something we produce and do. "Gender is constantly created and re-created out of human interaction, out of social life, and it is the texture and order of that social life . . . it depends on everybody constantly doing gender" (Lorber 1994, 13; 2000). Gender is a performance. Ethnicity and race can likewise be understood as social constructions, based on bodies but transformed by culture. Sport (in the broad sense of the term) is one of the few areas of our culture in which the body plays a decisive role: in enacting and exposing physical strength, endurance, power, and aggressiveness, but also grace and elegance. Sport always involves the presentation of the body and its capacities, the demonstration of physical performance, and the enactment of a person's image. Therefore, sport offers a stage where bodily differences, gender differences, and gender as a whole are re-produced and presented. Doing sport is always doing gender and doing race; it is always presenting oneself as male or female, as white or African-American. The changing roles of women, African-Americans, and various ethnic groups show, along with the "mainstreaming" of their sporting practices, that not biology but social and cultural conditions decide discourses and practices.

READING INSTRUCTIONS

The chapters of this book are self-contained, each dealing with a key issue. The different chapters provide contributions on various subjects (women's sport, the mass media, sport systems, the history of individual sports, etc.) and thus offer insights from different angles. Consequently, a number of key events and important figures are dealt with in different chapters in different contexts. We have been at pains to avoid repetition by providing references to the relevant passages in other chapters.

CHAPTER ONE

AN INTRODUCTION TO THE UNITED STATES

GEOGRAPHY AND SOCIETY

The United States of America occupies the central portion of the North American continent. It extends across four time zones from the Atlantic Ocean on the east to the Pacific Ocean on the west. It comprises forty-eight contiguous states of various sizes, as well as the large peninsula of Alaska, adjacent to northwestern Canada, and the islands of Hawaii, located in the mid-Pacific Ocean. (Alaska and Hawaii entail two additional time zones.) It covers an area of 3,718,685 square miles or 9,631,420 square kilometers (Essential World Atlas 2001, vi; http://en.wikipedia.org/wiki/United_States).

The population of the United States exceeded 300,000,000 in 2006, most of whom lived in urban metropolitan areas. The United States has nine cities with an excess of 1,000,000 inhabitants, and four of its cities (New York, Los Angeles, Chicago, and Houston) are considered global centers, cities which serve as commercial, technological, and transport hubs in the world economic system (Abu-Lughod 1999). The East Coast is the most densely populated area of the country; although there has been an increasing movement to the warmer climate of the south and west (known as the Sun Belt) over the last generation.

A nation of immigrants, the United States has a diverse racial and ethnic population. More than 74 percent of the population (215,300,000 people) identify themselves as white with German, Irish, and Anglo ancestry predominant; while 14.5 percent (41,900,000) claim Hispanic heritage; although some Hispanics identifying themselves as white. African-Americans or blacks comprise 12.1 percent of the population (34,900,000); Asian-Americans 4.3 percent (12,500,000); Native Americans 0.8 percent (2,400,000); and Native Hawaiians or Pacific Islanders make up 0.1 percent (400,000). A small percentage claim a mixed race ancestry. The largest number of immigrants in the past decade came from Mexico, China, India, and the Philippines (Wills 2005; http://en.wikipedia.org/wiki/United_States).

Owing to the particular historical evolution of the country, both race and religion remain major factors within American society which influence values, politics, and lifestyles decisively.[1] Almost 80 percent of Americans profess to being Christians. Of the many Christian denominations, Catholics claim 25.9 percent of the population, while a wide variety of

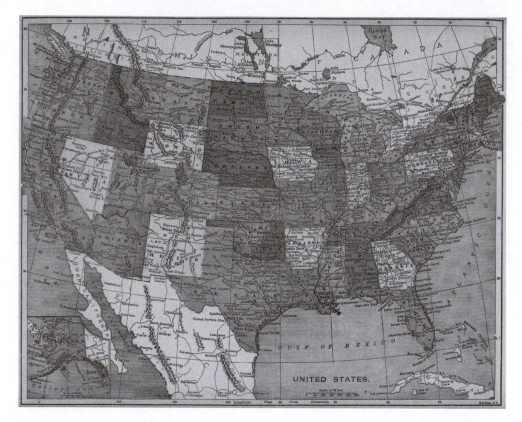

Figure 1.1 US map, 1902 (Northrope 1902, VIII)

Protestant sects account for the remainder. Among the Protestants, Baptists are most numerous with 17.2 percent, most of them living in the southern states, which are referred to as the Bible Belt. Evangelical Christian groups, though they represent only a small fraction of the population, wield an inordinate amount of political power as lobbyists and pressure groups. Jews make up 1.4 percent of the population; and Muslims, Buddhists, and Hindus each account for less than 1 percent. A growing number (15 percent) of US citizens are agnostics or atheists. As the US Constitution stipulates the separation of church and state, the non-believers have won several court cases relative to the public display of Christian symbols, such as crosses or Christmas nativity scenes on government property, and the teaching of religion in public schools. Still, they are considered to be an anomaly in the United States, which adopted the slogan "In God We Trust" as an official motto in 1956.

In the US population, females slightly outnumber males; women enjoy a life expectancy of over 80 years compared to 75 years for men. Although women have become the majority of college students and comprise the largest number of college graduates, men retain most positions of power in the government, commerce, and society.

The country has a 99 percent literacy rate, with mandatory attendance for school-aged children. Public schools offer a free education; however, 12 percent of children attend private, mostly religious schools, and another 2 percent are home-schooled by their parents, often for religious reasons. Slightly more than 27 percent of Americans have obtained a college degree, with 9.6 percent granted a graduate degree (http://en.wikipedia.org/wiki/United_States).

Economically the median income for American households is over $46,000 (over $67,000 for two-income families, which have become common since the 1960s). Twenty-five percent of Americans earn more than $77,000 annually, and 13 percent of Americans fall below the poverty line of $20,000 for a family of four. Racial and social class distinctions are evident; Hispanics earn, on the average, slightly more than $34,000; and blacks are paid an average of slightly more than $30,000. The latter two groups also have the highest unemployment rates at more than 9.4 percent for African-Americans and 14.6 percent for Hispanics.

The United States had the world's largest economy with more than $13 trillion in gross domestic production in 2006. Despite such wealth, economic inequality is more apparent in the United States than in European countries. One percent of Americans hold 33.4 percent of the nation's wealth, and 10 percent control 69.8 percent. The other 90 percent of the citizenry has declined in relative worth over the past decade (http://en.wikipedia.org/wiki/United_States).

GOVERNMENT

The federal government of the United States is comprised of three branches: the executive, the legislative, and the judicial. The executive branch is made up of the president, the vice-president, and a group of appointed administrators of various departments known as the Cabinet, who act as the presidential advisors and policy-makers. The president must be a native-born citizen of the United States, at least 35 years of age, and resident in the country for at least fourteen years. The president is elected for a term of four years and cannot hold office for more than two consecutive terms. He is the chief executive of the government and also serves as the commander in chief of the military forces. The vice-president succeeds to the presidency upon the death of a president or any other circumstance in which the president cannot fulfill his or her duties.

The legislative branch of the government is the Congress composed of two houses, the Senate and the House of Representatives. The Congress creates the laws which govern American society. The vice-president presides over the Senate, and the citizens of each state elect two senators, insuring a measure of equality regardless of the size of the state. Senators serve a six-year term in office and may be re-elected indefinitely. Election to the House of Representatives is dependent upon the population of each state. More populous states get

15

more representatives than less populated areas. Representatives are elected to two-year terms, but may be re-elected to office for an indefinite period. Either house of Congress may propose legislation; but both units must provide an affirmative vote before the proposed measures become law.

The judicial branch of the government is composed of a Supreme Court, which consists of nine judges and one Chief Justice, and a system of lower courts. Federal laws supersede the laws of the individual states. Supreme Court judges serve for the duration of their lifetime or until self-imposed retirement. They are appointed by the president and pass judgment on the legality of statutes and actions.

> The federal entity created by the Constitution is the dominant feature of the American governmental system. But the system itself is in reality a mosaic, composed of thousands of smaller units – building blocks that together make up the whole. There are 50 state governments plus the government of the District of Columbia, and further down the ladder are still smaller units that govern counties, cities, towns, and villages.
> (http://usinfo.state.gov/infousa/government/overview/ch7.html)

The United States has two major political parties, which provides limited choice for citizens. Both parties court celebrity (such as Hollywood movie stars) and corporate donors that supply the ever increasing finances necessary to run media dependent election campaigns.

The Republican Party is considered to be more conservative, favoring commerce and big businesses, as well as advocating right-wing social and moral issues (anti-abortion, private gun ownership, military expenditures). The Democratic Party is generally more liberal, supporting expenditure on social welfare programs and education.

POLITICAL ISSUES

One of the most debated issues in the US is welfare. In the US, each state has the authority to decide about its welfare politics.

> In practice, the US is pluralistic, rather than liberal. There are significant departures from the residual model – e.g. state schooling . . . In addition to federal and state activity, there are extensive private, mutualist and corporate interests in welfare provision. The resulting systems are complex (and expensive): the guiding principle is less one of consistent individualism than . . . "decentralized social altruism".
> (http://www2.rgu.ac.uk/publicpolicy/introduction/wstate.htm)

Welfare means a social commitment of the majority of the American population, as the following figures indicate:

16

About one million non-governmental, non-profit organizations are dedicated to welfare; more than 80% of all American citizens claim to be part of at least one such organization; about 60% of all American citizens do voluntary work in such organizations. The majority of Americans are against an expansion of the welfare state, but they want increasing efforts to fight poverty on a private level.

(Murswieck 1998, 42–45; http://tiss.zdv. uni-tuebingen.de/webroot/sp/spsba01_W98_1/usa1.htm)

Further issues confronting the populace are unequal educational opportunities and access to health care. Public schools are funded by real estate taxes, meaning that wealthier (often suburban) districts provide a greater budget and resources to their local schools than do small, rural, or inner city districts that accommodate poor neighborhoods. Thus poor children lack the same resources and opportunities for better schooling, higher education, and ultimately, social mobility in the American society.

Deficiencies in health care services afflict the poorer citizens, the elderly, and an increasing number of workers who lack health insurance and adequate pension plans. Infant mortality in the United States affects 6.37 of every 1,000 births, a figure higher than Western European countries. Likewise, teen pregnancies, at 79.8 per 1,000, supersede European figures. With two-thirds of Americans rated as overweight and one-third judged obese, both obesity and type 2 diabetes strain medical resources (Nye 2008; Orsega-Smith *et al*. 2008; http://en.wikipedia.org/wiki/United_ States).

In addition to educational and health concerns the unique American gun culture represents a distinct difference from European societies. The American Constitution guarantees the right to private ownership of guns and the National Rifle Association is one of the most successful lobbyist organizations in the United States, dedicated to maintaining that status. Proponents for and against guns debate whether such weapons promote or protect against criminal activities. The US murder rate of 5.6 per 100,000 inhabitants in 2005 was much higher than the rate, for example, in Germany (1/100,000). The United States also has the highest rate of imprisoned individuals among the world's developed countries (468/100,000), with an inordinate number of the prisoners being African-Americans, as the sentencing of criminals exhibits clear differences along racial lines. Blacks are often incarcerated with longer jail sentences than whites. Of the fifty states, thirty-eight enforce a death penalty for the most heinous crimes (http://en.wikipedia.org/wiki/United_States; http://www.gibbsmagazine.com/blacks_in_prisons.htm).

Despite social inequalities and the lack of a universal welfare system immigrants continue to flock to the United States in search of the American Dream. Unlike other nations of the world, which have a distinct national culture based on common traditions, American culture has been described as a "melting-pot" or a "salad bowl" in which migrants, ethnic, and racial groups retain elements of the cultures of their home countries as they integrate and finally assimilate into the American mainstream. Although a relatively young culture, the United

17

States exports its ideology and images throughout the world by virtue of its global entertainment enterprises, such as Hollywood movies, television, radio, music, and sports (Wills 2005).

AMERICAN HISTORY – AN OVERVIEW

Colonization

Prior to the European "discovery" of North America the continent was inhabited by numerous indigenous tribes of Native Americans. While many were hunters and gatherers, others practiced agriculture and lived in villages. Coastal communities proved adept at fishing. As communal societies with strong kinship ties, government took the form of tribal chieftains or a tribal confederacy among allied groups. They traded in a barter economy, practiced natural religions, and lived according to seasonal rhythms (Countryman 1996, 19–21).

Utilitarian sports, such as running and archery games that enhance hunting skills, were prominent among all tribes. Numerous ball games, especially lacrosse, were widespread throughout the continent as training for war, and a means to settle disputes with rival tribes. Gambling on such activities added interest and importance. Sports and games were often played in ceremonial contexts, and had religious meanings and significance for the social cohesion of the tribes (King 2004).

The arrival of Christopher Columbus in 1492 and the subsequent colonization of the Americas by the European powers decimated the ranks of the Native Americans and signaled a fundamental change in the indigenous cultures. The Spanish settled in the Florida peninsula in the southeast and moved northward from Mexico through south-west and coastal California, imposing the Catholic religion on subject peoples. The French took up residence in New Orleans at the mouth of the Mississippi River that drained central North America and brought the fur trade to the native tribes. French priests converted the "Indians" and lived among them in missionary outposts throughout central North America and Canada. The Dutch founded New Amsterdam (New York) before an English takeover in the seventeenth century. The British proved most influential, establishing colonies along the East Coast and the Atlantic seaboard (from the current states of Maine to Georgia).

The Jamestown colony, founded in Virginia on the mid-Atlantic coast in 1607 as a commercial enterprise, introduced the British class system to America. Many immigrants were sons of the aristocracy; they refused to work and whiled away their time, as they had done in their home country, at sport and gambling, to the peril of the starving colony. Indentured servants, immigrants contracted to work, performed much of the labor, until too many succumbed to sickness. By 1619 the British began importing slaves from Africa to replace the white indentured servants, fostering the plantation agricultural system in the

18

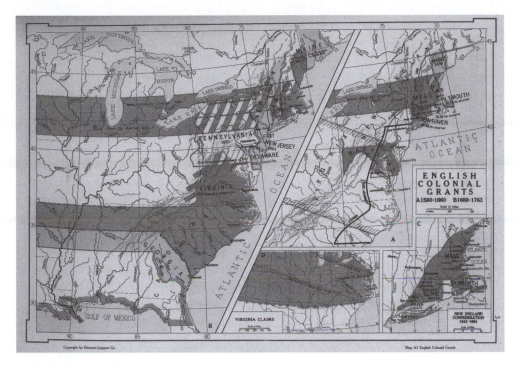

Figure 1.2 Settled areas in New England c. 1660 (Matteson and Bolton 1930, 5)

South. The Africans brought and preserved their values, beliefs and lifestyles. Thus elements of African cultures influenced and shaped modern American society. The establishment of slavery in the seventeenth century affected and continues to affect American economy, politics, and culture.

By 1630 the Puritans, reformers and separatists of the Anglican Church, founded colonies in Massachusetts in the northeastern United States known as New England. The Puritans' belief system, though diluted over subsequent generations, had a lasting impact on American culture. The Puritans saw themselves as a community of saints, God's chosen people, who were to found a "City on a Hill" to serve as a beacon for all mankind to follow. Their belief in predestination, the idea that one was destined for an afterlife in heaven or hell at birth, gave rise to materialism and wealth as a sign of favor from God. Puritans therefore valued a strong work ethic, self-discipline, and self-reliance in their quest for prosperity. Such views would later support Americans' belief in their "Manifest Destiny" to guide the world and in the "frontier thesis" through which men would develop the above-mentioned qualities during their conquest of the rough and "uncivilized" land in the west (Foner and Garraty 1991, 890–893; Countryman 1996, 13–15; McKnight 2003).

The Quakers, a faction that split from the Puritans after 1680, founded Pennsylvania, southwest of New England, as a "holy experiment" with a high measure of liberty including freedom of religion. Their strive towards reciprocal liberty, welfare and education, and their opposition to war and, eventually, slavery marked a departure from other European colonials who readily exploited, murdered, and enslaved Africans and Native Americans.

English Catholics found refuge in the tiny colony of Maryland, just north of Virginia, while British philanthropists began deporting debtors in 1733 from England to Georgia, a southern colony just north of the Spanish settlement in Florida. Their intention was to provide the destitute with a new opportunity to better their lives. That American Dream remained steadfast for millions of immigrants over the succeeding centuries (Garraty 1983, 23–24). The various groups of immigrants with their specific aims and interests, from the freedom of religion to economic endeavors, led to a variety of religious, economic, and social cultures in the different regions. Climatic conditions contributed to the different historical and cultural developments. New England soil proved too rocky for large farms; thus Boston grew into a mercantile and shipping center for trade with the motherland and its Caribbean colonies. In the South, rich soils proved amenable to agriculture and the wealthy acquired large tracts of land from the British crown that they developed into plantations by the sweat of slave labor, exporting crops such as tobacco, rice, and cotton to the homeland. As the colonists pushed ever westward, taking Native American land, a frontier society emerged, composed of the lower classes without means to acquire land in the east.

The encroachment of the British and French on Native territories to the north, south, and west and the desire to exploit the natural resources of the continent led to inevitable rivalries and conflicts between the Native Americans and the Europeans. As early as 1622 the Indians of Virginia rose up against the British settlers of the Jamestown colony. In New England attacks by white settlers upon the Indians provoked a retaliation and resulted in King Philip's War (1675–1676), which was titled after an American Indian leader named King Philip. Despite initial successes in both encounters, the Indians ultimately faced death, enslavement, and the expropriation of their lands. The Puritans assumed their victory as a providential sign of the righteousness of their cause, continuing their quest for land and conversion (Demos 1994, 7; Foner and Garraty 1991, 620).

The European concept of private property proved especially devastating to the communal societies of the indigenous tribes. Land belonged to all, particularly to the tribe, and could be used by the community. Individual landownership did not exist. Because the idea of land sales was alien to the tribes, they unknowingly sold their land for trinkets by signing treaties which they did not understand. As the indigenous peoples were drawn increasingly into the white economy and became dependent upon it, various tribes either resisted the white culture or allied with the colonists against rival tribes.

Rivalries between British and French colonists over the fur trade and Atlantic fishing rights, as well as religious differences between Catholics and Protestants resulted in the French and Indian War, the North American chapter of the Seven Years' War (1756–1763), a conflict about influence and power which involved all the major European countries and was fought mostly on European battlegrounds. In North America both the British and French laid claim to the western lands (eastern Canada and the Midwestern United States) that supplied much of the resources for the fur trade. Indian tribes aligned with one side or the other in the prolonged conflict. The eventual victory of the British enabled them to take control of both Canada and Florida (Catholic Spain allied with France in the losing cause), greatly expanding the British hegemony in North America (Brumwell 2004; Garraty 1983, 206, 619–620).

The struggle for independence and the constitution of the US

The resolution of conflicts proved brief, however, as the British colonists, angered over the taxation to pay for the colonial enterprises which they perceived as unfair, fomented a rebellion. Tensions escalated after the colonists, intent on breaking the British trade monopoly, dumped a shipment of British tea into Boston Harbor in 1773, an event which was called the Boston Tea Party. When the British authorities closed the port, the colonies banned together in Philadelphia to form a Continental Congress in 1774. The Congress did not strive for independence, but protested against the unfair treatment and addressed complaints to King George III.

Skirmishes between colonial militia and the British army throughout 1775 erupted into a revolutionary war in the following year. The American colonists declared their independence from Great Britain on July 4, 1776, a date now considered the most sacred holiday in the United States. A prolonged struggle ensued as the colonists waged both conventional and guerrilla warfare, aided by the French, traditional enemies and European rivals of the British. The decisive Battle of Yorktown in Virginia in 1781 assured an American victory. George Washington, commander of the American forces, was elected the first president of the United States in 1789. The United States, a coalition of thirteen colonies, embarked on an experiment in democracy and began forging a separate identity apart from the British monarchy.

The United States Constitution, the oldest written national constitution, was adopted on September 17, 1787 by the Constitutional Convention in Philadelphia. The Preamble states:

> We the People of the United States, in Order to form a more perfect Union, establish Justice, insure domestic Tranquility, provide for the common defence, promote the general Welfare, and secure the Blessings of Liberty to ourselves and our Posterity, do ordain and establish this Constitution for the United States of America.
>
> (www.gpoaccess.gov/constitution/pdf2002/006-Constitution.pdf)

In 1791 the Bill of Rights came into effect; ten amendments to the original United States Constitution which guaranteed individual liberties, such as freedom of speech, freedom of the press, or freedom of religion, that restricted the role of government in the lives of citizens. Various amendments to the Constitution have been endorsed and even withdrawn (the prohibition of alcohol) since then; but the original Bill of Rights has remained intact.

BOX 1.1 THOMAS JEFFERSON

About to enter, fellow citizens, on the exercise of duties which comprehend everything dear and valuable to you, it is proper that you should understand what I deem the essential principles of our government, and consequently those which ought to shape its administration . . . Equal and exact justice to all men, of whatever state or persuasion, religious or political; peace, commerce, and honest friendship, with all nations . . . the support of the state governments in all their rights, as the most competent administrations for our domestic concerns and the surest bulwarks against anti-republican tendencies; the preservation of the general government in its whole constitutional vigor, as the sheet anchor of our peace at home and safety abroad; a jealous care of the right of election by the people . . . absolute acquiescence in the decisions of the majority – the vital principle of republics . . . a well-disciplined militia – our best reliance in peace and for the first moments of war, till regulars may relieve them; the supremacy of the civil over the military authority; economy in the public expense, that labor may be lightly burdened; the honest payment of our debts and sacred preservation of the public faith; encouragement of agriculture, and of commerce as its handmaid; the diffusion of information and the arraignment of all abuses at the bar of public reason; freedom of religion; freedom of the press; freedom of person under the protection of the habeas corpus; and trial by juries impartially selected – these principles form the bright constellation which has gone before us, and guided our steps through an age of revolution and reformation.

(quoted in Peterson 1975, 290)

The fledgling nation doubled its size in 1803 when President Thomas Jefferson made the Louisiana Purchase from France. Spain had ceded the vast lands that encompassed the middle third of the continent from the Gulf of Mexico to Canada to Napoleon. In need of funds for his European campaigns, Napoleon sold the territory of 828,000 square miles (2,144,510 square kilometers) with the French name Louisiane to the United States for only $15,000,000 (Garraty 1983, 682). An exploratory party, the Lewis and Clark expedition of 1804–1806, traversed the new land to the Pacific Coast and back, reporting on the geography, flora, fauna, and Native inhabitants, thereby increasing interest and settlement of the rich western terrain (Ambrose 1996; Ronda 2001). Throughout the nineteenth century farmers, adventurers, and various groups of immigrants set off for the west in

22

covered wagons, on foot, and eventually by railroad to claim their share of the American Dream. The trek assumed legendary status in American history and enhanced the legacy of the American conquest of the continent.

The United States faced Great Britain in the War of 1812 (1812–1814) over the seizure of American commercial vessels, the impressment of American sailors, and Indian raids on the American frontier, which were instigated by British agents. Although British troops burned down the United States capital, the war ended in stalemate. The Americans won their biggest victory at the Battle of New Orleans; but unbeknownst to the combatants, a peace treaty had already been signed two weeks earlier.

This war had a major impact on the national sentiments of the Americans who identified increasingly with collective symbols and rituals of the new state. When the Americans successfully withstood the British siege in the battle for Baltimore, a city resident wrote the song "The Star-spangled Banner" in homage to the still standing American flag. The song, destined to become the national anthem, is played today before the commencement of every American sporting event.

BOX 1.2 "THE STAR-SPANGLED BANNER"

The first verse:

Oh, say can you see by the dawn's early light
What so proudly we hailed at the twilight's last gleaming?
Whose broad stripes and bright stars thru the perilous fight,
O'er the ramparts we watched were so gallantly streaming?
And the rocket's red glare, the bombs bursting in air,
Gave proof through the night that our flag was still there.
Oh, say does that star-spangled banner yet wave
O'er the land of the free and the home of the brave?

Expansion

In the nineteenth century the United States embarked upon a western odyssey in earnest, fostering the belief in the American "Manifest Destiny," the driving force behind the continental conquest and beyond.

By the 1830s American settlers had moved southwest into the Texas area, a part of Mexico. There they fomented a rebellion against the Mexican government, winning their independence in epic battles that added to the martial glory of frontier heroes. Texas briefly became an independent republic (1836–1845) before it was annexed to the United States on the eve of the Mexican–American War (1846–1848). Mexico had never recognized the independence of Texas and its acquisition by the United States sparked a war, resulting in an American invasion and the capture of Mexico City. The peace treaty gave a large portion of northern Mexico to the victors, with the new territory forming California and the southwestern United States.

Already engaged in the war with Mexico, the United States avoided a third conflict with Great Britain over the Oregon territory on the Pacific Ocean, which both jointly occupied. Nationalists clamored for the annexation of all of the territory which stretched well into Canada. John Quincy Adams, a former US president, invoked the religious zeal of the perceived American mission when he stated that it was the young nation's intention "to make the wilderness blossom as a rose, to establish laws, to increase, multiply, and subdue the earth, which we are commanded to do by the first behest of God Almighty" (Blum *et. al.* 1977, 263). Canada and the US reached a resolution in 1846 by dividing the land in half, whereby the American land gain marked the northwest corner of the United States until the acquisition of Alaska.

When gold was discovered in California in 1848 fortune seekers from around the world hastened to the area. Its rapid population growth allowed California to become a state in 1850. By the late twentieth century California's continuing growth made it the state with the largest population, its sunshine, beaches, and Hollywood movie industry still promoting the American Dream.

By the mid-nineteenth century Americans had developed their own cultural traits, increasingly independent from their English roots. A new American literature and music based on particular American historical experiences had emerged. Writers such as Nathaniel Hawthorne described in numerous short stories and several novels – the most notable of which is the "Scarlet Letter" (1850) – the Puritan experience, and Herman Melville portrayed the adventures of New England whalers. The most dramatic of American novelists, however, Harriet Beecher Stowe, wrote of the lives of slaves in *Uncle Tom's Cabin* (1852), a work that strengthened the abolitionist movement which called for the abandonment of slavery, and enflamed regional tensions which preceded the Civil War.

BOX 1.3 RUNAWAY SLAVE

Ranaway from the Subscriber, on the 22nd December last, his negro man MARTIN, aged about 23 years. He has a pleasing countenance, round face, is quick spoken, and can tell a very plausible story; he is shining black, stout built, with large limbs, short fingers, and small feet; the toe next to his great toe has been mashed off.

The above reward will be paid on his delivery to me, or at any Jail in North Carolina.
James R. Wood
Wadesboro', Feb. 5, 1844.
(http://scriptorium.lib.duke.edu/slavery/oldsouth.html)

Southerners favored the pre-eminence of individual states' rights over the dictates of the federal government, and individual rights to their slave property over the human rights to liberty favored by the abolitionists.

The contrasting regional economies produced further differences in values and opinions. After the turn of the nineteenth century the northern states experienced rapid industrialization processes, whereas plantations worked by slaves were the dominant pattern of the southern economy. Northern factories were manned by wage laborers, and the use of slaves raised fundamental questions about the nature of American democracy and the universal human right of freedom prescribed by the Constitution of the USA.

The conflicts erupted in a civil war (1861–1865) when the southern states attempted to secede from the union over issues of political difference and slavery. At the height of the war President Abraham Lincoln issued the Emancipation Proclamation, which freed all slaves. After a long and bloody struggle that cost the lives of 620,000 soldiers, the superior industrial power and greater population resources of the North proved victorious. As the war came to a close a southern sympathizer assassinated President Lincoln. Southerners bemoaned their Lost Cause for generations afterward, symbolically celebrating their military heroes in rituals and memorials (Countryman 1996, 198).

Reconstruction

The period immediately following the war was known as the era of Reconstruction in reference to the rebuilding of the political structure of the defeated southern states. White politicians from the North moved south to assume governmental roles and the freed blacks elected African-Americans to offices.

The disputed presidential election of 1876, however, enabled the Southerners, members of the Democratic Party, to return to local and regional power. When the corrupt manipulation of ballots by both sides resulted in a deadlocked election the rival parties reached a compromise. Southern Democrats agreed to the election of the Republican candidate, Rutherford Hayes, in return for a pledge that the federal government would not interfere in southern affairs (Garraty 1983, 412–415). The pact allowed the white residents of the southern states to enact restrictive voting covenants that prohibited blacks from

Figure 1.3 Confederate Memorial in Charleston, South Carolina

exercising their suffrage rights. In addition, veterans of the Confederate army founded a secret society of white vigilantes, a group known as the Ku Klux Klan, who terrorized the freed blacks into subservience (Foner 1983).

Without capital, the former slaves were forced to work for white landlords in exchange for a percentage of their crops. This arrangement virtually returned the blacks to a state of slavery. Although technically free they had little or no money and subsisted on the meager harvest of their small agricultural plots, which they had to share with the overlords who were no longer obliged to feed or clothe them. Later laws firmly established the social segregation of the races.

The Gilded Age

With the industrialized economy of the northern states triumphant, the post-Civil War years became known as the Gilded Age as unbridled capitalists strove to achieve commercial monopolies and amassed immense fortunes. Men like Jay Gould controlled the stock market, J.P. Morgan dominated investment banking, Andrew Carnegie cornered the steel industry, John D. Rockefeller established himself in the oil business, and Cornelius Vanderbilt and other railroad magnates reigned over the shipping networks. By 1892 the United States registered 4,047 millionaires, most of whom had made their fortunes in the Gilded Age (Blum et al. 1977, 464).

The excesses of employers and the exploitation of workers resulted in the formation of labor unions that opposed corporate greed, often in armed conflict. Like the exploited blacks in the South, industrial workers claimed that they were "wage slaves" without adequate protection or security. Ethnic and trade differences in the labor movement, however, factionalized employees and prevented a concerted and thus powerful opposition. Moreover, the federal government usually sided with employers, providing military forces to quell the workers' outbursts and intercede in the biggest strikes. However, the labor movement won some concessions, such as shorter working hours. Radical movements, such as socialists, communists, and anarchists, used freedom of speech to propagate their political messages, but they never gained the influence or the number of adherents as had the European socialist and/or communist movements. Despite the class conflicts, the Gilded Age provided a climate where sports, among others baseball and football, developed and flourished.

The Progressive Age

Middle-class reformers sought to cure the ills of American society based on their own perceptions of morality. Women continued to campaign for suffrage rights, and they were particularly prominent in the temperance movement, which sought to ban alcoholic beverages from the country, a crusade that clashed with the lifestyle of European immigrants.

The booming American economy lured millions of European immigrants to the United States after 1880 in the era known as the Progressive Age. The immigrant masses huddled in the tenements of urban slums, creating health and social problems. Their immediate needs were met by corrupt party organizations, called machines, in return for votes on election day.

BOX 1.4 HOW POLITICAL MACHINES WORK

One New York political boss explained his strategy . . .

> go right down among the poor families and help them in the different ways
> they need help . . . If there's a fire . . . I'm usually there with some of my
> election district captains as soon as the fire engines . . . I don't ask whether
> they are Republicans or Democrats, and I don't refer them to the Charity
> Organization Society, which would investigate their case in a month or two
> and decide they were worthy to help about the time they were dead from
> starvation. I just get quarters for them . . . (and) I can always get a job for a
> deservin' man . . . And the children . . . They know me, every one of them,
> and they know that a sight of Uncle George and candy means the same
> thing. Some of them are the best kind of vote getters.
>
> (quoted in Blum *et al.* 1977, 480)

Figure 1.4 Maxwell Street Market, Chicago, *c.* 1905; Photographer: Barnes-Crosby.
(Chicago History Museum)

28

In reaction to the corruption of politicians and the power of entrepreneurs and business-men, middle-class reformers, known as Progressives, made strident attempts to regain control of American society and remedy the problems caused by industrialization and urbanization. They envisioned the perfection of both the individual self and society in a program known as the Social Gospel that invoked religious zeal to enact social reforms. Progressive reformers established settlement houses (community social agencies) to live among the poor immigrants in the industrial cities. In such places they offered instruction in English and civics classes as they tried to assimilate the Europeans into the American culture. Legislators passed a series of laws, among others restricting child labor and introducing mandatory education, intended to Americanize the myriad ethnic groups who sought to better their lives in the United States (see Chapter 3).

Physical education laws insured that even those who could not yet speak English would be exposed to particular values and cultural traits, such as competition (the basis for capitalism) and cooperation (see Chapter 3). Physical educators introduced children to a compre-hensive array of sports and games. They believed and hoped that games taught deference to authority because the players had to obey rules and game officials. The best players won acclaim and might even graduate to the professional ranks, where they earned large salaries. Such lessons could be carried to the factories, where the most productive workers might gain advancement and serve as models to their fellow laborers.

Figure 1.5 Girls' school yard baseball game in Gary, Indiana (Curtis 2006 [1915], 124)

Employers, who supported these educational efforts with financial contributions, particularly hoped that the immigrant children who learned such lessons would become loyal workers and avoid the political orientations of their parents, many of whom filled the ranks of the labor unions.

Despite the benevolent intentions, these reforms were not as successful as the initiators hoped. For a variety of reasons, it was only a small minority of adolescents which were regular users of playgrounds and the activities offered (Wassong 2005).

Frontier and the frontier myth

For both American citizens and newly arrived immigrants the vast expanses of the American west promised free agricultural land for family farms; but required subjugation and incarceration on reservations for the indigenous tribes who inhabited the valuable territory. The western frontier offered a social and economic "safety-valve" for Americans as an alternative to the overcrowded cities and a chance for a new life based on one's work ethic and abilities. The frontier with its promise of meritocracy proved to be especially attractive for immigrants.

At the Chicago World's Fair of 1893 history professor Frederick Jackson Turner proclaimed that the frontier had created an exceptional American people who were self-reliant individualists, democratic in their outlook, and unique in their character (Turner 1935). It was a declaration that Americans too readily believed about themselves. Although relatively few people lived on the frontier it became an entrenched part of the American identity and Americanness (Bogue 1998).

BOX 1.5 THE SIGNIFICANCE OF THE FRONTIER IN AMERICAN HISTORY

Up to our own day American history has been in a large degree the history of the colonization of the Great West. The existence of an area of free land, its continuous recession, and the advance of American settlement westward, explain American development . . . Behind institutions, behind constitutional forms and modifications, lie the vital forces that call these organs into life and shape them to meet changing conditions. The peculiarity of American institutions is the fact that they have been compelled to adapt themselves to the changes of an expanding people – to the changes involved in crossing a continent, in winning a wilderness, and in developing at each area of this progress out of the primitive economic and political conditions of the frontier into the complexity of city life . . . But we have in addition to this a

---

recurrence of the process of evolution in each western area reached in the process of expansion. Thus American development has exhibited not merely advance along a single line, but a return to primitive conditions on a continually advancing frontier line, and a new development for that area. American social development has been continually beginning over again on the frontier. This perennial rebirth, this fluidity of American life, this expansion westward with its new opportunities, its continuous touch with the simplicity of primitive society, furnish the forces dominating American character.

(Bogue 1998)

The frontier myth and the belief in meritocracy engendered subscription to the doctrine of Social Darwinism. White, Anglo-Saxon, Protestant males (WASPs) assumed that they rested upon the apex of the evolutionary pyramid as superior beings. All others were ranked below in a hierarchical fashion that ascribed stereotypical characteristics to various ethnic and racial groups. The WASPs thus rationalized and justified their quest for dominance and the suppression of "others," the native population, the blacks, the immigrants, and the women, as the "survival of the fittest" (see Chapters 8 and 9).

Beliefs in American exceptionalism reinforced Turner's views on the hardiness of Americans and the conditions that elicited such traits. He cautioned, however, that the free land of the frontier had expired by 1893. Nevertheless, another historian (a former student of Turner), Frederic Paxson, predicted sport to be the new frontier. Professional sports, in particular, seemed to provide the means to social mobility based on one's physical prowess, not unlike the work ethic and discipline required of the pioneer farmers. The meritocracy of professional or semi-professional sports, which required physical skills, but not the education, social status, or wealth of more elite professions, made athletes into heroes for aspiring youths, especially young men of lower social class.

Colonialism

Americans invoked their sense of moral superiority and democracy to criticize Spanish imperial governance of Cuba and its brutal repression of the revolution at the end of the nineteenth century. When an American battleship mysteriously exploded in the Havana harbor, the incident erupted into the Spanish–American War of 1898. The United States' quick victory brought an instant empire in the form of Caribbean and Pacific Island territories, such as the Philippines, Hawaii, Cuba, and Puerto Rico. The acquisition of such colonies immediately placed the United States on the level of the global powers of Europe (Great Britain, France, and Germany) in the quest for world leadership.

31

At this time, America already had experience with colonial enterprises. As early as 1820 Protestant missionaries traveled to the Sandwich Islands (Hawaii) in the Pacific, converting the indigenous peoples, establishing residential schools and plantations that drastically changed the traditional lifestyle of the inhabitants. American commercial interests grew exponentially with the expanded territory with its mineral and agricultural resources; but even that proved insufficient for capitalist entrepreneurs.

In 1853 an American naval expedition sailed to Asia and forcefully opened the Japanese market to American trade the following year. American Protestant missionaries had long been active in China, but at first with little success. By 1877 Americans had established more than 200 Christian schools in China in an attempt to undermine Confucianism, in order to gain influence and to transfer Christian values (Gems 2006a, 19).

The American acquisition of the Philippines fostered a contentious debate in American society. Anti-imperialists argued against any colonies as a transgression of American democratic ideals. Adherents of colonialism argued for accepting "the white man's burden" to civilize more primitive people; while imperialists clamored for new economic markets for American goods and the naval stations that would allow the United States to compete with the imperial powers of Europe. The Republican government favored the latter viewpoint, and Protestant missionaries soon hurried to the foreign lands to convert the largely Catholic masses in the Philippines and the Caribbean islands to their presumably better brand of Christianity (Gems 2006a, 46–47).

Racism in American culture

The racial connotations of the Social Darwinian ideology permeated both the colonies and the American mainland culture. A strict separation of blacks and whites in the southern states had been legally affirmed by the US Supreme Court in 1896. Sporting practices, however, sometimes allowed for interracial contests, and the sport of boxing clearly challenged the tenets of Social Darwinism. When an African-American, Jack Johnson, defeated Tommy Burns and became heavyweight champion, the superiority of the whites seemed to be endangered. A search for the Great White Hope began, but Johnson, harassed and forced into exile, stayed undefeated for seven years. During that time Johnson's boxing skills and lifestyle directly challenged white authority and clearly tested the prevailing beliefs in racial supremacy (see Chapter 10) (Gems 2006a, 59–71).

As Johnson became a symbol of black power, southern black sharecroppers began to move to northern industrial centers in search of better lives. Encouraged by the African-American press in the northern cities, the exodus became a mass movement known as "the Great Migration" during the World War I years. The blacks settled in industrial centers like New York, Chicago, Detroit, and Cleveland, segregated in ghettos like the ethnic immigrant groups. Northern employers exploited the new labor force as strikebreakers and residence in segregated housing kept the blacks from interaction with their white ethnic co-workers. The living and working conditions caused conflicts within the working class as whites viewed the newly arrived blacks as competitors for jobs, leading to several urban race riots: in East St. Louis white rioters killed thirty-nine African-Americans in 1917, and a Chicago race war lasted for two weeks in 1919 and cost thirty-eight lives (Foner and Garraty 1991, 115; Grossman 1989).

World War I and the 1920s

With the United States' entry into World War I the government took drastic steps to homogenize the American culture and remove any threats to the political and economic system. In the years following the war communism was perceived as a threat, and a Red Scare precipitated a backlash against anyone, especially ethnic minorities, deemed to be anarchists, socialists, communists or disloyal to the United States. Thousands were arrested, imprisoned, and many deported to Europe in an attempt to purify the society. German-Americans were subjected to particular scrutiny, German language newspapers were suppressed, and German language instruction was eliminated from the public schools' curriculum. During the 1920s the United States Congress enacted a series of immigration quota laws, limiting the number of aliens permitted to enter the country (see Chapter 3) (Gems 1997, 138–141).

The American paranoia and a growing desire for isolation from European affairs was demonstrated at the close of World War I when the US Congress refused to ratify the Treaty of Versailles that would have established the League of Nations proposed by the American president, Woodrow Wilson. The United States thus turned inward by concentrating on its own affairs. The entrenched puritanical moral code reasserted itself and proved evident in the passage of a constitutional amendment that prohibited alcoholic beverages. Widely ignored and spawning criminal activities involving the production and smuggling of illicit beverages, Americans still reveled in a growing popular culture fed by alcohol, movies, dancing, radio, and sport. The cultural flow of black musicians from south to north spawned the Jazz Age and the proliferation of celebrity culture. The rise of mass media contributed to a surge in competitive sport, especially ball games, the construction of sport heroes, and growing audiences, developments which made the 1920s the "Golden Age" of sport. Moreover, the lack of fitness of many American soldiers during World War I placed an increased emphasis on improving physical health.

The golden 1920s ended abruptly with the Stock Market crash of 1929 that produced a worldwide economic depression with rising numbers of unemployed people. With no governmental mechanisms in place to avoid economic disasters and no form of financial support and medical help, poor Americans were reliant on charity. Many avoided starvation by standing in long bread or soup lines to gain a modicum of sustenance. With the ascendance of Franklin Delano Roosevelt to the presidency in 1932 numerous reforms took place. Among them he introduced a Social Security system that would provide workers with a pension in their old age. To address the enforced leisure of the economic downturn he created agencies that employed people on government construction projects (Marquis 1986; Cohen 1990; Folsom 1991, 231–431; Dawley 1991, 334–417).

World War II and the Cold War

As fascist powers gained prominence in Italy, Germany, Spain, and Japan, the United States elected Franklin Delano Roosevelt, a liberal Democrat, to the presidency. He served an unequaled four terms, leading the nation through the Depression and throughout most of World War II. The Allied victory in World War II pushed the United States into a position of global leadership; soon challenged by the rise of the communist bloc that divided Europe. The ensuing Cold War quickly became hot as the rival forces fought over Korea (1950–1953), resulting in the division of that nation into opposing political countries. The fear of communism sparked a second wave of the Red Scare in the United States, resulting in trials of suspected radicals, deportations, and even executions that effectively curtailed the leftist movement in America.

The spread of nuclear weapons and the space race consumed the rest of the decade with both super powers fearing an atomic holocaust. That possibility reached crisis stage in 1962 when the Soviet Union placed intercontinental ballistic missiles in Cuba, a communist ally on the doorstep of the United States. The peaceful negotiation of the removal of the missiles made President John Kennedy an American hero; but his assassination the following year devastated the populace and destroyed the hopes of the nation for a better world (Huntington 1996).

The Civil Rights Movement and the Viet Nam War

American culture faced drastic changes in the 1960s as the Civil Rights Movement and the rise of feminism challenged the established white, male, power structures. The assassinations of black activist Malcolm X, Civil Rights leader Martin Luther King, and presidential contender Robert F. Kennedy horrified the nation as a bevy of leaders faced death for exercising their right of free speech. The country increasingly divided over the meanings and values of American democracy (Verney 2003, 49–56). An athletic revolution, led by boxer Muhammad Ali, played a prominent role in effecting social change especially for African-Americans inside and outside sport (Miller and Wiggins 2004).

American entry into yet another war against communism in Viet Nam (1964–1973) polarized the society. In the global showdown both blocs scurried for allies in the ideological

34

confrontation. The US backed French efforts to resume control of its Indochinese colonies after World War II, and initiated its own efforts when the French forces were defeated in Viet Nam. US policy-makers subscribed to the domino theory, which predicted that if one country fell to communism its neighbors would follow, eventually reaching the shores of America (Karnow 1983).

The Americans lost 58,000 lives in Viet Nam; but fared little better than the French. Their troops had to leave the country. The loss of the war and so many soldiers proved a devastating blow to American self-esteem and the population's belief in the invincibility of the nation (Karnow 1983; Palmer 1978).

Sport assumed the role of a surrogate war as capitalist and communist nations grappled in the Olympic Games. The international festival became a political vehicle when the United States boycotted the 1980 Games in Moscow as a reaction to the Soviet invasion of Afghanistan. The Soviets responded by spurning the 1984 competitions held in Los Angeles. The American hosts commercialized the games to a hitherto unthinkable degree selling exclusive sponsor rates to the highest bidders, endorsing numerous and various products and producing a huge variety of "Olympic" items as memorabilia. These new marketing practices and the largesse acquired significantly changed the future organization of the Olympics as well as the disposition and power of the International Olympic Committee.

Despite the setback in Viet Nam the US government continued relentless and often clandestine operations against communists throughout the world. With the fall of the Soviet bloc in 1989, America became the leading economic and military power; and its enterprises increasingly market their products to a global market. Coca-Cola, Kentucky Fried Chicken and McDonald's restaurants, American cars, and cultural productions increased their market shares outside the United States. The Disney Company expanded its reach into Europe, and Hollywood movies and American fashions permeated the world. ESPN, a sports television station, and Rupert Murdoch, an Australian with American citizenship and business operations in the US, assumed global influence. American entertainers, such as Madonna, and athletes, such as Michael Jordan, became international icons and brand names. With the globalization processes, especially the global influences of the mass media, including the internet, media industry conglomerates threaten to homogenize cultures worldwide, as American business practices, social values, and sport forms encroach upon national, regional, and local communities. American military incursions into the Middle East over the past two decades represent not only the safeguarding of American business enterprises abroad but a reaction to the perceived threats to Americans' lives, values, and culture.

CONCLUSION

The specific conditions and experiences of the foundation and historical development of the United States have left their imprint not only on Americans' understanding of statehood, democracy, and civil society but also on the relationships between these three concepts. While European citizens had to fight for their liberty in class struggles, the United States was founded as a society of free citizens who, from the very beginning, placed greater value on freedom than they did on social equality. The term "American exceptionalism," based as it is on the experience of the nation's founding and the opportunities afforded by the expansion of its frontiers, refers, among other things, to a weakly developed welfare state. America is also exceptional with regard to the trust and expectation the state puts in its citizens' self-reliance, and the great importance it attaches to religion even today. A typical feature of the United States' Constitution is the separation of executive, legislative, and judicial branches and a horizontal and vertical sharing of power by a system of checks and balances, which weakens the state and puts the burden of responsibility on civil society. The church and welfare organizations fill the gaps that arise due to the lack of a social safety net. In this scheme of things, social inequality is not regarded as a political problem and is thus not combated by political means. Neither workers' movements nor left-wing parties have ever played a significant role in the United States, which can be explained by the historical absence of a feudal order and the great opportunities there are for geographic mobility. Finally, as a country of immigration and as a slave-holding society, the United States has been greatly influenced by the relationships between its various races and ethnicities. Coping with and integrating different cultures is always a challenge – but one which has also enabled positive developments in all social spheres, including sport.

CHAPTER TWO

THE EVOLUTION OF AMERICAN SPORTS

INTRODUCTION

This chapter presents an overview of the evolution of American sports from the pre-colonial period to modern sport in the twentieth century. It focuses in particular on the early years and the development of regional cultures and religious influences. In addition, it shows the close interrelations between physical activities/sports and political, cultural, social, and economic conditions in America. It provides background knowledge for the other parts of the book. The development of major sports, institutions, and events of the twentieth century, as well as racial, ethnic, and gender issues are covered in greater detail in separate chapters.

PHYSICAL ACTIVITIES AND SPORTS OF THE NATIVE AMERICANS

The European "discovery" of the North American continent led to some immediate and some more gradual changes in the lives of Native Americans. Among the more immediate transitions, the Europeans, mistakenly believing that they had reached Asia, termed the indigenous inhabitants of the continent "Indians." That designation signified them as "others," whose non-European features and lifestyles would relegate them to an inferior status. The more gradual change in the Natives' lifestyles occurred over succeeding centuries and included their assimilation to Anglo culture, including sporting practices.

During the adaptation and assimilation processes of the "Indians," the aims, meanings, and conditions of their sporting practices changed dramatically. For the Native Americans, hunting, fishing, archery, running, and swimming were everyday activities and entailed practical skills necessary for daily sustenance. The game of lacrosse, played by tribes throughout the continent, resembled sport in the European concept of the term; but it had social functions, religious meanings, and also served as training for war. In addition, other physical activities such as running or dancing hold ritual, religious, social, or symbolic importance more so than "sport" as understood by Europeans. Among the Native Americans of the southwest, California, and the Pacific Coast, running was a central element in puberty rites. Daily runs at sunrise were meant to test endurance and predict long life. Other southwestern tribes engaged in competitive relay races against other clans. The races could take the entire day and were believed to recharge the power of the sun. "There is no victory celebration or record of the winning side; rather, it is done as ritual and ceremony" (Collier 2004, 264–265).

Early European commentaries established the dual nature of archery as both a necessary skill and a sporting practice. William Wood, a British settler in the Massachusetts Bay Colony of New England, remarked in 1634 that

> for their sports of activitie they have commonly but three or foure: as footeball, shooting, running and swimming . . . For their shooting . . . such is their celerity and dexterity . . . that they can smite the swift running Hinde and . . . pigeon without a standing pause or left eye blinking . . . They are trained up to their bowes even from childhood . . . as these Indians be good markemen (*sic*).

Peter Lindestrom, a Swede in the Delaware area in the 1650s, stated: "He who is the sachem (chief) has a turkey placed very high in the air, whose entrails are removed and (the body) filled again with their money. And the one who then can shoot it down, he receives the money" (quoted in Altherr 1997, 38–39).

A century earlier (1530s), Cabeza de Vaca, an early Spanish explorer of the Texas region, indicated the different conceptions of sport in his report. "These Indians are so used to running that, without rest, they follow a deer from morning until night . . . They wear the deer down and then sometimes overtake them in a race" (quoted in Altherr 1997, 325–326).

In the southwestern area of what is now the United States the natives practiced various "sports;" among others, they ran relay races connected to fertility rituals (Guttmann 1988, 19–21). The Zuni tribe of the southwest played a form of shuttlecock, believed to be derived from the gods and for the purpose of bringing rain to give life (Meneses 2004, 280–281). The southwestern tribes also played a ball game, as related by a Spanish captain in the Arizona region in 1699. "They make round balls, the size of a football, out of a black pitch-like substance . . . They play with these balls and make bets. They kick the ball with the tip of the foot, run three or four leagues, and the party that goes around and comes back to the starting point wins" (quoted in Altherr 1997, 162). The captain mistakenly equated the use of the kicked ball in a race with the European equivalent of football; but an English boy captured by the Powhatan tribe in Virginia shortly after the founding of the Jamestown colony (1607) claimed that the Indians of that region engaged in a recreation similar to the British folk game. "They use beside football play, wch (*sic*) women and young boyes doe much play at. They make ther Gooles as ours only they never fight nor pull one another doune (*sic*)" (Altherr 1997, 160).

British commentators of the seventeenth century marveled at the natural abilities of the natives. One stated that

They are generally very quick on foot; and brought up even from their Mother's Brests to running; their Legs being stretch'd and bound up in a strange way in their Cradle backward, from their Infancy: Which makes some of them to excel in running, that they will run four-score or an hundred miles in a Summers Day: and they very often Practice running of Races (*sic*).

(quoted in Altherr 1997, 225–226)

With their ethnocentric biases the Anglos tried to rationalize and qualify such abilities, as evidenced by William Wood in 1634. "For their running it is with much celeritie and continuance, yet I suppose there be many English men who being as lightly clad as they are, would outrun them for a spurt, though not able to continue it for a day or dayes (*sic*)" (Altherr 1997, 225). Nearly a century and a half later (1777) a trader in the Great Lakes region of the Midwest maintained that "The savages are esteemed very active and nimble-footed . . . but it is well known the Europeans are more swift in running a small distance. Their chief merit, I am of opinion, consists in their being able to continue a long time in one steady pace (*sic*)" (Altherr 1997, 232).

Gambling often accompanied the games of the Native Americans. One of the first settlers of the Plymouth Colony in Massachusetts declared that the Native Americans "use gaming as much as any where . . . (and they) will play away all, even their skin from their backs;

INDIAN AMUSEMENTS—CANOE-RACE BETWEEN SQUAWS.

Figure 2.1 Native American women in canoe race (Northrop 1902, 223)

yea, and for their wives' skins also" (Struna 1996, 39–40). Perhaps one of the biggest gambles involved the game of lacrosse, seemingly played by all tribes across the continent. Often played by hundreds at a time, its violent nature could cause serious injury or death.

Lacrosse, so named because the French missionary priests who observed the game thought the sticks used by the players resembled the wooden cross symbolic of the Christian religions, served several purposes. Both men and women played the game; for men it served as training for war. It sometimes accompanied religious rites, provided opportunities for gambling, and could even be used to settle tribal disputes over land (Vennum 1994). Despite the European incursions into indigenous lives some native games persisted well into the nineteenth century. American explorer Zebulon Pike encountered the tribes of the Great Plains (c. 1806) and wrote about a hoop and pole game played by two players on a designated site 150 yards (137.16 meters) in length. He indicated that scoring was quantified, as in modern sports, as one game was won when a competitor reached a total of 100 points (Altherr 1997, 431–432).

Lacrosse, though a native game, had some appeal for the Europeans. In an example of the cross-cultural transfer of sport, Canadian settlers adopted then adapted the game for their own uses, forming the Montreal Lacrosse Club in 1856. Written rules, regulations, and a

Figure 2.2 Carlisle men's physical education class (Library of Congress)

governing body soon approximated the game with the characteristics of modern sports. The National Lacrosse League of 1879 initiated a championship in the United States that year; but the game remained a regional pastime, played mostly in the New England and Atlantic states until the late twentieth century (Gems 1996a, 372).

Despite numerous and various sports and games, Native American sporting and cultural practices had a very limited impact on white American society.

By the late nineteenth century the Native American tribes had been decimated by European diseases and Anglo conquests. Indian children were sent to residential schools where they were forced to speak the English language, cut their long hair, and adopt white clothing styles. They were taught vocational skills and American sport forms designed to fit them for roles as workers in a capitalist economy (Adams 1995; Bloom 2000; Hoxie 1989; Oxendine 1995). Such schooling produced the greatest male athlete in United States history. Jim Thorpe, a student of the Carlisle Indian School, won both the pentathlon and decathlon competitions at the 1912 Olympics in Stockholm. He played both professional baseball and professional football and served as the nominal president of the first professional football league, which later became the NFL. The stresses of living in the white world, however, resulted in alcoholism and self-destruction (see Chapter 12 on sports heroes). The "Indian" schools still operate in the United States, although many tribes now undertake their own education in tribal schools on reservation lands, where traditional languages and lifestyles are promoted (Adams 1995; Bloom 2000; Hoxie 1989; Newcombe 1975).

LEGACIES OF THE EARLY EUROPEAN COLONISTS – RECREATIONAL PASTIMES IN A PURITAN CULTURE

In contrast to Native Americans, the early European colonists left a lasting legacy for American culture. They emphasized individualism, sabbatarianism, and a strong work ethic, principles which remain prominent today in the United States. The desire to live according to their faith led the Puritans, religious dissenters in England, to found the Massachusetts Bay Colony in 1630. There they hoped to establish "a city upon a hill," a religious example for the world. Although they rebelled against other forms of Protestantism, they allowed for little diversion from their prescribed beliefs and practices. For example, when Thomas Morton, one of the early settlers, erected a maypole and frolicked with the Native Americans, causing "great licentiousness;" he was severely punished and sent back to England (Struna 1996, 48; Zuckerman 1977). Evangelical Christian groups in the United States continue to promote their particular views of morality and have little sufferance for those who disagree.

Puritan laws regarding the Sabbath meant to keep the "Lord's Day" a holy one without any distractions from worshipping. The Puritans enacted rigorous "blue laws" which precluded any labor, recreation, travel, "idle conversation," and even unnecessary walking during that time. Transgressions were severely punished as the following examples show. In 1656 when a sea captain who had been away for three years kissed his wife upon his return, he was sentenced to two hours in the public stocks for "lewd and unseemly conduct," which violated the Sabbath (Rader 1990, 7). Sporting pastimes were also prohibited. In 1630 a man was "whipped for shooteing att fowle on the Sabbath day" (sic). In Vermont, running, riding, jumping, or dancing on Sunday would earn practitioners ten lashes with the whip and a fine of forty shillings. The Puritans did, however, draw some distinctions between "sport" and the utilitarian pastimes necessary for sustenance and defense. In the Rhode Island colony a 1647 law required archery practice, stating that "every person from the age of seventeen yeares, to the age of seventy . . . shall have a bow and two arrows, and shall use and exercise shooting . . . every Father having Children, shall provide for every man-child from the age of seven years . . . a Bow and two Arrowes . . . to bring them up to shooting (sic)" (Altherr 1997, 36; Guttmann 2004, 118). Remnants of such sabbatarian laws remain in some American states, where the purchase of alcoholic beverages is restricted on Sundays.

BOX 2.1 SPORTS ON THE LORD'S DAY

Cotton Mather, an influential Massachusetts minister, declared in 1703: "Sports on the Lords day! Never did anything sound more sorrowfully or more odiously, since the day that the World was first bless'd with such a day [sic]."

A New York City law of 1707 stated: "And be it further Ordained by the Authority aforesaid, That no Children, Youths, Maids Or other persons whatsoever, do meet together on the Lords Day in any of the Streets or places within this City or Liberties thereof, and there sport, play, make noise or disturbance, under the penalty of One Shilling for each Offence, to be paid by the Parents of all under Age [sic]" (quoted in Altherr 1997, 7).

In the southern colonies the strong work ethic, sometimes referred to as the "Protestant work ethic," preceded the Puritans and became evident in the first successful English colony. Jamestown was founded in Virginia in 1607 but the settlement barely survived its early years. The immigrants were "gentlemen" of the upper classes and assumed the aristocratic rights that they had enjoyed in England, taking their leisure in various games and sports as well as gambling, rather than working (see Chapter 2). Under Captain John Smith they were forced to work for the benefit of the colony under pain of punishment, even death. Ironically, many British settlers criticized the Native American males' lifestyles as lazy and profligate, but assumed the right to be idle for themselves (Struna 1996, 39, 207). In the southern colonies plantation owners hired the Indians to work for them, and soon imported African slaves, whom they did not have to pay for their labors. Like the English aristocracy, plantation owners led a life of considerable leisure which included various pastimes imported from their home country (Struna 1996, 76–77).

Even the harsh Puritan attitudes in the northern colonies towards idleness dissipated over time (Struna 1977). In 1686 a British visitor to Massachusetts wrote to his wife in England about a football game played between two villages, as settlers in the new land began to construct their own sporting culture (Struna 1996, 74–76). Folk games brought from Britain occurred at harvest fests and county fairs, and taverns provided the sites and opportunities for activities which were called sports in the contemporary terminology. In 1751 a Virginia minister complained that in the taverns "not only time and money are vainly and unprofitably squandered away, but (what is yet worse) where prohibited and unlawful games, sports and pastimes are used, followed and practiced, almost without intermission, namely cards, dice, horse-racing, cock-fighting, together with vices and enormities of every other kind" (Rader 1990, 11). When the authorities tried to ban the game of ninepins, enterprising bowlers circumvented the rulings by adding an additional pin. The restriction of gambling and sport proved untenable, and by 1665 even the British governor of New York had established a course for horseracing (Rader 1990, 11).

For the colonists, the term *sport* referred to many activities they deemed to be playful or recreational, and might include gambling. So-called blood sports especially chagrined the religious leaders, although at least one historian claimed, "not because it gave pain to the bear; but because it gave pleasure to the spectators" (Guttmann 2004, 118). In these "sports" a bull or a bear was pitted against a number of dogs. Onlookers were not only thrilled by the bloody spectacle but also by betting. They might bet on the number of dogs or the time required to kill the beast, or even if the wild animal might emerge victorious. Tavern owners attracted customers with these early versions of a commercialized sporting spectacle.

BOX 2.2 BULL BAITING

Thomas McMullan advertised the following on August 29, 1781: "The Subscriber having procured a Stout BULL, proposes bateing him to morrow, at four o'clock in the afternoon, at his house . . . The bull is active, and very vicious, therefore hopes the spectators will have satisfactory diversion [*sic*]" (quoted in Altherr 1997, 75).

In the southwestern region and Mexico the Spanish custom might pit a bull against a bear or a matador might test his courage in a confrontation with a bull. Cockfighting, too, enjoyed particular favor as a sporting (gambling) activity among all classes; but drew particular ire from the clergy. An Anglican minister in Virginia in 1724 decried the lack of work ethic more so than the cruelty, when he wrote: "The common Planters leading easy Lives don't much admire Labour, or any manly Exersice, except Horse-Racing, nor Diversion, except Cock-Fighting, in which some greatly delight. This easy Way of Living, and the Heat of the Summer makes some very lazy, who are then said to Climate-struck (*sic*)" (Altherr 1997, 60). Cockfighting continues in the United States in a clandestine fashion; but complaints now revolve around cruelty to animals.

Winter sports, such as skating, sledding, or sleighing were practical means of locomotion, but also exemplified blurred borderlines between pleasure and necessity. Such activities might serve as transport, as colonists skated to and from the winter markets; but they might also be a means of recreation or leisure on a Sunday. In 1657 three defendants in New Netherland (New York) were brought to court for playing ice hockey on the Sabbath, clearly a transgression of the religious laws (Altherr 1997, 462). However, twenty years later a British minister in that same city in 1678 judged skaters to be not only lawful, but admirable, when he stated: ". . . and upon the Ice its admirable to see Men and Women as it were flying upon their Skates from place to place, with markets [food] on their Heads and Backs (*sic*)" (Altherr 1997, 463).

THE RISE OF SPORTS AND GAMES IN THE EIGHTEENTH CENTURY

The Great Awakening and its impact on sports and pastimes

The morality of play and leisure came under scrutiny again in the Great Awakening of the 1730s and 1740s, one of the periodic religious revivals which continue to appear in the United States. The itinerant ministers of the era railed against idleness, drunkenness, sport, and the taverns that permitted such unproductive pastimes (Struna 1996, 161–164).

BOX 2.3 QUAKER VIEWS ON SPORTS AND GAMES

The Society of Friends, known as the Quakers, admonished congregants in 1739:

> WE earnestly beseech our friends, and especially the youth among us, to avoid all such conversation as may tend to draw out their minds into the foolish and wicked pastimes with which this age aboundeth (particularly balls, gaming-places, horse-races, and play-houses) those nurseries of debauchery and wickedness, the burthen and grief of the sober part of other societies, as well as of our own; practices wholly unbecoming a people under the Christian profession, contrary to the tenor of the doctrine of the gospel, and the examples of the best men in the earliest ages of the church [*sic*].

> (quoted in Altherr 1997, 288)

Despite the successes of the evangelicals, not all people agreed with their admonitions because sports, play, and games, properly conducted, might be beneficial. John Adams, who became the second president of the United States, recalled his childhood of the 1740s.

> I spent my time as idle Children do in making and sailing boats and Ships upon the Ponds and Brooks, in making and flying Kites, in driving hoops, playing marbles, playing Quoits, Wrestling, Swimming, Skaiting and above all in shooting, to which Diversion I was addicted to a degree of Ardor which I know not that I ever felt for any other Business, Study, or Amusement [sic].
>
> (Altherr 1997, 88)

In the American colleges, faculty members assumed the responsibility for the moral education of students and regulated their leisure time and practices accordingly. The Harvard College laws of 1734 stated that "No Undergraduate shell keep a Gun or pistol in the College, or any where in Cambridge; nor shall he go gunning, fishing, or Scating over deep waters, without leave from the President or one of the Tutors, under penalty of three Shillings [sic]" (Altherr 1997, 464). Yale College also regulated students' games by declaring: "If any Scholar shall play at Hand-Ball, or Foot-Ball, or Bowls in the College-Yard, or throw any Thing against College, by which the Glass may be endangered . . . he shall punished six pence, and make good the Damages [sic]" (Altherr 1997, 82). These regulations did not restrict leisure activities altogether. They indicate that students engaged in various recreational activities during their leisure time and that they were allowed to do so if they kept the rules. However, prohibition or control of sport and games because of religious or moral reasons continued over the next two centuries.

Whereas sporting activities were increasingly accepted for boys and men, girls and women were excluded from most physical activities. Immigrant societies were a men's world, depending on individuals ready to fight and able to conduct hard physical labor, qualities which were denied to women. Women were considered as the "weaker sex" and should be restricted to limited tasks and roles. One of the earliest accounts of colonial life in 1612 stated that while the Native American men fished and hunted in Virginia, the women "as the weaker sort be put to the easier workes, to sow their Corne . . . dresse the meat brought home, . . . beare all kyndes of burthens (burdens), and such like [sic]" (Struna 1996, 39). Female Anglo settlers held similar duties in the house and fields; as the size of settlements grew women joined together in quilting, spinning, butter churning, and husking parties. While they were mostly excluded from physical contests, their activities might be both cooperative and competitive. A diary entry of the Yale College president listed

> 30 May 1770: This day a voluntary Bee or Spinning Match at my house. Begun by Break o'day, & in fornoon early were sixty-four Spinning Wheels going. Afternoon seventy wheels going at the same Time for part of the time. Ninety-two

daughters of Liberty spun and reeled, respiting and assisting one another . . . the Spinners were of all (religious) Denominations [sic].

(Altherr 1997, 19)

While such spinning matches would not be considered sports in the modern sense, they point to the early sense of competition among Americans and an understanding of sport as playful fun. While strenuous physical exercises were considered as inappropriate for females, they could participate in harmless recreations such as dancing, sledding, or skating (Ulrich 1990, 71, 146).

Southern lifestyles and recreations

Lifestyles, gender roles, and men's and women's access to recreation varied considerably according to region and social conditions. For both men and women work and leisure were intertwined in the northern colonies. In the south, plantation owners did not work manually and their wives enjoyed a genteel existence with servants and slaves to do the household tasks. Due to the dispersal of the rural population (Charleston in South Carolina was the only area with sufficient population to be deemed a city), wealthy plantation owners constructed their own recreational facilities. The men enjoyed bowling, billiards, and even cricket; but they had a special passion for cockfights and horseracing, which promoted gambling. The colonists built oval racing tracks, unlike the straightaways in England. This allowed for better views for the spectators. Men and women would be among the crowds around the racecourse and might even gamble on the outcomes. Gambling persisted among all levels of society, and in 1764 the North Carolina Assembly worried that the colony was in jeopardy due to "many idle disorderly, and evil disposed persons . . . who are frequently found Loitering, gaming, and misbehaving themselves [sic]" (Struna 1996, 159).

Although considered sports in the terminology of the time, gambling was a sedentary activity, and it may be questioned as to how many of the owners of the horses rode their animals during the races. However, horseback riding was a popular and widespread pastime, as well as a necessary form of travel.

Southern society rested upon a strict social stratification, where upper-class whites assumed superiority over lower classes, and both shunned blacks. A 1674 court case in Virginia carefully reinforced the proper roles. The sentence stated: "James Bullocke, a Taylor [tailor], having made a race for his mare to runn w'th a horse belonging to Mr. Matthew Slader, for twoe thousand pounds of tobacco and caske, it being contrary to Law for a Labourer to make a race, being a sport only for Gentlemen, is fined for the same one hundred pounds of tobacco and caske [sic]" (Altherrr 1997, 242). In 1691 the Virginia governor organized holiday competitions with prizes for shooting, wrestling, sword fighting, horseracing, and foot races; but he stipulated that such contests were open only to those who had established a measure of social capital (Gorn and Goldstein 1993, 22–23). Such prohibitions and practices served to reinforce Bourdieu's concepts of habitus and social fields in which sport promoted social class distinctions.

Horseracing and gambling assumed great importance in the establishment of social status and honor among the gentry. The possession of excellent horses signaled wealth and expertise, and the competition to own the best horses increased when thoroughbreds began to be imported by the early eighteenth century. Plantation owners wagered large sums on horses. A prominent Virginia planter even wagered an entire year's crop of tobacco in a losing effort, stating that he could afford to do so because he was the wealthiest of the contenders, thereby reinforcing his social capital (Gorn and Goldstein 1993, 22–30). Women, slaves, and men of the lower social ranks reinforced such status as spectators.

In the south, both horseracing and gambling were essential to manhood. Exorbitant, even risky bets ensued as southerners demonstrated the speed of their mounts in a ritual of manhood (Breen 1977). A member of the Carolina Jockey Club maintained that "horses were the impersonation of Carolina chivalry – the embodied spirit of Carolina blood and Carolina honor" (Guttmann 1988, 43).

Transgressions upon the honor of a gentleman often resulted in duels with swords or pistols that persisted into the nineteenth century. Men had to defend their honor, and their lives depended on their prowess as well as on their skills. Dueling proved their masculinity and gained social status. In gambling the code of honor also played a significant role, among other things, because gambling debts were debts of honor. Gambling maintained its excitement when fighting cocks or black slave jockeys assumed substitute roles for their owners (Struna 1996, 151). When gambling conflicts or other affronts of honor became perceived as insults, retribution was required in duels with swords or pistols. Alexander Hamilton, the first Secretary of the Treasury in the United States, was killed in a duel; and Andrew Jackson, owner of a Tennessee plantation, numerous slaves, and racehorses, allegedly fought several duels before becoming the US president in 1828.

By the early twentieth century football teams at southern colleges adapted the concept of honor, still seeking revenge for the defeat of the South in the Civil War (1861–1865) in their confrontations with northern schools (Gems 2000, 165–170).

Sports on the frontier

Confrontations and fights were frequent in the frontier regions, inhabited by the itinerant settlers who lacked education, social capital, and the means to purchase land. There, one's honor and reputation rested upon physical prowess rather than wealth or education. No-holds-barred wrestling, known as rough and tumble, allowed for biting, eye gouging, and even castration, as indicated by the following primary accounts. A 1734 match in

South Carolina ensued when "Two men being in liquor, they quarreled until they came to blows, when one had the fortune to throw the other down . . . bit off his nose, which made the other immediately let him go; upon which the fellow made his escape" (Altherr 1997, 95).

BOX 2.4 GOUGING

In Virginia in 1779 a traveler described how a

> gentleman was at play in the billiard-room; a low fellow who pretends to gentility, came in, and in the course of play, some words arose, in which he first wantonly abused, and afterward would insist on fighting Mr. Fauchee . . . the other flew at him, and in an instant turned his eye out of the socket, and while it hung upon his cheek, the fellow was barbarous enough to pluck it entirely out, but was prevented. This most barbarous custom . . . is peculiar to the lower class of people in this province.
>
> (quoted in Altherr 1997, 96)

The commentator, quoted in the sidebar, was mistaken, since the practice of gouging was so widespread that authorities in several colonies passed laws against such maiming. Another cruel "entertainment" was "gander pulling." Travelers through the southern states described this "sport" as follows: in Kentucky "they have another practice nearly akin to this [gouging], called 'gander pulling.' This diversion consists in tying a live gander to a tree or pole, greasing its neck, riding it at a full gallop, and he who succeeds in pulling off the head of the victim, receives the laurel crown" (Altherr 1997, 98).

In California the Hispanic settlers established ranches, where they met for festivities that often included "challenges for wrestling, leaping, running, shooting with their bow, and trials of strength; and in these and like sports, days and nights, weeks and months were often spent in times of peace" (Altherr 1997, 101). The work of the Hispanic cowboys produced another form of competition known as rodeo, in which roping skills as well as horseriding abilities were tested. Since the nineteenth century, rodeo developed into a modern professional sport with several disciplines reaching from bareback bronco (wild horse) riding to bulldogging (steer wrestling).

As early as the nineteenth century historian Frederick Jackson Turner theorized that the American frontier experience created a new society, marking out Americans as different from others in their individualism, aggressiveness, independence, and self-reliance (see Chapter 1).

Figure 2.3 Modern rodeo (Library of Congress)

EXCURSUS: TAVERNS AS SPORT ARENAS

In America, sport activities and sport consumption often centered around the tavern culture of the colonies, which exhibited distinct differences from their European counterparts. In the frontier areas colonial militia groups gathered at regular intervals known as muster days for shooting practice and other military skills. Social gatherings and physical competitions continued in the local taverns, often promoted by the tavern keeper who earned a profit from the participants as well as the spectators, all of whom might wager on the expected results. In addition to contests in shooting, wrestling, bowling, and horseracing, animals such as bulls, bears, dogs, or cocks were pitted against one another for the amusement of patrons. Taverns increased exponentially with the growth of the United States, and tavern keepers continued to extol a particular culture of sport and consumption.

By the mid-nineteenth century the urban saloons were offering the male fraternity a club-like atmosphere where they might indulge themselves in more luxurious surroundings. In New York City Kit Burns' Sportsman's Hall provided seating for 400. Harry Hill's Dance Hall, another of New York's most popular establishments, featured multiple bars for hard spirits, beer, and wine. It included a concert hall and a stage for boxing and wrestling matches. At the Prairie Queen in Chicago the winner of a boxing match received a house prostitute as a prize.

Some saloons had a back room where illegal boxing matches occurred. Proprietors skirted the law by staging "exhibitions," for which no decision was rendered. Patrons paid an entrance fee to become "members" in such "clubs." Betting on the participants provided a sense of adventure and risk in otherwise mundane lives. Harry Hill won national fame as a boxing referee and as a repository for large bets. Billy McGlory, a New York underworld figure, charged 15 cents as entry to his promotions. His Grand Scarlet Ball, held at Armory Hall in 1883, included a cake-walk by African-Americans, boxing matches between men and women, a beauty contest, and a masquerade ball (Gilfoyle 2006, 115).

THE ESTABLISHMENT OF SPORT IN THE NINETEENTH CENTURY

The industrialized economy that transformed Europe appeared in the New England factories by the turn of the nineteenth century. The spinning and weaving mills, powered by water wheels, were replaced by steam-engines and coal furnaces by the 1850s. Urbanization and industrialization produced new rhythms to daily routines, spawning distinct periods of work and leisure. The technology that accompanied industrialization also

50

transformed the nature of sport. Canals, waterways, and railroads transported goods and persons with increasing speed, and steamboats raced for both commercial gain and sporting honor (Gorn and Goldstein 1993, 50–53).

First sporting competitions

In urban areas gentlemen of the burgeoning middle class, who increasingly dissociated themselves from physical labor, used sport as compensation for the lack of physicality in their everyday life. They organized competitions according to the characteristics of modern sport by the 1820s. At the same time sport began to assume nationalistic tones and to serve nationalistic aims. In 1824 the crew of a British frigate in New York harbor challenged the locals to a rowing race.

> The boat race for $1000 . . . took place about half past 12 this day. The American Star came of [sic] victorious. She beat the English boat about three hundred yards. The concourse of spectators . . . was immense – not less than fifty thousand. – Time of running the four miles, 22 minutes. The White Hallers (Americans) made 46 strokes the minute, and English rowers only 39.
>
> (Menna 1995, 85)

The description of the race provides evidence of the emergence of modern sport practices, as characterized by Allen Guttmann (1978). The principles of modern sport include the quantification of performances as well as the quest for competition and records. Sport is organized and conducted by a bureaucratic administrative body, performances are registered, and competitors assume specialized roles. While the boat race included only some of these facets, historian Melvin Adelman (1986) contended that harness racing of this period met such criteria. The New York Trotting Club, established in that city in 1825, conducted regularly scheduled events held at a designated course with agreed-upon rules. Aside from the concerns of the clergy about gambling, horseracing became rationalized as a necessity for the improvement of breeding stock, and therefore more acceptable. The horseracing fever was fanned by the emerging sports media in the form of specialized newspapers that reported on the races by the 1830s.

The occasional competition on the race-track against British or Canadian foes elicited comparisons and nationalist emotions. Regionalism still occupied the minds of Americans; and the race-track was used as an arena for competitions and comparisons between the north and the south, both aiming at demonstrations of superiority. Southern planters favored fast horses, while northern owners bred horses for endurance. The rivalries clashed in a series of spectacles known as the North–South races. Initiated in 1823 when Eclipse, the northern champion, faced Sir Henry, the southern favorite, at $20,000 per side at a New York course, the contests continued for decades. The southern loss and blow to regional honor required a rematch at even greater stakes. Sir Henry's owner wrote: "Sir – I will run the horse Henry against the horse Eclipse at Washington city, next fall . . . for any sum from twenty to fifty thousand dollars; forfeit ten thousand dollars" (Menna 1995, 188). Such affairs became sporting spectacles that attracted enormous crowds. When Fashion, a northern thoroughbred, defeated Boston, a Virginia horse, in 1842, as many as 70,000, including forty US senators, witnessed the event (Kirsch 1992, 191). When Peytona reclaimed southern honor by defeating Fashion in 1845, an estimated 100,000 thronged to the course (Kirsch 1992, 199). The decline in horseracing thereafter terminated the regional contests, which paralleled the rising tensions between the northern and southern states that culminated in the American Civil War.

Sport was not only sport consumption, but also activity and recreation. Between 1820 and 1840 sports clubs were founded which met the taste of gentlemen and provided opportunities for social gatherings and conspicuous consumption.

BOX 2.6 WASHINGTON SOCIAL GYMNASIUM

At the beginning of the summer, a number of gentlemen (comprising such of members of the old Quoit club, as chose to unite) organized a new quoit and bowling club, under the name of the Washington Social Gymnasium. Having obtained a very eligible site for the purpose they erected an excellent bowling-house, and laid out two good quoit alleys, all well enclosed, and the whole costing about five hundred dollars. The regular meetings have been three a week (though many members attend every afternoon, to bowl or pitch) and these meetings have fully realized the objects of the association; namely health-giving exercise, and the cultivation of sociability and good feeling.

(*American Turf Register and Sporting Magazine*, 1838,
quoted in Menna 1995, 151)

Gymnastics, pedestrianism and sport competitions – tendencies in the mid-nineteenth century

The more liberal, rational thought spawned by the Enlightenment in Europe reached America and its sporting culture as well. A first gymnastic and health movement emerged, which promised to prevent or cure the diseases of inner city lifestyles (see Chapter 3). Women, too, began gradually to pursue calisthenics and gymnastics as a means to greater health in the first half of the nineteenth century (see Chapter 11) (Borish 1987).

At the same time pedestrianism became a fashion. It served as a means to find the limits of human potential, but also as a demonstration of national superiority and pride.

Pedestrianism involved long-distance walking or running races, which gained increasing interest by the 1830s. An 1835 account captured the great feat of endurance, quantified in accordance with the increasingly scientific, technological age.

> The great trial of human capabilities, in going ten miles within the hour, for $1,000, to which $300 was added, took place on Friday, on the Union Course, Long Island (New York); and we are pleased to state, that the feat was accomplished twelve seconds within the time, by a native born and bred American farmer, Henry Stannard of Killingworth, Connecticut. Two others went the ten miles- one a Prussian, in a half minute over; the other an Irishman, in one minute and three quarters over the time.
>
> (Menna 1995, 366)

Pedestrianism allowed for comparisons between races and ethnicities at a time when the United States was struggling to define its cultural identity. An 1844 spectacle drew as many as 30,000 spectators from as far away as England, in an attempt to see how great a distance could be covered in one hour (Menna 1995, 316). This race was enacted as a contest between whites and Native Americans.

BOX 2.7 PEDESTRIAN TRIALS

> It was a trial of the Indian against the white man, on the point in which the red man boasts his superiority. It was the trial of the peculiar American *physique* against the long held supremacy of English muscular endurance. It was a trial of middle age (in Major Stannard) against his own youthful achievements. *The White Man beat the Indian – the American beat the English*, and, with much better training, and much more mental stimulus, *the limbs of forty years failed to do the achievement of thirty!*
>
> (New York Clipper 1958, quoted in Kirsch 1992, 323)

The nativist sentiments apparent in the account became more distinct as greater numbers of ethnic immigrants fled the turmoil of Europe for the shores of America. The Irish potato famine created a wholesale exodus from that island, and the failed German Revolution of 1848 brought numerous immigrants, among them many turners, members of the gymnastic societies, to cities in the United States. The large-scale migration of "foreigners," who competed with the resident Anglos for jobs, elicited a continual and still ongoing debate over the nature of American society. White, Anglo-Saxon Protestants perceived themselves to be the true Americans, beset by the newcomers who threatened their religion, their rights, and their way of life (Riess 1995, 69, 87). The struggle for dominance in society was transferred to the sport arenas. Sport provided numerous occasions to show superiority which was believed to demonstrate or mirror social positions in "real life." Sport became an arena where conflicts could be enacted but not often solved.

The first of many ethnic confrontations in the boxing ring took on symbolic importance in an 1849 match between native-born Tom Hyer and the Irishman known as Yankee Sullivan. When Hyer won he declared himself "Champion of America" (Kirsch 1992, 129). Some immigrant groups assimilated more easily than others into the mainstream culture. The Scots, for instance, initiated their Caledonian Games in New York in 1857. The track and field events were soon incorporated into American competitions and adopted by the influential New York Athletic Club upon its founding in 1868. Cricket clubs, promoting the English pastime, competed for some time with the evolving game of baseball until the American Game achieved dominance in the latter half of the nineteenth century.

Status clubs, college sports, and professionalization

By the 1840s baseball clubs composed of a growing middle class and some craftsmen who had some control over their leisure hours proliferated in the New York and New Jersey area. By the 1860s baseball rose to prominence as the American national sport (see Chapter 4). In 1866 the New York Athletic Club (NYAC) was formed to promote track and field activities. These metropolitan associations used their recreational pursuits to establish status, or social capital, by restricting membership to equally affluent participants. Initiation fees soon amounted to $100 with annual dues of $50. To further distinguish their rank and eliminate "professionals" from their competitions in 1876 the NYAC only recognized individuals who had never accepted a prize or money, nor competed against a professional, or received compensation for having taught athletic exercises (Rader 1990, 87, 89). The NYAC furthermore rejected working-class athletes and, until the 1960s, African-Americans (Guttmann 2004, 125). In 1888, the NYAC spawned the Amateur Athletic Union (AAU) in conjunction with other clubs. For much of the next century the AAU controlled amateur sport in the United States. The AAU initially set the standards and eligibility requirements for amateur competitions in a host of sports. Its responsibility extended to the recruitment and organization of athletes for national teams and (until 1978) the Olympic Games. In the decades following the American Civil War the upper and middle classes organized athletic clubs in the pursuit of rowing, track and field, archery, tennis, cycling, and golf.

BOX 2.8 ON THE ROLE OF SPORT CLUBS

The development of modern sport with its orientation towards competitions and records was closely interrelated with institutionalization and bureaucratization.

In many countries, clubs and federations took charge of the establishment of rules, the registration of performances, and the control of competitions. In the US the principle of voluntary associations in numerous areas and with various aims was and is extremely popular, but sport clubs played a specific role among organizations. Sport clubs mushroomed in the nineteenth century. According to Rader (1977, 357), "the sport club of the nineteenth century provided a tremendous impetus to the growth of American sport." He explains the "take-off" of sport in the second half of the nineteenth century with the quest for subcommunities in a time of urbanization where identification with a small geographical area lost importance. However, sport clubs did not target the whole population. They were either ethnic sport clubs which helped immigrants to deal with the frictions of integration, or status sport clubs. Men's clubs served as meeting places for the elite; they offered networks, entertainment, and social distinction. Especially in the second half of the nineteenth century wealthy young men took an interest in athletics and founded men's sport clubs (e.g. the famous New York Amateur Athletic Club), which accepted initially only members of the upper classes. Both, ethnic and status sport clubs, were exclusive and thus could not become the responsible bodies for American sports.

At the same time, educational institutions took over the organization of competitions, and thus schools and colleges became – to a certain degree – the functional equivalent of European sport clubs.

(Gertrud Pfister)

Intercollegiate athletic competition began in 1852 when a railroad company enticed the crews of Harvard and Yale to compete at its lakeside resort for a prize and expenses. The scheme succeeded in publicizing the business venture and tying intercollegiate sport to a commercial enterprise. By the end of the decade college crews from several colleges tested each other in front of thousands of spectators, enhancing the rivalries between students (Kirsch 1992, 42). In 1869 the first intercollegiate football game took place, spawning the phenomenon that continues to enthrall students, alumni, and fans. Today more than 100,000 spectators crowd into the biggest college football stadiums each Saturday to witness the spectacle.

While the students initially adhered to the Victorian British concept of gentlemen amateurs, professionalism continued to develop in various sports. Championship billiards matches started in 1858, in which Michel Phelan won not only personal fame for his success, but publicity for his pool table manufacturing business as well. Other manufacturers would follow this model by assembling all-star teams to travel across the country advertising their wares and popularizing their sports. Both billiards and bowling utilized such a strategy as equipment manufacturers sought new markets; but the greatest success occurred in baseball. In 1869 Cincinnati businessmen organized a fully professional baseball team that embarked on a national tour, returning undefeated, bringing much acclaim to the Midwestern city. A regional rival, Chicago, fielded its own professional baseball team the following year and by 1876 a national league had been formed.

Professional athletes garnered a great amount of media attention and, in the eyes of critics, a disproportionate financial remuneration for their physical prowess. Their celebrity and salaries provided a measure of social capital while their physicality won admiration, especially among the working class. The first national sports hero, Irish-American heavy-weight boxing champion John L. Sullivan, bridged both class and ethnic divisions (Gorn and Goldstein 1993, 119–125).

Sport – struggles and unifications

The "Muscular Christianity" movement and the adoption of sport by such evangelical religious organizations as the Young Men's Christian Association (YMCA) showed the changing attitude towards sport but also the awareness of how sport could be used to attract and educate youth. By the latter part of the nineteenth century clergy extolled the benefits of wholesome athletic activities in combating sinful temptations. To that end organized sports programs might entice the bachelor subculture away from their traditional haunts, such as brothels and saloons. The belief that physical training might enhance willpower and build strong moral character had great appeal for Christian missionaries, teachers, and coaches (Putney 2001). Protestant reformers, known as Progressives, made use of sport and games to gain their objectives. They initiated the playground movement, public school athletic leagues, and urban settlement houses which offered education and physical activities in attempts to acculturate immigrant youth to the WASP value system.

While such initiatives tried to bring consensus to American culture, countervailing forces obstructed wholesale agreement. Ethnic groups sought to retain their European customs, languages, and lifestyles, among other things, by founding their own gymnastics and sport associations. Women sought greater rights, including sporting opportunities. By the mid-nineteenth century women were challenging the Victorian standards of decorum through their participation in recreational games and sports that precluded chaperones and allowed for a measure of freedom. Croquet, roller-skating, and cycling became fads throughout the remainder of the century. Cycling was more than a passing fashion. Its adherents formed a national organization, the League of American Wheelmen, that lobbied effectively for paved roads even before the advent of the automobile. In increasing numbers, men and women, too, joined the middle-class tennis and golf clubs that proliferated among the wealthier classes. The restrictive membership covenants of such associations, however, only reinforced the distinct ethnic, social class, and religious lines that separated American society.

56

SPORT DEVELOPMENTS IN THE TWENTIETH CENTURY

Although particular sport forms and restrictive sport clubs separated practitioners, the inclusion of sports within the public schools united disparate groups in a common interest as students and community residents began to identify with their school teams.

Divisions among the various groups of the American population became less distinct as mandatory education laws in the twentieth century delivered ethnic and working-class children from the workforce into the schools, where they were subjected to the Americanization efforts of teachers, coaches, and administrators. In the public high schools sport became a unifying force as school teams merged ethnic and even racial (in the northern states) members in the pursuit of a common goal.

By the 1920s media promoted athletes as heroes in the Golden Age of American sport and sport stars served as role models as well as diversions through the difficult years of the Depression and during World War II. The increasing importance of sport and athletes in American society can be judged by their popularity among youth.

By the 1920s the advent and popularization of radio and teeming sports pages in the myriad newspapers made local and national athletic heroes out of teenage boys and girls. Sociologists had already determined by that time that "the highest honor a senior boy can have is captaincy of the football or basketball team" (Miracle and Rees 1994, 66). Regardless of school size, geographical location, or social composition of the institute, interscholastic athletics dominated the school culture for the remainder of the century and continues to do so. Identification as an athlete far outweighed identification as a scholar with regard to popularity among peers (Miracle and Rees 1994, 66–67).

Even parents are likely to support athletic programs more so than the educational needs of their children due to the prestige and media attention accorded to athletes. In one case a town with a championship basketball team voted to build a new gymnasium, while the school remained without a library. Another town built a stadium and a large training facility for its football team despite an economic depression. In another location the school had no parent-teacher association but maintained a 1,200-member booster club for its football team (Miracle and Rees 1994, 165–168). Even junior high school students, both boys and girls, aim at a sport scholarship or a professional career, choose their sports, admire their heroes and model their appearance and lifestyles after their role models.

The growth of television brought greater ferment to the national sporting culture in the 1950s as fans opted to watch more talented professionals via television rather than support local or minor teams in person. The demise of minor leagues placed even greater emphasis on the professionalized, commercialized sport model. The competition among the teams encouraged professional franchises to leave their home cities and move to new locations where they enjoyed unrivaled television revenue and community support. Even the marriage of television and sport eventually proved a boon to team owners, broadcasters, and commercial sponsors. Only the players seemed left out of the financial bonanza, due to their restrictive contracts, which bound them to one team without the ability to negotiate their salaries (see Chapter 4).

The "athletic revolution" of the 1960s changed the face of top-level sport. Black athletes fought against discrimination, women demanded equal rights, and professional athletes joined together in labor unions, forcing owners to compromise their monopoly rights to labor. Charismatic athletes, like Muhammad Ali, challenged the racial, religious, and class foundations of American society (see Chapter 10). Women organized to gain access to so-called male sports and a fairer share of the profits in their professional sporting endeavors (see Chapter 11). In ensuing years athletes hired sports agents and lawyers to contest their grievances. Instead of fighting the commercialized structures of professional sports, they joined the system to reap even greater financial benefits.

BOX 2.9 HARRY EDWARDS AND THE REVOLT OF THE BLACK ATHLETE

There was, for God knows what reason, a generation of great athletes who came of age in a unique historical era around 1968 – Muhammad Ali, Curt Flood, Spencer Haywood, Smith and Carlos, Kareem Abdul-Jabbar, Mike Warren, Lucius Allen, the Harvard University Crew team, Jim Brown, and Bill Russell. To have such a collection of people come of age and speak out, and literally change the dynamics of an institution, to take up the struggle that was pioneered by Jackie Robinson, Joe Louis, and Jesse Owens, and elevate that struggle from a fight for access to a battle for respect and dignity and human rights – that was historic. That is what 1968 means to me as I look back on it. I was fortunate enough to have experienced it, to have been part of it, to know all of these people. I will always look back on this period as one of the greatest moments in my life and a watershed in the history of modern sports throughout the world.

("What Happened to the Revolt of the Black Athlete?" by David Leonard (http://www.colorlines.com/article.php?ID=118&limit=0&limit2=1000&page=1))

Alternative sports movements

Alternative sports allow the individual appropriation and expression of new forms of movement, promise authenticity, and bodily and emotional sensations by exploring new dimensions. They are an opportunity for the appropriation and demonstration of various skills. Participants find pleasure in the movement and the body itself, and experience thrills because of the risks involved in most of these practices (Rinehart and Sydnor 2003).

Alternative sports are intertwined with everyday lives and embedded in identities. In addition, they provide an arena to produce and demonstrate masculinity. The majority of participants are boys and men. However, women are increasingly involved in sports such as snow boarding or free climbing and they construct gender outside of the traditional gender order (Thorpe 2008). The new sports create rebellious images and provide status and prestige, at least among insiders. Adherents organize, at least for a certain period, their lives around their sports. These characteristics are typical for the "Californian sports," one "old" sport, surfing, and various new inventions such as hang gliding, skate boarding, mountain biking, and windsurfing, which emerged in the 1950s in a region where geography and weather present outstanding conditions for alternative living and sporting practices. Skate boarding is a child of surfing; the surf boards were equipped with rollers and the first skate boards were used by surfers when the ocean was too flat for "real" surfing. It soon spread throughout the States and is today popular among children and youth who rebel against the adult-controlled organized sports (Coakley 2004, 137–138). Another sport derived from surfing is wind surfing. The meaning of wind surfing for the participants is found in bodily sensations, in the creative and self-actualizing potential. Although participants invest heavily in their lifestyles and identities, this commitment is a commitment to pleasure, what they call the "buzz," the ecstasy of speed, being at one with the environment, the standing still of time, experiencing what Csikszentmihalyi (1990) describes as "flow" (Dant and Wheaton 2007, 10).

BOX 2.10 THRILL OF SURFING

"It's almost a spiritual thing, the feel good factor is so high – even if you've had a bad spell, it's better than not sailing at all – you know, like the buzz I get, the endorphin sort of buzz . . . and the mental spin-off . . . So I think it's terribly life-enhancing" (a windsurfer).

"Today, curiously a growing number of adepts share the attraction of the void and the extreme sensations it offers, through bungee jumping, skysurfing . . . Suicidal experiments on the inertia of a body . . . the relative wind of dizzying displacement, with no other aim than that of experiencing the heaviness of the body" (Paul Virilio).

(Rinehart and Sydnor 2003, 87, 127)

Not only the surf culture but also the landscape in California provided a playground for inventors and explorers of new dimensions. In 1961, Barry Palmer, an aeronautical engineer, inspired by a gliding wing developed by NASA, invented a gliding airfoil and tested various hang gliders east of Sacramento. Other enthusiasts with the dream of flying also experimented with gliding airfoils which developed into sport equipment in the 1970s. Hang gliding became especially popular among the Californian surf subculture (Wills and Wills 1984).

Another sport that spawns a sense of freedom is snow boarding, which developed in the 1970s. The first snow boards were inspired by sleds, skis, and skate boards and were produced in small workshops. Snow boarding developed swiftly as a form of resistance against the dominant culture of skiing and the values which it represented. Skiers demonstrate a high amount of economic, social, and cultural capital and enact it via their behavior patterns and skiing styles and their "taste" with regard to dress and equipment. Young people were attracted to the new sport, among other things, because of the similarity to skate boarding. They wear baggy clothes and enact a grunge/hip-hop/gangsta look (Thorpe 2008). With the spread of snow boarding, the media started to use, enact, and sell the notion of youthful rebellion, which triggered commodification processes. In addition, the quest of snow boarders for differentiation did not prevent the sport from sportification processes and adaptations to the demands of performance and records. The media, especially ESPN, produced the X Games to attract the more youthful, rebellious audience to the mainstream sport structure; and in 1998 snow boarding became an Olympic event. All alternative sports currently experience a huge commercialization process triggered and pushed by the mass media (Thorpe 2008).

Ever in quest of new markets the American sports machine continually repackages sport as entertainment, produces twenty-four-hour-a-day sports broadcasts, and continually invents new "sports" and new sports events to capture a seemingly insatiable American appetite. Championship games or tournaments are no longer singular events but mega-spectacles that require weeks of hype, constant analysis, and the continuous selling of products. Sport sociologists have claimed that "While we may be seduced into thinking that media outlets are providing a public service by satiating the nation's appetite for sport, the cold reality is the media have no inherent interest in sport. It is merely a means for profit making . . . For TV and radio, sport gets consumers in front of their sets to hear and see commercials; in effect, TV and radio rent their viewers' and listeners' attention" (Andrews, 2006, 9). (See Chapters 13 and 14.)

the evolution of American sports

CHAPTER THREE

A NATION OF IMMIGRANTS

INTRODUCTION

This chapter focuses on one of the most striking peculiarities of the United States – its emergence from small and distant settlements, small "islands" in the huge vastness of the American continent, to a superpower. It describes the growing together of various groups of immigrants, with numerous conflicts and struggles, to a nation with its inclusion and

THE TENEMENT PLAYGROUND.

Figure 3.1 Tenement houses (Curtis 2006 [1915], 5)

exclusion processes, its power struggles and its hierarchies, based among other things on the ethnic origins.

Each group of immigrants from the English Puritans in the sixteenth century to the Mexicans today brought their specific cultures and ideologies, but also body cultures, sport, and recreational activities. Previous scholars have interpreted the integration of immigrants as fusion in a melting-pot, similar to cooking an ethnic stew; but more recent analyses have characterized American society more like a salad bowl, in which the varied ethnic ingredients retain some of their distinct cultural flavors (Steinberg 1989).

This chapter explores the process of Americanization and the role of physical activities in this process, the contribution of the various groups of immigrants to the current dominant sport culture; but also the role of remaining "ethnic" sports.

Most immigrants brought the physical culture of their home country and continued to play their "ethnic" sports in America. Hurling for the Irish, *Turnen* for the Germans, and Sokol gymnastics for the Czechs were both recreation and entertainment, but also served as anchors of ethnic identity, and created and sustained social networks. Immigrants, especially the second and third generation, participated in American pastimes; many even excelled in sports like boxing, baseball, football, and basketball. Thus, sport participation, performances, and success could become a demonstration of Americanness, a symbol of social integration, and an opportunity for upward mobility, even if this way was open for only a very few. (For an overview of immigrants and their sports see Kirsch *et al.* 2000.)

In addition, in this chapter we will describe how physical activities and sport were used to assimilate immigrants into American society. Company sport served to Americanize the immigrant workers, and in so-called settlement houses, but also in playgrounds and in schools, reformers, teachers, and school authorities tried to educate immigrant children and youth with the help of sports and games.

SPORTING ACTIVITIES OF NATIVE AMERICANS AND EARLY EXPLORERS

A nation of immigrants seems to be a contradiction in terms. A nation usually requires a common language and culture to create a uniform identity. The United States, however, has always been and continues to be a country populated by an ongoing stream of immigrants. The first migrants arrived from Asia, traveling across the Bering Strait from Siberia to Alaska; but estimates on their sojourn vary widely from 12,000 to 70,000 years ago. They adapted to the new land as hunters, fishermen, and farmers, and by the 1500s an estimated 2,000,000 inhabited North America in various tribes, speaking as many as 300 different languages (*National Geographic* 1991, 2A; Josephy 1991). Most of these Native Americans resided on the East Coast of the continent. Anthropologists estimate that at least 1,000,000 inhabited the eastern woodlands at the close of the fifteenth century (*National Geographic* 2007). The ways of life, the provision of food, the cultural practices, differed by geographic location; but the tribes practiced physical activities like running or archery as utilitarian sports in tests of skill and endurance. Virtually all the North American tribes engaged in dances and some form of ball games. However, physical activities not only had "practical" benefits, they were a means to enjoyment; but they were also embedded in the Indians' spiritual lives and served as a means to social cohesion, as has been described more in depth in Chapter 2 (Anderson 2006).

The Vikings had reached North America by 1000 ACE, but did not establish any permanent settlements. Five hundred years later, Spanish explorers traveled through the southeast in the ensuing decades and by 1650 the Dutch, English, French, and Swedes sent traders and colonists to North America. The Dutch established trading posts and established a colony in the Hudson Valley south of New Amsterdam, today's New York. The Swedes, in striving to compete with the Dutch and English merchants, founded settlements in the same area, but their New Sweden was conquered after seventeen years by the Dutch. France claimed a large territory in today's Canada and in the area of the Great Lakes. French explorers followed the Mississippi to its delta and named the territory Louisiane after King Louis XIV. They controlled the Mississippi River and its vast drainage system, even into the Great Plains.

The European encroachment had disastrous effects on the Native population. Wracked by contagious diseases, the Indians, as they were mistakenly called by the Europeans, soon dwindled to fewer than 40 percent of their pre-European population levels. By 1890 the remaining Native Americans in the entire United States numbered only 228,000 (*National Geographic* 2007; Washburn 1991, 558).

European immigrants undertook the long, dangerous and exhausting passage over the Atlantic Ocean for various reasons and with a broad range of aims. Some of the European colonists migrated for economic reasons; others sought relief from religious persecution in their home countries. British nobles and entrepreneurs organized commercial ventures, while the French sought the lucrative fur trade with the Native tribes.

Indentured servants tried to escape the misery in their home country and traded their labor for periods usually ranging from four to seven years for the passage to the Promised Land. The indentured labor system was developed as a reaction to the shortage of farm laborers and the lack of skilled craftsmen. By contract, the indentured servants sold their labor, but in practice they were often treated as slaves. At the end of the eighteenth century, one half to two-thirds of the population of colonial America had arrived on the new continent as indentured servants (Galson 1981). A variety of religious dissenters or oppressed sects founded communities in the New World where they were able to practice their faith free of restriction. By the end of the seventeenth century the British had conquered the Dutch colony as the follow up of the second Anglo–Dutch War and absorbed the Dutch and Swedish settlers.

In the eighteenth century the British and French battled over control of the eastern and central portions of North America, while Spain pushed northward from Mexico and established a system of religious missions in southern regions, especially in California, where Native Americans learned Christianity and the methods of European farming. These self-contained Catholic communities were connected with streets and grew into towns like San Diego or Santa Barbara.

BRITISH SETTLERS, BRITISH PASTIMES, AND THE RISE OF AN ANGLO CULTURE IN AMERICA

The victory in the French and Indian War (1756–1763) gave England control over eastern Canada and all lands west to the Mississippi, and allowed for the ascendance of Anglo culture in the thirteen colonies along the Atlantic seaboard. In these colonies, despite some religious differences, the English settlers continued to practice the customs, language, and recreations familiar to their ancestral homeland. Also in the following periods, British immigrants continued to cross the Atlantic in search of a new life. The British heritage is the most important ingredient in the "salad bowl" of America. Approximately 78 percent of Americans derived their ancestry from the British Isles (English, Scotch, Irish) and 99 percent of the British immigrants adhered to Protestantism (Steinberg 1989, 7–8).

Excursus: sports, games, and merriment in Britain

Since the Middle Ages, a wide variety of sporting pastimes had developed in Britain, which became the "cradle and focus" of sportification processes and modern sport. During feudalism, sports such as tournaments, tennis, or hunting were a prerogative of people of the upper ranks who had leisure time and money to indulge in sporting activities. Physical education was part of the education of young noble men (Barber and Barker 1989; Carter 1988). The Tudors, especially Henry VIII (1509–1547), were sport enthusiasts. Henry VIII was famous for his strength and skill in, among other sports, wrestling, dancing, fencing, archery, and jousting. Other activities enjoyed by the noblemen were throwing a stone or a hammer, jumping, and running, but also less strenuous games like shuffleboard. It was fashionable to have a shuffleboard table in the great hall of the mansions.

Widespread and very popular "sporting" entertainments were fights between animals, like bear baiting or cock fighting, events which were referred to as sports in the terminology of the time (Krzemienski 2004; Townson 1997). Strutt (1802/1903)[1] describes in his overview about "Sports and Pastimes of the People of England" the large variety of shows, festivals, acrobatic performances, theaters, pageantries, merriment, and amusements; the largest shows, the most sophisticated enactments and most expensive festivities took place at the royal court.

Sport was a privilege to which commoners had limited or no access. In 1512, a law forbade ordinary people from participating in games like tennis, bowling, or skittles. In 1540,

64

football, a wild game without rules, was banned, because it endangered the lives and limbs of the participants.

With the dissolution of the feudal order, common people could enjoy a huge variety of leisure and sport activities. Strutt (1903) reports on the physical activities of Londoners in the eighteenth century: "The lower classes divert themselves at football, wrestling, cudgels, nine-pins, shovelboard, cricket, stowball, ringing of bells, quoits, pitching the bar, bull and bear baitings, throwing at cocks," and, worst of all, "lying at ale-houses." To these are added by Maitland, an author of a later date in his *History of London* (Maitland 1756), published in 1739, "Sailing, rowing, swimming and fishing, in the river Thames, horse and foot races, leaping, archery, bowling in allies, and skittles, tennice [*sic*], chess, and draughts; and in the winter seating, sliding, and shooting." Other sources mention even more physical activities and games. The pastimes here enumerated were by no means confined to the city of London or its environs: the larger part of them were in general practice throughout the kingdom.

In the eighteenth century, horseraces, cricket, and prize fighting developed into sporting spectacles and businesses, financed by gambling. At the same time sport began to move from the premodern to modern stages as it assumed the guiding principles of equal access, competition, and record orientation, and particular characteristics such as secularism, rationalization, bureaucratization, quantification, and commercialization, a greater sense of equality, and specialization (Guttmann 1978).

BOX 3.1 ENGLAND AS "CRADLE" OF MODERN SPORT

Long before the Industrial Revolution, horseracing, boxing, pedestrian races, and cricket in Britain were organized in a fashion decidedly different from the Continent. The reason . . . lays in England's distinct "social configuration". The early dissolution of feudalism in Britain left peasants free to pursue their rough games. More importantly, the relative independence of the aristocracy from the monarchy produced a wide range of rural pastimes rather than a narrow courtly style of sports. Finally, the unique balance of freedom and authority in the public schools, where peer standards rather than external authority counted most, encouraged boys to play, innovate, and govern their own games, games which subsequently served as the basis for the sports boom in the late-nineteenth century.

(Baker 1980, 333–335)

BRITISH IMMIGRANTS AND THEIR SPORTING PRACTICES

The British immigrants brought a wealth of physical activities and sports to their new home country; but due to the hardships of life, the lack of facilities and equipment, and the need to address the basic needs for survival, it was difficult to practice the pastimes and amusements of "merry England" in their new home country. Sports did not blossom initially in the new land. Activities such as hunting and fishing, which offered recreational pleasures in England, became utilitarian necessities in the New World.

Another reason for the relative scarcity of entertainments and amusements, especially in the northern colonies, was the commitment of many settler communities to various Protestant sects which had one thing in common: the contempt and disapproval of sports and games which did not serve useful aims. They were looked upon as a distraction from religious service and forbidden by law (see Chapter 2).

In spite of the restrictions caused by religious leaders, the upper classes in the southern colonies amused themselves with traditional British sports such as cricket, horseracing, and billiards (Altherr 1997; Struna 1996). As already described in Chapter 2, common sporting interests and practices in various regions over time helped to establish a sense of community, at least among the white settlers. Even in the New England colonies men gathered regularly for military muster days to train for defense, and on such occasions they engaged in sports and frequented the local taverns that offered a variety of amusements.

That sense of commonality grew stronger with the colonists' Revolutionary War (1776–1781) against their British overlords and the adoption of a democratic political ideology and practice. The Americans were proud of their system, which endeavored to establish justice, equality, and political rights. They were proud of their republic which offered so many more opportunities than the monarchies that ruled the rest of the world. Although wealthy aristocratic landowners had already emerged in the south during the colonial period and a burgeoning merchant class appeared in the north, the American citizens believed that they lived in a society devoid of social classes in which every man was the equal of another and endowed with inalienable rights (although women and slaves still held inferior roles).

The new United States of America had doubled both its territory and its population by 1820 (from 4,000,000 to 9,600,000); but only about 250,000 of that number consisted of immigrants. The relative dearth of immigration from countries other than Britain strengthened the Anglo roots of the nascent American culture. The British influence was also dominant in the emerging sport movement where sports and games of British origin were adopted and/or adapted to the needs of American society. Collective memories and "invented traditions" (Hobsbawn 1997) transformed especially football and baseball to America's own sports (see Chapters 4 and 5).

BOX 3.2 THE AMERICANIZATION OF BRITISH SPORTS

The British sport model had the biggest influence on the movement culture in America, because the British immigrants formed not only the dominant class but also mainstream society. But sport developed in the USA quite differently from its British origin. On the one hand, sport and its ideology were rooted in the British public schools and had a middle- and upper-class orientation. The British ideal was the gentleman amateur with a special definition of fair play and a special attitude relative to winning and losing. The Corinthians (London), the most famous amateur soccer team, resisted, for example, the penalty kick because they believed that gentlemen would never commit a deliberate foul. Winning was not a goal in itself; on the contrary, failure could be glorious if one had done his best. In America, these ideals soon changed into the winning-at-all-costs mentality, and the British sports of soccer and cricket had to be re-invented as American games in order to be accepted by American society.

The American Revolution had opened the frontier to the West. A new type of migration emerged. Fortune seekers and land-hungry pioneers became the advance element in the conquest of the West after the victory over the British. By 1820 more than 2,000,000 had migrated to the western frontier in search of free lands. The frontier experience would later be credited with the development of an exceptional American character that distinguished Americans from other nations (Garraty 1983, 184).

The migration to the West entailed both opportunities and challenges in the way of hardships, dangers, and strenuous work. The adventurers to the western lands had to be a hardy type, usually lacking the resources or education to become entrepreneurs in the East. Their pastimes often centered around local taverns (detailed in Chapter 2). One unique American sport, however, developed in the southwest, where the cowboys on Spanish ranches developed the rodeo as a means to practice their work-related skills in competitions.

IRISH, GERMAN, AND SCANDINAVIAN IMMIGRANTS AND THEIR CONTRIBUTION TO AMERICAN SPORTING CULTURE

The Anglo nature of American culture began to change after 1840 as immigration intensified. In the following decade 1,713,000 newcomers traveled to the United States, and another 2,598,000 in the 1850s. A million and a half of these new immigrants were largely illiterate, poor Irish peasants who fled the potato famine of their native isle. Nearly a million Germans arrived in the 1850s, many fleeing the failed revolution of 1848. The 48ers were politically engaged, adherents of socialist ideas, and well educated, and they became an influential group in American society (Blum *et al.* 1977, 311; Hofmann 2001).

The rising numbers of immigrants from countries other than Great Britain provoked resistance among the Anglo population who saw themselves as the rightful heirs to the American Dream and the defenders of American customs and values. As a reaction to immigration, a nativist movement emerged. Nativists (individuals born in the USA, who considered themselves the rightful heirs to its benefits) viewed newcomers with disdain, among other things, because the immigrants posed an economic threat to workers as a labor force willing to work for lower wages than the Anglos. Newspapers advertised for workers, but with the addendum that "No Irish need apply."[2] In addition, religious, moral, ethnic, and cultural differences as well as foreign languages were perceived as threats to the American community. Many of the new immigrants were Catholics, who were suspected of loyalty to the Pope and thus not faithful citizens of the new republic. In the mid-nineteenth century a secret nativist society was founded, called the "Know Nothings" for their refusal to divulge the secrets of their clandestine operations. Later, the nativist American party flourished for a short while.

BOX 3.3 CATHOLICS AS ENEMIES

William G. Brownlow, a nativist author, wrote in 1856:

> Every Roman Catholic in the known world is under the absolute control of the Catholic Priesthood . . . and cause a vast multitude of ignorant foreigners to vote as a unit, and thus control the will of the American people . . . It is this aggressive policy and corrupting tendency of the Romish Church; this organized and concentrated political power of a distinct class of men; foreign by birth; inferior in intelligence and virtue to the American people . . . which have called forth the opposition . . . to the Catholic Church.
>
> (quoted in Blum *et al.* 1977, 313)

The fear of immigrant incursions reached a peak in the 1850s as the Know Nothings won more than 100 seats in the congressional elections (Foner and Garraty 1991, 780; Wills 2005, 44). Although the American party split over the issue of slavery and declined, nativist sentiments continue to play a role in American society today.

Irish immigrants and their games

The Irish immigrants, many of whom were peasants or farmers in their home country, with few marketable skills, settled largely in the American urban centers, where they assumed the factory jobs previously held by young Anglo women, or offered their physical labor as construction workers and ditch diggers. The Irish maintained the connections with their ancestral homeland in Gaelic associations and had funneled as much as 4 to 5 million dollars per year to Ireland by 1860 (Handlin 1951, 260). With their ability to speak English the Irish were able to assume leadership roles in both politics and the burgeoning labor movement throughout the nineteenth century. The Irish were and remain a fixture in the guidance of the Democratic Party. The Irish dominated the police force and the fire-fighting departments because the urban politicians relied on political patronage and provided service occupations in exchange for votes.

The Irish brought their national sports, such as hurling and Gaelic football, to American shores. In both games teams of fifteen compete with each other. The aim is to hit the ball through the goal posts of the opponent. In hurling, a small ball is batted with a stick. Gaelic football is a combination of basket ball and soccer; players advance the ball with a combination of carrying, kicking, and throwing to their team-mates. Hurling and Gaelic football were played by Irish immigrants since their arrival in America. In the second half of the nineteenth century clubs were founded, many of them in the large industrial cities like New York, Cleveland, Chicago, or Philadelphia. According to Darby (2006, 60),

> Gaelic games had been woven into the fabric of Chicago's Irish community . . . For those of a sporting disposition, the significance of the Gaelic football or hurling club in smoothing the transition from what was in many cases a rural background to a fast-paced and often frenetic urban environment cannot be overestimated.

However, both games were played by immigrants of the first generation, but discarded by their sons in favor of American sports. Still, Irish culture has become closely integrated with the American mainstream, and the annual St. Patrick's Day festival is celebrated by Americans regardless of their ethnic heritage. Cities promote their St. Patrick's Day parades, taverns throughout America serve green beer, and in Chicago the river is even dyed green for the occasion.

Germans, German *Turnen*, and *Turner* clubs as "cradles of ethnicity"

The early German immigrants settled largely in the cities or farms of the Midwest. Many were skilled craftsmen, and Germans vied with the Irish and native Anglos for leadership of the growing labor unions.

Like the Irish, the German immigrants, too, retained ties to their roots; but Germany did not become a united country until 1870. "In 1837 there was a falling-out among the men planting a new settlement in Illinois. One faction wished the name of the township to be Westphalia, another, Hannover, each after its own native land. The compromise was significant – Germantown; the language took them all in" (Handlin 1951, 187). The unification of Germany as a nation-state was the dream of many Germans, and many of the refugees who came to the USA after the failure of the 1848 revolution had fought for a united Germany. The German refugees, called "48ers," brought with them a specific concept of physical activities, known as *Turnen*. *Turnen* and the *Turner* clubs typified the roles and functions of physical cultures and ethnic associations in the lives of immigrants as well as in mainstream society.

BOX 3.4 *TURNEN* – ITS PRINCIPLES AND PRACTICES

The *Turnen* movement originated in Prussia in the early nineteenth century as an educational and a political movement. The aims of Friedrich Ludwig Jahn and his followers were to liberate Germany from French occupation, to overthrow the feudal order, and to form a German nation-state. *Turnen* was a comprehensive concept of games and physical activities ranging from climbing to running and from wrestling to playing games. The principles of *Turnen*, though, differed fundamentally from those of the kind of modern sport that was developing in England (see p. 64). The *Turner* did not attach any importance to records and abstract performance; instead, they used a person's height, for example, as the criterion for judging a high jump; they preferred all-round exercising of the body to specialization; and they strove to improve the "nation's strength" rather than individual performance. The *Turner* movement aimed to include the whole (male) population. In 1820 *Turnen* was banned for being part of the liberal movement; in the 1840s it enjoyed a revival when the *Turner* played a vital role in the foredoomed bourgeois revolution.

(Pfister 1996)

The *Turnen* movement in the USA

Turnen had already been introduced to educational institutions in New England in the early 1820s by the German political exiles Karl Beck, Karl Follen, and Franz Lieber. Although *Turnen* had an enthusiastic start on the American continent, its success lasted for only a few years (Hofmann and Pfister 2004).

It was only a quarter of a century later, in 1848, that the first *Turner* clubs were founded in the US by the 48ers. In 1851, they joined together and established an umbrella organization, the "Socialistischer Turnerbund von Nordamerika," later Nordamerikanischer Turnerbund (North American Gymnastic Union).

The *Turner* movement saw itself as a nursery for revolutionary ideas, and it promoted a form of socialism that concentrated on the rights and freedoms of individuals, and opposed monarchy and the religious indoctrination of the people. The political attitudes of the *Turner* reflected the opinions of the freethinkers, an anti-religious movement that advocated rationalism and science. *Turner* and freethinkers joined forces in their fight against American nativism, the system of slavery as well as the temperance and Sabbath-day laws. Throughout the nineteenth century, the "*Turner* societies" had a strong political orientation.

In the nineteenth and early twentieth centuries the *Turner* association may be interpreted as a "subcommunity" (Rader 1977) and "cradle of ethnicity" (Conzen 1989). *Turner* clubs were places where German (later German-American) culture and traditions were fostered. *Turner* clubs offered physical activity classes according to the concept of German *Turnen*. The emphasis was on gymnastics on various apparatus, but also on gymnastic exercises without equipment, which had similarities with calisthenics. Athletics and games lost importance when *Turnen* was transferred from open grounds to *Turner* halls. But "*Turner* halls" were also places where not only the German language but also German customs and festivities were preserved. *Turner* clubs were social centers where people could meet, participate in political debates, listen to lectures, attend Sunday schools, and use the library. The attached restaurants or bars were popular places for networking and German *Gemütlichkeit* (sociability). Just like other ethnic groups, the Germans had to fight the hostility of native-born Americans who did not approve of the high rate of immigration into their country (Hofmann 2001, 140; Hofmann 2008).

In contrast to the *Turners* in Germany who refused access to women until the end of the nineteenth century, *Turner* classes for women were introduced in the USA starting in the 1860s and many societies established a "Ladies Auxiliary" during that time. As an auxiliary the women baked goods, arranged picnics and other social affairs, and raised funds for the welfare of the *Turner* clubs. However, they were not accepted as club members and had no influence on the *Turner* movement as a whole (Pfister and Hofmann 2004).

The *Turners* continued their political activities in their new homeland. Most of them supported the political goals of the Republicans during the 1850s and 1860s. They served as Lincoln's bodyguard during his first inauguration and they formed *Turner* regiments at the beginning of the Civil War in 1861. For the 48ers the participation in the war served as their "second fight for freedom" (Hofmann 2001, 152),

In the years after the Civil War the *Turnerbund* dropped "socialist" from its name in order to signal its depoliticization. The *Turners* then focused more on culture and education, although political topics continued to be discussed in the *Turner* organizations and some clubs were active in the American workers' riots during the 1870s and 1880s (Gems 2009).

The peak of the American *Turner* movement was reached in 1894. At that time 317 societies existed with approximately 40,000 members, more than 25,000 children and around 3,000 women participating in the activity classes (Hofmann 2001, 166). This boom had ceased by World War I, a time when the remaining radical and socialistic tendencies in the *Turner* movement had also declined. Reasons for this decline were the generation shift and the increasing integration of the Germans into the American mainstream.

The Americanization was intensified by the anti-German politics of the American government in the years between 1914 and 1918. Many Americans with a German background were accused of lacking loyalty to the American nation. This resulted in a prohibition of the German language in schools and universities, the elimination of German journals and newspapers, and the Americanization of German names, whether of individuals, streets, towns, organizations, or societies. In the years after World War I the *Turner* movement became more and more Americanized, and the number of *Turner* associations continued to drop.

In 2009 there were still fifty-four societies that belonged to the umbrella organization the American *Turners*. Today, social get-togethers dominate association life, and the former German-American associations have grown into multiethnic societies, mostly with members from different European immigrant groups.

The Germans had gained political power in midwestern cities, mostly espousing liberal and even socialist views, and their election to school boards allowed for the introduction of the German language, kindergartens, and German *Turnen* to the school curriculums. In the so-called struggle of the systems, the *Turners* tried to establish *Turnen* as the dominant concept in American physical education (Pfister 2009). Although they did not succeed,

Figure 3.2 German *Turnverein* class, Chicago 1885; Photographer: Schollz (Chicago History Museum)

some of the *Turner* principles and exercises survived in the physical education curriculums. As in other countries, gymnastics became a modern, competitive sport which gained a modest measure of popularity in the US.

German lifestyles and assimilation

The Germans maintained their European culture not only in the *Turner* societies, but also in choral groups, shooting associations, and beer halls, family recreational venues that differed sharply from the homosocial saloons of the Anglos, which catered to a bachelor subculture. The Germans differed not only in language and recreational practices from the native Anglos but in their observance of the Sabbath. While the Anglo Protestants favored a strict observance of church and prayer, the Germans sought recreation and entertainment.

Germans gained prominence in several fields, including newspaper publishing, the meat-packing industries of the Midwest, and as brewers. Adolphus Busch settled in St. Louis in 1857, where he established a brewery that featured lighter, lagered beers. The new pasteurization process and refrigerated railway cars enabled shipment of the product on a national basis and Busch's Budweiser brand became the most popular beer in the United States by the twentieth century (Wills 2005, 149). The Busch family and other German brewers, such as Chris Von der Ahe, would purchase American professional baseball teams as a mark of their Americanization. The already mentioned anti-German sentiments fostered by the American entry into World War I eventually forced many Germans to reach accommodation with the American Anglo culture, many even Anglicizing their surnames to gain greater acceptance in the mainstream Anglo society.

Skiing – the heritage of Scandinavians

Scandinavians reveled in the harsh winter conditions of the northern states. They introduced their old-world pastimes, such as snow-shoeing and skiing. In the 1850s, they delivered mail to the gold-mining communities in California by skiing on their "Norwegian snow-shoes" through the mountains. In addition, "itinerant preachers – usually of Norwegian heritage – used skis to bring . . . spiritual message to remote, snowbound communities" (Fry 2006, 5). Besides the mail delivery and missionary activities, snow-shoes were used for downhill races "that pitted individuals from several camps against each other for large sums of money" (Allen 2007, 217). Women, too, participated in ski races, a sign of the liberality of the frontier community.

The Scandinavians lived in agricultural, logging, and mining communities in the Midwest and imported their skis and the art of skiing, which consisted of cross-country skiing and the much more popular and exciting ski jumping. The ski-jumping competitions contributed decisively to the propagation of skiing in the US. Ski jumper Mikkel Hemmestvedt

Figure 3.3 Children sledding (Library of Congress)

claimed the championship of Norway before migrating to Red Wing, Minnesota in 1886, where he garnered the American record as well (Gems 1996a, 482). He was one of many Norwegians who gained fame and money. In the following years, Norwegian ski jumpers would entertain fascinated audiences in Barnum and Bailey's circus, thus making ski jumping known among the American population. In the 1930s, a Norwegian woman, ski jumper Johanne Kolstad, became famous in the USA. As Queen of the Skis she not only performed in the on-ice shows but jumped 72m (Hofmann and Preuss 2005). Competitions demand organization, and the Scandinavians began forming skiing clubs in the 1880s in Minnesota, Michigan, and Wisconsin. In 1891, ski jumpers founded one of the nation's oldest enduring ski clubs in Ishpeming, Michigan which would later spawn the National Ski Association.

Since the turn of the century an increasing number of Norwegians came to the ski areas of the US to work as skiing teachers. Ski schools enhanced their reputation if they had a European ski instructor on their payroll. In the 1920s and 1930s the Norwegians lost their dominance in this sport, and the Americans took over in developing skiing, even inventing new forms as free-style skiing.

THE WESTERN FRONTIER AS A MELTING-POT

The vast lands of the American continent and the government offer of free farmland were an attractive enticement to many immigrants. Europeans settled throughout much of the territory from the Mississippi River to the West Coast of California on small farms, ranches, and in the latter case, vineyards and wineries.

The Germans joined a variety of European ethnic groups as farmers on the western frontier. The federal Homestead Act of 1862 provided virtually free land in the west to anyone willing to commit to a five-year residence (Foner and Garraty 1991, 509–510). In 1864 the Kansas legislature established a Bureau of Immigration and sent special agents to Europe to promote the opportunities available in the state. Immigration companies in New York and Chicago also tried to attract Europeans to the United States and railroad companies promoted immigration as a means to sell surplus land grants, which had been awarded to them by the US Congress in reward for building the transportation networks. Swedes began arriving in the 1860s, followed by a group of Scots who settled in northern Kansas in 1869. In the1870s German-Russians (both Mennonites and Catholics) made their way to Kansas, followed by Bohemians, Norwegians, Dutch, Danes, and French. Three British settlements, appropriately named Wakefield, Victoria, and Runnymede, appeared on the Kansas prairies (Stratton 1981, 225–226).

Sir George Grant, a London silk merchant, embarked on an American tour in 1872, and liked the potential that he envisioned in Kansas. He bought 50,000 acres from a Kansas railroad company and subsequently founded a British colony at Victoria with immigrants of noble descent and more plebeian Scots and Irish residents. The noble English families

75

sent sheep, horses, and cattle to stock the farms of their children, who soon attempted to re-create the pastimes of their homeland. Both men and women engaged in fox-hunts dressed in proper attire; and if foxes proved in short supply, they chased rabbits and coyotes. By 1876, however, most had returned to England due to the frontier hardships; and by 1878 the whole colony was gone – moved to the new town of Hays (Stratton 1981, 225–230).

The hardships encountered on the frontier are evident in the remonstrations of an early settler, S.N. Hoisington, who had emigrated to the United States at age 7 in 1871. "In the summer of 1872 and '73, the gray wolves and coyotes were very numerous. It was not safe to go out across the prairies without a weapon of some kind" (Stratton 1981, 80–81, 283).

BOX 3.5 DAILY LIFE ON THE PRAIRIE

In its isolation, the pioneer family existed as a self-sufficient unit that took pride in its ability to provide for itself and persevere in the face of hardship. Men and women worked together as partners, combining their strengths and talents to provide food and clothing for themselves and their children. As a result, women found themselves on a far more equal footing with their spouses . . . Pioneer life was not all hardship and danger . . . And there was the compensation of contact with the great new West – a new world – theirs to develop from wild prairie to comfortable homes . . . The pioneer Kansas woman shared her husband's work and interest in the garden, the orchard, the crops and animals of the farm; she worked in the garden and gathered its products. She knew just how each vineyard or tree in the young orchard was coming in. She shared in the hopes for a bountiful crop as the field thing sprouted and grew green and tall. Did a horse, dog or other farm animal get badly gored, cut or wounded, hers was the task to cleanse the wound and take the stitches that drew the torn edges together.

(Stratton 1981, 57)

Settlers faced prairie fires in the summer, drought, winter blizzards, floods, swarms of locusts and hailstorms that destroyed their crops, rattlesnakes, and tornadoes. Winter temperatures reached between 0–20 degrees F (–18 C –29 C), and with no abundance of trees or wood on the prairies, many were forced to construct sod houses to withstand the elements (Stratton 1981). Harsh environment and hard work left not a lot of time and energy for sporting activities. Early settlers might hunt buffalo, deer, antelope, wild turkeys, quail, and prairie chickens for sustenance; and horse-back riding was a necessity, as settlers made regular trips to the nearest towns for their supplies.

Despite such trying conditions, the pioneers endured, often finding solace in their religion and communal festivals. Protestants tended to share religious services in makeshift accommodations in homes or small towns, while Catholics generally waited to form their own church parishes. Women often engaged in the jobs typically reserved for men, but this was often a double burden, doing the housework (which was tedious and heavy without any of the amenities of civilization like running water) and hard work on the farm. Sometimes they enjoyed more freedom in the West than women elsewhere. By the 1860s a Kansas community featured for example a horse-back riding contest for women, which had eight entrants (Stratton 1981, 142). From the 1880s, women also participated in the rodeos and Wild West shows, often as "bronc riders." They had learned their skills helping with the chores at their parents' ranches. As the sharp shooters and the professional weight lifters in the circus, "they defied traditional gender roles by becoming professional athletes in traditionally 'male' sports. Yet virtually all of them were married, and they enjoyed reasonably fair treatment from the press" (LeCompte 1993, 34). The western region would be the first to grant women the right of suffrage, with Wyoming, Utah, Colorado, and Idaho granting voting rights by 1896 (Garraty 1983, 571).

JEWS AND THE FIGHT AGAINST STEREOTYPES

Immigration and lifestyles

The repression of Jews in Eastern Europe led to a Jewish diaspora in the late nineteenth century. Eventually, by the twenty-first century, the United States would accommodate 6,000,000 Jews, more than any country in the world, including Israel (Wills 2005, 80). German Jews, Yiddish speakers (a combination of medieval German and the Hebrew language), settled in the urban centers throughout the United States, often establishing themselves as merchants and trying to assimilate into mainstream American culture. Their religion, however, marked them as different; and Jews often faced prohibitive restrictions to membership in business and athletic clubs.

BOX 3.6 ARRIVAL IN AMERICA

His heart had sunk at the sight of his wife's uncouth and un-American appearance. She was slovenly dressed in a brown jacket and skirt of grotesque cut, and her hair was concealed under a voluminous wig of a pitch-black hue . . . The wig, however, made her seem stouter and shorter than she would have appeared without it. It also added at least five years to her looks.

At length, when the secluded corner had been reached, and Jake and Gitl had set down their burdens, husband and wife flew into mutual embrace and fell to kissing each other . . . Their kisses imparted the taste of mutual estrangement to both. In Jake's case the sensation was quickened by the strong steerage odors which were emitted by Gitl's person, and he involuntarily recoiled.

Gitl, on her part, was overcome with a feeling akin to awe. She, too, could not get herself to realize that this stylish young man – shaved and dressed as in Povodye is only some young nobleman – was Yekl, her own Yekl . . . And while she was once more examining Jake's blue diagonal cutaway, glossy stand-up collar, the white four-in-hand necktie, coquettishly tucked away in the bosom of his starched shirt, and, above all, his patent leather shoes, she was at the same time mentally scanning the Yekl of three years before. The latter alone was hers, and she felt like crying to the image to come back to her and let her be *his* wife.

(Cahan 1896)

Under the leadership of Rabbi Isaac Mayer Wise, some American Jews practiced a reformed version of Judaism, rather than the strict, more conservative Orthodoxy favored by some Eastern European Jews. Many of the reformed Jews enjoyed considerable success as bankers in the United States. August Belmont (1813–1890), a native of Germany, a banker and politician, also became a renowned sportsman, owner of a racing stable, and founder of the Belmont Stakes, one of the most prestigious horseraces in America (Wills 2005, 82–83). His son, the second August Belmont, inherited his father's obsession with horses. He was chairman of the Jockey Club, founded Belmont Park (a famous racetrack on Long Island, New York), and owned many successful horses. As a student at Harvard he competed as a sprinter, and later became an excellent equestrian and polo player (*Time*, December 22, 1924 http://www.time.com/time/magazine/article/0,9171,719669,00.html).

Between 1880 and 1920 pogroms engendered waves of Jewish immigrants from Central and Eastern European countries; as many as 2,500,000 arrived in the United States. Many immigrants were peasants, but Russian Jews, in particular, arrived with experience in manufacturing, trades, and commerce that fitted them well for the American industrial economy (Steinberg 1989, 95–101, 161). Jews tended to migrate as whole families rather than as individuals. They settled in the cities, mostly in New York, where they accounted for nearly a quarter of that city's population (Wills 2005, 83). The new arrivals transplanted their customs, such as eating habits (kosher food), clothes, and religious rituals to the teeming urban enclaves in which they lived; but they also adapted to their new environment. Many Orthodox women got rid of their wigs, and women in general had to adapt to the beauty and slimness ideals of the mainstream population (though Hasidic Jews in Brooklyn, New York and other enclaves retain a thriving Orthodox culture).

The Jewish emphasis on education, and the opportunity afforded by American public schools, resulted in large numbers of Jewish students enrolling in colleges and universities by the early twentieth century. The educational success and the social mobility of Jews spawned anti-Semitic attitudes and practices. Fearing the loss of their privileged status, American Protestant administrators reacted by imposing restrictive enrollment quotas on Jews by the 1920s at such prestigious institutions as Harvard, Columbia, and New York University. Despite such prohibitions Jews persevered to obtain a disproportionate number of faculty positions in higher education after World War II and were well represented in professions that required college educations (Steinberg 1989, 146–149, 224–252).

Jews were especially prominent as entertainers on the vaudeville stages, as comedians, and in theater. As songwriters, musicians, and producers they had a major impact on American culture, especially the movie industry, which came to dominate popular culture by the 1920s.

Muscular Jewry

Physical fitness and sport did not play a large role in traditional Jewish culture, where the most revered men were religious scholars, not athletes or soldiers. Thus Jews did not bring a specific movement culture to their new home country. However, the stereotypes of the wry, weak and sneaky Jews as well as the discrimination of Jews in many social areas had sparked off a counter movement (Vertinsky 1994). Zionism, developed at the end of the nineteenth century, aimed at the establishment of a Jewish homeland in Palestine. Zionist leaders repudiated the Jew's alleged inferiority and stressed the necessity of physical fitness and prowess. Max Nordau, one of the Zionist leaders, coined the term "Muscular Jewry" in 1898. In the following years Jewish sport clubs, many of them in Germany, were founded, and in 1921 a World Maccabi-Federation (a Jewish sport federation) was established. In 1932, a first Maccabi World Games took place in Tel Aviv (Pfister and Niewerth 1999; Eisen et al. 2003).

In many countries, Jews began to fight off stereotypes and engage in sports of strength and risk. In the USA, the 1920s was a decade which witnessed the emergence of Jews as boxers. The procession of Jewish champions from the ethnic ghettos to world conquerors dispelled the stereotypical notions of Jewish debility. In the following decade so many second-generation assimilated youth starred in basketball that it became known as a "Jewish sport."

Figure 3.4 Boys boxing in front of Chicago Hebrew Institute gymnasium, c. 1915 (Chicago History Museum)

ITALIANS AND THEIR ROAD TO ASSIMILATION

The Italians followed a similar path to acceptance and assimilation as the immigrants from other countries. Between 1880 and 1924 more than 4,000,000 traveled to the United States in search of job opportunities which were lacking in their home country. Most Italian immigrants were peasants from southern Italy and Sicily, areas traditionally ignored by the central Italian government and regions where the majority of people lived in poverty. Initially Italians were considered non-whites by the Anglo population, suffering the indignities and lack of respect accorded to other groups deemed to be of inferior racial stock.

Italian immigrants, especially southern Italians, were considered to be racially "suspect" due to their imagined African ancestry. They were labeled by scientists, journalists, the authorities, and the general public as unreliable and prone to criminality. Although these prejudices led to various forms of discrimination, Italians were considered as "whites" by American laws (local courts sometimes differed on their interpretation of whiteness). This led, eventually, to naturalization and social inclusion. However, the first generations of Italian immigrants did not identify with "whiteness" but formed a specific Italian identity.

The second generation of Italian-Americans lived a hyphenated existence in two cultures, adhering to European customs and their native language within the family, but practicing English and playing American sports in the schools and among non-Italian friends.

Italians settled largely in ethnic neighborhoods among old-world neighbors, known as Little Italies, where they found camaraderie and assistance in communal societies, similar to their ancestral villages. Padrones, or labor bosses, found work for strong young men, often supplanting the Irish on construction crews as the latter found jobs which were higher up in the hierarchy of the American labor market. Like the Irish, the Italians gradually won acceptance and a measure of social mobility (Wills 2005, 164).

Italians who did not return to Italy with their earnings eventually became not only socially accepted, some even climbed to the top of the American society. Perhaps the best example is Amadeo Giannini, who made one of the greatest fortunes of all Italians as the founder of the Bank of Italy in San Francisco. His business catered initially to Italian immigrants; but by 1930 it had become the Bank of America, operating on a national scale. Other Italians established wineries in California, and the children of Italian immigrants soon won status in a variety of fields, including politics and sport. Fiorella La Guardia won election to Congress and then served three terms as mayor of New York City in the 1930s to 1940s.

Sport was not part of the traditional culture of the Italian immigrants; but they imported bocce to the US, a recreational activity which the men enjoyed in the neighborhood parks or open spaces. But Italians soon adopted American sports and used their successes as a way into the American mainstream. Boxing provided excellent opportunities to demonstrate the American values of toughness, aggressiveness, and willpower. Boxing matches symbolized the struggle of Italian immigrants for acceptance and Italian-American boxers succeeded the Jews as champions throughout the 1930s to 1950s; with a parade of top fighters in numerous weight classes, such as Tony Canzoneri, Rocky Graziano, Jake LaMotta, Carmen Basilio, and Rocky Marciano.

The rise of Joe DiMaggio as a baseball hero and temporary husband of movie star Marilyn Monroe symbolized the acceptance of Italians in American culture (see Chapters 4 and 12). DiMaggio's rise to baseball stardom exemplified many immigrants' belief in sport as a meritocracy and the aspirations of the working class. DiMaggio stated that "A ball player's got to be kept hungry to become a big-leaguer. That's why no boy from a rich family ever made the big leagues" (Dickson 2008, 141).

IMMIGRANTS FROM EASTERN EUROPE: THE FALCONS AND THE SOKOLS

Polish immigrants

The Poles had a long attachment to the United States. A Polish noblemen, Casimir Pulaski, led an American cavalry unit in the revolution against Great Britain, and gave his life in the cause of liberty. This made him an American hero. On the first Monday of March, an annual holiday in commemoration of his deeds is celebrated in Illinois, which has a large Polish population in Chicago. Pulaski was one of the most renowned military leaders in Poland. He fought for years in vain against the Russian forces stationed in Poland and emigrated to America in the 1770s (Wills 2005, 115).

In the course of the eighteenth century, Poland became the playing field of the powerful nations Prussia, Russia, and Austria, which divided the country three times. Each time Poland lost territory, and the third partition in 1795 led to a dissolution of the country. Despite the attempts of the three "superpowers" to impose their cultures on the Poles, they retained a strong sense of national identity until they regained their independence in the wake of World War I. By that time nearly 2,000,000 Poles had migrated to the United States in search of better lives. They settled largely in the cities of New York, Chicago, and Detroit, and the smaller towns of Pennsylvania, working in the steel mills and auto plants.

The Poles brought their gymnastic and sport movement with them to their new home country. The "Falcons" were an off-shoot of the pan-Slavic Sokol movement (Sokol means falcon) which had been founded in Prague in 1862. The Polish branch was formed in 1867. The Falcons practiced gymnastics according to the model of German gymnastics (*Turnen*); they aimed at health and fitness, and engaged in the national revival and reunification of Poland. The local units of the Falcon organization were called nests.

The first nest in the United States was organized in 1887 in Chicago. More followed, and in 1894, representatives from nests from Chicago founded the "Alliance of Polish Turners of the United States of America." In the beginning of 1914, the Falcons added to their charter: "The object of the Polish Falcons Alliance of America is to regenerate the Polish race in body and spirit and create of the immigrant a National asset, for the purpose of exerting every possible influence towards attaining political independence of the fatherland" (http://www.polishfalcons.org/). During World War I, large numbers of the Polish immigrants, many of them Falcons, followed President Woodrow Wilson's call for volunteers and fought in the war against Germany. Falcon clubs, similar to the German *Turner* societies, served as the meeting place, support agency, and social network for Polish immigrants. The other "cradles of Polish ethnicity" were neighborhood churches. Poles adhered to a strong Catholicism, fostered by old-world clergy, which gave them support and a feeling of belonging, but impeded their integration into mainstream society. Throughout the twentieth century Chicago remained a major refuge for Poles, where the Polish language, food, and culture survived assimilationist attempts.

Czech and Slovakian immigrants

In the second half of the nineteenth century, the Czechs faced suppression from the Austrian monarchy, as did the Slovaks from the Hungarian government. The Czech lands, the former Bohemia and Moravia, had been ruled by the Habsburg kings since the sixteenth century.

The Slovaks, who share their language with the Czechs and – partly – their culture had been part of the Hungarian kingdom since the eleventh century. Both countries became part of the Austro-Hungarian Empire (1867–1918), where the Czechs faced Germanization, and the Slovaks were subjected to Magyarization policies. The Hungarians and Austrians denied these countries autonomy and tried to impose their culture and language on their subjects. Political oppression together with economic depression resulted in large numbers escaping to America, beginning in the 1840s and peaking in the 1890s (Wills 2005, 112–113). The Czechs arrived mostly in the big cities like New York, Cleveland, or Chicago, but many went westward, following the dream of free and fruitful land at the frontier. Many of the Czech immigrants were peasants and they settled largely in the Midwest. The Slovaks began their migration to the USA in the 1870s, most of them driven by the poor economic conditions in their home country.

The relative freedom of America was especially beneficial for art and culture. It provided Czech composer Antonin Dvorak with his most fruitful period, from 1892 to 1895, when he combined classical music with Native American and African compositions to create unique works. Another Czech immigrant, Milos Forman, later became a famous Hollywood movie director (Wills 2005, 265, 272, 281).

Like other immigrant groups, the Czechs and Slovaks quickly established churches, organized mutual aid societies, and founded theater groups and choirs; but the main centers of immigrant life were Sokol clubs. As already stated, Sokol (Falcon) was a pan-Slavic gymnastic movement, founded in Prague in 1862 by Jindrich Fügner and Miroslav Tyrs. The exercises aimed at health and fitness were "borrowed" from German gymnastics and focused to a high degree on exercises in groups, drills, and exercises with light equipment (Nolte 1993). The highlights were the gymnastic festivals, called "slets" (flying together) where mass gymnastics demonstrated the strength and skill of the participants. Women held particularly prominent roles in some of the Sokol clubs. As in the German gymnastic movement, the Sokol was a political nationalist movement. The various Sokol associations of Slavic countries aimed at the religious, cultural, and political unification of all Slavic people. The American Sokol organization supported the Free Thought movement and advocated, among other things, women's and worker's rights. In 1893 it stated: "we declare ourselves . . . against any type of hierarchy and any limitation to the personal freedom and rights of citizens" (Nolte 1993, 23).

Sokol clubs in the USA emerged in the 1860s; the first club was the Gymnastic Association Sokol St. Louis in 1865. By 1878, the US had thirteen Sokol chapters, and a national federation was founded in New York City in 1896. The Sokol federation is divided into districts. Each district conducts a slet every year; a national slet is organized every fourth year. As with the German gymnastic clubs, the Sokol associations served the various needs of the immigrants, and they altered their philosophies and programs in accordance with the changing situation of their members. In addition to the Sokol activities, Czech and Slovak immigrants formed athletic teams, mainly soccer teams. Today, European immigrants are among the most avid soccer fans in the US.

THE INTEGRATION OF MOVEMENT CULTURES

Each group of immigrants not only brought their hopes and their willingness to work, their languages and cultures, but also their physical activities and sporting practices to America. For the first generation of immigrants their native sports and sport associations served as a support of ethnic identity and a support network which alleviated the hardships of immigrant lives.

The movement cultures of the various groups were ingredients in the American "salad bowl"; however, the opportunities to contribute decisively to the taste of the salad varied according to ethnicity. The American sport culture is clearly dominated by the sporting heritage of Great Britain. British immigrants had not only the benefit to be the first settlers, but were also the huge majority of the American population throughout history. However, as Chapter 4 about baseball and Chapter 5 about football show, British pastimes were refashioned into American sports. In contrast, the physical activities and sports of other immigrants had high importance for the various groups, but only for a restricted period of time. In the process of assimilation to the dominant Anglo culture, the Germans, Czechs, and Irish participated increasingly in American sports like baseball and basket ball, not the least as a symbol of their new American identity. The popularity of modern sport and games in ethnic communities may also be explained by the worldwide propagation and fascination for performance, competition, and record orientation, the typical features of American sport. Ethnic sport associations became marginalized and survived only as nostalgic "places of remembrance" or as social clubs. However, some of the physical activities of immigrants from skiing to gymnastics became integral parts of the American sport movement.

Table 3.1 Sport associations of immigrants

1809	Boston Cricket Club (British immigrants)
1836	First Caledonian Games (Scottish Highland Society, New York)
1848	First *Turnverein*/gymnastic clubs (German immigrants)
1850	Socialistischer Turnerbund (Socialist Gymnastic Union)
1850	First YMCAs
1853	First Caledonian Society in Boston
1865	First Sokol Club in St. Louis
1878	National Unity Sokol
1884	Gaelic Athletic Association
1887	Polish Falcons of America

Source: Hofmann (2001, 93).

IMMIGRANTS – EDUCATION AND ASSIMILATION POLICIES

American racial attitudes colored the prescribed remedies for the real and imagined problems connected with immigration. While nativists in the east were alarmed by the increasing flow of European immigrants, white Europeans were considered to be somewhat more acceptable than Asians who were perceived as threatening aliens. Concerted efforts to assimilate the Europeans began in the 1880s when a pair of college graduates, Jane Addams and Ellen Gates Starr, both from upper-middle-class families, embarked on a new profession for women, the social worker. After their college graduation, and uninterested in the traditional roles available (wife, mother, nurse, teacher), both women toured Europe. In London they became interested in Toynbee Hall, a so-called settlement house, where the residents worked for social reforms and for the improvement of the lives of the poor. After their return to Chicago they founded Hull House as a neighborhood center and a social agency. Settlement houses, situated within the teeming urban ethnic neighborhoods, intended to bring about social reforms and to assimilate foreigners into American society. Addams and Starr were part of a widespread group of largely white, Anglo-Saxon Protestants known as Progressive reformers, who intended to refashion American society in a more equitable way based on ideals of democracy and their own WASP perceptions of social justice (Carson 1990).

BOX 3.7 HULL HOUSE

Hull House, established in Chicago by Jane Addams and Ellen Gates Starr in 1889, served as a national model for settlements in the inner city. Settlement houses provided a new occupation for women as social workers. In that context they combined the previous acceptable roles of teacher, nurse, and mother as they nurtured and instructed immigrant families in the assimilation process. Settlements offered educational classes, safe playgrounds for children, social services, nurseries, libraries, and athletic teams among their myriad activities. At Hull House resident sociologists from the University of Chicago conducted research on the lives of immigrants, which led to new laws, juvenile courts, political reforms, and better living conditions. Jane Addams became one of the most famous woman in America and the recipient of the Nobel Peace Prize in 1931.

(Gerald Gems)

Assimilated German Jews, hoping to maintain their social status within American culture but desirous of retaining their religion, founded Jewish settlement houses to acculturate the Eastern European Orthodox Jews who had to shed traditional habits and clothes in order to fit into mainstream American society. Sport and physical education were a major component of the acculturation process in the Jewish settlement houses. The Chicago

Hebrew Institute, organized in 1903, boasted some of the finest athletic facilities in the entire nation (Gems 1995b).

The process of assimilation focused largely on children, as the social agencies had less success with adults who were set in their cultural ways and suspicious of Anglo impositions. The Progressive Movement, initiated by social reformers, worked for the acculturation of immigrants by enacting three laws, which were adopted in many states: the child labor laws, which removed young children from the workplace; mandatory education laws, which required that children attend school; and laws which required physical education, meant to teach American games and values. Because many poor immigrant and Anglo working-class families relied on child labor for sustenance, many children worked long and dangerous hours in industrial plants, suffering severe injuries or even death. In addition, parents had no time to supervise children. If children did not have to work they often played on the city streets, which was very dangerous owing to the increasing traffic. Numerous uncontrolled children turned to juvenile delinquency. The mandatory education law required (and allowed) children to attend public schools without cost, where teachers might educate them and instill American middle-class values through history, civic education, and English language classes. Such education was meant to prepare children for labor market which demanded increasing knowledge and skills, but also intended to draw children away from the radical views of many European parents who had left Europe because of political oppression and a life in servitude and who favored socialism, communism, or even anarchism. By 1900 most states had enacted laws stipulating the mandatory education of youth (Blum et al. 1977, 486).

Physical education became a prominent means of instruction in the schools, but also in the playgrounds, particularly for children who did not speak English, but who might still absorb the prescribed values through sports and games. Reformers and the school authorities alike believed in the educational benefits of sport, not least because competition, the basis for the capitalist economy, permeated all athletic activities. For them, baseball, the national game, symbolized yet helped to explain some of the seemingly contradictory values in American society. According to the belief of influential educators, the communalism of the immigrants, practiced in their close-knit families and villages of Europe, could be symbolically retained in team sports, especially baseball, where all players had to cooperate on defense; but the prized individualism of Americans seemed to be clearly evident when each batter faced the opposing team alone. Employers, many of whom financed the athletic programs, hoped that students would learn to respect authority in the person of game officials or referees because failure to follow the rules or to question authority figures might result in expulsion from the game (or from employment).

At the turn of the twentieth century, extracurricular sport began to flourish at high schools, and coaches served as PE teachers in order to train the children for competitions like intercity football matches. By 1903 adults in New York City took control of students' extracurricular athletic activities by organizing the Public Schools Athletic League, which fostered competition in city championships for baseball, basketball, track and field, riflery, soccer, cross-country, tennis, crew, lacrosse, and swimming (Riess 1995, 137). Over the next two decades the competitions would extend to both boys and girls in an even greater number of sports as other cities adopted the New York model.

Outside of the schools the playground movement, adopted from Germany, was modified to include trained supervisors who regulated play in the parks and playgrounds, prescribing the same values taught in the schools which were thus reinforced during the children's leisure time. During the school year Chicago playgrounds were open between 3 p.m. and 10 p.m. and during the summer from 9 a.m. to 10 p.m. (Curtis 1915, 130).

In Chicago, city officials built large "field houses" in the parks throughout the first decades of the twentieth century. These buildings offered gyms for both boys and girls, as well as rooms for arts and crafts, and meeting rooms for a variety of social and recreational clubs depending on children's interests that were supervised by adults even during the winter months. The concept of playgrounds and field houses was soon adopted by other American cities as a means to train and acculturate (immigrant) youths (Gems 1997). In the United States during 1913, there were "6318 (playground) workers, of whom 774 were employed for the year. The numbers, both of permanent and summer workers are increasing at the rate of about twenty per cent per year" (Curtis 1915, 127).[3]

The athletic programs of the settlement houses, public schools, parks, and playgrounds thus initiated concerted efforts to control and educate youth, especially youth with an immigrant background.

Assimilation and resistance

Despite the high investments and the benevolent intentions, the efforts of the capitalists as well as the progressive reformers were not entirely successful. The playground movement managed to increase the number of playgrounds, but failed to attract the majority of children and youth for a variety of reasons (Wassong 2005).

Ethnic and working-class families needed the labor of their children to survive and resisted the impositions of the government authorities. In Chicago a 1900 survey found that 50 percent of children aged 10 to 12 still worked, with the immigrant children being five times more likely than the Anglo children to be employed (Gems 1997, 69). Nor did Catholics take readily to the education of their children in public schools, because they were afraid that their children would be indoctrinated with Protestant religious doctrines and values, and lose their faith. Consequently, Catholics formed their own parochial school system as a parallel structure to protect and preserve their religion. The Catholic schools, often operated by priests and nuns sent from Europe, reinforced not only Catholicism, but European customs and values until the American Catholic Church could train Americanized clergy. Even then, ethnic groups such as the Germans, Poles, and Italians resisted the impositions of the largely Irish-American church hierarchy. The Catholic schools did, however, adopt the athletic interests of their students rather than lose them to the Protestant influences of the YMCA and settlement houses. The athletic competitions between Catholics, Jews, and their Protestant counterparts ensued throughout the twentieth century, which brought divergent groups together in a common cause.

Non-Protestant groups reacted defensively to proselytizing efforts by initiating their own sports programs. Catholic priests often threatened their parishioners with excommunication from the church for the use of YMCA facilities. Catholic fraternal organizations offered track and field competitions in the nineteenth century and Catholic churches sponsored their own baseball teams and athletic leagues. Local Catholic efforts became national in 1930 when a Chicago bishop founded the Catholic Youth Organization (CYO) with the intention of supplying athletes for boxing competitions. The program soon encompassed a wide array of sports and social programs, including the world's largest basketball league. The boxing team made international tours and sent its members even to the Olympics. The founder, Bishop Bernard Sheil, became a labor activist and advisor to President Franklin Delano Roosevelt. Unlike the race-segregated YMCAs, the CYO welcomed African-Americans and other minorities. Sheil became a champion of the working class, and sport served an assimilating function among previously divergent groups as CYO teams competed with non-Catholics (Gems 1993b).

BOX 3.8 CATHOLICS ON THE FOOTBALL FIELD

While Catholic private schools competed with each other in their own athletic leagues, they also played against public school opponents in the public school leagues. The most telling of such encounters occurred in Chicago where Catholic high schools challenged the public schools' football champions starting in 1927. For Catholics, football became a means to win greater respect or to avenge perceived wrongs, since they assumed that the public schools promoted Protestant values. In the 1937 game for the city championship, played at Chicago's mammoth Soldier Field, more than 120,000 spectators came to cheer their favorites. The game was so important for the Catholics that their star player competed despite a severe injury. Still, the public school team prevailed with a player who had scored more points than any other in the USA that year. Ironically, he was a Catholic who attended a public high school.

(Gems 2000, 136)

Jewish groups, too, safeguarded their offspring in Jewish settlement houses in New York and Chicago as early as the 1890s. The Chicago Hebrew Institute offered a comprehensive athletic program and some of the best facilities in the United States by World War I. The B'nai B'rith Youth Organization (BBYO), a Jewish fraternal organization, adopted an official youth program in 1925. A basketball tournament was introduced in 1927 with numerous other activities to follow. Sports such as basketball, and particularly boxing, enabled Jewish boys to overcome the stereotypes that depicted them as cerebral but weak. By the 1920s Jews proliferated among the world's boxing champions. BBYO teams and athletes competed with Christians as sporting interests brought factions together in a common interest (http://www.bbyo.org/index.php?c=56&kat=The+History+of+BBYO).

Although ethnic and religious groups organized their own sport and education programs they used the same recipes, especially sport, to attract and educate young people. Thus they contributed more or less willingly to the assimilation of immigrants into American society.

Company sport – education on the sporting grounds

Starting in the 1880s employers began to organize large-scale industrial recreation programs to teach the lessons about American values, attitudes, and behavior to their employees. In addition, they founded company teams in a wide variety of sports. Organized by company officials, sport competitions not only benefitted the health and fitness of the participants, but the teams represented the company in competitions against teams of rival enterprises (Park 2005). Business owners got free publicity as newspapers covered their athletic teams and the commercial rivalries might translate into greater production and profits as workers instilled with company pride tried to outperform their business competitors not only in the sport field but also in the workplace.

BOX 3.9 THE PULLMAN INDUSTRIAL RECREATION PROGRAM

George Pullman, whose company built palatial sleeping cars for the railroads, established the first industrial recreation program in his company town outside Chicago in 1882. Pullman offered his employees (many of whom were immigrants) housing, stores, a library, and a comprehensive athletic program that included rowing, soccer, baseball, football, cricket, tennis, ice-skating, billiards, boating, and riflery. The Pullman Company's outstanding athletic facilities allowed it to host national championship events. The national rowing championships, held on a nearby lake, brought 15,000 spectators to the town in 1883. Such events and the Pullman teams generated much positive publicity for the company. Pullman's intention, however, was not an altruistic one. He intended the recreation program as a means of socially controlling his workers. For example, alcohol was banned from the town except for the hotel bar, where workers were not allowed.

89

Pullman reasoned that by keeping his workers away from alcohol and engaged in wholesome activities during their leisure hours they would be more efficient and more productive in the workplace. Moreover, the wages that he paid to the workers were at least partly returned to him in the form of rents and purchases at the company store. The arrangement worked well until the economic depression of 1893 resulted in one of the most famous labor strikes in American history. Many other employers adopted the Pullman model well into the twentieth century (Pesavento 1982; Park 2005).

(Gerald Gems)

These programs were especially beneficial for women. Whereas the women's colleges did not support competitive female athletes after 1900, the company programs provided ample opportunity for working-class and immigrant women to engage in competitive sports. Many of the early female Olympians on the American squads had learned and trained for their sport in the municipal and commercial recreation programs (Park 2005).

Company sport aimed at increasing the profits of the enterprises, but it had at the same time integrating effects as it shaped social networks outside of the ethnic groups, and it transferred American habits and values. In addition, company sport reached people, especially women, coming from cultures which did not favor sport and games.

IMMIGRATION – AMERICAN POLITICS AND POLICIES FROM THE LATE NINETEENTH AND THE TWENTIETH CENTURIES

The mélange of peoples flooding American shores in the late nineteenth and early twentieth centuries posed a distinct problem for the Anglo residents of the United States. With liberal voting rights (at least for men) the Anglos feared the loss of not only their political power but their culture. Politicians addressed the issue by passing the Chinese Exclusion Act in 1882. About 60,000 Chinese resided in the United States by that time, most drawn by the California Gold Rush of 1848. Most of the Chinese still resided in California in segregated "Chinatowns," apart from the other residents who saw them as competitors for jobs. Bowing to pressure from nativist protestors the Congress passed restrictive legislation that banned further immigration from China (Wills 2005, 154–155).

Playwright Israel Zangwill's 1908 theatrical production, *The Melting Pot*, declared: "Understand that America is God's Crucible. The great Melting Pot where all the races of Europe are melting and reforming!" (Wills 2005, 270). As already stated, more contemporary observers consider America to be more of a salad bowl with ethnic groups retaining their cultural flavors and a measure of difference. That salad, however, lacked Asian ingredients. The ban on Chinese enacted in 1882 was followed by the "Gentlemen's Agreement" of 1907 with Japan, which stemmed the flow of Japanese workers to the United States (Garraty 1983, 559). The US government authorized the Congressional Dillingham Commission that same year to study the immigration problem. In 1910 the commission ascertained that "immigrant hordes" comprised 58 percent of the workforce, including 67 percent of the mining industry, 76 percent of those engaged in the clothing factories, 53 percent of tanneries, and 51 percent of steel mill workers (Steinberg 1989, 36). A year later the commission judged there to be at least forty-five different racial groups with varying degrees of acceptability (Gems 2006a, 5). In 1924 the US Congress acted upon the commission judgments to pass the National Origins Act, which placed annual immigration quotas that discriminated against Southern and Eastern European groups who lacked the desirable "racial" characteristics ascribed to Anglo-Saxons (Blum *et al.* 1977, 635). The foreign-born population fell from 13 percent in 1920 to 4.7 percent by 1970 (Garraty 1983, 623).

The Red Scare (fear of communists) which followed World War I and the Russian Revolution led to further isolation of the US when the US Congress refused to ratify the League of Nations treaty. The lack of a continual flow of European migrants to reinforce old-world values, customs, and languages accelerated the acculturation of second- and third-generation European Americans. Second-generation children were caught between two cultures, speaking their European tongue at home with parents and grandparents but using English with Americanized friends in the schools, parks, and playgrounds of the urban centers. The third generation, although they retained some European customs, such as culinary preferences, had generally lost any ability to speak their grandparents' native language.

The Depression further limited immigration and 500,000 Mexican workers were deported in an attempt to save jobs for American citizens during the 1930s. The Cold War that ensued after World War II brought 400,000 European refugees to the United States. The communist control of Cuba after 1959 resulted in an exodus of more than 500,000 refugees to the United States, most of whom settled in Florida, where they gradually assumed political power in the city of Miami. As the United States became more embroiled in Asian affairs in the 1950s, the flow of Asian migrants surpassed that of Europeans after 1966 (Foner and Garraty 1991, 536–537).

The Immigration and Nationality Act of 1965 rectified the restrictive and discriminatory 1924 legislation by enacting a new immigration focus that allowed for the reunification of family members of US residents and acceptance of those with particular skills regardless of their national origin. As a result, the numbers of Asian immigrants increased substantially; by 1975 they accounted for one-third of the total number of those relocating to the United States. Numerous Latin Americans, particularly "boat people," fled Cuba and Haiti for asylum in the United States. In addition, transient workers from Mexico crossed the Rio Grande River boundary illegally. To curtail such unwanted migrants the US Congress passed legislation in 1976 that again limited the number of visas granted to some countries. Still, those seeking work from Mexico, Central and South American countries entered the US clandestinely, with estimates ranging from 4,000,000 to 8,000,000 illegal aliens by 1980 (Blum *et al.* 1977, 882–883).

The American immigration policy with regard to Mexico has been a contentious and ambiguous one. In more stable economic periods throughout the twentieth century, the American government welcomed the cheap labor provided by Mexican workers. In more dire times, American critics charged that the Mexicans took jobs from American workers. In reality, many of the Mexican workers occupied menial positions that were unwanted by the vast majority of Americans. The Mexicans especially populated the ranks of farm workers, who planted and harvested the crops on corporate farms at low wages and in dreary living conditions. In the1960s Cesar Chavez, the son of such immigrant workers, organized the laborers into the United Farm Workers Labor Union to address the exploitative conditions and better their lives (Wills 2005, 172).

Economic woes caused numerous Dominicans to leave their island for life in the United States. After the overthrow of the Dominican dictator and a consequent revolution in the 1960s, the instability of the nation and the concurrent poverty brought on an evacuation. Between 1990 and 2000 half a million Dominicans arrived in the United States, joining another 500,000 already resident there (Wills 2005, 179).

In addition to the economic conditions, political issues brought numerous other refugees who sought freedom from persecution and oppression. Civil wars within Central America throughout the latter half of the twentieth century brought many refugees from Guatemala and El Salvador. Few, however, were awarded asylum and most were deported. New legislation in 1990 granted temporary sanctuary to Central Americans for renewable periods of time. Nicaraguans were treated with more leniency. With the installation of a communist government from 1979 to 1990, the 20,000 Nicaraguans residing in the United States were granted refuge (Wills 2005, 128–129). Political ideology superseded humanitarian concerns as the basis for asylum.

The aftermath of US involvement in Viet Nam also affected immigration policies. With the victory of the communist forces, millions fled the country, many as "boat people" on makeshift rafts or overloaded cargo ships. Many of them languished in relocation camps for extended periods of time while foreign governments debated whether they were economic or political refugees. By the late 1970s the US government began accepting 14,000 individuals per month, accounting for 988,000 residents in the country by 2000. Laotians, Cambodians, and Hmong numbered another 616,000 refugees from Southeast Asia by 2005 (Wills 2005, 212, 215, 216, 220). These groups, from communal, agrarian societies, have experienced difficulties in adjusting to the individualistic and technological culture of America.

The Iranian Revolution of 1979, which deposed the Shah and installed a rigid Islamic government, resulted in more than 100,000 fleeing to the United States. By 2005 an estimated 1,000,000 Iranians had settled in their newly adopted country. Continual turmoil in India between Hindus and Muslims, in the Middle East between Jews and Arabs, between

a nation of immigrants

Christians and Muslims in Southern Europe, and between African nationalists accounted for new waves of Muslim immigrants during the latter decades of the twentieth century. By 2005 approximately 7,000,000 Muslims resided in the United States, adding greater religious diversity to the country (Wills 2005, 94–96).

With the fall of the Soviet bloc in 1989 nearly 2,000,000 people from Poland, Hungary, Romania, Czechoslovakia, Yugoslavia, and the Soviet Union made their way to the United States, and perhaps many more arrived illegally. Like the Mexican workers, many of the illegal aliens are exploited as low-wage workers. The Immigration Act of 1990 permitted the legal migration of those with desirable skills, particularly technicians and engineers (Wills 2005, 186–187).

In 2002 the US Census Bureau determined that 11.5 percent of the US population was born outside the country (Wills 2005, 8). That number is compounded by the estimated 7,000,000 to 10,000,000 illegal aliens (70 percent from Mexico) who reside in the US (Wills 2005, 54). These numbers fuel the ongoing immigration debate in the United States and resurgent nativist sentiments. Immigration has followed a continual pattern over the history of the country. Immigrants came and continue to come to the United States in the belief that they will enjoy the American Dream of prosperity and freedom. Americans, in turn, expect the newcomers to assimilate and acculturate to the predominant value systems and develop a national rather than an ethnic identity.

CONCLUSION

Carl Degler, a distinguished American historian, has surmised that:

> Americans . . . came from elsewhere, and what they came for was not really a place or a location, but an idea; their physical destination began as a wilderness stretching along the edge of a continent and ended as a country of farms and cities. Their identity had to be self-created, drawn not from where they had been, but for what they hoped. (Only later were Amerindians and African Americans let into the pattern.) Working out American identity took a long time, perhaps over a century and a half, after which Americans discovered that they were no longer subordinates of Britain, but a new people. What they had learned in the process was not only the freedom and independence that they had gained from Britain, but also the religious freedom that diversity had bestowed on them . . . Americans arrived at the principle that "all men are created equal." In short, rather than being a people of a place or locale, Americans became and remain an attitude of mind, a set of ideas that determine what it means to be an American. It is a set of ideas that knits together the diversity of peoples to which America has come, and from which American identity has been forged.
>
> (Degler 1998, 12–13)

This set of ideas was and is part of the American Dream which motivated immigrants to embark on long, often dangerous journeys to the Promised Land although not all of them were always welcome. The metaphor of the "melting-pot" obscures the fact that the various groups of immigrants had and still have a different impact on American society. However, it also refers to the fact that strong assimilation processes formed an American identity and a mainstream culture which is more and more shaped by the mass media. However, it is a question as to whether or not the assimilation processes described in this chapter will continue, or if the US will stay a diverse society with divisions along the lines of race and ethnicity. This question is very topical at a time when the position of English as the unifying language is endangered.

Part of the American Dream was and is the notion of meritocracy and the conviction that everybody, including the immigrants, can obtain the position in society which he or she deserves. America was never a society which enforced equality; on the contrary, Americans emphasize differences which are considered as outcomes of abilities and efforts. Today the gap between rich and poor is even widening, with African-Americans and (Hispanic) immigrants at the bottom of the hierarchies.

Sport serves to demonstrate the justice of the unequal distribution of resources as well as the importance of the American values of competing and winning. Thus it may have unifying effects, not the least because sport fascinates people from various race, class, and ethnic backgrounds. In the US, there is a particular focus on team sports, which is believed to promote an ideology of democracy, equality, and self-sacrifice for the good of the whole in a performance-oriented society, which rationalized competition within the capitalist economic framework.

As in American society, American sport may be interpreted as a "salad bowl" with a major input from the British immigrants. In the process of distanciation from the British roots, Americans developed a new identity and Americanized British sports and pastimes. Many immigrant groups inscribed their physical cultures on the American sport landscape. In some cases, gymnastics and sports were used – for a period of time – as "cradles of ethnicities"; in other cases ethnic sports, such as skiing, were adopted quickly by the American mainstream population. But immigrants were also confronted with American sport, and physical activities were used as a means to educate the new Americans and make them familiar with American values and practices. Here the playgrounds, the schools, and the companies played a decisive role. Today the common interest in and the media consumption of the American national games of football, baseball and basketball seem to unify Americans of the various classes and ethnicities.

CHAPTER FOUR

THE RELEVANCE OF BASEBALL

INTRODUCTION

> I think about baseball when I wake up in the morning. I think about it all day and I dream about it at night. The only time I don't think about it is when I'm playing it.
>
> (Carl Yastrzemski, professional player, cited in Plaut 1993, 390)

Baseball is *the* American sport, constructed as the national pastime, played by numerous American boys, but also big business and a media attraction watched by millions. Baseball became a professional sport in the nineteenth century and influenced the professionalization processes of American sport decisively. The game is at the center of the American culture and provided the blueprint and business model for the other professional sports.

This chapter has a twofold intention. It describes the transformation of a children's ball game into a national pastime and the transformation from a game played by amateurs to a sport where the players earn millions of dollars. In addition, we try to explain the popularity of baseball and explore the fascination of this sport for numerous and various groups of the American population.

BACKGROUND

French-born historian Jacques Barzun once observed that "whoever wants to know the heart and mind of America had better learn baseball" (Riess 1980, 1). Innumerable players, writers, journalists, politicians, and the general public discuss the role of the game in their lives and in American society. Henry Chadwick, sports writer and inventor of baseball statistics, wrote, for example, in *Beadle's Dime Base-Ball Player*, 1860: Baseball "requires the possession of muscular strength, great agility, quickness of eye, readiness of hand, and many other faculties of mind and body that mark a man of nerve . . . Suffice it to say that it is a recreation that anyone may be proud to excel in, as in order to do so, he must possess the characteristics of true manhood to a considerable degree" (Dickson 2008, 102).

Sportswriter Jimmy Cannon declared 100 years later:

> It is the best of all games for me. It frequently escapes from the pattern of the sport and assumes the form of a virile ballet. It is purer than any dance because the actions of the players are not governed by the music or crowded into a formula by a director. The movement is natural and unrehearsed and controlled only by the unexpected flight of the ball.
>
> (Plaut 1993, 385)

As a country of immigrants America had to find its national identity, and Americans constructed images and self-concepts as well as political myths in order to distinguish themselves from Great Britain, which had assumed the role of motherland as it tried to retain the American colonies. The historical remembrance of the Boston Tea Party and political myths such as the frontier experience, or the imagination of a "manifest destiny" for the American people, served as tools which bound the people together, supported the invention of an imagined American community, and the development of an American identity (see Introduction). The power of these constructions becomes obvious when taking the vast territories and the different backgrounds, ideologies, and living conditions of the immigrants into consideration. Baseball played a major role in the process of Americanization; it became a game where Americans with various ethnic and social origins could eventually find a common interest and a means of identification.

Playing the game is an initiation, a rite of passage for American children, and its mytho-logical ties to American history are well known to Americans even by early childhood. Writer Luke Salisbury stated that "Baseball is more like a novel than like a war. It is like an ongoing, hundred-year work of art, peopled with thousands of characters, full of improbable events, anecdotes, folklore and numbers" (Plaut 1993, 387). Its cultural meanings are constructed and reproduced by numerous collective symbols, rituals, and memorials that tie it to patriotism and past heroes and make it a part of the national identity. The myth, however, is problematic and the claim that baseball is a wholly American game is historically inaccurate. It is, as Eric Hobsbawm (Hobsbawm and Ranger 1983) might say, an invented tradition which may serve community-building as well as nationalistic purposes.

The history of baseball reveals another crucial development in American sport, the early professionalization and the way in which American sport was and is shaped according to the demands and rules of the market. The history of baseball tells the story of the development of a specific system of professional sport involving resistance and power struggles. The resultant business model became a stimulus and the model for all other professional sports.

Hobsbawm stated that there is probably no time and place which has not seen the
"invention" of tradition, although he also argued that invented traditions occurred more
frequently at times of rapid social transformation when "old" traditions were disappearing.
He therefore expected an especially large number of "new" traditions to be invented over
the past two centuries, in both "traditional" and "modern" societies (Hobsbawm and Ranger
1983, 4f.).

BASEBALL, CONTESTED ORIGINS, AND INVENTED TRADITIONS

The origins of baseball were an issue of long and intense conflict between historians,
baseball officials, and fans. Some historical sources and evidence (since disproven: Block
2005) supported the assumption that baseball had its roots in the English children's game
of rounders. However, this did not fit into the imaginations and constructions of a specific
American identity and destiny.

In 1907, amidst a continuing controversy over the origins of baseball and a growing rivalry
between the US and Great Britain, a six-man committee was established to clarify the
provenience of the game. The driving force behind the search for the "truth" and the
construction of the baseball myth was Albert G. Spalding (1850–1915), a sporting goods
magnate with major profits coming from the sale of baseball equipment and a former player
and executive leader of the National Baseball League. He handpicked the members of the
committee and chose his personal friend, Abraham G. Mills, former president of baseball's
National League, as chairman. In its December, 1907 report the committee declared that

"First: Base Ball had its origin in the United States. Second: That the first scheme for playing it, according to the best evidence obtainable to date, was devised by Abner Doubleday at Cooperstown, N.Y., in 1839" (Riess 1998, 64). The evidence consisted of a letter from a person named Abner Graves, supplied to Albert G. Spalding, that entailed the remembrances of an old man's youth. Graves was born and spent his childhood in Cooperstown, New York. He claimed that Doubleday, allegedly a childhood friend and subsequently a Civil War hero and army general, invented the game at the above-mentioned time and place. In 1939 upon the centennial of the supposed creation of the game, the National Baseball Hall of Fame was founded in the tiny village of Cooperstown in the State of New York, commemorating the game's importance in establishing an American cultural identity.

The idyllic setting and its small town values contributed to the rural image of baseball which transferred its imagery to the large cities where the park-like baseball grounds enticed urban Americans by their "good old-time" charm.

Sport historians have since pointed to numerous implausible factors in the decision by the Mills Commission. Graves, the letter writer, was only five years of age in 1839; he became an adventurer and was later judged to be criminally insane (Guttmann 2004, 127). Doubleday, the alleged inventor of baseball, was in fact a cadet at the United States Military Academy at West Point, and not in Cooperstown during 1839. Although he and Mills were members of the same club, the supposed inventor had never mentioned his role in baseball history to Mills.

The Doubleday-story was not the only etiological tale about the origins of baseball. Henry Chadwick, considered at that time to be "the father of baseball," had always contended that the game evolved from the British game of rounders. Chadwick, an ardent supporter of baseball and a sportswriter of fifty years, was a British immigrant, familiar with both games. However, the Mills committee and the American public disregarded the contention of a British origin of their national game.

Spalding's views on the matter were much more in line with the growing American nationalism. Besides nationalism, he had specific personal reasons to repudiate any connection between baseball and British games. He revered baseball. As a star player, head of the National League, and as a sporting goods manufacturer, he had become a millionaire. He had attempted to spread the game on a global tour in 1888 to 1889 but was much chagrined by the refusal of the British cricket players and the British public to take baseball seriously. For them, baseball was an unmanly boys' game. Spalding adamantly denied that his beloved sport had its origin in children's play; he believed that it was the ultimate sport for men. Spalding insisted and tried to prove that "baseball was of purely American origins and no other game or country has any right to claim its parentage" (Kirsch 1992, 67; Lamster 1992, 67).

The Doubleday myth was proven false by a journalist, Will Irwin, in 1909 and again by a New York librarian, Robert Henderson, in 1939 as the Baseball Hall of Fame opened in Cooperstown.

Despite irrefutable evidence to the contrary, the media and the public, encouraged by the flag-waving bluster of the baseball industry, clung to the Doubleday Myth. It seemed they simply preferred the "immaculate conception" of baseball by the war hero Abner Doubleday to the messy evolution that the historical evidence clearly indicated.

(Block 2005, xiv)

The significance and sharpness of the debate must be placed within its historical context. Drawing on Bourdieu's concept of space and various forms of capitals, the struggles about the origins of baseball may be explained as a competition for positions in various political and social fields in the US.

During the nineteenth century the fledgling United States was a new nation and its inhabitants were in search of a cultural identity. Without its own language, literature, music, or art, Americans had few cultural or technical attainments that had not been transferred from Great Britain. It was British taste which ruled in American society, and neither Indian nor later immigrant cultural influences had great impact on mainstream habits and tastes.

Having fought two wars against the mother country to gain and maintain their independence, Americans sought to distance themselves from their British roots in the areas of culture and everyday life. Like a petulant teenager in search of itself, America wanted something to call its own. Sport was and is highly suitable for the creation of collective symbols and "places of remembrance." Sporting events and heroes easily gain entry into the collective memory of a nation because they are highly visible and provide rituals, where participants and audiences can join together in the common celebration of superiority. While upper-class Americans enacted their British roots and played cricket, citizens identifying with the United States chose baseball, an allegedly American game.

BOX 4.2 BASEBALL PLAYER OR PRESIDENT?

"When I was a small boy in Kansas, a friend of mine and I went fishing . . . I told him I wanted to be a real major league baseball player, a genuine professional like Honus Wagner (star of the Pittsburgh team). My friend said he'd like to President of the United States. Neither of us got our wish" (Plaut 1993, 42). The narrator of the story, Dwight D. Eisenhower, never became a professional baseball player; but he did become the thirty-fourth president of the United States, the job desired by his friend.

Current sport historical research has found evidence that games termed "base ball" had been played in the United States, Canada, but also in several European countries (e.g. in Germany) earlier than 1839 when the game was allegedly created in Cooperstown (Menna

1995, 152; Block 2005, xiii). Sport historians, on the basis of systematic research, are in general agreement that baseball evolved from a variety of bat and ball or base games played in Europe and imported to the colonies.

One of these games was stool ball, in which chairs sufficed as bases, described in the "Little Pretty Pocket-book" (1744) by the British author and publisher John Newberry:

> THE *Ball* once struck with Art and Care,
> And drove impetuous through the Air,
> Swift round his Course the *Gamester* flies,
> Or his Stool's taken by *Surprise*.
>
> (Newberry 1744)

Rounders, the British boys' game, which has distinct similarities to baseball, is also described and depicted in this book.

In 1786 a Princeton College student wrote in his diary that it was "A fine day, play baste [*sic*] ball in the campus but am beaten for I miss both catching and striking the ball" (Altherr 1997, 76). Another British children's book published in 1802 also in Baltimore, compared the game unfavorably to cricket, which was considered a more manly diversion. "Bat and ball is an inferior kind of cricket, and more suitable for little children, who may safely play at it, if they will be careful not to break windows" (Altherr 1997, 76).

In America boys played a game similar to rounders called "old cat," which assumed the moniker of "townball" as informal teams or clubs organized in towns and challenged each other to games. A townball club played in Philadelphia as early as 1831 (Kirsch 1992, 68). Variations of the game were played throughout the northeastern states, with differing sets of rules and on different playing fields.

BASEBALL RULES

In the process of sportification, the baseball rules underwent considerable changes which all aimed to increase the standards of performance and to make the game more thrilling for the spectators and efficient for players. As a background to the understanding of the development of the game, we present here the basic idea of the game and the most important current rules.

Baseball is a game with numerous rules and a specific terminology. Those who have not grown up with the rules and terms may have problems understanding the game. Baseball is a game of two teams, each with nine players. The playing ground is a square, called the diamond, with a base on each of the corners. Bases are safe places for the runners. One corner is the home plate, the place of the batter. In the middle of the diamond is a mound, the place of the pitcher. The diamond is placed in a large field.

The players of the offensive team take turns batting. It is their goal to score a run, which means to run around the diamond, touch all the bases, and reach the home base. The game starts when the pitcher, a player of the defensive team, throws the ball to the batter, who tries to hit the ball as far as possible. If the batter does not hit a correctly pitched ball it is called a strike. After a hit, the batter starts running; he can stop at every base and wait for another hit. If the pitcher throws the ball four times outside a designated zone, the strike zone, the batter proceeds to the first base. If the batter manages to hit the ball over the fence beyond the outfield he gets a home run. He and all runners at the bases can proceed to the home base.

The goal of the defensive or fielding team is to prevent the players of the offensive team from reaching the bases. Defensive players try to get hold of the ball and throw it to each other in order to put runners out. When they are in possession of the ball they can put runners out when they touch (tag) them outside a base or when they touch the base before the runner is able to get there.

Batters are out after three strikes or if they hit the ball and it is caught in the air. After three outs the offensive team has to switch to the defense. When each team has had a turn at the bat and in the field it is called an inning. A baseball game consists of nine innings, and the winner is the team with the most runs. If the score is tied, the game continues until one team scores more runs than its opponents.[1]

Baseball differs from the other popular ball games in that it has no time restriction. Because of its natural breaks after each half-inning, it offers an excellent opportunity for television commercials. Thus games often last for more than two-and-a-half hours without putting off the fans. The tension and excitement of baseball fans is augmented by baseball statistics which register all actions of all players and allow them to compare the games and the players beyond space and time.

BASEBALL – FROM AMATEURISM TO PROFESSIONALISM

The amateur years

In New York, the Knickerbocker Club, composed largely of middle-class members, formed in 1842. The members developed a set of baseball *rules* formalized by Alexander Cartwright which are considered the basis of the rules of the current game. The Knickerbocker rules differed from a version which was used in Massachusetts.

Teams in both New England and New York proliferated by the 1850s. A virtual baseball mania transpired by the 1850s with some clubs composed of clerks and others of working-class laborers or craftsmen. By 1857 a National Association of Base Ball Players (NABBP) was organized in New York City. By 1861 it had seventy-four clubs as members, which adopted the Knickerbocker Club's version of the rules, which were modified in 1863 in

Figure 4.1 Baseball field (North Central College Archives)

order to make the game faster and more efficient. A major decision was that the association opted for amateurism and banned professional players (Kirsch 1992, 78–79). The importance of winning and the subsequent prestige of the clubs had enticed some club officials to offer monetary inducements to the best players by the 1860s; however, amateur clubs deemed such a practice to be unacceptable.

Spread by migrants from New York and the media, the New York Knickerbocker version of the rules triumphed over those of Massachusetts to become the national model. Baseball had been played by the soldiers during the Civil War, and the returning soldiers brought the games and the rules to their home towns. The adoption of one set of rules placed baseball on course to become the "national game." With a few modifications, the game is played essentially the same way today.

A series of matches in 1858 between rival cities in the State of New York produced an athletic spectacle attracting large audiences, and this type of competition was widely copied by organizers and promoters in later years. Each city chose its best players to represent it as an all-star team for the matches, fostering public and media attention on the event.

Figure 4.2 Baseball pitcher and hitter (North Central College Archives)

BOX 4.3 THE GREAT MATCH

The great match, which has been in contemplation for several weeks past, has, in connection with Base Ball, had the effect of directing the public mind to the great question of athletic sports for the people, and it has been growing and growing until the excitement has become so intense that it has been made the chief topic of conversation, and every one met with has had opinions to express as to who would be the ultimate victors in this grand contest. Such untoward interest being manifested by the public, caused the Committee of Arrangements to change their original plan of operations, and, instead of having the match played on their usual playing grounds, it was deemed expedient by them to pay more attention to public convenience, consequently the Fashion Race Course, L.I. (Long Island, New York), being neutral ground, and considered the place most suitable to accommodate the thousands that were expected, as well as combining the requisites for play, it was secured.

(New York Clipper 1858, quoted in Kirsch 1992, 86)

In the 1860s, the intercity matches were no longer restricted to local areas. In 1862 a team from Philadelphia traveled to New York for matches that drew 15,000 spectators and the New York team consequently played in Philadelphia, extending the scope of competition (Kirsch 1995, 60). Regional matches became commonplace as teams sought greater competition and glory. In 1864 a contest between a Canadian team and an American contingent "for the championship of the American continent" ended with the Americans triumphant (Kirsch 1995, 60).

However, the interest in cricket continued and some men engaged in both sports; but baseball clearly gained ground. Nationalistic comparisons with British cricket had been drawn after a British team toured the United States.

Baseball is better adapted for popular use than cricket. It is more lively and animated, gives more exercise, and is more rapidly concluded. Cricket seems very tame and dull after looking at a game of base ball. It is suited to the aristocracy, who have leisure and love ease; base ball is suited to the people . . . Both games seem suited to the national temperament and character of the people among whom they respectively prevail.

(Kirsch 1992, 93–94)

As industrialization took hold throughout American cities in the later nineteenth century, spawning pollution, immigrant ghettos, and corruption, baseball served a nostalgic longing for the good old days, small town values, and healthy open spaces.

the relevance of baseball

Professionalization processes

In the years after the American Civil War baseball consolidated its place as the national pastime, and became at the same time a professional sport. The Civil War resolved not only the issue of slavery but, to a great extent, the form of the US economy as well, as the urban, industrialized north defeated the rural, agricultural south, setting the future of the nation on an industrial path. Modern sports would thereafter conform to a particular commercialized, business model developed by the baseball teams (Guttmann 2004, 130).

The better baseball teams began constructing their own enclosed playing spaces in the 1860s, enabling them to charge admission fees to spectators. As teams with their own grounds accumulated money they began recruiting the best players by offering them cash payments or a percentage of gate receipts, in effect professionalizing the game.

BOX 4.4 THEODORE ROOSEVELT ON AMATEURISM

In England the average professional is a man who works for his living, and the average amateur is one who does not; whereas with us the amateur usually is, and always ought to be, a man who, like other American citizens, works hard at some regular calling, it matters not what, so long as it is respectable, while the professional is very apt to be a gentleman of more or less elegant leisure, aside from his special pursuit . . . the amateur, and not the professional, is the desirable citizen, the man who should be encouraged. Our object is to get as many of our people as possible to take part in manly, healthy, vigorous pastimes, which will benefit the whole nation; it is not to produce a limited class of athletes who shall make it the business of their lives to do battle with one another for the popular amusement . . . In baseball alone, the professional teams, from a number of causes, have preserved a fairly close connection with non-professional players, and have done good work in popularizing a most admirable and characteristic American game.

(*North American Review*, August, 1890, Issue 405, Volume 51)

While most teams remained on an amateur basis, the best players, however, enjoyed a free market and "jumped" or "revolved" from team to team, earning their living with their physical skills and depending on the increasing money offered by the teams. By 1869 the businessmen of the city of Cincinnati, in competition for the hinterland trade with midwestern rivals Chicago, St. Louis, and Milwaukee, secured the first fully professional team to gain visibility, and prestige, with the hope that the performance of the team would demonstrate and promote the economic power of Cincinnati. The Cincinnati team went undefeated in a series of national tours, gaining wide media attention and thus bringing fame to the city. Chicago responded by hiring its own professional team the following year and other cities soon followed. The organization of the National Association of Professional Base Ball Players in 1871 divided the clubs between professional and amateur contingents.

In 1871, ten professional teams formed an association dedicated to arranging national championships based on the NABBP rules. The league, however, was poorly organized, and players switched teams after each season, which diminished fan loyalty. Between 1871 and 1875 twenty-five teams competed in the professional league; but only three retained a constant presence. Weaker teams, no longer in contention for the championship, simply refused to finish their scheduled games, disrupting the organizational coherence. Two of the top teams, Boston and Philadelphia, traveled to England in 1874 to engage in both cricket and baseball games in an attempt to generate interest abroad; but the venture proved the first rebuff for baseball in Great Britain (Kirsch 1995, 67–68).

Dissatisfied with the operations of the NAPBBP league, the officers of the Chicago team instigated a revolt in 1875. The following year eight defectors from the players' league (NAPBBP) formed the National League, an organization of entrepreneurial owners, in an attempt to "rectify" the problems of the previous association. Control of the teams reverted to the owners rather than to the players. Owners agreed not to hire players from opposing teams until they had fulfilled their contracts and a board of directors, similar to a business enterprise, directed league business and adjudicated any disputes. In addition, the new constitution required that teams represent only larger cities (75,000+) to insure an adequate fan base. In 1879 the team owners introduced the infamous "reserve clause" into player contracts, which reserved players for their entire careers only to the team that signed them to an initial contract, until that team (i.e. the owner or owners) desired to trade or dismiss the player. By reserving players to one team the owners removed the players' ability to negotiate better contracts with other teams, thereby giving the owners a monopoly. The unified ownership of the National League thus operated as a cartel, excluding new/other teams/owners, limiting player salaries, and dictating the terms of employment.

The owners took further steps to promote the game to the WASP middle class, to appeal to its value system, and to safeguard morality and propriety. They banned Sunday games and forbade the sale of alcohol during the games (1880), expelled players accused of accepting bribes to throw games (1877), and insured the protection of umpires, who were often accosted by fans. Thus, they restored public confidence in the honesty of the contests.

Baseball statistics and the popularity of the game

Newspapers gave increasing coverage to the National League and the famous sportswriter, Henry Chadwick, devised a number of ways to increase the interest and commitment of fans by quantifying the games and abilities of the players, such as the batting average which measured the number of hits obtained per number of "at bats" (chances to hit). The league office also kept records of team performances and the course of matches required an equal number of games for each team in all cities. The variety of numerical analyses and statistics added interest for fans. They allowed comparisons beyond individual games, supported the evaluation of each player and changes in the course of his career, and the ranking of players independent of space and time, enabling comparisons across different historical eras (Kirsch 1995, 70–74, 78–99).

Excursus: baseball statistics

In the US, in sport as well as society, quantitative performance plays a central role. Audiences peak when records are about to be broken, and athletes turn into stars when they set new and, as far as possible, spectacular records. In team games, though, it seems to be impossible to set records and measure individual and quantitative performance. However, this is not true in football, and especially in baseball, where the performances of each and every player are recorded and appraised. Ever since baseball began to be played professionally, statistics have been compiled, and they are still an integral part of the game today.[2]

Baseball comprises short, self-contained episodes of play in which the actions of each of the players involved are exactly quantifiable, such as the number of hits by means of which the batter reaches first base, the runs, the home runs, the bases reached, and the runs "batted in," i.e. the runners who were able to score runs as a result of a batter's good hits. Negative actions are also recorded, for example, strike-outs (when the batter fails to hit three correctly thrown balls). Successful actions are defined for each role in the game (batter, pitcher, runner, fielder) and are included in the statistics. Around forty different actions are noted for batters and ten for the defending players.

Many actions are described in the form of "rate statistics," which place actions in relation to opportunities. The most important figure for batters, for example, is the batting average, i.e. the number of hits (where the batter reaches first base) in relation to the number at bat (the times he faces the pitcher). If the batter, for instance, was at bat ten times and scored three hits, his batting average is .300 (an above-average value). Babe Ruth had a batting average of .342, thus holding tenth place in the list of "all-time leaders." With 714 home runs, he also holds third place in the list of home-run hitters. Statistics are also compiled for the performance of each team and for the various leagues.

The compilation and publication of ever more complicated statistics has developed into a million-dollar business. SABR, the Society of American Baseball Research (which was founded in 1971 and has around 7,000 members), has developed what it calls Sabermetrics, an objective analysis of the game on the basis of the statistics with the use of mathematical tools. Sabermetrics does not only aim at determining the "value" of a player in the past but also at predicting his development in the future (www.sabr.org). Statistics are used by team managers to gather information about the abilities of players, and this influences, among other things, the make-up of a team. This knowledge also plays a major role in recruiting new players.

Coaches and players use statistics in the analysis of games and the evaluation of players as well as in tactical decision-making. Fans are obsessed with statistics since these allow them to compare the achievements of contemporary players with those of baseball legends like Babe Ruth or Joe DiMaggio. However, cases of doping uncovered in recent years have raised doubts about the whole value of statistics and records (see Box 8.3).

But statistics are most important for the players themselves, for they can rise to immortal fame as a result of record achievements. As players' salaries are also tied to performance, the rise in the use of performance-enhancing drugs has been one of the negative consequences of the fascination with quantification and records (http://www.btcavemen.de/statistik.html).

Baseball engendered the extensive quantification and emphasis on records that characterizes much of American sport. Baseball statistics allowed fans to build up expertise and background knowledge, which increases the tension of spectatorship, and provides social and cultural capital in the sports-addicted American society.

BOX 4.5 BASEBALL ADDICTION

Baseball is famously known for the almost religious devotion of its fans, writers, and scholars. Walk into any large bookstore, and you will see many more feet of shelf space for baseball books than for books on other American sports. There are currently more than seven thousand members of the Society for American Baseball Research, or SABR. The game has been studied, analyzed, dissected, poetized, theorized, and obsessed upon. There is a book that lists the uniform number of every player ever to have worn one. Another book tells what happened on each and every opening day for the New York Yankees. There are books about small town teams and leagues so obscure that almost no one besides the author recalls them.

(Block 2005, xvi)

Historian Steven Gelber has theorized that the explosive popularity of baseball coincided with the rise of American business in the late nineteenth century and that the game reinforced values and practices prevalent in the US economy in its bureaucracy, specialization of roles, work discipline, and application of scientific principles. He claimed that ball players replicated their work lives in their recreational habits (Gelber 1983). As the nation moved towards rapid industrialization in urban centers the game also provided people with a compensatory nostalgia for rural spaces and rhythms. Today the most popular ballparks are still those that offer an open-air environment and natural grass. Unlike the timed contests of other professional sports, baseball games defy the clock. As already mentioned, games have no time limit and a tie game continues indefinitely until one team outscores the other, heightening the drama for fans. Later historians have discredited Gelber's thesis because the early players had not yet encountered the dominant influence of corporate practices on their lives, and the quantification of sport did not become commonplace until the 1880s (Adelman 1989; Riess 1995, 62). Nevertheless, the explanation suited the proponents of the American Doubleday myth.

Baseball and the cities

As team owners built new enclosed ballparks in the 1860s to garner more profits from the growing fan base, they became increasingly involved in the political life of the cities. They had to negotiate with politicians for building permits, sites, licenses, taxes, the construction of transport networks, and the security of fans which had to be provided by the municipal police. In such negotiations owners transferred and still continue to transfer the costs of their private enterprises to the public domain, i.e. having taxpayers fund the construction and maintenance of new stadiums, or the additional police security outside the stadium (Delaney and Eckstein 2003). Michael Burke, President of the NY Yankees, said at a town council meeting, "A baseball club is part of the chemistry of a city. A game just isn't an athletic contest, it's a picnic, a kind of town meeting" (Dickson 2008, 86).

In some cases, the politicians owned the teams in their cities. Baseball, as the "national game," provided owners with a civic-minded image (Riess 1984a). Despite the machinations of the owners, fans perceived and continue to perceive professional teams as community treasures that vicariously represent the city. Robert Coover, a contemporary writer, stated,

> I felt like I was part of something there, you know, like in a church, and I joined in the scorekeeping, hollering, the eating of hot dogs and drinking of Cokes and beer, and for a while I even had the idea that ball stadiums, and not European churches, were the real American holy places.
>
> (Dickson 2008, 120)

The lucrative opportunities available to team owners spawned rival leagues which had only temporary success. Smaller towns and cities could not compete with large cities, whose fan base enabled them to attract the best players. Although limited by the "reserve clause," the salaries paid to professional baseball players far surpassed those of the working class. This made the game attractive for Irish and German-Americans, who were increasingly drawn to the game as players and fans.

Labor struggles – conflicts between players and owners at the end of the nineteenth century

Mike "King" Kelly, a fan favorite and star of the Chicago team, particularly resented the owners' impositions on personal freedoms. In addition to the limits on salary, owners expected "proper" deportment during the players' leisure time. A Chicago newspaper reported that

> Mike Kelly says he will not play base ball with the Chicago club during the year
> 1887 . . . The boys were to receive a certain sum of money in addition to their
> salaries if they won the championship and abstained from drink. Well, they won
> the championship, but they never got the money that was promised for abstaining
> from liquor.
>
> (Gems 1996a, 132–133)

The owners' emphasis on sobriety, work discipline, productivity, and a middle-class morality conflicted with the working-class physicality and lifestyles of many players. With Kelly's refusal to abstain from alcohol the Chicago ownership promptly sold him to Boston for, at that time, the astronomical sum of $10,000.

The limits on players' salaries and the rules regarding their lifestyles, however, spawned a revolt. In 1885 the athletes organized the Brotherhood of Professional Baseball Players, an early labor union. In 1890 they formed their own professional league with financial support from disgruntled financiers who had sought National League franchises (the right to own a team) but were rejected. The league was organized on the principle that profits were to be shared by players and financiers. The National League, bereft of most of its best players, went on an offensive. Led by Albert Spalding, the chief executive of the National League, it scheduled its games in direct competition with those of the Brotherhood League, forcing fans to choose between the two. The National League had greater financial resources to draw upon and could sustain temporary losses. Through bribery and coercion, some of the rebellious players returned to the National League teams and the financial backers of the best Brotherhood franchises merged with the more established league, bringing demise to the rebellion after only one year. With the dissolution of the Brotherhood players had to "work" under the conditions which the owners dictated.

The birth of the American League and the growth of Major League Baseball (MLB)

In the later nineteenth and early twentieth centuries social reformers, known as Progressives, attempted to rectify the perceived ills of American society. White, Anglo-Saxon Protestant (WASP) morality was evident in the campaigns for temperance (the abolition of alcohol) and the elimination of gambling, which was tightly connected with sports (see Chapter 2). With the successful bans on boxing and horseracing in many states after the turn of the twentieth century, baseball gained even greater popularity as the owners attempted to ban alcohol and thus constructed an acceptable image for their game.

The growing interest in baseball initiated another professional circuit, known as the American League, which started play in 1901. Its permanent success led to competition for players, which in turn led to escalating salaries and the post-season series of games for the national championship between the two league champions in 1903. Americans ethnocentrically and grandiosely termed it the "World Series." This tournament became an annual tradition, and an athletic spectacle that further enhanced interest in the sport, and thus was a benefit for both leagues.

BOX 4.7 THE POPULARITY OF THE "WORLD SERIES"

Will Rogers, an American humorist and satirist: "My idea of conceit would be a political speaker that would go on the air [radio] when the World Series is on." John F. Kennedy, thirty-fifth president of the United States: "No presidential campaign can seriously begin until after the World Series" (both in Plaut 1993, 324).

Attendance at the games of the two major leagues doubled to 7,000,000 throughout the USA from 1903 to 1908. Ten new Major League ballparks were built by 1916 at an average cost of $500,000 (Riess 1998, 48, 50). A popular magazine reported in 1912 on the business of baseball:

> Fifty million people pay $15,000,000 a year to see baseball games. One hundred and seventy-nine thousand paid $350,000 to see on(e) series of baseball games. Baseball magnates pay salaries of $10,000, $12,000, $15,000 and $18,000 to their managers and players. One baseball magnate paid $22,500 for the right to employ a single player. Millionaires . . . invest in baseball franchises as they do in railroads and industrials, Baseball is a business – a wonder business.
>
> (Riess 1998, 70)

The profits and popularity of the game even extended to the minor leagues, which, in a dozen years, expanded from thirteen in 1900 to forty-six (Riess 1998, 48, 50). The extent of popularity may be seen in the 1914 amateur championship game which drew 83,000 fans in Cleveland (Riess 1998, 95).

Baseball and national identity

Journalists portrayed baseball in idealistic terms, emphasizing the Americanness of the sport, contributing to the increasingly popular myth of baseball as part of American identity, drawing parallels between alleged American virtues and the idealized characteristics of the players. Educators, politicians, social reformers, and even missionaries believed in the socializing effects of baseball and saw it as a means not only to educate young Americans but also to assimilate the myriad immigrant groups flooding the American cities. Physical educators, park and playground supervisors taught the game to children in the schools and community recreation spaces (see Chapter 3). As second-generation ethnic youth adopted the game and began to forsake their ethnic pastimes the European gymnastic societies, such as the German *Turner*, Czech Sokols, and Polish Falcons, organized teams in order to retain their membership. Military commanders even introduced the game to colonized peoples with the intention of acculturating them to American values. General Franklin Bell, the military commander of Manila in the Philippines, claimed, for example, that "baseball has done more to civilize Filipinos than anything else" (Seymour 1990, 324–325). The American-owned *Manila Times* concurred in stating that "Baseball is more than a game, a regenerating influence, or power for good" (Gleeck 1976, 39).

BASEBALL IN THE FIRST HALF OF THE TWENTIETH CENTURY – STRUGGLES, SCANDALS, AND INNOVATIONS

Struggles for monopoly

The enthusiasm for baseball spawned a third major league in 1914, known as the Federal League. The competition between the three circuits for top players further increased salaries; but the Federal League was short-lived. The more established leagues joined forces in order to get rid of the unwanted competitor. The Federal League owners could not compete financially with the owners of the other teams, who decided to buy out their new rivals and to integrate the surviving teams and players into their leagues. The Baltimore team, however, refused the agreement and sued the two established leagues as a business monopoly. The case reached the United States Supreme Court in 1922, which decided that baseball teams were not truly a business but a civic enterprise run by well-meaning individuals. The ruling, despite challenges by the players, remained in effect until the end of the twentieth century, guaranteeing monopoly powers to the owners and the entrenchment of the reserve clause that continued to bind players to one team.

Baseball scandals and triumphs – from the Black Sox to Babe Ruth

With the onset of World War I few professional players joined the military and many found employment in war-related industries, such as shipbuilding, which allowed them to continue to play baseball. To counter perceptions of baseball players as "slackers" who failed to support the war effort, owners had players demonstrate their readiness to fight for their country by marching in military formations before the start of games. In addition, they decorated the seating areas with bunting in the national colors. At the 1918 World Series they introduced the playing of the "Star-Spangled Banner," the song that glorified American fortitude and that would officially become the National Anthem in 1931. Such militaristic displays tied the game to nationalism, patriotism, and militarism. Playing the National Anthem is a symbolic gesture that continues before all games today. Even high schools maintain the practice.

After two generations in which baseball had been laden with idealistic and nationalistic notions it came as a cultural shock when it was discovered that Chicago White Sox players had purposely lost games during the 1919 World Series after being bribed by gamblers. Due to the cheating of the players and the tainted reputation of baseball the affair was dubbed the Black Sox scandal. Despite the disgrace and public disgust, a Chicago jury refused to believe the evidence and acquitted the players when their confessions were "lost."[3] The scandal caused the baseball owners to abandon the national commission, which had previously ruled baseball, in favor of a single commissioner, who ruled the game as an autocratic dictator. They chose a controversial Chicago judge[4] for the position, who announced:

> "Regardless of the verdict of juries, no player who throws a ball game, no player who undertakes or promises to throw a ball game, no player who sits in confidence with a bunch of crooked ballplayers and gamblers, where the ways and means of throwing a game are discussed and does not promptly tell his club about it, will ever play professional baseball."
>
> (Gropman 1988, 201)

He soon banned forever all the alleged conspirators. The edict restored some faith in the besmirched national game, and all other professional leagues (NFL, NBA, NHL) adopted the lone commissioner system; although subsequent commissioners have been selected by the owners (and worked for the owners). While the commissioner system seemed to guarantee fair play in the professional leagues, baseball found greater redemption in its heroes, especially in the person of Babe Ruth.

Babe Ruth was the incorrigible son of a German tavern owner, who was sent to an orphanage at the age of 7. There he excelled at baseball and gained a professional contract with the Boston Red Sox. The Boston owner sold him to the New York Yankees, where his prodigious home runs (balls hit out of the park, allowing the batter to run safely around all

114

bases and score) made him a legendary figure. His prowess revolutionized the game of baseball, transforming the strategy from what had been a progression of successive hits to generate scoring (runs) to a reliance on the home run with one big blast of power. In 1920 he hit more home runs than any entire team in MLB (Rader 1990, 134). His production spawned greater interest in statistical analyses of the game, which appealed to (and continues to appeal to) more intellectual fans. The general public became fascinated with Ruth's home runs, as well as his exuberant lifestyle, and his zest for life. Ruth's feats and daily activities were chronicled by the popular media of the 1920s that created an American celebrity culture. Ruth became the biggest celebrity of all. The new technology of radio broadcast sporting events to millions and made athletes like Ruth into idols. By the end of the decade Ruth's salary surpassed that of the president of the United States and he earned much more in a bevy of commercial endorsements. For many he represented the promise and the dream of America, the working-class hero who became a millionaire through his physical prowess. Ruth upheld the belief in sport as a meritocracy even as the conspicuous consumption of the 1920s and the Depression questioned the American value system.

Figure 4.3 Baseball player Babe Ruth, New York Yankees, during game against White Sox at Comiskey Park, Chicago 1929 (Chicago History Museum)

Hard times and innovations

The hardships of the Depression, caused by the global economic collapse after the Stock Market crash of 1929, had a negative impact on the attendance in baseball. People lacked money to buy tickets, which forced sports promoters to innovate. Team owners offered doubleheaders, i.e. two games for the price of one, and ladies' days, which allowed free entry to any female spectators on selected days of the week. Some teams adopted the practice of the Negro League by playing games at night under electric lights to attract those lucky enough to have a job during the daytime hours. Minor league teams affiliated with the richer MLB franchises in order to survive and funneled their best players upward through the organization. In 1934 the sports editor of a Chicago newspaper devised a plan for an all-star game that would bring all the best players from both leagues together at one site for an unprecedented spectacle which would attract a huge crowd of fans. The spectacle proved so popular that it became an annual event that continues today as the All-Star Game (Littlewood 1990, 67–76).

According to the beliefs of the time, baseball helped to alleviate the hardships in other areas of life. The sporting press declared that the game "promoted the cardinal virtues of the nation – team play, discipline, and sportsmanship. It developed clean-minded, clear-thinking citizens, while acting as a powerful instrument for combating juvenile delinquency" (Baldwin 2000, 49). Even President Franklin Delano Roosevelt proclaimed that "major league baseball has done as much as any one thing in this country to keep up the spirit of the people" (Baldwin 2000, 49).

BOX 4.9 THE SOFT SIDE OF BASEBALL

Softball was invented in Chicago in 1877 as indoor baseball. The diminutive version of baseball was adapted for use in the playgrounds as a means to acculturate immigrant children. Although identical to baseball in most rules, the game is played on a smaller field with larger balls ranging from 12–16 inches (30.5 cm–40.6 cm), which are thrown underhand to the batter. This makes it easier to hit the ball. The rules became standardized in 1934. There are two different versions of the game. In the slow pitch version the ball has to be thrown in an arc to the batter. The other version allows for fast pitches. This version is played by high school girls and college women in interscholastic competitive leagues. From 1996 to 2008 softball teams competed at the Olympic Games.

(Gerald Gems)

During World War II, baseball owners considered suspending operations for the duration of the hostilities. The president beseeched the owners to continue the competitions for the good of the national morale. Unlike World War I, the players readily joined the military services, with nearly 1,000 in uniform by 1943 (Davies 2007, 190). Baseball continued with lackluster performances by substandard players; but in 1943 Philip Wrigley, owner of a Chicago team and a chewing-gum empire, devised another innovation, the All-American Girls Baseball League. During the war women assumed unconventional roles, leaving the home and working in factories or at other traditionally masculine occupations; thus playing men's sports did not seem so extraordinary. Women had long played baseball, and more recently softball, the indoor and playground variation of the game. Wrigley held tryouts for players and organized four teams in a professional league representing three midwestern states. Each team required a female chaperone and the women had to attend charm school and cosmetics classes to project an appropriate image of femininity. They also played in skirts. The quality of play was high and the league expanded to ten teams by 1948, a season in which it drew nearly a million fans; but with the return of men from the war interest in the women's games diminished and the old order in baseball as well as in American society was soon resurrected. In addition, the growing influence of television hurt attendance of women's as well as minor league baseball games, as audiences concentrated on the top male teams. The All-American Girls Baseball League disbanded in 1954 (Davies 2007, 191).

Baseball, race, and ethnicity

The post-war event that had the greatest impact on baseball was the desegregation of MLB, meaning the acceptance of African-American players (see Chapter 10). Sports writers had clamored for decades that African-American players had the abilities to play with whites as equals. Satchel Paige, who had been confined to the Negro League teams and foreign leagues, was widely regarded as the best pitcher in the United States; yet the commissioner and team owners disregarded him despite his skills. World War II and the commitment of African-Americans as soldiers raised the question of civil rights and the integration of the African-American population into American society, including sport.

As the national game, baseball was a very visual symbol for race relations in the United States. When the Brooklyn Dodgers signed military veteran Jackie Robinson to a baseball contract it signaled a new era. Robinson had previously played for one of the Negro League teams, and soon became a star in the National League despite widespread hostility among white players and fans. African-Americans, however, swarmed to the stadiums to cheer their new hero. Once Robinson took the field in 1947, a few other teams signed black players. By the end of the 1947 season five blacks appeared on team rosters and Satchel Paige, despite advanced age, played for Cleveland in 1948 (Davies 2007, 215). Robinson's stellar play despite the many cases of discrimination won him not only many honors but also the respect of white team-mates and fans. Through baseball he had demonstrated that integration could be a positive factor in American society. Seven years after his MLB debut the Supreme Court of the United States agreed in a landmark decision in the case of Brown v. Board of Education, in which the judges voted to end segregation in the public schools. The decision opened all government schools in the United States, including universities, to people of color.

While Jackie Robinson marked the gradual acceptance of African-Americans in baseball, the game had similar ramifications for other minority groups. Irish-Americans had gained prominence in the sport as early as the nineteenth century; while Eastern Europeans made headway in the early twentieth century. Others, such as Jews and Italians, had to gain a standard of whiteness (i.e. adapting to the middle-class values and norms of white society) before full acceptance into American society. Italian-Americans reveled in the accomplishments of Joe DiMaggio, who succeeded Babe Ruth as star of the New York Yankees team in the 1930s. A high school drop-out, his magnificent physical abilities earned him celebrity and wealth, reinforcing the perception of baseball as a symbol of American meritocracy. In 1941 he set a record considered by many to be the greatest feat in American sports: hitting safely in fifty-six consecutive games.[5] DiMaggio had ninety-one hits in 223 at bats during the stretch, a hitting average of .409. This feat was called "The Streak," and added to the glory of the legendary baseball hero. Yet when war broke out DiMaggio's parents were classified as enemy aliens because Mussolini sided with Hitler and Italian loyalty became suspect. DiMaggio joined the army air corps, proving his patriotism, and then returned to the Yankees until his retirement in 1951 (see Chapters 3 and 12).

RECENT DEVELOPMENTS – BASEBALL AS BIG BUSINESS

The power of mass media

The greatest influence on the business of baseball, and American sport in general, occurred with the introduction of television. Baseball games were broadcast as early as 1939; but the marriage of sport and television was a post-war development. At first, television presented a problem for the owners of sports teams. They feared that televised contests would diminish the number of spectators at the games. The minor baseball leagues, the Negro Leagues, and the AAGBBL (women's league) all declined after the onset of televised MLB games. The teams initially used "blackouts" (refusal to broadcast the game on television) to insure that fans would have to come to the stadium. The courts, however, ruled such a tactic illegal, as it restrained the business of the broadcasters. Soon, the team owners and broadcasters reached agreements that proved lucrative for both parties. Teams sold broadcasting rights to television networks, who passed the costs along to commercial sponsors that promoted their advertisements to the television audience. The many stoppages in baseball games proved ideal spots for the commercial ads (see Chapter 13).

BOX 4.10 THE BUSINESS OF BASEBALL

In 1953 *Sporting News*, considered the "Bible of Baseball," published an account of the financial arrangements at that time.

> Upwards of ten million dollars will be spent this season in broadcasting major league ball. Yet . . . it can be safely said that this phase of the entertainment industry is barely past its adolescent stage . . . Television studios have been springing up all over the landscape, making it certain that more than $10,000,000 will be spent on major league broadcasts this year. In addition, another $10,000,000 will be accounted for by minor league broadcasts, bringing the grand total to something over $20,000,000. Even in the free-spending broadcasting industry, this sum is impressive . . .
>
> The idea has become fairly general that sports of all kinds enjoy the largest audience among owners of television and radio sets. This, however, is true only in the daytime when as many as 35 per cent of the sets are tuned in on a sports event . . . At this point, the question naturally arises whether the sponsor gets value for money paid out while providing armchair fans with free games . . . But there is little doubt that if the sales were not commensurate with the outlay, breweries, gasoline companies, and cigarette makers would not long be tossing their money around.
>
> (Franks 2004, 52–54)

By 1960 90 percent of Americans owned television sets and the New York Yankees, baseball's richest team, earned $1,000,000 in television revenue (Davies 2007, 230). Other teams, however, had to compete for fans and television contracts. Unlike the owners of other professional leagues, MLB owners do not share their revenue equally, which puts smaller cities at a disadvantage in their ability to obtain a team with high-priced players. Large cities, such as New York or Chicago, offered large markets and greater opportunities for television contracts and advertising sponsors than smaller cities. In the early 1950s most baseball teams were located in the Northeast and Midwest. New York alone had three teams in MLB; but as rich teams got richer, owners began to move their franchises to areas without competing teams where they could monopolize the television market. By 1958 even two of the New York teams moved to Los Angeles and San Francisco in California, a populous state with no Major League teams. By 1987 television and radio rights averaged almost $6,000,000 for each team (Rader 1990, 256).

While the league tried to curtail the stockpiling of top players by the rich teams by introducing a salary cap for all teams, rich teams such as the Yankees still overspend and willingly pay the required fine. Consequently, the Yankees have been a dominant team in the American League for decades. The success of a team is interrelated with the salaries of the players. The highest paid player in baseball, Alex Rodriguez of the New York Yankees, was paid $28 million in 2008. The entire Florida Marlins baseball team made only $21 million for the 2008 season. The average MLB player (there are 855) made $3.15 million per year for 2008 (*Chicago Sun-Times*, April 6, 2008, 62A).

In the competition for media attention, visibility, and prestige, American cities pin their hopes on professional sport. Because cities without professional sports franchises are not considered prime urban centers, aspiring locations are more than willing to attract established teams by building new stadiums for them and offering extravagant financial incentives. Only one of many examples is the case of the Chicago White Soxs[6] who were offered a new stadium to move to Tampa, Florida in 1991. Chicago countered by building a $150,000,000 stadium, a guarantee against financial losses, the purchase of 300,000 tickets annually, and another $2,000,000 per year to maintain the edifice (Guttmann 2004, 138). Since 1992 seventeen of the thirty MLB teams have obtained new stadiums, largely at public expense (Delaney and Eckstein 2003, 2).

The team owners legitimize a city's support by professing the benefits gained through such constructions; for instance, the enhancement of the city's image, the creation of jobs, and the economic boost that results. Sports economists, in general, disagree with such assertions (Delaney and Eckstein 2003, 30). The jobs created are only temporary and the stadium is used for only a proportion of the year. Many cities use sports stadiums to anchor urban entertainment zones with a mélange of shopping malls, cinemas, and restaurants designed to gentrify decaying inner cities and generate tourist dollars.

Owners and players – power struggle, Part II

The cash flow accruing to team owners has caused continuous labor issues. Players, discontented with the reserve clause that had bound them to one team and limited their salaries, formed a labor union, the Major League Ball Players Association, in 1953. It made little headway until Marvin Miller, a lawyer for the Steelworkers' Union, was hired as executive director in 1966. Thereafter the players assumed a more militant resistance, including strikes. Their solidarity won concessions, such as greater pension contributions, salary increases, the right to representation by sports agents (usually lawyers who represent the players and negotiate on their behalf), and the right to arbitration to settle disputes. In 1969 an African-American player legally challenged the reserve clause "as a vestige of slavery," but failed to sway the US Supreme Court (Davies 2007, 295). Miller, however, managed to legally subvert the clause when owners did not uphold all conditions of the contract or if players performed for one year without a contract, thus making them free agents, able to negotiate with any other team. In effect, the reserve clause was overcome by such maneuvers by 1975. The baseball owners, unable to act in a concerted fashion and desirous of winning games, soon made ever larger salary offers to star players who had become free agents. Charles Finley, owner of an American League team, stated that "Good stockbrokers are a dime a dozen, but good shortstops (the central defensive players) are hard to find" (Plaut 1993, 92). When owners did try to take uniform action and refused to negotiate with free agents in 1985 the players appealed the issue to an arbitrator and won their case (Guttmann 2004, 138). As a consequence, by 2004 the average MLB baseball player salary reached nearly $3,000,000 with top players making much more (Davies 2007, 296). The escalating salaries and the additional performance bonuses precipitated new problems for baseball. Intent on improving their worth, players turned to steroids and other drugs, which resulted in record-breaking accomplishments but tainted the game. Writer Dan Gutman noticed the problem as early as 1990 when he wrote that "The general public will forgive them for cheating much more quickly than they will for losing. If they can't perform, there are a hundred guys dying to take their place. It's the perfect atmosphere to encourage breaking the rules" (Plaut 1993, 189). MLB had no official policy on such matters and resisted imposing any substantial penalties on guilty players until the US Congress interceded with formal hearings into the matter in 2005 (see Box 8.3).[7]

Over the course of the 2006 and 2007 seasons, Barry Bonds pursued and eventually surpassed the all-time home-run record of Hank Aaron (who had exceeded Babe Ruth), the most sacred statistical feat in baseball history. But he accomplished the goal with an unequaled surge of home runs over a prolonged period of years after the age of 35, normally a time of reduced performance in aging athletes. In 2001 Bonds hit seventy-three home runs in a single season at the age of 37, surpassing the admittedly drug-induced record of sixty-six set in 1998. The previous record of sixty-one had stood since 1961. Bonds had noticeably gained forty-five pounds (twenty kilos) of muscle since his entry into MLB, almost assuredly through the use of steroids. Though cheered by his hometown fans as a hero, Bonds was roundly booed in other ballparks as a cheater. The issue gnaws at the traditional idealistic American assumption of sport as a character-building activity and athletes as role models. Sport is now readily recognized as big business, an entertainment industry, and the audiences even seem to accept that the heroic performances of physical excellence are attained by illegal means and thus questionable in their veracity.

BASEBALL BETWEEN HISTORY AND FUTURE

Baseball is part of American identity and a symbol of American values. It has a cherished tradition which is reconstructed in and through a continuous flow of publications. More books are published on baseball than any other sport in the United States each year. Via collective memories, crystallized in baseball statistics, Americanness is reinvented and enacted in every game.

Americans grow into this sport from early childhood, not only by watching baseball but by playing it. A national survey in 2003 found that baseball is the game most played by boys and girls aged 9–13 (http://www.cdc.gov/mmwr/preview/mmwrhtml/mm5233a1.htm). Little League baseball, and its younger version known as tee-ball, introduce both boys and girls to the game as early as 6 years of age. Children's leagues modeled after the professional teams exist in virtually every American community, an indication of the entrenched and continuing hold of the game on the American psyche. Thus, the tradition of interest in the "national game" is secured.

CHAPTER FIVE

FOOTBALL GAMES

INTRODUCTION

Non-Americans watching American football would be dismayed. For them the scenes would be very similar and very violent. During the attempt to move towards the goal, the ball carrier is thrown to the ground, often in a violent manner, and sometimes disappears under a pile of opponents. This stops the action, while the teams meet in a huddle to discuss their next strategic move. After half a minute they regroup at the scrimmage line and the action repeats itself all over again. Why Americans are so fascinated with their teams and why they invest so much time, money, and emotion in this sport is hard to understand for non-Americans.

In this chapter, first, we will reconstruct the development and rise of football and examine the relationships between the game and national identity. We will focus on college sport and describe pro football and the NFL later in the context of professional leagues in Chapter 8. We will then explain the rules of American football. A main focus will be on the hegemony of football within the sporting culture of the USA and the fanaticism of its fans. Finally, we will provide a short overview of the development and situation of the "other football game," soccer.

BACKGROUND

In America, football is part of the hegemonic sport culture, which means it is one of the sports which, promoted by the media, plays a central role in the lives of large parts of the population. Football is the number one sport at colleges and universities, which use football as a means to enhance identification with the school, to gain prestige, and to market the institution. Following Bourdieu, Markovits and Hellerman (2004c) developed the concept of the "sport field" which has a dimension of time and place. The specificity of the era and the region influences the significance and the position of a sport in the hierarchically constructed field of sports. Here, time plays a distinct role in a number of ways. On the one hand, the amount of time available for sport activities and sport consumption is limited. Playing and/or consuming sport depend, among other things, on the amount of leisure,

which is influenced by class, race, and gender. This means that only a small number of sports can become "national pastimes." On the other hand, the timing of a sport's introduction is significant, because latecomers face a distinct disadvantage competing with already established sports. This can be explained, at least partly, with the "consumption-capital hypothesis," which states that an increase of consumption means an investment in "cultural and social capital" in the sense of Bourdieu (see Introduction). The interest in a sport grows together with the amount of involvement because this leads to a deeper understanding and knowledge. Therefore it is difficult for new sports to displace sports which people have known and played since their childhood (Schellhaaß 2003).

Sport fields are contested cultural territories where various groups with different interests and resources meet and compete for influence and power. Thus the "sport field" mirrors the power relations in a society (Markovits and Hellerman 2004, 9). In the US, the key period for the establishment of sports was between 1870 and 1930, a time when rapid modernization processes changed the values and structures, but also everyday life of Americans, decisively. Sports established during that period had a more favorable chance of becoming a national sport. In this period the rules, the practices, the values, the symbols, and the images of American football were invented and constructed. This phase is also important because during the establishment of the game, the interpretations and meanings were discussed, negotiated, and generally fixed.

FOLK FOOTBALL

Soccer and football have the same roots in the wild and chaotic folk games which were played during religious holidays according to local customs and with a minimum of rules in many European countries. Often a whole village competed with another village and large crowds tried to move the ball by any means possible to a predetermined goal. Because of the destruction to property and injury to people, authorities tried, often in vain, to ban the game. In the wake of the modernization processes at the turn of the eighteenth into the nineteenth century folk football lost its importance. Among other things, the increasing effectiveness of the public administration, the secularization, the urbanization, and the "enlightened" patterns of thinking and acting provide an explanation for the gradual disappearance of this game (Marples 1954; Walvin 1994).

However, it continued to be played in the British public schools where football coincided with the rowdiness and aggressive behavior of the upper-class students (Williams and Wagg 1991; Walvin 1994). In the course of the civilization process as described by Norbert Elias (see Introduction) and the reformation of the public schools, the students' behavior was expected to meet more refined standards of decorum. Within that process the game assumed rules and regulations designed to achieve better deportment and greater self-control of the players.

BOX 5.1 FOOTBALL AND THE CIVILIZATION PROCESS

Norbert Elias (1897–1990) emphasizes the links between social conditions and the human psyche, taking as his example the changes in both rules and behavior in post-Middle Age Europe. The growth of the towns and the establishment of royal courts led to increased "chains of interdependence," which in turn led to the concentration of power in the sovereign state and an internalization of control in individuals/subjects.

In an article on the "Genesis of Sport as a Sociological Problem" Elias applied the basic principle of his civilization theory to sport, demonstrating that the norms and rules of physical cultures are dependent on the particular level reached in the civilization process.

Since the nineteenth century, rules in football were successively introduced to reduce the dangers to life and limb. Numerous regulations, for example, with regard to protective equipment, such as padding and helmets, transformed football from a serious fight into a sport which meets the standards of civilized conduct in industrial nation-states. However, in comparison to other sports, football still allows a high measure of violence, which may signify a regressive step in civilization (Elias and Dunning 1986).

(Gertrud Pfister)

At several schools, such as Eton or Rugby, variations of the rules evolved which were codified in the 1840s. Eventually two different styles of play emerged: soccer and rugby. Soccer disallowed the use of hands by all players except for the goalkeeper. The British Football Association, founded in 1863, adopted this form of the game. The term "soccer" comes from the word "association." At Rugby school a different version of the game developed which allowed players to grab the ball and run with it (Harvey 2001).

British immigrants brought folk football to the American colonies where sources report the game being played in the seventeenth century. A Boston ordinance of 1658 stated that "Forasmuch [sic] sundry complaints are made that several persons have received hurt by boys and young men playing at football in the streets, these are therefore to enjoin that none be found at that game in any of the streets, lanes, or enclosures of that town, under penalty of twenty shillings for every such offense" (Altherr 1997, 161). The folk version of the game was also played at American colleges as early as the eighteenth century. Football was one of the entertainments of the young men who lived on the campus and who spent their free time not only studying but also drinking or fighting. According to Gems (2000, 12), football was an "excuse to throttle each other in intramural contests" (see also Waddington and Roderick 1996; Guttmann 2006).

COLLEGES AND FOOTBALL – EARLY HISTORY

The development of higher education in America

Since the inception of higher education in the American colonies in 1636 with the founding of Harvard College, schools were defined and identified themselves as institutions not only responsible for intellectual education but also for the moral development of their students. The moral mission can be explained by the character of these colleges as religious schools. Brubacher and Rudy, historians of higher education in the United States, stated that "the desire of important religious denominations (such as the Anglican and Calvinist) for a literate, college-trained clergy was probably the most important single factor explaining the founding of the colonial colleges" (1997, 6). While the colleges also trained men for public administrative roles and professions, religion remained central to their mission. "To the early Harvard scholars, the university man was in direct line of succession to the original prophets and apostles" (Brubacher and Rudy 1997, 7). Religious organizations directly or indirectly controlled all of the American colleges founded before the Revolution. All but one institution stated as its purpose "the training of students for the Christian ministry" (Brubacher and Rudy, 1997, 7). Harvard, the first and most prestigious college, stated: "Every one shall consider the Mayne End of his life & studies, to know God and Jesus Christ, which is Eternall life [sic]" (Brubacher and Rudy 1997, 8).

In the American colleges students lived on a relatively self-contained campus that included not only their classrooms but residential dormitories and dining facilities. Due to the small number of colleges, students whose families did not live in the immediate vicinity of the school would be forced to live in the dormitories and pay a fee for their room and board in addition to the costs of tuition and books. College campuses became like small villages in which the students amused themselves with pranks, and provided their own recreation. With such liberty the faculty eventually took on the responsibility of safeguarding the students' activities outside the classroom, acting as surrogate parents and overseers.

The early colleges stressed philosophy and language arts, not unlike medieval European institutions. All required prayer, church attendance, and the study of theology. Faculty members, usually clergy, comprised the early colonial intelligentsia and were also entrusted with the moral development or at least care of their young charges. They often did so in a dictatorial and authoritarian manner. Students were expected to show deference not only to their instructors but to elder classmates, who subjected them to hazing and servile conditions. The domineering relationships imposed by older students led to riots and rebellions by the 1830s. A growing list of rules, regulations, and punishments aimed to enforce proper deportment in a never-ending struggle, as students found creative ways to avoid the authorities and their restrictions (Brubacher and Rudy 1997, 41–56). Sport provided a ready antidote and served as a means of social control. By the end of the nineteenth century many college administrators believed that sport provided training in leadership and character building. Sport seemed also to foster a martial spirit, a competitive attitude, and a will to win which was believed to be important for the young men of a young nation intent on achieving its place among the world powers.

With the advent of Enlightenment thinking in the late eighteenth century the religious requirements began to ease; but occasional religious revivals restored the moral influences on campuses. The president of Brown, a Rhode Island college, recalled the Puritan concerns for morality and work ethic when he admonished his students. "But a few men fail for want of intellect. There are two sources of failure in the world, first moral deviation, second indolence" (Brubacher and Rudy 1997, 51). Today, proselytizing evangelical groups continue their efforts on almost all college campuses. Many private colleges or universities maintain their affiliations with religions in a less stringent manner; but may still require some religious instruction or course work.

BOX 5.2 FELLOWSHIP OF CHRISTIAN ATHLETES (FCA)

The close interrelations between colleges, sport, and religion becomes evident in Christian associations who use sport as an arena for spreading their religious messages. The largest interdenominational Christian sport organization is the FCA, established in 1954. The organization promotes Christian values in the schools by enlisting athletes and coaches as a means of Christian evangelism. The FCA organizes summer camps featuring sports activities and uses Christian athletes at colleges around the country to promote its ideals. According to the report on its webpage, the FCA reached more than 356,250 people on 7,125 campuses and worked wth more than 46,000 coaches and athletes at camps across the globe.

(http://www.fca.org/AboutFCA/)

After winning independence from Great Britain, the American Congress provided lands for schools in its western territories. The influences of the Enlightenment and the need for practical knowledge led to early attempts to create public, state colleges, free from religious influence in the late eighteenth century.

The first technical institute was founded in 1824 as a "School of Theoretical and Practical Science to prepare teachers who would instruct the sons and daughters of local farmers and mechanics in the art of applying science to husbandry, manufactures, and domestic economy" (Brubacher and Rudy 1997, 61). Schools with an emphasis in engineering and science were established on other campuses thereafter. The University of Virginia, founded by Thomas Jefferson and opened in 1825, was the first to achieve true freedom from sectarian influence. In 1862 the federal government passed the Morrill Act, which provided land grants to states in order to establish schools that focused on agricultural and mechanical engineering.

After the American Civil War, separate colleges for women, blacks, and Native American Indians addressed marginalized groups of the population but provided a second-class education. As women and blacks gained increasing freedoms, including the permission to attend schools, they were segregated, with a few exceptions, from the mainstream institutions in separate schools. Native Americans, too, faced an isolated academic education in lower level residential schools that separated them from their tribes. They lost their own cultures and were forced into assimilation on the whites' terms. Their limited contact with white schools occurred largely through their athletic teams (Brubacher and Rudy 1997, 63–83, 143–173).

Body cultures and physical education at colleges

The ideas of the Enlightenment, especially the conviction of the juncture of body and mind as a precondition of learning, led to a new perspective on physical activities as well. In addition, the Civil War accentuated the necessity of fitness and health. The clergy began to preach the idea of a muscular Christianity that merged spirituality and physicality. As the housing of the soul, the body should be strong and competent. In the wake of these ideas, health and physical development became a concern of the colleges and universities by the mid-nineteenth century.

Some universities established departments of physical training, whose heads were often physicians (Park 1987, 50). It would be an interesting question to ask why physical education was provided in American colleges and universities whereas European universities had nothing to do with physical training or with athletics. They understood themselves as institutions of science where research and teaching should be confined to scientific disciplines, and they did not see themselves as socialization agencies.

In contrast, teachers at American universities felt responsible for their students' moral and physical health. Therefore, tests and measurements, the science of anthropometry, were developed and used in order to identify the health status of the students. Students who did not reach the defined norms and standards were assigned to medical gymnastics classes in order to correct deficiencies. This was the root of physical education at colleges, and led to structures, positions, and institutions which later became known as physical education departments.

Amherst College in Massachusetts appointed a medical doctor as a professor of hygiene and director of the gymnasium as early as 1861. Yale and Harvard established scientific institutes that included the study of human performance, especially the influence of nutrition. The scientists used athletes as subjects for their experiments, aimed at explaining physical efficiency. Philosophers, adherents of "pragmatism," such as John Dewey, espoused learning by doing. They claimed the potential of sport to learn teamwork, leadership, and social skills. Thus sport and games became acknowledged as physically and morally rewarding. By the 1880s the universities utilized different gymnastic systems as a means to enhance the physical development of their students (Van Dalen and Bennett 1971, 424–427).

football games

The newly founded women's colleges in the 1860s soon included anthropometric measurements as well. Delphine Hanna, a medical doctor at the coeducational Oberlin College in Ohio, became a well-known practitioner of anthropometry. In the women's schools of the Northeast the students rowed boats, skated on the ice in winter, played baseball and tennis, and even developed specialized clothing for their athletic pursuits and gymnastics classes (Warner 2006).

As the American version of football consumed the school rivalries by the end of the nineteenth century, specialization and rationalization of the game even encouraged scientific study. On the other hand, science could be used for the performance enhancement of the athletes. The Sheffield Scientific School at Yale embarked, for example, on nutritional studies of athletes to determine the best fuel for human engines. Athletes in various sports became laboratory subjects and photographic analysis of sporting activities fostered kinesiological studies of physical skill development. At the same time, the coaches developed proper training regimens based on scientific results, and the strategies on the football field assumed the level of championship chess matches (Mrozek 1983, 18–22, 196–202).

Athletics and football – a student's affair

Early athletic encounters at colleges and universities were often soccer games between classes that gave upper-class men an excuse to pummel and kick their younger classmates as a form of initiation. The first "intercollegiate" competition occurred in 1852 when Harvard and Yale agreed to a rowing match for a pair of silver oars as a prize. A railroad company sponsored the event as a means to promote a lakeside resort and a thousand spectators turned out to watch a Harvard victory (Rader 1990, 97). By 1858 four New England Colleges had formed the College Rowing Association (Guttmann 1988, 103). Yale students soon hired a professional coach to insure victory.

The commercialization of sport and its transformation to a business enterprise proved a harbinger of the future. Regattas maintained students' interests for the remainder of the century; but intercollegiate baseball and football, as well as track and field competitions, gained favor.

In 1869, male students organized the first intercollegiate football contest played according to soccer rules. Thereafter intercollegiate competitions became increasingly popular. The top schools of the northeastern states, like Princeton, Harvard, and Yale, known as the Big Three, played a leading role in the propagation of the game and in the negotiations about the rules (Davis 1911; Waddington and Roderick 1996; Watterson 2000).

In the beginning, football was based entirely on the initiative of the students. Its development and propagation was due to the specific learning and living conditions on the campus (u.a. Riesman and Denney 1951; Smith 1988; Miracle and Rees 1994; Guttmann 2006). Whereas in England teachers used football as a means to tame and educate students, in the US students used it as a refuge from the educational process. Annual intramural games established a class hierarchy and provided an excuse to batter younger students or their older oppressors. College presidents and professors reacted with dismay and alarm. They looked upon playing as a waste of time and they detested the violence and brutality of football. At Harvard, officials banned the game in 1860 and threatened persistent students with expulsion. The game was nevertheless quickly resurrected (Weyand 1955, 5, 10–11; Danzig 1956, 7; Rader 1983, 80–81; Gems 2000, 12).

Further concerns referred to loss of class time due to travel, and the betting and drinking associated with the games. The president of Cornell, a New York school, refused a request by the football team to get leave for a competition by stating: "I will not permit 30 men to travel 400 miles (660 km) merely to agitate a bag of wind (the football)" (Gems 2000, 13). However, as an extracurricular activity the game was outside of the control of the faculty who could not thwart the football enthusiasm of the students (Smith 1988; Gems 2000, 89; Watterson 2000).

The football teams commonly used the names of their schools to issue challenges to other schools and the faculty deemed their behavior as detrimental to the prestige of their institutions. The overemphasis on winning eventually led to the recruitment of players who were not students as well as to clandestine compensation to the players. These practices legitimated the attempts of the faculty to gain control of the athletic teams; but at the same time, as football became an important weapon in the rivalry between academic institutions some professors began to support the game. Football victories elicited a great deal of school pride and championship games soon became national spectacles, held in large urban arenas, that allowed for the greatest number of seats to be sold. Pride and profit led to the employment of professional coaches, undue alumni involvement in the way of financial or recruiting support, and the use of illegal players. College administrators tried to enact greater control over student activities – especially games and competitions – by incorporating them within the formal structure of the school. They did so by hiring athletic coaches as faculty members and forming administrative governing bodies to create, regulate, and apply common standards of participation for all football teams under their jurisdiction.

The new role of football may be shown in the competition between Yale and Harvard on and off the field. Harvard was the chosen institution of elite American families; whereas Yale, founded in 1701, attracted the newly rich. Both aspired to academic excellence but Harvard had the longer pedigree. Yale used football to close the gap. Between 1880 and 1905 Yale beat Harvard twenty-three out of twenty-five times (Smith 1994, xv). Her victories generated great school spirit and bragging rights, especially among the Yale students and alumni (graduates of the school). The Yale system, developed under Walter Camp, a former player (and head of the football rules committee), included organized practices in training, specialized roles for players, and strategic innovations. It also included the systematic recruitment of the best athletes from American prep schools. Walter Camp was one of the initiators of the above-mentioned commercialization of football. Under Camp's guidance the student managers rented large stadiums in big cities, New York in particular. The generated money derived from admission fees eventually resulted in a very large secret fund which served to provide gifts and pay for players' expenses (Watterson 2000).

BOX 5.3 RECRUITMENT PRACTICES

In June, 1905 Henry Beach Needham published an exposé of recruitment practices in *McClure's Magazine* (pp. 115–128).

> Hogan entered Exeter [a prep school], a poor boy, at the age of twenty-three . . . Harvard joined Yale and Princeton in competition for this great prep athlete. . . . Hogan went to Yale . . . [he] occupies a suite in Vanderbilt Hall – the most luxurious of the Yale dormitories . . . He takes his meals at the University Club . . . an expensive undergraduate organization similar to any social club. The initiation fee and dues are remitted . . . Hogan made a ten-day trip to Cuba. The athletic association paid for the excursion, which cost . . . $25 per day for Hogan . . . Hogan receives $100 a year, the income of the John Bennett Scholarship. In addition, according to the dean, his entire tuition is abated. The baseball association gives to Hogan (and two teammates) the score-card privilege.[a] From the sale of the cards at intercollegiate games and from the advertising, these athletes take the entire proceeds; the athletic association gets nothing . . . Hogan's income is further augmented by commissions paid him by the American Tobacco Company.

[a] The players received a percentage of the sales of the scorecards which were sold at the game at a time before they had electronic scoreboards. People enjoyed keeping score for themselves and many have kept the scorecards as nostalgic souvenirs of the games they attended.

Harvard retaliated by hiring a professional coach at a salary nearly double that of a professor; but he succeeded in defeating the Yale football team in only one out of three matches (Rader 1990, 175). Other colleges desirous of Yale's success employed more than a hundred former Yale players as coaches. In most cases these coaches were employed on a temporary basis and were paid by the students. The Yale system of training, preparation, and management, and the use of professional coaches spread quickly throughout the United States (Smith 1988).

The University of Chicago, founded in 1892, sought immediate status. The first president of the University, a former Yale professor, hired Amos Alonzo Stagg, a recent Yale star, as football coach and gave him the title of "athletic director." Stagg became the first professional coach to gain faculty status. Employed as head of the new department he answered directly to the president, who aimed to gain institutional control over the students' sports, promote his new university, and realize the financial benefit of the football games (Lester 1995). Harper told Stagg: "I want you to develop teams which we can send around the country and knock out all the colleges. We will give them a palace (railroad) car and a vacation too" (Brubacher and Rudy 1997, 133).

Stagg's salary in 1892 was $2,500 per year, which was 40 per cent higher than that of the average professor. In the following years the salaries of coaches escalated. In 1901 the University of Michigan, a rival of the University of Chicago, hired Fielding Yost, despite a negative reputation, at a salary of $2,000 plus expenses. Yost served only as the football coach and had no academic responsibilities. In 1904 Georgia Tech University awarded Coach John Heisman not only a salary of $2,200 plus expenses but 30 per cent of the gate revenue of football games as well. By 1905 Stagg's salary at Chicago had reached $6,000 when that of a full professor was only $4,500. In 1918, Hugo Bezdek, one of Stagg's former players, was hired at Penn State University as the coach and department head at a cost of $14,500. Two years later Stanford University in California attracted Glenn "Pop" Warner with a salary of $7,500, the same as a full professor; but Warner also received $2,500 in "expenses" and another $2,500 bonus when his team was invited to the Rose Bowl game in the post-season (Smith 2007). The escalation of coaching salaries continued throughout the twentieth century, and top coaches' salaries now surpass those of the university presidents. In addition, famous coaches enjoy academic honors. Joe Paterno, the current coach at Penn State University, with a stadium that accommodates more than 100,000 spectators, has full professor status, although he has never taught a class nor authored a scholarly book (see Chapter 12).

Athletic departments – faculty gains control

The integration of athletics with the Physical Education Department created a new model in American higher education, which initiated very ambiguous processes. The idealistic notion of sport as a means to build character suffered in the realistic world of competition and the need to win. Universities, established to promote high ideals and greater intellectual achievements, willfully accepted and coddled unsatisfactory pupils who masqueraded as student athletes. The increasing commercialization of college sport, especially football, meant compromising educational principles for financial gain (Sperber 1990; Thelin 1994; Byers 1997; Shulman 2001; Duderstadt 2003). A good example is the University of Michigan, one of the main competitors among universities in the search for national prominence. In 1901, it hired a professional coach, Fielding Yost, who had been successful at Kansas and Stanford in California by importing experienced, even professional players. The Stanford president related the following story:

> A young fellow came in from the mines who wanted to study mining-engineering – a tremendously big and strong fellow. He was admitted . . . as a special student . . . failed in his studies, and was dropped. Yost carried him to Michigan, where

he has become the center of a strong team which is the pride of Michigan University; and this man, who was not able to pass any examinations (while at Stanford) . . . has been playing some ten or fifteen games a year at Michigan . . . All of us who have ever had a Yost or any Yost-like man about are not to be counted as sinless.

(Rader 1990, 177)

The growing numbers of spectators since the 1880s enticed more and more university administrations to build concrete stadiums, whose mortgages had to be paid, thus committing them to the commercialization of sport. Harvard built a concrete stadium seating 40,000 in 1903, and Yale nearly doubled the size of this facility with a 75,000-seat arena in 1914 (Gems 2000, 29; Guttmann 2006). Harvard named this stadium Soldiers Field as a memorial to the Civil War dead, thus promoting the image of nationalism and patriotism.

The attempts of the professors to gain control over the increasingly violent game succeeded, to some degree, with the foundation of the National College Athletic Association (NCAA) in 1906. In 1905 the representatives of sixty-eight schools met in New York to address the violence and cases of deaths on the football field and to discuss solutions, thirty-eight of which formed a governing body in 1906 (eventually regulating most college sports). Another thirty-three players died in 1909, necessitating further reforms. Despite the brutality of football, schools were reluctant to give up the game. The University of California, Stanford

Figure 5.1 Football melée (National Police Gazette, December 20, 1884; Library of Congress)

and Northwestern University turned to rugby as an alternative; but soon returned to football. Swarthmore College even denied a bequest worth millions of dollars rather than abort its athletic program (Gems 2000, 29, 61–62).[1] Resistance against the game proved in vain, among other things because of the popularity of football among the students, the alumni, and powerful members of the schools' boards of trustees. The colleges and universities had also constructed football as a signifier of status and prestige, and it seemed to be impossible for single institutions to resist the myths of sport as an incorporation of American values, to establish a counter-discourse, and to enforce other symbols of academic superiority.

BOX 5.4 CONSIDERATIONS OF A COLLEGE PRESIDENT

We are the university, was the attitude of the Dupont faculty. Consequently, they resented not only the vast amount of money that went to sports, they also resented the glory. Why should a collection of anabolic morons such as the Dupont basketball team, led by a man who goes by the ridiculous name of Buster, be idealized at one of the world's greatest institutions of learning? The President had wondered about the same thing himself, for years . . . It wasn't until he was promoted from chairman of the history department to provost of the university that he began to understand. Contrary to what most people believed . . . big-time sports did not make money for the university, did not help to underwrite the academic depart-ments, etc. National championship teams receiving big postseason television fees lost still more money, more than all the minor sports, baseball, tennis, squash, lacrosse, swimming, the lot put together. Big-time sports were a stupendous drag on the financial health of the university . . . Nor did alumni donations increase or decrease with the fortunes of the teams. It was something subtler and grander at the same time. Big-time sports created a glorious aura about everything the university did and in the long run increased everything sharply – prestige, alumni donations, receipts of every sort, as well as influence. But why? God only knew!

(Wolfe 2005, 559–560)

Rules of the game

In the beginning, various versions of soccer and/or rugby were played at the different universities. Therefore, long and sometimes difficult negotiations took place before competitions. By 1873, the students who served as team captains or managers organized meetings and tried to develop and enforce common rules. Not the least because of the rivalries between the universities, it took until the early twentieth century until a consensus about a body of rules was reached. This was the result of numerous negotiations and power struggles in which not only values and meanings of the game but also the prestige of the universities was at stake. In the following years numerous changes of the rules were necessary, partly as reactions to the violence on the football ground, partly with the aim of increasing the attractiveness of the game (u.a. Riesman and Denney 1951; Nelson 1994; Waddington and Roderick 1996; Guttmann 2006).

The current football rules can be condensed as follows. The official playing time is sixty minutes, divided into four quarters with a half-time intermission, but because of the numerous interruptions a game can last for more than three hours. The name "football" is misleading, because "normally" the ball is thrown or carried.[2] The ball can be kicked over and through the goal posts (a field goal); or punted (kicked) away from one's own goal. In contrast to most of the modern ball games, the players can be pushed, thrown, or tackled (pulled down) to the ground.

The basic idea of American football is simple: there are two teams, each with eleven players, which start the game on opposite halves (sides) of the field. The game is initiated with a kick-off, and the recipient of the kick-off is determined by a coin toss. The aim of the game is to bring the ball into the opponent's end zone. Six points are awarded if the ball is carried in the end zone (touchdown), three points if the ball is kicked from any location/distance on the field through the goal posts in the end zone (field goal). After each touchdown the ball is placed two yards from the goal line (NFL rules) and another opportunity to score is awarded (known as an extra point or point after touchdown (PAT)). One point is awarded if the ball is kicked through the goal posts (as in a field goal) or two points if the ball is successfully run or passed across the goal line (the end zone). In addition, points are given if the defensive team manages to stop (tackle) a member of the offensive team with the ball in his own end zone (safety: two points).

Every play begins with the opposing teams lining up on opposite sides of the scrimmage line. The ball may be advanced by running and carrying it. Like rugby, the ball can be handed or tossed backward while running at any time; but forward passes must be thrown from behind the line of scrimmage. Once the ball has passed the scrimmage line it can no longer be thrown or tossed forward.

The defensive team tries to tackle the ball carrier as soon as possible. As soon as the player with the ball is brought to the ground, the play stops, which establishes a new scrimmage line. The players come together in a timed "huddle" (thirty seconds) and the quarterback gives the directions for the next play based on the yardage gained or lost and the distance to the end zone.

The offensive team has to advance the ball at least ten yards (9.14 meters) in four tries. If it is successful, the team continues until a score is attained, the team loses the ball through a fumbled ball recovered by the defensive team or an intercepted pass, or if they fail to gain the required ten yards. If the offensive team determines that it cannot gain the required

Figure 5.2 Huddle (North Central College Archives)

Figure 5.3 Running play (North Central College Archives)

ten yard's it may punt (kick) the ball to the opponents; but as far as possible away from its goal. A touchdown or field goal requires the team which has scored the points to kick the ball to their opponents, who then assume the offensive role.

Because of the need to advance into the opponents' territory, football means a struggle for space whereby tactics are of major importance. The players have different and exactly defined roles and specific tasks on both offense and defense. This leads to a very high specialization and to the development of different types of players from the heavyweight offensive and defensive linemen to the fast, agile, and versatile running backs. The coaches are the conductors of the game. They transfer their tactical instructions to the quarterback via signals with their hands, through incoming players, or via an intercom in the player's helmet. The quarterback has the final decision, announces the plays, and transfers the ball to a runner or receiver by a hand-off or a pass. Besides these basic rules of the games there are numerous additional regulations and penalties for individual or team offenses which make the game rather complicated and hard to understand for people who have not grown up with American football.

Football rules allow direct bodily contact and body blows; but prohibit fighting. During tackling of the ball carrier, the size and velocity of colliding players results in a high rate of injuries and makes football the most dangerous team sport. As studies have shown, two out of three players have to live with a permanent handicap after finishing a professional football career (Guttmann 2006; Oriard 2007, 207).

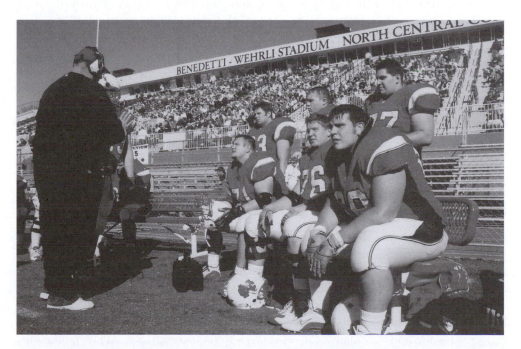

Figure 5.4 Sideline coach's instruction (North Central College Archives)

BOX 5.5 FOOTBALL VIOLENCE

Last Saturday, Stanford quarterback Tavita Pritchard was struck in the head by an opponent so violently that his helmet was ripped off, his bare head snapped back and forth and his skull slammed to the ground with a thud. Hawaii quarterback Colt Brennan, a Heisman Trophy contender, was knocked unconscious by a crushing hit three weeks ago. The Oklahoma freshman quarterback Sam Bradford sustained a concussion while being trampled in a game two weeks ago.

Each impact triggered the delicate and controversial process of determining when the athlete is fit to return to the field . . . College players operate in a murky zone: their bodies are between youth and manhood, they play in quasi-professional environments on national television – unpaid but with the riches of professional careers dangling before them – and no rules govern how concussions are treated in college football. Coach Harbaugh said he expected both Pritchard and Ostrander to play Saturday because both are capable and of similar talent. He said he would decide how much each plays, and who starts, solely on how they perform in practice . . . He added that unless Pritchard displayed the effects of the concussion in practice, which he had not through Tuesday, the injury would not be a consideration.

(Alan Schwarz, *New York Times*, November 30, 2007 at
http://www-tech.mit.edu/V127/N58/concussions.html)

Football rituals – marching bands and cheerleaders

Together with the rules, numerous symbols and rituals were added to the game which contributed decisively to the attractiveness of football. Thus, "marching bands," especially in the collegiate games, accompany the teams to the playing ground. They also entertain the audiences during the half-time intermission.

The cheerleaders play a specific role in the spectacle of football. In the early years of the game, the task of calling on the spectators to cheer was strictly a man's domain, as male spectators would not be expected to follow the directives of a woman. By the 1920s sexual allure became a prominent form of advertising and attraction for males, and women began to assume the role of cheerleaders at athletic contests (Hanson 1995, 15). Cheerleading has become a display of femininity before and during football and basketball games, displays of aggressiveness and masculinity. Cheerleading is a controversial issue: Whereas feminists interpret the exhibitions of the cheerleaders as a demonstration of the inferior and

Figure 5.5 Marching band (North Central College Archives)

sexualized role of women, cheerleaders themselves tend to understand their activities, consisting of tumbling, dance, and stunting, as a serious sport which also has a competitive side. Since the 1980s, cheerleading teams emerged whose main objective was and is competition.

In American schools, cheerleading is an essential part of the extracurricular activities with millions of young women involved. There is hard competition for membership on the cheerleading squad which consists of well-trained, but mostly also pretty and slim students. However, the training is compensated by the chance to perform in front of large audiences and stand, at least for a short time, in the center of attention (Adams and Bettis 2003).

BOX 5.6 MARCHING BANDS AND CHEERLEADERS

Chip told me that the Wildcats had one of the best marching bands in the State with over 40 kids playing different instruments. The band had its own leader who was also a music teacher at the school. It performed in the half time shows during football games and practiced almost as much as the football team. Chip was rather surprised when I asked him what cheerleaders were, and couldn't believe we didn't have them in German schools. As far

Figure 5.6 Cheerleading (North Central College Archives)

as I can make out they are mostly attractive girls who dress up in uniforms and do dances and chants on the sidelines while the game is going on. Chip said that for a girl, being a cheerleader was about the most important thing there was. Over 100 girls tried to make the squad and they only took ten, it was very competitive. He may be right because the girls were very pretty. Watching cheerleading practice is a lot more fun than watching football practice . . . The coolest girls are the cheerleaders, but some are a bit stuck up and only hang around with the football players.

(Brettschneider and Brandl-Bredenbeck 1997, 14)

FOOTBALL AND THE VALUES OF AMERICAN SOCIETY

Football as an American game

The arguments and the numerous statements about football show the close intertwinement between football and American culture. From the nineteenth century up until to today, journalists, coaches, players, authors, pedagogues, and politicians constructed football as an American game using collective symbols and remembrances. They emphasized over and over again that football could produce and demonstrate the state-supporting credos and the allegedly endangered values of the "New World." Football became a means of orientation and self-assurance which were especially important in periods of change and insecurity (u.a. Oriard 1993; Gems 2000; Mandelbaum 2004). Sean F. Brown has charged that football retains and even strengthens its popularity in the United States relative to baseball and basketball because most of the players are Americans (Brown 2005).

Football was and is not the only national sport of the Americans. Until the 1960s, baseball had more adherents than football, but football had dominated at the colleges and universities since the 1890s. Football fascinated especially the elites, among other things, because the game fitted with their visions about America as a world power and was looked upon as a vehicle to transport their norms and values, as well as a reassurance of their own virility. When high schools and colleges began to become accessible for lower classes and immigrants of the second generation after the turn of the century, football gained acceptance also in the wider American society (Riesman and Denney 1951; Smith 1988; Watterson 2000). With the establishment of the first professional teams, members of the working class were also attracted to the sport due to its obvious physicality.

Football developed in the period after the Civil War (1861–1865) and experienced an upswing at the end of the century at a time when numerous societal changes occurred. During this period, the USA was transformed from an agrarian to an industrial society which was connected with processes of modernization and urbanization, with new forms of struggles between the classes and the races, including the confrontations with and the integration of numerous and various groups of immigrants. The turn of the century was also a period when the women's movement gained ground and when gender relations changed. In the 1890s there was a growing divide between rich and poor, and poverty seemed to threaten larger circles of society. The problems of the farmers – not the least owing to surplus production – financial crises and strikes also endangered the position of the middle and upper classes. In the midst of such changes the United States began to compete with the European powers for world leadership (Zimmerman 2002; Traxel 2006).

The social problems caused intellectuals to especially engage themselves in the reforms of the so called "Progressive Era." They fought against *laissez-faire* capitalism and stood up for democracy and social justice. In many American states the activities of the reformers caused changes in the laws, which improved the working conditions and restricted the power of the monopolies. Other conflicts continued to be prevalent between the North and the South. Although the Civil War was over, there were still economic, political, and cultural tensions between the southern and the northern states. The different traditions and cultures, but also the different economic systems and ways of production as well as the different conditions of life in the various areas in the USA resisted homogenization.

During this period, football offered opportunities for identification, especially to the elites whose power was endangered by the reforms as well as by the crises mentioned above. Football began to be looked upon as a symbol of the "New World" – geographically and metaphorically. Since the 1880s, the conformity between the values and messages of football and the ideologies of American society was one of the most often evoked topics of the influential upper classes. James Knox of Harvard explained that "Football . . . embodies so many factors that are typically American . . . virile, intensive, aggressive energy that makes for progress is the root which upholds and feeds American supremacy" (Gems 2000, 20). Waddington and Roderick expressed the coincidence between football and American identity as follows: "Baseball and American football draw upon and express – or at least, and no less importantly, are commonly believed to draw upon and express – a set of values and characteristics which are uniquely American" (Waddington and Roderick 1996, 34).

The establishment of national identity made it necessary for Americans to gain distance from the "mother land" and to develop specific characteristics: "Americanness." This was also an issue of sport. The emancipation from the British games of soccer and rugby, and with this symbolically from Great Britain, was accomplished and demonstrated by a successive change of the football rules (u.a. Riesman and Denney 1951; Waddington and Roderick 1996; Guttmann 2006). Walter Camp, head of the rules committee until 1925 and considered to be the "father of American football," stated: "Our players have strayed away from the original rugby rules . . . they have built up a game and rules of their own, more suited to American needs" (quoted in Gems 2000, 20). American football differs from rugby among other things by the concept of the scrimmage line; that means the formation in two lines after each "down," the concept of gaining space, and the high importance of tactics.

Football and American myths

In an immigrant country like America, a common culture and a national identity cannot be created as in the "old world" by a common language, tradition, and history. The Americans of various origins constructed their collective remembrances beginning with their arrival on the American continent, whereby the collective memories about their home countries and the experiences in their new country combined with specific places and cultures of remembrance.

The experiences of immigration and settlement were evoked over and over again as constitutive of the American identity. The political myth of the "frontier"[3] emphasized the importance and the challenge of the outlying regions, which separated civilization and wilderness and which was moved continuously throughout the nineteenth century to the West (u.a. Slotkin 1985, 1992). The myth evoked the historical designation of the Americans, their "manifest destiny" to conquer frontiers and to civilize the wilderness. It was/is believed that the allegedly typical features of the Americans developed during the move towards the West and the colonization of the country. The "virtues" of the settlers, trappers, and cowboys were believed – as espoused by Theodore Roosevelt – to guarantee America's magnitude (see Chapter 12). Following the civilization of the wilderness in the 1890s, sport was imagined as the "new frontier" and took over the task of character formation, community building, and a release of urban tensions in the overcrowded cities (see Chapter 1) (Paxson 1917; Riess 1995; Dyreson 2005).

The concept of sport as a frontier might be envisioned in other ways as well. Sport is per se a challenge because it requires performances to be surpassed over and over again. The imminent call of sport to overcome boundaries made it easy to imagine sport as a frontier area and this is especially true for football because the fight for space could be imagined as the conquest of land. Thus football could be used as a collective symbol of America. For some, the professionals and the recipients of college athletic scholarships, football offered a means to socioeconomic mobility, as promised by the frontier.

In addition, football seems to demonstrate the popular Social Darwinist doctrine about the "survival of the fittest," whereby "fit" in the sense of Darwin refers to the ability to adapt, but in football ideology fit was associated with strength and dominance. In a 1900 *Outing* magazine article, Harvard coach and later American Governor-General of the Philippines W. Cameron Forbes asserted that football "is the dominant spirit of the dominant race" (cited in Guttmann 2006: 537).

Football, like other sports, was believed to serve as a "melting-pot," where immigrants, especially the second generation, could learn the "American way of life" and prove themselves as genuine Americans. An excellent example of the rise of an immigrant to national fame as an exceptionally gifted football coach is Knute Rockne (see Chapter 12; Sperber 1993; Waddington and Roderick 1996). Last but not least, football and football matches had great importance for the accommodation of the heterogeneous regions of the USA.

Football as a bastion of masculinity

With the civilization of the "Wild West" the needs for real men were met. The rise of the middle classes and the increase of white-collar jobs led to a devaluation of physical exertion and strength in the workplace. This and the emerging women's movements rendered traditional concepts of masculinity obsolete and jeopardized the positions of the WASP (white Anglo-Saxon Protestant) males, who imagined themselves as the pride of creation. At the turn of the century, women sought paid employment and political rights. A new ideal was the athletic Gibson Girl who embodied the freedom and the new opportunities available to women, including the opportunity to play sport. In short: women intruded continuously in areas previously reserved for men (see Chapter 11) (Guttmann 1991).

Football was one of the numerous answers of men to the threatening incursions of women. The football field was and remained a domain of men (Nelson 1996; Gems 2007). According to Guttmann (2006: 536), "football had . . . a long career as the chosen sport of Ivy League athletes eager to prove that they were real men and not 'mollycoddles' . . . Within the tight confines of rationality, football allowed for bravado and demonstrations of rugged masculinity." Messner decribed the gender relations on and off the football field, as follows:

> Football, based as it is on the most extreme possibilities of the male body . . . is clearly a world apart from women, who are relegated to the role of cheerleaders/sex objects on the sidelines . . . in contrast to the bare and vulnerable bodies of the cheerleaders, the armoured bodies of the football players are elevated to mythical status and as such, give testimony to the undeniable "fact" that here is at least one place where men are clearly superior to women.
>
> (Messner 1988, 202)

BOX 5.7 CHEERLEADERS AS AWARDS?

"That's what cheerleaders are all about." "What is?" said Camille. "Well, you know – they're a chorus line," said Edgar. "They kick their legs like cancan dancers, they show you the inside of them – thighs, their breasts are hoisted up like missiles waiting for someone to push the button, they're wiggling their hips, they wear these skimpy outfits . . . you know what I mean." Camille said, "I know what you mean, but I don't get it." Edgar hesitated before saying, "They're the sexual reward – or they represent the sexual reward." Running out of patience: "Whose sexual reward?" "The athletes'," said Edgar, "or that's what they represent."

(Wolfe 2005, 312–313)

The majority of the football spectators were men, but the game also attracted women, although or perhaps because football was a demonstration of values and practices which enhanced masculinity and reproduced the gender hierarchy. Only very few women offered resistance. Sometimes the mothers of the players who feared for the health or even the life of their sons protested against the violence on the football field. But there have been exceptions. In 1897 Richard "Von" Gammon was killed in a football game between the universities of Georgia and Virginia, two southern states where male honor was held paramount. When the State of Georgia attempted to ban the sport, Mrs. Gammon, the mother of the deceased player, protested against the ban to the state legislature (Gems 2000, 59–60).

Up until today, football produces and demonstrates masculinity. The mascots and the names of the teams (i.e. Rams, Jaguars, Lions, Panthers, Vikings) symbolize strength and aggressiveness. Names such as the Cowboys or the Buffalo Bills transport collective memories about a glorified past and tie in with the "Frontier Myth" (Messner and Sabo 1990; Guttmann 2006). The bodies of the players, with their broad shoulders and muscular thighs, are shaped like a triangle and comply thus with the ideal of hypermasculinity. Today this shape is exaggeratedly emphasized by the clothes and equipment. Tight trousers make each muscle visible, pads exaggerate the broadness of the shoulders, and the helmets add the image of a warrior.

The aggressive masculinity which the players demonstrate with their bodies, their habitus, and their behavior patterns are also a means of social distinction. Since the nineteenth century, football players have enjoyed the status of heroes on the college campuses. They enact masculinity not only on the football field but in everyday life, at parties, as well as in drinking rituals (u.a. Crosset and McDonald 1995; Coakley 2004, 2007).[4]

BOX 5.8 FOOTBALL, MASCULINITY, AND POLITICS

Over the next three weeks, America will be in thrall to its cult of masculinity. Weekends will be defined by the NFL playoffs, culminating in the Super Bowl Feb. 3. What remains of the nation's attention, after football, will be seized by presidential politics, leading up to the decisive primaries on Super Tuesday, Feb. 5. The first process is a celebration of a peculiar notion of manliness, while the second is a prisoner of it.

It does not take an anthropologist to understand that professional football occupies its central place in the American imagination as a sublimation of violence. That may be its main virtue. Indeed, games in which males draw up lines on fields and then contest those lines with balls date to the dawn of history, when such activities took the place of actual combat. Struggles between tribes were ritualized with primitive games, sometimes to the death. The first balls may have been decapitated heads.

In America, football is a last preserve of "manhood" . . . one remaining source of gender bonding that has withstood the pressures of the feminist revolution. Indeed, football players remain the beau ideal for girls who hope only to be some guy's trophy. And football, with its culture of unashamed physicality, butt slapping, and hugging, offers release from the otherwise too-threatening impulses of the homoerotic.

(James Carroll, *Boston Globe*, January 14, 2008 at http://www.boston.com/bostonglobe/editorial_opinion/ oped/articles/2008/01/14/electoral_politics_as_sport/)

With the control of the game by the faculty, football promised (and still promises) character formation, the education of real men. "The game is a thorough education in all the qualities that go to make a manly man. It teaches obedience, self-restraint, unselfishness + calls for the greatest amount of pluck, self-denial, quickness of thought + action," claimed lawyer John Poe in 1894 (quoted in Gems 2000, 53; see also Miracle and Rees 1994). President Theodore Roosevelt, a sportsman himself, accepted only a man "who is actually in the arena, whose face is marred by dust, and sweat, and blood" (quoted in Gems 2000, 53).

A central ingredient in the enactment of masculinity was and is violence, which was at first only restricted by few and ineffective rules (Guttmann 2006). In the Yale versus Princeton game in 1884 the "elevens . . . hurl themselves together . . . in kicking and writhing heaps . . . throttling, wrestling, and the pitching of individuals headlong to the earth . . . savage blows that drew blood, and falls that . . . crack the bones" (quoted in Gems 2000, 18). Hits, punches, and choking were the order of the business. The spectators cheered for the players with calls like: "kill him, break his neck, slug him." It was a popular tactic to injure, as soon as possible, the best player of the other team and thus put him out of action. Injuries and even deaths were commonplace. In 1905, for example, eighteen deaths and 156 severe injuries occurred, and in 1909, as many as thirty-three players lost their lives on the football grounds. The brutality of the game led, as already mentioned, to the foundation of the NCAA and caused the governing bodies of some universities to demand that football be banned (Gems 2000, 26).

The adherents of the game reacted to these demands with arguments based on Social Darwinism. They claimed that football would prepare young men to thrive in a world in which only the strongest could survive. In addition, America needed men with the drive for victory in order to fulfill its "manifest destiny" (Zelinsky 1988; Gems 2000, 26). Violence was looked upon as catharsis and as a necessity in the face of the alleged effeminacy and feminization of society (Gems 2000, 97). According to Waddington and Roderick (1996),

American football mirrors the relatively low level of pacification and the relatively high propensity of violence in American society, although various changes in the rules, especially the prevention of mass collisions, led to a decrease in the number of injuries. However, violence is still a central problem in football (Gems 2000, 29). Guttmann (2006) interprets the development of football as a civilization process with an increase of rules and a decrease of violence. However, football may become increasingly dangerous because of the growing weight and strength of the athletes.

Masculinity means the readiness to make sacrifices, self discipline, and the willingness to bear pain without complaint (Gems 2000, 56). Injuries were (and are) not a reason to sit on the bench. Coaches, the other players, and the audiences expect "team spirit" and full commitment regardless of casualties (Sabo 1989).

Football was and is imagined as war on a "mimic battlefield," on which two teams act as "two armies, managed on military principles" (Whitney 1892, quoted in Gems 2000, 3). Thus it is no wonder that numerous war metaphors were/are used in order to describe the game.

Governor Wolcott of Massachusetts was one of the many who drew a comparison between war and football. He stated in 1898 in the *Boston Globe* that "the thing that makes a man a strong, fearless and clean athlete makes him also a good citizen of his country, a gallant soldier" (quoted in Gems 2000, 75). Football was looked upon as surrogate warfare and as a preparation for the country's call, a state of readiness for future military actions (Wolcott 1898, quoted in Gems 2000, 73). In compliance with these ideologies, in the short Spanish–American War in 1898, numerous football players fought as volunteers in the "Rough Riders" regiment, led by Theodore Roosevelt (Zimmerman 2002; see Chapter 12). Infected by the war metaphors, the football players would later go enthusiastically to both World Wars, where many former players lost their lives and gained heroic status (Gems 2000, 79).

BOX 5.9 FOOTBALL PLAYERS AS PATRIOTIC HEROES

In the most celebrated recent case, Pat Tillman, a player for the Arizona Cardinals of the NFL, abandoned his $3.6 million contract after the 2001 season to join the US Army Rangers. In 2004 Tillman was killed in a fire-fight with al-Queda forces in Afghanistan. The US government and the NFL quickly eulogized and honored Tillman as an exemplary hero with memorial services; but that fanfare was soon exposed as a cover-up when journalists discovered that Tillman had actually been killed by friendly fire (a mistake by American troops). Despite the circumstances of Tillman's death (and his personal disagreement with the US invasion of Iraq) the NFL and the general public continue to fuse football, military service, and heroism.

(Gerald Gems)

Figure 5.7 Homecoming (North Central College Archives)

Winning is everything

Football embodies the "winning is everything mentality" dominant in the USA (see Chapter 1). "By contrast to the British, the Americans demonstrated a high degree of interest in winning games and winning one's way to high production goals," wrote Riesman and Denney in their article about "Football in America" (1951). "Americans play to win," stated General George S. Patton in his speech on the D-day invasion of the allied forces at Normandy during World War II. That sentiment can already be found in a magazine article in 1905, which emphasizes the parallels between sport and business in the USA. The writer claimed that the Americans were far more serious than the British in both business enterprises and sports, which accounted for US ascendance in both spheres (quoted in Gems 2000, 28). The famous coach of the Green Bay Packers during the 1960s, Vince Lombardi, overemphasized winning and he is often attributed with the phrase "winning isn't everything, it is the ONLY thing" (quoted in Maraniss 1999, 365; see Chapter 12). Winning is so important that the rules prevent a game from ending in a tie. Winning at all costs also means that violations of the rules are interpreted as tactical maneuvers, even if health is put at risk. This is demonstrated by the numerous players who paid for their football career with serious health damage or even invalidity.

As early as 1890 *The Nation* stated that "The spirit of the American youth, as of the man, is to win . . . by fair means or foul; and the lack of moral scruple which pervades the struggle of the business world meets with temptations equally irresistible in the miniature contests of the football field" (quoted in Gems 2000, 97).

Football and the American economy

Football exemplifies the processes of industrialization and economic development as well as the scientific approaches to the bodies.

> The mid-field dramatization of line against line, the recurrent starting and stopping of field action around the timed snapping of a ball, the trend to a formalized division of labor between backfield and line, above all, perhaps, the increasingly precise synchronization of men in motion – these developments make it seem plausible to suggest that the whole procedural rationalization of the game was not unwelcome to Americans, and that it fitted in with other aspects of their industrial folkways.
>
> (Riesman and Denney 1951, 318)

The development of football also fits the "spirit of capitalism" in the sense of Max Weber, which dominate American society. Already at the end of the nineteenth century, football had developed into a prosperous commercial enterprise in which the college players, because of their supposed amateur status, were and are not allowed to participate (at least, they were not allowed to be paid for their performances) (Smith 1988).[5]

BOX 5.10 THE LITTLE GIFTS TO ATHLETES

There – right in front of him – there it was! . . . a brand-new Chrysler Annihilator SUV pickup . . . Jojo stood still on the sidewalk about fifteen feet away from this awesome manifestation of beauty and power and slowly withdrew from his right-hand pocket . . . sure enough, a set of keys on a ring that also bore a little black remote-controlled transmitter and an inch-long, lozenge-shaped tab with a piece of white enameled metal – just like the car's – on one side and a license plate number on the other. On the passenger seat was what looked like a small white leather album . . . and inside . . . but he really already knew: the vehicle's registration and insurance cards in the name of his father, David Johanssen. It was no doubt the same arrangement they – the booster club, known as Charlie's Roundtable – had made for the Dodge Durango he had, in fact, driven over to the Buster bowl this afternoon.

(Wolfe 2005, 54–55)

Wealthy alumni (graduates of the school) often join a booster (fan) club of the football or basketball teams. They donate large sums of money to the schools and often try to induce high school athletes to come to the college, sometimes with expensive and illegal gifts. Schools endeavor to keep all alumni involved with the school through regular correspondence, emails, and social gatherings. Each year the school provides a major festival, known as a homecoming, to attract former students back to the school and maintain their lifelong loyalty in the hope that they will support the institution with monetary gifts (see Chapter 6) (Sperber 1990; Thelin 1994; Byers 1997; Shulman 2001; Duderstadt 2003).

Conclusion

Today, in a time of modernization and globalization and all the insecurity connected with rapid changes, football provides Americans with a means of identification because the game symbolizes both tradition and progress. The physicality of the game recalls times in which real men and atavistic fights existed, while the elaborate tactics and the scientifically calculated systems of the game portray the rationality of modernity (see e.g. Riesman and Denney 1951; Waddington and Roderick 1996).

As a conclusion one can state that football was and is a product as well as a motor of Americanness. "The symbols, rituals, and meanings inherent in the game resulted in a clear definition of the United States as an aggressive, commercial, patriarchal culture ready to promote its ideals on the world stage" (Gems 2000, 7).

American football is the biggest sport attraction in the USA (for professional football, see Chapter 8), whereas it has not established itself with a firm foundation in Europe, although businessmen tried to import the game and although the National Football League (NFL) invested considerable resources to market football in various European countries (Dzikus 2004).

Why is football not attractive for Europeans? The complex body of rules and regulations, especially the long list of breaches of the rules, the numerous interruptions of the game, the long duration, the counting of points gained in various actions, the extreme specialization of the players which allows only players of certain positions to become stars – all this contravenes the "taste" of European and South American soccer fans. They perceive football as difficult to understand, long-winded and, because of the high level of aggression, as pre-modern.

THE "OTHER" FOOTBALL GAME – SOCCER IN THE USA

With the rise of football as a national sport, a domain of men, and a demonstration of masculinity, soccer was pushed to the sidelines, but it did not disappear. It became a game of women and of youth and was played by schoolboys in several American cities in the nineteenth century (Abrams 1995). In addition, in the USA, soccer was popular with Polish, Jewish, Irish, German, Italian, and also English immigrants, most of them industrial workers, who founded soccer clubs according to the European model, such as the First German-Americans SC in Philadelphia or the Shamrock SC in Cleveland.

In the wake of "Americanization," many immigrants, especially the second generation, played "American" sports, while others stood behind their cultural heritage and used sports, among others soccer, as a place of support and a "'symbolic umbrella,' which served to unite an immigrant community that was otherwise divided along regional, dialect, class, political and religious lines" (Abrams 1995, 12). Among the Anglo-Americans "soccer became conclusively identified as an urban pastime that was alien, multi-accentual ethnic, and hence definitely non-American" (Andrews 1999, 34; Markovits and Hellerman 2001).

The anti-German emotions during World War I and the Cold War in the 1950s intensified the distrust in and disapproval of "others," and at the same time fostered American patriotism and nativism. This favored the emphasis on American sports, baseball and football, which became a major content of the increasingly powerful mass media. Media sport focused on American heroes and their performances, and anchored the notion of American superiority in the heads and hearts of the increasing crowd of sport consumers.

The concentration of men on American football opened the way to soccer for girls and women. At the end of the nineteenth century, the female students, especially at women's colleges, participated in various forms of calisthenics, but also in games like basketball, field hockey, and soccer. Soccer was very popular with the students of the elite "Seven-Sister-Colleges," seven women's liberal art colleges in the New England region, founded between 1837 and 1889. In 1923, a book about hockey and soccer rules for women was published. Whereas in the beginning women's soccer was purely recreational, in the 1920s intramural competitions took place. However, the resistance of the female physical educators prevented women's soccer from developing as a competitive sport (see Chapter 11) (Markovits and Hellerman 2003).

Since World War II various attempts have been made to interest Americans in soccer, leagues were founded, mercenary players from Europe or South America were imported, but this did not have a resounding success, at least not at the professional level. However, the "missionary work" of the National American Soccer League got children and young people involved. The organization of the Soccer World Cup in the USA in 1994 and the foundation and successful operation of Major League Soccer (MLS) in 1996 brought the sport a measure of popularity.

In 1997, soccer ranked second among the sporting activities of the 6–11-year-olds, and third among the 12–18-year-olds. In both age groups basketball was number one; but eighteen million Americans (70 percent under age 18) were playing soccer, twenty-seven million are "involved family members," and fifty million are "soccer literate," which means that they know the rules and can follow the game. In 2001, members of the various youth soccer leagues numbered around 3.9 million. This number more than doubles if one takes into consideration those children who play soccer sporadically (Markovits and Hellermann 2004, 17). In the last decades, soccer has become extremely popular among kids in the suburbs. Here soccer is part of "conspicuous consumption."

Andrews (1999, 40) interprets suburbs as landscapes of consumption as a means of social distinction whereby the various social groups compete for status and prestige.

> The late twentieth-century American suburb represents a complex social space, comprising multiple interrelated fields and sub-fields (housing, décor, diet, employment, education, dress, leisure, sport). Within this setting, individual agents compete for various types of capital . . . which underpin their lifestyle practices and are regulated by the codes of suburban taste cultures.
>
> (Andrews 1999, 45)

Andrews emphasizes especially the competitive nature of these practices and the performative character of consumption.

At first sight, it is not clear in what way soccer can contribute to the competitive lifestyles and cultural capital of the players and their families. A ball and an empty field is practically all that children and adolescents need to play soccer. However, to play the game "just for fun" does not provide prestige (and is not the American way of playing sport). "Real" soccer teams are the traveling teams which compete on high levels and train up to five times per week during the season. Children and parents are highly motivated or even overambitious in this matter, not the least because they hope for a college grant.

Playing soccer in this way is quite expensive – $3,000 to $4,500 per year for membership fees, travel costs, and so on – and thus is also socially exclusive. Being a member of such a team promises visibility, image, and "cultural belonging," in addition it provides social and cultural capital, and signals the "right" taste. Parents use their soccer-playing children for demonstrative consumption and understand soccer as an educational program which conveys middle-class values. Soccer is an alternative to the aggressive American football and to basketball with its "bad boy" image. Markovits and Hellermann stated that soccer was accepted among the "American professional and commercial classes who desired a game for their children that was allegedly nonconfrontational, non-violent, 'multicultural' often coeducational . . . and different from what many of the upscale and educated viewed as the crass and crude milieu of the big Three" (Markovits and Hellerman 2001; 2004).

According to Andrews (1999, 31) youth soccer has emerged as a status symbol of the American middle class.

> Indeed, such has been youth soccer's material and symbolic penetration of the suburban landscape, that the game presently enunciates the dominant rhythms and regimes of suburban existence every bit as naturally as the single family home, ballet classes, sport utility vehicles, lawn sprinkler systems, The Gap, and the imperious Martha Stewart.[6]

Recreational and competitive soccer for middle-class children is organized by various national leagues as the American Youth Soccer Organization (AYSO), the United States Youth Soccer Association (USYA), or the Soccer Association for Youth (SAY). In addition, there are associations such as the Super Y-League and US Club Soccer which focus on competitive sport.

BOX 5.11 A BLACK GIRLS' TRAVELING SOCCER TEAM

Warrington could be any soccer-crazed suburb in any city in the United States. Except in this particular game the players on one of the teams are non-white. In just about any country in the world that wouldn't be worthy of notice. But this is America, where soccer is played by an estimated 24 million people, a vast number of them kids. And a huge percentage of those kids are girls . . . Philadelphia Area Girls Soccer – the biggest local girls' league, which has been around in one form or another since the '80s – runs soccer leagues from as far away as Baltimore and Harrisburg, and from all over Philadelphia, a city that's 43 percent African-American. The league has 9,200 girls, 85 clubs and 556 teams. But only one of those teams is predominantly African-American . . . In fact, as far as anybody can figure, the Anderson Monarchs are the only predominantly black girls' traveling soccer team in the country.

By American youth soccer standards the Monarchs' home field – Smith Playground at 24th and Jackson in Point Breeze – is a dump . . . Some weeks the girls have to spend the first half-hour of the training session clearing dirt, rocks, broken glass and worse.

Since the girls split away from the also successful Anderson Monarchs boys in 1998, they've relied on handouts, parental contributions and whatever they can scrape together from street collections. Stewart – who's unpaid and works part-time as a teacher – makes up the difference out of his own pocket most weeks, paying for gas; van payments; ref, field and league fees; and a dozen other expenses. Week in and week out the Monarchs play better-funded and -equipped teams. And more often than not, they beat them.

The Point Breeze-based Anderson Monarchs are the Bad News Bears of girls' soccer. And they routinely beat the pants off their well-heeled suburban rivals.

(Steven Wells at http://www.philadelphiaweekly.com/articles/14977)

Today, soccer is more and more a game for girls and women. For a long time, high school girls and college women had to be content with intramural games and play days. This changed in 1972 with Title IX (see Chapter 11), which finally guaranteed girls and women equal sporting opportunities and resulted in an increase of girls' and women's soccer, a game, which is "not like baseball and football, a long established bastion of masculinity, a male secret society where machismo reigns" (quoted in Fields 2003, 317; see also Markovits and Hellerman 2003).

Today, the gender relations in youth soccer are nearly even. In 2001 AYSO counted 348,000 girls and 317,000 boys (between 6 and 18 years) in its federation. Among the 12- to 17-year-olds, 24 percent of the boys and 25 percent of the girls played soccer at least sporadically. From 1980/1981 to 2000/2001 the number of girls participating in soccer competitions in high schools increased 700 percent to 292,000 (Fields 2003).

In the 1980s, women's college sport was reorganized and finally integrated in the NCAA. At the same time philosophy and practices changed which opened the way for inter-collegiate soccer competition (see Chapter 11). In 1975, universities started to bestow varsity status on women's soccer teams. However, only 3 percent of colleges offered soccer teams for women; but 90 percent did so by 2004. Today, there are more women's than men's soccer teams at the American colleges and universities.

The phenomenal growth of women's soccer in the United States has produced significant successes, including World Cup championships in 1991 and 1999, as well as Olympic gold medals in 1996 and 2004, considerably surpassing the achievements of male soccer players. Men's focus on football, but also on baseball and basketball, has provided a niche for women in which they can compete and excel. However, the male domination of the media, essential to the success of professional sports, has not been so amenable to the women's professional leagues in the United States. After the World Cup championship of 1999 in front of 90,000 fans in Los Angeles, the victorious American women players launched their own professional league, known as the Women's United Soccer Association (WUSA). The women had equal shares, along with other investors, in the eight-team league that recruited international stars, including Germany's Birgit Prinz and Maren Meinert. The unstable financing of the league and the inability to attract major television network coverage doomed it to failure. It ceased operations after three seasons and resumed an exhibition schedule in 2004, pending reorganization and a new business model. The retirement of its most celebrated star, Mia Hamm, along with the greater popularity of basketball and volleyball for girls and college athletes, leaves a questionable future for professional women's soccer in the United States. Despite the attainment of international glory in only one generation of athletic competition, American women still struggle to overcome patriarchal domination in their homeland.

CHAPTER SIX

COLLEGE SPORT

INTRODUCTION

This and the following chapters provide an insight into the various institutions which organize sport and sport competitions in the USA. In contrast to other countries, there is no umbrella organization governing the various sports on different levels and in different contexts. The main sport providers (sport according to the American terminology) are high schools, colleges and universities, and the professional leagues, and they refer to a very different clientele. Schools are responsible for a large number of children and young people, and have, besides organizing sport, an educational responsibility, whereas professional sport is limited to a very small group of extraordinarily gifted and successful athletes. In the following chapters, we will explore the organizations and their structures, the discourses and practices as well as the opportunities and problems of the American sport system.

As described in Chapter 5, there are close connections between the development of football and the rise of college sport. This chapter deals with colleges and universities as the most important sport providers on the amateur level in the United States.

ORGANIZATION

American football was the catalyst for a unique organizational framework for sport. With the propagation of football at the end of the nineteenth century, a sport system was established which uses educational institutions as an organizational basis (Hums and MacLean 2004). Colleges and universities are the main sport providers in the US; they organize intramural programs for their students and they provide the framework and the basis for competitive sport on various levels.[1]

College sport is governed by three organizations: the National College Athletic Association (NCAA), the National Association of Intercollegiate Athletics (NAIA), and the National Junior College Athletic Association (NJCAA). As early as 1895, representatives of midwestern colleges formed an athletic association (known as a conference or league) to regulate their students' extracurricular activities, especially football games. Eighteen deaths on the football fields in 1905 caused so much outrage that college representatives from sixty-two institutions met, and decided to found an organization which would regulate and control sport competitions between colleges and universities. This association became the NCAA in 1910 (Rader 1990, 180–181; see Chapter 5).

The NCAA is the primary administrator of collegiate sports in the United States. It sets, publishes, and enforces the rules for athletic participation. It keeps the statistical records for collegiate athletic performances and conducts the national championship events. Although technically a nonprofit organization, the NCAA produces an extraordinary amount of revenue, largely from television rights, which is shared among member institutions (Hums and MacLean 2004, 186). More than 1,000 schools hold NCAA membership and more than 40,000 collegiate athletes competed under the auspices of the NCAA in 2003 (Uhle 2005, 63).

Although the NCAA is the largest of the collegiate athletic governing organizations, it does not enjoy monopoly status. The National Association of Intercollegiate Athletics (NAIA), initially organized to regulate basketball games, assumed its current name and the responsibility of intercollegiate athletics in 1952. Its members are mostly smaller schools that have less focus on sport and share the "principle that participation in athletics serves as an integral part of the total educational process" (http://naia.cstv.com/member-services/about/). Still, like the NCAA, it provides national championship competition and shares revenues with its members. The NAIA is divided into fourteen regions and has more than 300 members, some of which are junior colleges (Hums and MacLean 2004, 189–194).

The last organization dealing with college sport is the National Junior College Athletic Association (NJCAA). Junior colleges provide vocational training as well as two-year associate degrees of general higher education transferable to colleges and universities for completion of bachelor's degrees. By 2007 the NJCAA had grown to approximately 550 members in twenty-four regions throughout the United States (http://www.njcaa.org). Athletes whose high school grades or test scores are inadequate for entry into colleges or universities often attend junior colleges to improve their grades in order to be able to get an athletic scholarship.

Since 1973, NCAA member colleges have been divided into three divisions (I, II, III), generally based on the size of the school or the ideology and the degree of emphasis on sport in order to equalize competition. Division I is further subdivided into three divisions depending on the size of its football program. Division I-AAA schools do not field football teams. College teams compete only with others of the same division. Division I institutions invest incredibly large resources in sport, especially in football and basketball, and they are the top players in this field. They also produce most of the revenue from the television networks.

Division I colleges and universities offer a specified number of athletic scholarships in various sports to student-athletes that represent the school on its teams. Scholarships which cover the cost of tuition, room, and board are the dream of high school sport stars and their families, as they provide a virtually free college education (worth up to $200,000). Division

II schools have smaller athletic programs and offer fewer athletic scholarships. Division III colleges, the largest group with more than 400 members, do not award any athletic scholarships, but they offer training and competitive opportunities in various sports for large numbers of athletes and teams (Hums and MacLean 2004, 184–189).

Schools and their teams are grouped into leagues which are called conferences. They may also be described as associations of sports teams that organize matches for their members. They provide a ready-made schedule for athletic contests, and distribute television revenues among NCAA schools. Conferences are usually organized by region, so that travel distances for games at opponents' locations are limited. Among the biggest conferences of Division I schools are the Atlantic Coast Conference with ten members, the Big Ten, which covers eleven schools in the midwestern states, the PAC 10, with ten schools along the Pacific Coast and Arizona, and the Southeast Conference with a dozen members. Most conferences organize competitions between their members in several sports; others do this only in football or ice hockey.

Schools are not obligated to join a conference, but most do. Independent teams which are not part of a conference must seek games with opponents who are willing to accommodate them on their schedule. Among the independent football teams the United States Military Academy, the United States Naval Academy, and Notre Dame University play each other, as well as other teams in football; but they belong to leagues for all other sports. The three institutions maintain their independence for football for various reasons. By playing teams around the whole country each institution gains national rather than just regional TV exposure, a benefit when recruiting student athletes. In the case of Notre Dame, the most popular Catholic university in the United States, its national fan base allows it to negotiate its own television contract with broadcast networks, apart from the packages arranged by conferences. Notre Dame appears on national television each week during the football season, more than any other team, and thus garners a broadcast revenue which it does not have to share with other schools.

Within each school a board of trustees has oversight for all operations within the institution. The president serves as the chief executive with overall jurisdiction, and an athletic board may formulate and recommend policy relating to intercollegiate athletics. Each school has a faculty athletic representative whose responsibility it is to provide a watchdog function to insure that schools comply with NCAA rules (e.g. with regard to the eligibility of the athletes). An athletic director is the head of the athletic department and serves as the day-to-day administrator of the entire sports program, and may have several associate or assistant athletic directors, depending on the number of sports offered. Coaches of each sport report to and are supervised by the athletic director. Large institutions employ numerous coaches; even small colleges may have as many as thirteen football coaches and four basketball coaches for one team (men).

Coaches not only train the athletes but are also responsible for the recruitment of student athletes. In addition to the coaches, each college employs several trainers, medical personnel who treat and rehabilitate injuries.

Depending on the sport, the performance level, and the success, coaches have a high status at the university, enjoy various privileges, and earn a lot of money. The average head football coach at a Division I school in 2006 had a salary greater than $900,000 annually (http:// finance.myway.com/jsp/mw/nwdt_rt_top.jsp?news_id=ap-d8oer2jgO&.html). At universities with a high emphasis on sport, the salaries are much higher. For example, at the University of Oklahoma the football coach earned $3,500,000 per year, ten times what the school president received (http://finance.myway.com/jsp/mw/nwdt_rt_top.jsp?news_id=ap-d8oer2jgO&.html).

BOX 6.1 THE INCOME OF A COACH

Buster Roth, a big-time college coach who made more than a million in salary plus at least twice that in endorsements, public appearances, life-is-like-a-basketball-game motivational speeches for businessmen, and swoosh deals, as they were known because of the swoosh symbol of the Nike company, still the biggest swoosh dealer of them all. In a swoosh deal, the coach dresses the entire team; from top to bottom – jerseys, shorts, basketball shoes, and socks – in the company's products, with each item identified by a logo – in return for . . . nobody ever seemed to know exactly how much . . .

Coach's domain took up the entire third floor. There was a screening room with a sloping theater floor . . . solely for the analysis of Dupont basketball games. Behind the fence, at workstations, as they were called, was Coach's harem of secretaries and assistants, all of them young women with short skirts.

(Wolfe 2005, 197–198)

Coaches' contracts and benefits extend well beyond their salaries. It is typical to get a car, a country club membership, and free tickets to other athletic events. There are bonuses for winning games, meeting graduation rates for players, and simply for preventing players from engaging in disreputable activities. Some coaches even get private jets, low interest loans or vacation homes. The University of Texas football coach received a birthday present of $1,600,000 in 2004 and the University of Oregon coach received 10 percent of the revenue from ticket sales in 2005, which amounted to an additional $631,000 (Upton and Wieberg 2006). In addition, coaches can earn substantially more than their assigned salaries through endorsement deals with shoe companies or other businesses. Many coaches also have their own radio shows. "The insatiable desire of 24-hour sports networks to fill air time has created a cottage industry for coaches [sic] shows. News Corp's FSN, which reaches 82 million homes through 21 regional sports channels, offers a smorgasbord of [coaching] shows" (McCarthy 2006, 2B).

Sport programs at universities – investments

The cost of sport programs and the construction of athletic facilities can be enormous. Athletic department budgets at large universities can approach $100 million annually. Indiana University maintains a $42 million endowment[2] just to cover its athletic scholarships (http://newsinfo.iu.edu/news/page/normal/2600.html). The Ohio State University built excellent facilities for football, baseball, basketball, ice hockey, track and field, gymnastics, wrestling, fencing, soccer, lacrosse, and a golf-course. The construction or renovation of football stadiums alone can exceed hundreds of millions of dollars.

The most prestigious sports are football and basketball which is mirrored by the university-owned stadiums or arenas, the grants for the players, or the above-mentioned salaries of the coaches. In the past it was possible for some universities to make a profit with successful teams. Today, intercollegiate athletics are often a losing deal. The Ohio State athletic department, for example, has a debt of $200 million to be paid off over thirty years. Still, the president and the whole school are extremely proud of their athletic accomplishments. In the local newspaper the deeds of the university football team get front page coverage; while the announcement that two faculty members were elected to the National Academy of Sciences appeared on Page 4 (http://library.osu.edu/sites/archives/manuscripts/oral history/geiger.htm).

BOX 6.3 **THE REPUTATION OF A UNIVERSITY**

For years the university had built up and promoted its reputation of being a national power in football, basketball, ice hockey, and even minor sports – track and field, baseball, lacrosse, tennis, soccer, golf, squash – without

> compromising academic standards by so much as a millimeter. A case indicating that Dupont had tutors who wrote the athletes' papers for them would explode all that in the public eye. It might, he had hinted in guarded terms, open up a whole can of worms. Where did the players' new SUVs come from? What about this list of "friendly" courses? What about these rumors that four of the team's players had SAT scores of under nine hundred? The President thought about that. For a start, it would knock Dupont from second, behind Princeton, in the U.S. News & World Report rankings down to . . . God knew where.
>
> (Wolfe 2005, 558)

Colleges and universities go to great lengths to promote their athletic programs and bring media attention and national exposure to their institutions. In 2001 the University of Oregon paid $250,000 to create a mural of its star player in New York City, the site of voting for the Heisman trophy, which is awarded annually to the best football player in the collegiate ranks (Falk 2005, 50). Despite the effort, the player did not win this trophy, which is awarded annually to extol the merits of young athletes. This promotion of a single player shows the high value schools attach to their athletics and their sport stars who are in the center of attention and treated as celebrities by the colleges, the administration, the faculty and the fellow students, but also by the general public. In contrast, few efforts are made to promote student scholars or prize-winning professors at the universities.

Sport programs – why universities are and stay involved

Athletic departments and intramural and intercollegiate sport are an intrinsic part of American colleges and universities. Since the nineteenth century, the emphasis on sport has been perceived as anti-intellectual and often disparaged by many faculty members as antithetical to the academic purposes of the institutions. However, the NCAA and coaches have ascribed particular advantages and values to athletic activities, such as gaining media attention and prestige, maintaining alumni ties, attracting students, securing financial resources, improving social cohesion, and contributing to the students' education (Gems 2000; Mandelbaum 2004). Visibility, status, and prestige are of decisive importance for educational institutions in the USA. Private but also public universities are financed to a large extent by tuition fees which forces them to compete for students, and the prestige won via sport can be a decisive factor in the choice of a university. In addition, sport increases the prestige of the institution which improves job opportunities and life chances of the alumni.

What has the scientific quality of teaching and research and the scientific prestige of a university to do with the successes of a football team?

How can athletes combine extensive training with acceptable standards of scholarship? What becomes of athletes who after four or five years are no longer eligible to play and /or what happens to those who fail to graduate? Despite the commercialization, why are the players still considered amateurs?

Further problems are the recruitment of players who do not meet acceptable academic standards, the dominating role of sports on the campus, and the social transgression of the athletes, who have been involved in numerous violent acts, including sexual harassment (u.a. Miracle and Rees 1994; Coakley 2004).

(Gerald Gems, Gertrud Pfister)

Another important source of income of universities is the donations of former students (alumni), who finance, among other things, professorships, buildings, or grants (Brubacher and Rudy 1997). The ongoing relationship with alumni and the quests for support started early. In 1878 the president of Princeton University (in New Jersey) wrote to a graduate who then lived in the state of Kentucky:

> You will confer a great favor on us if you will get . . . the college noticed in the Louisville papers . . . We must persevere in our efforts to get students from your region . . . Mr. Brand Ballard has won us great reputation as captain of the football team which has beaten both Harvard and Yale.
>
> (Lasch 2007, 438)

BOX 6.5 ALUMNUS DONATES MILLIONS

> In 2007, Richard Jefferson, a professional basketball player, has pledged $3.5 million toward the University of Arizona's future basketball and volleyball practice facility which will be named after Jefferson. He wanted to make a gift to an institution that had supported him as a student.
>
> (The University of Arizona Alumnus, Fall 2007, 70)

Alumni are intrinsically integrated in the college community. They are regularly contacted by the college administration, among other things asked for donations, and/or invited to sport or cultural events. Successes of the sports teams enhance the identification of the students and the alumni with the team and with the university, which increases their willingness to pay and/or donate money. Yale organized alumni giving in the 1890s, and by the 1920s its graduates were donating nearly $500,000 a year (Brubacher and Rudy 1997, 379). In its Annual Report for 2007, North Central College a small liberal arts school, reached a "gift income" of 16 percent of its total revenues of around $65 million. The "Honor Roll of contributors" and the *Alumni News* filled many pages of the report.

American football and basketball are not only the most popular sports on college campuses, they also draw numerous fans from the towns and cities where they are located. This is particularly important for schools in rural areas where the schools and their teams are important ties for the construction and sustenance of collective identity. The popularity of the contests is mirrored in the size of the audiences. In 2003 the Division I schools attracted thirty-five million spectators to their football games; while the smaller divisions drew eleven million fans. The University of Michigan averaged 110,918 at each home game, and Penn State University, the University of Tennessee, and the Ohio State University averaged more than 100,000 per game. The Division I basketball schools had twenty-five million paid admissions to their men's games in the 2003 to 2004 season, and another 5.1 million at the lower divisions. Women's teams in all divisions drew ten million fans (Uhle 2005, 62–63). These numbers show that college sport is a major attraction with huge audiences who bring prestige and revenues to the universities and the cities/towns as well. The college athletes represent the community, and the communities support the athletic programs, among other things, via the booster clubs.

At Division III-level schools, which do not offer athletic scholarships, the sports teams provide playing opportunities for high school athletes (the vast majority) who were not recruited by the major universities. Athletes at Division III schools may comprise as many as half or more of the residential students on small college campuses and are essential (as tuition-paying students) to the financial health of the school. It is not unusual for even small colleges to have more than twenty different sports teams to attract students (Princeton University has thirty-eight varsity teams). For those students who lack the physical abilities or choose not to participate on the school teams, a vast program of intramural sports is available for recreational purposes, with activities that mirror all of the athletic teams (i.e football, basketball, volleyball tournaments) to recreational pursuits. Even small schools might offer more than sixty intramural activities throughout the year which contribute to the attractiveness of the institution for the students (and the parents who often pay the tuition fees and therefore have a say in the choice of institution).

Besides financial considerations, health promotion and the widespread conviction about the pedagogical values of sport play a considerable role in the maintenance of the sport pro-grams. Coaches, athletes, and pedagogues contend that sport, especially football, educates players to become good American citizens. Although this argument is contested, it has many believers and is thus very powerful (u.a. Miracle and Rees 1994; Pope 1997). Last but not least, sport and sport competitions offer numerous opportunities on the campus to create, enact, and celebrate community. Sport is an essential component to life on the campus.

COLLEGE LIFE

College and university students live in a vertically and horizontally structured community with various groups, cliques, and cultures and with numerous unwritten ideals, norms, and rules. College life is heavily influenced by the fact that American universities are mostly situated on a campus where teaching, living, and leisure take place. Depending on the school, a more or less high percentage of the students live on the campus in school dormitories. The members of exclusive students' associations – called fraternities for men or sororities for women – live near the campus in large houses with multiple occupants. These associations are very selective in their membership, require fees, and conduct initiation rituals which are often connected with harassment, called hazing. "Frat brothers" are well known for their weekend parties, their anti-intellectual attitudes, and their ardent support for the athletic teams. Not all colleges allow these associations (Nuwer 2001).

BOX 6.6 HAZING

Although hazing has often been thought to exist primarily in fraternities and sororities, a 1999 study by Alfred University and the NCAA found that approximately 80% of college athletes had been subjected to some form of hazing. Half were required to participate in drinking contests or alcohol-related initiations while two-thirds were subjected to humiliating hazing. Additionally, much of the reported hazing in high schools occurs during initiations related to athletic teams with many problems arising during pre-season sports camps.

(http://www.alfred.edu/sports_hazing/introduction.html)

As already mentioned, almost all educational institutions offer numerous sport programs, and many students at Division III colleges are engaged in one or more sports.

In the USA, children dream of a sport scholarship or at least of being on a college team. Students who excel in a sport already get special treatment by the time they enter high school. One of the tasks of the coaches is the recruitment of promising athletes who are addressed and "courted" before they leave high school. The colleges invite them to the campus and they are often pampered in order to entice them to come and play for the school.

Students are eligible for intercollegiate sport "normally" for four years, and the athletes have to maintain a certain academic standard. Those who fail a course are not eligible for a sporting team in the following term. In large schools, student athletes receive considerable support in their academic work; among other things they are supported by tutors. Because the first priority is performance in sport, athletes with low academic competencies are often admitted. It is difficult to balance training, competition, and study. Normally student athletes train every day and have a game on weekends for football and two to three games per week for basketball.[3] Athletes, especially football and basketball players at Division I schools, do not care so much for academic success; many of them dream of a professional career, although the chances of thousands of college players being picked by one of the few professional teams are minimal.

BOX 6.7 FAME AND AMBITION

Nobody, not the president of the university or anybody else, was nearly so recognizable or awesome as the starting five (players) of the national champions. Go go, Jojo. Of course, Dupont was just a stop on the way to the final triumph, which was playing in the League. In the meantime, being at Dupont was cool. Everybody was impressed that you were playing ball for Buster Roth. For that matter, everybody was impressed that you were even attending Dupont . . . If the unthinkable happened and you didn't make it to the League, it was pretty good credentials. Just to be able to say you graduated from Dupont – assuming you managed to keep your grades above water and did graduate. Well, that was what tutors were for, wasn't it?

(Wolfe 2005, 56)

Good athletes enjoy a privileged status and receive numerous benefits depending on the sport, the success, and the school. The most prestigious sports are men's football and basketball; women's teams attract considerably less attention and support. Although privileges for athletes are not allowed according to NCAA rules, players in Division I schools may receive money, are provided with cars, and live in luxurious accommodation.

BOX 6.8 LUXURY FOR BASKETBALL PLAYERS

The lockers were made not of metal, but of polished oak in its natural light color with a showy grain. Each one was nine feet high and three and a half feet wide, with a pair of louvered doors and all manner of shelves, shoe racks, beechwood hangers, lights that came on when the doors opened, and a fluorescent tube near the floor that was on twenty-four hours a day to keep things dry. Above the door was a brass strip with the player's name engraved on it, and above that, framed in oak, a foot-high photograph of

---

the player in action on the court . . . Under NCAA regulations, you could no longer have special dorms for athletes. They had to be housed with the general student population. So the basketball players were all put at one end of a big hallway on the fifth floor of Crowninshield. For the basketball players, they had knocked down the walls between the two bedrooms on either side of the suite's common room, so that each player had one large bedroom, with a private bath.

(Wolfe 2005, 46, 59)

There are various special events to celebrate the athletes such as the festivities revolving around homecoming, including a dance in the evening. There is an athletic awards dinner where the athletes are celebrated, and awards for the best, most valuable, or most improved players are handed out. The portraits of the best male and female athletes in various sports are exhibited in athletics departments. The best college athletes have the chance to be selected to a virtual All-American team. However, the grandeur of college sport has a dark side: the high emphasis on winning puts a lot of pressure on the athletes and may contribute to the use of legal and illegal performance-enhancing means in American schools.

The campus as community and a social field

A college may be interpreted as a field in the sense of Bourdieu: a vertically and horizontally organized system of social positions and power relations, as well as an arena where individuals and groups compete for the appropriation of economic, social, or cultural capital. Social and cultural capital in a college are closely intertwined with popularity. Popularity is of decisive importance for the students because it influences, among other things, image, status, friendships, and dating (with whom, how often). Besides academic work, extracurricular activities such as discussion groups, playing in a band, dances, and so on play a central role for prestige and the placement of students and groups in the college field.[4]

Students who are members of one of the various clubs and groups, especially fraternity/ sorority members, command a high status and are popular among their peers. Good students who are not interested in sport are called "nerds" and they are not very popular. In a recent study Ashmore et al. (2007) identified ten types of students, from "in-crowd," "status-oriented" students to "derogated females" and "stigmatized outcasts." On the basis of a multidimensional structuring configuration, they reconstructed the place of these groups with regard to social and academic involvement.

Playing sport, especially being on the school team, contributes decisively to one's symbolic capital. Jocks, male students well known for their athletic abilities, are on the top of the popularity hierarchy. However, status also depends on the sport and the gender. American football and basketball convey prestige to male students, whereas cheerleaders are among the most popular female students. Not only active participation in sport, but being a sport fan or even an expert adds to the social capital of male students (End *et al.* 2004).

BOX 6.9 THE FANS

The fans descended from the stands in a pell-mell rush and thronged the players. So easy! No security guards to impede their worship! They could touch them! Jojo was surrounded. He was mainly aware of the crop of ballpoint pens and notebooks, notepads, cards, pieces of paper . . . Jojo kept walking slowly toward the locker room as he signed autographs, carrying a great buzzing hive of fans with him. There were a couple of obvious groupies, their bosoms jacked up by trick bras, who kept smiling and saying "Jojo! Jojo!" and searching his eyes for a look deeper than the ones he gave to ordinary fans.

Consciously, the players regarded this hiving as a tedious fate that befell them as part of their duty as public eminences. Unconsciously, however, it had become an addiction. If the day should come when the hives disappeared and they were just a group of boys walking off a basketball court, they would feel empty, deflated, thirsty, and threatened.

(Wolfe 2005, 44)

Besides sport, social class, clothes, and appearance denote one's social position in the field. The appearance of young women necessitates traditional features of femininity, especially a slim and trained body; men need to have muscles, and therefore anabolic steroids seem to offer a quick means to build up the dream body with an abdominal six-pack. While the drug issue affects relatively few students, it is a growing problem.

BOX 6.10 MUSCLES AS A FAD

The muscular students . . . were merely subscribing to the new male body fashion – the jacked, ripped, buff look. They were all over the place here on the weight-lifting floor! Ordinary guys with such big arms, big shoulders,

---

> big necks, big chests, they could wear sleeveless T-shirts and strap-style I'm-Buff shirts to show off in! What were they going to do with all these amazing muscles? . . . Nothing, that's what. They weren't going to be athletes, and they weren't going to fight anybody. It was a fashion, these muscles.
>
> (Wolfe 2005, 267)

Sport, fans and the enactment of community

Sports events are a major component of students' leisure lives. Attendance at football or basketball games is a weekly focus for many students and is a primary means of building community spirit. Numerous students and teachers are loyal fans who not only attend every game of their team, but also encourage the players, conduct campaigns, and organize victory ceremonies. Before and after the game fans throw tailgate parties in the vast parking lots adjacent to the football stadium (see Chapter 5).

The emphasis on sport and the emotional involvement of the majority of students can be at least partly explained by their situation. American college students have particular pressures, caused above all by the high tuition costs which might range from a 2007 average of $5,836 per year at public universities to more than $45,000 per year at private institutions ($22,218

Figure 6.1 North Central College homecoming parade, 1917 (North Central College Archives)

on average), requiring students to take out loans and work in local jobs during their educational years.[5] For many students it is their first taste of independence, no longer living at home with their parents, and the last chance before beginning a career and the loan repayments to feel truly "free." Sports events provide an opportunity for relaxation, identification, and entertainment as well as the venue and the excuse to show emotions, and to engage in rowdy behavior.

BOX 6.11 HOMECOMING AT NORTH CENTRAL COLLEGE, NAPERVILLE

The 2007 weekend homecoming activities for North Central College, a small Division III school, included campus tours of new buildings and facilities, a trolley tour of the local town, a barbeque, a "powder puff" (tag rather than tackle) football game for women, historical exhibits at the library to enhance nostalgic remembrances, a men's soccer game and a social gathering with the team, a musical concert with orchestra and choral groups, special reunions for particular classes, an alumni basketball tournament, and a game of the women's volleyball team. All of this occurred on Friday. Saturday started with an early morning jog with the men's and women's cross-country teams, and a special breakfast for those who had graduated fifty years ago, while others could have a breakfast with the faculty. After the breakfasts the alumni basketball tournament continued, along with alumni football and volleyball games, as well as a special alumni awards ceremony. A parade then led to a pep rally before the highlight of the weekend, the afternoon football game. After the game different graduating classes met their old friends at assigned locations to relive their college days. In the evening a musical band of alumni played at a local bar in the town.

The festivities of Friday and Saturday were followed on Sunday morning with a church service and a brunch before the tired but happy alumni headed back home after renewing their attachments to the school.

(Gerald Gems)

Alumni are, as mentioned above, closely connected and emotionally involved with their former schools. They are an intrinsic part of the school community, and sport is part of the alumni's collective memory.

A 2007 pamphlet for Texas Tech University, entitled *Shaping America*, stated that

> The fabric of America is stitched by athletic competition . . . Nostalgia stirs the spirit, allowing us to relive the athletic experiences of yesteryear and to realize the lessons learned in the sweat and toil of a bright day in the springtime of our lives have stayed with us to the present.
>
> (Texas Tech 2007, n.p.)

Figure 6.2 Crowning of the homecoming king and queen (North Central College Archives)

Many alumni return to the campus to bask in collective memories and to re-enact their youth by watching football games.

Each season a particular game is chosen as a symbolic "homecoming," with parades, social events, dinners, planned remembrances, and festivities, including a popularity contest to choose the "king" and "queen" from among the current students. The elected monarchs are often a football player and a cheerleader. Some alumni arrive days before the game with ample supplies of food and liquor to enjoy in the commemoration of the glorified past. Collective memories, invented traditions, and annual re-enactments tie the graduates to an imagined community that centers on the school. In these ways the universities consciously fashion lifelong loyalties with their graduates, inferring a debt of gratitude.

Mega-events of college sport

The two biggest athletic spectacles in collegiate sport revolve around football and basketball. In football all NCAA divisions except Division IA (the biggest schools) conduct national championship tournaments. Division IA teams, however, are the most popular and draw the greatest number of fans. The media, which stand to benefit most by a national football championship, and fans, have long clamored for a tournament which determines the absolutely best college football team in the US. In a society where winning is everything it is astonishing that this dogma does not count for the most popular game: football. College presidents have resisted such a championship with the argument that it would prolong the season by a month, necessitating a greater loss of educational time for the student-athletes. The television networks have managed to arrange a pseudo-national championship by incorporating the bowl games into the football schedule, at the end of the fall football season. In the 2007 season, more than sixty of the 119 Division I teams played in one of the bowl games in which two teams are paired according to their ranking.

The bowl games have been entrenched in American culture for more than a century. The Rose Bowl, the first of the football spectacles, originated in southern California in 1902 as a means to promote tourism (Hibner 1993). Other bowl games, such as the Orange Bowl, Sugar Bowl, and Cotton Bowl appeared during the Depression years to draw similar attention to the regions where those games took place. Numerous smaller bowls proliferated to accommodate as many teams, fans, and parochial interests as possible in the pursuit of revenue and fame. The bowl committees of each city invite top teams and try to match those teams which promise a thrilling match.

In order to identify which teams should play each other in a "national championship" game, the media corporations devised a plan to use rankings at the beginning of the 1990s. Two separate polls, one by the sports writers and another by the football coaches, rank teams according to their performances. The committees of the four most prestigious bowl games agreed to host the game between the top two teams on a rotating basis, insuring that each would get the game of most interest every four years. This way to finding a nation's champion is a unique American practice.

College basketball, however, does have a national championship tournament at the end of each spring season, known as "March Madness." Each team that wins its conference championship is ranked and arranged in one of four regional tournaments, culminating in the "Final Four" which play for the national title. Teams are seeded in each of the regional tournaments to allow the best teams a greater opportunity to advance; but upsets occur regularly, making the tournament quite unpredictable. The unpredictability of the event results in millions of dollars wagered in betting pools at work or online, where the unknowledgable non-sports fan has a fair chance of winning a lucrative jackpot.

Collegiate sport issues

Currently, collegiate sport and the individuals, groups, and institutions involved face numerous problematic issues. The widespread gambling on college sport has corrupted some players, with periodic scandals involving point shaving/match fixing in both football and basketball. Performance-enhancing drugs have become commonplace. One of the means of the fight against doping is unscheduled testing of athletes to catch those seeking an advantage, but drugs, especially steroids, are also common among body-conscious male students.

Athletic budgets have grown exponentially despite the fact that few schools show a profit. Most spend more on sports than they make each year, but the pressure from alumni and booster clubs to produce winning sport programs is immense.

> There is enormous pressure for [college] presidents to stay in this arena, even when the logical choice for an institution may be to pull back. A president who stands up and says "This is ludicrous. We can't compete at this level" may very well find him- or herself out of a job.
> ("Assessing the Arms Race" 2007, 8 (http://www.athleticmanagement.com/2007/03/assessing_the_arms_race_1.html))

Many American universities have become better known for their athletic teams than for their educational programs. The out-of-scale promotion and emphasis on sport in many colleges and universities may have negative effects on those students and staff who focus on academic work. They may be marginalized. In addition, the need to be "popular" and the high prestige of "being on the team" can divide the college community and lead to social tensions.

CHAPTER SEVEN

PHYSICAL EDUCATION AND SPORTS IN AMERICAN SCHOOLS

INTRODUCTION

The aims of this chapter are to show the specific role of physical activities, education, and sports within the American school system and the opportunities and issues incurred in such a framework. We will explore the development of physical education (PE) as a school subject, the evolution of extracurricular sports and games, and the interrelationships between sport and PE which are both intertwined with particular cultural values and embedded within the social context of schools, and society at large. A main focus will be the (in)significance of PE in the American society, in spite of its fascination with and its commitment to sports. Another emphasis will be laid on the importance and meanings of extracurricular sports as well as on the reasons for the integration of sport competitions in the schools.

BACKGROUND INFORMATION – THE AMERICAN SCHOOL SYSTEM

In the US, individuals are required to attend at least ten years of primary and secondary education (although twelve years are necessary to graduate with a diploma), usually starting with kindergarten. Some urban school districts require eight years at the primary level and four years at high school. In suburban school districts students attend either two or three years of junior high and four years of high school. They graduate with a US high school diploma.

Unlike the school systems in many other countries, in the US the school system is nomadic, which means that schools are not segregated in different branches with different performance levels. All students attend the same types of schools. Typically in the US, public services, including education, are decentralized. Thus, the individual states determine and control the course work at the schools within their borders, and decide about requirements that students must meet. State laws generally require all students to stay in school until the age of 16; but independent school districts in all states can formulate their own curricula based on the state guidelines. This can lead to problems if one wants to transfer credits from one school to another.

Schools are financed and controlled at the local level. More than 15,000 independent school systems exist, financed by various taxing arrangements, each with a board of education, and specific aims and objectives. Public schools are free of charge; however, the quality of the education depends on the amount of funding, which is generally allotted from the real estate taxes of the region/area. Such a funding arrangement generally benefits wealthy communities to the detriment of poor areas. Private schools demand a tuition fee, but they are very popular because they provide better education, among other things, by offering advanced mathematics and science courses, a variety of language courses, or a better athletic program. The quality of the students' course work in the high schools determines their admission to colleges and universities.

Elementary schools provide PE, but do not organize activities outside the realm of the normal curriculum. In junior high schools and high schools extracurricular activities play a central role for the students, but also for the school communities. There is a broad variety of activities ranging from producing a school newspaper to acting in the theater. The participation is voluntary, but many students participate in such activities in the course of a school year. Some of the activities are provided by the school, others are organized by the students, often under the guidance of teachers. Athletics are the most important programs, since they not only benefit the students, but interscholastic competitions also bring visibility and status to the school.

In American educational institutions, physical education and extracurricular sport activities are separate entities. While PE in the upper grades often includes the teaching of sport skills, the extracurricular sport programs have much greater influence and interest within the school community. They focus on training and interscholastic competitions in various sports. Recreational activities do not play a central role in the school system, although some schools are adapting their curriculums to promote lifetime activities as well as sports. As a result, PE curriculums merge a variety of theoretical frameworks and models. The elementary schools usually focus on movement education. Sport skills start in the junior high, and high schools teach sports, recreational activities, and fitness (Darst and Pangrazi 2008).

HISTORY OF PE – THE BATTLE OF THE SYSTEMS

In 1890, only half of American children enrolled in a public school but attendance at school became compulsory in all states in 1918. At the same time, the living conditions of children in the big cities, but also the long hours in school, appeared to endanger the health and development of the students. As a recipe against the over-exertion of the brain and the lack of physical activities PE was introduced in schools and colleges. An overview of physical training in public schools in 1884 showed that only 1 percent of pupils had any form of physical training.[1] At the turn of the century cities and schools increasingly began to integrate PE in the curriculum. However, guidelines and teachers were needed. During most of the nineteenth century there were no centralized and prescribed guidelines for the different subjects, no uniform teacher education, and no rules and regulations for PE. Because of the widespread belief that physical activities had important effects on health, education, and socialization, the question of aims, contents, and methods of PE was important and topical. PE became a "hot issue" with long and intensive debates among experts and the adherents of different movement concepts, such as Swedish gymnastics and German *Turnen* (Pfister 2009).

German *Turners* were among the first to introduce their system of training to the American schools in the nineteenth century. They were particularly successful in the cities of the Midwest, where many Germans had settled and gained political influence. In Chicago, schools introduced German gymnastics in the 1870s (Miller 2000). Friedrich Ludwig Jahn, grandson of the founder of the *Turner* movement, served as one of the first public school instructors in Chicago (Gems 1997, 66). According to Hartwell, the system "worked admirably, and to the satisfaction of the board, the teachers, and the pupils alike" (quoted in Pfister 2007a, 104).

BOX 7.1 GYMNASTICS AT THE SCHOOLS IN KANSAS CITY

Carl Betz, a German *Turner*, was made director of physical training. He taught drills to the principals of the different ward schools on Sunday, they drill their assistants, the regular teachers on Monday. The assistants take up the drill for the week on every Tuesday: "at ten a clock all principals strike a gong and at this signal the teachers take up the drill at once (daily). Thus at the same time all school children throughout the city have the same exercise" (Leonhard 1922, 117).

The *Turners*, convinced of the benefits of PE, helped to pass state legislation to make it an obligatory subject in schools. The first laws were passed in the 1890s (Van Dalen and Bennet 1971, 405; Welch and Lerch 1996, 103). The need for teachers led to the foundation of normal schools (teacher education institutions) for PE – institutes of very different quality – where numerous and various "systems" were taught from *Turnen* to Sandow's exercises. In addition, the "scientific" level of these schools was very different; at some schools the education included experiments in several sciences, while others taught only the practical skills (Park 1987, 56). These diverse developments led to disagreements and challenges over which system was best suited to the needs of American students.

The American Association for the Advancement of Physical Education (AAAPE)[2] and the battle of the systems

The "battlefield," but also the "highest court" in PE questions was the AAAPE, founded in 1885. Physical educators at colleges, teachers in the YMCA or the US Military Academy, eleven physicians, among them some professors, and others participated in the first meeting (Park 1987). Because there was no education for gymnastic teachers, physicians were the most important experts on the body and its training. Women, especially physical educators at women's colleges, played a considerable role in this organization. From the very beginning, they participated in discussions and activities.[3] Very soon the AAAPE became the most important forum for information, presentation of ideas, and discussions about PE.

The aims of the AAAPE were: "to awaken a wider and more intelligent interest in Physical Education; to acquire and disseminate knowledge concerning it; and to labor for the improvement and extension of gymnastics, games, and athletic pastimes in the education of children and youth" (according to the revised constitution of 1895: Park 1987, 29).

Parts of the AAAPE's initiatives and activities could be described using the paradigm of professionalization: its members working in the same field formed a pressure group which aimed at a specialization of knowledge, rules for eligibility, control of access, and the right to define their aims and means. Professions detect and develop a demand for their services and try to prove that they are indispensible to society. As "rewards" they expect power and resources (Park 1987).

Benefits of PE and the scientific legitimation

At the center of the debates was the question which is still relevant today: Why should educational institutions include PE in their curriculum? What are the demands for PE with regard to the mission of schools? Which of the different concepts and the different physical activities have the best effects?

The experts in the AAAPE believed that PE could enhance hygiene, health, and rehabilitation, have a positive impact on moral virtues, and provide personal and intellectual development. However, these imagined effects of PE were not taken for granted, as, for example, in Germany, but became topics of scientific reflections and studies. One major focus of AAAPE activities was to gain knowledge, but also legitimization through science. The establishment of various committees for research and methods shows the importance of science in the organization.

The first scientific approach of AAAPE members was anthropometric measurement which seemed to provide scientific tools to show the effects of PE on the body. One of the leading experts in this area was Dudley Sargent, who developed a system of exercises with equipment which could be adapted for individual use (Park 1987, 44). Another central question was about the role of PE in education. It focused on the connection between bodily movement and muscular training on the one hand, and the functioning of nerves and brain on the other (Park 1987, 46).

> Brain cells grow, like other parts of the body, by exercise. The sensory cells . . . can be exercised only by the use of the senses. In like manner the motor cells can be exercised and developed by making them contract the muscles. Muscular exercise . . . is therefore absolutely essential for the healthy growth of the brain.
>
> (T.M. Balliet 1898, quoted in Park 1987, 35)

The physiological discourse was not superseded, but added to by psychological concepts, based among others on G. Stanley Hall's *Adolescence* (1904). From this perspective the play instinct, necessary for the development of children, could only be satisfied in games, not in gymnastics. Therefore adherents of this approach recommended athletics, but with educational aims and in an educational setting.[4]

All in all, the AAAPE promised expertise, functioned as a referee, gave recommendations, and defined itself as a pressure group with regard to PE.

Gymnastics and athletics

From a European perspective, one would question why the physical educators did not focus on games and athletics which had already been established. Students had started to engage in various sports, especially football, and to organize intercollegiate competitions which gained increasing popularity and publicity (see Chapter 5). PE was clearly a latecomer in colleges and universities, and it did not include athletics – to the contrary, there was a segregation and tension between the ideology and the practices of both movement cultures.

This appears more astonishing if one reads the claims, hopes, and promises of athletics which were quite similar to the hopes connected with PE. One reason for the separate development of PE could be that athletics, with an emphasis on competition and winning, had already established itself and it was too late to change it and to include educational aims and values.

The AAAPE was at first not very interested in athletics; later a more or less intensive debate began which focused on criticism of the deficiencies and excesses of the existing system. It was clear that students liked athletics more than gymnastics, but the fun orientation of games and athletics made it difficult to legitimize their integration in the curriculum. The majority of AAAPE members were convinced that gymnastics provided harmonious development of body and mind, whereas athletics led to specialization. "There is a sharp and clear distinction to be drawn between athletics and gymnastics . . . this distinction was made in the Grecian period, athletics implying even then a contest . . . while gymnastics meant more practically discipline or drill" (quoted in Park 1976, 353). This distinction is still valid today.

The search for the right "gymnastic system"

The AAAPE seemed to be the right group of people to play the referee in the "battle" in which military drill, Swedish gymnastics, *Turnen*, Sargent's exercises, educational athletics, and other systems were involved. Since its foundation, the discussion about the various gymnastic systems was a central topic of the AAAPE's meetings. The most intensive debate with all different groups and an audience of more than 2,000 people took place in 1889 during the conference on physical training in Boston which was presided over by the United States Commissioner of Education.[5]

The German *Turner* had a strong voice in the discussions, not the least because they were united in the North American Gymnastic Union and had even established a normal school for gymnastic teachers. In one of these meetings the representative of the *Turner* called upon the participants to adopt the German *Turnen* as the best system of PE. "The German system has been established now for over fifty years and built up by the genius, industry and experience of a century. It covers all the ground."[1] *Turnen* offered a ready-made concept which had already been tested. This concept included a system of exercises with clear rules, methods of teaching, and a connected philosophy including promises of the effects and benefits. The promises of *Turnen* were far-reaching and included character building and military preparedness, and this was one of the major concerns after the Civil War because of the poor fitness of the Union soldiers (Miller 2000).

In addition, German gymnastics seemed to have fulfilled the wish of the AAAPE for "educational" athletics, as the *Turner* included in their system athletics and games without the overemphasis on performance, and the negative effects of winning at all costs. However, this aspect of *Turnen* seems not to have played any role in the "battle of the systems." *Turnen* was identified only with apparatus work, drill, and calisthenics. *Turner* exercises on apparatus and drill were not very popular with young men who found them strenuous and boring. Also in the *Turner* clubs, the number of members dropped at the turn of the century (Hofmann 2001, 209). Despite the positive evaluations and the introduction of *Turnen* in the PE of several cities, *Turnen* did not have a real chance to become mainstream. During the Boston conference, mentioned above, some speakers emphasized that *Turnen* was not American. "But our American needs are peculiar," said Dr. Seaver from Yale University, an "advocate for outdoor work." And if there is a need for one of the foreign systems, then they have to be "Americanised" (quoted in Pfister 2007a, 106).

In addition, the political orientation and ideology of the *Turners* were different if not strange, and did not fit with American beliefs and attitudes. The *Turners* resisted the commodification, record orientation, and professionalization of sport. The *Turnerbund* also adhered to principles of socialism and individual freedom which contravened American virtues and values. Religion was for the *Turners* an individual choice, as were the drinking habits. Therefore they fought against the power of the churches, enforced Christianity, and temperance laws, all of which were strong influences in American society (see Chapter 2).

The other "foreign" system which aimed at an integration in schools was Swedish gymnastics, and there was strong competition between the German and the Swedish concepts. Swedish gymnastics was not imported by immigrants but by single persons, like Nils Posse, who sought opportunities for work. Looking for possibilities to improve the health and fitness of children, the wealthy Boston philanthropist Mary Hemenway and her assistant, Amy Homans, favored the Swedish system and they introduced it in the schools in their city (Spears 1986). Swedish gymnastics in the form it was taught in Boston consisted of a series of exercises which aimed to strengthen different parts of the body and improve balance, posture, and respiration. From Boston Swedish gymnastics spread to other areas, and it was introduced in many cities and schools all over the country. Swedish gymnastics had some advantages in comparison to *Turnen*: it seemed to be especially appropriate for girls and women. Therefore female physical educators favored the Swedish system. In addition, it seemed to be easy to learn and to teach, it could be conducted in the classrooms, and it claimed to be scientific.

Like *Turnen*, Swedish gymnastics was considered to be "foreign." In 1930, Wood and Cassidy judged that "Physical education should be . . . suited to the nationality and the demands of the environment. To take a system of exercises fitted to the needs of the Swedish, Danish, or German nation and use it without change in the United States is a mistake" (quoted in Miller 2000).

The battle of the systems had advantages because it brought the issue of PE into the limelight, supported discussion, and produced insights. But it also had negative effects, because each system claimed to be the best and accused the others of being useless, if not dangerous, as is stated in a government report:

> With what confidence can an American board of education adopt the one system of gymnastics when a large and able body of experts pronounce it "without rational or physiological foundation" and with what trepidation will they approach the other system when an even larger number of equally able men assert . . . that only the half educated are impressed by it?
>
> (quoted in Welch and Lerch 1996, 107)

The resistance against the German and Swedish systems led to an increasing demand for physical education which was orientated towards American needs based on science (Park 1987, 43). At the turn of the century a "New PE" developed with a shift of paradigm from the focus on the exercises to the needs of children: child development became the rationale. This was accompanied by a shift of scientific legitimation as psychology became more important than physiology. The outcome of the debates and the research was a mixture of ideas and practices based, among other things, on the psychology of play. Edward Hartwell, the best American expert on German *Turnen*, ventured a prophetic statement at the 1889 conference on physical training: "A careful study of the German and Swedish systems . . . will be found an indispensable preliminary step for those who propose to organise a natural, rational, safe and effective system of American physical education" (quoted in Pfister 2007a, 107). In the following decades sport skills would assume a considerable role in the physical education curriculum, and remain so today.

BOX 7.2 AMERICAN ALLIANCE FOR HEALTH, PHYSICAL EDUCATION, RECREATION, AND DANCE

The American Alliance for Health, Physical Education, Recreation, and Dance (AAHPERD) is the oldest and largest professional organization of its kind in the United States. Established in 1885, AAHPERD counts 25,000 members among its various groups. It serves as an umbrella organization of five national and six district associations of educators, health care practitioners, fitness, dance, and recreation specialists intent on promoting healthy lifestyles. It includes teachers at all levels from elementary schools to universities. The allied organizations include the American Association for Health Education, the National Dance Association, the American Association for Physical Activity and Recreation, the National Association for Sport and Physical Education, and the National Association for Girls and Women in Sport. AAHPERD also includes a Research Consortium to disseminate scientific studies involving sport, health, and physical activity (http://www.aahperd.org/aahperd/). In addition to an annual convention AAHPERD offers a multitude of programs, workshops, publications, and events aimed at the professional development of its members. It formulates policies and national standards for its disciplines, debates issues within the health domain, and promotes its particular agenda by advocacy and lobbying efforts at local, regional, and national levels.

(Gerald Gems)

PHYSICAL EDUCATION TODAY

The heritage of the battle of the systems and the segregation of PE and sport is still influential. As described in other chapters of this book, sport played and plays a huge role in the history, the identity, and the everyday life of Americans. But the enthusiasm is directed at competitive sport and PE was often pushed to the sidelines. While sport remains an abiding interest among Americans, the interest does not equate to their own physical activity or their children's PE. Americans are largely spectators rather than active participants. However, the sedentary lifestyle and the high rate of obesity has fostered a nationwide discussion and placed a greater emphasis on PE.

In spite of the current discussions, the high interest in sports, and the general awareness of the benefits of physical activities, PE does not play an important role and is not considered to be a core subject of equal importance to other courses in most schools. At the elementary level (ages 5 to 11) physical education generally promotes the learning of basic movement skills, low-level games, and activities. Some districts have middle school or junior high schools for children aged 12 to 14, where physical educators begin to teach fitness and sport skills. High school-aged students (14 to 18) may learn more fitness, health, sport skills, and lifetime activities; but, as mentioned above, there is no national curriculum (Darst and Pangrazi 2008).

The National Center for Disease Control has long demanded that PE should be obligatory and that the hours should be expanded. The Congress reacted to these demands with a program which offers support for initiatives aiming at an improvement of PE; however, this did not have a huge impact, not least because the states are independent with regard to their educational policies. But there are national associations, such as the National Association for Sport and Physical Education, which have developed national standards for physical education that are in use in many states.

The available statistical material in the "Shape of the Nation Report 2006"[6] shows the marginalization of PE in the American school system. In 70 percent of the states PE is obligatory for elementary schools, in 65 percent for middle schools and in 83 percent for high schools, but this does not mean that PE is offered in all grades. Only two of the fifty States, Illinois and Massachusetts, require PE from kindergarten to grade 12; and New Jersey and Rhode Island from grades 1 to 12 (see also the overview in McCullick and Hofmann 2009).

In 2003, throughout the USA, only 56 percent of high school students were enrolled in PE classes (71 percent 9th grade, 61 percent 10th grade, 46 percent 11th grade, and only 40 percent in 12th grade). The recommendation of health experts to be physically active for thirty minutes at least five days a week is not met by the schools. Only 8 percent of the elementary schools, 6.4 percent of the middle schools/junior high schools and 5.8 percent of the senior high schools offer PE daily (150 minutes per week for elementary schools and 225 minutes for the other schools).

In addition, in most states, there is no regulation about the amount of time for PE (eleven states have these regulations and the time varies between 30 and 225 minutes per week). Only in Illinois is daily PE obligatory; but even there exemptions or waivers are granted to individual students who petition the school board. In more than 50 percent of the fifty states other activities can be substituted for PE (e.g. participation in the marching band or on athletic teams). Fifteen states (29 percent) demand a student assessment in PE, eleven an assessment of physical fitness, ten an assessment of knowledge, nine of motor skills, and two of personal/social interaction in PE (McCullick and Hofmann 2009).

PE and interscholastic sports

The numbers provided by the Shape in Nation Report indicate that in most American states, PE does not seem to have a high priority. In spite of many discussions, programs, and projects, PE is marginalized in schools. This is also shown by the fact that students do not have to attend PE lessons if they participate in sport-related activities. Parents and school administrators often want more time for other classes, such as science or math, and they reduce PE hours accordingly. In addition, since the No Child Left Behind law passed by the Bush Administration, which requires all schools to meet minimum standards in certain subjects or face penalties, time for PE is even considered as less important. PE is not included as an essential subject in this law! This overall picture should not conceal the fact that there are schools with excellent PE programs. For example, researchers at Harvard University have determined that the PE program in Naperville, Illinois schools has a relationship to brain stimulation and learning abilities. In Naperville, teachers use heart rate monitors and track individual fitness progress which proved to be very motivating for the students (Ratey and Hagerman 2008).

However, these schools are a minority and restricted to affluent communities, whereas minority and/or working-class children who are endangered by inactivity and obesity have to attend schools which are at a disadvantage in facilities and resources. In most schools, there is a much greater emphasis on interscholastic sports than on PE.

EXTRACURRICULAR SPORT ACTIVITIES IN SCHOOLS

History of interscholastic sports

Unlike Europe, the most popular sports teams emanate from American school systems rather than sport clubs. School teams are formed as early as junior high; but they assume their greatest influence and interest at the high schools and colleges. Virtually all secondary schools, as well as colleges, or universities (see Chapter 6), field teams that represent their institution in numerous sports and extracurricular activities (e.g. chess, debate). This alliance between sport and the school system started in the nineteenth century (see Chapter 6).

At both high schools and colleges students provided their own recreation and entertainment. Teams, loosely organized by high school students, began challenging other secondary schools, particularly in baseball and football, by the late nineteenth century. Chicago high school students formed their own league for such purposes in the 1880s. Emulating the college students they developed athletic rivalries and a consequent emphasis on winning that included the use of non-students as players. As sports, particularly football, gained greater interest and influence among the students and led to greater abuses such as brutality, cheating, and the use of ineligible players, faculty felt a moral responsibility to take control of the students' extracurricular activities. In the 1890s, Midwestern states moved to organize the high schools into more formal associations headed by adults (Gems 1997).

In 1903, Luther Gulick, formerly a teacher at the YMCA teacher training school in Springfield, Massachusetts, was appointed director of physical training in the New York City public schools. A firm believer in the character-building qualities of sport, Gulick soon organized the Public Schools Athletic League (PSAL) under adult guidance. The Athletic League aimed at social control by redirecting youthful energies away from criminal activities and into sports. It also aimed to assimilate immigrant children through athletic lessons in a wide variety of competitions. In 1905 the League added a division for girls. By 1907 more than 100 high school baseball teams vied for the city championship, watched by 15,000 spectators at the stadium of a professional baseball team (Rader 1990, 221–222). Other American cities soon developed similar programs for their high school students. "High school sports helped give an identity and common purpose to many neighborhoods, towns, and cities which were otherwise divided by class, race, ethnicity, or religious differences . . . High school sport could become a community enterprise" (Rader 1990, 227). Sport thus united the factions within American communities against athletic rivals. The increasing importance of sport and the fierce competitions caused schools to employ coaches, who assumed greater importance than other teachers in the school and were paid higher salaries.

Athletic rivalries had already extended beyond the local areas as high school teams traveled extensively in search of regional and even national honors by the turn of the twentieth century. A New York team traveled to Chicago in 1902, where the Midwesterners triumphed by a score of 105–0. When New Yorkers complained that Chicago had not faced their best team, a different Chicago team traveled to New York the following year and handed the home team a 75–0 defeat (Gems 1997). A study conducted between 1905 and 1907 indicated that 78 percent of high schools fielded a football team (Gems 2000, 185). The football frenzy reached a crescendo in 1937 in Chicago when 120,000 spectators witnessed the city high school championship game between the winner of the Catholic League and its public school counterpart. Despite the ongoing economic depression the game held great symbolic meaning for the various religious, ethnic, and social class factions within the city, and more widely within American society (see Chapter 5). The public school star, still a high school student, was enjoying national celebrity by that time (Gems 1997).

BOX 7.4 HIGH SCHOOL BASKETBALL AS STATE RELIGION

In 1936 *Time* magazine estimated that 20 percent of the top 500 college basketball players came from the State of Indiana, where basketball was considered "a state religion." The state high school athletic association had 850 members and each one had a basketball team.

> There are literally dozens of communities where the high-school gym seats more than the population of the town . . . The desire to win is so great that the luring and capture of high-school athletes has become a great problem . . . Since it's against the rules for a boy to live in one town and play in another, they arrange that little matter by transporting the whole family. There was a fine young player in a junior high-school team . . . His father drove a gasoline truck and had no objection to a better job. One town offered him a job paying $125 . . . and (then) . . . another offered him $150 . . . and the boy is on the team.
>
> (Crichton 1937, 13, 38)

SPORT AT HIGH SCHOOLS TODAY

Over the remainder of the twentieth century interscholastic competitions increased and gained significance and public attention. Today, high school students from 14 to 18 years old have more opportunities for extracurricular activities than ever before and engage in one of the numerous athletic teams, theatrical societies, political clubs, chess clubs, and so on. Due to the limited sport facilities, teams often have to share the gymnasium space, especially during the winter. While most activities are conducted in the afternoons after school, some of the athletic teams practice before school, arriving two hours or more before the start of academic classes.

Each state has its own governing body to regulate high school sports. The state associations organize state championships, set ethical standards, establish eligibility requirements, publish rules, provide awards, and discipline schools that do not adhere to their standards. Both public and private schools are members of the state associations. Funding for each of the state organizations differs. Some receive appropriations from the state governments;

while membership dues, revenue from state championship events, or corporate sponsorships may provide additional support (Hums and MacLean 2004, 84–85).

Virtually all high schools provide facilities and staff for extracurricular sport. School districts or individual schools hire the coaches and administrators, such as athletic directors. The latter schedule sporting events, arrange for officials, monitor students' eligibility, supervise all coaches, and have general supervisory responsibilities for the school's program. Each school provides the facilities for its athletic contests and many schools have their own arenas, stadiums, gymnasiums, swimming pools, and running tracks for such events. In the poorer public schools students sometimes have to supply some of their own equipment; but generally the schools supply the uniforms, equipment, training facilities, transportation, and meals when traveling.

As mentioned previously, schools in the United States are funded by the real estate taxes of each district. Students living in poor areas, such as many inner cities, generally have less funding for facilities and services than those in more affluent suburban locations. This influences the whole of school life, not only the quality of the scientific courses, but also the opportunities to play sport.

A survey conducted by the National Federation of State High School Associations in 2005 to 2006 indicated that participation in interscholastic sports programs had increased for seventeen consecutive years. More than seven million students took part in the athletic competitions, including around three million girls. The girls' activities with the most participants were: basketball, track and field, volleyball, softball, soccer, cross-country, tennis, swimming and diving, competitive cheerleading, and golf (in this order); while boys were most interested in football (with over one million participants). Basketball, track and field, baseball, soccer, wrestling, cross-country, golf, tennis, and swimming and diving followed in the number of athletes. Most schools offered more than ten sports each for boys and girls, with the largest number of participants in the more populous states: Texas, California, New York, Illinois, Michigan, Ohio, Pennsylvania, New Jersey, Florida, and Minnesota (JOPERD, January, 2007, 4).

Some schools have teams at various performance levels, usually two or three, to develop younger players. They must play the other teams in their league to determine the league champion; but on certain dates, usually before the league games start, they can play teams of their choice. Some states restrict interstate games; others do not. The Naperville, Illinois high school played, for example, a team from Ohio with a million dollar budget, which brought along its band and a live tiger. Some rich high school teams even have their own plane.

The following examples may not refer to the majority of high schools but they show how much importance can be assigned to sport and how many resources schools are willing to invest in order to gain fame and prestige in interscholastic competitions. As in colleges, football is also the top sport in the high schools.

The importance of sport may be seen, among other things, in the number and the salary of the coaches and other sport-related staff or in the size of the football stadium and the

184

audiences. By the 1980s the city of Massillon, Ohio had only 30,000 residents; yet it supported its high school football team with 2,700 members in the booster club, eleven coaches, a full-time trainer, a statistician, and an information director. In 1985 the fans of a Texas high school football team chartered nine Boeing 727 jets to transport them to the state championship tournament (Rader 1990, 341–342). In Odessa, Texas, a town with less than 96,000 inhabitants, the football coach had a salary of $81,000; while the teachers with twenty years of service earned only $44,000 (Falk 2005, 19). By the twenty-first century a number of high school coaches had their own radio shows, teams played in multi-million dollar stadiums on national television, and traveled on airplanes in search of national exposure. In the state of Texas alone, four million residents attend high school football games each weekend. In 1995 an Ohio high school team drew more than 120,000 fans. High school sports have become big business in the United States (Gems 2000, 185–186).

BOX 7.5 NATIONAL FEDERATION OF STATE HIGH SCHOOL ASSOCIATIONS

In 1920 five states formed the Midwest Federation of State High School Associations, which expanded to a national governing body in 1923. All fifty states had become members by 1969. The establishment of the NFSHSA was and is the quest to control and direct students' activities. Like the NCAA, it provides services to coaches, officials, and administrators. The NFSHSA has more than 17,000 member schools and is organized in eight geographic sections. The National Council is composed of a representative from each state. The Board of Directors has a representative from each of the eight sections, plus four members elected at large. An executive director and staff conduct the daily business. The organization's revenue is derived from its publications, as well as membership fees, conference fees, and royalties.

(Hums and MacLean 2004, 81–82)

FUNCTIONS OF INTERSCHOLASTIC SPORT

For non-Americans it is astonishing that high schools invest so many resources in sport and that interscholastic competitions are prioritized over PE with its potential educational and health benefits. In addition, they wonder why high school sport attracts so much public attention.

High school sport was and is supported or at least legitimated by its educational values. Teachers, coaches, parents, and the general public are convinced that playing sport has numerous positive effects on the morale, but also on intellectual development. Some empirical studies showed correlations between school-based activity participation and the development of adolescents. However, "the picture becomes mixed once moderator variables are included." Correlations do not detect cause–effect relations and insight into the mechanism of a potential impact of activities is lacking (Feldman and Matjasko 2005).

BOX 7.6 SPORT AND EDUCATION

Myth or reality? Most Americans believe that sport builds character . . . There is an overwhelming emphasis on winning in American sport. Moreover, it is believed by some that winning demonstrates moral superiority . . . Apparently we have not been concerned that all youth build their character through sport, just those with superior athletic talent . . . Americans' beliefs about school sport seemingly require no proof. Certainly if we look for scientific evidence to support popular, cherished beliefs about sport, we shall be disappointed.

(Miracle and Rees 1994, 221)

High school sports serve economic, social, and psychological functions, and many of the purposes of school sport are similar to those of other sport competitions (see Chapters 6 and 13).

Scholars emphasize the positive effects of sport consumption and mention, among other things, that it can entertain, fascinate, and dull the stresses of daily life. "When the school team wins, the community feels good about itself, even if economic or social conditions are bleak" (Miracle and Rees 1994, 155). A football coach stated that "I think it gives them [the community] a shot in the arm on Friday night and Saturday night, because they can forget all their worries about, I've got to pay the electric bill on Monday" (Miracle and Rees 1994, 153). In addition, "representational sport" provides means for identification (Guttmann 1986). Sociologist James Coleman claimed that diverse community residents rarely experience common goals that "engender a communal spirit and make members feel close to one another" (Anderson 2006, 260). Sport provides one area of common interest and a collective goal for the members of a high school and its community.

BOX 7.7 PEP RALLY

From a letter of a German exchange student:

The last class in the afternoon was canceled and all the teachers brought all the students into the auditorium for a pep rally. It was incredible, the football team had their first game the next day and this was a kind of ritual in which

---

the whole school came together to give them support. When I walked in the first thing I saw was Chip and the rest of the team up on the stage along with the cheerleaders, Coach Macho and the Principal. The marching band was also there in uniform playing the school fight song. After the cheerleaders had done their cheers the Principal addressed the whole student body and told us how proud the community was of our school and especially the football team who were the State Champions, and how football really demonstrated school spirit and solidarity. Everyone clapped and cheered . . . Then he called the name of each team member who stood up and got a huge cheer from the crowd. Then he called on all the athletes, male and female, to stand to be recognized, so I got up too as part of the soccer team. By that time everyone was going crazy and chanting "WE'RE NUMBER 1, WE'RE NUMBER 1". It was really wild.

(Brettschneider and Brandl-Bredenbeck 1997, 13)

That sense of pride is particularly strong in small or rural communities that lack any allegiance to the college or professional teams. In such places, high school sport is the major form of community entertainment. The patriotic and communal rituals conducted at such sporting events tie participants and spectators to both the community and the nation as they are repeated across generations (Miracle and Rees 1994, 153–163). One of the most powerful enactments of patriotism is the playing of the national anthem which precedes every game.

In African-American or ethnic communities, however, high school sports teams may serve as agents of retribution in a power struggle against the dominant white society. Historically oppressed groups, such as Native Americans and African-Americans, enjoy beating the wealthier and more privileged white schools at their own games. For such teams sporting success is a matter of racial pride (Anderson 2006).

As in colleges, in high school sport plays a considerable role in the lives of the students and has a big influence on the atmosphere, the culture, and the image of the school. In addition, in high schools popularity is extremely important and the popularity and status of male students depends to a high degree on being on the team, especially on the football or the basketball team. Studies since the 1950s consistently show athletes to be the most popular students in the school (Yiannakis and Melnick 2001, 91ss). For girls, appearance and conspicuous consumption (e.g. the fashionable outfit) are more important than being an athlete. The girls with the highest prestige are the cheerleaders (see Chapter 5).

The most important function of sport for American schools, however, is in determining the student social structure within the schools. Groups are formed and prestige is bestowed largely on the basis of sport. Traditionally, athletes have occupied positions of higher status

187

in American schools than those who excel in academic subjects, art, music, and any other skill area. Similarly, the impact of sport on school/community relations can be enormous. Parents and the general citizenry in the community can participate in school athletics through booster clubs and other support groups (Miracle and Rees 1994, 225). In addition, high school sport serves as a reservoir for college sport because successful high school athletes can get scholarships and this is the aim of many students.

BOX 7.8 FOOTBALL AND SCHOLARSHIPS

From a letter of a German exchange student:

> Chip Junior is my age and we should get along OK since we are both interested in football. Well Chip actually doesn't know much about real football, they call it soccer over here . . . He told me that last year when he was a junior he was the starting tackle (whatever that is) on his school football team (the American kind) which won the State Championship. This year is his final year and he thinks that the team will be just as good. He says if he plays well as a senior he has a chance of being picked as one of the members of the All State team (its just an honor, they never play any games), and might be recruited on a four year scholarship to play football at university. This scholarship would actually pay for all your books, tuition costs, room and food and everything for four years! I've never heard of anything like that before and cannot see why a university would give a scholarship to someone just to play sports but Chip seemed to think it was quite normal.
>
> (Brettschneider and Brandl-Bredenbeck 1997, 13)

HIGH SCHOOL SPORT ISSUES

Numerous sport issues confront the state associations and the school administrators as well as the students. Parental involvement in school athletic programs, the overemphasis on winning and consequent recruitment of athletes (similar to abuses at the collegiate level), eligibility issues, the use of performance-enhancing drugs, athletes' and fans' inappropriate conduct at games, and the proper role of sport in the educational process present ongoing concerns. In addition, the hierarchical construction of the school's social field with the stigmatization and exclusion of groups and individuals can cause academic failure and a high drop-out rate for sport programs.

BOX 7.9 BOOSTER CLUB

One example of how parents and other adults who are not employees of the school district can influence the school sport programs occurred in the state of Washington after the 2006 football season. At one high school, which has won the state football championship five times in the last six years, the head football coach is paid a stipend of $5,753 in addition to his teaching salary. The booster club (usually composed of parents, local businesses, and other fans) awarded him another $55,000 as a gift for his coaching success. Such awards raise ethical questions regarding who controls the school program, school administrators or fans?

("WIAA School to Monitor Gifts", 2007, 10)

The decrease of educational funding and the pressures of Title IX, a federal law that seeks to achieve gender equity, have caused some schools to reduce the number of sports programs in the schools. Private club teams now challenge the school programs for the best athletes and increasing numbers choose to pursue possible individual benefits rather than promote community pride.

CHAPTER EIGHT

PROFESSIONAL SPORT

DEVELOPMENT AND ORGANIZATION

INTRODUCTION

This chapter builds on the chapter about baseball (Chapter 4) and explains the organization of professional sports in the USA today. In addition, advantages and problems connected with the professional sport leagues in general and the dominance of pro sport in the US are presented and discussed. Baseball was not the only sport which experienced professionalization at a much earlier period than in other countries. Professional rowers and harness racers competed already during the antebellum era, and in the 1840s pedestrianism became a spectacle for large audiences and an opportunity to earn huge sums of prize money for the athletes. As early as 1844 thirty-seven competitors registered for a foot race in New Jersey that offered $1,000 in prize money. "The contest was to determine who could run the farthest distance in one hour . . . Between 25,000 and 30,000 spectators turned out to watch this event" (Kirsch 1992, 316–322). In the second half of the nineteenth century, athletes competed for salaries in a large number of sports, from billiards to boxing and track and field.

BOX 8.1 SALARIES IN THE EARLY PHASE OF PROFESSIONALIZATION

In 1859 Michael Phelan won a reported $15,000 in a single billiards match (Rader 1990, 42) and baseball players, began to be paid by the 1860s (Riess 1984a, 291). Mike Kelly's salary reached $15,000 in 1887 (Gems 1996a, 133), and John L. Sullivan won a $5,000 prize and another $1,000 in a side bet for his two-round victory over Paddy Ryan in 1882 (Rader 1990, 51). Lon Myers profited as a professional track star in the 1880s, and Walter "Pudge" Heffelfinger, the first known professional American football player, received $500 for his services in one game in 1892 (Gems 1996a, 332).

(Gerald Gems)

In the twentieth century, commercialization became a central issue in sport: the number of professional sports and athletes as well as the amount of salaries and as a whole the amount of money involved in sports increased to incredibly high figures.

PROFESSIONAL SPORTS

Semi-professional leagues

Whereas professional sports are in the limelight, semi-professional teams are no longer at the center of public attention, although those teams proliferated in a wide variety of sports in the United States during the first half of the twentieth century. The recreation programs of companies produced widespread working-class interest in sport and opportunities to play on teams. While semi-pro leagues and teams still exist they have difficulty attracting spectators due to the prevalence of professional and college teams, and widespread television sports programming. Semi-pro players may or may not be paid, depending on the revenue stream of the franchise/team. Teams that rely on ticket sales may not generate enough income to pay the players regularly or at all. Semi-pro sport is not a primary source of income and players generally have a full-time job in addition to their athletic participation. Most lower level boxers, but also baseball, football, and basketball leagues are "semi-professional": the athletes compete more for the love of the activity than any financial remuneration. Sports adapted for television, such as arena football (indoor football), box lacrosse (indoor lacrosse), or ultimate fighting provide similar opportunities to the participants. Professional wrestling, though more entertainment than competition, is the most successful of the new TV sports with a large fan base and some of the actors have gained fame and considerable sums of money.

The major sports

While numerous sports organizations declare the professional status of their sport, four governing bodies dominate the American sport culture: Major League Baseball (MLB), the National Football League (NFL), the National Basketball Association (NBA), and the National Hockey League (NHL). These leagues share certain common organizational characteristics. All teams, also called franchises, playing in these leagues have an owner or a group of owners, who form, in each league, an owners' committee or a board of governors that sets the policies and determines business decisions, such as franchise relocations or television contracts. Each league has a commissioner who, in some cases, has nearly dictatorial powers, although commissioners are hired by the team owners. The commissioner influences the development of the game, since he proposes rule changes, approves player contracts, resolves disputes involving the players, the teams, or the league, and may discipline any personnel, including owners, for conduct detrimental to the league (Hums and MacLean 2004, 320–322).

League offices employ specialists as administrators and other personnel to address the daily business of marketing, sales, licensing, scheduling, security, public relations, finances, officials, and so on. Owners of individual teams conduct their own team offices in a similar fashion (Hums and MacLean 2004, 322–324). These leagues are powerful businesses with enormous resources and strong political connections at local and national levels.

Each of the major leagues also has a players' association, which acts as a labor union to regulate working conditions and safeguard players' rights. For example, both the NFL and NBA have mandated particular uniforms and the way in which they must be worn in order to generate a "middle-class" image, which has been challenged by some of the players. The players' associations may also represent their members in disputes with owners, and unresolved matters have led to disastrous strikes and lockouts in the past. Health insurance, retirement benefits, and marketing of the athletes for revenue enhancement are other responsibilities of the unions. Each team elects a player to serve as its representative to the players' association (Hums and MacLean 2004, 325–327).

The NFL Players' Association through Players' Inc., its marketing arm, generated $42, million in 2000, based on the sale of merchandise. Such collective contracts benefit all players. Players also have their own sports agents who negotiate contracts individually between the athletes or the teams and sponsors. Agents get a maximum of 3 percent of NFL players' contracts, but may get as much as 20 percent of the endorsement fees (Falk 2005, 185–188).

Player development and recruitment differs by sport. In each sport the potential labor force (reservoir of athletes) has become global as agents scour the world in search of athletic talent. For the NFL and NBA the college teams serve as a training academy, without getting acknowledged or paid for it.

Both MLB and the NHL operate a system of minor leagues for the training of young players. Only the best players reach the NHL or MLB and most have short professional careers. Although winning is very important to American fans making money is the important issue for the owners. However, fans continue to support their team even if it shows mediocre performances. The Chicago Cubs, for example, a National League baseball team, have not won a World Series since 1908; yet they are one of the most profitable franchises in MLB.

Unlike the European soccer leagues, poor performance of a professional team does not relegate it to a lower division. Even the worst team stays in the league, which has a major interest in keeping the performance of the teams at a similar level. Poor teams are embarrassments to their cities (although they are privately owned), and fans of bad teams have come to games with paper bags over their heads to avoid recognition. The worst teams, however, get the first choices of the best college players in the annual draft, which theoretically provides them with the means to better their team for the following season. Professional leagues strive for parity (i.e. equality in competition), so that most teams will remain in contention for playoff spots throughout the season; thereby enhancing fan interest and television viewership. In addition, they have introduced regulations that prevent the salary of all players from exceeding a given sum. Thus rich teams cannot buy all the good players and dominate the competition.

The emphasis on increasing revenues becomes evident by the movement of teams to the city which offers the best conditions. The owners do not take the investments of their home city or the disappointment of their fans into account.

Major League Baseball (MLB)

As described in Chapter 4, the oldest of the national sports, the National League, was formed in 1876. A number of rival leagues faltered until the establishment of the American League in 1901. Its success led to a playoff to determine the professional champion in 1903, presumptuously titled the World Series. The two leagues are collectively known as Major League Baseball (MLB). Until the 1970s players labored under the "reserve clause" in their contracts, which required them to provide their services only to the team that had signed them to a contract. Baseball owners also enjoyed the legal benefits of a monopoly because the Supreme Court ruled in 1922 that baseball, as the national pastime, was not actually a business, and therefore not subject to commercial laws. The establishment of a viable players' union in 1954 eventually curtailed such practices and led to escalating salaries as players became free agents (see Chapter 4).

Today, Major League Baseball is divided into two separate leagues with further divisions arranged by region. The National League has a total of sixteen teams; while the American League has fourteen teams. Some larger cities, such as New York, Chicago, and Los Angeles, have teams in both leagues. At the conclusion of the baseball season (April to October) the regional winners, three in each league, and the team with the next best record are matched in a playoff consisting of two rounds. The tournament starts with four teams in each league, and losers are eliminated. The league champions meet in a best of seven games series known as the World Series. The high number of competitions between the two teams increases the interest and the thrill of the fans, and thus increases the revenues of the owners. An innovation, introduced in 1997, allowed for interleague play with a limited number of games during the regular season. This new schedule was meant to regain fans' interest after a disastrous labor strike had caused the cancellation of the World Series.

Baseball team owners do not share their revenue equally as in the NFL; therefore teams located in big cities with a large audience often dominate the quest for the best players due to greater resources. Team salary caps, namely agreements about the maximum sums which can be spent on the salaries of a team, are intended to balance the financial inequalities of the teams; but such measures are anathema to the players, because this means that each player is competing against his team-mates for a better salary. The team of the New York Yankees, perennial contenders for the baseball championship, is the most highly valued in American sport at $1.2 billion (2007). If the owner were to sell the lowest valued baseball team, the Florida Marlins, he would still get $244,000,000 (http://abcnews.go.com/Sports/wireStory?id=3058636). Despite gambling and doping scandals baseball is still a very profitable business. The interest of the audiences did not decrease in spite of various doping cases; some fans obviously do not care how the performances are obtained.

National Football League (NFL)

Professional football began in the 1890s when star players were offered cash to appear in selected games between rival athletic clubs in which considerable sums had been wagered (see Chapter 5). At the same time workers, and later European immigrants became increasingly interested in football. Semi-professional and fully professional teams appeared, particularly in the Midwestern states, after the turn of the twentieth century (Ziemba 1999; McClellan 1998).

In 1920 the Midwestern teams formed a league known as the American Professional Football Association, which became the National Football League in 1922. Throughout the decade a number of towns and small cities fielded teams in the league without continuous success. They could not draw enough fans to cover their expenses. Green Bay, Wisconsin, a city of slightly more than 100,000, remains the only remnant of such franchises in the early years of the league. The Green Bay Packers are owned by the people of the city as shareholders in the corporation. Green Bay can compete with the teams situated in much larger American cities because the NFL teams share revenue equally, enabling Green Bay to offer comparably competitive salaries to the players. All other teams in the four professional leagues are owned by individual businessmen or shareholding companies.

As professional football slowly gained popularity in the 1920s rival leagues began to emerge. Such enterprises either failed or were absorbed in mergers with the NFL. The ascendance of the new American Football League after 1959 resulted in a merger with the NFL in 1966. The top teams of the two leagues competed for the national championship known as the Super Bowl. They consolidated as one league with thirty-two teams in 1970; but maintained two separate conferences with regional divisions.

A professional sports franchise, particularly a pro football team, is a highly desirable symbol of the prosperity and expression of pride, and part of the identity of cities. Therefore, franchise moves have caused considerable turmoil and resulted in litigation.

BOX 8.2 FOOTBALL AND IMAGINED COMMUNITIES

Indianapolis lured the Baltimore football team in 1984, which stirred Baltimore to attract the Cleveland team in 1995. Cleveland offered the team $175 million for a

---

new stadium, despite the fact that eleven schools in that city closed that year for lack of funding (Falk 2005, 65). Baltimore countered with an offer of $200 million for a stadium, which the team got rent-free for seven years, and the team soon departed (Falk 2005, 124). Cleveland residents sued the NFL, and managed to keep the historic symbols and official history of the team. They gained a new franchise in 1999 which took, literally and symbolically, the place of the departed team. This does not only make clear the profit-orientated logic in the professional leagues; it shows how the "imagined communities" of the fans are constructed.

By the 1970s football had superseded baseball as the national pastime surpassing it in both attendance and interest (Gems 2000, 189). By the twenty-first century nearly half (48 percent) of Americans (and 43 percent of women) watched football on television and 35 percent of them attended the games in person (Falk 2005, 98, 134). The physicality of the game, its aggressiveness and martial spirit, its corporate structure, and complex strategies resonate with American culture. The Super Bowl, played between the two conference champions after a playoff system as described above for baseball, is a two-week-long national festival of media hype and civic hope, mixing sport, capitalism, and musical entertainment (see Chapter 13).

National Basketball Association (NBA)

Professional basketball players appeared soon after the invention of the game in 1891. Professional leagues languished for half a century; but individual barnstorming teams proved successful. The New York Rens and the Harlem Globetrotters, African-American teams, won the first two professional tournaments in 1939 and 1940 respectively. The merger of the Basketball Association of America and the National Basketball League in 1949 resulted in the NBA. As in football also in basketball the teams in smaller cities failed to survive. The growing popularity of the game led to the establishment of a rival league, the American Basketball Association, in 1967. Its success fostered a merger of the two leagues in 1976. Since then the NBA has a similar structure with two conferences like the other professional team sports. Each conference has two regional divisions, with a total of twenty-nine teams in the NBA. A playoff system similar to baseball and football results in a national championship series of the two best teams.

The NBA sponsors the WNBA, the women's professional league, which began in 1997. The women compete in an abbreviated schedule in the thirteen-team league and salaries are considerably lower than for male players. The top salaries in 2004 for female professionals in the WNBA were $90,000, while NBA players earned millions) (Baroffia-Bota and Banet-Weiser 2006).

195

National Hockey League

A professional hockey league first appeared in the United States in 1904. The NHL originated with only five Canadian teams in 1917 and spread to the United States in 1924 (http://www.nhl.com/nhl/app?service=page&page=NewsPage&articleid=280069). Only the teams in large cities survived the Depression. Like baseball players, professional hockey players were saddled with a reserve clause that bound them to one team and, as a consequence, limited salaries (Baldwin 2000, 224–225). This resulted in labor disputes. In 2004, the owners locked out the players in a conflict over a salary cap and the amount of pay which the players found too low. It took nearly a year until an agreement was reached.

From 1942 to 1967 the NHL consisted of only six teams. Six more American franchises were added for the 1967–68 season (http://www.rauzulusstreet.com/hockey/nhlhistory/nhl history.html). The World Hockey Association, a rival league that began play in 1972, merged with the NHL in 1979. Like the other professional leagues, the NHL has two conferences. Each conference has three regional divisions with five teams each, which makes a total of thirty teams. Despite the continual addition of American franchises, hockey is still perceived as a Canadian game and has failed to displace the entrenched American interest in football, baseball, and basketball. During the above-mentioned labor conflict over 200 NHL players competed in Europe and an entire hockey season was abandoned in the United States with little concern shown by Americans (Davies 2007, 316).

National Association of Stock Car Auto Racing (NASCAR)

The National Association of Stock Car Auto Racing (NASCAR) has grown from rural southern roots to a national phenomenon. Stock cars are "normal" cars used in races. Modern stock cars resemble family cars or pick-ups, but are racing machines built according to strict regulations which intend to guarantee identical cars and equal chances for all drivers. The races take place mostly on oval courses, but some are conducted on road courses.

The family of William France has controlled the NASCAR circuit since its inception in 1949, and under his guidance garnered a multi-billion dollar contract with the television networks (Davies 2007, 309–316). Americans are not so much interested in formula one racing, as NASCAR is considered an indigenous sport. NASCAR races first appeared on national television in 1979, and by the 1990s its television audience had overtaken that of baseball and basketball. Only American football has higher television ratings inside the US (Cobb 2005, 324)(see Chapter 13). Every year over 1,500 NASCAR races at over 100 tracks take place in thirty-nine American states, as well as Canada and Mexico.

Winners of NASCAR races are accorded points, with the top ten scorers allowed to compete in the championship competition. The owners, NASCAR drivers, and their fans promoted a distinct working-class, southern, and rebellious image that assumed more mainstream characteristics as its popularity spread to the rest of the country. NASCAR drivers are heroic figures to their fans, perhaps replacing the iconic American cowboy of a previous era. Their prowess as drivers, stereotypical masculine figures who demonstrate a reckless courage, draws admirers of the brawny American car culture (Newman 2007) (see Chapter 13).

Other professional sports

While the United States hosts a wide variety of professional sports and minor leagues, none can compare with the NFL, MLB, and NBA. Major League Soccer (MLS) has had difficulty gaining a solid fan base, despite the Olympic and World Cup success of the national women's team. The MLS started play in 1996 with ten teams. In 2003 it attracted 2.2 million spectators to its games, an average of only 14,898 per game. The United States Soccer Association, the women's professional league, began play in 2001 with eight teams. In the 2003 season it had a total of only 560,000 spectators for the entire league and was forced to disband after that year (Uhle 2005, 65).

Professional golf and tennis circuits have a devoted but small following. Sports such as professional bowling or beach volleyball attract a regional fan base and get a minor share of the television market (see Chapter 13).

PROFESSIONAL SPORT ISSUES

Professional sports face many but similar issues in the United States. One of the concerns refers to the relations between the cities and the teams or the team owners. In the competition to attract professional teams, cities promise and provide various benefits. Team owners continually lobby for and often get public subsidization of new stadiums by threatening to move the franchise to another city. Tampa, Florida built a new stadium in the hope of attracting at least one of five major league teams in the 1980s and 1990s, before it was finally awarded a franchise in 1995. More than half of the professional baseball and professional football team owners have managed to get new stadiums constructed since 1992 (Delaney and Eckstein 2003, 2). Even the renovation of an existing stadium can cost a staggering amount of money. The cost of an upgrade for Chicago's historic Soldier Field amounted to $660,000,000; two-thirds of that sum was publicly financed. This means that cities withdraw resources from other important areas such as schools or parks and invest them into sports.

Although the professional teams are perceived as belonging to the community, they are privately owned, and public taxes are often diverted to the owners' coffers. In a continual effort to maximize profits, ticket prices continue to rise, inevitably excluding many working-class fans. The Chicago football team made an estimated $201,000,000 for the 2005 season. Like other teams it gains revenue not only from television rights and ticket sales and the rental of special seating or luxury suites, but from food and drink concessions and stadium advertising as well. Chicago nearly doubled its ticket prices by 2006 from the $42.70 charged in 2001. The New England (Boston) franchise built a new stadium in 2002 at a cost of $325,000,000; and then raised the average ticket price to $160 by 2004, beyond the means of most fans (Falk 2005, 192). Still, the Chicago team ranked only tenth in franchise value among the thirty-two professional football teams. Five of the teams were worth more than a billion dollars in 2005 (Bergen 2007). When the Chicago team reached the Super Bowl in 2007 its head coach was the lowest paid in the league at $1,450,000 per year. His new salary approached $5,000,000 the following season; but that did not approach some coaches who made $8,000,000 per year (Bergen 2007). A baseball player for the New York Yankees makes more than $28,000,000 per year, more than the total of the poorest team ("Extra Bases"; http://asp.usatoday.com/sports/baseball/salaries/player detail.aspx?lname=Rodriguez&player=53). The team values and the salaries of coaches and players show the rampant commercialization of sport, an incredible increase in the revenues on the one hand, but also in the salaries on the other. The escalating team revenues have owners battling coaches and players for the brunt of the revenues. The NFL's television revenue for 2006 was estimated at six billion dollars, with 59.5 per cent of that going to the players (Bergen 2007) (see Chapter 13). The major problem with these developments is that the costs are being passed on to the consumers (fans) and to the cities, where the poorest inhabitants are the most affected.

The hierarchical structure in the professional leagues, the dominance of the owners, but also the growing self-confidence of the players, who know what they are worth, led and lead to conflicts, and in the case of baseball and hockey also to serious and long-lasting labor conflicts with strikes and lockouts of the players. Owners have sought to impose salary caps on team spending to lower the expenses, and thereby preserve more profit for themselves. Players feel that they are the main attraction for fans and wish to be compensated accordingly. Benefits and pensions present another concern, particularly for NFL players. The violent nature of the game can result in career-ending injuries (the average career lasts for 3.2 years: Falk 2005, 70), disabling conditions requiring multiple surgeries, and shortened life spans. The health problems, injuries and early deaths, especially of football players, are major problems, whereby the health risks are one side, and the denial of an adequate covering of health care expenses after the sport career has ended are another side of the same issue. The body of an athlete is seen as invincible, pain has to be overcome, invalidity has to be risked, but this is imagined as a heroic deed and not a matter of health insurance (Hewitt 1993).

Despite the risks, players, and the youth that idolize them, aspire to the wealth, privileges, and celebrity that accompany a professional sports career. In order to perform at that level many have resorted to the use of steroids or other performance-enhancing drugs. Doping scandals in baseball reached such proportions that the US Congress intervened and threatened sanctions in 2004, forcing the league commissioners to invoke standards and harsher penalties.

Other issues are gambling and cheating which have affected each of the major sports. For example, Pete Rose, one of baseball's greatest players from 1963 to 1986, was banished from the game and denied entry into the Hall of Fame due to gambling on his own team. Sports gambling in the USA is a multi-billion dollar industry ($380 billion in 2002: Falk 2005, 196) (see the Black Sox scandal described in Chapter 13).

Aggressiveness and an emphasis on masculinity, as well as the fascination with a "bad boy" image may have contributed to the problems of some athletes with the law, the police, and society at large. Pro basketball and football players have been involved in numerous cases of violence perpetrated against women and criminal cases including murders. One study claimed that 21 percent of NFL players had been indicted for major crimes (Falk 2005, 199–200). The commissioners of each league have taken actions to protect the image (and the profits) of the association by suspending players; but they often assess lenient penalties. Courts have sometimes spared professional athletes as well; although some have gone to prison. In either case, questions have been raised about the societal responsibilities of athletes as role models. However, professional athletes are problematic role models in any case because they and their allegedly glamorous lives instigate millions of children and youth to dream of a professional career and disregard education.

The dominance and ubiquity of professional sport in American society has a major impact on American culture. It shapes the picture of sport and its actors, the athletes, the coaches, the owners, as well as the interrelationships among them. The mass media convey the impression and shape the conviction that professional sport is the blueprint for all other sporting activities and thus relegate other sport cultures to the sidelines.

CHAPTER NINE

FITNESS AND RECREATIONAL SPORT

INTRODUCTION

Today, a multitude of experts and professional organizations, but also scientists in the area of sport and health, provide evidence of the importance to be fit and active. In addition, there are numerous recommendations on how to become or how to stay slim and fit. Dieting has become nearly an obsession for many Americans, a result of the so-called obesity epidemic.

On the one hand there is a growing concern about health issues in the USA; on the other hand the physical activity rates are relatively low, although a variety of organizations and institutions provide physical activities for different groups of the population. In this chapter, we explore opportunities and challenges of various groups of society to engage in physical activity and sport (in a broad sense), and provide capsule descriptions of major providers of sport, as well as of organizations and governing bodies for the regulation of athletic activities. Given the elitist nature of many American sporting practices, one might question whether or not there are enough opportunities and enough encouragement for everybody (without talent or ambitions) to play sport. We also inquire into the habits and tastes of the American population relative to physical activity, and discuss potential reasons for the rather sedentary lifestyle in the US.

SPORT FOR ALL – GENERAL CONSIDERATIONS

Sport for all is not a concept known in the United States where the term "sport" is strictly connected to performance-oriented and competitive activities. But terms are not just words; they are intertwined with structures, meanings, and practices. The lack of an overall term for sport and physical activities indicates not only that there is no umbrella structure for sport (in a broad sense), but also that the various physical practices including sport for all are not conceived of as a unity, as belonging to the same social field or the same discourse.

Whereas top-level sport has a high significance and embodies American values as equal chances, reward for performances, and opportunities for social advancement, the emphasis on a strong work ethic in the US conflicts with recreational physical activities. The Puritan belief in non-work time as wasted time is still strong. When Americans take time from work to exercise they call it a "workout," and generally do so before or after employment hours. Fitness is thus gained through working at it, not through a leisurely activity which is meant to be fun (Volkwein and Zohner-Nassi 1998, 252; Smith Maguire 2007).

BOX 9.1 SPORT FOR ALL FROM THE PERSPECTIVE OF AN AMERICAN SOCIOLOGIST LIVING IN EUROPE

The U.S. has no central authority or organization devoted to sport, unlike many other countries of the world. Instead, sport and Sport for All (recreation) programs exist in a complex, largely uncoordinated network of private and public agencies and organizations at the local, regional and national level.

To continue team sports into adulthood is difficult to manage. Factors such as the lack of time, access to facilities, coaching, equipment aid in the decline of participation with age. As adults age they often move . . . to individual and pair sports, and to participation in outdoor recreation . . . Time and money and scarce environments tend to limit participation in outdoor recreation to weekends and holidays.

Sport for All faces serious challenges in modern U.S. society. Hopefully the time will draw near that individuals, communities and governments will see the need for Sport for All as an antidote to a host of society's problems. We urgently need Sport for All's contribution to social integration, the cultural understanding and celebration, play and games and health producing physical involvement.

(Jones-Palm 2002, 713, 715, 721)

AN OVERVIEW OF PHYSICAL ACTIVITIES

Some peculiarities of American culture determine the opportunities for sport for all. As described in Chapter 6, American sports revolve around the school system, rather than around sport clubs as is the case in many European countries. In the United States children play sports and games as recreational amusements; but they also participate in extracurricular sport activities provided by schools for pupils aged 10 years and older. The older the students, the more competitive and selective the program. The most talented and skilled students are selected for the school teams and the best athletes may later get an athletic scholarship at a college or university (see Chapter 6).

Since the 1980s, an increasing amount of community-based programs have organized sport for children and adolescents, in soccer, baseball, swimming, and other sports. Most of these programs focus on competitions which take place especially during the summer. Good athletes or teams reach high levels of the various leagues which can attract the attention of coaches who recruit athletes for college scholarships. Competition and winning are the main focus of sport and games, and those who want to play for fun do not get a chance to join a team. Such an elitist framework awards only a handful of players/athletes; the majority of adolescents are relegated to spectator status. At each level of education (high school, college, university) more participants are weeded out, until only a select few athletes reach the level of Division I university teams or ultimately the professional ranks.[1]

Besides children, young adults also have various opportunities to play sport. At the university, students can participate in intramural sports, which have some similarity with the sport-for-all activities of clubs in countries where the sport system operates outside of educational institutions. American colleges and universities organize programs in a large number of sports for their students. Intramural sports are mostly competitive but low-level sporting activities are conducted *intra muros* (inside the walls), namely between the members/teams of the institutions on a relatively informal basis (see Chapter 5).

After leaving college, sport-for-all opportunities decrease decidedly and depend to a high degree on the environment and on the living conditions, especially the financial resources, of individuals and groups. There are community-based activities for adults, mostly financed by public funds and membership fees, as sport-for-all programs are hard to sell to sponsors, who are focused on top-level sport. Many large companies initiated corporate fitness programs for their employees, not as a humanitarian interest but as a cost-cutting measure to limit health insurance claims. In the US, employers of more than twenty employees must pay a proportion of the health insurance for their workers. Employees are also responsible for a part of the health costs; but because many (especially low-waged) workers cannot afford to pay their share, they go without insurance. Healthy workers not only save money for the employer, they prove to be more productive and have less absenteeism. In 1999, about 25 percent of employees in knowledge-based industries were in workplaces that provided fitness and recreation services (on- or off-site). The corresponding numbers for other goods-producing industries, professional and other services, and retail trade and consumer services were 15 percent, 17 percent, and 5 percent respectively.[2]

Private clubs offer a wide range of sports from tennis to golf or martial arts. However, many of these clubs ask for high enrollment and membership fees, thus restricting the access to the middle or even upper classes. A special form of a private club is the country club which offers a variety of recreational facilities, social events, and sport opportunities to its members. Well-tended tennis courts and attractive golf-courses are assets for most clubs. Access to membership is restricted by high membership fees which can be more than $300,000, in addition to annual dues.[3] The exclusivity of these clubs may also be guaranteed by a limited number of memberships and restrictive admission rules. Thus clubs can decide to admit only those persons who are proposed by an existing member. Country clubs used to secure their social status by the exclusion of minority groups such as African-Americans, Hispanics, or Jews. Although these practices are usually illegal today, the self-selectivity of these clubs ensures their "whiteness." Country clubs are more than a sport association; they are meeting places in often exclusive environments, they provide selected social networks, and contribute to the symbolic capital of members.

The most popular activities are unorganized, often together with family or friends, such as hiking, jogging, fishing, or swimming. However, these activities depend on the environment as described later in detail. Whereas rich communities offer recreational areas such as biking paths or jogging trails, people living in poor neighborhoods have limited or no access to recreational facilities. A solution for inner city residents may be mall walking. Mall walkers are small groups of mostly older adults who use the huge shopping malls for their workout as an alternative to parks and streets. Thus they avoid hot or cold weather and traffic, and in addition gain security, because the streets of inner cities are often not safe for pedestrians. A Mall Walker's Association of America represents the interests of the walkers and the malls involved (http://www.mallwalker.org/index.php?option=com_content&view=frontpage).

PHYSICAL ACTIVITIES AND SPORT – PROVIDERS

Children and youth

Community sports programs

In the US numerous organizations provide sports and activities for non-elite athletes, especially children and adolescents. Administrators of local park districts,[4] community clubs, fraternal organizations, and church groups offer athletic programs and sponsor competitive teams (Hums and MacLean 2004). Communities provide organized competitions for both adults and children in a variety of sports within a league structure as a public service. More than 3,000 boys' and girls' clubs, often in the inner city, provided activities for over 3,000,000 children in 2002 (Hums and MacLean 2004, 126).

Parents or other adults organize teams or clubs for competition in local leagues. A 2006 report indicated that 41,000,000 American children participated in youth sport activities (Carney 2006). Often such programs provide general instruction, training, and participation in competitions, but some also offer recreational opportunities where children can shoot baskets, hit baseballs, or swim. The coaches are often parents, many of whom lack any formalized training. The more ambitious or more competitive coaches recruit the best children and adolescents for travel teams that play in regional tournaments in baseball, softball, basketball, volleyball, and soccer. The travel clubs are funded by the parents and many have become profit-minded businesses that attract young players with expectations of winning athletic scholarships to universities (see Chapter 5). Players on such teams receive exposure to college coaches or recruitment agents, who measure their performances against

204

other highly talented players in the tournaments and select the best for their schools. Players on high school teams have increasingly withdrawn from participation on their interscholastic teams in favor of the exposure offered on the travel teams, some of which play or practice on a year-round basis.[5] Youth travel teams may play more games than professional teams, and the consequent expenses for parents, the problems with injuries, and the loss of school or personal time are high in comparison to the slim chance of winning a scholarship.

Little League baseball

Little League baseball, founded in Pennsylvania in 1939, has become an American institution. It is a non-profit organization dedicated to promoting baseball and softball for children. Until the passage of Title IX, a federal law guaranteeing gender equity in 1972, girls were prohibited from joining Little League baseball teams. The "Little Leagues" mirror the American professional leagues with teams dressed in uniforms and adopting the names of their major league counterparts. The more affluent leagues play in miniature stadiums, while others may compete on local park district baseball fields. Playing Little League baseball is a rite of passage for American boys as the game, once the national pastime, has great resonance in American culture. (It has since been superseded by American football.)

The baseball leagues are arranged by age groups in an attempt to equalize competition. Tee ball leagues are generally for 6- to 8-year-olds and allow players to hit the ball off a stationary pedestal (the tee) rather than attempt to hit the more difficult pitched (thrown) ball. Tee ball players graduate to "minor" leagues for ages 9 to 10, where the ball is thrown to the batter (hitter), who attempts to strike it with the bat. Eleven- and 12-year-old players compete in the "major" league, with three more categories of leagues for older players (juniors, seniors, big). Little League also offers a "Challenger Division" for children with disabilities (http://www.littleleague.org).

Little League baseball has transcended the United States and has been instituted in many areas where Americans have had a global presence. In 1939 only forty-five boys played in the initial league; but by 1964 that number had reached 1,066,600 in all fifty states, the American territory of Guam, and twelve foreign countries (Carriere 2005, 352). American military bases that house families, for example, often have a Little League baseball organization. Numerous other nations in Latin America, the Caribbean, Asia, and even in South America, Europe, and Africa field teams (Rogers 2007b). The highlight of each year is an international World Series between regional played in Williamsport, Pennsylvania, the founding site of the organization (http://www.littleleague.org).

Participation in baseball leagues has decreased 1 percent annually since 1996, yet 2,200,000 American children, almost all boys, still play the game (Carney 2006).

Pop Warner football

The Pop Warner football program is the correlate to Little League baseball, although founded earlier, in 1929. At that time it was established in Philadelphia and named for a famous college football coach. Like the Little League program it organizes local, regional, and national competition for boys aged 5 to 15. The football competitions are further categorized according to weight due to the physical nature of the game (http://www.popwarner.com/football/pop.asp). Leagues are locally organized by adults, and champions may continue to compete for regional and national honors with the national championship being broadcast on television. Like the children's baseball leagues, the football leagues emphasize somewhat contradictory values. Winning is important, but winning as a team. Individual statistics are eschewed in favor of team accomplishments. Some leagues require playing time for each team member regardless of ability; yet many coaches concentrate on winning the games as the most important issue. Stereotypical gender roles are reinforced, as girls are relegated to cheerleaders for the boys' teams. The growing ascendance of football in American culture may be measured by the number of participants in the Pop Warner leagues, which has increased 100 percent since 1987 (Carney 2006). As many as 350,000 players and 40,000 coaches are active in youth football (Falk 2005, 17).

Basketball

Like baseball and football, youth basketball leagues are organized by a variety of groups: park districts, schools, churches, social agencies, and the organizers of independent travel teams. Organizations, such as Biddy basketball, operate similarly to Little League baseball in that they accommodate the needs of younger children by using smaller balls, lowering the height of the basket, and playing on smaller courts. Still, competition is highly valued and teams may compete for international honors.

Basketball travel teams that seek out the best players and travel to regional and national tournaments have become quite popular, but also, as mentioned above, problematic. While many players aspire to participate on such teams, basketball is most popular in its "streetball" version. Streetball developed on urban playgrounds over the course of the twentieth century in impromptu games organized by neighborhood youths who regulated the games themselves. A predefined number of points determined the winner of the game and the winning team was allowed to continue playing until defeated. Various versions of the game might involve a limited number of players, such as 1 vs. 1 or 3 vs. 3. Such competitions often feature individual brilliance and spectacular plays that have made some participants local and even national legends. Streetball teams travel across the United States and challenge other urban contingents with some games broadcast on the ESPN television network. A cable television station has even created a traveling streetball team that plays in many cities and is presented like a Big Brother show in which players get voted off the team.

Streetball is often associated with race; it is most often played by African-American boys, although not all players are African-American. Numerous professional players have brought

206

the streetball style of play to the National Basketball Association; but its emphasis on individual stardom is often condemned by coaches.

BOX 9.2 BLACK BASKETBALL

The playground game wasn't so much a team sport as a series of duels. If you had the ball and passed it to the open man under the basket, nobody considered that admirable. All you'd done was throw an opportunity away. The game was outdueling the man guarding you. Making a terrific jump shot from outside didn't get the job done, either. The idea was to fake your man out or intimidate him, outmuscle him, drive past him "into the hole," soar above him, score a layup or dunk the ball if you were that tall, and then give him the look that said – this was where Jojo first learned it – "I'm kicking your ass all over the court, bitch."

(Wolfe 2005, 49–50)

Basketball has a historic relationship to particular rural areas as well. The states of Indiana, Kentucky, and North Carolina are well known for their rabid fans and their devotion to school teams. In Iowa, girls' basketball supersedes even the popularity of the boys' teams.

American Youth Soccer Organization (AYSO)

The American Youth Soccer Organization originated in Los Angeles in 1964. It has since become one of the fastest growing youth sports groups in the United States with more than 50,000 teams and 50,000 players (40 percent of whom are girls). AYSO endeavors to limit the American overemphasis on winning by guaranteeing that each player on the team gets to play half of the game regardless of individual ability. Teams are restructured every year to balance the players' abilities and insure that one team does not become a dominant power. Like Little League baseball, AYSO provides a division for children with impairments (http://soccer.org/home.aspx). Overall participation in youth soccer leagues, including the local community programs, numbered 17,500,000 children in 2003, the largest number of participants in any sport (Carney 2006) (see Chapter 5).

National Police Athletics/Activities Leagues (PAL)

Police athletic leagues are organized by urban police departments for the social control of young men.[6] They intend to keep youth busy in order to detract them from criminal activities, as well as establish more harmonious relationships between police officers and young people. The leagues provide recreational and educational opportunities; but their athletic components attract more media attention. Boxing competitions or "midnight" basketball leagues intend to keep gang members off the streets during the later hours and to teach positive values, such as teamwork, discipline, and a strong work ethic that might be transferred into job skills. Similar to the other programs' emphasis on competition and winning; PAL even offers national championships (http:www.nationalpal.org/).

Excursus: sport clubs and academies for talented children

Besides the non-profit organizations, commercial clubs and academies train children aiming at elite sports, for example in gymnastics, tennis, or ice-skating. Highly renowned and very successful are the International Management Group (IMG) academies, located in Florida. IMG prepares students at the same time for college and for top-level sport, offering two boarding-schools, excellent facilities, and state-of-the-art training in various sports. Famous is the Nick Bolletieri Tennis Academy which has produced hundreds of players gaining at least a college scholarship and which has the crème-de-la-crème of tennis among its alumni. College-aged students can participate in postgraduate programs (http://www.imgacademies.com/hq/default.sps?itype=7939).

The potential awards and financial gains in top-level sport entice parents to pay the high fees for the professional training of their children. In some cases, parents even act as stockholders and sell shares of the future success of the young athletes.[7]

Youth sport issues

There are several problems connected with these types of sporting activities and organizations: the "professionalization" of children's sport, the high costs and the lack of consistency, as well as financial uncertainty. The focus on highly talented children fails to take account of the less skilled youngsters who actually need physical exercise. The overemphasis on winning in American sport has caused many children to forgo participation in sports programs. In addition, there are few sports initiatives in rural areas and poor neighborhoods. Further problems are caused by the great ambitions of parents and children who dream of sport scholarships (free tuition, board, and accommodation) at colleges and universities. Over-exertion, injuries, or burn-out syndromes of young athletes can be the consequences. Traveling teams, but also the training centers for gymnastics and ice-skating, have been accused of misusing the children through long periods of training, punishments, or disregard of injuries (Ryan 1995).

fitness and recreational sport

The programs offered by parents are also not without problems and conflicts. Volunteer coaches, often the parents themselves, have little or no coaching education which impedes the quality of the training and may even endanger the health of the children. Parents of players often charge that coaches favor their own children, by granting them more playing time or choosing them for leadership positions. Coaches or parents may publicly berate young players for poor performances in their quest to win the contests. The behavior of parents towards coaches, officials, and other parents has often been not only derogatory but violent. Brawls involving more than a hundred spectators have, for example, erupted at youth football games over referees' decisions (Falk 2005, 18).

Travel teams and sports academies, which offer specialized training, are increasingly operated as private businesses that charge expensive fees but cannot guarantee the expected results. Youth sport programs often duplicate the offerings of the interscholastic programs, which some taxpayers see as a waste of money.

Programs and opportunities for adults

On the community level, recreational activities and especially competitions are also
organized for adults. Park districts provide beaches, swimming pools, and golf-courses for
recreational use. Local governments support such facilities and programs with usage or
rental fees and funding via taxes.

Health and fitness as business

Within the commercialized capitalist American society, health and fitness are commodities.
Like beauty operations and wrinkle creams, they are products promising eternal youth to
be bought in the quest for longevity (Smith Maguire 2007). It is no wonder that the "number
one" physical activity of the adult population is working out in a health club, with the fitness
industry currently experiencing a tremendous boom. In addition, bowling alleys, tennis
centers, golf-courses, and other facilities are available for paying users. They promise fitness
together with recreation and fun.

In commercialized fitness centers operators sell services, clothing, food, and a variety of
membership plans to attract new customers with the intent of maximizing profits (Sage
1998a). Fitness, as a business, is a lucrative industry.

Health and fitness is also "sold" by the YMCA (Young Men's Christian Association), which
curtailed its religious mission in the latter part of the twentieth century and assumed the
role of a fitness company (Hums and MacLean 2004, 123). America's 2,686 YMCAs are
collectively one of the largest not-for-profit community service organizations in the US
(http://www.ymca.net/about_the_ymca). However, YMCAs are not voluntary associations,
but function like commercial health and fitness centers.[8]

Between 1992 and 2002 the number of commercial health clubs in the United States increased by 40 percent and membership grew by 60 percent. The health club owners pursued different strategies to attract patrons. Some offered low membership fees aimed at lower or middle-income clients, others targeted particular demographic groups, such as women. High-priced clubs, which proved to be more recession-proof, attracted wealthier clients with plush amenities, personal trainers, masseuses, and the projection of greater social status ("Industry Will Continue to Prosper", 2002). By 2005 at least 23,500 health clubs were serving more than 39,000,000 members. Women comprised 52 percent of the members. Selling fitness had become a $14.8 billion industry with prospects for even greater future success. The patrons had an average annual income of $75,000. But these figures should not cover the fact that about 90 percent of adult Americans had not joined a club, and that not all of those who joined use the facilities regularly (http://www.golds gym.com/golds/franchising/facts.php).

BOX 9.5 SPORT FOR ALL IS NOT FOR ALL

The increasing split between the rich and the poor in the U.S. and the shrinking middle class places access to Sport for All critically important in a society hungry for healthy leisure pursuits. It is a sad commentary on U.S. culture that so much emphasis is placed, in our service orientated capitalist economy, on preparing people for their work and consumer roles and such little emphasis is placed on how to enjoy life, how to join with others in play and games, how to develop attachments with others and in the appreciation of culture and nature . . .

Sport for All is a complex and often contradictory landscape. On the one hand, the U.S. is the cradle of globally successful activities like jogging, walking, aerobics, wellness, body-shaping, of new sport equipment enhancements like windsurfing, snowboards and inline skates and in producing evidence of benefits in scientific research. On the other hand, in the U.S. access to sport is limited for the less affluent, the minorities, the indigenous, physical education is less and less an obligatory part of school curriculums, particularly at the young adult level. The U.S. has no national program that combines the forces and institutions of sport, recreation and health for giving the benefits of sport and physical activity to everybody.

(Jones-Palm 2002, 721)

National initiatives, policies, and organizations for health and fitness

The United States has no universal national health insurance program. Citizens must rely on private health insurance to meet their medical needs. Health care providers have historically assumed a restorative or remedial role rather than a preventative one in dealing with maladies, also with the increasing lifestyle diseases. The onus for health care generally lies with the individual; this is true for the prevention and cure of diseases. In spite of the lack of concrete health promotion politics, the US government has adopted health and physical activity as an issue.

United States government

Any federal policies or directives pertinent to health emanate from the United States Department of Health and Human Services, headed by a Secretary with Cabinet-level status.[9] The federal government declares national health objectives each decade (Healthy People 2010), which include topics such as diseases, injuries, safety, substance abuse, nutrition, dietary guidelines, and fitness. It provides guidelines for achievement, but lacks any national policy for the solution of health problems (Sage 1998a).

The Surgeon General, who operates under the Office of Public Health and Science, is the chief "health educator" of the United States. He is appointed by the president for a four-year term and serves as an advisor to the president and the Secretary of Health and Human Services. The Surgeon General heads a corps of health professionals organized and structured in a military framework. (The position originated as a service to sailors.) The Surgeon General may set health standards and develop research priorities.

The President's Council on Physical Fitness and Sports also operates under the auspices of the Office of Public Health and Science. Originally established in 1956 as the President's Council on Youth Fitness as a reaction to the dismal showing of American children on international fitness tests, the position enjoyed Cabinet-level status, and was chaired by the vice-president of the United States. A year later a national fitness test was initiated for children between the ages of 5 and 12, which has continued annually for elementary school students. Testing of secondary school students began in the 1960s. In 1966 the council was transferred to the Department of Health, Education, and Welfare (later to become the Department of Health and Human Services). In 1961 President John F. Kennedy appointed Bud Wilkinson, a famous college football coach, to chair the council and act as consultant to the president on fitness matters. Thereafter presidents generally chose coaches and athletes to chair the position, including Arnold Schwarzenegger from 1990 to 1992 (http://www.fitness.gov/about_history.htm). In 1970 the council extended its scope to include community recreation departments, boys' and girls' clubs, and company fitness programs. Throughout the 1980s and 1990s American children showed little improvement in fitness levels, and obesity rates among children and adults increased despite the council's efforts to enhance public awareness. As chairman of the council, Arnold Schwarzenegger visited all fifty states to advocate daily physical education classes in the schools; but only the state of Illinois requires five PE lessons per week. In the 1990s initiatives to improve the fitness levels of senior citizens had some success; but most Americans remained inactive (http://www.fitness.gov/about_history.htm).

Other governmental entities responsible for the general welfare of Americans include the National Institutes for Health, comprising twenty-seven research institutes devoted to various maladies. The Centers for Disease Control and Prevention assume both a proactive and reactive function relative to health care in the United States.

The U.S. states may have their own health and fitness initiatives, but few have established formal policies.

Associations addressing health and fitness issues

The American College of Sports Medicine (ACSM), established in 1954, serves more than 20,000 member professionals in the fields of education, medicine, clinical practice, exercise science, and athletic training. Unlike in Europe an athletic trainer in the United States is not a coach, but a certified medical practitioner who treats and rehabilitates athletic injuries. Athletic trainers are employed by secondary schools, colleges, and universities, as well as hospitals, therapeutic centers, and fitness clubs. The ACSM develops the certification standards and sets the national curriculum for licensure of trainers and various other health-related professions such as health/fitness instructors or exercise physiologists. The association provides professional development and continuing education to its members in the form of clinics, workshops, and a national convention, disseminates knowledge via professional publications, and provides research grants to scientists. The linkage between sciences and practices is emphasized in ACSM's Mission Statement:

> The American College of Sports Medicine promotes and integrates scientific research, education, and practical applications of sports medicine and exercise science to maintain and enhance physical performance, fitness, health, and quality of life. Working in a wide range of medical specialties, allied health professions, and scientific disciplines, our members are committed to the diagnosis, treatment, and prevention of sports-related injuries and the advancement of the science of exercise.
>
> (http://www.acsm.org/AM/Template.cfm?Section=About_ACSM)

The American Heart Association (AHA) is the largest and most important among the many voluntary organizations that address health and fitness concerns. Starting as a local group in New York City in 1915, it became a nationwide organization in 1924. Its purpose is to decrease cardiovascular diseases and strokes through research, education, and community programs. It particularly opposes the use of tobacco and promotes physical activities, good nutrition practices, and healthy lifestyles. The AHA offers information about health and fitness, provides advise for a healthy everyday life, gives exercise tips for different groups of the population, conducts campaigns, and offers various programs. In the 1970s, the AHA promoted rope jumping as an easy and healthy physical activity. Similar to the traditional children's exercise, rope jumping with various tricks became an attractive sport. The public elementary schools hold an annual national competition known as Jump Rope for Heart (http://www.americanheart.org/presenter.jhtml?identifier=10860).

Another non-profit organization focusing on fitness is the American Council on Exercise (ACE) which provides educational materials and training for fitness personnel. It certifies personal trainers and weight management specialists and offers resource guides and consulting services to schools (http://www.acefitness.org/aboutace/factsheet.aspx).

The world-renowned "fitness institute", the Cooper Institute, was founded in Dallas, Texas in 1970 by Dr. Kenneth Cooper. Cooper is author of numerous books on health and lifestyle. He introduced the term "aerobics" to the English language and is often credited with starting the jogging boom of the 1970s. The institute is a non-profit foundation dedicated to research and education. Particular areas of research include exercise physiology, nutrition, obesity, aging, and children's health. Cooper introduced the "Fitnessgram" in 1982, assessments of flexibility, body composition, strength, muscular endurance, and aerobic capacity widely adopted by physical educators in the schools. The scientific research conducted at the institute is often cited in professional journals and has greatly influenced fitness activities throughout American culture. The Cooper enterprises also include a fitness center, a lavish resort and spa facilities providing services, consultations, weight management programs, classes, workshops, personal trainer certification, and corporate-team building activities that merge very profitable business enterprises which sell health and health products to affluent customers (http://www.cooperinst.org/research/index.ctm).

HOW ACTIVE ARE THE AMERICANS? PARTICIPATION RATES

"To many Americans, 'sport' is something one watches on TV, reads in the newspapers, or is an event attended" (Jones-Palm 2002, 707). Americans are largely a nation of spectators. Many become sedentary, especially after completing their education. The high numbers of sport consumers are discussed in Chapter 13.

Despite the multitude of sport programs in the United States, described above, most recreational activities of the 302 million Americans are spontaneous and unorganized pursuits. A 2004 survey by the Sporting Goods Manufacturers Association determined that 96.4 million Americans over the age of 6 go swimming each year, and another 53.7 million cycle. There were 55 million bowlers; but only 3.2 million did so in organized leagues. Bowling is especially popular in the Midwestern states. Another 35.4 million Americans played basketball; but only 5.6 million did so on a weekly basis. Tackle football had

214

Table 9.1 Sporting leisure activities

Most popular sports for men (aged 6 and over) based on "frequent" participation, 2003

Activity	Year 2003	(Age 5 to 69) % of Population
1 Fishing (freshwater/other)	9,169,000	7.5
2 Free weights: Barbells	8,484,000	6.9
3 Free weights: Dumbbells	7,878,000	6.4
4 Stretching	7,569,000	6.2
5 Calisthenics	6,748,000	5.5
6 Fitness walking	6,626,000	5.4
7 Billiards/pool	6,381,000	5.2
8 Running/jogging	6,209,000	5.1
9 Weight/resistance machines	5,812,000	4.8
10 Basketball	5,640,000	4.6
11 Golf	5,552,000	4.5
12 Treadmill exercise	5,375,000	4.4
13 Hunting (shotgun/rifle)	4,327,000	3.5
14 Day hiking	4,260,000	3.5
15 Bowling	3,783,000	3.1

Most popular sports for women (aged 6 and over) based on "frequent" participation, 2003

Activity	Year 2003	(Age 5 to 69) % of Population
1 Stretching	10,710,000	8.6
2 Fitness walking	9,788,000	8.0
3 Treadmill exercise	6,160,000	5.0
4 Free weights: Hand weights	4,587,000	3.8
5 Running/jogging	4,247,000	3.5
6 Weight/resistance machines	4,073,000	3.3
7 Calisthenics	3,921,000	3.2
8 Day hiking	3,749,000	3.1
9 Bowling	3,552,000	2.9
10 Recreational vehicle camping	3,373,000	2.8
11 Fishing (freshwater/other)	3,103,000	2.5
12 Free weights: Dumbbells	3,011,000	2.5
13 Billiards/pool	2,973,000	2.4
14 Other exercise to music	2,942,000	2.4
15 Abdominal machine/device	2,208,000	1.8

215

Table 9.1 Continued

Most popular sports for youth (aged 6 to 17)[a] based on "frequent" participation, 2003

Activity		Year 2003	% of Population
1	Basketball	4,127,000	8.4
2	Fishing	3,472,000	7.0
3	Inline skating	3,467,000	7.0
4	Running/jogging	3,054,000	6.2
5	Stretching	3,052,000	6.2
6	Calisthenics	2,704,000	5.5
7	Baseball	2,531,000	5.1
8	Outdoor soccer	2,435,000	4.9
9	Skateboarding	2,107,000	4.3
10	Touch football	1,998,000	4.1
11	Scooter riding	1,954,000	4.0
12	Court volleyball	1,894,000	3.8
13	Tent camping	1,880,000	3.8
14	Billiard/pool	1,879,000	3.8
15	Tackle football	1,840,000	3.7

Most popular sports for seniors (aged 55 to 69) based on "frequent" participation, 2003

Activity		year 2003	% of Population
1	Fitness walking	6,277,000	16.7
2	Stretching	4,011,000	10.7
3	Treadmill exercise	3,059,000	8.1
4	Golf	2,966,000	7.9
5	Fishing (freshwater/other)	2,625,000	7.0
6	Recreational vehicle camping	2,189,000	5.8
7	Free weights: Hand weights	1,735,000	4.6
8	Bowling	1,647,000	4.4
9	Weight/resistance machines	1,493,000	4.0
10	Day hiking	1,414,000	3.8
11	Calisthenics	1,161,000	3.1
12	Fishing (saltwater)	1,147,000	3.1
13	Free weights: Dumbbells	1,040,000	2.8
14	Stationary cycling: Upright bike (regular)	1,031,000	2.7
15	Hunting (shotgun/rifle)	960,000	2.6

[a] The number of the population in the age group 6 to 17 is estimated based on figures 5–19 in the census.
Source: Uhle (2005, 11, 12) (http://www.census.gov/popest/national/asrh/NC-EST2007-sa.html)

5.8 million participants; but most opted for safer versions such as touch or flag football. There were 14.1 million participants in the touch/flag games. Soccer showed an increasing number of players with 17.7 million; and softball had nearly as many participants with 16 million (Uhle 2005, 64). These numbers seem to indicate a high level of physical activity; however, they refer to individuals who do this activity at least once a year. A survey of the choice of activities since 1987 shows a decline of traditional sports such as baseball, touch football and other team sports, as well as aerobics and an increase of new activities like pilates, various fitness exercises on stationary equipment, and "alternative sports" like mountain biking or snow boarding (Uhle 2005, 8–10).

A more accurate picture of the sporting activities of the US population is given in the SGMA study on "frequent" participation (see Table 9.1).[10] The most popular activities for males (aged 6 and over) were fishing followed by weightlifting and stretching. Basketball was number 10, golf number 11, hunting number 13, and bowling number 15 on the list. Women preferred stretching, fitness walking, and treadmill exercises. Seniors, both men and women, reported activity patterns which were similar to the activities of women. Youth (aged 6 to 17) reported more strenuous and playful activities than adults. Basketball was their number 1 activity, followed by fishing and inline skating. They also participated in baseball, outdoor soccer, touch football, volleyball, and tackle football (in that order).

All activities reported by the adult population were to a high degree fitness exercises and informal activities which did not necessarily need to be conducted in specific facilities (exceptions are bowling and billiards). If we relate the numbers of sport participations to the number of the different age groups of the American population, it becomes obvious that only a relatively small percentage of Americans are active. The percentages of participants in the various sports (aged 6 and over) are under 10 percent, and most involve less than 5 percent of the population (see Table 9.1).

The frequency of fitness activities reported in the surveys is supported by the reports of the fitness centers. Commercial fitness centers reportedly have 39.4 million and the YMCA 20.2 million members; this would mean that around 20 percent of the American population (including babies and old people) are members of a fitness club. However, membership in a club does not necessarily mean that one also trains more or less regularly there (Smith Maguire 2007).

Surveys about the amount and frequency of physical activities, too, give insight into the activity patterns of the various groups of the US population. According to information provided by the National Centre for Health Statistics (NCDC 2007), children and adolescents are the most active groups among the US population, with 77 percent of children aged 9 to 13 reported participating in free-time physical activity, and 39 percent reported participating in organized sport.[11] The Youth Risk Behavior Surveillance (2005) showed that 68.7 percent of high school students (75.8 percent of boys and 61.6 percent of girls) had been vigorously or moderately physically active and met previously recommended levels of physical activity (http://www.cdc.gov/mmwr/PDF/ss/ss505.pdf). However, only 36 percent of the students

(27.8 percent of girls and 43.8 percent of boys) had participated in at least sixty minutes per day of physical activity on five or more of the seven days preceding the survey and had met the currently recommended activity levels. Activities in physical education and extracurricular sporting activities at schools are included in these figures.[12]

A recent study revealed some progress in girls' physical activities and fitness but did not give the all-clear:

> Adolescent girls participate in a broader array of physical activities, ranging from informal, playlike environments to the pressure-cooker world of Olympic sports, than ever before in our history . . . Despite the rise in participation for some sports, significant declines in team sports . . . pick-up play, and multi-sport participation are evident among youth . . . pressures of early sport participation, intensive training expectation at young ages, and selection or funnelling processes that, among other things, eliminate lesser-skilled girls and often discourage future participation in physical activities . . . so while 1 in 3 girls are active through sports participation . . . one-third of girls barely meet minimal physical activity standards, and the remaining third are completely sedentary.
>
> (Tucker Center 2007, 1–3)

A 2006 report indicated that around forty-one million American youngsters play competitive youth sports (Hilgers 2006).

However, there is also bad news. The percentage of students attending PE classes daily from 1991 to 2001 declined from 42 percent to 32 percent. A major source of activity could be the way to and from school. However, only 57 percent of families with children live in areas where schools are within walking distance, and many children do not walk or bike to school because of the danger from traffic (Brownson et al. 2005, 438).

Physical activity is a privilege of youth. According to the National Center for Health Statistics the percentage of adults engaged in vigorous physical activities is 48 percent, but only 24 percent take part in vigorous activities three or more times a week as recommended by the health experts. Around 40 percent of adult residents in the USA have adopted a totally sedentary lifestyle.

The frequency and intensity of physical activities is correlated to race, gender, and the level of education. Men are on average more active than women, whites more so than Hispanics and blacks. Thirty-eight percent of the white, 51 percent of the black, and 53 percent of the Hispanic population are not engaged in any physical activities (Bernstein et al. 2006). Only 15 percent of the population with fewer than twelve years of education, but 34 percent of people with a college education, are physically active. Huge differences occur as well in the different states, and low activity levels may be found especially in the Southern states where poverty is higher and resources lower than in the North (Brownson et al. 2005, 424).

Besides everyday physical exercises, outdoor activities have to be taken into consideration. Americans love the outdoors, and the parks and beaches are very popular on weekends and holidays. Hiking, fishing, swimming, camping, and picnicking are among Americans' favorite activities. In 2003, 36 percent of the adult population reportedly engaged at least once a month in outdoor activities (Uhle 2005, 33). One of the best ways of enjoying the outdoors is visiting one of the national parks which attract 266 million visitors every year. Outdoor recreation is correlated with class, race, and ethnicity. Whites with a college degree have the highest, African-Americans the lowest participation rate.

BOX 9.6 NATIONAL PARKS

There is nothing so American as our national parks . . . The fundamental idea behind the parks . . . is that the country belongs to the people, that it is in process of making for the enrichment of the lives of all of us.

(President Franklin D. Roosevelt)

During the 1930s, the Park Service became involved with areas intended primarily for mass recreation, including parkways and waterways. Since 1933, other parks and monuments have been placed under the jurisdiction of the National Park Service, including National Seashores, National Recreation Areas, and National Lakeshores.

Currently the National Park Service System includes more than 380 parks covering more than eighty-three million acres, in nearly every state and US possession. The Park Service supports the preservation of natural and historic places as well as promoting outdoor recreation outside the system through grant and technical assistance (http://www.u-s-history.com/pages/h1605.html).

LIFESTYLE CONDITIONS

Obesity

Currently, the lack of physical activity is connected in many ways with obesity. On the one hand, obesity is the trigger for numerous projects and programs aimed at activating the American population. Fitness and sport for all has become – at least on paper – a central issue for the whole nation. On the other hand, being overweight or obese inhibits participation in physical activities and sports.

Weight, food, and physical activity are the intertwined topics of the fervid health discourses in the USA. Physicians, politicians, scientists, (physical) educators, and mass media conjure an "obesity epidemic" which allegedly threatens American society. Eighty-five percent of Americans believe that obesity is an epidemic, according to a new poll conducted by the Trust for America's Health (Zieff 1994). Fitness operators hope to capitalize on the obesity concerns in the United States. They present evidence that one-third of American citizens are obese, with another third being overweight, and that treatment amounted to nearly $100 billion a year by 2005 (http://www.goldsgym.com/golds/franchising/facts.php).[13] Studies showed a correlation between obesity and numerous diseases such as heart disease, diabetes, stroke or cancer.[14]

BOX 9.7 OBESITY AND PHYSICAL EDUCATION

(*CBS*) With obesity at near epidemic proportions among our young people, you'd think physical education would be at the top of schools' priority lists. But you'd be wrong. Only six percent of schools in the United States offer daily physical education classes, reports *The Early Show's* Debbye Turner. *The problem, she explains, is money. To start a phys ed program costs a school approximately $500,000. And increasingly, schools just don't have that kind of money to spare.*

(http://www.cbsnews.com/stories/2005/01/27/
earlyshow/contributors/debbyeturner/main669760.shtml)

Americans understand and treat obesity mostly as the responsibility of individuals, without taking the social and material environment into account. Americans are confronted with ambiguous messages: they should be slim and healthy, but food advertisements suggest happiness via eating, chain restaurants offer cheap meals, restaurants serve huge portions, and fried food is among Americans' favorite meals. Fast food chains such as Kentucky Fried Chicken or McDonald's have operated since the mid-twentieth century. Numerous imitators proliferated, and eating out became a habit. "Unhealthy" food is cheap and easy to get, whereas healthy food is expensive and hard to find. No wonder that in the US there is the highest per capita intake of fat and carbohydrate – at the same time energy-saving devices are widespread and physical activity rates are relatively low. The laments about the obesity epidemic are one-sided and do not lead to concrete policies. A good example is PE: in spite of the knowledge about the importance of physical activities, the number of PE lessons in schools has declined.

Environment

Car country

In the past decade, in American discourses about health and lifestyle, not only recreational, but transport and work-related physical activities came to the center of attention. This caused a shift of scientific perspective: the attention of the public health experts is focused today on environmental factors and their influences on people's lifestyles. This means that urban design and transportation studies complement the different areas of physical activity and lifestyle research. Here it has also to be taken into consideration that recreational physical activities and walking/cycling as means of transport can overlap. People can choose to cycle to work in order to get some activity and they can enjoy the bike ride. With regard to health, there is today a consensus that positive effects depend on an increase in the amount of activity. Thus the focus is now, among other things, on workplaces, the design of cities, transportation, and accessible green areas.

An important form of non-recreational physical activity (PA) can be utilitarian transportation, but America is a car society. The majority of households (57 percent) have more than one car, 34 percent have one car, and only 9 percent have no car (Brownson *et al.* 2005, 431). In the past fifty years, the daily vehicle miles per person have continuously increased. Currently, on average, an American travels forty miles with the car daily, 45 percent of the time for personal/family reasons. Since 1950 the number of people who travel to work by car has increased from 67 percent to 88 percent, whereas walking to work or using public transport has decreased. Today, 87 percent of all utilitarian trips are made by car, 3 percent by public transit, and only 9 percent by walking (Brownson *et al.* 2005, 431).

According to the American Housing Survey (2001; http://www.census.gov/hhes/www/housing/ahs/ahs01/ahs01.html), 37 percent of Americans have no shopping opportunities nearby, and 45 percent have no access to public transportation. This means that a considerable percentage of Americans have to use cars for shopping and other business. Using cars as the main vehicle of transportation leads to a high waste of energy/gasoline, increasing costs and air pollution. The annual gasoline consumption is over 500 percent higher in Phoenix, Arizona (5.6 million inhabitants) than in London, UK (7.5 million inhabitants) (Duany *et al.* 2000, 92).

On the basis of the relevant surveys, Brownson *et al.* (2005) described the overall PA trend over the past fifty years. They came to the conclusion that recreational PA among the American population was level or slightly increasing, but that work-related and especially transportation PA, as well as PA in the home and garden, had declined substantially; whereas sedentary activities, especially TV consumption, had increased, with the effect that the total amount of PA had declined. Large differences with regard to gender, race, and class have to be taken into consideration. The environment is a major impact on lifestyle, including PA.

Suburban lifestyle

Eighty percent of Americans live in urban areas and around 50 per cent live in the suburbs.[15] As one's lifestyle is dependent on the social and ecological environment, for half of the American population their way of life is connected with the opportunities and challenges in the suburbs.

222

"Suburban sprawl, now the standard North American pattern of growth, is an invention, conceived by architects, engineers and planners [as well as businessmen] and promoted by developers in the great sweeping aside of the old that occurred after the Second World War" (Duany et al. 2000, 4). Suburban sprawl is the spreading out of a city over rural land, and this occurred and occurs with all large American cities.[16] Since the 1950s more and more people have migrated to the suburbs driven by the American Dream to move out of noisy and crammed cities to the countryside, in a single house with a garden, a quiet neighborhood, and a safe place for children. But when the masses began to live out this dream, it turned, at least in some areas, into a nightmare. The idyllic countryside has been lost to an encroaching urban sprawl, which does not provide "bucolic serenity," but uniformity, segregation, and isolation. In addition, the permanent building of new suburbs led to the decline of the infrastructure in the inner cities. Some cities such as Chicago, New York, and San Francisco managed to gentrify the downtown areas and to make them attractive for middle- or upper-class residents. They succeeded with the revitalization of parks and recreational areas that contribute to the (new) image and the attractiveness of the city.

The effects and evaluation of the sprawl are highly debated and a contested issue in the USA. In the following, we present only the most notable characteristics which may be found in a broad variety of suburbs.

Today, the large American cities are surrounded by rings of suburbs which spread out often more than 100 km and are spreading ever farther. The above-mentioned rise of a car culture was both the product and motor of suburbanization. Suburbs are connected via freeways with urban or suburban centers, and cars provide the transport to work (to the joy of the car industry). Because public transportation in and to the suburbs is only very seldom available, a high percentage of people use their cars, which leads to many traffic jams and many hours of transportation to and from work. Seventy percent of urban freeways are clogged during rush hour (Duany et al. 2000, 92). Adding new lines to existing highways does not help; it leads to "induced" traffic because a decrease in commuting time encourages people to move further away, which in turn increases the traffic again.

Living in a suburb means living in an urban area but with a low population density, far away from the urban centers. People live in single houses surrounded by lawns or gardens. The houses are of different sizes and assets depending on the money invested, but houses in the same communities are usually in the same price ranges and quite uniform, designed by home-building companies with the same taste and the same rationale. Americans move on average every six years, and "moving up" to a more expensive type of home and a "better" neighborhood is a sign of success. A new trend is going to "gated communities" where the rich can feel safe in a walled development.

Suburbs are constructed according to the rules of single-use zoning, which means a rigid separation of residential, commercial, and industrial areas. Thus shops, restaurants, and banks are concentrated in shopping centers, so-called strip malls, surrounded by huge parking areas. In the strip malls large chain stores dominate and there are everywhere the same chains, the same franchised restaurants, especially fast food restaurants, which provide the cheapest and easiest accessible opportunity to get food. Workplaces are in separate zones as well as civic institutions like schools, town halls, and churches – all of them also surrounded by large spaces, mostly used for parking (Duany *et al.* 2000; Ewing *et al.* 2003).

This segregation of areas is caused by the laws of zoning which means the regulation of land use according to mapped zones of the property. Throughout the USA the state, via its municipalities, has the authority to decide about the land use and destination of the various zones. One of the main aims of zoning is to protect the residents against the alleged harm coming from other users like industry and business. Therefore the housing subdivisions are often surrounded by fences and accessible by broad access streets. Only the names of the subdivisions, (e.g. Turtle Crossing, Lakeview) nostalgically remind one of the "good old times" before the sprawl destroyed the natural surroundings. Whereas many European cities try to integrate life, work and recreation, in the USA the different zones are like islands.

Access to the various destinations of daily life in the different zones is often possible only by cars. This is one of the reasons why people living in the suburbs depend to a much higher degree on cars than do the inhabitants of cities. Public transportation is often not available in the suburbs; thus everything is adapted to car traffic – large streets, numerous parking places, oversized garages and long distances from one zone to the other. However, the fact that everybody uses a car and that there are few access streets to the many culs-de-sac often causes traffic jams even in the suburbs. The problem is that "nearby is still far away" (Duany *et al.* 2000, 24): culs-de-sac and fences around the residential areas make even nearby places unreachable by walking. In suburbs cars are not luxury goods but mostly essential for shopping, going to work, visiting friends, and using a fitness center.

BOX 9.9 NOT WITHOUT A CAR

There are five of us in our family, and I am sad to say that we own five cars. This costs us over $27,000 a year. I have a car for business and pleasure. My ex-wife works; she has a car. Our son, away at college in Fort Worth, has a car; our eldest daughter has to have a car for college and her part-time job. Our youngest daughter recently got her driver's license and has to have a car to drive to school and to her music lessons. Cars are essential to my children's social lives. Neither I nor my ex-wife can afford to take time off from work to chauffeur the children, which they don't want or expect anyway. Even more horrifying, we can't afford to buy collision insurance for our children's cars. So if one has a wreck and is at fault, the repair bill will be astronomical; if a car is totaled, it will need to be replaced somehow.

(Duany *et al.* 2000, 127)

224

Although almost everybody is affected by the urban sprawl, there are groups of the population which suffer more than others, such as people without a car, either those who cannot drive because they are too young or too old, or those families who cannot afford the necessary one (or more) cars.

Currently, there are numerous discussions and studies about the impact of "urban sprawl" on rates of physical (in)activity. The main question is how the design of the suburbs and the transportation systems affects the behavior, especially physical activities, fitness, and health of residents. More than fifty studies are available which focus on the correlations between (sub)urban design and utilitarian transport (necessary travel) (Ewing et al. 2003). Whether or not people choose walking or cycling as transport depends, among other things, on the distance to schools, shops, or work. Here zoning has a decisive negative impact. The design of most suburbs, especially the long distances between the various zones and the lack of sidewalks and cycle lanes, prevents walking or cycling as means of transport (Brownson et al. 2005, 422). According to all the studies, walking or cycling for utilitarian purposes is more common in densely inhabited "mixed-used" areas where houses, shops, restaurants, cinemas, and schools are easily reached. Pedestrian life depends on reasonably short distances and safe and interesting street space – all of this is lacking in the suburbs with their large residential areas and their low density of inhabitants.

"Poor accessibility is the common denominator for the urban sprawl – nothing is within easy walking distance of anything else" (Ewing et al. 2003, 48). This is also true for sport and fitness facilities. Chains of fitness studios are available in many strip malls. Some suburbs provide cycle and jogging paths, swimming pools, or skateboard parks. A study based on available representative surveys came to the conclusion that the living area

> could be significantly associated with some forms of *physical activity* and with some health outcomes. After controlling for demographic and behavioral covariates, the county sprawl index had small but significant associations with minutes walked, obesity, BMI, and hypertension. Those living in sprawling counties were likely to walk less, weigh more, and have greater prevalence of hypertension than those living in compact counties.
>
> (Ewing et al. 2003, 56)

The sprawl not only revolutionized the lifestyles of millions living in suburbs; it also had a decisive negative impact on the inner cities.

Lifestyle and physical activities in inner cities

Whereas those groups of the population who could and can afford it left the city centers, the poor were forced to stay. The concentration of poor, largely minority people changed the inner city neighborhoods dramatically. With the exodus of people, businesses also left the cities. Corporations, stores, and entertainment services and numerous jobs moved to the new suburban centers. Because around 40 percent of the population in the central cities do not have a car and because of the poor public transportation system, the urban poor cannot reach workplaces in the suburbs.

The concentration of the poor in the city centers means that numerous cities have an inadequate tax income, which leads to inadequate services and infrastructure including run-down streets and buildings or under-financed schools. Schools are financed by the tax income of the communities. Thus good (and bad) education is "socially inherited". Rich communities attract well-off families whose taxes finance excellent schools and recreational facilities, whereas poor families have to stay in poor communities which cannot afford to invest in schools and recreation. This enlarges racial and ethnic segregation and the divide between rich and poor in the new towns of the urban sprawl and the inner centers of many "old" cities.

> Most old American cities have been abandoned by the middle class. Detroit, St. Louis, Cleveland, Buffalo, Newark, New Orleans, and Baltimore, for example, have been on life support for decades. Their central business districts are forlorn, their crime rates are high and their public schools are dysfunctional. Their once thriving neighborhoods are now characterized by abandoned buildings, littered streets, and an eerie silence.
>
> (Jackson 2006, 11)

Parks or malls are open to everybody for recreation, but the question remains whether or not the "urban poor" have the resources to pay for access to a fitness club or a swimming pool. Is access also available to PA opportunities for those who do not have a car? Are there programs and resources for PA for poor people? In addition, it can be a question of security: if places in inner cities are not safe, people, especially women, but also children, cannot go out and use existing spaces like parks for their physical exercise. This problem is also a concern for middle-class people living in inner cities.

CONCLUSION

Sport for all is not an idea or a concept in the US. In spite of the enthusiasm for sport, a sedentary lifestyle is widespread among the adult population. However, the inactivity rates depend to a high degree on class, race, and gender. In addition, there are large regional differences dependent on the economic situation of the states and regions. Another important factor is the environment, and living in a city, a suburb, or in the countryside supports or impedes recreational, but also transportation-related physical activities. The majority of the adult population engages in recreational sports rather sporadically on an informal level. Whereas children play the typical American sports and games, adults focus on fitness-related exercises. The marketing of health and fitness clearly left its imprint on the tastes and habits of the population. In addition to indoor exercise, Americans love the outdoors which may provide an escape from their mostly sedentary everyday life. Where indoor exercise may be regarded as a chore, outdoor recreational activities are fun.

CHAPTER TEN

SPORT AND RACE

INTRODUCTION

American history is shaped by the fact that it was once a slave-holder society. This determined politics, economy, and legislation, and also led to the most decisive event in US history, the Civil War. The emancipation of African-Americans did not mean the end of discrimination, and even today racism is still a fact. Sport and race were always closely intertwined. When African-Americans were excluded from sport or certain sports, they formed their own organizations and events, but fought at the same time for integration into "mainstream" sport. They are under- or overrepresented in sports today, depending on the type of sport and performance level, and they were, and still are to some extent, portrayed as the "others" in the mass media. Sport played an important role in the conceptualization, discussion, and enactment of black- and whiteness; it was a means to demonstrate superiority, a struggle for capital (in Bourdieu's sense of the word) and power in an important social field of American society.

In this chapter we describe the physical activities of black slaves and the long struggle of African-Americans to gain access to the world of "white" sport. Racism was a major issue in top-level sport, especially in popular games. Segregation and desegregation processes in the three big American sports will be the focus of this chapter. In addition, we will discuss current issues and problems related to sport and race.

WHO IS BLACK? DEFINITIONS AND BACKGROUND

While the social construction of race and racism affects all groups, including whites, discussions of race and sport in the United States have focused largely on African-Americans. This chapter will not deviate from that discourse because racism had the greatest impact on this group and has long determined their chances of participating and excelling in sport and society. African-Americans are among the groups which show the lowest participation in sport at the "sport for all" level but compose the largest percentage of the various minority groups active in sport at the professional level (see Chapter 9). While the proportion of

African-American, though not "black" athletes, is less than 10 percent in MLB, African-Americans make up nearly 67 percent of NFL and 80 percent of NBA players (Reaves 2007). In addition, black athletes remain prominent in boxing and track and field. In both sports, the participation of blacks has a long tradition, and in both sports black athletes competed for a long period of time primarily, but not exclusively, among themselves.

The murky designation of "black" might include Afro-Caribbeans, but also people designated as Latinos, Hispanics, or of other ethnic origins such as Cuban, Dominican, or Puerto Rican. Racial categorization is beset with issues and controversies about definitions, categorizations, and meanings. Legally (race is defined differently by the states) the "one-drop" rule has been generally and historically applied, meaning that if a person has one drop of black blood, he or she has been/is considered "black." Important judicial cases, such as Plessy v. Ferguson (1896), which legalized race segregation in the United States, have rested upon this doctrine. In another case, genealogical records were traced through eleven generations to ascertain a person's blackness.[1]

Scholars have termed the labeling of a group or groups as non-white "others" to be part of the concept of "whiteness" (Ignatiev 1995; Allen 1998; Jacobson 1998; Roediger 1999; Guterl 2001). Whiteness entails not only skin color but the standards, values, and decorum (i.e. the social capital) required to obtain acceptance in mainstream society. By the mid-nineteenth century scientists rationalized a Social Darwinian racial pyramid, assuming white, Anglo-Saxon male Protestants (WASPs) to be at the apex of civilization. All other groups were in inferior positions, based on ascribed characteristics of difference with the WASP population. The focus on "differences" rather than similarities assumed physical, social, and moral deficiencies and the consequent inferiority of the "others." Professor Daniel Brinton, president of the American Association for the Advancement of Science in 1895, claimed that "the black, brown and yellow races differ anatomically so much from the white . . . that even with equal cerebral capacity they never could rival its results by equal effects" (quoted in Baker 1998, 27).

The perception of race characterized the earliest relationships between Europeans and Native Americans who were designated "Indians," a denomination which marked differences or "otherness." In the seventeenth century, the Puritans considered themselves to be "God's chosen people," picked to spread their particular religious message. With the success of the colonists' war for independence, the new nation assumed its supremacy as the only democracy in the world.

The perception of WASPs' social and moral superiority fostered belief in the "Manifest Destiny" of the United States by the mid-nineteenth century, i.e. the responsibility to spread its democratic, republican form of government and its promotion of individual rights to the rest of the world. Ironically, these rights were reserved for those who were white or had gained whiteness, and numerous immigrant groups have pursued that status with varying levels of success throughout American history (Horsman 1981; Brodkin 1998; Guglielmo 2003).

Africans were not voluntary migrants but captured slaves, shipped under terrible conditions to America, where they were sold to the highest bidder. Dutch traders brought the first slaves to market in Virginia in 1619. They were usually destined to work the agricultural fields of the Southern colonies. By 1700 black slaves accounted for one-third of tobacco workers, and nearly two-thirds of the labor force by 1750 (Struna 1996, 111). All had to serve the wishes of their masters unconditionally, and they and their children might be sold at whim. In an 1857 Supreme Court case involving a runaway slave, the Chief Justice ruled that "Negroes were beings of an inferior order with no rights which any white man was bound to respect" (Blum *et al.* 1977, 334).

BOX 10.1 A SLAVE NARRATIVE

You see there was slave traders in those days, jes' like you got horse and mule an' auto traders now. They bought and sold slaves and hired 'em out. Yes'm, rented 'em out. Allotted means somethin' like hired out. But the slave never got no wages. That all went to the master. The man they was allotted to paid the master . . .

"Allotments made a lot of grief for the slaves," Aunt Sally asserted. "We left my papa in Kentucky, 'cause he was allotted to another man. My papa never knew where my mama went, an' my mama never knew where papa went." Aunt Sally paused a moment, then went on bitterly. "They never wanted mama to know, 'cause they knowed she would never marry so long she knew where he was. Our master wanted her to marry again and raise more children to be slaves. They never wanted mama to know where papa was, an' she never did," sighed Aunt Sally.

(http://xroads.virginia.edu/~HYPER/DETOC/FEM/
education.htm to racism and slaves)

PHYSICAL ACTIVITIES AND SPORTS OF THE SLAVES

The leisure time of slaves was largely determined by masters, and utilitarian practices such as hunting and fishing might be both work and recreation. In coastal areas, slaves learned how to swim, but even swimming could entail labor as slaves dived for pearls or salvaged sunken goods. Their duties could include hunting sharks, or safeguarding the master's children (Struna 1996, 77). When at leisure, slaves tested each other in physical contests as they ran and jumped. Dancing, singing, and storytelling, as well as gambling at cock-fights and horseraces, perceived as sports in the terminology of the time, were other recreational activities of slaves (Wiggins 1977).

230

Slaves and their sporting abilities were used in the service and for the entertainment of their owners. Among other things, they took care of the horses. In the rural southern states horses were a necessity for travel and transport, a symbol of social status, and interwoven with the lifestyle of the gentry. Owners of thoroughbred horses demonstrated wealth, but also expertise and a noble lifestyle, and thus enjoyed great social and symbolic capital. It was often slaves, however, who trained the horses of their masters and rode them in the races.

Slaves entertained masters not only with songs and dances, but also with physical feats, some of which might be coerced, such as boxing. In the early nineteenth century, a black slave, Tom Molyneaux, allegedly won his freedom as a pugilist, then traveled to England.

BOX 10.2 TOM MOLYNEAUX, FORMER SLAVE AND FAMOUS BOXER

An 1811 account reported that "A boxing match took place in Morisly Hurst, in the neighborhood of London, on the 21st of May, for one hundred guineas. The champions were Molineaux (the famous black man from New York) and a young Englishman named Rimmer. In the course of fifteen rounds, the black pounded his antagonist most tremendously . . . There were at this brutal exhibition about fifteen thousand spectators of all ranks" (Altherr 1997, 2, 132). While Molyneaux gained fame in England, he eventually lost two matches to the British champion Tom Cribb. He died on a tour of Ireland aged 34.

(Gerald Gems)

Although black athletes might prosper as surrogates for whites at horse races and/or entertain them with boxing matches, sporting confrontations between the races were outlawed in the Southern states. Sport was, and still is, an arena where dominance and masculinity are presented and produced. The participation in sports and potential victory of slaves would have endangered white hegemony; thus it seemed self-evident and no legitimacy was needed for the fact that blacks were excluded. Physical activities and sports could contribute to make the everyday life of slaves slightly more enjoyable, but sport, even sporting successes, had no impact on their general situation, which was determined by an entrenched racial hierarchy.

THE FALSE HOPE OF LIBERATION

With the formal liberation of slaves by President Abraham Lincoln during the American Civil War (1863) the social relations between "blacks" and "whites," as well as the situation of both groups, began to change. Given the right to vote, blacks elected representatives to the US Congress in the decade after the Civil War. Southern whites, who had lost not only the war but also their means of production, feared the loss of privileges and social domination and brokered a political deal during the deadlocked presidential election of 1876. In return for their support of the Republican Party candidate, southern Democrats regained control of the political offices in their states. They soon passed and enforced restrictive voting laws that prohibited the newly freed blacks from exercising their suffrage rights. The racist and clandestine Ku Klux Klan organization reinforced these edicts and secured white rule with threats, intimidation, and violence, which even went as far as lynching. Between 1889 and 1898 a lynching occurred, on average, every other day (Putnam 2000, 375). From 1885 to 1921 a total of 4,096 African-Americans were tortured to death in lynchings, at a rate of more than nine per month over that period (Falk 2005, 212). Freed blacks, without an education, resorted to sharecropping, in which white landowners rented small portions of their land in return for a percentage of the crop. This strategy provided the blacks with a bare subsistence, virtually returning them to a state of slavery without the food, clothing, or support of their previous masters. This practice resulted in the utmost poverty among the vast majority of African-Americans. Furthermore, in 1896 the US Supreme Court legalized the segregation of the races, which affected not only African-Americans but many other groups, such as Asians, designated as non-white as well. Public transport, recreational facilities, and schools in the Southern states were designated for whites or for coloreds (a generic term that included all non-whites) only. Even at the higher education levels blacks went to separately established colleges and universities that still operate in the United States. Race was also an important issue with regard to immigration. By 1911 a Congressional committee determined that there were forty-five separate races of varying desirability, which eventually resulted in immigration quotas and varying levels of acceptability in American society throughout the twentieth century (see Chapter 3).

The separation of whites and non-whites, while strictest in the South, extended to other parts of the United States as well. In Northern cities segregated housing patterns, while not legal, were enforced with violence (such as the fire bombing of black homes) or resulted in the flight of white home owners from neighborhoods where blacks were moving in. Such strategies confined blacks to the least desirable living areas, the poorest schools, menial jobs, and limited opportunities for advancement.

SPORT AS A HARBINGER OF CHANGE

The general exclusion of blacks from white sport did not extend to all areas. Blacks continued to excel in horseracing, but soon faced resistance. After Isaac Murphy, a black jockey, won three of the première Kentucky Derby races, he was driven from the sport by false allegations in the 1890s. At the turn of the century the black cyclist, Major Taylor, held the American championship as well as several world records. White riders banded together to obstruct and endanger him, forcing Taylor to seek his fortune on European tracks thereafter (Wiggins 2006).

Baseball, the national pastime, was a symbol of American (white) culture and a contested terrain for African-Americans. At the professional level, white baseball players refused to play against teams with black players, effectively excluding them from the National League in the 1880s.

One of the few sports that permitted interracial competition, boxing, did so due to the Social Darwinian beliefs that blacks lacked by nature the endurance, stoicism, and courage necessary to succeed in this sport. When the black Australian Peter Jackson traveled to the United States and proved otherwise, white boxers refused to fight him. Heavyweight champion John L. Sullivan even enacted a racial ban after 1882 in order to maintain the symbolic status attached to the best boxer as the world's toughest man for the white race. A New Orleans athletic club staged a "Carnival of Champions" in 1892 featuring two championship bouts. "Gentleman" Jim Corbett took the heavyweight crown from John L. Sullivan. Thereafter, he too refused to fight any black fighters in order to protect the imaginary supremacy of whites, even though he had previously fought a sixty-one-round draw with the black boxer Peter Jackson. In the second bout the black featherweight champion, George Dixon, badly bloodied a white challenger, which caused protest in the media and among white boxing fans.

BOX 10.3 RACIAL EQUALITY IN THE BOXING RING?

We disagree with the policy of the Olympic Club, and that is in respect to the match between Dixon and Skelly; and we sincerely trust that this mistake – and it was a mistake and a serious one to match a negro and a white man – will not be repeated . . . a mistake to bring the races together on any terms of equality, even in the prize ring . . . We of the South who know the fallacy and danger of this doctrine of race equality, who are opposed to placing the negro on any terms of equality, who have insisted on separation of the races in church, hotel, car, saloon and theatre; who believe that the law ought to step in and forever forbid the idea of equality by making marriages between them illegal, are heartily opposed to any arrangement encouraging this equality, which gives negroes false ideas and dangerous beliefs.

(New Orleans Times-Democrat on
September 7, 1892 (quoted in Gems 1996a, 225))

Figure 10.1 Jack Johnson defeats Jim Jeffries, Reno 1910 (Nevada Historical Society)

The strategy known as the "color ban" forced black boxers in the heavyweight rank to fight each other until 1905, when the undefeated white champion, Jim Jeffries, retired.[2] A tournament among the white boxers to find his successor resulted in the Canadian Tommy Burns emerging as the new title holder. Initially he, too, refused to fight the black champion, Jack Johnson. But when Burns embarked on a global tour, Johnson followed him in quest of a true title fight. In Australia a promoter guaranteed Burns a large sum of money for a fight with Johnson. It proved a mismatch as Johnson toyed with and pummeled Burns until the fight was stopped in the thirteenth round and Johnson was declared champion. However, Johnson had only succeeded in the boxing ring, and his accomplishments did not provide him a place in white society. His biography shows clearly that racism was unconquerable at that time. The more he claimed full access to the freedom and the pleasures of life, the more he became a pariah to whites (see Chapter 12) (Wiggins 2006; Miller and Wiggins 2004).

Johnson defied white standards of social decorum. He took great pride in his blackness, and flaunted his physicality and his rights, much to the chagrin of white society. He even challenged the champion white racing car driver to a race. When stopped for speeding through town in his flashy roadster, he paid the fine with a large dollar bill and then told the policeman to keep the change because he would be returning in a similar fashion. But the worst of his "crimes" was that he courted and married three white women.

sport and race

BOX 10.4 RACE AND BOXING

Black boxers from the time of Jack Johnson (the first and most flamboyant of the world's black heavyweight champions, 1908–1915) through Joe Louis, Sugar Ray Robinson, Muhammad Ali, Larry Holmes, Sugar Ray Leonard, and Mike Tyson have been acutely conscious of themselves as racially *other* from the majority of their audiences, whom they must please in one way or another, as black villains, or honorary whites. (After his pulverizing defeat of the "good, humble Negro" Floyd Patterson, in a heavyweight title match in 1962, Sonny Liston gloated in his role as black villain; when he lost so ingloriously to Muhammad Ali, a brash new-style black who drew upon Jack Johnson, Sugar Ray Robinson, and even the campy professional wrestler Gorgeous George for his own public persona, Liston lost his mystique, and his career soon ended.)

To see race as a predominant factor in American boxing is inevitable, but the moral issues, as always in this paradoxical sport, are ambiguous. Is there a moral distinction between the spectacle of black slaves in the Old South being forced by their white owners to fight, for purposes of gambling, and the spectacle of contemporary blacks fighting for multimillion-dollar paydays, for TV coverage from Las Vegas and Atlantic City? When, in 1980, in one of the most cynically promoted boxing matches in history, the aging and ailing Muhammad Ali fought the young heavyweight champion Larry Holmes, in an "execution" of a fight that was stopped after ten rounds, did it alleviate the pain, or the shame, that Ali was guaranteed $8 million for the fight? (Of which, with characteristic finesse, promoter Don King cheated him of nearly $1 million.) Ask the boxers.

("The Cruelest Sport" by Joyce Carol Oates
(http://web.usfca.edu/~southerr/boxing/cruelest.html))

Johnson opened a café in Chicago where rebellious jazz music was played, and whites and blacks intermingled freely. A hero to downtrodden blacks, whites considered him to be the devil incarnate. A campaign ensued to find the "great white hope" who might defeat the flamboyant Johnson and return the heavyweight crown to its rightful place. When a series of contenders failed to accomplish the mission over a period of two years, the undefeated Jim Jeffries was forced out of retirement. The showdown took place on Independence Day, July 4, 1910, and drew an international audience of 20,000 to the desert town of Reno, Nevada. Johnson wrote that "it wasn't just the championship that was at stake – it was my own honor, and in a degree the honor of my race" (Davies 2007, 198). Johnson dominated the fight, knocking his opponent through the ropes. A white reporter admitted that "James J. Jeffries' efforts to regain the heavy weight pugilistic championship from Jack Johnson here yesterday was farcical [*sic*]." The referee declared: "I could not help but feel very sorry for the big white man as he fell beneath the champion's [*sic*] blows. It was the most pitiable sight I ever saw" (Riess 1998, 155–156). Jeffries' loss sparked off race riots throughout the United States as blacks celebrated and whites retaliated.

Unable to dethrone Johnson in the ring, the federal government took steps to curtail him in 1913 by indicting him on an anti-prostitution law for transporting his white female consorts across state lines. Johnson fled the country for Europe, but when World War I broke out he was unable to arrange significant fights to cover his lavish spending. In 1915 he agreed to a fight in Havana, Cuba with Jess Willard, who finally returned the crown to white America. Johnson claimed that he agreed to throw the fight in return for readmittance to the United States, but the US government failed to comply. In 1920 he returned to the United States and served his one-year prison term. He was never granted another opportunity to fight for the championship.

The great migration and opportunities in sport

Like Johnson, many African-Americans left the South in the "great migration" to the industrialized Northern cities in the early twentieth century in search of a better life. The white working class, however, often perceived the newly arrived blacks as competitors for jobs as employers pitted one against the other to lower wages. This led to race riots, which accounted for the deaths of 500 African-Americans between 1915 and 1919 (Falk 2005, 212). Forced to live in urban ghettos, blacks formed vibrant neighborhoods that spawned creative music, dance, literature, and sports teams. In New York the eruption of black pride and black creativity was known as the Harlem Renaissance[3] that spread throughout much of the United States and Europe (e.g. Paris) and attracted intellectuals on both continents. Adventurous whites traveled to the so-called black-and-tan cabarets for excitement and listened to the new forms of black music such as the blues and jazz. At the same time, Marcus Garvey, a politician and publisher, leader of a "Back-to-Africa movement," preached the need for black separatism and reliance on their own economic capital ventures in order to succeed. The US government deported him to his native Jamaica, but African-Americans found heroes and opportunities, also in sport, where black entrepreneurs heeded Garvey's message, founded black organizations, and built a parallel black economy that merged popular culture, such as music, dance, and gambling with sporting enterprises (Grossman 1989; Lomax 2003).

Ball games

Unable to cross the race barrier in baseball and gain entry into the white major leagues, Rube Foster, a migrant from Texas to Chicago, founded the Negro National League in 1920 to provide baseball opportunities to black players and owners. The organization paralleled the MLB model with franchises in most cities with sizable black populations. The Eastern Colored League soon followed, providing more opportunities for black athletes. The Negro Baseball Leagues took on an even greater importance as opportunities for African-Americans dwindled in football. The fledgling NFL allowed African-American football players to join its teams until 1934, when its owners conspicuously failed to renew any contracts for black players until 1946, when the unwritten agreement was finally lifted. Black athletes, both men and women, also found limited opportunities in the barnstorming basketball teams of the East Coast and Midwest (Gems 1995a).

Invented by James Naismith on behalf of the YMCA in 1891, basketball soon spread throughout the world. In the United States ethnic and black teams readily took to the new sport. The Buffalo (New York) Germans of that city's YMCA won the national amateur championship and the demonstration games played at the 1904 Olympics before turning professional. The New York Celtics, an Irish team, gained fame throughout the following decade (Riess 1998, 103–104). By the 1930s basketball was considered to be a Jewish game, and sports writers freely used racist stereotypes in rationalizing the game with the "temperament of the Jews" in placing a "premium on an alert, scheming mind . . . flashy trickiness, artful dodging and general smart aleckness" (Baldwin 2000, 73). African-American teams were organized by YMCAs, churches, and social clubs in New York, Washington, DC, and Chicago early in the century and began to feature a faster style of play with crisp passing and ball-handling skills. Both men's and women's teams drew widespread interest in the black communities, particularly in interracial games, which allowed blacks to measure themselves against their white opponents (Gems 1995a).

Whereas it was (and still is) taken for granted that baseball and football were men's games, women had access to basketball, and this game offered one of the few opportunities for black women to take part in sports. In the African-American schools of the South, women formed basketball teams despite the efforts of school administrators to eliminate competitive ventures as unladylike. In the Southern states competition with whites remained prohibited (Liberti 2004; Grundy 2004, 2006).

A Chicago men's team renamed itself the Harlem Globetrotters in honor of the black pride movement in New York and embarked on a barnstorming (traveling) tour in 1927. The top eastern black team, the New York Renaissance, won the first professional basketball tournament in the United States in 1939. The Globetrotters won the following year, proving that black athletes could compete successfully with whites on the basketball court. However, professional basketball leagues and teams still practiced racial segregation. After the Globetrotters beat the Minneapolis Lakers, the best team in the NBA, in 1948 and 1949, the white professional teams began to offer contracts to the best black players.

BLACK ATHLETES REPRESENT THE NATION

After the ostracism of Jack Johnson black boxers were again unofficially but effectively banned from heavyweight championship bouts. This changed with the rise of a boxer who had reached a certain degree of whiteness. After a nearly unblemished record as an amateur boxer, Joe Louis was carefully tutored by his coaches to adapt to expected norms of propriety and decorum and not to transcend the limits set for African-Americans.

A white sports writer described him in 1935 in "A Revealing Close-up of Joe Louis, the Sensational New Menace to the White Man's Supremacy in the Prize Ring" as follows: "He neither drinks nor smokes. He dates no girls . . . Louis avoids white friends" (quoted in Baldwin 2000, 118–119). In short, he acted in a way which made him acceptable to whites. Louis served as a symbol of American democracy even among many white Americans when he defeated Primo Carnera, who represented fascist Italy in 1935. A year later the undefeated Louis met the German boxer Max Schmeling. When Schmeling won with a twelfth-round knockout, Americans were stunned, and Germans, especially the Nazis, rejoiced, as the fight seemed to prove the doctrine of Aryan supremacy. Louis avenged that defeat with a first-round knockout of Schmeling in 1938. All of his fights held great significance for African-Americans.

BOX 10.5 MAYA ANGELOU ABOUT JOE LOUIS

Maya Angelou, a famous black writer, recounted that if Louis was knocked down My race groaned. It was our people falling. It was another lynching, yet another Black man hanging on a tree. One more woman ambushed and raped. A black boy whipped and maimed. It was hounds on the trail of a man running through slimy swamps (trying to escape slavery). It was a white woman slapping her maid for being forgetful . . . If Joe lost we were back in slavery and beyond help.

It would all be true, the accusations that we were lower types of human beings. Only a little higher than apes. True that we were stupid and ugly and lazy and dirty and, unlucky and worst of all, that God Himself hated us and ordained us to be hewers of wood and drawers of water, forever and ever, world without end.

(quoted in Baldwin 2000, 122)

Lena Horne, an African-American singer, claimed that "Joe was the one invincible Negro, the one who stood up to the white man and beat him down with his fists. He in a sense carried so many of our hopes, maybe even dreams of vengeance" (quoted in Baldwin 2000, 115). Such sentiments expressed the pent-up frustrations of millions of African-Americans in the United States, and showed the importance of heroes for the black community.

The defeat of Joe Louis was quickly rectified by another black athlete. Only two months after Louis's devastating knockout, Jesse Owens restored American pride by winning four gold medals against Germany's and the world's best athletes at the 1936 Olympics in Berlin, overturning the Nazi doctrine of Aryan supremacy. Owens' achievements were supplemented by a corps of black stars in the track and field events at the 1936 Games, but the American reliance on black athletes as symbols of democracy belied the truth. While Owens and the other black track stars seemingly personified equal opportunity, African-Americans had still not gained a full measure of equality in the United States. They lived in segregated housing, worked for lower wages, and were still exposed to racist assults. Between 1935 and 1936, twenty-six African-Americans were lynched in the United States (Rader 1990, 203).

When Owens refused to participate in a post-Olympic exhibition tour of Europe, the Amateur Athletic Union (AAU) suspended him from competition (Dyreson 2006). After his Olympic feats he was reduced to running exhibition races, even against cars and horses. Louis held the heavyweight title for twelve years. During World War II he joined the US Army and donated his winnings to orphans whose fathers had been killed in the war. The US government later sued him for back taxes and he died in poverty (Margolick 2005).

Steps towards racial integration

During the "war for democracy" (World War II) African-Americans served in segregated military units and gave their lives for their country, where they still suffered discrimination inside and outside the sporting arena. A stronghold of segregation was baseball, the national game. Black as well as some white sports writers called for the racial integration of the MLB, and one of the army veterans became the key figure in the momentous change in American sport and society as a whole. After the war Branch Rickey, the general manager of one of the white teams, the Brooklyn (New York) Dodgers, devised a surreptitious plan to integrate the MLB. A New York law required that military veterans be re-employed in their previous occupations upon their return. Rickey founded a black professional baseball league with no real intention of initiating play. He signed Jackie Robinson, who starred in four different sports in college, then a member of a Negro Baseball League team, and a military veteran, to a contract. When the imaginary league disbanded, he assigned Robinson to the Dodgers minor league affiliate in Montreal, a rather cosmopolitan Canadian city in the International Baseball League, where he would not be subject to as much overt discrimination as in the US. Robinson became the star of the league and was called to the Brooklyn team in 1947. Being the first black in the major leagues since the 1880s, he faced relentless hostility, racial taunting, segregation from his teammates, and even death threats. He answered with superb play that won him individual honors and league championships for his team over the next decade (see Chapter 4). African-Americans flocked to the baseball stadiums to honor their new hero (Joe Louis lost his boxing title in 1948). More importantly, Robinson's stellar play and stoic demeanor helped to ease race relations in America and proved that whites and blacks could coexist and cooperate several years before the United States Supreme Court ended racial segregation in the nation's schools.

Rickey's courageous act of bringing Robinson to MLB was honorable but not entirely altruistic. It made good business sense. By being the first team to sign a black player, he had access to the wealth of talent in the Negro leagues and the Dodgers benefited immensely over the following decade from such foresight. All other previously white teams were forced to sign black players as well in order to compete successfully with their rivals. Boston, one of the most segregated of American cities, was the last to do so in 1959. The entry of black players into the MLB had dire consequences, however, for the black leagues. Depleted of their talent, the Negro leagues soon disintegrated.

Racial progress also occurred in professional football. A new organization, the All American Football Conference (AAFC), started play as a rival to the established NFL in 1946. The AAFC initially prospered, and its dominant team, the Cleveland Browns, employed black players. When the NFL moved a team to Los Angeles, that city required integration for the use of its stadium, and the owner promptly signed two blacks to contracts.

After two professional basketball associations merged to form the NBA in 1949, team owners began employing African-Americans (shortly after baseball and football), many of whom achieved star status in the 1950s. The rival American Basketball Association (ABA) started play in 1967, fueled by the exploits of African-American Julius Erving, whose spectacular dunks signaled a transition in the style of play. By the time the ABA merged with the NBA in 1976 a more flamboyant "black style" permeated the game and drew increasing numbers of fans. While fewer than two million fans attended NBA games in 1960, the number of spectators reached ten million by the end of the 1970s (Rader 1990, 272). In basketball, black players changed the style of play, and the image of the game began to assume an increasing "blackness."

Intercollegiate basketball, especially the national championship tournament of the NCAA, became a national sensation known as "March Madness." In 1966 the tournament generated only $180,000 in television revenue, a figure that reached $58,000,000 by 1988 (Rader 1990, 288). Such lucrative opportunities led coaches to recruit a host of excellent African-American basketball players. A small college from Texas won the national championship in 1966, the first team to use five blacks as the primary players. College coaches increasingly recruited black players with athletic scholarships thereafter, and sport became a vehicle towards higher education for African-Americans (see Chapter 6).

In the decades following World War II African-American women became the backbone of the Olympic track and field team. Alice Coachman became the first black American female to win an Olympic gold medal in 1948, her Olympic debut (Lansbury 2006). She had been the American high-jump champion for ten years. Of the twelve women that comprised the US track team in 1948, nine were African-American, four of whom represented Coachman's school, the Tuskegee Institute (Lansbury 2006, 156). Tuskegee and Tennessee

State, black colleges in the American South, provided numerous Olympians for the American teams during the Cold War (Cahn 2004).

From the perspective of mainstream society, athletics were competitions of strength, speed, and endurance, capacities reserved for the stronger sex. Female physical educators, both black and white, discouraged their students from participating in masculine sports which would destroy their attractiveness, if not their health. The beauty and femininity ideals of the whites were not entirely shared by the black community, but middle-class and educated blacks who aspired to whiteness, or at least greater acceptance in white society, adhered to white norms.

Sport and the civil rights movement

Sport became a vehicle for civil rights in the 1960s. Muhammad Ali rose to prominence as a critic of American hypocrisy, using the boxing arena as his oratorical stage. Reminiscent of Jack Johnson, Ali challenged the democratic rhetoric of civil rights, religious and personal freedoms, and questioned the validity of the Viet Nam War that engaged the US in Asia. After winning the heavyweight championship in stunning fashion, he rejected Christianity in favor of a black separatist sect. He refused induction into the US Army, which caused boxing commissions to suspend his professional license and career. Ali jeopardized his future for his beliefs, losing four years of his athletic life before reinstatement. Ali's courageous stance factionalized American society along political and racial lines (see Chapter 12).

BOX 10.6 DISCRIMINATION: THE SITUATION OF BLACK ATHLETES DURING THE 1960S

The segregation was awful. You couldn't live in approved housing if you were black because they were afraid white students would move out. There were restaurants we couldn't eat in . . . If you went to a dance, you almost always danced with white women because there were virtually no black women on campus. But the minute you did that you could be in big trouble. I knew athletes who believed their scholarships were taken, who were kicked off campus, because they were accused of dating a white woman.

Blacks faced academic inequities. If blacks wanted to major in something outside of social welfare, physical education or criminology, they had to go through all kinds of changes . . . Black athletes were not graduating. There were about 70 blacks on campus, out of 22,000 students, and 60 or so were athletes, or former athletes trying to finish their degrees.

(From an interview with Harry Edwards, student athlete, later professor and one of the organizers of the athletic revolt (http://www.colorlines.com/article.php?ID=118))

The racial tensions in the United States erupted in 1968. Blatant discrimination against non-whites persisted throughout the United States and overt suppression engulfed the South. In April Martin Luther King, the African-American preacher who advocated a non-violent approach to gaining civil rights and obtaining racial harmony, was assassinated by a racist white. Shortly afterwards, presidential candidate Robert Kennedy, a liberal with the ability to assuage the racial discord, was also murdered. The Black Panther Party retaliated against white oppression with armed resistance as civil unrest approached open warfare in urban areas set ablaze in riots and gunfire (Verney 2003).

African-American athletes revolted by staging strikes and protests against the lack of respect on college campuses and the injustices in the larger society. In some cases they refused to play football until their oppressive white coaches were replaced or until better services were provided for all black students. Black athletes boycotted the Olympic team in 1968, but among those that competed, Tommie Smith and John Carlos, medalists in the 200-meter race, performed the most grandiose statement. They used the podium to silently raise their gloved fists in the Black Power salute, informing a global television audience of their dissatisfaction with American racism. They were summarily dismissed from the team and sent back to the USA. Despite magnificent performances in Mexico City the 1968 Olympic team was not invited to a presidential reception at the White House.

BOX 10.7 THE OLYMPIC PROJECT FOR HUMAN RIGHTS (OPHR)

The Project was not just about athletic goals. We recognized that the black athlete was inextricably embedded in and reflective of the community circumstances from which these athletes emerged. We felt we had to speak not just about the predicament of athletes, but to the interests of their communities. To simply speak to athletes' interests would not only have been short-sighted, but self-serving. We had to understand the broader context and configuration of the black struggle for freedom and justice.

(Harry Edwards; http://www.colorlines.com/article.php?ID=118)

Racism disguised: opportunities and challenges of African-American athletes

In many ways, African-American athletes were, and still are, to a certain degree discriminated against by the mass media, as described in Chapter 13. The media coverage of black athletes mirrors their situation on sports fields.

In the 1960s and 1970s, in both the collegiate and professional ranks, black athletes protested the practice of "stacking," in which coaches placed talented African-Americans

Figure 10.2 Black Power salute at 1968 Olympics (Library of Congress)

in positions that required physical abilities, but little intelligence or opportunity for leadership. At both the professional and intercollegiate levels there were few black coaches, and black players rarely held strategic positions. In 1976 a study revealed that among black professional baseball players most played the outfield or first base, where their biggest responsibility was to merely catch the ball. Only 4 percent of pitchers and catchers, the central and strategic positions, were African-Americans; and none were shortstops, the players who handled the ball most often. Similarly, in football there were few black centers or quarterbacks, the positions that held leadership and determined strategy (Rader 1990, 317). Although racial discrimination with regard to team positions has decreased in recent decades, the labeling of African-American athletes as unfit for leadership still persists to a certain degree (Lewis 1995; Coakley 1998; Woodward 2004).

In the professional leagues, African-Americans received lower salaries than white players. "The dean of American sports writers, Sam Lacy, sports editor of the Baltimore Afro-American, noted in 1967 that 'the African American player was much quicker to sign a contract than white players, and in comparison, was woefully under paid'" (Walter 1968). During the 1980s and 1990s the situation changed dramatically, and today African-Americans are among the highest paid athletes in professional sport.

The restrictions on black high school and college athletes extended beyond the playing field. Coaches even dictated players' personal lives by indicating acceptable clothing styles, hair lengths, and, at the collegiate level, dating partners. Black players might be dismissed from the team simply for dating white women.

Athletes sought, and colleges provided, athletic "scholarships" to attend universities (see Chapter 6). Such grants provide free tuition, room and board to gain a college education in exchange for participation on a university athletic team. The term "scholarship," however, has proven a misnomer. Many of the athletes are ill prepared for the educational rigors of the college classroom, with poor study skills and little background knowledge. Moreover, coaches demand extensive hours of training and conditioning, often at the sacrifice of class time. Travel to away games means further loss of educational time and many athletes spend more time in game preparation than they do in study. The focus on sport prevents academic success, especially for black athletes who might come to the university with limited education or deficient study skills.[3] At some schools few athletes ever meet graduation requirements and only a relatively small percentage of black athletes graduate from college. Even athletes who manage to obtain degrees are not seldom functionally illiterate due to conspiratorial professors and administrators who overlook the deficiencies of the student-athletes. Blacks comprised 14 percent of all college students in 2000 (about the same percentage as blacks in the general population) (http://factfinder.census.gov/jsp/saff/SAFFInfo.jsp?_pageId=tp5_education), but the graduation rate for African-Americans reached 43 percent by 2006, still 20 percent lower than that of the white students (http://www.jbhe.com/preview/winter07preview.html).

Many black youths had, and still have, unrealistic aspirations with regard to professional athletic careers in the NFL or NBA. They see the college or university not as an institution of learning but as a stepping stone to the professional ranks. Increasing numbers of basketball players drop out after only one or two years to seek careers as pro athletes. Such a practice has raised numerous issues regarding intercollegiate athletic programs in the United States. Are they simply training programs for the professional leagues? Are intercollegiate athletes being exploited by the schools for their athletic abilities if they do not get a degree? Why do universities accept student-athletes who are incapable of fulfilling the necessary academic requirements? Should collegiate athletes be paid for their services, considering that they generate millions of dollars in revenue for the schools (see Chapter 5)?

Whereas African-Americans are favored as athletes, they are not invited to share the power. In 2005, among the Division I universities, African-Americans comprised 57.8 percent of the basketball players and 45.4 per cent of the football players. On female basketball teams, black athletes accounted for 43.7 percent of the team members (Lapchick 2006, 3). With regard to positions of power, such as the administrators who direct and control the leagues, however, all the conference (league) commissioners were white men. In Division I, 25.2 percent of the men's basketball coaches were African-Americans, but as of 2006 only six of the 119 football coaches at that level were black. Only twelve African-American men held the position of athletic director and, at the highest level of the hierarchy, more than 94 percent of university presidents were white (Lapchick 2006, 3–5). At the professional level the league commissioners of all the major sports are white men.

The struggle for images and cultures

The league commissioners have attempted to incorporate aspects of black popular culture into the staging of games for financial gain. In the NFL black players introduced new forms of expression, for example, dancing after scoring a touchdown, while African-American basketball players initiated the dunk shot and individualistic street ball-dribbling skills. Under David Stern, who became NBA commissioner in 1984, the league has tried to find a balance between black street culture and the values of the white middle-class mainstream audience, a primary revenue base. Under Stern's guidance the NBA achieved a 1,600 percent growth rate in its annual revenues during the first ten years after he took office (Hughes 2004, 167).

The enormous profits made by the NBA are largely the result of black talent. Unlike the colleges and the supporting media, who continue to extol intercollegiate sport as an educational rather than a commercial entity, the professional leagues operate as fully capitalist enterprises without any veil of disguise for their actions. The NBA All-star Game encompasses an entire weekend as an entertainment extravaganza that includes a slam dunk contest, musical groups, parties, and a host of celebrity appearances. The NFL Super Bowl dwarfs the NBA production in a two-week media orgy of consumption (see Chapter 13).

The NBA found its ideal merger of black and white cultures in the ascendance of Michael Jordan. In the words of sport sociologist David Andrews, "Jordan was constructed as a racially neutered (hence, non-threatening), popular, representation of black male athleticism" (Andrews 2006, 20; see Chapter 12). The term "constructed" is apt, since the professional leagues have unofficially scripted texts and characters (players) which resemble the dramatized television shows, music videos, and Hollywood films that produce a celebrity culture of "good guys" and "bad guys." Jordan, marketed by Nike and numerous other corporate sponsors "as embodying personal drive, responsibility, integrity, and success," personified the American Dream (Andrews 2006, 73). That image, reinforced by his individual brilliance and team success, transcended racial boundaries and enabled him to gain "whiteness" in a sport that increasingly emphasized blackness in its playing styles.

With Jordan's retirement, his successor as NBA scoring champion, Allen Iverson, caused concern for the NBA white corporate mentality because of his tattooed body, corn-rowed hairstyle, and thug image. One survey showed that 41 percent of fans no longer attended games due to players' perceptively negative behaviors, but other fans, especially black and white kids, love the "bad guy" image. Younger players who have grown up in the hip-hop generation assume a rebellious attitude and are not so readily acquiescent to white authority. They present an image management problem for the NBA, which faces the dilemma of "the need for discipline, the need to deal with racism, and the recognition of the formula that Black equals cool equals revenue" (Hughes 2004, 172).

Like the college coaches described above, the NBA has also attempted to control the image of the game as one that is acceptable to white America by dictating players' behavior and clothing on and off the court. Aggressive behavior towards fans, verbal assaults on referees, and innovative fashion accessories to official uniforms are no longer tolerated and severely punished with fines and suspensions. Even injured players who are not participating in the game are required to attend the game in "business attire," a euphemism for clothing that is acceptable to the corporate community. An alternative strategy of team owners is the drafting of non-American (usually white European) players, whose perceptively conservative, team-oriented values are more acceptable to coaches and mainstream white spectators than blacks enacting black culture. Coaches, social critics, and politically conservative commentators have blamed a string of US losses in international play on the individualism of the black style, thereby rationalizing and justifying the new strategy.

Likewise, the NFL has encountered problems with the thug or gangster image so prominent in hip-hop culture. It has reacted with similar authoritarian measures as the NBA. Both the NFL and the NCAA prohibit particular types of celebration after scoring; this measure seems to be neutral but is directed at African-American athletes. Black culture has been historically oral and expressive, but players can no longer enact their culture and express joy by dancing in ball games. When the original ruling outlawed all forms of celebration an evangelical minister successfully sued the NCAA, making it permissible for all players to kneel in prayer, which can be interpreted as an appeasement to Christianity. The NCAA thus made accom- modations for religious expressions but not for cultural displays.

The NFL has made rule changes not only to decrease the level of violence in the game but also to protect players who represent a valuable investment for owners. In addition, the NFL attempts to promote an acceptably white middle-class image by limiting players' gestures and attire. Players are required to wear official clothing and equipment (safe- guarding the brands of its corporate sponsors), and any deviations are punished with sometimes exorbitant fines. A player in the 2007 Super Bowl incurred a $100,000 fine for wearing unauthorized gear. Sideline inspectors act as police to insure that players' socks are the appropriate color and suitably pulled up to the desired length. Even shoe color is regulated. Uniformity and standardization are prized over individuality. One scholar has reprimanded: "That [white] Americans neither seem to care about, understand, or wish to celebrate all the African American moves and grooves that make football (and American life) swing suggests an anxiety of influence at the deepest levels of our society and culture" (Dinerstein 2005, 187).

BLACK FEMALE ATHLETES

Despite significant gains made in the wake of the civil rights era, black women still suffer from double discrimination, as women and as African-Americans. In American society, they are overrepresented among the poor and the sick. High rates of obesity, diabetes, and cardiovascular disease and low rates of physical activity contribute to their low health status (see Chapter 11). However, black women have increasingly gained a college education, and have achieved high positions in society. Oprah Winfrey, a media mogul, is the richest woman in the United States; and Condoleezza Rice has carried considerable political capital as the US Secretary of State. African-American female athletes, however, have not gotten a high level of respect or media coverage. While black females maintain prominence in track and field and basketball, they face economic and social barriers in other sports, where expensive equipment, lessons, or facilities are of benefit.

Black female athletes are also exposed to the critical gaze of whites. Venus and Serena Williams captivated the tennis world with their powerful play which fostered not only positive reactions. Even the prestigious *New York Times* described the sisters in football terms, claiming that Venus had a "wide receiver physique," while Serena looked more like a "running back" than a tennis player (Davies 2007, 375). The media chastised the girls' father for the unorthodox (non-white) way in which he developed their talents and managed their careers. Upon reaching the apex of the sport, the women turned to other interests, such as fashion design. Critics assailed their on-court attire and denigrated their new-found interests as a distraction that hindered their performance. But not all commentators saw the Williams sisters in negative terms. One declared that

> their ascendancy in tennis and in corporate sponsorships has helped change the way Americans view African American women, women athletes, and women in general. The sisters, young, spirited, intelligent, fun-loving, confident, strong, and beautiful, were seen as role models for women in the new century.
>
> (Davies 2007, 377)

While the Williams sisters have made some headway in overcoming negative stereotypes, others, such as track star Marion Jones, have only exacerbated the negative image of female black athletes with their involvement in doping scandals.

RACIAL PLURALISM

Very few blacks have been able to succeed in "upper-class" sports like in the white world of golf, but Tiger Woods became the heir apparent to Michael Jordan as a golf prodigy. The golf country club, bastion of the upwardly mobile suburbanite and essential consumer, had to take notice of the Woods phenomenon. His multiracial ancestry, adroitly marketed by Nike, and a subsequent host of corporate sponsors gave him a multicultural appeal (Andrews 2006, 75–80). His prodigious accomplishments seemingly marked him as possibly the greatest golfer in history. Even more importantly for the celebrity-obsessed media and corporate benefactors, he portrayed a wholesome, middle-class, moral image at odds with the popular perception of football and basketball players. He resurrected popular interest in golf that crossed racial, ethnic, and class lines, i.e. a corporate marketer's dream. Still, despite the sales of endorsed products, the achievements and the accolades, there remained golf-courses in America that were not open to Tiger Woods, an indication of the continuing and contested blend of racism, sport, and capitalism in American culture.

However, the ascendance of non-white athletes in the white bastions of sport has not translated into more power for non-whites in the general population, whose health status, physical activity levels, educational, and occupational opportunities remain below the level of whites. Black youth has lost interest in baseball, and there are few fields to play on in the inner cities. As a result, black athletes in professional baseball have decreased significantly. African-American males continue to star in football, but the sport of choice for both black boys and black girls is basketball. Nevertheless, less than 1 percent of high school players will be offered a college athletic scholarship. Even among those who are offered such opportunities, some cannot meet the college entrance requirements due to academic deficiencies. In the largest cities in the United States fewer than 50 percent of the students graduate from high school.[4] The focus on entertainment or sports careers as the historical path to social mobility is misplaced, but such beliefs continue to stimulate the hopes of many black children.

CHAPTER ELEVEN

WOMEN AND SPORT

THE LONG ROAD TO LIBERATION

INTRODUCTION

In this chapter we not only follow the women on the long road towards liberation in sport and society at large; we also show the wide variety of women's lives and their opportunities and challenges in physical activities and sport in different periods of time.

The diversity of the country and the hugely different circumstances of life (e.g. in the plantations in the South, the western frontier, or the cities of the North) also determined the situation of the women who might be elite peacocks of the upper class, hard-working farm wives, or industrial workers. America was the country of opportunities – also for some women, but the women's case was ambivalent: on the one hand there was a society, especially in the South, which restricted women to roles as decorative objects; on the other hand, women enjoyed freedom (and hardship) in periods of transitions and in situations where they had to take their fates (and the fate of their families) in their own hands.

Women's lifestyles influenced or even determined their leisure activities and their participation in sports which varied greatly. However, the opportunities of women were influenced in the whole country by rules of morality, religion, and decorum as well as by a hierarchical gender order which restricted the opportunities of girls and women in physical activities and sport.

Specific to women's sport in the US was the strong influence of female physical educators who tried to develop and establish women's sport as something which differed greatly from the professionalized and commercialized sport practices of men. The close connection of the sport and the education systems provided a unique way for women to influence the structures, content, and development of physical education and sport. Since women's colleges were established as separate institutions in the nineteenth century, the female teachers and administrators gained opportunities and abilities to determine women's activities and objectives in the colleges, in the area of sport, and in society at large. The integration of sport and education made the intervention of the state with respect to women's rights possible. In 1972, Title IX, a part of a federal education law, guaranteed women opportunities equal to those of men relative to education including athletic participation. This law changed the situation of women and the gender relations in sport decisively.

In this chapter we will explore the interrelations between gender, living conditions, and sport cultures with a specific focus on the early periods of American history. In addition, we will discuss current issues of physical activities and sports of girls and women.[1]

WOMEN'S SITUATION IN THE US – FROM COLONIAL TIMES TO THE TWENTIETH CENTURY

Throughout American history women have been restricted, not only by their gender but by race, class, ethnicity, and religious factors. The European colonists brought the gender-specific division of work and associated gender roles and myths to North America. The gender relations were rooted in the conviction of gender differences which crystallized in the myth of male strength and female weakness. From real or alleged physical differences, the "nature" and "destiny" of women and men, the "gender characteristics" which were perceived to be normal, natural and unchangeable, and thus the tasks and position of men and women – the gender order – were derived. Because characteristics like rationality and aggressiveness were attributed to men, they seemed to be determined for the public sphere; whereas women, due to their emotionality and passivity, seemed to be destined for tasks within the family and for maternity (Park 1978). In the "New World" the roles of women varied among different ethnic groups, different regions, and different social classes. However, throughout the country women were in many ways the "inferior sex." In all areas of public life – society, politics, education, and the economy – men shaped the lifestyles of women and defined the proper sphere of their activities, which were the home and the family. In spite of the pride of the Americans in their democratic constitution, women were not granted any universal political rights until 1920. They were considered to be intellectually inferior, might be easily swayed by their sentimentality or specious arguments, and incapable of making wise decisions.

BOX 11.1 ON THE PROPER OCCUPATIONS FOR WOMEN

To me, woman appears to fill in America the very station for which she was designed by nature. In the lowest conditions of life she is treated with the tenderness and respect that is due to beings whom we believe to be the repositories of the better principles of our nature. Retired within the sacred precincts of her own abode, she is preserved from the destroying taint of excessive intercourse with the world . . . she is often the friend and adviser of her husband, but never his chapman.

(Cooper 1824)

The submissive role of women in patriarchal American society had a legal basis. Until the middle of the nineteenth century, wives were subordinate to their husbands, who virtually owned them (including her property) and their children. Concerned women organized a national convention at Seneca Falls, New York in 1848, in which they called for equal rights, including suffrage (Flexner and Fitzpatrick 1996).

A first step for more equality was the Married Women's Property Act passed in 1848 in the State of New York. This law gave a married woman the right to possess her own property, which she had either inherited or earned. Previously, it had automatically gone to her husband (Salmon 1988). As each state formulated its own laws, this enactment had limited effect, but signaled the rise of feminism and the changes to come. In 1869 women established the National Woman [sic] Suffrage Association and began a crusade that continued for half a century (Flexner and Fitzpatrick 1996).

Women were not only restricted by laws, but more so by rigid rules of propriety, the "moral decorum," which was especially important in the cities. This could even lead to gender segregation, as the British writer Frances Trollope reports:

> In America, with the exception of dancing, which is almost wholly confined to the unmarried of both sexes, the enjoyments of the men are found in the absence of the women. They dine, they play cards, they have musical meetings, they have suppers, all in large parties, but all without women.
> (http://xroads.virginia.edu/~HYPER/DETOC/FEM/entertain.htm)

Beauty and grace were extremely important to women of the higher bourgeoisie because, unlike men, they were not valued for their work and efficiency, but for their decorative and representative qualities. While southern women and the wives and daughters of the northern bourgeoisie were expected to conform to European models of gentility, working-class women, farmers' wives, and females on the frontier assumed more active lives and social roles. In the petty bourgeois and proletarian milieus as well as in the country the ideals of femininity and the gender-specific division of work could not be put into practice. Here, weak women were not in demand, but women who could contribute to the living conditions of their families were. However, most women worked in and around the house (Kessler-Harris 1982; Strasser 1982).

As a rule, most women would arrive in America with their husbands or families. Here, women could and often had to make money, which gave them a greater measure of independence than in their home countries. One way to earn money was to open or work in a boarding-house or a tavern. In Boston, for example, women held 45 percent of the tavern keepers' licenses by 1690 (Struna 1996, 83). Other women served as midwives, especially in rural areas. After the "civilization" of the environment and the "normalization" of life, American women in the cities followed traditional blueprints. The Christian religion, which regulated life in many areas of the colonies, prescribed different and complementing characteristics, tasks, and roles for men and women. Men were considered to be the head of the families and the breadwinners, the main role of women was to be mothers and housewives. However, some of the domestic skills like cooking, washing or making clothes could become the basis of small businesses in growing cities.

Because women could own property in the West, some owned and ran farms and ranches; others shared farm work with their husbands. Depending on the region and the situation, women's lives could be very hard and lonely. Often they lived in deplorable circumstances such as sod houses, far away from neighbors or towns, or medical help, and in fear of Indian attacks. Women had not only to care for the house and bring up numerous children, but also to do men's work owing to the shortage of farm hands. Women plowed, planted and weeded, fought fires, took care of cattle, and built homes (see Chapter 3). They participated actively in festivals in the countryside, where they baked goods and sometimes provided entertainment as musicians or singers. As early as the mid-eighteenth century, the American emphasis on competition became evident in butter-churning and yarn-spinning contests at communal harvest festivals, or barn raisings where neighbors came together to build a barn (Struna 1996, 123). Although gender relations in the South were even more closely tied to the myth of male strength and female weakness (and beauty) than in other parts of America, wives ran plantation affairs in the absence of their husbands.

The introduction of industrialization with the factories established in New England during the late eighteenth century led to the segmentation of time into work hours and the little time left for eating, sleeping, and leisure. Many women worked in factories, and, for them, Sunday afternoons, after church services, were their only leisure time. In 1834, the French economist Michel Chevalier wrote about the situation of female workers in one of the factories: "The making of cotton fabric in Lowell employs six thousand women. Of that number, close to five thousand are young girls from seventeen to twenty-four years old, daughters of farmers from many different New England states." They had to follow strong rules, such as abstinence from alcohol and games of chance or attendance of church on Sundays. They saved money for a dowry, and quit the fabric industry upon marriage (http://xroads.virginia.edu/~hyper/detoc/fem/employment.htm). However, women earned much less than men and there were not many jobs available. "The low rate of female labour (in America) is a grievance of the very first magnitude, and pregnant with the most mighty ills to society" (http://xroads.virginia.edu/~HYPER/DETOC/FEM/employment.htm). Similar statements are reported by numerous contemporary scholars, writers, and travelers.

By the end of the nineteenth century it was not unusual for American women to work. The majority of them belonged to the lower classes and had to earn money, no matter whether they were single, married, or widowed. Their wages, although lower than men's, were needed to support their families (Kerber and De Hart 1999; Friedman et al. 1984, 116–117). In contrast to Europe, where lower class women continued to form a majority of the industrial working class, many American women worked at home. A popular source of earning money was taking in paying boarders, as between 20 and 30 percent of American women did in the mid-nineteenth century. In the case of immigrant women this number rose to over 50 percent in the early twentieth century. Other common jobs were service occupations such as domestic servants, washerwomen, midwives, and nurses. During the nineteenth century another job opportunity emerged with teaching, a job typically allotted to women at the elementary levels. By the end of the nineteenth century, in the wake of industrialization and urbanization, the number of white-collar jobs for women rose, too. Quite frequently women were employed as telegraph operators, secretaries, and library workers (Friedman *et al.* 1984, 266, 268). In 1920 American women got suffrage rights, their participation in the workforce increased, and they gained a measure of influence and power in American society.

EDUCATION AND PHYSICAL TRAINING IN EARLY GIRLS' SCHOOLS

Throughout the nineteenth century, many Americans did not get a formal education at all. This is especially true for poor people and the population in the South and the West. Those families who could afford education for their children enrolled them in private academies or parochial schools. Affluent parents could also send their children to cities in the North or even to Europe for schooling. In most states a public school system developed in the second half of the nineteenth century. However, a formal education seemed to be of much more importance for men than for women.

Both women and a few enlightened men called for the education of females at the end of the eighteenth century; and a Boston High School for Girls was established in 1821 (Park 1978). That same year Emma Willard founded a female academy in Troy, New York (Brubacher and Rudy 1997, 64).

Women were the driving force for an improvement of girls' education, and the fact that females could get a secondary education and that some upper-class families cared for the intellectual education of their daughters increased the competencies and opportunities of women to be advocates of education and also physical education for girls.

At the beginning of the nineteenth century, Frances Wright, an early feminist, called for "the union of bodily and mental vigor," that women "might, with advantage, be taught in early youth to excel in the race, to hit the mark, to swim, and in short to use every exercise which could impart vigor to their frames and independence to their minds." In 1829 she declared that "girls have equal claims to the development of all their faculties" (quoted in Park 1978, 14). By the 1820s Catharine Beecher, one of the daughters of a highly influential New England family, began founding girls' schools and advocated calisthenics (exercises) to improve health (Guttmann 1991, 91).[2] When Mary Lyon opened Mt. Holyoke Seminary for women in 1837 she prescribed daily exercises for the students.

The widespread gender segregation in American higher education and the foundation of women's colleges offered the opportunity for women to gain leadership roles. From the very beginnings of the discourses about (physical) education, women, especially the teachers at colleges, had a voice and a strong influence on the development of physical education of girls and women. The first college to admit women was Oberlin College which was established in Ohio in 1833 as a coeducational institute. Separate colleges for women appeared in the South soon afterwards, such as Wesleyan Female College in Macon, Georgia in 1836, Judson College in Alabama in 1838, and Mary Sharp College for Women in Tennessee in 1852. In the Midwest, Rockford College (Illinois) opened for women in 1849, and a Milwaukee, Wisconsin school for girls and women was established in 1851. Elmira College (New York) for women opened two years later. At that time, higher education for women often meant teacher training.

Women's colleges in New England, such as Vassar founded in 1865 and Wellesley in 1875, intended to put women on an equal intellectual footing with men and, like the male institutions, also offered a great variety of physical training and recreation (Spears 1986, 20, 23). Even Harvard established an "Annex" for women, that eventually became Radcliffe College (Brubacher and Rudy 1997, 64–66).

Whereas Catharine Beecher had introduced domestic chores and gymnastic exercises in her schools, colleges in the second half of the nineteenth century offered more active recreations and sports to their students. Such efforts indicate that American women preceded their European counterparts in the quest for physical education. In contrast to their European sisters, women in the US could not only get a college education, but could also participate in physical exercises. The initiatives in America aimed not only at girls, but also at (young) women. The progressive attitude with regard to the physical exercises of women can be explained with the education at colleges, the life on a campus, and the influence of female physical educators. In most European countries women were accepted at universities only after the turn of the twentieth century.

Schools for girls and women challenged the established norms and conventional anthropological theories based on biology that presumed women to be inherently inferior both physically and intellectually. In 1850, the leading figure for the women's rights movement, Elizabeth Cady Stanton, wrote that "We cannot say what the woman might be physically, if the girl were allowed all the freedom of the boy, in romping, swimming, climbing, and playing hoop and ball . . . Physically as well as intellectually, it is *use* that produces growth and development" (quoted in Park 1978, 21). Educated and physically active women posed a threat to the dominant patriarchy and challenged the traditional domestic roles that restricted women's participation in society. After the Seneca Falls Convention of 1848, mentioned above, annual conventions throughout the remainder of the nineteenth century clamored for property rights, suffrage, higher education, and jobs for women. Such campaigns infringed previously male prerogatives, and met with stubborn resistance by the male hierarchy (Flexner and Fitzpatrick 1996).

PHYSICAL ACTIVITIES OF WOMEN – FROM COLONIAL TIMES TO THE END OF THE NINETEENTH CENTURY

The sources about the early sports and pastimes in America are scarce and far between, and this refers especially to daily physical activities. Girls and young women participated in recreational activities such as skating, sledding, and dancing. However, women may have been much more physically active than we know (Park 1978; Struna 1997).

In colonial times, sporting deeds and the exhibitions of sporting performances were often part of fairs or shows. Women participated in these events as spectators, and some may have even earned a living as performers. At least one female entertainer, known as "the female Sampson" [sic], performed as an acrobat and weightlifter in New York City in 1752 (Struna 1996, 174). But these women were, even more so than the male showmen, outsiders. They did not influence the physical exercises and activities of the general American population.

PASTIMES OF MIDDLE-CLASS GIRLS AND WOMEN

Sources indicate that girls and women of the middle classes, of "proper" families, could participate in some of the recreational games like bowling which did not demand a lot of strength or endurance and which could be played in fashionable costumes. Above all, the norms of propriety and fashion greatly restricted the spheres of living and moving of girls and women. Although fashion was changing, the corset, a piece of armor made of steel, fishbone, and solid fabric, which pressed the body into prescribed forms and made it

256

appear "feminine" and fragile, was considered both in Europe and the United States as indispensable.[3] To fulfill the ideal of beauty so strongly connected with the myth of the weaker sex, women accepted the corset despite its inconvenience and pain. "Proper" women's sporting endeavors were confined to activities which could be conducted in long skirts and corsets. Most of these activities, such as the bowling game nine-pins, were not only entertainment but also social events, meant to see and meet people (also of the other sex). Frederick Marryat, an English novelist, described his experiences with nine-pins and American ladies as follows:

> The game of nine-pins is a favorite game in America, and very superior to what it is in England . . . The ladies join in the game, which here becomes an agreeable and not too fatiguing exercise . . . There were some very delightful specimens of American females when I was this time at Niagara. We sauntered about the falls and wood in the day time, or else played at nine-pins; in the evening we looked at the moon, spouted verses, and drank mint juleps.
>
> (Niagara Falls, August 1837)
> (http://xroads.virginia.edu/~HYPER/DETOC/FEM/entertain.htm)

Recreation and entertainment were also the main aims of croquet, which was imported from England in the mid-nineteenth century. The "croquet craze" was partly due to the clever marketing of the manufacturers who met the taste of large parts of the middle-class population. "In less than a decade from its first public notice, the manufacturers of equipment and the publishers of guide-books had transformed croquet into a semi-organized and codified pastime" (Lewis 1991, 367). Croquet became especially popular in the US. "Supporters suggested . . . because it matched the spirit of the aggressive, achievement-minded nation, 'and nowhere else is the family circle so certain to appreciate its purity, and give it full patronage'" (Sterngass 1998, 3).

However, the game also had opponents who criticized its competiveness, the fanaticism, and the frequent attempts to cheat (Sterngass 1998, 402). When croquet became a fashionable recreation among the middle class it not only made sporting pastimes available to women, it also fostered the beginning of change in Victorian courtship patterns. Formal introductions and chaperoned social meetings gave way to mixed groups of young men and women playing the game in public view on the lawns of their parents or in established clubs. Croquet was a game which was "manly" enough to be enjoyed by men, but the majority of the players were women. It provided the opportunity to demonstrate skill but also to show a pretty foot or a small ankle. Authors praised the beauty of the women players, but many others complained about their violations against the rules.

Her figure was faultless – nor tall, nor petite –
Her skirt barely touched the top lace of her boot;
I've seen in my time some remarkable feet,
But never one equalling that little foot.
Its tournure was perfect, from ankle to toe –
Praxitiles ne'er had such a model for art –
No arrow so sharp ever shot Cupid's bow;
When poised on the ball it seemed pressing your heart!

(Sterngass 1998, 404–405)

One of the strategies of the ladies was to surreptitiously move the balls with their hoop skirts to gain an advantage. Cheating on the croquet ground became commonplace in contemporary literature. A good example is an article in *Harper's Bazaar* about "The Immorality of Croquet." The author described a game in which "such words as liar, cheat, brute, scoundrel or viper have passed into currency. Rules are improvised as the game proceeds, and the basest subterfuges resorted to in order to gain a point" (quoted in Sterngass 1998, 407).

Sterngass concludes his considerations about cheating and gender roles:

> Women may have cheated at croquet, but ultimately the game ended, and everyone returned to the strictures and boredom of everyday life. But for a moment, with the grass closely cut and the turf smoothly rolled, with mallet in hand and dress cut short, with steady eye and practiced stroke, women occupied the same moral plane as men, for better and for worse.
>
> (Sterngass 1998, 414)

Croquet did not change the gender hierarchy in American society, but it provided a space for the middle class to enact ambivalent gender images and to try out new gender relations.

Roller-skating became a fad in the 1870s and joined croquet as an outdoor activity. It was also a primary means of interaction between the sexes as it too allowed for gender mixing similar to ice-skating. Roller-skating rinks were constructed in urban locations, serving as public meeting places, not unlike parks, but involving a recreational form of physical activity (Gorn and Goldstein 1993, 102). Skating allowed women to enjoy their bodies, experience new forms of movements, and show off their skills and their fashionable outfits. It allowed women to visit public areas, helped to break down the Victorian rules of propriety and

decorum, and gave women a measure of freedom which included informal gatherings with other women, but also with men.

At the end of the nineteenth century, cycling became a popular pastime that replaced roller-skating. For the first time in history, a sporting activity gained large popularity among American women. Wealthy women had sought some recreation on expensive tricycles; and the high-wheeled cycles proved too dangerous for all but the most skilled individuals. The introduction of the "safety" bicycle with two equal-sized wheels and a more affordable price made cycling attractive to the middle class as well. Whereas the first bicycles had to be imported from Europe, in the 1890s a number of manufacturers accommodated the growing demand for bicycles. At the turn of the century about a million bicycles were produced annually valued at more than $31 million (http://www.vintagebicycleposters.net/ bicycle-history.html). For the bicycle industry, women were an excellent target group which was heavily addressed by advertisements. Glossy pictures with ladylike women riding their bicycles contributed to the acceptance of this new sport equipment. Numerous cycling clubs proliferated throughout the United States, which arranged mixed road rallies in the 1880s. Courting couples might evade even an assigned chaperone on extended journeys. By 1896 four million cyclists were traveling on American roads, a figure which rose to ten million only four years later (Gorn and Goldstein 1993, 170; Riess 1995, 40).

Cycling changed the lives of women who could now explore the environment, enjoy the company of like-minded people, and were independent of other more bothersome means of transport. The pioneer of the US women's rights movement, Susan B. Anthony, interpreted the bicycle as the best tool for emancipation:

> Let me tell you what I think of bicycling. I think it has done more to emancipate women than anything else in the world. I stand and rejoice every time I see a woman ride by on a wheel. It gives a woman a feeling of freedom and self-reliance.
> (1896; http://cyclingsisters.org/node/3242)

Even recreational female cyclists completed century runs of 100 miles. Such endurance adventures challenged the accepted notion of females' limited physical abilities (Gems 1997, 38–40). However, physicians did not reach a consensus about the judgment of cycling. Some warned that cycling could cause exertion and thus take away the energy which women needed for birth and child rearing, others praised cycling as a proper fitness activity at least if it was not done in excess (Merington 1897; Marks 1990). Cycling not only gave reason for health concerns but also for moral indignation, raising the assumption that women engaged in the activity for masturbatory purposes by bouncing on the seat. In such ways women who did not accept their assigned roles and challenged the patriarchal system were accused of being unfeminine or even castigated as immoral or rebellious. In spite of the warning of doctors, female cyclists even took part in bicycle races. These cyclists earned their living as professionals; their achievements will be described in the context of professional women's sport.

Figure 11.1 Archery contest (Smith College Archives)

The history of cycling reveals how sport developed as a contested field with various meanings and practices; it shows the struggle for power as well as the gendered inclusion and exclusion processes. The new fashionable recreational activities provided opportunities for both sexes to meet, to play together, and to get to know each other without a chaperone. In addition, they freed women from being restricted to the house, allowed them to explore their bodies and bodily capacities, and encouraged them to pursue a new, more active lifestyle. Some of the pastimes which became fashionable in the second half of the nineteenth century, such as croquet and roller-skating, lost the interest of the Americans; but others, like archery, became a competitive sport. All of the new sports could be played as recreational activities, and most women participated in sport on a "sport for all level," but at the same time, some women developed their abilities to play competitive sport, which was dominated then as it is now by men.

FROM RECREATIONAL ACTIVITIES TO COMPETITIVE SPORTS

Ice-skating perhaps best fits the concept of sport for all. Since colonial times it had been enjoyed by both sexes as a pleasant winter recreation. Males and females might mingle in

public view without upsetting the traditional norms of separate spheres for men and women. Skating began to assume a more competitive approach with the organization of skating associations for figure-skating and speed-skating in the later nineteenth century. Newspapers in big cities like New York and Chicago organized speed-skating contests for both men and women (City of Chicago 1916, 34; Bureau of Recreation 1930–1931, 10). In 1892 the International Skating Union was founded which organized competitions in figure- and in speed-skating. In 1902 the British skater Madge Syers entered the figure-skating world championship for men and finished second. This gave reason for the creation of a world championship for women in 1906. However, the vast majority of skaters enjoyed their sport on an informal level as recreation (Hampe 1994).

Women gradually intruded upon the male domain in a number of sports that required skill and training, as well as a measure of exertion (Struna 1984). Both men and women sought recreation in archery by the mid-nineteenth century. A relatively passive sport, it posed no immediate danger to women's health and decency. By the 1870s, however, archery developed into a more serious sport, and men and women engaged in separate competitive tournaments. In 1879 the National Archery Association was established and a first national tournament was organized. Fifty-four men and twenty women competed for the national championship (Bulger 1982, 5). The participation of women in championships meant a removal from the traditional roles and ideals, which required women to be delicate, passive, and charming, to avoid public attention, and to favor cooperation instead of competition. Archery became an Olympic sport in 1900, but only men participated. In 1904, it was the only event for women at the Olympic Games in St. Louis. Six American women competed in this event (Guttman 2002).

With the introduction of lawn tennis to the United States in 1874, women adopted not only the game, but more active and competitive roles in sport. Mary Outerbridge observed the game on a trip to Bermuda and returned to the United States with equipment

Figure 11.2 Tennis match on Allen Field 1909 (Smith College Archives)

for play. Her brother, as manager of the Staten Island (New York) Cricket and Baseball Club, allowed her to set up a court on the premises. The game soon enjoyed popularity among the middle and upper classes, who founded country clubs for recreational purposes (Riess 1995, 56).

The already mentioned restrictive nature of women's fashions at the time greatly limited play to a leisurely pace. This caused discussions which show exemplary contemporary opinions about and practices with regard to clothes as well as the conflicts when women had to choose between femininity and functionality.

BOX 11.4 PLAYING TENNIS IN CORSETS

A sportswriter for *Outing* magazine, the most popular sporting publication of the era, advocated a more active role for sportswomen by 1885:

> Of all the womanly recreations out-of-doors there is most hope in lawn tennis; there would be more – a great deal more if the game were as popular for purposes of exercise; as it is for bringing the young people of both sexes together . . . however, it is useless to expect them (ladies) to dress as they should to enjoy the fullest possibilities of physical exercise. Once in a while a red-cheeked, bright eyed girl may be seen completely absorbed in the game and dressed so as to give her arms and lungs full play, but . . . the advent of man . . . causes women to quickly encase herself in the feminine substitute for a strait-jacket.
>
> (Bulger 1982, 6)

The allusion to a strait-jacket refers to the corset that bound women's bodies into tightly wrapped figures of the feminine ideal.

As women increasingly began to appear in competitive tournaments another writer warned about the loss of femininity in 1888:

> In the opinion of some impartial critics the woman who is unfortunate enough to defeat all others and win a tournament "plays like a man," and is too ungraceful for anything . . . It does not seem impossible that a woman should be able to smash and smash skillfully too. But can she learn to smash, volley and play all the other difficult strokes of lawn tennis without sacrificing a certain amount of grace?
>
> (quoted in Bulger 1982, 6–7)

Despite these concerns, tennis became one of the first and few sports which allowed women to compete under similar conditions to men. The initiation of a national women's championship tournament in 1888 marked the beginning of a continuous and successful development of women's tennis; although it took some time until dress reform allowed fiercer competitions and better performances (Struna 1984; Hult and Trekell 1991; Beran 1993; Markels 2000; Liberti 2004).

By the 1890s women had also taken up golf, like tennis, a sport of the middle and upper classes whose members had the time and the resources to engage in idle pastimes as sport (Guttman 1991). Golf was one of the most attractive activities in country clubs which provided various forms of recreation not only for rich men but also their families. In the safe surroundings of the clubs, the daughters could engage in a healthy recreation which did not offend beauty and femininity ideals. The first national championship for women took place in 1895. In 1896, the 16-year-old Beatrix Hoyt won the first of three consecutive United States Women's Amateur Golf Championships. She proved exceptional in her abilities, which drew even comparisons with men. In 1899 a sports writer reported that "Miss Hoyt can outdrive, on the average, seven out of ten of her ordinary masculine rivals. She has acquired the knack of getting the ball away clean and can count upon an average distance of one hundred and twenty to one hundred and sixty yards" (Bulger 1982, 9). In 1900 Margaret Abbott, a female golfer from Chicago, accompanied her mother on a study visit to Paris. There she entered and won the women's Olympic golf tournament as well as the women's French Championships, aided by her more practical choice of apparel, as the other competitors showed up in high heels and tight skirts (Riess 1995, 56).

THE QUESTION OF (SPORTS) CLOTHES AND THE FIGHT FOR TROUSERS

"Your dress movement involves the whole woman's rights case. The woman, whose soul is capable of casting from her person the absurd and degrading dress, in which fashion has bound it, can aid that cause. No other woman can" (Gerrit Smith on motivations of the female dress reformers) (quoted in Riegel 1963, 390).

As early as the 1850s women had campaigned for less restrictive and more functional garments by proposing the controversial bloomer costume that consisted of a short skirt and pantaloons. Amelia Bloomer, a feminist and adherent of the temperance movement, and other like-minded women advocated for this costume in 1851, which would free women from the restrictions of the corsets, the petticoats and the heavy and constraining long skirts and allow them an active participation in work and politics. One of the "bloomer girls," feminist Susan B. Anthony remarked: "I can see no business avocation in which a woman, in her present dress, *can possibly* earn *equal wages* with a man" (quoted in Riegel 1963, 391; Park 1978, 22; Guttmann 1991, 90).

Some audacious members of the women's movement wore bloomers in public; however, they were subjected to laughter, derision, and even physical aggression. Trousers were not only garments, they were a symbol of male power, and men did not tolerate any attacks to their superior position in society. Soon the bloomers disappeared from public sight.

Bloomers experienced a revival in the 1880s in the wake of the bicycle craze. To avoid getting their skirts caught in the bicycle spokes women adopted bloomers or pants as a precaution. Again, wearing trousers was perceived as a transition to ascribed male attire which caused great consternation especially among men. Some clergymen claimed that female cyclists wearing bloomers or pants were possessed by the devil; while male magistrates tried to ban female cyclists from their city streets (Gems 1997, 39–40). However, the new clothes also found support. Dudley Sargent, a renowned physician, felt a dress reform was overdue. "When we reflect that woman has constricted her body for centuries, we believe that this fashion alone is due much of her failure to realize her best opportunities for [physical] development . . . the girls' corsets must be taken off . . . As to skirts . . .They have hampered the progress of civilized women for three thousand years . . . during exercise the skirt should be worn to the knee, or should be changed for the bloomer" (Sargent 1889, 184).

Dress was a matter of morality. As young college women raised their hemlines to play basketball the appearance of a naked ankle caused concerns about illicit temptation. Men were banned from women's basketball games except for college presidents, who were assumed to be above temptation. As female swimmers rid themselves of the cumbersome attire worn in the nineteenth century, swimsuits that exposed flesh also became an issue. Policeman patrolled city beaches and arrested women who thwarted the acceptable standards of decorum (Gems 1997, 109).[4]

By the dawn of the new century women in various sports had made headway in effecting changes not only with regard to clothes but also with regard to their participation in more active forms of recreation and their changing roles in society.

Frontier women and outdoor life

On the western frontier and on farms women had to be more physically active by necessity. For generations they had been engaged in hunting and horseback riding, and in some cases even horseracing. Women of frontier Indiana, noted William C. Smith (1867), "could handle the rifle with great skill, and bring down game in the absence of their husbands" (quoted in Herman 2003, 465). Recalling her antebellum childhood in northern New York State, Livonia Stanton Emerson similarly testified that "it was not long after we moved into this wilderness before father brought mother a very nice rifle." Mother "took lots of game with that rifle," added Emerson, and even taught her 10-year-old son to hunt deer at night (Emerson n.d.)

Men attempted to minimize women's abilities and prowess in such traditional male
activities. "Women cannot conveniently become hunters or anglers," wrote popular essayist
Wilson Flagg in 1871, "nor can they without some eccentricity of conduct follow birds and
quadrupeds into the woods" (cited in Keeney 1992, 69–72).

Many of the female hunters

> did not cross-dress in the field; they wore silk sashes and ankle-length dresses and
> sometimes permitted themselves "to tremble, or even faint" after the kill. Yet in
> taking up hunting and shooting, women sought to break down the barriers of
> middle-class patriarchy.
>
> (Herman 2003, 465)

Despite the widespread conviction that women were not able to fish or to hunt, the sporting
journals of the period refer to increasing numbers of women engaged in shooting for
sustenance or sport. Good sharpshooters could turn their skill into a profession and make
a lot of money.

WOMEN AS PROFESSIONAL ATHLETES

The shooting star of the late nineteenth century was Phoebe Mozee, who learned to shoot
by hunting small game as a young girl in Ohio. Her skill, especially her trick shooting, gained
her fame and social mobility. Hired by Buffalo Bill Cody to perform in his traveling Wild

West Show in 1885 she took the stage name of Annie Oakley. Presented as a re-creation of the vanished American frontier, the exhibition traveled throughout the United States and Europe until 1916 as a popular form of entertainment. The success of the enterprise spawned many imitators (at least eleven) who sometimes competed with Cody for customers. The spectacles also provided opportunities for numerous other female experts to find commercial employment for their skills. In addition to target shooting, the women shot glass balls or other objects tossed into the air, shot while riding horses, and even shot cigarettes out of the mouths of male accomplices (Kasson 2000; McMurtry 2005). Besides the female shooters the traveling performances also employed female horseriders who were adept at racing, trick riding, or cowboy skills, such as bronco busting (the breaking of wild horses by riding them). Women began competing in western rodeos as early as the 1880s if not before. Buffalo Bill Cody hired his first female rider in 1887 and by the 1890s a host of professional female rodeo stars appeared in the demonstrations of the Wild West shows (Jordan 1984, 188–189; LeCompte 1993, 32–33).

BOX 11.6 BARREL RACING – A FAST-GROWING WOMEN'S PROFESSIONAL SPORT

Barrel racing is a horse-riding contest in which riders must gallop at breakneck speed around three barrels placed in the form of a triangle. Each rider negotiates the clover-leaf shaped circuit alone, and at the end of the race the times stopped for each rider are compared. The best times are around 14 seconds. Barrel racing makes great demands on a horse's agility and speed as well as on the rider's equestrian skills.

Barrel racing has its origins in the world of rodeo. The classic rodeo disciplines, such as bull roping or bronco riding, were work-related skills of cowboys and were for the most part a men's preserve. Even so, women did take part in rodeos, and contests were held for them in the classic disciplines, a few women even acquiring fame and fortune. The contest that women mainly took part in was barrel racing.

In 1948 women rodeo riders formed the Women's Professional Rodeo Association (WPRA). Since then further barrel-racing organisations have been formed, among them the Professional Women's Barrel Racing Association and the National Barrel Horse Association with 23,000 members and a Hall of Fame.

These organisations hold numerous contests throughout the United States at differing levels of skill and with prize money amounting to several million dollars. Barrel racing is one of the fastest growing professional sports for women, and successful barrel racers can earn $1.5 million. One of the most famous riders is Charmayne James, who is not only the all-time leading money earner but has also won more world championships than any other woman in sport. She is listed in the Guinness Book of World Records.

The growing popularity of the sport and the earning potential that goes with it has increased men's interest in barrel racing, and today men account for 5% of all competitors. However, they face opposition both from "real" cowboys and from women riders.

Rodeos and barrel races are firmly rooted in American culture. They represent the frontier myth, but they also symbolise the gender order, where the men demonstrate courage and strength while the women show off their skills and add a touch of glitter in their brightly coloured shirts.

(Gertrud Pfister; see http://www.rodeohouston.com/hmagazine/02nov/barreloffun.pdf)

Women in the Wild West shows and rodeos were not the only females who earned their money with professional sports. Professional sportswomen appeared nearly as early as professional sportsmen. Both were performing in the same way as acrobats who presented exceptional skills, but it was the show not the performance per se which counted. Because women were less likely to develop these skills and display them in public, they may have attracted even larger audiences than their male colleagues. The borderlines between professional sportswomen and circus women were blurred as, among others, strong women such as Katie Sandwina, a famous performer in weightlifting competitions during the early twentieth century, shows.

> Women performed athletic feats as circus performers, swimmers, boxers, baseball players, wrestlers, bicyclists, and professional long-distance walkers. Although several athletic performers were highly skilled, many were portrayed as women with questionable reputations. Their activities were considered popular and vulgar entertainment.
>
> (Shaulis 1999, 32)

As with circus performers and actresses, the sexual purity of female professional athletes came into question as they endured the "male gaze" and public assumptions by flaunting their bodies.

Professionalism and athleticism for women presented negative perceptions because it violated two principles: women should not participate in competitions and women should stay at home rather than pursue a profession. Competitions were looked upon as especially unfeminine as they demanded strength or endurance, skills and aggressiveness, all characteristics which were considered to be lacking in women. Women who were strong, competent, and aggressive were not looked upon as real women. Still, some women pushed the boundaries of gender prescription as not only sportswomen but as professional athletes in such sports as pedestrianism, boxing, and even baseball (Gems 1993b; Shaulis 1999).

In the 1870s, there were a variety of professional rowing events for men at various distances and with different numbers of crew members. It was the most popular sport at that time, already very commercialized with cash prizes which attracted women as well. Female rowers appeared in 1867 and female swimmers in New York City competed for jewelry prizes in the following decade (Gems, Borish and Pfister 2008, 157).

A clear transgression into a male domain was women's entry in professional baseball. It caused much attention because baseball was the national game. Professional women's baseball teams, such as, among others, the Blondes and Brunettes, took the field in 1875, and spectators paid 25 cents each to watch their performance. Players might earn $15 to $25 per week. However, when the attractiveness of the sensation wore off, the teams were dissolved. The players were accused of soliciting attention not for their performance but because of their appearance. Some women, however, clearly excelled at baseball by the turn of the twentieth century. Lizzie Stroud used the pseudonym of Lizzie Arlington to play with men's teams; but Alta Weiss gained fame and prospered as a pitcher. As a member of a men's team she earned enough money to attend medical school and graduate as a physician. Another woman, Amanda Clement, even acted as an umpire, a rarity for a woman to be accorded a position of authority, especially in the area of men's sport (Kovach 2005).

Females were an integral part of pedestrianism, which became a worldwide fashion and attracted large crowds of followers in the second half of the nineteenth century; but it also drew criticism when women walked themselves into exhaustion or raised doubts about their femininity and propriety. By the end of the 1870s at least a hundred women had engaged in pedestrian contests. Ada Anderson, an English immigrant, gained fame for her endurance by walking 750 miles (1,207 km) in 750 hours, and Bertha von Hillern, from Germany, earned celebrity status for her feats as well. The New York Times (November 14, 1877) gave her front-page coverage in an article entitled: "Bertha von Hillern's Walk: One Hundred Miles Inside of 28 Hours the Latest Sensation in Philadelphia."

Interest in pedestrianism declined in the course of the 1880s. "Organized social pressure by temperance officials, religious conservatives and doctors against women's sporting entertainment appears to be a major factor in their marginalization" (Shaulis 1999, 43). Some pedestrians, among them Bertha von Hillern and Louise Armaindo, switched to professional cycling.

Most women engaged in cycling for recreational reasons and for transport. Because of the high demands on speed and endurance, all cycling events from long-distance road competitions to races on cycling tracks and velodromes were men's affairs. Women were believed to lack the necessary physiological capacities for participation in cycling races; in addition, as already mentioned, racing was considered to endanger women's health, especially their ability to give birth.

However, cyclists such as Elsa von Blumen, Annie Sylvester, or Louise Armaindo, who participated in various types of shows and competitions, drew large crowds of spectators, got positive press coverage, and became stars. Sylvester was primarily a trick and fancy rider; Armaindo, who claimed to be the world champion female bicycle rider, even defeated men in six-day endurance events (http://cyclingsisters.org/sheroes).

After the turn of the century, cycling lost some of its excitement. It became a children's toy and means of transport for those who could not afford a car which quickly became the fetish of American society. Concerns about women's health, beauty, and morality contributed to the decline in popularity of female cyclists and women's competitions. Interest in men's cycling continued until at least 1930 with a growing fascination for the sprint and endurance races in velodromes.

BOX 11.7 LOUISE ARMAINDO, THE WORLD CHAMPION FEMALE CYCLIST

The Lady whose portrait we give in this issue, Mlle. Armaindo, claims and maintains the distinction of being the champion female bicycle rider of the world . . . Mlle. Armaindo was born near Montreal, Canada, is 5 feet 2 1/2 inches in height and weighs about 135 pounds. She has defeated Prof. Fred Rollinson, the American champion, in three 20-mile races, Rollinson allowing her a 2 miles start. At St. Louis, she rode 617 1/2 miles in 72 hours, 12 hours per day for six days. She won a race for the championship, and she is willing to ride against any lady in America, or will take fives miles start in a fifty mile race from any man in America. Mlle. Armaindo elevates an 80 lb. dumb bell, lifts 700 lbs. dead weight, and is a natural athlete.

(*National Police Gazette*, New York, July 29, 1882, 12)

Even more disconcerting for middle-class adherents than women running, cycling, and playing ball was their engagement in boxing. The following statement may represent a widespread attitude towards female boxers and their male onlookers:

Prize fights between men are beastly exhibitions, but there is unutterable loathsomeness in the worse brutality of abandoned, wretched women beating each other almost to nudity, for the amusement of a group of blackguards, even lower in the scale of humanity than the women themselves.

(Chicago Tribune 1868, quoted in Gems 2000, 50)

The early female professional athletes, however, were largely working-class women, who were motivated by the prize money. They posed no danger to the dominant social structure.

The competitors on the Blondes and Brunettes baseball teams, for example, had been circus performers, actresses, and vaudeville performers, all of whom were not held in high esteem by the middle and upper classes. The male promoters of such events focused on the commercial aspects, attempting to make money by displaying the physical attractions of the women in risqué costumes rather than their athletic abilities. Middle-class newspaper writers derided them accordingly (Lieberman 2006). One account of an 1883 game concluded that the women "did not cover themselves with glory – much as they stood in need of some kind of covering" (Lieberman 2006, 25). But the professional sportswomen influenced, at least to a certain degree, the everyday convictions about the weaker sex.

BOX 11.8 A FEMALE PEDESTRIAN

I went to see Madame Anderson on her walk . . . and was completely fascinated by her gracefulness, her modest and business-like deportment, and dignity . . . I believe Madame Anderson has done a good thing in demonstrating the ability and endurance of one woman, at least, beyond what a man is capable of. She has made speeches occasionally in her periods of rest, in which she has given utterance to her belief that women are committing daily suicide in not using more freely their powers of locomotion . . . She has gained the respect of all who have witnessed her performance.

(*Woman's Journal*, 1879; quoted in Shaulis 1999, 40)

WOMEN AND ADVENTURE SPORTS

Like women on the frontier and the professional sportswomen, females engaging in adventurous activities such as mountain climbing and flying an airplane were perceived as threats to the gender order, even though or perhaps because they were members of the middle and upper classes. Despite the criticism of "unfeminine" conduct and the attempts to restrict the "weak sex" to their "destiny," a number of women, mostly from the upper class, disproved the myths about female weakness engaging in sporting adventures. Because dangerous sports produce (male) heroes, they are considered taboo for women who allegedly lack the bravery, determination, strength, and endurance needed to survive in high-risk sports like mountain climbing.

In the mid-nineteenth century, pioneering mountain climbers conquered natural boundaries previously insurmountable by human beings. The mountains of the American west posed formidable obstacles which attracted women as well as men. As early as 1858 Julia Archibald Holmes climbed Pikes Peak in Colorado, followed by Isabella Bird's success on nearby Longs Peak in 1873. Annie Smith Peck, perhaps the most distinguished of the

American female climbers, reached the top of several mountains in the United States before climbing in Europe. She wore pants to ascend the Matterhorn and eschewed the restrictive corsets worn by more traditional women. She then set her goals on Mexico, where she was the first woman to summit Mt. Popocatepetl. In South America she made numerous attempts before conquering Mt. Huascaran in Peru at the age of 58 in 1908, and upon reaching the top of Mt. Coropuna she planted a suffragist flag (Miller 2000, 37–46). Smith had been a teacher at Smith College for women in Massachusetts, and it was at the new women's colleges that such confidence, discipline, determination, and independence were nurtured.

As mountaineers, the pilots in the first period of motor flying aimed to reach new dimensions and to overcome their earth-bound existence. With the building of the first airplane able to fly in 1903, the American brothers Orville and Wilbur Wright contributed to a development which revolutionized human life. In the first period, flying was considered a sport. The fragile airplanes were tested in numerous competitions and record attempts. American women were among the first and most successful female pilots in the world. In 1911, journalist Harriet Quimby became the first female to gain a pilot license in the US. Soon she was joined by Mathilde Moisant. Both became members of the "Moisant International Aviators," a group of pilots who engaged in performances and competitions. In 1911, Quimby, Moisant, and Blanche Scott entered a flying competition on Staten Island, the first organized race for women. In 1912, Quimby was the first woman to cross the English Channel from Dover to Calais, which secured her a place among the most distinguished pilots, women and men. After her return to the US, the "Queen of the Channel" participated in the Third Annual Boston Meet, admired by spectators and thronged by journalists. Shortly before landing, her airplane dipped, the pilot was ejected, and fell to her death in the waters of Boston Harbor. Quimby, who combined cold-bloodedness, flying skills, and an attractive appearance, paved the way for numerous other American women who learned how to fly for various reasons, among other things to fulfill their dream to soar like a bird or to earn money in an exciting job (Pfister 1989).

BOX 11.9 POWDER PUFF DERBY

One of the highlights of the history of female pilots is the so called Powder Puff Derby, a transcontinental race over 4500 km and 8 days for women pilots in 1929, in which 18 of the 20 competitors were Americans. Immediately after the race the pilots met and founded the Ninety Nines, an association which represented the interests of its members, 99 of the 117 American women pilots. In the following time, Amelia Earhart, the first president, and the organization stood up for women's rights in aviation.

(Jessen 2002)

271

1904

Tremont Temple, Wednesday, February 17th
at eight o'clock, p. m.

Miss Annie S. Peck, A. M.

will give for the first time her Illustrated Lecture
with 150 original views, on

Travel and Mountain Climbing in South America

Panama
and the Isthmian
Canal.
Peru and Bolivia.
Highlands and low-
lands.
15,000 ft. in a day.

**Ascent of
El Misti**
(19,200 ft.) and
descent into the
bottom of the
crater.
The highest lake
and railroad in the
world.

**The greater
Andes**
and their wonder-
ful scenery.

Mt. Sorata
still unconquered.
Shut in by the
plague.
Seventy miles
horseback across a
desert.
Cities alive and
dead.
Tiahuanaco, of
prae-Inca civiliza-
tion.
Huaccapuna; was it
a Pigmy city?
LaPaz, Lima, Are-
quipa and the
Harvard Observa-
tory.
Opportunities for
business.
Life and dress
of the Indians and
others.

MISS PECK IN CLIMBING COSTUME

Tickets, with Reserved Seats, 50 Cents and 25 Cents
For sale at the Temple Box Office and at Herrick's on and after February 8th

MISS PECK, whose fame as a mountain climber extends over this country and Europe, is called
by the Redpath Bureau one of its most entertaining lecturers. With a pleasing personality, an unusu-
ally graceful manner, a charming voice which easily fills the largest halls, and a story of strange
countries and adventure, Miss Peck will doubtless give a lecture rivalling, if not surpassing, in interest,
her Matterhorn, which has been given thirteen times in this city.

Figure 11.3 Broadside of Annie Smith Peck in climbing gear, 1904 (Sophia Smith
Collection, Smith College Archives)

SCIENTIFIC DISCOURSES ON WOMEN'S ABILITIES AND WOMEN'S SPORTS

Transitions in women's roles, including their intrusion into male domains such as sport, inevitably caused concern and discussions in which anthropologists and physicians, but also the clergy were heavily involved. Physicians, allegedly experts on the body, had a major influence on everyday knowledge about women and their abilities and weaknesses. Thus they were also opinion-makers with respect to women's sport and physical activities. Many doctors (almost entirely males) emphasized sex differences and identified women as the "weaker sex." Physicians defined women's primary role as biological (i.e. motherhood) and claimed that any other physical or intellectual pursuits might impair the ability to reproduce. Edward Clarke, who published the influential *Sex in Education: or a Fair Chance for Girls* in 1874, even argued against higher education for females. Another physician, A. Lapthorn Smith, wrote in 1905 that "the development of the brain 'was a decided barrier against the proper performance' of the duties assigned to the wife and mother" (Zieff 1994, 153). Both physicians and the popular media blamed the "new women" for the declining birth rate in the United States, which had decreased by nearly half over the course of the nineteenth century (quoted in Zieff 1994, 156–157). While some doctors condoned a certain amount of physical activity for women by the end of the nineteenth century, the concerns persisted. Even a champion of women's physicality, Dudley Sargent, M.D., asked in 1912 "Are Athletics Making Girls Masculine?" in which he stated:

> Heretofore women have been more creatures of the kitchen and fireside than of the great outdoors, and the present generation of young women who will become the mothers of the next generation have more muscle and more lung capacity than their own mothers. The growth of athletics for girls is largely responsible for this.
>
> (Sargent 1912, 255)

However, he also cautions that

> Physically all forms of athletic sports and most physical exercises tend to make women's figures more masculine, inasmuch as they tend to broaden the shoulders, deepen the chest, narrow the hips, and develop the muscles of the arms, back and legs, which are masculine characteristics.
>
> (Sargent 1912, 260)

Luther Halsey Gulick, a doctor and an influential physical educator, proposed in 1906 that

> athletics for women should for the present be restricted to sport within the school; that they should be used for recreation and pleasure; that the strenuous training of teams tends to be injurious to both body and mind; that public, general competition emphasizes qualities that are on the whole unnecessary and

undesirable. Let us then have athletics for recreation, but not for serious, public competition (Gulick 1906, 158).

The proclamations of physicians were supported by psychologists who stressed the "weakness" of women's brains which prevented women from engaging in intellectual work, but influenced as well their sporting performance. G. Stanley Hall, a college president and the first president of the American Psychological Association, declared that "it was a pity to spoil a good mother to make a grammarian"; while a Harvard professor claimed that women's delicate brains would suffer from intense study, causing a nervous breakdown. *Popular Science Monthly* (1887) explained females' alleged deficiency by rationalizing "that the average brain weight of women is about five ounces less than that of men . . . we should be prepared to expect a marked inferiority of intellectual power in the former" (quoted in Gems 2000, 49).

Medical professionals believed that overemphasis in any traditionally male pursuits might be damaging. "Within the framework of psychoanalytic theory, for example, nonconformity to traditional roles and stereotypes was considered pathological. Hence, women's interest and involvement in business, engineering, athletics, or other 'masculine' activities were clinically suspect" (Sabo 2007, 64). Still, in 1929 Frank Rogers, writing in an educational journal, stated that "Intense forms of physical and psychic conflicts tend to destroy girls' physical and psychic charm and adaptability for motherhood" (quoted in Guttmann 1988, 148).

HIGHER EDUCATION FOR WOMEN AND THE WOMEN'S SPORT CONCEPT

Despite any male misgivings, the public universities of the western states, established by a federal land grant law in 1862, provided for the coeducation of women as equal citizens. The taxpayers who funded the schools had daughters as well as sons; and by 1900 more than 71 percent of American colleges served women as well as men (Brubacher and Rudy 1997, 68). Such opportunities gave women aspirations beyond the traditional occupations of wives, teachers, or nurses. At the end of the nineteenth century over 5,000 women graduated from American colleges per year, the majority of them subsequently taking up employment (Friedman *et al.* 1984, 268). However, these were still very low numbers, and only middle- and upper-class women could take advantage of such an education because of the high tuition fees. Nevertheless, despite the admonitions of the medical profession, women proved that they could perform as well as men in the classroom. This posed a threat to male students. As early as 1877 male students at Amherst complained that

> we appreciate (women's) excellent qualities . . . peculiar powers, peculiar charms
> . . . but we are hardly ready to admit that the opposite sex surpasses in intellect,

and it is not very flattering to our pride to have our professors continually stirring us up, by telling how much more the "Smith College girls" are doing . . . and how much more readily they grasp difficult points.

(Harvard Advocate 1877, 80)

The establishment of coeducational, and eventually all-women's colleges in the nineteenth century exposed women not only to the intellectual challenges but also to more active physical lives as well. Vassar College for women opened in 1865 with a gymnasium, bowling alley, and a riding stable, and young women soon formed their own groups for baseball, boating, and gymnastics. Radcliffe College included gymnastics for its students; while Wellesley provided for gymnastics and ice-skating on a lake, which also stimulated intramural boating competitions. By 1884 students at Smith College and Mt. Holyoke had formed baseball teams, and Bryn Mawr, which opened in 1885, eventually held competitions in basketball, field hockey, and track and field events. All competitions at the women's colleges were intramural, meaning that they took place between teams of the same school (Gems, Borish and Pfister 2008, 214).

Shortly after James Naismith invented basketball at the Springfield, Massachusetts YMCA school in 1891, Senda Berenson, a teacher at the nearby Smith College, adapted the game for women (Shattuck 1991). She addressed the concerns of physicians, who feared that running and overexertion might damage reproductive capabilities, by dividing the court into three zones, each of the zones to be occupied by two players from each team. The rules limited players' movements to their assigned zone and prevented body contact. Within a few years, women's basketball, as a specific form of the game, gained widespread popularity across the entire country. Intramural games between class teams at the women's colleges soon evolved into interscholastic contests with other schools. Stanford University and the University of California engaged in the first intercollegiate contest between female students in 1896.

However, the best basketball team of the new century was a team of Indian girls from Ft. Shaw, in the far western state of Montana. Their performances disproved the Darwinist claim of the superiority of whites. In 1904 this team became the national champion in a tournament which was conducted during the Olympic Games held in St. Louis (Peavy and Smith 2007). The extension of competition beyond the confines of the women's campuses followed the pattern of men's sport that had led to rivalries, commercialization, and an overemphasis on winning.

Sport competition presented a dilemma not only for physicians, as mentioned above, but also for the female physical educators at the colleges and some physicians, who felt that aggressiveness was unladylike and that rough play endangered the health of the students and their ability to give birth. They disagreed with the commercialization, and the emphasis on winning that permeated the sporting practices of men with numerous negative consequences. The female physical educators offered a number of alternative

Figure 11.4 Senda Berenson officiating at a Smith College basketball game, 1903 (Smith College Archives)

ways of playing sport for women that focused on widespread participation without the allegedly negative aspects of excessive competition. Their motto was: "A girl for every sport, and a sport for every girl" (Guttmann 1991, 135).

Schools held field days that engaged the women in intramural contests in which classmates played among themselves; or they might invite other schools for a "play day," in which the two institutions mixed players to avoid rivalry. "Sport days" involved the mixing of players from several schools at one site. The athletic contests might be followed by a shared social event that developed camaraderie, such as a tea party or picnic. A more competitive option allowed for telegraphic meets where the schools did not actually face each other; but sent their scores to a central location that determined the winner (Guttmann 1991, 135ff.; http:www.westga.edu/~coe/phed2602/American.html; Everhart and Pemberton 2001, 3).

The debate over competitive activities for women and their proper role in society continued throughout the twentieth century, and women were active participants in these discussions and negotiations. The growth of women's colleges, of which there were 119 by 1901, and the increasing numbers of physically active and educated women allowed them to challenge the established stereotype of the weaker sex. However, these women did not assume that men and women were alike. The cohort of female physical educators, who formed a network in opposition to the male model of sport, had a conception of womanhood that allowed for biologically founded social, emotional, psychological, and physical differences between men and women. They admitted the physical superiority of men, but felt that male aggression was an inferior quality and should not be an aspiration of women (Zieff 1994). In addition, they disapproved of intensive training because it allegedly produced large, masculine muscles that destroyed grace and beauty. Female teachers, particularly in the eastern women's colleges, disavowed competitive inter-scholastic activities and advocated for intramurals because "the strain on the players would be too great . . . interclass contests afford all the advantages of the intercollegiate games without the objectionable feature of the latter." In addition, it was suspected, that "raising the standard of excellence of play" would discourage "the less expert players" (Bulger 1982, 13).

Mabel Lee, a professor at the University of Nebraska until 1952, and the first female to preside over the American Association for Health, Physical Education, and Recreation, stated:

> Because of the particular physical conformation and physical makeup of girls let us promote for them an athletic program free from emotionalism, free from intense competition, free from heart and pelvic strain, free from all attempts to imitate the boys . . . Let us build for girls a sports realm of their own . . . founded on physical safeguards and moderation.
>
> (quoted in Verbrugge 1997, 278)

The female physical educators had some success in propagating and enforcing their views at the collegiate and high school levels where they placed their students and adherents as teachers. They held positions of dominance in the eastern women's colleges and regional pockets in the San Francisco area, and in Nebraska. In 1917 they formed the Committee on Women's Athletics of the American Physical Education Association, which set standards for the schools and in 1923 they established the Women's Division of the National Amateur Athletic Federation, which addressed sport issues outside of the schools. These American women greatly opposed the iniatives of the Federation Sportive Feminine Internationale and its president Alice Milliat to promote competition for females, especially participation in the Olympic Games (Pfister 2000).

The "play day movement" showed that a group of influential women could develop original ideas and implement a specific concept of women's sports in the colleges. Although their arguments were shared by some women (and men) in Europe, it was, among other things, the specific situation of women's colleges in the USA which allowed the realization of their plans. Here one has to take into account that the colleges and universities were and are the main sport providers in the USA.

The concept of female educators was based on a gender anthropology rooted in biology. The glorification of women's destiny, motherhood, legitimized their claim of "equal worth" and at the same time it provided arguments for a specific education for women which also justified their own positions without having to compete with men.

The American women's sport concept brought opportunities, especially for students without sporting talents, and it avoided the problems of the intercollegiate sport of the men. However, it also restricted women and barred access to competitive sport for those women who wanted to participate in sport competitions and enjoy the benefits of a successful athletic career. Thus the power of the physical educators and the confinement of female students to intramural competitions are ambiguous issues: they eased the access of women into physical activities, but prevented their commitment to "serious sports." Despite their insight into the dangers of men's sport the female educators did not try to gain influence and change the male sport system. The women's vision of a parallel gender-based sporting concept lacked universal approval, however, eventually causing a schism in the ranks of physical educators and sport administrators. Opponents of the "play day movement" advocated the access of girls and women to competitive sport. A good example is girls' basketball in Iowa. There, men gained control of the girls' high school basketball leagues in the 1920s, making the games so competitive that the girls surpassed the boys' teams in fan interest.

"NEW WOMEN" AND WOMEN'S SPORT AFTER THE TURN OF THE CENTURY

At the turn of the century, young, middle-class women turned increasingly to outdoor activities to promote their health and to enjoy a measure of freedom. By the 1890s artist Charles Dana Gibson portrayed such "new women" as independent, athletic, and vivacious, a departure from the domesticated women of the past.

Women on bicycles, female tennis players, but also professional sportswomen represented a movement which at the turn of the century contributed to a gradual change of the gender order.

> Women rapped more insistently on the door of equality. Middle- and upper-class women – called "new women" – increasingly insisted on going to college, working

outside the home, voting, wearing less restrictive clothing, and practicing birth control. Women – at least some women – would no longer be mere helpmates and mothers, asexual creatures linked more closely to the realm of angels than that of humans.

(Herman 2003, 466)

The "Gibson Girls" proliferated in the mainstream media publications, inspiring untold numbers of women to adopt a new image and to become slim, sporty, and fashionable at least before they married and had children. The enthusiasm about this new woman easily obscures the fact that the majority of women still aimed for marriage, and that numerous women had to work to support their families; for them the new women lived on another planet. One of the most radical "new women" was Emma Goldman, a labor activist, anarchist, atheist, and advocate of free love and birth control. She urged women to take greater control over their own bodies. Her radical feminism resulted in the revocation of her citizenship by the US government and deportation to her native Russia in 1919. A year later American women won a measure of equality with the ratification of the nineteenth Amendment to the Constitution, which gave them the right to vote and to run for office in national elections.

Body cultures

The emphasis on the "new" woman, the wider exposure to physical activity, and the importance of sport in society spawned a new body culture in the United States. An early prototype and propagator was Eugen Sandow, who traveled around the country exposing his mesomorphic body as the classical ideal to discerning and adoring fans. From the turn of the century, Bernarr Macfadden, one of the leaders of the body culture movement, organized competitions for both men and women to display the most perfectly developed bodies. Macfadden was an inspirational and influential advocate of a natural approach to living, namely natural food, physical fitness, outdoor life, and the natural treatment of diseases. He recommended regular exercises such as brisk walking, calisthenics, and training with light weights. His initiative for a healthier lifestyle referred to both sexes, and his wife, a former champion swimmer, his six daughters and two sons presented themselves as a perfect physical culture family who would train together with dumb-bells or swim in ice-cold water. After their divorce, his wife Mary would accuse her former husband of using the children as guinea-pigs for his theories (Todd 1987; Ernst 1991; http://www.bernarr macfadden.com/macfadden4.html).

Macfadden's initiative was revolutionary, especially with regard to women. It was not only that he emphasized the importance of health for women and recommended sporting activities like swimming and tennis, it was most of all his campaign against corsets, high-heeled shoes, and old-fashioned swimwear which hindered free movements. Women posed in skin-tight body stockings for "body-building" competitions in Macfadden's *Physical Culture* magazine, which caused curiosity, but also indignation. The publication had more than 100,000 monthly subscribers by 1903; but its contents were often deemed to be pornographic by the puritanical American censors. Throughout his long life, Macfadden, the "father of physical culture," published extensively and inspired millions of people to follow at least some of his advice. For women Macfadden's concept offered a new lifestyle. However, he still portrayed women as passive objects of the "male gaze," an image which was in contrast to the strong-willed, independent, and active "new women" who controlled their own destiny (Ernst 1991).

Sportswomen and female Olympians

Since playing sports had become a fashion among the middle classes, the "new women" were often sportswomen. By 1901 women had formed their own athletic clubs in cities such as New York and Chicago. The club in Chicago offered facilities for billiards, swimming, gymnastics, basketball, and bowling. Women competed in a national bowling tournament by 1907, and organized the Woman's [sic] International Bowling Congress as the first national sport organization formed specifically for promoting women's sports in 1916 (Gems 1997, 148–149).

Swimming was an increasingly popular recreational activity, and the beaches became crowded on sunny weekends. However, women still had to observe the norms of morality and propriety. In 1920, Charlotte Epstein founded the Women's Swimming Association of New York (WSANY). She promoted the health benefits of swimming and coached female swimmers for competition. Epstein's swimmers won thirty national championships and set numerous swimming records. She contributed decisively to the popularity and the high performance level of women's swimming in the US. Even more revolutionary than her activities as a coach was her fight for women's emancipation inside and outside of sport and her successful battle for a reform of the heavy wool bathing suits (Borish 2004). This was a major issue in prudish America where Ethelda Bleibtrey, winner of three gold medals at the 1920 Olympics, was arrested for nude swimming on New York's Manhattan Beach because she had taken off her shoes and stockings (Warner 2006, 96).

Besides bowling, swimming, and the upper-class sport of golf, tennis gained status as an appropriate competitive sport for women. Around World War I female tennis players adopted clothing that allowed for greater freedom of movement and more powerful strokes, including the overhead serve used until the turn of the century only by men. One of the tennis champions, Eleanora Sears, was, in 1910, proclaimed as the best "all-around athlete in American society."[5] Besides tennis she played squash and golf, but also participated in men's games like football and baseball, and excelled in many other sports (http://www.hickoksports.com/biograph/searseleanora.shtml).

Table 11.1 Women's participation in the Olympics – a comparison between the USA and the United Kingdom

Year	Host city	Overall participants	% Overall women	US athletes	% US women	% UK athletes	% UK women
1896	Athens, Greece	241	0 %	14	0	15	0 %
1900	Paris, France	997	2.2 %	90	7.8 %	93	1.1 %
1904	St. Louis, MO	651	0.9 %	542	1.1 %	3	0 %
1908	London, England	2.008	1.8 %	126	0 %	744	4.5%
1912	Stockholm, Sweden	2.407	2.0 %	174	0 %	279	3.6 %
1920	Antwerp, Belgium	2.626	2.5 %	277	4.7 %	226	5.8 %
1924	Paris, France	3.089	4.4 %	296	7.8 %	261	10.0 %
1928	Amsterdam, Holland	3.883	9.6 %	220	16.8 %	197	14.7 %
1932	Los Angeles, CA	1.332	9.5 %	275	12.4 %	72	19.4 %
1936	Berlin, Germany	3.963	8.4 %	309	13.3 %	212	17.5 %
1948	London, England	4.104	9.5 %	301	12.6 %	313	15.0 %
1952	Helsinki, Finland	4.955	10.5 %	291	14.1 %	258	17.1 %
1956	Melbourne, Australia	3.314*	11.3 %	305*	15.4 %	197*	14.7 %
1960	Rome, Italy	5.338	11.4 %	294	17.3 %	253	18.2 %
1964	Tokyo, Japan	5.151	13.2 %	345	22.9 %	204	21.6 %
1968	Mexico City, Mexico	5.531	14.2 %	356	23.0 %	223	22.4 %
1972	Munich, Germany	7.134	14.8 %	404	20.8 %	286	25.9 %
1976	Montreal, Canada	6.084	20.7 %	394	29.9 %	241	27.4 %
1980	Moscow, USSR	5.179	21.5 %	NA	NA	220	31.8 %
1984	Los Angeles, CA	6.829	22.9 %	522	34.9 %	334	31.7 %
1988	Seoul, Korea	8.391	26.1 %	443	43.3 %	349	36.1 %
1992	Barcelona, Spain	9.356	28.9 %	537	35.0 %	369	38.2 %
1996	Atlanta, GA	10.318	34.0 %	649	41.6 %	298	38.9 %
2000	Sydney, Australia	10.651	38.2 %	586	43.2 %	310	41.6 %

*Including the Equestrian Games in Stockholm the same year.
Source: IOC homepage; Decker 2004.

Sears defied convention by her choice of sports, but also by her high performances and by her unorthodox clothes. She played polo with men, participated in car races, and wore trousers whenever she wanted. On the one hand, Sears was the prototype of the new sportswoman; on the other hand, she was also an exception. First, she was outstanding because of her talents and skills. Second, as a wealthy, upper-class woman she could thwart the accepted standards of the day without reproach due to her social status. However, she provided a model which middle-class women could follow in their quest for greater freedom.

Rich women could afford to be "gender troublemakers." The same is true for working-class women. Whereas the sporting opportunities at schools and colleges were restricted, girls and women found athletic competitions in the settlement houses, parks, and playgrounds of the inner cities. Likewise, employers provided a wide array of athletic opportunities through industrial recreation programs (Park 2005).

After the turn of the century, the Olympic Games gradually became the most important and prestigious meeting place where the best athletes of the (Western) world could compete against one another. The Olympics were considered to be a male preserve, as they had been in ancient Greece. Throughout his life, Pierre de Coubertin, the founder of the modern Olympics and a typical man of his times, thought that women should not sully the games with their sweat but should merely crown the victors (Leigh 1974; Simri 1977; Boutilier and San Giovanni 1991; Welch and Costa 1994; Wilson 1996).

In the USA, the issue of women's participation in the Olympics was highly contested. As already mentioned, many physicians and psychologists, but also sport officials like James Sullivan, the president of the AAU, and influential female physical educators, opposed the participation of women in top-level sport competitions (Guttmann 1991, 163). In 1917 the Athletic Conference of American College Women had objected to intercollegiate contests and favored, as already described, widespread rather than elitist participation. The resistance against female athletes competing in the Olympic Games increased in the 1920s. Female members of the American Physical Education Association withdrew from the Amateur Athletic Union (AAU) in protest after the AAU sent a women's swim team to Paris in 1922. A year later they formed the Women's Division of the National Amateur Athletic Federation (NAAF), which also rose in opposition to any form of national or international competition (http:www.westga.edu/~coe/phed2602/American.html; Guttmann 1988, 148–149).

Especially controversial were the track and field events which were discussed throughout the 1920s and included in the Olympics in 1928. Relevant groups, such as the women's committees in the American Physical Education Association (since 1917) and the NAAF, objected strongly to the participation of women especially in track and field:

> If any sport was picked to be condemned, it appeared to be track and field for it came to symbolize in women's sport what were considered to be the evils of a

system of athletics in which a few might gain prominence, though exploited, at the expense of the masses of girls and women.

(quoted in Lucas and Smith 1982, 244)

In 1929 the Women's Division of NAAF decided to discourage participation by women in the next Olympic Games (quoted in Pfister 2000). It applied to the IOC to cancel the women's competitions (Gerber et al. 1974, 151). However, this initiative was not very successful, and even faced considerable resistance in the USA. Thus, the American Amateur Athletic Union did send women to the Games and even stood up for the continuation of the Olympic women's program with inclusion of the contested track and field events (Leigh 1980; Guttmann 1991, 169).

American women participated in the pre-war Olympic Games more or less accidentally (see Table 11.1). Women were excluded from the Olympic Games in 1896. Since the following games in 1900 and 1904 were connected with World Fairs, the selection of events to be included in the Olympic program was mainly in the hands of the fairs' organizing committees, and thus to a large extent beyond the control of the IOC (see for the Games in 1900, Lennartz and Teutenberg 1995; Odenkirchen 1995/1996; Kluge 1997; Mallon 1998). Therefore, in many respects, a move was made away from the ideas and ideals of Coubertin and his adherents. In 1900, women took part in the Games for the first time, and at least sixteen female players took part in tennis and golf competitions, typical upper-class sports. Six of them were Americans, and all six came from rich families; they had come to Europe more or less by chance and regarded golf and tennis mainly as social events (Welch and Costa 1994, 124). Besides tennis and golf, women participated in various other events such as croquet, dressage, and ballooning. However, some of these competitions may not have been included in the official Olympic program.[6] The American Helen Barbey, married to Count Herman de Pourtales, was the first woman to gain an Olympic victory. She was a member of the crew of one of the winning yachts. At the St. Louis Games in 1904 only six or eight American women represented their country, this time in archery,[7] however IOC members, who were strong opponents of competitive sport for women, declared the archery competition to be an exhibition only (Welch and Costa 1994, 124).

In 1908 no American woman traveled to London to participate in the Olympics. In 1912, in the Olympics in Stockholm, swimming, considered a healthy sport suited to women, was added to the Olympic program. James Sullivan, president of the Amateur Athletic Union who helped determine the composition of the US team, disapproved of women's sports and did not permit American women to swim in the Games of 1912. In the following years, the battle about women's participation in competitions persisted. Sullivan confirmed the position of the AAU in a letter which was published in the New York Times: "Of course you know that the Amateur Athletic Union of the United States does not permit women or girls to be registered in any of its associations, and does not sanction open races for women in connection with Amateur Athletic Union events." In her answer, the captain of the New York Female Giants baseball club attacked the AAU president as follows:

[Sullivan] is always objecting, and never doing anything to help the cause along for a girls' AAU. He objects to a mild game of ball or any kind of athletics for girls. He objects to girls wearing a comfortable bathing suit. He objects to so many things that it gives me cause to think he must be very narrow minded and that we are in the last century.

(quoted in Warner 2006, 95)

In 1914, Sullivan asked the AAU committee members to vote for a resolution "that the AAU does not and will not recognize the registration of women athletes (Warner 2006, 95). The death of Sullivan in 1914 opened the way for women's competitive sport.

Whereas at the 1912 Olympic Games in Stockholm only European women competed in swimming and diving, thereafter the United States, largely through the efforts of team manager Charlotte Epstein in New York, produced a bevy of star swimmers that garnered Olympic medals over the next two decades (Borish 2004). In 1924 Sybil Bauer even surpassed the men's world record in the backstroke. Tennis star Helen Wills won Olympic gold in 1924 and monopolized amateur laurels throughout that decade in the United States. Many of the Olympians emanated from the industrial recreation programs and private sports clubs. Bertha Severin, founder of the Illinois Women's Athletic Club in 1918, recruited working-class girls "to bring fame and enhance the name of the club" (Gems 1997, 145). They were allowed to train at the club and use its facilities as long as they adhered to middle-class standards of modest dress and decorum. In addition, they could not violate the rules of amateurism. Betty Robinson, a Chicago schoolgirl, member of a private club, won the 100-meter race at the 1928 Games. The results of the 800-meter race in 1928, however, stalled women's progress in track and field for decades. After the 800-meter run several of the athletes sank to the ground. Their exhaustion at the end of the race seemed to confirm the arguments of all those opposed to women's sports: "This distance puts too great a demand on feminine strength," wrote the New York Times on August 3, 1928 (quoted in Daniels and Tedder 2000, 72). The runners recovered quickly, and one of the two Canadians involved even set a world record in the 4 × 100-m relay three days later. Despite this evidence, the behavior of the athletes was regarded as proof that women were not made for sports which required stamina. The 800 meters, moreover, provided the IOC with an occasion for reconsidering the whole question of women's track and field events. Even if the track and field events for women stayed in the Olympic program, the 800 meters were excluded from the following Games until 1960 (Messerli 1952, 11). In the ensuing years American delegates in the IOC strongly supported the case for women's athletics, not the least because they hoped for medals in the 1932 Olympics.

These expectations came true when America's greatest athlete, Mildred "Babe" Didrikson, became the heroine of the games in Los Angeles. A working-class woman, she honed her skills in an industrial recreation program. Leading her company basketball team to undefeated seasons and a national championship. As a one-person track team she also

Figure 11.5 Bathing costumes, bathing beauties (Smith College Archives)

garnered the national track championship of 1932, setting four world records. At the 1932 Olympics she won three medals: gold medals in the javelin throw and hurdles, and a controversial silver in the high jump.[8] Her jump would have won gold, but the officials ruled it illegal because they had never before seen a woman jump with her head first over the bar. The Olympics 1932, conducted in a period of economic depression, meant that a limited number of foreign athletes made the long journey. Still, the triumph of Didrikson, hailed in the mass media, made her a celebrity. After the Games she was paid to exhibit her abilities as a baseball player before embarking on a career as a professional golfer. Apart from the great controversy about her amateur status, her appearance, behavior, and especially her athletic performances did not comply with the current ideals of femininity, although the public speculation about her (homo)sexuality diminished following her marriage to a professional wrestler, George Zaharias (Borish 1996).

In 1936 the question of proper behavior for women again became an issue when Eleanor Holm Jarrett, the best backstroker on the women's swimming team, was banished from the squad for drinking alcohol on the ship transporting the team to the Games. Avery Brundage, head of the AOC, deemed her to be a bad example. Race also became an issue. As African-American male track stars led the American teams to victory in 1932 and 1936, the two African-American women who qualified for the women's track team in 1932 were replaced by white runners. Both Tidye Pickett and Louise Stokes qualified for the team again in 1936. While Pickett broke her foot in a hurdles race, Stokes was again replaced by a white runner on a relay team and could only watch as a spectator (Wrynn 2004).

The Depression, however, curtailed many of the industrial recreation programs that accommodated the female athletes. White colleges did not offer athletic programs for women because athletics were not considered to be feminine and attractive. Thus,

Figure 11.6 Babe Didrikson (far right) at the 1932 Olympic Games (Library of Congress)

women and sport

after World War II the women's Olympic track teams relied largely on African-American athletes from the historically black colleges in the South. In 1960 Wilma Rudolph became the first American woman to win three gold medals at the Olympic Games. The black women faced the double discrimination of gender and race; yet their successes quietly attacked the hegemonic and patriarchal social framework (see Chapter 10).

Developments during and after World War II

The World War II era brought changes to the patriarchal sport structure. Not all women agreed with the non-competitive dictates of the largely eastern leadership. Girls and women had continued to engage in strenuous activities in the midwest and western states. In 1941 at Ohio State University Gladys Palmer openly disdained the PE professors in the AAHPERD by offering a golf tournament for women. Female physical education leaders objected to this tournament, which included thirty participants; but despite their misgivings the number of colleges offering competitive women's sports grew from 16 percent in 1943 to 26 percent in 1951 (Rader 1990, 321).

As in the labor market, also in sport women substituted for the drafted men and took on tasks and duties which had been considered male domains, most noticeably in baseball. When many professional baseball players joined the military service it provided a window of opportunity for women. From 1943 to 1954 the All American Girls Professional Baseball League operated with success in the midwestern states and even drew more spectators than a men's pro team in 1948.

Throughout the turbulent years when African-Americans fought for civil rights, sport became a means for women and African-Americans to address questions of equality in American society. The acceptance of female and black athletes in sports that were formerly reserved for white men signaled progress toward equal treatment of both sexes and black and white. Still, the women's baseball league, like the professional white male teams, did not accept any black players.

The attempt of women to enter the main domain of men's baseball was met with rebuke when, in 1952, a professional baseball team in a minor league attempted to use a female player. The national *Sporting News* reported:

> Take it from Ford Frick, as commissioner of Organized Baseball, a woman's place is not on the diamond (baseball field) . . . Following press reports that the Harrisburg club had entered into a contract with a woman player, the National Association office contacted the club . . . I am notifying all clubs that signing of women players by National Association clubs will not be tolerated and . . . will be subject to severe penalties . . . It just is not in the best interests of professional baseball that such travesties be tolerated.
>
> (quoted in Franks 2004, 140–141)

287

Black athletes had been excluded from many sports, or they had been relegated to competing in their own separate leagues and competitions (see Chapter 10). Besides the track and field athletes, Althea Gibson, an African-American tennis player, became one of the gender and race barrier-breakers. She became the first African-American woman to play in the United States Lawn Tennis Association national championship in 1950. Gibson was supported by a former white champion, Alice Marble, who wrote an editorial in favor of Gibson for the July 1, 1950 issue of *American Lawn Tennis Magazine*. This article shows that Gibson was still looked upon as an outsider, but it also shows that the initiative of individuals could be effective.

BOX 11.10 TENNIS, A GAME FOR BLACK WOMEN

The article read, in part:

> Miss Gibson is over a very cunningly wrought barrel, and I can only hope to loosen a few of its staves with one lone opinion. If tennis is a game for ladies and gentlemen, it's also time we acted a little more like gentlepeople and less like sanctimonious hypocrites . . . If Althea Gibson represents a challenge to the present crop of women players, it's only fair that they should meet that challenge on the courts.
>
> (http://www.all-about-tennis.com/alice-marble.html)

In 1956 Gibson won the singles and doubles at Wimbledon, as well as the French Open. She repeated her success in the French Open the following year and the Associated Press named her Athlete of the Year in 1957 and 1958, the first black woman to gain the honor (Davidson 1997). In 1960 she won the women's professional championship and her dignified demeanor dispelled stereotypical notions of black Americans.

Tennis was not only the sport that signaled the liberation of black female athletes, it also provided a stage for demonstrative feminism and for challenges to men's superiority. Billie Jean King made formidable statements on the tennis courts in the cause of feminism. In 1968 she exposed clandestine payments to men in the prestigious Wimbledon tournament, forcing greater equality for women in the form of more substantial prize money. She led other female tennis players in a boycott of the pro circuit over unequal prize money and the formation of a women's professional tour in 1970. With the success of the women's game and increasing interest and revenue, King became the first female athlete to earn $100,000 a year in 1971. Her most symbolic victory, however, occurred in 1973 when Bobby Riggs, a 55-year-old former tennis champion and an avowed chauvinist, issued a challenge to all women. Riggs declared that he could still defeat any female tennis player and then beat the highly ranked Margaret Court. Billie Jean King responded to the challenge

when a $100,000 stake was offered. The spectacle, called the "battle of the sexes," one of the most famous tennis events of all time, held in the Houston Astrodome before the largest crowd ever to witness a tennis match and broadcast to thirty-six countries around the world, ended in Riggs' defeat (Rader 1990, 327; Gutmann 1991, 210). King's triumph was a symbol of women's empowerment and gender equality. She became an idol and a role model for millions of women who had to confront oppression by men in everyday life in the family as well as in the workplace (Spencer 2000). King would subsequently take equally courageous stands in the cause of feminism and sexual orientation as the champion of women's rights throughout her career as a player, administrator, and social activist.

College sport and Title IX

The increasing interest in women's sports led to the gradual acceptance of competition in the schools (at all levels) as well as in society. Intercollegiate championships for women began in the 1960s and the Association for Intercollegiate Athletics for Women (AIAW) was organized by female physical educators as the governing body for such events in 1971. The AIAW created a separate division of women's intercollegiate sports with a gender-specific ideology and practice. The organization offered competitive events for elite college athletes, but eschewed the granting of athletic scholarships and the recruiting of athletes, strategies which were so prominent in the men's programs of intercollegiate sport. A rivalry for the governance of female athletic programs soon developed between the AIAW and the NCAA, which ended with the abolishment of the women's organization. Ironically, the law which was meant to guarantee gender equality, the so-called Title IX, facilitated the victory of the NCAA (Hult 1980; Wu 1999).

The passage of Title IX of the Educational Amendments Act (1972), a federal law guaranteeing equal opportunity for all students in federally funded educational programs, further complicated the discourse relative to the appropriateness and scope of women's sport (Gutmann 1991, 212ff.). Perhaps one of the most contentious laws in the United States and certainly the most important for interscholastic athletic programs, the brief passage reads: "No person in the United States shall, on the basis of sex, be excluded from participation in, be denied the benefits of, or be subjected to discrimination under any education program or activity receiving Federal financial assistance" (Carpenter and Acosta 2005, 3). Although not specifically directed towards athletic programs, the law has often been invoked to rectify inconsistencies as well as blatant injustices in relation to equitable sports participation of female and male students (Fields 2005).

As an effect of Title IX the participation rates of girls and women increased dramatically. In 1971 before the passage of the law, only about 294,000 girls played sports; this was 5 percent of the high school athletes. By 2003, thirty years after the legislation, more than 2,856,000 girls were members of high school teams, comprising 41 percent of secondary school athletes (Carpenter and Acosta 2005, 168). At the college level 30,000 women played sports in 1972, only 15 percent of the athletic population. By 2003 women accounted for 42 percent of the athletes at the NCAA institutions (Carpenter and Acosta 2005, 171).

Title IX intended to create equal opportunities regardless of gender; but it also had unintentionally dire consequences for both males and females. Males (coaches, athletes, athletic departments, and the NCAA), unwilling to surrender their dominant position and the revenue inherent in the sport hierarchy tried repeatedly to contest Title IX. In 1974 they lobbied the Department of Health, Education, and Welfare to exclude athletics from the law. Their efforts proved futile. In another 1991 court case (NCAA v. Califano) the NCAA argued that the law was unconstitutional. Again it lost (Everhart and Pemberton 2001, 4).

All institutions receiving federal financial aid in any form were required to comply with the Title IX directives by 1978. The federal government failed to punish offenders, but published standards for compliance in 1979. Still, 80 percent of the colleges did not comply with these rules as of 2003 (Priest 2003, 29). Conversely, male administrators, rather than upgrade women's programs, continued to pour money into men's football and basketball programs, the premier sports on college campuses and the only ones that produce revenue. As of 2008 female students made up more than 57 percent of the student body in the colleges; but women's teams were awarded only about one-third of the athletic budget (Carpenter and Acosta 2008, 6). Athletic directors chose to practice "roster management," i.e. limit the number of male athletes in order to improve the gender ratio among the athletes or to eliminate some male teams altogether. As a rule they chose to eliminate those sports which are not as popular in the United States as the big games. In 2002, this strategy resulted in an unsuccessful lawsuit by the National Wrestling Coaches Association, which charged that Title IX enforced a quota system that ironically denied male athletes the opportunity to engage in their specific sport. The court decided that the individual schools rather than the law itself should decide as to how each institution would comply. While men's wrestling, swimming, gymnastics, track, and cross-country programs faced extinction, schools continued to increase the number of football teams during the 1990s (Crepeau 2003, 1).

A 1992 court case (Franklin v. Gwinnett County Public Schools) changed the enforcement power of Title IX lawsuits decidedly. In this case, a female student accused an employee of the school of sexual harassment and filed a Title IX lawsuit in the federal court. The court declared the availability of monetary compensation in Title IX lawsuits. The cost of lawsuits have caused many schools to give in and to upgrade women's sports programs. The ongoing struggles with Title IX resulted in a presidential commission to address the issues in 2002 to 2003 that left the law essentially unchanged; but critics claim that the guidelines for compliance have significantly weakened the intent.[9]

Despite the widespread and ongoing debates over Title IX it has clearly been a boon to female athletes. In terms of participation and achievement American women have made significant strides owing to Title IX. By 2008, more than 180,000 women competed in intercollegiate athletics on 9,101 teams, with 98.8 percent of schools providing a women's basketball team, 95.7 percent offering volleyball, and 92 percent of colleges sponsoring women's soccer teams due to the increasing popularity of that sport. The increased opportunities for girls and women have proven very effective, and contributed to successes of US teams in international competitions. The US women's soccer team won the World Cup in 1991 and again in 1999 as well as the Olympic gold medal in 1996 and 2004. The women's ice hockey team captured the gold medal at the Winter Olympics in 1998 (Carpenter and Acosta 2008, 1, 10).

However, Title IX also proved to have negative or at least problematic consequences. This was especially true for the Association for Intercollegiate Athletics for Women. The AIAW provided championship competition for women in seven sports in the school year 1972 to 1973. In 1973, however, a female athlete sued the AIAW over its refusal to grant athletic scholarships on the grounds that it discriminated against women because they were not given the same opportunities as male athletes. The successful suit forced the AIAW to forgo its opposition and adopt the men's sports model (Rader 1990, 325). However, this did not guarantee the survival of the organization.

Both the NCAA and the NAIA initiated their own national championships for women by 1981. The NCAA offered travel expenses for athletes and controlled television revenue; while the financially strapped AIAW lacked the resources for a successful fight against its more powerful opponent. With the demise of the AIAW in 1982, the formerly separate women's physical education departments and athletic programs were absorbed by the existing men's departments in the colleges. Female administrators and coaches lost their power if not their positions. Whereas females held more than 90 per cent of administrative and coaching roles in women's sport in 1972, those numbers dwindled to 21.3 percent of administrative positions and 42.8 percent of the coaches in 2008. More than 57 percent of the women's teams are coached by men (Carpenter and Acosta 2008, 1).

Women, sport, and leadership

Despite major changes and an increasing inclusion of women in the 1990s, equality has not yet been reached in the NCAA, which is governed by a male president and an executive committee with eleven male and four female members (http://www.ncaa.org/). In 2006, on the next level of leadership, among the forty-one NCAA chief aides/directors, the percentage of women was 48 percent. However, 90 percent of the powerful conference commissioners (Division 1) are (white) men (Lapchick 2006, 106).

A national study has provided data about gender relations in the athletic departments of their member colleges (Acosta and Carpenter 2008). In the NCAA member institutions women hold 21.3 percent of the Athletic Director positions, an increase from 18.6 percent in 2006; but only twenty-nine (8.4 percent) women are athletic directors at the Division I (largest) schools (Acosta and Carpenter 2008, 2).

The percentage of women increases in the positions as associate/assistant athletic directors, but also here the percentage of women decreases with the importance and prestige of the Division. In women's Division I 30.2 per cent, Division II 36.2 percent, and Division III 46 percent of assistant athletic directors are female.[10] However, 11.6 percent of schools have no females at all on the administrative staff (Acosta and Carpenter 2008, 6). Analyzing and interpreting these data, we have to take into consideration that traditionally men's and women's athletic departments had been segregated. That meant that at the beginning of the 1970s, not only the majority of the athletic directors but also 90 percent of the coaches in the women's athletic department were women. Today the percentage of women coaching women's teams has dropped to 42.8 percent – partly because women's athletics gained importance as a result of "Title IX" – and only 2 percent of coaches of male teams are female (see Lapchick 2003; Acosta and Carpenter 2008, 1).

Also in the American Athletic Union (AAU), the power is in the hands of men. The five national officers – president, two vice-presidents, general secretary, and treasurer – are all men. Of the thirty-one National Sports Chairs five are held by women (trampoline and tumbling, soccer, field hockey, dance, and cheerleading).[11] The Board of Directors of the United States Olympic Committee, too, is dominated by men. It consists of eight men and three women (http://www.usoc.org/).

Whereas women have gained some power in intercollegiate athletics, the male dominance in professional sport is still unbroken.[12] The teams in the six professional leagues are owned mostly by a group of investors, sometimes also by a single individual. Owners are, to a high percentage, men. In 2003, among the majority or primary owners of teams in basketball and baseball there were no women (currently the baseball commissioner's daughter owns the Milwaukee team), and among the majority or primary owners of teams in football and hockey the percentage of women is 9 percent. One hundred of the 102 teams of the five men's leagues have a male chief executive officer/president; only two women hold this position. There are around 200 team vice-presidents in each of the four big men's leagues and 24 team vice-presidents in soccer. The percentage of women as vice-presidents is between 0 percent for soccer and 15 percent in NBA (Lapchick 2003, 37). No woman is employed as a general manager (principal in charge of day-to-day team operations) in the five men's professional sports. In the Women's National Basketball Association, nine women (56 percent) hold this position. The percentage of women among senior administrators in the four big men's leagues is between 15 percent and 29 percent.

In recent years, the professional leagues and the NCAA have started several "diversity initiatives"; among other things they train the staff to take race and gender into account when hiring new employees. The NCAA also conducts diversity education workshops for athletic personnel or gives grants for minority women coaches to develop their expertise (Lapchick 2003).

Another "taskforce" with respect to women's rights and leadership is the Women's Sport Foundation, founded by Billie Jean King in 1974. Like the early female physical education

women and sport

teachers, women activists have banded together in this organization to address concerns such as female sports participation, equal opportunities, and women in leadership roles.

BOX 11.11 WOMEN'S SPORTS FOUNDATION

The Women's Sports Foundation is the trusted voice of women's sports and physical activity because our work is anchored on fact-based research and 34 years of experience in the design and execution of award-winning education and public policy programs. Founded in 1974 by Billie Jean King, the Women's Sports Foundation is a national charitable educational organization dedicated to advancing the lives of girls and women through physical activity . . . An educated public is the strongest form of advocacy and research is key to demonstrating that sports and physical activity lead to healthier, happier and more productive lives.

Our vision is a society in which parents understand the benefits of sports and physical activity participation for both their daughters and their sons and equally encourage them to be active and healthy. Together we want to create a society in which girls and women of all ages fully experience and enjoy sports and physical activity with no barriers to their participation. Our success depends on people around the world who work with us to help every girl and woman believe that she can be fit, confident and healthy in a body of any size.

(http://www.womenssportsfoundation.org/About-Us/Our-Work.aspx)

CURRENT ISSUES

American female athletes have excelled in a number of sports. They have dominated Olympic and world championships in basketball and softball, and won numerous titles in track and field, swimming, beach volleyball, gymnastics, and a variety of winter sports, such as figure-skating, bobsled, and skiing. As youth league, interscholastic, and professional programs continue to expand sports participation by females will continue to grow. However, it is an open question if the increase of female athletes in various sports and on different levels will influence the sport for all participation rates of the female population (see Chapter 9). In addition, the increasing numbers of female athletes obscure the fact that in many sports American women are not participating or are a small minority, especially in the team sports such as football and baseball; although increasing numbers are engaged in ice hockey at the high school and collegiate levels. As women have adopted the male sports model the pressures to win have also gained prominence. Some of the issues that concerned the educators and physicians of the past still remain. While research has validated the benefits of exercise for women, new concerns have emerged. For example, gymnasts, long-distance runners, and all female and, to an extent, male athletes, in sports where low weight has an impact, are particularly susceptible to eating disorders such as anorexia and bulimia in their attempts to gain competitive advantages. Female athletes, like their male peers, have also turned to doping. Marion Jones is the most famous of several female track stars who were engaged in doping scandals. She was convicted in 2007 and faced a prison sentence.

The commercialization of women's sport requires the women to compete with the men for media attention, spectators, and revenue. This causes a sexualization of female (and to a lesser degree male) athletes who appear nude or scantily clad in magazines like *Sports Illustrated* or in *Gear Magazine* in order to attract public attention, advertisement contracts, and sponsors. Professional golfers and tennis players have become more renowned for their physical attributes than their playing abilities. Likewise, Olympic swimmers, such as Amanda Beard and Jenni Thompson, or beach volleyball players have attracted viewers with skimpy attire or no attire at all. *Sports Illustrated*, the popular American sports magazine, continues to publish its famous swimsuit issue with alluring female models each spring, focusing on women as sexual objects rather than as athletes (Pfister 2004). Feminists decry the sexual portrayal of feminine bodies but many athletes and also some federations see this as the only way to make female athletes and women's sport visible and place them better on a contested market.

Chapter 13 shows the concentration of media coverage on men's sport and the marginalization of women. However, the question is whether sexualization is the right way to get publicity, because it transfers the focus from sporting performances to appearance and sexuality.

BOX 11.12 ATHLETES AS SEXUAL OBJECTS

If the media present women as sexual objects and men as stars then this is a double standard that objectifies women. Because *Sports Illustrated* seldom covers women for their athletic exploits and frequently portrays women as sex objects rather than athletes, such coverage is objectionable and demeaning to female athletes . . . The male or female athlete's decision to appear in this magazine [*Esquire*] nude or semi-nude is one that reflects on her image. Does he or she wish to be remembered as an athlete or a model posing unclothed? . . . There are many ways in which women choose to "reclaim their bodies" after being objectified in the media for so many years. Displaying their strength and their muscles is one such method and should be recommended. Male and female athletes can do this in minimalist athletic wear (swimsuits, compression shorts, sports bras) in authentic athletic poses without displaying or attempting to accentuate genitalia in "sexy" ways . . . For the female, who has been the victim of portrayal as a nude or semi-nude sex object for many years, one would think that the decision to appear naked should be carefully considered, especially when her male counterpart is not similarly displayed. Why is this important? In the end she can't ignore the fact that she is most likely a role model for thousands perhaps millions of young girls.

(Wosport Weekly, September 13 2000,
The Women's Sport Foundation newsletter)

While women and girls have earned recognition for their athletic achievements since the passage of Title IX, the reins of power in American sport are still held by men, and there seems to be no change in sight.

CONCLUSION

During the various periods of US history, women met specific conditions which supported or impeded their participation in physical activities and sports. On the one hand, there was the frontier where it was possible to leave traditional roles and enjoy a measure of freedom in spite of the hard and often dangerous life. In many historical periods, people sought popular entertainment and paid for the performances of professional sportswomen. On the other hand, restrictions by religious laws and social expectations, such as in the upper-class circles of the South, impeded women's range of movements, both verbally and literally.

Specific to women's sport development in the US was the strong influence of female physical educators who tried to develop and establish women's sport as an activity which differed greatly from the professionalized and commercialized sport practices of men. Therefore the colleges did not provide a basis for women's competitive sport, which became a domain of female athletes in the industrial recreation programs and private clubs. Competitive sport thus became a privilege of rich women who could easily confront limits or women from the working classes who did not conform to the ideals of femininity and propriety.

The integration of sport in the education system also allowed for the enforcement of gender equality by law. In 1972, Title IX, a part of a federal education law, guaranteed women opportunities equal to those of men relative to athletic participation. Title IX led, without doubt, to an advancement of women's sport in the US.

Women's issues are also addressed in the other chapters which deal, among other things, with the coverage of women's sports in the mass media, men's and women's patterns of sport consumption, and the sport activity rates of the male and female population (see Chapters 9, 12, and 13).

CHAPTER TWELVE

THE CULTURAL IMPORTANCE OF SPORTS HEROES

INTRODUCTION – THE NEED FOR HEROES

All societies seem to revere gods and/or heroes, who are rooted in the myths of origin and the value system. As the type of heroes in a society mirrors its values, dreams, and needs, the reconstruction of American sport heroes not only gives an insight into sport developments, but also into the aims and values of American society.

Historians, sociologists, and anthropologists have all offered theoretical explanations for the necessity of heroes, and sports heroes in particular. *Webster's Dictionary* defines a hero as a person recognized for his courage, nobility, or exploits; or admired for qualities and achievements which make him a role model or an ideal (Guralnick 1970, 657; Whannel 2002). However, the concept of heroism depends on the cultural context and it is

> troubling and ambiguous. Statements about heroism, the heroic and heroes are frequently statements not just about the society in which we live, but statements which carry a marked positionality, inscribing both the perspective from which they are made and the frame through which we should perceive society.
>
> (Whannel 2002, 41)

In everyday theories and discourses, the concepts of heroes, stars, and celebrities are often blurred. "Stardom is a form of social production in which the professional ideologies and production practices of the media aim to win and hold our attention by linking sporting achievement and personality in ways which have resonances in popular common sense" (Whannel 2002, 51). Today, heroes and stars are constructed by the media; they select, emphasize, frame, and narrate the deeds and events, provide explanations, and thus create meaningful biographies. Not (only) do the characteristics of an individual make a star, but the constructed and mediated images and narratives as well. The legends of heroism are very often told as metamorphoses, such as the rise of a person from poverty to fame based on skill and efforts.

With the spread of modern mass media, promotion and fame became significant issues in elite sport. Sport heroes and stars sharing the public attention and celebration gained increasing social importance although we never meet or truly know them. According to Andrews and Jackson,

> the virtual intimacy created between celebrity and audience often has very real effects on the manner in which individuals negotiate the experience of their everyday lives . . . Celebrities are public entities, responsible for structuring meaning, crystallizing ideologies, and offering contextually grounded maps for private individuals as they navigate contemporary conditions of existence.
>
> (Andrews and Jackson 2001, 2)

Celebrities can assume the role of intermediaries, in whom individuals with mundane lives could enjoy the vicarious experiences of their heroes. Sport offers numerous occasions for admiration, emulation, and identification (see Chapter 13).

In each historical period, heroes were presented with the help of the available tools of communication, such as pictures, books, and newspapers. However, the enactment of heroes gained a new quality through TV where everybody is constantly consuming celebrities. "As a consequence, social institutions, practices and issues are principally represented to, and understood within, the popular imagination through the action of celebrated individuals" (Andrews and Jackson 2001, 4). But one has to emphasize that audiences are not passive consumers, but actively involved in the process of "celebrity appropriation." Current sport celebrities (including heroes) are products of public culture and commercialism; symbols of social values, they arouse emotions, stimulate identification, address the audiences with various messages, and call on the population for consumption. The high media consumption in the US is closely interrelated with an overemphasis of stars and heroes.

The invention of heroic traditions and the construction of collective myths has to be interpreted against the background of the specific history of the US. As a relatively new culture the United States may have a greater need for heroic figures than other, more established societies. Historians have asserted that heroes are a necessity in societies undergoing change, as they represent stability in uncertain times. Susan Douglas claimed that the adulation of heroes and the excoriation of villains became a dominant feature of American journalism during the late nineteenth century, when many aspects of American life were in flux. As the society navigated, and sometimes drifted, towards new horizons, heroes served as fixed points during an uncharted voyage (Reel 2006, 18). In America several regional cultures developed, some with their own distinct heroes. With the end of the American Civil War in 1865, there was an additional need to reunite the country and develop a sense of unity via political myths. As a country of immigrants, the United States had to find and shape new idols which could represent America as a whole or one of the different class, ethnic, race, and gender groups. American culture, therefore, has heroes and sports heroes in abundance, perhaps more so than other cultures.

Sport was and is an excellent arena for the creation and presentation of heroes, and the huge importance and popularity of sport in America made sport stars predestined to become national heroes. The phenomenon of sports heroes and sports spectatorship is a relatively recent one, and seemingly a result of modern sporting practices (Pfister 2007b; see also Chapter 13). In this chapter we will introduce the heroes that both mirrored and established American values during the struggles for the creation of the American nation and show how sport stars increasingly took on the role as American idols. Archetypical idols were soon joined by athletes who represented the various groups, classes, ethnicities, and genders in the USA. However, in more recent decades the male – and to a lesser degree also the female – "subcultural" heroes increasingly became the representatives of the whole nation, a process which contributed to the integration of the various groups of the population, and signaled a more cohesive national identity and pride.

BOX 12.1 CELEBRITIES, HEROES, STARS

Heroes and stars are celebrities. Sport celebrities without heroic status achieve their prestige, often temporary, by virtue of their athletic abilities and their media exposure. Almost all professional athletes and many college athletes enjoy a measure of celebrity due to media publicity about their athletic deeds. It is a condition of momentary fame and must be sustained to reach the level of star, hero, or idol.

Stars shine brightly, but may have a brief and limited lifespan. An athlete may be a star for one game or one season; but few retain their luster over an entire career. It is a temporary condition and often a fleeting honor.

A hero is distinguished by unforgettable deeds and services to society. Sport heroes gain fame for their athletic abilities accompanied by valued characteristics, such as courage, tenacity, and an indomitable spirit. Heroes have lasting qualities and may serve as role models and idols.

AMERICAN HEROES

Soldiers, politicans, and cowboys

Like in other nations, the original heroes of the American people were military figures who represented perceived ideals of the populace (Jackson and Ponic 2001). Generals, later presidents, like George Washington or Andrew Jackson, represented liberty and equality, courage and manliness, which was a precondition of heroism. Washington, the military leader in the American Revolutionary War and the first president of the United States, is known as "the father of his country." His refusal to seek a prolonged term in office despite the support of the people marked him as a democratic republican who voluntarily left a position of power in contrast to the emperors and monarchs of other countries. Andrew Jackson, the most esteemed military leader of the War of 1812, which enabled the young United States to maintain its independence from the British, also became president. As such he curtailed the power of the National Bank, which exercised control over the monetary system and increased the wealth of commercial and industrial entrepreneurs at the expense of farmers and laborers. Thus he offered hope and a perception of equality to the common man, despite his own stature as an aristocratic plantation owner.

The conquest of the West, starting in the eighteenth century, created new national characteristics and new heroes who symbolized the new Americans: the frontier pioneers. The frontier thesis of Frederick Jackson Turner promoted the perception of American cultural exceptionalism. It proclaimed that the particular character of Americans, their independence, resourcefulness, self-reliance, individualism, and their belief in democracy had all been forged by their experiences in settling the western regions.

BOX 12.2 DANIEL BOONE

Daniel Boone (1734–1820) served in the military during the French and Indian War (1756–1763). In 1767 he conducted exploratory expeditions to the Kentucky region, and he began leading settlers to the area in 1773. He rescued his daughter and others from capture by the Indians in 1776. Boone's own capture and induction into the local Shawnee tribe of Native Americans enhanced his knowledge and stature within both cultures; but his escape settled his ultimate allegiance with the settlers. His arduous adventures in Kentucky were immortalized by the publication of *The Discovery, Settlement, and Present State of Kentucke* [sic], a romanticized account by John Filson in 1784. Widely read in America and England, it established the prototype of the frontier hero. Boone served briefly in the Virginia assembly in 1781, and again in 1787 and 1791; but his love of the wilderness led him back to the west. In 1799 Boone led his family to settlement in Missouri, which became part of the US in 1803. He died in 1820 and was buried in Missouri; but in 1845 Kentuckians dug up his body and brought the remains back for reburial in their state. In his lifetime and thereafter Boone was glorified in numerous books, poems, and paintings that presented him as an exemplary and heroic frontiersman.[1]

(Gerald Gems)

the cultural importance of sports heroes

The heroization of Daniel Boone and his adventures in the frontier regions led early settlers across the Appalachian Mountains into an unknown wilderness, braving capture or death at the hands of allegedly uncivilized savages, in order to fulfill the American Manifest Destiny. This is a political myth and a story familiar to American schoolchildren. Boone's capture and escape from his native American captors was attributed to his supposedly superior guile, fortitude, and extraordinary marksmanship, thus rationalizing the American conquest as a consequence of white superiority. Such stories cast the Native Americans as uncivilized heathens, or noble savages at best. Boone's physical abilities were augmented by his individualism, service to others, and virtuous character in a legend that defies the encroachment of urbanization into Indian lands and its concomitant ills which finally erased the Indian nations.

After the death of Daniel Boone, Davy Crockett became his replacement as a frontier hero. A product of the frontier settlements of Tennessee, Crockett's rise from common man to Congressman exemplified the possibilities of social mobility in the United States. In 1836, Crockett traveled to Texas (a Mexican territory largely inhabited by Americans) and participated in an ill-fated crusade to help the allegedly mistreated Anglos win their independence from Mexico. His death at the famous Battle of the Alamo made him a martyr and solidified his legacy as a freedom fighter who made the ultimate sacrifice for the liberation of Americans. The Crockett story has been retold in numerous books, songs, movies, and television shows that (as political myths generally do), obscure or completely ignore other perspectives, such as the significant role and the perspectives of the Tejanos (Mexican Texans).[2] This story also negates the fact that Texas was not a neutral territory, but a legitimate province of Mexico. The focus of popular historians on the "white" Americans and their reluctance to take the perspective of the Catholic Mexican Tejanos not only cast a racial dimension on the narratives of the independence movement but advanced the Anglo notion of the Manifest Destiny of white, Anglo-Saxon, Protestant Americans.

The political myth[3] of America's destiny was further established at mid-century in the American Civil War which emerged as a debate over slavery and freedom, and which clarified the meaning of American democracy as a "land of the free." In the aftermath of the war and the assassination of President Abraham Lincoln, which made him a martyr, historians have characterized his nobility, courage, and self-sacrifice as distinguishing qualities, perhaps, of the greatest American hero. Lincoln, too, was born in a log cabin in the frontier. Through diligence and hard work, he achieved social mobility and political office, even election to the presidency. His steadfastness in the face of the country's greatest crisis, the Civil War, and his compassion for and magnanimity towards the conquered southern states legitimated his decisions and actions as the righteous use of force for the greater good of all. Controversies still ensue over the nature of the war, its aftermath, and the psychological composition of Abraham Lincoln, but these historical debates do not affect his image as a hero. He is ranked among the greatest presidents in US history and he is immortalized in one of the most renowned "places of remembrance," the monument with the faces of the four most important presidents, Washington, Jefferson, Roosevelt, and Lincoln, at Mount Rushmore.

Systematically, throughout the remainder of the nineteenth century, American soldiers conquered the Native American tribes of the West, incorporating their lands into the United States. These western lands were opened to farmers and ranchers, whose fates and deeds in a hard environment became epic tales about manliness, courage, self-reliance, and independence. The icon of the frontier hero was and is the cowboy, who tamed the land and the "wild Indians," displaying legendary skills on horseback with the lasso and with guns. Cowboys were infamous for their gambling and drinking habits. Their reputation and the image of the cowboy culture covered the fact that they were underpaid laborers which ranked low in the social structure of the time. The gradual government control and settlement of the new territories enabled their integration within the growing democracy. The "civilization" of the country also changed the character of its heroes and created new myths about the imperial power of the US, which began to contend with European states for worldwide influence and dominance.

Theodore Roosevelt, soldier, politician, and sportsman

The Spanish–American War of 1898 offered another opportunity for the Americans to garner territories in the name of liberation. The conflict arose over the issue of Cuba's independence from Spain. With this victory the US acquired the former Spanish colonies of Puerto Rico, the Philippines, and Guam, as well as other Pacific territories. The brief war produced yet another American hero: Teddy Roosevelt (1858–1919), who embodied an assortment of often conflicting American ideals. A wealthy socialite from an established New York family, Roosevelt had many talents and served the state in many roles, among others as historian, explorer, and politician.

In the 1880s Roosevelt moved to the Dakota Territory and became a frontier cowboy to cure his physical problems, such as asthma and general weakness brought on by a sickly childhood. A regimen of hiking and gymnastics rewarded him with health and hardiness, and the rough life as a western rancher who could ride, rope, and hunt enhanced his self-confidence. His experiences led him to an appreciation of sport, especially football, a rough game which promoted aggressiveness and a martial spirit. Roosevelt lived what he was preaching: he proved his male prowess and martial spirit in the Spanish–American War, where the Americans supported Cuba in their fight for independence. Like Crockett, he left his Washington post as Assistant Secretary of the Navy in order to organize the so-called Rough Riders, a volunteer cavalry contingent of mostly athletes and cowboys.[4] Under his command, the Rough Riders captured San Juan Hill, a fortification near the city of Santiago. This battle, glorified in odes and a famous painting, made Roosevelt a household name, and sped his ascent to the vice-presidency and eventual presidency of the United States (Jeffers 1996).

the cultural importance of sports heroes

As president, Roosevelt lived up to his fame as charismatic leader: his decisions benefitted the whole nation, also the "common man." He championed legislation that prohibited economic trusts and the monopolization of industries in the hands of a few capitalists. This fostered competition between oil, steel, and railroad corporations, with resultant benefits – lower prices and higher salaries – for farmers and workers.

Theodore Roosevelt gained his fame as a military and political leader, but his athletic prowess contributed to his heroic image. As a student at Harvard he was active in rowing and boxing; later he became a famous hunter and a mountaineer (he led a party to the summit of Mont Blanc during his honeymoon in 1886). His love for sports did not stop after his election to the presidency – he continued not only boxing, but in 1904 he also started to learn Judo (http://ejmas.com/jcs/jcsart_svinth1_1000.htm). His publications about sport and physical exercises and his active involvement in the development of sport, especially American football, conferred a measure of social acceptability on sporting pastimes.

BOX 12.3 THEODORE ROOSEVELT AND AMERICAN FOOTBALL

Theodore Roosevelt is sometimes credited, erroneously, with the founding of the NCAA, the governing body for intercollegiate sports in the United States. In fact, the violence and deaths that occurred in early football games caused some schools to discontinue the sport or substitute it with the less injurious game of rugby. Concerned that young, American men might lose their courage and aggressive martial qualities, Roosevelt called the coaches of the top teams to the White House for a conference in 1905 after his own son was seriously injured in a football game. Roosevelt urged the coaches to foster rule changes in order to save the game. Although the coaches made only minor changes, the college presidents soon organized the NCAA to gain greater control over all of the students' athletic competitions.

(Gems 2000, 29, 83)

For many, Roosevelt was the American hero who embodied typical American values. His fame was based on his military prowess and political deeds but also on his personality: his broad array of interests, his competencies and achievements and not the least his physical prowess, his cowboy image, and his love of sports made him a model of masculinity and martial spirit.

Political myths simplify history and focus attention on the hero. The glorification of Roosevelt and the Rough Riders obscured the contribution of African-Americans, who had fought in the African-American 10th Cavalry Regiment in the battle for Santiago (http://www.buffalosoldiers.com/). The marginalization of blacks and their accomplishments in this and many other cases reproduced the dominant WASP culture with its focus on white heroes.

The construction of American heroes over the course of the nation's early history favored particular characteristics involving leadership, courage, manliness, whiteness, and social mobility that became engrained in Americans' perceptions of themselves and their burgeoning national identity. Heroes were imagined to have led the American people through crises and changing times, and improved the situation of the country. With the changing challenges – wars, race conflicts, economic depression – the characteristics of the charismatic leaders also changed accordingly.

CURRENT HEROES

In the twentieth century, the range of potential heroes was enlarged considerably – scientists and actors, black Americans, and women gained heroic status. At the same time, heroes did not have to be perfect any more; weaknesses and faults, as in the case of Elvis Presley or Bill Clinton, were and are accepted, and also the term *hero* became contested and replaced by terms like *celebrity* or *star*.

Historians, but also media such as *Life Magazine* or the Discovery Channel collected and presented American heroes, which included a wide range of very different people, among many others Martin Luther King, Bob Dylan, John F. Kennedy, or Oprah Winfrey. However, these lists are hardly authoritative, depending, among other things, on the questions and samples of this "research" (http://dsc.discovery.com/convergence/greatestamerican/greatest american.html).

SPORTS HEROES TAKE THE FIELD

In conjunction with the changing nature of American society in the later nineteenth century, such as urbanization, industrialization, and a culture of consumption, sport emerged as a field where heroes were made. America was and is an Eldorado for sport stars who gained earlier fame, earned much more money, and emerged in much larger number than in other countries.

Since the nineteenth century, sport has become an increasingly important part of popular culture, gaining a growing number of adherents (see Chapter 2). Athletes and their achievements are visible, their performances may be measured and compared, and their heroic status seems to be justified by verifiable deeds.

The development of sport (and watching sport) as a popular American pastime and the emphasis on record orientation and professionalization drew attention to excellent athletes who became famous at first among the adherents of their sports, and later in their regions, or even in the whole country. Some of the sport stars gained attention and adoration among the whole population, while others (e.g. black athletes or immigrants) gained fame primarily among African-Americans or their ethnic groups.

National sport heroes – from the mid-nineteenth to the mid-twentieth century

Heroes of the nation did not only excel in their sport, they also represented American values, as described above. This means that only white and male athletes who achieved outstanding success were able to ascend to heroic status. In addition, the fans loved biographies and deeds which made the hero human and superhuman at the same time. Heroes represented the American dream that wealth, status, and prestige are distributed according to ability and effort, i.e. that the USA is a meritocracy.

One of the first athletes who became a symbol of the American Dream and an embodiment of the American ideology that fortune favors the bold was John Morrissey (1831–1878). An Irish immigrant, Morrissey was a successful bare-knuckle fighter in a time when boxing matches were so violent that they were illegal in most places of the US. In 1853 he managed to get a fight for the American championship with Yankee Sullivan (another Irishman) who dominated the thirty-seven rounds of the fight but violated the rule not to hit his opponent when he was on his knees. This brought Morrissey the victory and made him a hero, especially among the Irish. Morrissey parlayed his winnings into a New York gambling house, and expanded his business into several gambling parlors. He had a stake in the construction of the famous Race Track at Saratoga Springs, New York. His ventures as a boxer and as businessman won him friends not only among the working classes but also among the affluent, and Morrissey enjoyed election to the US Congress where he served two terms. The socioeconomic mobility which Morrissey obtained through boxing (and gambling) supported the ideology of sport as a meritocracy where one might obtain the promise of America based on one's abilities rather than birthright. Sport thus became a symbol of American democracy (Gems, Borish and Pfister 2008, 99).

Sport heroes flourished in the Golden Age of American sport in the 1920s, promoted by an eager and enthusiastic crowd of sport reporters. One of the greatest American sports heroes of the era, maybe of all time, was George "Babe" Ruth (1895–1948), who unified the nation in the admiration of his performances on the baseball field. Ruth's dissolute lifestyle (see Chapter 4) was largely hidden from the adoring masses by discrete journalists, who focused on his prodigious displays of physical prowess. Ruth was seen by his audiences as "one of the crowd," having similar tastes and weaknesses as his admirers. His amazing performances fascinated middle-class bureaucrats and earned him a salary in excess of the US president. When a sports writer questioned such remuneration, Ruth replied matter-of-factly, "So what? I had a better year." (Dickson 2008). Ruth's records for home runs in a season stood for thirty-four years, and for home runs in a career for thirty-nine years. The players who finally surpassed these records in the latter half of the twentieth century suffered death threats from devoted Ruth fans. For several reasons, Ruth held a top position in the American sporting pantheon. Not only was baseball the national game at which Ruth excelled but he did so at a time of cultural transition.

BOX 12.4 BABE RUTH

The Ruthian image of home-run blasts ran counter to the increasingly dominant world of bureaucracies, scientific management, and "organization men." Ruth was the antithesis of science and rationality . . . [Ruth] also ran counter to Victorian rules . . . He drank heroic quantities of bootleg liquor . . . he sometimes ate as many as eighteen eggs for breakfast and washed them down with seven or eight bottles of soda pop . . . In each town . . . Ruth always found a bevy of willing female followers . . . His astonishing success reassured those who feared that America had become a society in which the traditional conditions conducive to success no longer existed. He transcended the world of sport to establish an indefinable benchmark for outstanding performances in all fields of human endeavor.

(Rader 1990, 135, 137; Davies 2007, 126–130)

Ruth's fame could be easily turned into money, as he was hired by numerous companies to act as spokesperson for their products. He became the "prototypical sport celebrity endorser" (Andrews and Jackson 2001, 7).

Biographies of Babe Ruth continue to be written, sports broadcasters annually invoke his name, and continual comparisons are drawn any time a new power hitter approaches any of Ruth's records. He remains an enduring icon in American sport (Creamer 1974; Montville 2006).

Johnny Weissmuller (1904–1984) represented another type of hero. He was, in various ways an exception, a transitional figure both because of his ambivalent ethnicity and his move from an athlete to an actor. In addition, Weissmuller gained fame in swimming, which was and is not one of the "big" sports in the USA. Born in today's Romania, he grew up in Chicago and claimed to be an American. Weissmuller who, as child, was often sick, started swimming allegedly at the advice of his doctor. He became famous because of his five gold medals at the Olympic Games of 1924 and 1928. He established numerous national and international records, "invented" a new swimming style, the American crawl, and was – without any doubt – the best swimmer in the 1920s. In 1922, he broke the record of Duke Kahanamoku and became the first swimmer to swim 100 meters in under a minute. He never lost a race, and such feats fascinated Americans, who still believe that "winning is everything." Weissmuller managed to transfer his "cultural capital" as famous swimmer to the world of celluloid dreams. After working as a model, he was selected as an actor for the role of Tarzan and played the role of the jungle hero in twelve Hollywood movies. Weissmuller became Tarzan and Tarzan conquered the world (Weissmuller and Reed 2002).

For a brief time in the 1920s daring pilots enjoyed a measure of celebrity and fame for their demonstrations of courage and endurance. Since the American brothers Orville and Wilbur Wright had conducted the first twelve-second heavier-than-air flight in 1903, aircraft technology as well as the distance and the height reached by airplanes advanced rapidly and enormously. But also in the 1920s flying was still more of a sport than a means of transportation: various competitions with different types of airplanes were conducted and records in distance, speed, and height were broken. The most spectacular deeds were long-distance flight, and hundreds lost their lives when flying new routes, especially when it included the crossing of oceans (Corn 2002). Due to the high standard of technology and the excellent aircraft industry, the US was among the leading nations in aviation. No wonder that the most famous male and female pilots of all times were the Americans Charles Lindbergh and Amelia Earhart (Pfister 1989). Lindberg demonstrated not only his mastery of the new technology but displayed his courage by conquering the aquatic frontier with the first solo flight across the Atlantic Ocean in 1927. Like their earlier frontier heroes, Americans greatly admired his adventurous spirit and gave him a huge ticker-tape parade in New York upon his return. The tragic kidnapping and murder of his child in 1932 further endeared him to the American public in his sorrow before his sympathy with Nazi Germany tarnished his image.

Amelia Earhart followed Lindbergh, proving that heroines could be as brave as men when she soloed across the Atlantic Ocean in 1932. Three years later she completed a solo flight from Hawaii in the mid-Pacific Ocean to California. Her modesty in the face of such accomplishments won favor with Americans' self-perceptions. She was one of the few female pilots who may be considered a feminist, and she became a role model for numerous girls and women. She was lost in an attempt to circumnavigate the globe in 1937, but her mysterious disappearance on her last and most daring flight made her unforgettable. Her fate is still a matter of public interest and stories about her life or death continue to make news (Pfister 1989).

SPORT HEROES AND THE AMERICAN DREAM: THE INTEGRATION OF ETHNIC, CLASS, AND RELIGIOUS GROUPS

While previous military and political heroes bridged the often large gaps between social classes, sports heroes served the various racial, ethnic, and religious groups as well as both genders as icons, models, and targets for identification.

During the 1840s the large-scale immigration of Germans and Irish to the United States threatened the economic, political, and social hegemony of the "Anglos" who viewed themselves as the rightful heirs of the American enterprise. The Anglo-American working class, those most threatened by the influx of European laborers, reacted in violent fashion, and riots and street fights occurred in industrial cities like Chicago on a regular basis.

Boxing and baseball as a means to social mobility

The clash of cultures continued in the boxing arena, which served as substitute battle-grounds where working-class immigrants could fight their Anglo protagonists. Since the 1850s a series of matches featured Irish pugilists against their American counterparts, with John Morrissey (mentioned above) emerging as a great American success story.

That lesson and that legacy solidified itself in the career of John L. Sullivan (Gorn and Goldstein 1993, 121–124). Born in 1858 to Irish immigrant parents, the "Boston Strong Boy" achieved a measure of fame among the bachelor subculture by walking into saloons and announcing "I can lick any son of a bitch in the house." (Isenberg 1988). In 1882 he easily defeated Paddy Ryan to claim the heavyweight championship of the United States, and then embarked on a series of national tours. Sullivan offered $1,000 to anyone who could last four rounds with him. His antagonist, Richard Kyle Fox, another Irish immigrant and publisher of the *National Police Gazette*, a weekly newspaper with a largely working-class readership, crusaded for a challenger to dethrone the champion; but his promotions only enhanced Sullivan's celebrity. A picture of the first national sports hero allegedly adorned every working-class saloon as Sullivan held the title without defeat for a decade. His 1889 defense against Jake Kilrain took seventy-five rounds and proved to be the last of the bare-knuckle championships. Sullivan lost his title in 1892 to "Gentleman Jim" Corbett under the new Marquis of Queensberry rules that required boxing gloves. Corbett, a middle-class bank clerk who had attended college and learned to box in an athletic club, represented a transition in American culture as the dominant values and myths of the frontier, with its connotations of brute force and individualism, gave way to the ideal of a more genteel, societal progress which was embodied in the educated middle class (Rader 1990, 51–53). In that sense, boxing proceeded through a measure of what Norbert Elias called a "civilizing process," as it became "tamed" by rules and as it transcended class lines in the recruitment, habits, and tastes of its heroes (see Introduction).

BOX 12.5 CORBETT DEFEATS SULLIVAN

For a $50,000 prize they fought on September 7, 1892, before ten thousand fans, many of them in formal evening wear, in a grandly lit New Orleans arena. William Lyon Phelps, a professor of English at Yale, recalled in his

---

> *Autobiography* that next day he read the newspaper to his elderly father, a minister. "I had never heard him mention a prize fight and did not suppose he knew anything on the subject, or cared anything about it. So when I came to the headline CORBETT DEFEATS SULLIVAN, I read that aloud and turned the page. My father leaned forward and said earnestly, 'Read it by rounds.'" Sullivan's rise to national celebrity status bespoke the changing role of sports in American society. No longer was boxing mainly the preserve of the old bachelor subculture, that collection of men who lived as outlaws from bourgeois respectability. Prizefighting had moved toward the cultural mainstream.
>
> (quoted in Gorn and Goldstein 1993, 124)

The transition in the evolution of boxing and its growing interest among the upper class is noted by the popularity of the John L. Sullivan–James J. Corbett fight. Despite his defeat, Sullivan remained a celebrity on the vaudeville circuit. His dissolute lifestyle and alcoholism contributed to his downfall; but his temperance lectures in later life provided an element of redemption for American moralists.

Historian Ben Rader claimed that sports heroes of the second half of the nineteenth century had a compensatory function. During a period of declining Victorian values and an increasing control of society by politicians and corporations, sport heroes provided the population with entertainment, suspense, and models for identification (Rader 1990, 132). Sullivan and Corbett, at least, represented two different social groups vying for prominence in the American culture in a period of time when progressive reformers from the middle classes attempted to bring greater regulation, control, and morality to both sport and society. As bosses controlled people's work lives and social reformers increasingly passed legislation that regulated leisure time, boxing still retained the physical qualities cherished by the working class. A procession of black, Jewish, Italian, and later Hispanic champions maintained racial, ethnic, and class pride in a changing, "more civilized" society which tended to marginalize immigrants and the working class.

As in the nineteenth century, boxing matches retained their attractiveness as vicarious battles after the turn of the century. Historian Elliott Gorn has described the clash of class cultures in a series of symbolic boxing matches, which featured the working-class hero Jack Dempsey, and the middle-class upstart Gene Tunney. Dempsey, the son of poor Irish-Americans from a Colorado mining town, won the heavyweight championship in 1919 when he knocked down the giant titleholder, Jess Willard, five times in the first round. A brawler and slugger, Dempsey's style exhibited the hardships of working-class life. The media portrayed subsequent fights in nationalistic terms, posing Dempsey as an American hero against invading foreign boxers. After defeating the European light heavyweight

Figure 12.1 Pugilist Gene Tunney after being knocked down by Jack Dempsey (Chicago History Museum)

champion, Georges Carpentier, in 1921, in the first million-dollar gate (revenue derived from the number of spectators at the arena), Dempsey engaged a giant, Argentinian Luis Firpo, in a memorable slugfest in 1923. The encounter featured twelve knockdowns in the first four minutes before Dempsey scored a knockout in the second round. He spent the next three years collecting nearly $500,000 a year in endorsements, movie roles, and stage fees as one of the biggest celebrities of the decade (Rader 1990, 148; Davies 2007, 172). Dempsey was one of the most popular athletes of the era. He was "written in boxing mythology" (Whannel 2002, 86). His fame enabled him to gain large sums from exhibition fights, public appearances, or as spokesperson for various products.

Tunney, in contrast, displayed a "scientific," defensive fighting style. He read Shakespeare, married a rich socialite, and disdained sportswriters. His aloofness and his social circle clearly set him apart from the masses. In the initial meeting with Jack Dempsey set in Philadelphia in 1926, more than 120,000 spectators witnessed a surprising decision for Tunney. The result begged a rematch in Chicago the following year, which is believed to be the most famous bout in boxing history. More than 104,000 fans packed the stadium and produced a $2,658,660 gate, while another fifty million Americans listened to the radio broadcast

(Rader 1990, 149). Dempsey scored what appeared to be a decisive knockdown in the seventh round but failed to retire to a neutral corner, as prescribed by the new regulations. The referee motioned Dempsey to the corner before beginning his count, which reached nine before Tunney regained his feet. At least fourteen seconds had gone by in what has become known as "the long count"; yet Tunney managed to finish the fight, and he was proclaimed the winner by the judges. Dempsey's fans, outraged at the result, felt cheated by the judges and by the rules which obviously supported middle-class values like self-control. They protested long and loudly to no avail (Gorn 1985). Tunney's middle-class lifestyle denied him any chance to gain heroic status among the working class. He retired from boxing and became a successful businessman, while Dempsey could transfer his fame into retirement. He was politically active, opened a New York restaurant, wrote books about his life, and enjoyed celebrity status for the rest of his years.

Not only boxers, but also other athletes represented their ethnic origin and/or social class and contributed to the inclusion of various groups in American society. Because baseball was the national sport, good baseball players could easily gain visibility and fame.

One of the most famous ethnic baseball players was a fleet-footed young Italian-American from San Francisco who assumed the mantle of stardom in the 1930s. A son of a fisherman, Joe DiMaggio (1914–1999) succeeded Babe Ruth on the New York Yankees baseball team, and his unique performances and records placed him among the best players of all times (see Chapters 3 and 4). His biography is presented as the typical hero story, the transformation from a nobody to a superstar. He was mythologized as a "gentleman" and he strengthened his status as an American hero by serving for three years in the Army Air Corps during World War II. His short marriage to Marilyn Monroe was the ultimate proof that he, and with him the Italian community, had arrived in American society (Cramer 2000).

Football and religion

Before World War I, numerous sport heroes represented specific groups of immigrants, especially the Irish, and broke the ground for their integration into mainstream society. At least as much as ethnicity, religion divided American society, and there was a clear "religious hierarchy" with regard to reputation and status with Protestantism at the top, and others such as Catholics and Jews at lower rungs of the social hierarchy. The hostility against Catholics was still virulent in the 1920s. Thus, in 1928, for example, a Catholic candidate for the US presidency was defeated largely on the basis of his religion. In the same way as ethnic communities, religious groups used sport as a means to demonstrate their prominence on the athletic fields and with this gained visibility and respect.

In the case of Knute Rockne and the rise of Notre Dame football, ethnicity, social class, and religion became intertwined (Davies 2007, 143ff.). After the turn of the century, football experienced a transformation from the province of elites to the area of working-class. By the 1920s Rockne declared that "western supremacy" (the supremacy of the teams of the midwest) in football "is a triumph of the middle class over the rich (the teams of the elite universities)" (Gems 2000, 113; Lester 1995, 121). Rockne contributed decisively to this change in the social placement of American football.

Knute Rockne learned the American sport forms as a Chicago youth. He played football and ran track at Notre Dame, a small Catholic college in Indiana that attracted working-class students. After graduation Rockne remained at the school and rose to the position of head coach of the football team in 1918. A brilliant coach, Rockne built the small institution into a national sport power over the next decade. He taught his players innovative techniques, developed new tactics, and incited his teams with impassioned pep talks to improbable victories. Rockne arranged a national schedule of games that saw his team travel from coast to coast in order to play large universities. These games and the exposure by the media brought numerous athletic recruits to Notre Dame who contributed to the further advancement of the team and the school. Rockne's success on the football ground, but also his affable personality and his excellent connections to the media, gained him lucrative endorsement contracts and widespread celebrity status which he also used to promote Notre Dame. He is regarded as one of the best college football coaches in American history (Sperber 1993; Phinizy 2006).

America's craze for statistics reveals Rockne's and Notre Dame's success story: he reached an "all-time winning percentage of 88.1%, still the best percentage in Division I-A. During 13 years as head coach, he oversaw 105 victories, 12 losses, 5 ties, and 6 national championships, including 5 undefeated seasons" (http://en.wikipedia.org/wiki/ Knute_Rockne# Notre_Dame_coach). The Notre Dame football team heralded the school as the champion of American Catholics, underdogs in Protestant America. Raised a Protestant, Rockne converted to Catholicism, which brought him additional sympathy with the Catholics. He died in a plane crash in 1931 during the production of the movie "The Spirit of Notre Dame". Almost a martyr to the cause, he has been sanctified by Notre Dame football fans. Notre Dame's success was seen as the symbol for the rise of Catholicism and the intrusion of Catholics into American sport and society. This caused distrust in and resistance of those who believed in the superiority of WASPs and wanted to maintain the existing social hierarchy.[5] Nativist groups objected to the encroachment of Catholics into American culture; and the Ku Klux Klan even organized marches of protest against the college.

Catholic high schools around the country adopted the Rockne strategies and challenged public schools, which they perceived as Protestant foes. In 1937 more than 120,000 fans attended the Chicago city championship game between a Catholic and public high school. That is the largest number of spectators who have ever attended a football game in the United States, including the Super Bowl (Gems 1996b).

Even more than Catholics, Jews were marginalized in American society because of religion and "race". They too used sport as a means to gain a measure of acceptance. In 1933 Jews comprised half of the boxing champions (Guttmann 2004, 123). By the 1930s Jews excelled in basketball, and Hank Greenberg, a Jewish star, emerged in baseball. Jewish

the cultural importance of sports heroes

athletes destroyed the myth of the feeble and degenerate Jews which they had brought with them to America. In the following periods Jewish boxers would be supplanted by Italian, African-American, and Hispanic athletes (Levine 1992).

NEIGHBORHOOD CELEBRITIES AND THE PROFESSIONALIZATION OF SPORT

Sport promised to provide men with some control over their lives, and for some, even a measure of wealth based on their physical prowess. The successful boxers and baseball players not only provided material for the making of heroes, but they also laid the foundation for the professionalization of sport, which began in the United States much earlier than in other parts of the world. At the end of the nineteenth century, boxers and baseball players in particular could earn considerable sums of prize money or salaries. Examples are John L. Sullivan, who won a $5,000 prize and another $1,000 in a side bet for his two-round victory over Paddy Ryan in 1882 (Rader 1990, 51), or Walter "Pudge" Heffelfinger, the first known professional American football player who got $500 for his services in one game in 1892 (Gems 1996a, 332).

Even semi-professional athletes, who held a full-time job during the week and played their games on evenings or weekends, earned substantial sums. Henry Penn, a local star on a Chicago team, turned down contract offers from four professional baseball teams in 1914 because he was already making more money than they offered him. Such players became local heroes, "objects of admiration and emulation" and role models for youth (Mandelbaum 2004, 11, 13). The importance of local celebrities should not be understated, because they maintained a belief in social mobility and meritocracy, and embodied the physicality of working-class culture. Physical prowess counted more than wealth or education, since the lower classes could expect little of either.

The confrontations between labor and capital reached their peak in the latter decades of the nineteenth century, as workers struck for greater rights, wages, and an eight-hour day. Local and federal politicians, often indebted to the rich and powerful, usually sided with the company owners, even providing police or military personnel to break the strikes. For immigrant and working-class children sport offered a way out of the ghetto and promised social advancement. Charles "Hoss" Radbourne, the son of immigrant parents, could not write, which made him of little value in the clerical world of the middle class, but as a star baseball pitcher he stated: "I get ten times the money I used to get for working sixteen hours swinging a twenty-five pound sledge by playing ball for two hours a day" (Holst 1988, 263). However, only few made it into the ranks of professional athletes (Riess 1984a, 293). Still, a host of ballplayers attested to the "easy" money in baseball compared to their previous jobs. Burleigh Grimes called it a "picnic" compared to farming, and work in the lumber and steel mills. Al Bridwell got $150 a year working in a shoe factory, but garnered $2,100 as a major leaguer with the Cincinnati Reds baseball team (Fox 1994, 106–109).

313

The belief in sport as a means to social mobility and the rise of working-class athletes to fame continued throughout the twentieth century. By the late twentieth century Sparky Anderson, a professional baseball team manager, declared:

> This game [baseball] has taken a lot of guys over the years, who would have had to work in factories and gas stations, and made them prominent people. I only had a high school education, and believe me, I had to cheat to get that. There isn't a college in the world that would have me. And yet in this business you can walk into a room with millionaires, doctors, professional people and get more attention than they get. I don't know any other business where you can do that.
>
> (quoted in Plaut 1993, 390)

Although pecuniary benefits often proved temporary in the "sport business," the physical feats of the athletes and their remembrance by devoted followers earned social capital that lasted a lifetime as sports fans debated (and still debate) the merits of newer generations of athletes compared to those of the past. Such memorials are consciously constructed and reconstructed in the commercialization of sports memorabilia and sports Halls of Fame that enshrine the sport stars and their deeds in the collective memories of Americans.

Whereas in the nineteenth century sport had served various groups as a primary means of identification, in the 1920s sports heroes gave visibility and prestige to ethnic, racial (see Chapter 10), and gender groups (see Chapter 11), previously stereotyped and caricatured as inferior in the mainstream and popular media. Heroes always instilled a sense of pride in the fans, who reveled in their victories. Now "ethnic" or working-class heroes gained more and more acceptance in society as a whole which contributed to the inclusion of a variety of social groups. In addition, the glorification of athletes – independent from their origins – reinforced the belief in sport as a meritocracy, where the chances are equal and where underdogs, such as Catholic or working-class teams, might defeat their supposedly socially superior opponents.

THE CONSTRUCTION OF HEROES

The role of the mass media

The 1920s was a period of urbanization when most Americans eschewed the farm for urban residency. Urban occupations, particularly those of the growing middle class, were often sedentary, and men with "white-collar jobs" did not live up to the ideals of traditional masculinity. In addition, all the land in the West had been settled by the end of the nineteenth century and the "loss of the frontier" removed an essential factor in the composition of American identity. Professor Frederic Paxson, a former student of "frontier theorist" Frederick Jackson Turner, proclaimed sport to be the new frontier in 1917, which might serve as an antidote to urban ills (Riess 1995, 179–180).

Sport heroes gained a new status and a previously unthinkable popularity owing to the alliance between sport and mass media. Sportswriter Paul Gallico characterized the 1920s as follows:

> Never before had there been a period when, from the ranks of every sport, arose some glamorous, unbeatable figure who shattered record after record, spread eagled his field and drew into the box office an apparently unending stream of gold and silver. We had lived through a decade of deathless heroes.
>
> (quoted in Davies 2007, 162)

Gallico described his own writing as superficial and uncritical, "spinning a daily tale in the most florid and exciting prose . . . part of the great ballyhoo . . . swallower of my own bait" (quoted in Davies 2007, 163). Whereas in former periods the newspaper and magazines had presented a reflective analysis and narrative accounts of sporting events and athletes (as well as a vicarious experience of masculinity (Reel 2006, 35)) after the occurrence of the event, the new technologies of the 1920s changed the form of sport coverage dramatically. Radio allowed for the instantaneous transmission of information by sports broadcasters who provided often embellished and dramatic accounts of sports contests and the athletes that participated in them. Movies, too, provided scripted and edited portrayals of athletes that fashioned public opinions, creating new sports heroes (or villains) that might appeal to various segments of the population.

> The twenties ushered in a brave new public world, a more homogenized, consumption-oriented culture, the "Golden Age" of American sport. In this emerging mass society, public relations experts and publicity agents, reporters and promoters, hustlers and go-betweens all looked to promote and profit by sports heroes.
>
> (Gorn and Goldstein 1993, 195)

The reporting of sport began to assume an entertainment function that moved beyond journalism as provision of information. The characters in the various sports dramas assumed heroic or villainous roles often representing social, ethnic, racial, religious, or gender groups.

The 1920s produced a multitude of athletic heroes, some of whom have been already presented in the sections above. Their performances, marked by remarkable production, characterized a new industrial age which conferred its values and characteristics as well its technologies to the world of top-level sport. In addition, as described above, heroes emerged in new types of sport such as football, flying, and swimming, but also in golf, track and field or tennis, and seemed to transcend many of the social divisions within American society.

The biographies, achievements, personalities, and images of the sport stars, as well as the way they presented themselves and were presented by the media, varied considerably.

They depended among other things on the type of sport. The most popular sport was baseball, followed by American football. In these sports, excellent athletes could easily gain celebrity status.

Baseball heroes

Baseball is a sport in which each activity and the success of every single player can be systematically registered and evaluated. This allows for a comparison of the players beyond place and time, and makes baseball thrilling and fascinating for the fans (see Chapter 4).

Baseball requires both teamwork and individualism, as the batter has to demonstrate his individual hitting skills. Many baseball fans consider the ability to hit a pitched (thrown) ball, which may travel at varying speeds of up to 100 miles per hour (160.93 kilometers per hour), and to curve, drop, or float unpredictably, to be the most difficult task in all of sport. Excellent batters, such as Babe Ruth, have often become heroes; however, their fame was sometimes short-lived when other players broke their records (e.g. in home runs or batting percentages). An average batter hits the ball about 25 percent of the times at bat, a star over 30 percent. Ruth's career batting percentage (hits per chances) of .342 (he got a hit more than 34 percent of the time while batting during his career) placed him among the all-time leaders in that category as well as in home runs (see Chapter 4).

Joe DiMaggio followed Babe Ruth as star player of the New York Yankees, where his performances gained fame and fortune (see Chapters 3 and 4). He played centerfield (the central position of the outfield, requiring speed and a strong throwing arm) with great versatility. Writer Donald Honig described the role of the centerfielder as follows. "It is an unwritten decree that when the centerfielder calls for the ball, all others cease pursuit . . . No other player has so imperative a mandate. He is a player whose boundaries are defined solely by his speed and daring" (quoted in Plaut 1993, 95). DiMaggio could run, catch, and throw effectively; but he won most acclaim with his bat. Like Ruth, he could hit for power (so far that the ball landed outside the field) and batting average (the percentage of hits per times at bat). The Yankees won ten league championships and nine World Series titles in the thirteen seasons (1936–1951) that DiMaggio played for the team.[6]

In the 1941 season he hit successfully at least one time in fifty-six consecutive games, a record that has never been approached. When the streak finally ended due to two outstanding plays by an opponent he embarked on another streak of sixteen games with at least one hit (Davies 2007, 184, 187). DiMaggio took his status as a role model seriously, stating: "There is always some kid who may be seeing me for the first or last time. I owe him my best" (Plaut 1993, 58).[7] DiMaggio was not the only athlete who rose from working class to celebrity; but his amazing productivity in an age that admired efficiency, production, and quantification as well as his humility endeared him to Americans (Cramer 2000).

Figure 12.2 Joe DiMaggio with Marilyn Monroe (Library of Congress)

the cultural importance of sports heroes

The 1941 baseball season produced another legendary feat by Ted Williams, an outfielder for the Boston Red Sox, arch rivals of the New York Yankees in the American League. Williams possessed exceptional eyesight and the ability to hit a baseball consistently. Like Ruth and DiMaggio he could hit the ball very far and he was consistent in hitting. His lifetime percentage of .344 (hits per chances) even surpassed that of Ruth. Few possessed his confidence or his brashness, which led to a love-hate relationship with the Boston fans and sports writers; but none could deny Williams' abilities. While DiMaggio hit the ball successfully in numerous consecutive games, Williams hit it more consistently throughout the entire season, a feat which gained him admiration and fame among the baseball fans. On the final day of the 1941 season Williams' batting average stood at .39955 (hits per attempt). The official scorers would have rounded off the figure to an even .400, a mark achieved by only a small handful in baseball history; but Williams chose not to accept the easy way out. Boston was scheduled to play a doubleheader (two consecutive games against an opponent on one day) on that final date, and the team manager offered to let Williams sit out the two games to preserve his record. Williams, a proud man, refused the choice as a dishonorable way to achieve the mark. He played in both games, batting eight times, and hitting safely six times, raising his season average to .406. Such a display appealed to the American sense of honor and fair play. No player has ever approached .400 since that time and Williams is placed among the leaders in most statistical categories (Whitley 2007). Like DiMaggio, Williams entered the military service as a pilot in World War II, and flew combat missions again in the Korean War. Despite his problems with the Boston fans most Americans admired Williams' sense of nationalism, patriotism, and dedication to the country in times of war, as well as his astounding pride, his physical abilities, and his performances.

Football heroes

In the 1920s the media spotlights moved beyond New England and New York, the former strongholds of the game, to create national football heroes. Harold "Red" Grange garnered national attention as a collegiate football player well before he entered the professional ranks. A sportswriter dubbed him "the galloping ghost" for his elusive running style. Grange's handsome appearance combined with a modest demeanor and abstemious personal habits (he neither drank alcohol nor smoked cigarettes) made him "everybody's darling" and, according to the media, a perfect role model for American youth. He represented traditional virtues in the Roaring Twenties, a period of excess marked by libertine attitudes that espoused drinking, dancing, smoking, and sexual freedom.

Grange had already attained All-American status; but surpassed his own legendary exploits on October 18, 1924. Grange played for the University of Illinois team and on that fateful day Illinois faced an arch rival, the University of Michigan, which had not lost a game over the previous three years. Moreover, it was to be the first game to inaugurate Illinois' new Memorial Stadium, which honored the school's students who had sacrificed their lives during World War I. A multitude of 67,000 filled the stadium seats and its adjoining walls for the occasion. Grange took the opening kickoff 95 yards for a touchdown and then proceeded to score three more times on runs of 67, 56, and 44 yards – all in the first twelve minutes of play! He returned in the second half of the game to score on yet another run and passed for a sixth touchdown (Davies 2007, 140). For those who may not be familiar with football and might have difficulty grasping the enormity of such a display, an equivalent example might be if Cristiano Ronaldo had scored four goals in the first twelve minutes against Arsenal, then added a fifth and an assist in the second half for good measure, all on the Queen's birthday as a party gift.

Grange tarnished his image as the perfect athlete by turning professional after his last college game. At that time the world of professional football held little esteem and the upper classes still considered it a business for gamblers, crooks, and other undesirables. However, the popularization of Grange was spurred on by sport journalists like Grantland Rice, who presented his heroic deeds to an estimated sixty million movie goers (Andrews and Jackson 2001, 6). He was one of the "compensatory heroes" who helped to distract the people's attention from the social problems of the time.

Upper classes, amateurs, and contested heroes

Some middle- and upper-class families still adhered to British notions of gentility and social class into the twentieth century, including the ideal of the amateur athlete, who competed in sport for the love of the game rather than for private gain.

Upper-class athletes, such as Bill Tilden, who ruled the tennis courts during the first half of the 1920s, and Bobby Jones, who dominated golf throughout the decade, appealed to the traditionalists, those who still cherished the ideals of the amateur gentleman. The working class found it difficult to identify with people so unlike themselves as heroes. People like Tilden and Jones lived in large homes, owned cars, and had money and leisure time to pursue their hobbies, among other things their sport.

In addition, sports like tennis and golf that lacked the physical contact of team sports seemed effeminate to the workers. George Lott achieved international stature as a tennis star; but lost the favor of his childhood friends, who considered his sport to be less manly than boxing, baseball, or football (Gems 1997, 159).

Big Bill Tilden dominated men's tennis between 1920 and 1930. Among his successes were three Wimbledon titles and seven victories in the US Open. He ranked in fifth place on the list of winners of Grand Slam titles (all-time), and second place when only the titles in singles are taken into account. He refused to play mixed doubles because women allegedly "emasculate genius." He was an excellent all-around player with great tactical skills, high self-esteem, convinced about his abilities, a controversial figure, arrogant, and flamboyant, who used the tennis court as his stage (Davies 2007, 167).

> For him, tennis was more than just a sport. "It's an art like the ballet, or like a performance in the theatre. When I step on court, I feel like Anna Pavlova. Or like Adelina Patti. Or even like Sarah Bernhardt. I see the footlights in front of me. I hear the whispering of the audience. I feel an icy shudder. Win or die! Now or never! It's the crisis of my life".
>
> (http://quotationsbook.com/quote/38641)

As an amateur, Tilden earned and spent large sums of money. But he was also a tragic figure, a hero who was knocked off his pedestal. In a time when homosexuality was looked upon as a sin, a deformity, and being gay and an athlete was an irresolvable conflict, his sexual orientation made him an outsider. "In the policing of sporting masculinity, no feminization, no public sentimentality, and of course, as tennis player Bill Tilden found out to his cost, not the slightest hint of camp or male desire for another man can be tolerated" (Whannel 2002, 92). In 1930 he turned professional, and his sexual orientation became an open secret. In 1946 and in 1949 he was arrested and convicted for sexual acts with boys. He served several months in prison ignored by the tennis circle, excluded from tennis places, and treated as an outcast. He died at the age of 60 of a heart attack, destitute and forgotten.

320

In contrast to Tilden, Jones was the ideal of the amateur gentleman (Lowe 2002). Bobby Jones (1902–1971) was born into a successful southern family but experienced a sickly childhood. Access to a local country club enabled him to engage in an outdoor physical activity that improved not only his health but his talent. By the age of 9 he had won a local golf tournament and was soon acknowledged as a golf prodigy. Well educated and a practicing lawyer, Jones maintained a purely amateur standing until he retired from competition in 1930.

Although not physically imposing at 5′ 7″ (1.70 meters) and 165 pounds (74.84 kg) he possessed a handsome appearance, charm, and a modest personality despite his immense achievements. Jones overcame a petulant manner that caused him to throw his clubs after a poor shot, eventually displaying the ultimate sportsmanlike behavior. He often penalized himself for rule infractions, and did so in the 1925 US Open, which cost him the championship that year. Despite that loss, Jones dominated golf during the period, winning the US Open Championship four times (1923, 1926, 1929, 1930), the US Amateur championship five times (1924, 1925, 1927, 1928, 1930), the British Open three times (1926, 1927, 1930), and the British Amateur Championship in 1930. His victory in all four major events in 1930 is considered the first Grand Slam in golf history. He won 62 percent of the competitions he entered.

Jones retired from competitive golf after 1930. He authored instructional golf books, and endorsed golf products thereafter. True to his heroic image, Jones enlisted in the US Army during World War II, serving as an intelligence officer. In 1948 he suffered a crippling spinal disease that eventually claimed his life in 1971 (Lowe 2002). In 2004 a movie was made about Bobby Jones, the golf legend.

Athletes and their fight against racism had gained fame and were revered as heroes – at least for some time – as early as 1912. The 1912 Olympic team included the Native American Jim Thorpe, who won both the pentathlon and decathlon (Newcombe 1975). The Swedish King, rewarding him with his prize, addressed him as the greatest athlete in the world. When he returned to the USA he was heralded as a hero, and received with a parade on Broadway.

An Olympic teammate, the Hawaiian Duke Kahanamoku, won a gold medal as a swimmer in 1912, adding several other gold medals in subsequent Olympic Games (Nendel 2004). The inclusion of Kahanamoku and Thorpe on the American team allowed American journalists to extol the liberty, democracy, and equality of the American republic.

Kahanamoku, bronze-skinned, muscular, and good-looking, was a bridge between two worlds. "He is alternatively characterized as a noble representative of a vanquished race, a dark skinned inferior, an American representative from Hawai'i and a symbol of the American melting pot" (Nendel 2004, 33). A Hollywood actor and Hawaiian folk hero, a lifeguard, and sheriff, he popularized the traditional Hawaiian sport of surfing and was granted "whiteness," or acceptable status within the white mainstream society.

This was not the case with Thorpe. When it was discovered that Thorpe had earned small sums of money playing baseball, his medals were revoked and his name disparaged. He became a professional football player and continued to play sport, but he had to endure discrimination and racism, among other things, when the media presented him as a "Redskin" and emphasized his "Indianness," thus marginalizing his performances. Native Americans were not considered full citizens and were granted the right to vote as late as 1954. He ended his sporting career at the age of 41, and had to struggle to earn enough money to survive. He died in 1953, according to his third wife, with "nothing but his name and his memories" (http://en.wikipedia.org/wiki/Jim_Thorpe).

BOX 12.7 JIM THORPE AS PLACE OF REMEMBRANCE

During the emergence of racial pride in the 1960s and thereafter, non-white athletic heroes were remembered, treated as icons, and given a place in America's collective memory. In Thorpe's case, two neighboring Pennsylvania towns to which he had no previous affiliation bought his body from his widow, then merged and renamed the combined location "Jim Thorpe" in his honor in 1957. They memorialized his burial site as a place of remembrance and a tourist attraction. Many other honors were later bestowed on Jim Thorpe reaching from his induction in the Pro Football Hall of Fame to the nomination as America's Athlete of the Century by the United States House of Representatives. In October 1992, even the IOC decided on the rehabilitation of Jim Thorpe, returning his honor to his family.

(Gerald Gems)

The vaunted American equality did not extend to African-Americans. When Jack Johnson (Chapter 10) won the heavyweight boxing championship in 1908 it provoked a national search for the "Great White Hope" who might return the laurels in real and symbolic meaning to the WASPs who claimed superiority in all areas. According to Social Darwinism, one of the most popular theories of the time, competition was the driving force of evolution, which was based on the survival of the fittest. And who presents better the "crown of creation" than the man who is able to beat all opponents in a boxing match? That the African-American Johnson wore this "crown" caused major problems for many white Americans. Johnson was a notorious celebrity and represented a hero to the poor and downtrodden blacks, especially because he stood up to white transgressions against and the disrespect of blacks. In the moment of his victory over Jim Jeffries, "symbolically millions of African Americans stood beside him" (quoted in Davies 2007, 199). It was claimed that a boxing ring was the only venue in which a black man might hit a white man without going to jail or risk being lynched. For most whites and many aspiring blacks, however, Johnson was anathema. Black clergy and the white bourgeoisie decried his unconventional lifestyle,

the cultural importance of sports heroes

his arrogance, and his defiant behavior. Breaking taboos and claiming privileges of whites challenged white hegemony (Roberts 1983).

It would be another generation before African-American athletes were accorded the opportunities for heroism. In the 1930s Joe Louis, the son of Alabama sharecroppers, emerged as America's best boxer who knocked out the German Max Schmeling in 1938 (p. 238). Louis and Jesse Owens, gold medal winner at the Olympic Games of 1936 (p. 239) seemed to prove that America was a democracy which provided equal rights and opportunities to its citizens and, thus, a blessed country superior to other nations. The African-Americans' performances, especially when competing against German athletes in a symbolic battle with fascism, were acclaimed, at least as long as the athletes were successful. Louis and Owens adapted to the expectations of white audiences and acted accordingly, i.e. with humility. They gained acceptance by minimizing their blackness. "The perception of Louis held by whites changed . . . At first he was viewed through the prism of well established racial stereotypes . . . when he met Schmeling again in 1938, he carried with him the hopes and prayers of white America" (Davies 2007, 207). But both were treated with disdain when their usefulness expired.

When African-Americans increasingly questioned the "war for democracy" (World War II) as one which failed to deliver basic liberties to them, a new hero emerged in Jackie Robinson, who satisfied the requirements for heroism among both blacks and whites (Chapter 10). His stoic persistence in the face of racism, overcoming the social obstacles of segregation of the races, and displaying an individual brilliance on the athletic field won widespread admiration and at least a grudging respect by virtually all baseball fans (Davies 2007, 210ff.).

SPORTS HEROES IN HARD TIMES

The Great Depression, after the crash of the stock market and the collapse of the economy in 1929, had changed American life: loss of savings and investments, high rates of unemployment, shattered dreams, and uncertain futures led to massive political protests and to a "somber and frightened mood" among the population. Sport journalists and fans found out that even the greatest sport events were only "the playing of games . . . In such depressing times, it was difficult to get excited about a new home-run slugger" (Davies 2007, 176). However, heroes such as Joe Louis attracted huge media attention; his race, his fight against Aryan supremacy, and his successes guaranteed a high amount of public attention. His enlistment in the US Army added to his popularity. This was also the case with other sport stars who demonstrated patriotism by participating in World War II.

During the 1950s, the United States was engaged in a Cold War with the Soviet Union and its allies. As the space technology of the Soviet Union equaled and, at times, surpassed that of the United States, Americans worried about their ability to win a potential nuclear war and sustain their way of life.

BOX 12.8 SPORT AS AN ARENA FOR HEROISM

In a world where religious, military, and political leaders are often contested, top-level sport provides an ideal arena for the production of heroes because sport highly valued and athletes are not involved in problematic decisions and developments with potentially negative consequences for the society, as for example politicians. Sport heroes represent the world of fun and entertainment, they deliver easily comprehensible top performances, and they and their deeds are real and authentic. Sport with its competition and record orientation provides suspense, creates numerous dramatic situations and offers opportunities for identification. In addition, the alliance between the sport and the media systems offers a stage for (self)presentation and guarantees visibility. Sport heroes are a specific category of prominence: They are conspicuous by physical and psychological capacities as well as by spectacular performances and skills, which they have acquired by many years of hard work. Thus they represent meritocracy, the legitimization of modern societies. They distinguish themselves from those celebrities whose reputation is based on their willingness to make her private life a public affair.

(Gertrud Pfister, see Bette 2007)

Sports promised to provide a diversion from worries and preoccupations with political tensions. Boxing was an especially powerful "opiate" because the fights could be easily imagined as substitute wars. Successful boxers like Rocky Marciano could fuel the American dream of superiority. His performance as heavyweight world champion reassured Americans of their values and their prowess in a time when the dominance of the US was threatened. The son of a Italian shoemaker, Marciano was born into poverty and sought comfort in sports, playing American football and baseball. He learned to box as a soldier during World War II. After a failed tryout in professional baseball, he turned to boxing as a profession. Although undersized for a heavyweight, Marciano possessed endurance, toughness, and a devastating punch. He battled his way through the heavyweight ranks, winning the championship in 1952. He held the title until his retirement four years later, compiling an undefeated record of 49–0, with 43 victories by knockout (http://www.rocky marciano.net/about/achievements.htm). His fortitude, courage, ability to overcome impending defeat, and humility in victory were the attributes that Americans identified with and perceived as typically American. Therefore they granted (and grant) sport stars with those characteristics heroic status (Sullivan 2002).

For many years the African-American press and some liberal white sports writers had called for the inclusion of black athletes in sports, especially professional baseball. The emergence of a multitude of African-American stars in the professional baseball, football, and basketball ranks seemed to indicate that the United States had finally achieved true equality for all of its citizens in the 1950s. That notion changed abruptly with the rise of Muhammad Ali in the following decade (Chapter 10).

THE EMERGENCE OF HEROINES

The primary American games of baseball, football, and basketball had dominated the sporting culture for a century, becoming firmly entrenched as masculine activities. The popularity of these ball games with the media and the fans was transmitted to the players who could quite easily become stars if they showed excellent performances. Heroism in sport was based on characteristics such as strength, endurance, aggressiveness, and courage which were defined as male, and being a hero meant to embody and to enact masculinity. Until the 1970s, few women participated in the popular sports (at least not on the intercollegiate and professional levels); thus they had much less opportunity than men to gain visibility and fame. In addition, the prerequisites of sporting success, namely strong bodies and tough minds, augmented men's and diminished women's chances to become stars because these qualities were considered, at least until the end of the twentieth century, as unfeminine.

Female athletes such as Gertrude Ederle, the first woman to swim the English channel, tennis star Helen Wills, or multi-sport star Babe Didrikson had won acclaim and were glorified as heroines – at least for some time. However, their glory was always overshadowed by the fame of male stars. After a short time in the limelight, Ederle led a long and lonely life, forgotten by most Americans (Davies 2007, 168).

For a long time, the success of female athletes had little effect in changing the gender order, not the least because most of them did not, at least not actively, support the women's movement. Billie Jean King is the exception; she became a sports heroine because of her success in tennis, but also because of her dedication to women's emancipation on and off the tennis court. Her accomplishments (among others her victory over a male player, described in Chapter 11), occurred during the period of athletic rebellion (1960s–1970s); but her legacy continues to grow. King established the Women's Sports Foundation in 1974, which promotes sports and physical activity for females and advocates initiatives for gender equality (http://www.womenssportsfoundation.org/cgi-bin/iowa/index.html). King's significance has endured and even increased in retrospective. The United States Tennis Association recognized King's impact on women's tennis and did not accept a large amount of corporate money to name its major New York facility after a company; instead it named it after Billie Jean King (Smith 2006). King's legacy continues in her activism and that of the Women's Sports Foundation, among other matters, over the still contentious issue of Title IX.

Currently, strong and successful female athletes such as soccer player Mia Hamm or Venus and Serena Williams are cultural icons, at least among women (Heywood and Dworking

Figure 12.3 Billie Jean King (Library of Congress)

the cultural importance of sports heroes

2003). The Williams sisters and other female tennis players get the most public attention in the United States, but this does not make them into heroes of the nation. It would need a change in media politics (and in the taste of American audiences) to bring women into the limelight and into the collective memory of the Americans.

COACHES AS AUTHORITARIAN HEROES

The sporting careers of athletes are relatively short, depending on the type of sport; they often last for less than ten years, and only few sport stars with outstanding achievements become heroes with lifelong glory. The addiction to quantification, evaluation, and analysis of sporting performances brought some athletes such as Babe Ruth or "Red" Grange eternal fame, but the baseball or football statistics, and the public memory, pushed athletes back onto the second row of stardom, when new stars emerged who broke their records.

In contrast to the athletes, coaches have much longer careers, and they were and are legendary figures in the American culture. This is especially true for football coaches, because it is the coach who decides about the tactics and thus about the success in American football.

The series of famous coaches started with Walter Camp (1859–1925), the father of American football, who is still considered as one of the most accomplished persons in this sport (Chapter 5). He was Yale's first football coach, but contributed even more to football by working all his adult life on the football rules committee. He shaped the game that became the most popular American sport and he propagated football in numerous books and articles.

Knute Rockne became the coach of Notre Dame in 1918, and supplanted Walter Camp as the sport's greatest figure. Rockne's rise from immigrant, working-class roots to fame and fortune personified the American Dream held by the lower classes (p. 311).

As described above, Rockne became a new type of hero that represented ethnic class and religious groups, but he was also an icon of the American mainstream population. In addition, he was a new type of coach. One historian stated that he "demonstrated that the big-time college football coach had drifted from the company of professors . . . The activities of recruiting, promoting, and public speaking, along with the lures of endorsements, indicated that by the 1930s the role of the big-time college coach had evolved very differently from that of the university faculty" (Davies 2007, 147).

Two other football coaches, Vince Lombardi (1913–1970) in the professional league, and Paul "Bear" Bryant (1913–1983) in collegiate football, have top positions in the hierarchy of American heroes. Both reached the peaks of their careers in the 1960s, in a time when young people protested against the conservatism of the 1950s, developed a subcultural lifestyle, joined the hippie movement, and changed the cultural fabric of American life.

A school without football is in danger of deteriorating into a medieval study hall.

Winning isn't everything, it's the only thing.

Winning is not everything, but wanting to win is.

Winning is not a sometime thing; it's an all time thing. You don't win once in a while, you don't do things right once in a while, you do them right all the time. Winning is habit. Unfortunately, so is losing.

Perfection is not attainable, but if we chase perfection we can catch excellence.

Football is like life – it requires perseverance, self-denial, hard work, sacrifice, dedication and respect for authority.

If you can accept losing you can't win. If you can walk you can run. No one is ever hurt. Hurt is in your mind.

The difference between a successful person and others is not a lack of strength, not a lack of knowledge, but rather a lack of will.

(http://www.brainyquote.com/quotes/
quotes/v/vincelomba127517.html)

Against the spirit of the age, both coaches exerted an authoritarian leadership style. The declaration that "winning isn't everything, it's the only thing!" is often attributed to Lombardi; it captures the spirit of the traditionalists who believed in discipline, hard work, and determination as the core of American success. Lombardi's Green Bay Packers represented distinct underdogs in American society as the only small town team, a remnant of the early days of the NFL, which had to compete against the teams of major cities within the United States. Yet Lombardi's teams, spurred on by his indomitable leadership, won five NFL championships due to the military precision of the play of the team and the unquestionable authority of the coach. In Green Bay, Lombardi is still revered as a demi-god, and a street is named in his honor.

Similarly, Coach "Bear" Bryant, another authoritarian coach and a symbol of strength and righteousness, produced a legendary record at the collegiate level at the University of

Alabama (Davies 2007, 258ff.). Beginning in 1959, his teams played in twenty-four consecutive bowl games, which means that they had been among the best teams of the season for twenty-four consecutive years. Six of those teams won national championships. Bryant's success was due to the aid of the university board of trustees and a very generous booster club. Although Alabama was poor and ranked among the lowest states in expenditures for education, Bryant had excellent facilities, and he stockpiled athletic talent with 125 football players who had athletic scholarships and dozens of "walk-ons" (non-scholarship players). The coaching staff numbered seventeen assistants, not including numerous graduate assistants, who served apprenticeships (Davies 2007, 262).

Alabama, located in the deep South and, in the nineteenth century, the heart of the slave-holding Confederacy, was still mired in the lost cause of the Civil War and still practiced racial segregation. "The southern legacy of poverty, defeat and outsider status within the larger American polity left the state with a powerful longing for a symbol for success and virility. There is abundant evidence that the University of Alabama football team had pleased this symbolic role" (Doyle 1996, 72). Alabamians understood Bryant's all-white teams, and their successes, as a source of collective pride and a justification of white supremacy. They revered Bryant as a demi-god and cultural icon because he seemed to restore the honor and self-respect of Southerners. After a significant loss to a University of Southern California team with outstanding black athletes, however, Bryant led the South in the recruitment of African-American athletes, who greatly aided the Alabama quest for respect and national glory. When Bryant retired in 1982 he had amassed a record with 323 victories, the most by any coach at the Division I level, and the NCAA named its Coach of the Year trophy after him upon his death in 1983 (Davies 2007, 263).

THE CONTENTIOUS ROLE OF SPORTS HEROES FROM THE 1960S TO TODAY

Today cultural relativism, the collapse of authority, and the crisis of masculinity continue to stress American society. Heroes in other areas have lost credibility during the fragmentation of modern society (see also Bette 2007). Sport, too, lost its innocence (which it never had), due to cheating, doping, and corruption.

Americans began to question the idealistic perceptions of sport and its practitioners in the 1960s. Journalists revealed the human faults, such as gambling, drinking, whoring, wife sharing, drugs, and the sexual harassment of some of the top athletes who had previously been considered as role models. A number of athletes openly challenged the bureaucratic and authoritarian systems of ownership and governance in top-level sports that limited their personal freedom to sell their abilities and increase their salaries.

While the excesses of athletes reduced their prestige among the mainstream, their perception as rebels enhanced their heroic stature among particular groups, especially young people, who opposed the dominant ideologies and policies. However, in the struggles against traditional values and practices athletic heroes lost much of their exalted status, falling to mere celebrities whose larger salaries distanced them from their fans, who could no longer identify with them.

The conflicts in the athletic world reflected the larger conflicts in American society which started with the anti-communist pursuits in the McCarthy area, followed by the movement against the Viet Nam war and the struggle of African-Americans for civil rights and racial equality represented by Martin Luther King and Malcolm X. Black athletes, too, protested against discrimination, speaking out on their own behalf, but also supporting the case of their race (see Chapter 10). The black athletic revolt peaked in 1968 with the black power demonstration at the Olympic Games.[8]

Symbol and protagonist of the fight of African-American athletes for justice, equality, and inclusion was and is Cassius Clay who became Muhammad Ali. Ali's story is the narrative of a metamorphosis: the rise, the fall, and the catharsis (Zang 2001, 96–118). Ali's crusade as an athlete and as a leader of the Civil Rights Movement made it apparent that African-Americans in general, even professional athletes, suffered discrimination. In addition, black activists made clear that the success of the athletes did not improve the fortunes of the vast majority of non-whites in America. Like Jack Johnson, Ali fractured American society along racial lines and within the African-American community. Ultimately he reached acceptance as an American hero, when he was chosen to light the Olympic flame at Atlanta in 1996. By that time a historical perspective enabled Americans to recognize his stance for the basic principles of freedom and his willingness to sacrifice personal gain for a greater good. Ali's example illustrates how heroes change images, how they are continuously re-enacted, and how their mythologies are permanently rewritten.

BOX 12.10 MUHAMMAD ALI

In a secular, yet pseudo-religious and sentimental nation like the United States, it is quite natural that sports stars emerge as "heroes" – "legends" – "icons." Who else? George Santayana described religion as "another world to live in" and no world is so set off from the disorganization and disenchantment of the quotidian than the world, or worlds, of sports. Hauser describes, in considerable detail, the transformation of the birth of Ali out of the unexpectedly stubborn and idealistic will of young Cassius Clay: how, immediately following his first victory over Liston, he declared himself a convert to the Nation of Islam (more popularly known as the Black Muslims) and "no longer a Christian." He repudiated his "slave name" of Cassius Marcellus Clay to become Muhammad Ali (a name which, incidentally, the New York Times, among other censorious white publications, would not

---

honor through the 1960s). Ali became, virtually overnight, a spokesman for black America as no other athlete, certainly not the purposefully reticent Joe Louis, had ever done – "I don't have to be what you want me to be," he told white America. "I'm free to be me." Two years later, refusing to be inducted into the army to fight in Viet Nam, Ali, beleaguered by reporters, uttered one of the memorable incendiary remarks of that era: "Man, I ain't got no quarrel with them Vietcong."

(Joyce Carol Oates, "The Cruelest Sport"
(http://web.usfca.edu/~southerr/boxing/cruelest.html))

The athletic revolution brought greater numbers of African-Americans into the top levels of sport which spawned a "black style" of improvisational play in both football and, especially, basketball (see Chapter 10). Since the 1980s, hip-hop culture intruded upon the NBA with its distinctive styles of dress, tattooed bodies, and inner city image. This produced different types of heroes, who appeal to different groups of audiences. These types include the "thug," a gangster who reflects the harsh conditions of the tough, urban life and who appealed to black inner city youth and a growing number of white suburban emulators.

In basketball, Allen Iverson, whose abilities and successes as a player are undoubted, effected such an image. Iverson was several times arrested by the police, among other things, for possession of drugs, death threats to his cousin, and urinating in public. A distinct feature and seemingly a part of the enactment of "bad guys" is male chauvinism. Several athletes were accused of sexual harassment or even rape. As the case of Kobe Bryant shows, this does not necessarily destroy a career, since Bryant won the Most Valuable Player award[9] in 2008 despite an earlier indictment for rape (Smith and Hattery 2006).

BOX 12.11 PATERNITY: NO LAUGHING MATTER

Lance Briggs, linebacker of the Chicago Bears, "ought to be hit with personal foul for irresponsible babymaking" (three daughters with three different women). "This after totaling his $400,000 Lamborghini at 3 a.m. last September on the Edens Expy, then fleeing the crash scene for unspecified but oh-so-suspicious reasons. This after pleading guilty to leaving the scene and not reporting the accident and being ordered to serve 120 hours of community service, only to admit recently that he had served only two hours."

(*Chicago Sun-Times*, May 18, 2008, 74A)

the cultural importance of sports heroes

Players enacting underclass or black images during the game are at odds with the image of whiteness and correctness preferred by the owners of professional leagues. White media and league bureaucrats decried the language, dress, appearance (such as corn rows, a distinctive black hairstyle, baggy jeans, or Timberland boots), and deportment of the new breed of black players. Both the NFL and NBA enacted regulations which dictated dress, appearance, and conduct more suitable to their tastes and that of their largely white, middle-class audiences and corporate sponsors (see Chapter 10).

Michael Jordan represented the antidote to drugs, crime, and violence as television advertisements urged American youth to "be like Mike." Jordan merged hero and celebrity and his image was celebrated on a global scale, skillfully marketed by multinational corporations to achieve the greatest profit. Jordan's socially constructed and idealized persona combined reality and illusion, attributing personal and generic American values of perseverance, work ethic, discipline, and intensity to Jordan who led the Chicago Bulls to six NBA championships, was awarded five Most Valuable Player awards, and won ten NBA scoring championships and two Olympic gold medals (Andrews 2001, xiii). Jordan is one of the most marketed athletes in history, being the spokesman for a large number of brands, among others Nike, McDonald's, and Coca Cola, and he earned several hundred million dollars with endorsements. He contributed decisively to the global consumption of American products (Andrews and Jackson 2001, 20, 272–276). Jordan gained hero status beyond the confines of American culture; but the "Jordan myth" had specific, unintended ramifications in the United States, as a multitude of youths abandoned education as a goal, with the unrealistic expectation that they could "be like Mike" (a song in a Gatorade advertisement) and become the next NBA and global superstar.

Golfer Tiger Woods (Chapter 10) succeeded Jordan with a similar image, embodying American perceptions of the US as a country of work ethic, discipline, morality, social mobility, and equal opportunity. Woods also represented the racial pluralism that American society had featured in the last decades, but struggled to manage and accept (Cole and Andrews 2001). Woods' pre-eminence suggests that the United States has finally conquered its racial problems; but like athletes in former times such as Joe Louis or Jesse Owens, both Jordan and Woods must still fit the dominant white standards of acceptability. While both may be judged as sport and corporate superstars who forged new economic opportunities for athletes of color, neither has aimed at or effected the societal changes of Muhammad Ali (see Chapter 10).

American sporting culture has proved to be inclusive of a variety of divergent groups represented by their heroes reasserting the belief in cultural and regional pluralism. NASCAR represents the South. It is the fastest growing sport in America, and has spread well beyond its southern rural roots, but continues to embrace evangelical religion and traditional values (see Chapter 13). NASCAR has its heroes which stand for these values, the most famous being Dale Earnhardt. A North Carolina farmer, Earnhardt earned the nickname "The Intimidator" for his aggressive driving style, which won him seven championships on the racing circuit and a total of seventy-six victories (http://en.wikipedia.org/wiki/Dale_ Earnhardt). In 2001, Earnhardt was killed in a crash at the prestigious Daytona 500 race, and he has been commemorated in films, songs, articles, and even a novel. Fans rationalize Earnhardt's death by placing a decal on their autos with Earnhardt's car number 3 enfolded in an angel's wings and bearing the inscription "God needed a driver."

INSTEAD OF A CONCLUSION: HEROES AND PLACES OF REMEMBRANCE

The history of American heroes mirrors the respective social situations, the needs and aspirations, but also the struggles for power and the conflicting norms and ideals in American society. Heroic soldiers, cowboys, and politicians were joined by sportsmen (later women) who represented the nation or various ethnicities, classes, races, and both genders. Athletic success caused identification and facilitated inclusion in mainstream society. Not only the feats of athletes but the timing of their occurrence was important in the construction of heroes. In periods of insecurities and conflicts such as the Depression or the "Cold War," heroes seemed to be used for diversion and/or self-assurance. Both DiMaggio's and Williams' achievements took place on the eve of America's entry into World War II.

A characteristic of heroes is their long-lasting fame and their embeddedness in popular culture and collective memories. Heroes are the material of political myths and they are embodied in "places of remembrance" which celebrate the past, but are relevant in the present circumstances. The heroization of sport stars fueled a specific memory culture which combines hero-worship with business (see Introduction).

In the United States professional sports leagues and teams, as well as intercollegiate teams and sport associations, towns, and cities have increasingly turned to the power of nostalgia to gain visibility, strengthen identity, abut also to retain fan bases and produce additional income through sport tourism and the sale of memorabilia. Virtually every sport has a Hall of Fame in which heroes are commemorated, memorialized, and honored. Halls of Fame transform heroes to myths, decide about remembrance and oblivion, and provide ideals, norms, and guidelines for the people.

Many Halls of Fame (e.g. the baseball, football, boxing, basketball, and soccer Halls of Fame) are located in small cities or even villages and provide the major attractions to that locality. Fans go to such places on annual excursions, spending dollars and greatly aiding the local economies. The multitude of stadiums and athletic arenas constructed over the past two decades are designed with nostalgic features and often include museums, artifacts, and memorials. Many are ornamented with a phalanx of statues or images that pay tribute to the heroes of the past. The Michael Jordan statue that adorns the exterior of the United Center (United Airlines bought the corporate naming rights) in Chicago, where the Bulls won their NBA championships, suggests a superhuman figure soaring over mere mortals. Its four-sided base lists a litany of Jordan's records and achievements, a tribute to the cherished American value of production. The statue has become a major tourist site in the city.

Athletic sites not only showcase but also enact collective remembrances. Sport organizers take care to create a sense of nationalism and to form a patriotic community by producing memories and stimulating identification. The athletic events conducted at the United Center (it is also home to the Chicago Blackhawks' pro hockey team) and other sports venues around the United States are inevitably preceded by the National Anthem and often accompanied by symbolic decorations such as bunting in the American colors, and American flags that promote patriotism. Some teams have substituted the National Anthem with the song "God Bless America" since the tragedy of September 11, 2001, and special occasions are celebrated with flyovers by military combat jets. Numerous "memorial" stadiums throughout the country commemorate war victims, tying sport to nationalism, patriotism, and self-sacrifice. Baseball, the most traditional of the American professional sports, maintains its oldest stadiums as revered sites. Not only local fans, but devotees from around the country flock to New York's Yankee Stadium, Boston's Fenway Park, and Chicago's Wrigley Field as if on a holy pilgrimage. Such symbolic and ritualistic practices indicate an ongoing relationship between sport, heroism, religion, patriotism, and the American spirit that is continually re-energized by the production and commemoration of new heroes that perpetuate the belief in the core values of the culture.

CHAPTER THIRTEEN

SPORT, MEDIA, CONSUMPTION

INTRODUCTION

In this chapter we examine the role of the mass media and media sport in American society. Media are omnipresent and media consumption fills many hours of the every-day lives of Americans. Sport has a prominent place in all types of media, and sport consumption via the media or life in the stadia is one of the most common leisure activities. Media have transformed sport in many ways, from the change of rules to the construction of new sports and new events. Media sport[1] has changed the leisure habits of Americans. We will explore the coverage of various sports and the interests of sport consumers as well as the gendered and racialized media discourses. Major issues in this chapter are the sports consumers and/or sports fans, their behavior, and the reasons for their addiction.

According to the definition given on p. 4, one of the characteristics of sport is physical activity. Active participation in sport has increased significantly since the nineteenth century, but sportsmen and women are outnumbered by far by those people who consume sport, although sport participation and sport consumption are often closely intertwined. We understand sport consumption to mean selecting, buying, and using goods and services related to sport.

Consumption is embedded in cultural contexts and is today part of our (post) modern culture. Currently, not only is the practical value of goods important but also their meaning for consumers who use consumption for the construction and enactment of images and identities; via their tastes they aim to acquire and demonstrate economic and cultural capital. According to Ohl and Taks (2007, 160),

> goods reveal values, social networks and consumption patterns which are an integral part of the sport culture. The consumption of sporting goods is often used to shape an identity . . . to obtain recognition and to have new social and bodily experiences. We argue that sporting goods consumption is related to social presentations, representations, and narratives that express the symbolic boundaries of one's self and are a resource in the construction of subcultures.

Consumption has often been criticized as an addiction, and consumers have been described as victims of capitalism. There may be some truth in this judgment with regard to the power of markets and the media, but it neglects, among other things, the huge variety of consumers and their tastes as well as the possibility of redefinitions and resistance. Here we use sport consumption as a neutral term for buying and using media products and sporting goods. Often both forms of consumption are closely intertwined. According to Underwood *et al.* (2001), sport audiences comprise a distinct subculture whose consumption patterns (as a distinct subgroup that identifies with certain activities or products) give meaning to their lives.

MEDIA AND SPORT CONSUMPTION – AN HISTORICAL PERSPECTIVE

By the 1820s a few American newspapers had begun reporting the results of horseraces. The telegraph soon provided nearly instantaneous results to pool rooms (gambling parlors) where bettors parlayed wins and losses like the upper classes, who gambled in the stock market. By the 1880s the print media had started to specialize in sporting interests, with the *Sporting Life* (1883) and *The Sporting News* (1886), for example, focusing attention solely on baseball. The expansion of professional baseball, college and professional football, and basketball in the ensuing years exacerbated the symbiotic relationship of sport and the media. In 1946 *Sport Magazine* began publication as a very popular general interest magazine, only to be superseded by imitators such as *Sports Illustrated* and *ESPN The Magazine* in later decades (Bryant and Holt 2006, 25, 31). Today, in addition to the general coverage of sport provided by the print and broadcast media, a host of individual sporting activities are represented by specialized magazines. Among these are adventure sports, archery, baseball, basketball, cycling, billiards, boating, fishing, fitness, golf, gymnastics, hunting, running, scuba diving, skateboarding, skiing, snowboarding, soccer, tennis, and track and field; and the list is hardly all-inclusive (Lipsey 2006, 93).

The print media seemed to be eclipsed by the advent of newsreels and radio in the 1920s. Newsreels, short documentary films about the news shown in movie theaters, provided attractive visual images, and radio announcers brought drama and suspense to their delivery that enhanced viewer interest and appeal. A radio survey in Philadelphia revealed that in the 1920s 63 percent of male and 30 percent of female users already listened regularly to sporting events (Hettinger 1930).

BOX 13.1 A GAME OF HEROIC PROPORTIONS

The popular American writer, James Michener, recounted his early experience with sports reporting on the radio in 1936:

336

It was a football game between two western universities, late in the final quarter. It was obviously a game of heroic proportions, with players from the home team . . . performing heroic miracles . . . and the announcer was breathless in his excitement over the performance of his heroes. Then the game ended and he revealed the score. His miracle players had lost, something like 42–0, and I realized . . . that the announcer's job was to create suspense, sustain tension, and give the listener the feeling that he had participated in a game which had been decided only in the final seconds.

(quoted in Raney and Bryant 2006, 30)

Because it offered visual impressions and created the illusion of being at the game, television began to overtake radio coverage in consumer appeal in the 1950s. As the technology became more advanced and the pictures on the screen clearer, more and more Americans purchased TV sets. Radio, however, remained a mainstay at the workplace, in offices, and in the cars of large numbers of suburban commuters. In the past decade, the success of the internet has increased competition between the various media. By the end of the twentieth century radio had adopted new broadcasting forms with the expansion of sports talk shows that followed the successful shows of the ESPN cable television network (Owens 2006, 123–124). Newspapers reacted to the competition from seemingly more attractive media by, among other things, presenting background information or human interest stories. In all, media sports programming departed further from simple reportage of "reality" in favor of creating suspense, telling heroic narratives, and constructing sporting myths in order to provide the frame for the messages and products to be sold.

The close alliance between sport and the media

has occurred because each has been able, synergistically, to supply the other with important benefits. For sport to become professional in character and national, international and then global in reach, it could no longer rely on physical spectator presence in stadia that was its economic staple until the mid twentieth century.

(Rowe 2007)

Sport provides

the broadcast media with passionate followers (and so enthusiastic advertisers and sponsors), "live" action, constant and cyclical news, replays, studio discussion material, and so on. Sport, at first reluctantly and then enthusiastically, traded media access to events and audiences for broadcast rights revenue, in the process creating the foundation of a celebrity sport star system, and advancing the development of commodity logic within sport.

(Rowe 2007)

337

AMERICANS AND MEDIA CONSUMPTION

Today, the United States is a media-entrenched society. Over the past four decades, technological progress and epoch-making inventions in communication technologies have intensified the use of the media dramatically.

> These new delivery options include innovations in real-time television pro-gramming (cable and satellite television), television programming on demand (on-demand services and playback devices including videocassette recorders, TiVo, etc.), movies on demand (videocassettes, digital video discs, and pay-per-view), and audio media (compact discs, satellite radio, MP3, etc.).
>
> (Maibach 2007, 354)

Currently, 98 percent of American households have at least one television, and 75 percent have two or more TVs, making an average of three per home (Maibach 2007; Brownson *et al.* 2005, 435). In some homes the televisions are permanently switched on; they screen, among other things, soap operas, reality shows, sport, and many commercial advertise-ments. The majority of Americans also have access to computers and the internet in their homes or elsewhere, and many have mobile phones which are multifunctional and can also be used to listen to music and access the internet. Cars are equipped with radios and digital video disc players. Because of the amount of time the average American spends in the car, the radio is still an important source of information and entertainment.

Since the 1970s, Americans have spent an ever increasing amount of time consuming media, including TV, video, and the internet: daily consumption has increased in the past twenty years by 26 percent, which means two hours more per day. In 2007, on average, US residents spend 3,874 hours per year using various media, more than ten hours per day, including a daily dose of five hours of television (Maibach 2007, 355). This is an enormous amount of time, even if one assumes that there is a lot of "multi-tasking," such as reading a newspaper or cooking while watching TV.

Time for media consumption is found by spending less time at paid work, less time doing housework or working in the garden, and less time for other leisure activities. Health experts agree that the increasing time spent on media consumption has negatively influenced the amount of physical activity (e.g. Buckworth and Nigg 2004; Marshall *et al.* 2004).

Children and adolescents are a specific target group for the media, as they spend an incredible amount of time with old and new technologies which are often available for their private consumption. In numerous children's bedrooms there are TVs, videocassette recorders, digital video devices, computers, and internet access (Maibach 2007, 355). On average, children spend six hours and twenty minutes per day primarily with media use. Because they often use more than one medium at a time and do other things beside using media, their total media exposure is much higher, around 8.5 hours per day.

But media are not only consumed in private environments; they are omnipresent in waiting areas, buses, shopping malls, restaurants, and bars. "Referred to as 'captive audience networks,' these media delivery systems are becoming more pervasive because they offer their host organizations a new source of revenue. To an ever-increasing degree, the world is becoming a screen" (Maibach 2007, 355).

SPORT AND THE MASS MEDIA

Media sport – proliferation

The ever increasing levels of sporting performance on the one hand and the growing competition among the media (the print media, radio, TV networks, cable TV, and the internet) on the other have led to a development which may be characterized as the era of commodification and mediatization of sports (Crawford 2004). In the USA, more than twenty broadcasting networks transmit their programs nationwide. The four major commercial networks are ABC, CBS, NBC, and FOX, all of which use high-profile sport to attract a loyal audience, especially 18- to 34-year-old male consumers, the preferred target group for corporate advertisers.

Insight into the amount and the content of media sport available for consumers is given by an analysis of the sports programming of a mid-sized metropolitan area in North Carolina. This study, based on the *TV Guide* magazine, showed, for example, that broadcast and basic cable stations aired 532 sports programs comprising nearly 645 hours of coverage per week. This means that sports fans have a wide choice of sport at any of the 168 hours that make up the week. Twenty-nine percent of the sports programs and nearly half of the time was given to sporting events, while sports journalism programs accounted for 30 percent of the programs but covered less time (Brown and Bryant 2006, 77–79). The survey did not include cable stations which offer even more sports programming.

A historical and nationwide perspective reveals the enormous growth of media sport. Whereas in the 1970s 1,000 hours of media sport was programmed in the USA, in 2005 more than 60,000 hours of sport were aired by four major networks, cable television, various digital channels, and local cable networks (Jeanrenaud and Késenne 2006). The most popular and most successful sports channel, ESPN, covers sport throughout the entire day and night with a variety of sports talk shows offering contest results, analysis, discussion, predictions, news, and pre-game and post-game commentary. ESPN's most popular show, *SportCenter*, is presented as a live show three times a day, which is taped, repeated, updated, and broadcast throughout the day. The show "has become a part of the larger sport culture, transcending the mundane updates of sports scores and news to become a daily ritual for millions of people" (Brown and Bryant 2006, 82). During the week twenty-eight million people access *SportCenter*, while twenty-two million watch the show on the weekend. Men comprise 78 percent of the viewers of the 11 p.m. shows, compared with 45 percent of viewers during the day, indicating the broad appeal to both sexes (Brown and Bryant 2006, 82).

Other networks, such as Rupert Murdoch's Fox, compete with ESPN by offering regional programs such as *Around the Track* and *NASCAR This Morning*, which appeal to auto-racing fans. Fox's answer to ESPN's *SportsCenter* program is entitled the *Best Damn Sports Show Period* (BDSSP) with celebrities and former professional players as hosts who conduct the discussion in a loud, brash, and rowdy manner that especially appeals to young men. "Blending sports, comedy and an irreverent tone, BDSSP takes a humorous look at the sports happenings of the day, and features special guests" (Brown and Bryant 2006, 82).

This enormous sports programming has numerous consumers: in 2000, the members of American households spent, on average, 201 hours per year watching sport, men 172.5 and women 91.5 hours watching nationally televised sport (Downey 2001). In addition, regional sports networks, pay-per-view, and satellite TV services have their share of sports consumers. It is safe to say that the viewing time has, if anything, increased since then.

Table 13.1 Average household ratings and hours spent watching nationally televised sport per year

	Households		Men		Women	
	Rating	Hours	Rating	Hours	Rating	Hours
1998						
Network	5.0	93.9	4.1	76.4	2.4	44.2
Syndication	6.2	6.0	4.8	4.6	2.3	2.2
Basic cable	0.5	83.2	0.4	66.3	0.2	30.4
Total without Olympics		183.1		147.3		76.8
Total with Olympics		194.6		154.1		85.8
1999						
Network	5.0	99.2	4.1	81.8	2.3	46.0
Syndication	6.7	24.0	5.1	18.1	2.6	9.1
Basic cable	0.5	82.5	0.4	66.2	0.2	30.4
Total		205.7		166.1		85.5
2000						
Network	4.7	103.6	3.9	85.6	2.1	47.0
Syndication	5.9	22.1	4.6	17.2	2.3	8.6
Basic cable	0.5	74.7	0.4	61.5	0.2	27.1
Total without Olympics		200.4		164.3		82.7
Total with Olympics		213.5		172.5		91.5

Source: TN Media analysis of Nielsen Data (Downey 2001)

Contents of the coverage and consumers

Since the turn of the century the mass media's interest in sports has increased decisively. According to Lever and Wheeler (1984), who analyzed the *Chicago Tribune* from 1900 to 1975, sports coverage grew from 9 percent to 17 percent of the space of the paper. In 1975 half of the general news stories were devoted to sports.

At the same time, the space provided for team sports increased from 30 percent in 1900 to 60 percent in 1975 mainly at the cost of horseracing and boxing (Lever and Wheeler 1984). Valgeirsson and Snyder (1986) found that the *New York Times* (1984/1985) printed, on average, twenty-two sports articles per day, 7 percent of the total newspaper space, and that 65 percent of the articles covered baseball, football, and basketball. A recent international press survey showed that 53 percent of the sports articles in the five American newspapers covered the "Big Three" (Schultze-Jørgensen 2005).

American football is the top sport on television, with an NFL game on Sunday night on ESPN attracting 8 percent to 9 percent of US households (Brown and Bryant 2006, 83). *Monday Night Football* on ABC reaches up to twelve million households, 19 percent of the turned-on televisions. In 2003 sixteen of the eighteen highest rated sports programs were football contests, and the top six were NFL games. Besides football two Major League Baseball playoff games were in the top eighteen. The football craze is most obvious in cities which host a professional team. Especially fanatical are the approximately 100,000 inhabitants of Green Bay, Wisconsin, which has the only city-owned professional team in the NFL, the Green Bay Packers. When the Packers play, 80 percent of the turned-on televisions in this area are tuned in to the game (Brown and Bryant 2006, 85).

College football also receives a huge amount of coverage and fan attention. Thus the Fiesta Bowl game in 2003, which featured Ohio State University against the University of Miami, was viewed in more then 18.4 million households (i.e. 29 percent of TVs switched on were covering this game). On average, broadcasts of NCAA games in prime time are viewed in 9.5 million households (Brown and Bryant 2006, 85).

TV coverage of a football game is not a simple showing of the game but a careful and strategic composition and enactment, with an emphasis on offering multiple opportunities for commercial sponsors to sell their products. A telecast of a college football game on ABC in 2004 included

> 111 replays, 163 informational graphics, 262 changes in the corner score box (down and yardage, statistics), 86 crowd or marching band shots, 120 cuts to coaches, 28 shots of cheerleaders and 20 sideline reports . . . Only 16 minutes and 28 seconds of action, 7.3% of the 3 hour and 43 minute contest . . . were shown on TV. The typical play of the 161 plays (offensive run, pass, kick or kick off) consumed only 8.1 seconds. In the 25 breaks 79 commercials were shown.
>
> (Brown and Bryant 2006, 86)

The highlight of the football season is the NFL championship game, known as the Super Bowl, which is a blockbuster. In 2004, it was viewed by 137.6 million fans in 43.4 million households (61 percent of the televisions in use at that time), and garnered $170 million in advertisements (Brown and Bryant 2006, 83–84). In 2008, a thirty-second commercial at the Super Bowl cost $2.7 million.[2]

The professional baseball championship, the so-called World Series, attracted between 68 and 121 million viewers between 2004 and 2007 (http://en.wikipedia.org/wiki/World_Series_television_ratings). Regular games throughout the season draw considerably less, often depending on the ongoing success of the team. With regard to TV audiences, baseball is clearly behind American football. According to the "Professional Sports Attendance and TV Viewership" report published by the National Sporting Goods Association in 2006, slightly more than 106 million adults viewed at least one NFL game on TV (each team plays sixteen games) versus 76.7 million who viewed a Major League baseball game (each team plays 162 games each season). The National Basketball Association (NBA) attracted 60.9 million viewers (each team plays eighty-two games) (http://www.nsga.org/public/pages/index.cfm?pageid=1497).

College basketball, particularly the month-long men's national championship tournament known as March Madness, draws great fan interest, especially among college students and alumni. The 2008 tournament averaged more than eight million television viewers per game (a 7 percent decrease from 2007), but another 4.3 million fans watched games online during the early rounds. Internet viewers showed a 147 percent increase (Learmonth 2008).

As shown above, media sport in the US focuses attention on very few sports, primarily American football, baseball, and basketball. However, currently three other sports, NASCAR, X Games, and professional wrestling, attract an increasing crowd of (male) fans and supporters.

NASCAR, the professional stock-car racing circuit, is the fastest growing television sport. Two of its major 2003 events (Daytona 400 and the Budweiser Shootout) appeared in prime time, broadcast by major networks (see Chapter 8). Major races draw a television audience of more than five million households, mostly in the South, where 37 percent of survey respondents reported that they were NASCAR fans (Brown and Bryant 2006, 90). Beside the TV networks, cable television stations cover car races. The TV guide magazine listed twenty-nine motor sports shows on various television stations during one week in June 2004 (Brown and Bryant 2006, 89–90). On the webpage of "Race Jesus Motorsports," a race car team, it is even stated that 71 percent of the American population has an interest in motor sports (http://www.racejesus.com/about.htm). The name of this team indicates the close ties of NASCAR with religion. NASCAR represents American nationalism and conservative values. Its fans are largely evangelical Christians. The race circuit has a traveling preacher who accompanies the drivers, and it allows a "Jesus car" in the races to advertise religion. Non-Christian drivers do not feel welcome. The close ties to religion may add to the popularity of stock car races, given the emphasis on religion in the US. However, the popularity of NASCAR also may be explained, at least in part, by its promise and enactment of an American life which the fans feel entitled to but which is threatened or already lost (Newman 2007).

BOX 13.2 NASCAR NATION

NASCAR races are colorful spectacles, expressions of a specific American lifestyle, embedded in current economic, social, and political formations of US society. Scholars paint colorful portraits of "a culturally significant mélange of gas-guzzling race cars, Confederate flag insignia, the omnipresent tang of smoldering oils and burnt tire rubber, and the intermittent hum of roaring engines and Lynyrd's Skynyrd's 'Freebird' – all set against an ubiquitous backdrop of American flags and corporate logos" (Newman 2007, 289). Lynyrd Skynyrd is a legendary Southern American rock band, revered by the "NASCAR Nation," the millions of predominately white, male, working-class fans.

NASCAR fans spend billions in buying licensed merchandise which is sold in temporary shopping malls around the race-track. As spectators they are exposed to more than 40,000 corporate logos at the race-track and their brand loyalty makes the investment of the sponsors/advertisers a good business. The commodification of NASCAR spectacles is intertwined with a promulgation of conservative ideologies and politics. Fans and drivers have an interest to protect the southern heritage and culture as well as the privileges of white male Americans. The NASCAR Nation feels a sense of entitlement which "is underwritten by a history of white privilege . . . a reverie for communal opulence sans taxation, a commitment to the forged logics of faith and nationalism, and a sense of obligation and unconditional support for American imperialism" (Newman 2007, 299).

Christianity and politics are closely intertwined: "In the opening moments of today's race, a local minister evoked the 'Lord's prayer', through which he called on 'Jesus as our savior' to 'protect our American way of life.' Then, a 'special social guest', Republican Senator George Allen took the microphone. Allen applauded the sea of 'patriots' . . . and called on those same NASCAR fans to hold fast to their 'patriotism' by supporting our troops."

(Newman 2007, 299)

The X Games are spectacular action sports events shaped after the model of the Olympics. The disciplines of the Summer Games include BMX downhill, sky surfing or speed climbing, and the Winter Games include snow BMX racing or ice climbing. The X Games were invented and are promoted by ESPN, whose management decided in 1993 to invest considerable resources in an action sport event. ESPN adapted the rebel images of skateboarding, snowboarding, BMX, and motorcycle racing within the X Games in order to capture the youth market (Wimmer 2001).

Networks also successfully promoted pseudo-sports, such as professional wrestling. Professional wrestling is not a conventional sport in the way that the fight decides victory and defeat. It is rather a choreographed play or soap opera where the roles of the wrestlers are fixed although the pretension of an open end is maintained. Without doubt professional wrestlers display strength, speed, skills, and an element of courage; but they are actors more so than athletes. The violence, aggressiveness, and danger as well as the (traditional) masculinity enacted in these events contribute to their popularity, especially among young men and boys (Messner et al. 2000; Tamborini et al. 2005).

The television networks, especially ABC, also garnered a larger audience share by creating pseudo-sport shows, such as actors or celebrities competing in sports events. ESPN further promoted poker in televised national tournaments with substantial prize money. Other networks, like Fox, have promoted ballroom dancing as a televised sport, with great popularity.

Evaluating these last-named developments, one has to take into consideration that sport is a product and the media have to sell it at a time when globalization and new technologies intensify competition for readers, users, and audiences. Among television stations, too, the contest for audiences, advertisements, and TV rights is becoming fiercer and fiercer. Viewers are greedy for sensationalism and intimate insights into other people's lives, and a collective voyeurism generates numerous reality shows. It thus seemed logical to use the popularity of sport, sports events, and sport stars, and to increase the identification of audiences with the athletes, but also with the network by "human interest stories." Thus, in some media, the borderlines between sport shows and soap operas have become blurred. "Sport has risen to become the great dramatic metaphor of media society, the global soap opera . . . achievement, success and career, victory and defeat, joy and sorrow – the ultimate serialisation of life's drama" (Mohr 2000, 150).

Media sport consumption – children and adolescents

Sport consumption starts at an early age: Children and adolescents are "heavy" consumers of media sport, as the "Children and Sports Media Study" conducted in 2001 revealed.[3] The aim of the study was to explore the exposure of 8- to 17-year-old children to sport in eight different media, among them TV, radio, print media, movies, video games, and the internet. Results showed that 93 percent of the children, 97 percent of the boys and 89 percent of the girls, watch, read about, or listen to sports-related information/entertainment. Forty-two

344

percent of all boys and 13 percent of girls consume sport via the media every day; 89 percent of the boys and 52 percent of the girls do this every day or at least two days a week.

TV was the most frequently used medium, with boys more likely than girls to be viewers. Boys were also more likely to mention videogames than girls, who were more interested in sport-related movies. The general patterns of sport consumption did not vary greatly by age or race/ethnicity sub-groups (AAF/ESPN 2001, 21). Among children, the Olympic Games are quite popular: 88 percent of the girls and 84 percent of the boys reported watching them on TV. However, Olympic Games are singular events, conducted only every fourth year. In everyday life, the most popular media sports on TV are (in this order): NLF Football (89 percent boys, 68 percent girls), NBA basketball (74 percent boys, 67 percent girls), professional baseball (71 percent boys, 54 percent girls), X Games (74 percent boys, 45 percent girls), college football (68 percent boys, 50 percent girls), men's college basketball (57 percent boys, 56 percent girls), and professional wrestling (46 percent boys, 43 percent girls). Less than 50 percent of children, but in some cases more girls than boys watch (in this order) gymnastics, soccer, ice-skating, auto/motorcycle races, boxing, swimming, NHL hockey, and tennis. Among other sports, 37 percent of the girls, but only 23 percent of the boys are interested in women's professional basketball. Golf takes the last place in the popularity hierarchy.

There were considerable differences according to race and ethnicity: children from African-American households tended to favor basketball in all forms (pro and college, men's, but also women's, in that order). In addition, they were more likely than white kids to watch professional wrestling and boxing. Children from Hispanic households tended to favor pro basketball, wrestling and boxing, and, to a lesser degree, soccer, whereas white children were more interested in the NHL, baseball, extreme sports, and motor races compared with African-American children. The results show clearly that the different sporting traditions of the races/ethnicities, and also their lifestyles, influence children's tastes.

Among children of all races/ethnicities, boys and girls, the most popular media sports are men's sports. Boys prefer, to a high degree, competitive and aggressive sports, whereas girls are also interested in individual, aesthetic sports like gymnastics, skiing, diving, and figure skating. But the "big three" are also girls' favorites (Sergent et al. 1998). The results of the AAF/ESPN study show that media sport contributes to socialization into American culture and to a preference for American sports.

Gendered sports coverage

Quantitative findings

The popularity of professional and college ball games and of other professional sports like wrestling and stock-car racing leaves little space for women in the sports coverage of the various media. The only professional league in women's sport is the WNBA, but it struggles to survive, with funding provided by the men's NBA. As shown in Chapter 11, sport was invented by men for men; women were latecomers and were only slowly and hesitatingly accepted by the men in power. This is true not only of admission to sports grounds but also to media coverage. The marginalization of women's sport in the media has been impressively proven by numerous studies on the coverage of female athletes which have been conducted in the USA since the 1980s (Pfister 2004; for gender worldwide see Bernstein 2002). Title IX and the connected discussions on gender equality in sport have also directed attention to the media coverage of male and female athletes and have encouraged quantitative and qualitative research.

Lever and Wheeler (1984) analyzed, for example, the sports pages in the *Chicago Tribune* from 1900 to 1975 and discovered that women's sports coverage increased from 1 percent in 1900 to 4 percent in 1975. Valgeirsson and Snyder (1986) found in their content analysis of the *New York Times* (1984/1985) that only 3 percent of sports coverage was devoted to women's sport. In 2005, an "International Press Survey" showed that, in the five American newspapers examined, 7 percent of the articles covered women's sports; but 80 per cent focused on male athletes.[4] The study reported that 33 percent of women's sports coverage was dedicated to golf, 20 percent to basketball and 16 percent to tennis.

Gender relations are only slightly better in the sports coverage of university newspapers: male athletes and events were given 73 percent of space in sports articles in the print media, and even 82 percent of TV sports coverage (Huffman *et al.* 2004). Not much more attention is paid to women in the most widely read sports publication, *Sports Illustrated*, with eighteen million male and five million female readers. The magazine devotes only 10 percent of its coverage to women (Fink and Kensicki 2002; Duncan 2006, 234f.).

Tennis, which is considered "gender neutral," is the sport in which women get the most attention. However, even here female athletes do not attract the same amount of coverage as men. This was the result of a study on the coverage of female and male tennis players competing in the 2004 Wimbledon Championships in three national newspapers which included the *New York Times* (Crossmann *et al.* 2007).

Among the few media with a nearly "fair" gender ratio in its coverage is the *NCAA News*, a non-profit paper published as a service for NCAA members. Women receive coverage according to the proportion of female athletes, although women's teams are not adequately presented. The high visibility of women in the *NCAA News* may be the result of numerous initiatives and decisions at colleges and universities to improve gender equality with regard to participation, funding, and also media coverage in college sport (Cunningham *et al.* 2004).

Not surprisingly, there is a clear emphasis on women in women's sport magazines, but they have found it impossible to survive on the market. The bimonthly *Sports Illustrated for Women* (later *Sports Illustrated Women*, *SI Women*) was launched in 1997 and targeted young women with a "passion for sport" (Fink and Kensicki 2002). In 2002, *SI Women* reached 400,000 readers, which was not enough to survive. The same fate befell the *Real Sports Magazine*, founded in 1998, which exists today on the web: "Since the magazine's launch, seven women's professional leagues have gone out of business (along with four competing women's sports magazines). The lack of advertiser and reader interest in building a market for women's sports created an environment whereby Real Sports had to change in order to stay viable" (http://www.realsportsmag.com/). This and other women's sports magazines have found a niche and exist online.

Female athletes are not very visible in the print media, but the situation on TV is not much better, although some outstanding women's events, like the NCAA women's basketball championship, attract considerable attention. The coverage of the 2004 championship game reached nearly four million households (Brown and Bryant 2006, 88).

According to Messner, Duncan, and Cooky (2003), who analyzed the sports coverage of the three network affiliates in Los Angeles and ESPN's *SportsCenter*, the network affiliates gave women's sport less than 10 percent of their coverage, and around half of the newscasts contained no information about female athletes at all. ESPN's *SportsCenter*, one of the top sport shows in the United States, aired an even smaller percentage of women's sports coverage. In 2002, *SportsCenter* showed in one month 778 stories about males and only sixteen stories about female athletes (Adams and Tuggle 2004).

A longitudinal study of the Amateur Athletic Foundation of Los Angeles (AAF) on "Gender in Televised Sports" in the USA found: "In 1989 women's sports received only 5% of the coverage. The 1999 numbers show an insignificant increase to 8.7%. What coverage does exist still too often treats women not as athletes, but as sex objects."[5]

In her report on the results of the study in 2004 Anita DeFrantz stated:

> On local Los Angeles sports news shows, only 6.3 percent of all stories deal exclusively with women's sports. On ESPN's *Sports Center*, only 1 in 20 stories is on women's sports. The continued paucity of women's stories occurs against the backdrop of a significant growth of girls' and women's sports nationally and internationally, a development that is simply ignored by television sports news.
>
> (quoted in Wilson 2005, 3)

The media explain the marginalization of female athletes in media sports with the disinterest of (male) audiences. However, the networks do not make great efforts to promote interest in women's sport. According to Duncan (2006), TV networks focus on men's sport with their audience-building strategies. For example, nearly all previews, called "teasers," draw attention to men's events.

Like television, sports radio talk shows generally feature men as hosts and as telephone discussants. A recent study claims that sports talk shows on the radio offer a male bonding experience and a comfort zone, or male refuge (Kaufman 2007).

All studies concerned with the gender ratio in media coverage show that the "symbolic annihilation" of women in and through media sports has not changed decisively in recent decades – at least in its everyday coverage.

Olympic Games

During international events, especially the Olympic Games, women attract much more attention than they normally do. Here, the usual arguments for neglecting female athletes (e.g. the unattractiveness of the sport or the small number of women participating) are not valid: Since the 1990s more than 40 percent of Olympic participants have been women, and medals are of public interest, regardless of the sex of the athletes. During the Olympics, furthermore, a high percentage of television viewers in the USA are women. In 1996, Olympic female viewership was 65 percent and viewership among the most desirable female consumer demographics (18–34 years old) increased by 40 percent from Barcelona (1992) to Atlanta (1996).[6]

On the basis of a study of selected print media, Vincent et al. (2002, 320) have pointed out that "longitudinal content analyses have indicated that the deficit in the coverage of female athletes is gradually being reduced." Studies such as the analysis of NBC's coverage of the 1996 Olympic Games – dubbed as the "Women's Games" – showed that men were given 53 percent of coverage time while women were given 47 percent. NBC and other media had detected girls and women consumers as a niche in a quite saturated market. They adapted to the tastes of female viewers, aired individual and aesthetic sports, and emphasized human interest stories. In spite of the high female television audience during the 2000 Olympic Games, women's coverage decreased from the coverage of the 1996 games (see also Eastman and Billings 1999). Tuggle, Huffman and Rosengard (2002, 361) examined the NBC's 2000 Olympics coverage and found out

> that women received proportionately less coverage in 2000 than they did in 1996 on the U.S. network, and that coverage focused on individual events, with women competing in team sports receiving relatively little coverage. As was the case in 1996, women who competed in 2000 in sports involving power or hard physical contact received almost no attention.

Gendered discourses

What are the discourses which frame the performance of the athletes and which messages and images do the media disseminate about men and women in sport? The studies carried out on the constructions and enactments of gender in the media have made use of various methods, mainly quantitative and qualitative content analysis which are often supplemented by hermeneutic interpretations.

A common feature of the media discourses is the emphasis on gender difference which is culturally constructed but presented as natural and real. "Since the masculine is the default position in our society, the feminine is seen as *'the Other'*" (Duncan 2006, 238).

Frequently the following hypotheses were examined: the interest of the media in the private lives of female athletes; the trivialization of sports women, for example, by giving them nicknames or pet names; the attribution of their success to chance or luck; and the concentration on their outward appearance, with an emphasis on their good looks, their eroticism, and their sexual aura. The hypotheses with regard to male athletes included the concentration of the media on their sporting performance and the attribution of their success to achievement and commitment.

These hypotheses were confirmed in numerous studies, at least with regard to the tendency of diminishing women's performances and emphasizing their appearance (Billings and Eastman 2002, 355).

Researching print media coverage of US women's Olympic gold medal-winning teams, Jones, Murrell and Jackson (1999, 183) stated:

> Female athletes in male sports were described by the print media using frequent male-to-female comparisons and comments that had little to do with sports or the athlete's performance. Print media coverage of female athletes in female sports focused on performance while reinforcing female stereotypes.

Research into the television coverage of women also found considerable gender asymmetries. The title of a study by Messner *et al.* (2003) stands for the content of women's coverage in network affiliates and ESPN's *SportCenter*: "Silence, Sport Bras and Wrestling Porn." The focus when dealing with women's sport was on humorous stories about non-serious women's sport and sexual allusions. In the period of the investigation, thirteen feature stories dealt, for example, with the wrestler, celebrity, and *Playboy* magazine model, Sable, who was often the only woman appearing in the program.

Sexualization of female and, to a lesser degree, male athletes has become a major issue in recent decades. A good example is coverage of the 1999 Women's World Cup Soccer Championship in US newspapers (Christopherson *et al.* 2002). Nearly one-third of the articles referred to the eroticism, bodies, and appearance of the players. However, when the media present erotic images and messages, the athletes are not (only) victims. Many athletes, such as the soccer player Brandi Chastain, the Olympic swimmer Jenny Thompson, or tennis player Anna Kournikova, used their sex appeal to gain visibility, become celebrities, and attract sponsors (see Chapter 11). The sexualization of female athletes in the mainstream media always means "heterosexualization." Especially in "male" sports like basketball and soccer, the players are portrayed as "real women" with traditional female qualities and boyfriends, husbands, and families. If the athletes do not measure up to these expectations they are often ignored, if not rejected. The coverage of women's sport thus mirrors and (re)produces homophobia and compulsory heterosexuality in American sport and society (Duncan 2006).

The latest study in the series of AAF-sponsored studies "Gender in Televised Sport," conducted in 2004, revealed progress: the quality of reporting on women's sport has improved and in most cases female athletes are taken seriously and treated with respect. Humorous stories about female athletes have become exceptions, but the quantity of reporting on women's sport has not increased (Duncan *et al*. 2005).

All in all, the coverage of women's sport in the US media frequently contains ambiguous messages. Female athletes are often portrayed positively, but subtle messages can lead to a trivialization of their performances. Kane and Greendorfer (1994, 39) suggested that ambivalence allows "those in power to acknowledge (and therefore accommodate) the social changes that have taken place within the last two decades while simultaneously offering resistance through the maintenance of the status quo."

Sport coverage also reproduces traditional images of masculinity. In a textual analysis of the most popular TV sport programs among boys (football, basketball, extreme sports, wrestling) Messner *et al*. (2000) extracted recurrent themes concerning gender, race, aggression, violence, militarism, and commercialism, and concluded that "televised sports . . . consistently present a narrow portrait of masculinity" which the authors call "Televised Sports Manhood Formula," i.e.

> a real man is strong, tough, aggressive and a winner in what is still a Man's World. To be a winner he has to do what needs to be done. He must be willing to compromise his own long-term health by showing guts in the face of danger, by fighting other men when necessary, and by "playing hurt" when he is injured.
> (Messner *et al*. 2000, 390)

Reasons for and effects of gendered sports coverage

Asked about the reasons behind the marginalization of women's sport in the mass media, journalists and media producers use the imagined taste of the audience as a seemingly convincing argument (Duncan 2006). The target group of sports reports are men, and only sports (like American football, baseball, basketball, and motor sports) which interest a male audience have the chance of gaining a measure of media attention. Here, it must be assumed that interest in particular sports and identification with teams grows with the length and intensity of consumption and is thus on a relatively constant high level among adults (Wann 2006). Contact with or reports on a particular sport or team arouse interest, and the taste and interest of audiences have, in turn, an effect on the reporting in a reciprocal process. Sports journalists who are sport fans themselves orient their articles towards other male fans and both develop similar attitudes and preferences. But the "right" sports do not guarantee coverage; the athletes also have to have the right gender. Women playing male sports like American football do not attract the interest of the media and their male audience: "real" football and women's football seem to be two different types of sport.

Little is known about the effects of the (gendered) representation of athletes and teams. It may be assumed that the focus of the media on men's sport renders women's sport second rate. This may influence sponsors and make female athletes less attractive for advertising, although a few female top stars in tennis or golf earn millions of dollars. The lack of sponsors minimizes the development potential not only of athletes but also of sports and the opportunities for women to compete at an elite or professional level. The failure of the professional soccer league is a good example of the lack of media (and audience) interest in women's sport.

In addition, gendered media sport provides specific role models which are especially important for children and adolescents. The "Televised Manhood formula" identified by Messner et al. (2000) suggests that media sport can – under certain circumstances – teach violence and reproduce gender and race stereotypes. It provides for boys models of masculinities which combine traditional with postmodern traits.[7] Girls can identify with relatively few female athletes and this may influence their sport participation in a negative way. On the other hand, some successful female athletes have become cultural icons and media coverage of powerful soccer players, basketball players or track athletes may provide positive role models, may challenge gender stereotypes, provoke resistance against or subversions of hegemonic images, and deconstruct gender dichotomy (Heywood and Dworkin 2003). However, a "degendering" of sport would require that men's sport practices and coverage also have to move away from traditional images and messages.

Sport spectators – live events

Spectators attend sports events for a variety of reasons. Promotions bring fans to the arenas; but most fans attend events because they are emotionally attached to, identify with "their" athletes and teams, and want to support them (even if the performance of athletes does not depend on fan attendance) (Wann 2006). More spectators will attend if their favorite athlete/team is performing well (i.e. winning) or has a chance to get to the playoffs for the championship. Fans also like to see star athletes perform; but the biggest reason for attendance seems to be the chance to be "a part of history" and be witness to an event where a record is broken. This is at least true for the numerous fans, especially baseball fans, who track records (e.g. in home runs via statistics) (Lu and Pitts 2004, 146–147). Some research suggests that Americans exhibit more enthusiasm and spend more money on sport consumption than people in other countries (Summers and Morgan 2004, 202). An indicator for the high level of sport consumption is the huge number of sport spectators.

According to James and Ridinger (2002), the "Big Three and a Half," professional baseball, football, basketball, and ice hockey, attracted more than 116 million spectators in 1999. Baseball draws the most spectators in the stadia, but it also provides many more competitions than the other sports.[8] In 2006, major league baseball with its thirty professional teams had nearly eighty million spectators, an average of around 33,000 per game (*Chicago Tribune*, October 7, 2007, 2). Taking only the adult population into consideration, the following figures of a survey emerge: between April 2005 and March 2006, 29.5 million Americans attended a professional baseball game, 15.6 million a NFL football game, and 12 million a NBA basketball game (http://www.nsga.org/public/pages/index.cfm?page id=1497).

The high numbers of Americans attending sport events or watching sport on TV are an indicator of a widespread fan-aticism. According to a national survey 67 percent of the US population were reported to be fans of the NFL; 62 percent of the MLB, 54 percent of the NBA, and 35 percent of the Women's National Basketball Association (WNBA) (Frank 2000) (see Table 13.2).

Not only the professional, but also the college football teams lure tens of thousands to the stadia, and the home games of many teams are sold out for years – in spite of the high ticket prices. In 2006, for example, tickets for the game between Notre Dame University and Penn State University were sold for $3,500 by scalpers (black market dealers). Similarly, a courtside ticket (nearest to the players) to watch the Los Angeles Lakers of the NBA during the 2007 to 2008 season cost $2,300 per game (Tucker 2007, 16).

According to Wilson (2002), 62 percent of the adult American male and 49 percent of the female population had attended an amateur or professional sport event in 1993. More affluent and more educated people are more likely to attend sport events. Sport attendance is clearly based on cultural and economic capital and that is true for both sexes. Whereas, for example, 69 percent of women in the highest income category had visited a sport event, only 34 percent of women with low incomes did so. Wilson (2002) found similar differences in sport attendance with regard to education.

This is confirmed by the results of a survey of sports fans done between 2000 and 2001 which discovered the demographic profiles shown in Table 13.2. The figures in Table 13.2 indicate that a considerable percentage of spectators are women. However, with the exception of women's basketball, the majority of fans are male. The gender differences in men's favor are most significant among the spectators of aggressive sports like football, ice hockey, and NASCAR.

Fans seem to have a higher social status than the average American population, where only 35 percent have an income of $50,000 or more; and 54 percent (age 25 years and over) have at least some college education.[9] The fans with the lowest income are those of women's basketball, which may be explained by the high percentage of women who have on average a lower income than men. In addition, soccer and NASCAR fans earn considerably less than fans of other sports. Thirty-four percent of the NASCAR fans, but only 23 percent of the NHL fans shop regularly in Wal-Mart (a discount store) and 60 percent versus 73 percent have internet access (Frank 2000). Soccer has a mixed fan base. It is

Table 13.2 Fan base in percent

Fan base

January through June 2000	US population	Males 12–24	Males 25–44	Males 45 +	Females 12–34	Females 35 +
Fan-NFL	67.3	86.0	78.1	74.4	65.1	52.2
Fan-MLB	61.7	69.6	67.0	68.3	54.6	56.4
Fan-NBA	54.4	75.6	58.7	52.0	60.6	42.2
Fan-NHL	36.6	54.1	51.1	32.9	36.3	24.8
Fan-college football	54.7	70.0	63.2	67.1	48.1	41.3
Fan-college basketball	49.8	64.6	52.9	57.1	49.5	38.7
Fan-pro golf	38.6	39.6	47.7	51.1	22.2	35.4
Fan-pro tennis	35.3	34.0	38.7	37.3	34.6	33.3
Fan-auto racing	40.3	49.1	51.9	48.6	33.0	30.7
Fan-pro soccer	29.0	39.7	31.1	24.4	37.2	21.8
Fan-pro figure skating	51.7	18.4	28.3	43.6	66.9	72.7
Fan-pro boxing	38.9	69.2	57.4	43.6	34.4	17.5
Fan-pro wrestling	27.7	61.9	34.7	18.8	32.0	13.6
Fan-WNBA	35.0	41.0	30.8	35.1	41.8	31.2
Fan-horseracing	31.6	18.9	29.1	37.5	27.4	36.7
15 Sport average	43.51	52.78	48.05	46.12	42.91	36.57

Based on approximately 12,000 interviews with a random representative sample of the US population aged 12 and older: 65.5 percent of those interviewed in 1999 said they were an NFL fan.

Source: ESPN Sports Poll, a product of TNS Intersearch: Frank (2000, 47).

popular with the suburban middle class, but also with the Hispanic population. In the suburbs soccer is a youth sport, and therefore it attracts especially young fans (see Chapter 5).

Sports like stock-car and motorcycle races seem to appeal especially to working-class
males.[10] This is true for the TV coverage (see above) but also for the spectators at the race-
tracks. Wilson (2002) identified stock-car racing as a proletarian sport where speed,
violence, and driving skills are crucial, abilities which are familiar and highly valued in
lower classes. The Wilson study (2002) indicates that there is a close connection between
interest in motor racing and education. In 1993, only 2 percent of women and 6 percent
of men with a postgraduate degree attended races, but 14 per cent of the least educated
women and 32 percent of men with only a high school degree did so. "Prole" sports do
not fit in with the preferences, tastes, images, and identities of the American cultural elite.

Fan behavior

I argue that in contemporary America sport is an ever present component of social
life. Consequently, Americans are all sport fans/consumers of varying degree.
Although some fans are more ardent than others and some Americans do not
consider themselves fans at all, sport surrounds us in ubiquitous inclusion in both
material and non-material culture. We experience sport like the landscape in a
painting that includes us and like the air we breathe, we absorb sport through
osmosis.

(Levy 2005, 1)

The numbers of media sport consumers, mentioned above, indicate that America is a
country of sport fans with various levels of addiction, ranging from occasional spectators
to fans or enthusiasts who would virtually give their lives for their club or team.[11]

Results of a representative survey showed that 73 percent of the Americans were either
"very interested" or "fairly interested" in watching sports (Lieberman 1991). In a study
about sport fans among students, 73 percent of female and 83 percent of male respondents
did so (Dietz-Uhler et al. 2000). "Real" fans are not only an interested but also an active
audience. For them sport is a major part of their daily lives; they spend considerable time
and energy on sport consumption, get information from a variety of media, use sport as a
major topic of conversation, participate in live events, play sport video games, travel long
distances to matches, and spend a large amount of money on their "obsession," for travel,
tickets, merchandise, and memorabilia (Aaron and Smith 2007). Hardcore fans know
everything about their sport, identify with the athletes/teams, and are, to a higher degree,
more emotionally involved than the average audiences (Gantz 2006). Among the clubs with
a high number of extremely loyal fans are the Cubs, one of the two professional baseball
teams in Chicago. Their emotional attachment to their team is evident in the emotional
statements about the continual defeats of the Cubs. After another loss a major newspaper

354

interviewed the fans, who lamented that "it [the loss] just rips the heart right out of me," or "it is like a punch in the gut" (*Chicago Tribune*, October 2007, 27). The frustration of Cubs fans has lasted a full century, for their team last won the World Series in 1908. Still, the team enjoys a devoted following and sells all of its seats for nearly every home game. Anthropological studies of a group of Cubs, fans attest to their loyalty, camaraderie, and sense of family. This group, known as the "bleacher bums," have occupied the same seats for decades (Swyers 2005; Miller and Gillentine 2006).

Before sports events, fans are encouraged to conduct "tailgate" parties in the vast parking lots adjacent to the stadium or the open fields near the car racing track. Tailgating also attracts the unfortunates who do not get or cannot afford tickets. Participants open the tailgates of their cars or trucks and serve food and drinks. Although fans of numerous sports use tailgaiting to make the sport event into a whole-day experience full of fun, it is most prominent in collegiate football games. Some fans arrive long before the events with ample supplies of food and liquor. Food is grilled on outdoor barbeques and alcohol is iced in plastic coolers, as music plays, team "fight songs" are sung and all is shared in celebration of the football teams. Fans of college sport, particularly those in states which have no professional sports teams, are especially rabid. At the University of Alabama, for example, fans begin arriving in their house trailers three days before the Saturday football games. Some drive hundreds of kilometers each week to get there. One couple missed their daughter's wedding because she scheduled it during a game; while another fan regularly attended the games despite the risk of missing the appointment for a heart transplant. A sports talk show host who criticized a team received death threats from fans. Other fans harassed a college president at the grocery store until he replaced an athletic director whose football team made a poor showing (the athletic director hired the coach responsible for the loss). Even a clergyman was so fanatical that he delayed weddings at his church until the half-time intermission and had a television installed in the sanctuary so that he could watch the games during the church service (St. John 2004).

BOX 13.3 ASHES OVER THE STADIUM

Even though he's only 37 and in good health, Nathan Davis has already made out his will. In it, he bequeaths money to the University of Alabama athletic department and his ashes to Bryant-Denny Stadium. Davis, whose heavily tattooed body is a living tribute to his beloved school, wants his remains to become an actual part of it. "I spell it out in my will," Davis said. "My first choice is to spread my ashes at the stadium, second is on the Walk of Champions, and third is on Bear Bryant's statue."

Davis is one of an apparently large number of people who feel there's no better place to spend eternity than the place they cheered on the old home team or otherwise celebrated their favorite sport. A couple of years ago Christopher Noteboom ran across the field during a Philadelphia Eagles game scattering his mother's ashes as he went. Noteboom said Mom was a big Eagles fan and he couldn't think of a more fitting tribute.

George Helms' family had the urn holding his ashes strapped onto a car at the Las Vegas Motor Speedway where it rode during practice laps. Afterward they scattered some of the NASCAR fan's ashes over the track so he could remain part of his favorite sport.

(Foster 2008)

Americans demonstrate their sport craze openly and wherever possible. The logos of "their" team adorn baseball caps, jackets, T-shirts, and assorted other articles of clothing. Team or school flags are flown on houses and cars. Another popular place to announce loyalty to a team is by placing a team logo on one's car or the license plate holder, which can be engraved with team and school names. Even babies wear sleepers with the symbol of Notre Dame, a college football team, or the Chicago Cubs, a professional baseball team, on the breast.

The ubiquity of sport makes it a substantial topic of conversation among family members, colleagues, friends, and acquaintances. Important games are a very welcome opportunity for family gatherings or parties where everything centers around food and television (Gems 2000, S. 192). Very popular are the "March madness" basketball games, the World Series in baseball and the "bowl-games," contests between selected college teams after the end of the regular football season, where much money and even more prestige is at stake. An excellent example of the football craze is the "Super Bowl mania," the incredible enthusiasm for the championship of the NFL (Barber and Didinger 1996, 245; Martin and Reeves 2001; Hopsicker and Dyreson 2006). More than 200 million Americans follow the game on TV. According to Hopsicker and Dyreson (2006) the "Super Sunday" is the most popular holiday in the USA and is celebrated by more people than Christmas. Because the football season is in autumn and winter, the traditional holidays like Thanksgiving, Christmas, and New Year are dominated in many families by football. These holidays are celebrated with a big family dinner accompanied by watching the nationally televised football games.

THE AMERICAN "SPORT TASTE" AND THE MOTIVATIONS OF FANS

Like the soccer fans in many countries of the world, the fans of American football, baseball, or NASCAR see their fascination with their favorite sport as self-evident and natural. But just the fact that Americans love football and Germans (for example) love soccer shows that interest in a sport depends on traditions and social conditions. Sport is a social construction and is embedded in the culture of a society or social group. Sport and the consumption of mediated sport developed within the contested terrain of values, norms, rules, and ideological orientations. Sport depends on social structures, lifestyles, and environmental conditions and is closely intertwined with the habitus and taste of groups and nations (Bourdieu 1984).[12] Emphasis on winning, conviction of American superiority and patriotism characterize American society and American sport as well as the value system of American sport consumers.

A further question still to be answered is: What characterizes those sports which are in the public gaze? What, for example, makes football so much more popular in the US than artistic gymnastics, team handball, or fencing? Attempts to answer this question with arguments referring to the "natures" of the different sports, with their aesthetic qualities, their rules, or the skills required to play them, soon lead to a dead-end, not least since the same sport is regarded as attractive and exciting in one country but as boring and tame in another. In the USA, for example, baseball brings huge crowds to the stadiums and mass audiences in front of the television (see e.g. Mandelbaum 2004). In many European countries, however, baseball is virtually non-existent. It is not the sport but the "taste" of audiences which determines the attraction of a sport or game, and this "taste" is determined not only by individual preferences but also by cultural and subcultural codes and scripts. In the USA, it is surprising that the interest of the fans focuses on two very different sports. Baseball is a sport with limited body contact. In contrast, American football is a demonstration of aggressiveness, brutality, and masculinity (Mandelbaum 2004; Szymanski and Zimbalist 2005).

Who are the fans and why are they fanatics?

A wealth of research focuses on the question: Who are the sport fans and why are they so committed to sport (for an overview see Gantz et al. 2006; Raney 2006)? In a review of the existing research, Stewart, Smith and Nicholson (2003, 206) conclude that fans are not a single group and a static parameter, but "display a bewildering array of values, attitudes, and behaviours." Fans live and express their loyalty to athletes/teams in different ways; they may change their rituals and activities and adapt to the social environments and conditions.

Since sport became "big business" with a billion-dollar turnover, fanship has developed into a favorite issue among economists, who look upon audiences as consumers and thus as addressees of advertisements and potential buyers of various products (see e.g. Dietl et al. 2003; Kühnert 2004; Schumann 2004). The main questions of economic studies are concerned with the impact of several easily accessible variables on the number of spectators: these variables are, for example, the types of sports and events, scheduling of games, accessibility, performance levels, the athletes and teams, competing programs, and the weather, but this type of research does not address the reasons and motivations of the fans.

Further information is provided by quantitative surveys on demographic characteristics and the motivations of spectators. The aim of this type of research is to gather information for the advertising industry. Fans are a steady base of viewers who have to be known in order to be "sold" to advertising agencies. Studies identified different reasons for being interested in sport, ranging from emotional to cognitive and social motivations (Raney and Bryant 2006). Numerous psychological and sociological studies revealed the following reasons for becoming and remaining a sport fan: psychological motives are a striving for tension and excitement (in psychological terms, eustress), for the release of emotions, and for drama and entertainment, the wish to escape the everyday routines, and the aesthetic attraction of sport events. In addition, opportunities to spend time together with family or friends and/or to belong to a group may influence sport consumption (Raney and Bryant 2006; Aaron and Smith 2007). However, the next question, i.e. *why* watching sport is fun, relaxing, or exciting, is not asked.[13] This question is even more important given the fact that sport is "only" a game and that successes and failures of athletes and teams have no effects on "real" life, such as economic conditions, family relations, or job situations of the fans. According to Wann (2006) and many others, one of the reasons to become or remain a fan is the quest for identification: fans identify more or less with the athletes or teams, thus "getting involved" in the action and fulfilling the need for affiliation. Being excited or thrilled and suffering with the players or competitors is one of the main attractions of watching sport. Identification is more likely to occur when the fans perceive the athletes/players as attractive and similar to themselves (Wann 2006). The identification hypothesis raises the question of the meaning of "identifying." Is identification with players or competitors the viewers' way of compensating for their own incapability? Studies indicate that fans gain a sense of accomplishment (Wann 2006, 341). In addition, there is evidence that identification with athletes and teams has positive influences on self-esteem and that fans "bask in reflected glory," at least when their team wins (Raney and Bryant 2006). The civic parades conducted in cities that win professional championships often draw more than 100,000 fans for a communal celebration of civic pride. In addition, being a fan also conveys social status – at least for male college students (on the benefits of sport consumption see Armstrong 2007).

Allen Guttmann (1986) emphasized the importance of "representational sport," pointing out that sport is looked upon as a representation of groups, institutions, races, religions, or nations:

> In "representational sport" individual identification with the athletes and collective membership in the community combine. There is . . . an apparently irresistible impulse to allegorize sports contests and to feel that collective identity is somehow represented by five or eleven or fifteen men or women doing something with a ball.
> (Guttmann 1986, 182)

"Representational sport" is based on the imperturbable conviction, not only in the USA but worldwide, that the success of athletes or teams is evidence of the qualities of the group, institution (college or university), or nation they represent. However, this is an illusion. Victories or defeats of athletes or teams have no predictive value for the state and success of groups, institutions, or societies in areas such as the economy, science, or democracy.

Fans are part of a community or network which provides social identity, and being a sport expert contributes to "social and cultural capital."[14] Watching sport takes place in "social settings" (this is true not only in the stadium but also in front of the television – be it at home or in pubs or other public places) where specific relations among the spectators (family, friends, or strangers) are produced and enacted. Media sports provide a frame and social space for contacts, a sense of belonging, communication, and feeling at ease. Sport consumption is always connected with a broad variety of practices and is part of complex interactions and rituals in the stadium, but also outside, when tailgating in the parking places around the stadia, celebrating victories in one of the ubiquitous sports bars, or sitting with the family in front of the television (on sport fan communities see e.g. König 2002; Crawford 2004).

BOX 13.4 SPORT BARS

"Viewing television in public places . . . is an established phenomenon in American culture through which communication rules, in general, and public viewing rules in particular are created, molded and practiced" (Goffmann 1971, 779). Bars are such public places; they are as a rule equipped with TV screens and entertain their clients mostly with never-ending series of sport programs. Sport bars have a special focus on fans; they feature numerous TV sets, often projection TV systems, and allow their clients to choose between various programs or simultaneous coverage of multiple events. Most sport bars are decorated with sport memorabilia and/or photos of stars which convey the proper atmosphere. All cities and most towns have sport bars which differ widely in size, equipment, and the available food. A large menu and a restaurant-like atmosphere attract more women than bars with a focus on drinking. In the latter, men dominate, sometimes even using the sport bars as "refuges from women" (Eastman and Land 1997, 161).

The atmosphere also depends on the program. When a game of the home team is on, the bar is packed with shouting and drinking fans who enjoy membership in a community of like-minded people and create a stadium-like atmosphere by wearing fan clothing, cheering, betting, and celebrating.

New forms of sport bars even include active participation in sports. The ESPN Sports Bar in New York City is full of various TV screens with different programs which may be watched from three levels, each with a bar, a private lounge, and an activity hall where people can compete in various sports with automated interactive videogames. This "total immersion concept" is now widely copied throughout the cities and towns in the US. Eastman and Land (1997, 161) assume that the sports bars may even be an attractive alternative to the stadium.

(Gertrud Pfister)

The interest in sports is widespread and worldwide, but the interest in American football (or soccer or team handball) is a product of American socialization. In numerous accounts or recollections fans talk about their first encounters with "their" sport, which in most cases took part in the family (see Crawford 2004; Wann 2006). American studies indicate that "fathers have a particularly powerful effect as a socialization agent and that parents can influence the team identification of children as young as five" (Wann 2006, 335). In addition, children develop a liking for media sports and a knowledge of certain sports sitting and watching television with their families or friends. Current constructivist concepts of socialization are an excellent basis for the description of the "appropriation" of a sport and integration into a spectator or fan culture. Here, the active role of children and adolescents is emphasized, and socialization is understood as the appropriation of the social and physical environment, including mass media and sport, in and through social practices (see e.g. Horne et al. 1999).

Interest in a sport can be also triggered off by active involvement, and here, watching sport and doing sport are, especially for children, closely interwoven. Watching sport can encourage sporting activities such as playing baseball in the cul-de-sac streets of suburbs or joining one of the flag football teams organized by the church. Playing sport is often followed by watching with the desire to learn from the athletes and imitate the stars.

Socialization into media sports also means gathering knowledge. According to the "consumption capital" hypothesis sporting events are all the more interesting, the more information about the sport, the club, the team, or the athlete is available (on the consumption-capital theory see Schellhaaß 2003). Such knowledge and analysis is readily supplied by the numerous daily sports talk shows on television and radio stations. The more background knowledge one has, the better one can understand, interpret, and evaluate the actions on the field. Furthermore, competitions are more thrilling if one knows, for example, what is at stake. Well-informed audiences can explain the line-up of players, anticipate actions, and evaluate results. The longer the "appropriation" of a sport takes and the more time and energy that is invested, the higher the "consumption capital." This is also one of the reasons for the thriving interest of Americans in sport statistics, especially baseball statistics. In the USA collecting knowledge, often in form of statistical material, seems to be an addiction: 750,000 books about baseball find readers, and each year the collection of baseball books gets larger. Fans can use their knowledge in fantasy leagues which have emerged in the major sports. In these leagues, fans pretending to be owners choose players for "their" team and then compete with other "owners". The outcome of these competitions depends on the performances (based on statistical comparisons) in the real games. There are even money prizes for the "champion" at the end of the season.

BOX 13.5 SPORT AS A FANTASY

Fifteen million American adults own a fantasy team, often a football team; but basketball, baseball, NASCAR, hockey, and other sport fans can also engage in their sport with an imaginary team. The participants, often colleagues or friends, choose their players according to certain rules from the existing leagues and compete with between seven and eleven other team owners in a league. In some cases, money prizes are awarded according to the league finish. Each fantasy player gets points according to the performances of the player in the real world, necessitating regular perusal of the statistics of the players.

In the US, the competition with friends has turned into a business with internet pages and media involved in promoting or sponsoring fantasy sport. Information about the players and strategies is marketed and is worth around three billion dollars a year. Owners spend around three hours a week managing their teams, but more than half an hour a day thinking about "their" fantasy teams.

According to the Fantasy Sport Trade Association most participants are men (93 percent), white (93 percent), college educated, and married. "In fantasy sport the valued commodity is statistics. Complicated statistical analysis packages designed to predict fantasy baseball success are marketed to owners" (Levy 2005). Many participants compete in several leagues and develop an interest in these leagues which come close to an addiction. The engagement in fantasy sport could be interpreted as an ultimate form of fandom, as an attempt to be part of a world which includes only a chosen few. Interest in fantasy sport could also be explained with the quest of fans to make use of their insight and to show off their cultural capital of expertise.

SPORT CONSUMERS – GENDER ISSUES

Sport is "doing gender," which means to say that the athletes and the consumers and fans always present themselves as men and women, both demonstrating, more or less dramatically, masculinity and femininity. Sport consumption experiences are complex and intertwined with gender, race, and culture (Crawford 2004). However, many American studies describe and analyze fan behavior and motivations without reflecting about potential impacts of race and gender on sport practices and sport consumption (see e.g. Wann (2006) about team identification).

As many indicators and the following examples show, sport consumption is highly gendered. Seventy-eight percent of the readers of *Sports Illustrated* are male (Bishop 2003), and the audiences of the sports shows are also dominated by men. In 1995, *Sports Tonight* had an audience of 44 percent women and 56 percent men, and only 22 percent of those who watched *SportsCenter* were women (Tuggle 1997).

Although many of the existing studies have small samples of college students, findings suggest that men and women have different reasons and different experiences when consuming sport. Women seem to be more likely to watch sport on television in order to be with friends or family, and they are more often "multi-tasking" (doing something else besides viewing) than men (Raney and Bryant 2006, 324). Men seem to be attracted to sport consumption more by "eustress" (identification, self-esteem and escape motives) as well as gambling. In addition, Raney (2006, 324) assumed that men have the power over the remote control and decide about programs in their living rooms according their own tastes (McGinnis *et al.* 2003).

Several more recent studies indicate that the patterns of women's media sport consumption are becoming similar to those of men. Thus, a study conducted by Dietz-Uhler *et al.* (2000) examining sex differences in fan behavior of college students showed that as many female as male students considered themselves to be fans. However, if being a "sport fan" is defined more strictly and includes variables such as enjoyment, time spent, and interest in sport news, then a large majority of fans are male. In a study of college students which compared TV sports fans with fans of other program genres, Gantz *et al.* (2006) found out that 28 percent of the sample were dedicated sports fans and 86 percent of them were men. There is clear evidence that men are more committed and addicted consumers/fans than women, they spend more time with sport, have more knowledge about sport, are more emotionally involved, and identify to a higher degree with athletes and teams. Being a sports fan is part of their image and identity (Tajfel and Turner 1986; James and Ridinger 2002; Gantz *et al.* 2006).

Women and men have different "tastes" with regard to media sport consumption as has already been shown in the paragraph about children's sport interests (p. 344) and the paragraph about the demographic variables of sport spectators (p. 352). Boys and men tend to prefer ball games, boxing, martial arts, extreme and motor sports, while girls and women are attracted to individual sports, like gymnastics, skiing, diving, and figure skating. Whereas males seem to enjoy aggressive fights, females seem to favor, besides the "Big three", sports with aesthetic appeal (Sargent *et al.* 1998). Women are a minority among audiences at ball games, but there is one exception: the audiences at women's basketball are predominantly female (James and Ridinger 2002). According to the study by Armstrong (1999), who explored the supporters of a professional women's basketball team, females made up to 70 percent of the audience (Fink *et al.* 2002). However, women's interest in men's sport seems to be increasing, as the growing numbers of female football or NASCAR fans indicate (McGinnis *et al.* 2003).

But there are still men's domains in mediated sports consumption, one of them being sports talk shows in radio. By 1996, there were more than 4,000 talk shows on 1,200 stations which attracted one-fifth of the adult audience. By the mid-1990s one hundred twenty-four-hour sports talk stations entertained their listeners. Sports talk shows invite everybody to join in the discussions about various sport-related topics. Thus sport coverage and consumption merge, and the producers and users of such sport talk shows continually change their roles. The talks circle around men's sport and male sport stars, and both – those on the air and the listeners – are men. Sport talk creates "imagined communities " of like-minded, like-thinking souls, gated circles of virtual friends where misogynist statements are accepted like "Women's professional basketball, what a joke. You wouldn't catch me dead watching it." Goldberg concludes: "Sports talk radio facilitates (masculine) self-elevation, the ideological reproduction of hegemony – risk- and cost-free but for the toll call . . . Sports talk has become the leading forum for expressing White maleness" (Goldberg 1998, 219).

Since the beginning of modern sport, women have been a minority in the baseball and football stadia. As Table 3.2 indicates, men are still dominant in the stands. Watching sport "live" as a fan and being one of the crowd is often connected with male behavior, along with a great variety of signs and symbols of masculinity, such as drinking, painting one's body, cheering as a means to yell louder than opponents, or taunting opposing fans. One may question if the football stadium is attractive for men because this is a place where men can still be "real men" (on fans and the construction of masculinity see Crawford 2004).

Media sport, consumption, and race

Numerous studies over the past three decades (1977–2001) have consistently determined racial biases of the media relative to African-American athletes (Rada and Wulfemeyer 2005). Newspapers and broadcast personnel reinforced racial stereotypes by promulgating African-Americans' success as a result of natural abilities, while successes of white athletes are attributed to intelligence and hard work (Eastman and Billings 2001; Hardin et al. 2004; Rada and Wulfemeyer 2005). Blacks are disproportionately covered in strength sports such as football and boxing; black women are nearly invisible, and defeminized in passive photos, except for track and field athletes, such as the flashy FloJo with her long fingernails and eccentric outfits, or the Williams sisters in tennis (Hardin et al. 2004). Venus und Serena, highly talented and successful, are presented by the media as a combination and interaction of gender, race, and sport. Their "blackness" in the "white sport" as well as the strength and aggressiveness which they seem to radiate makes them different from other women tennis players. This difference is highlighted by the media, whether they describe the sisters as "giants" or as "intimidating." Following the logic of racial differences their performance is regarded as being "natural athleticism." Media also frequently report about their "weird" hairstyles and clothes. "These narratives reinforce the notion that the sisters are trespassers, whose presence undermines the cultural integrity of women's tennis" (http://physed.otago.ac.nz/sosol/v5i2/v5i2_3.html).

363

Television announcers, who are overwhelmingly white, continue to characterize black athletes, especially football and basketball players, in more negative terms than white athletes (Niven 2005, 687). The media focus especially on the aggressiveness, violence, misconduct, and crime of black athletes on and off the playing field. The "bad boy" image created by some players is also reproduced by the media which are just waiting for any form of sensational news. Thus journalists basked in the rape case of basketball star Kobe Bryant and the dogfighting scandal that resulted in the imprisonment of football star Michael Vick.

Recent studies have detected a diminished amount of negative coverage of African-American athletes (Billings 2004; Niven 2005). It may be assumed that the increased participation rates of minority athletes and their successes will contribute to a more positive picture in the media. This trend seems to hold true, as the achievements of Michael Jordan, and then Tiger Woods, have brought increasingly positive coverage since 1988 (Billings 2003; Niven 2005, 688). Niven's examination of more than 10,000 newspaper articles found no significant differences in praise or criticism relative to white and black football players (Niven 2005). Billings (2004), too, found that whites are no longer praised and blacks faulted among broadcasters. Rada's and Wulfemeyer's study (2005) of the announcers of intercollegiate football and basketball games agreed that negative attributions in general have decreased; but that the remaining offensive attributes are still directed at African-American athletes. The power of television announcers is substantial in that regard because they "frame issues and interpret behavior immediately to enormous audiences" (Hoberman, cited in Rada and Wulfemeyer 2005, 1), giving them the ability to influence particularly young viewers. Grainger, Newman and Andrews (2006, 447) conclude:

> Mass-mediated sport is a site where ideologies of race (and racism) are both constructed and negotiated . . . the central role of mediated sports within the mass-media entertainment complex means that athletes, and athletes of color in particular, are increasingly important actors in the construction and reproduction of racial and ethnic identity.

Although images of African-Americans have changed, they are

> produced for mass consumption by dominant interests and have illuminated the larger cultural politics of race, advertising, and consumption. Understood in the context of the structural inequalities of American society, African American consumption is not in and of itself different from normative (white, middle-class) consumption. Rather, it is enacted within constraints, pressures, limits, and opportunities that give that consumption particular form and content.
>
> (Chin 2007)

There is little research about the amount and the patterns of sport consumption among African-Americans. Studies indicate that they are in general emotionally and behaviorally more involved in sport than whites although their attendance rate at professional and college sport is relatively low (Armstrong 2002; Baba 2003). A survey of black college students revealed a considerable difference between their media sport consumption and attendance at games (Baba 2003). Female students were significantly less interested in both TV and attending sport events. When dealing with race, social class also has to be taken into account, and the ticket prices restrict access to sport events to those who can afford them.

The most popular sport among African-Americans is basketball, followed by football and boxing. They are ardent and frequent consumers of sport offered by "historically black colleges/universities," where sport events "foster a distinct atmosphere reflecting African heritage, culture and tradition" (Armstrong 2002, 288). Football games are "a country revival and a family reunion all set to the funky tempo and sultry gyrations of black college marching bands and dance teams" (Armstrong 2002, 268). Eighty-six percent of the spectators of a black college event reported in a survey that they attended the event with friends or family (Armstrong 2002, 279). Most of them identified highly with their ethnic group. Since identification is influenced by similarity between athletes and consumers (see p. 358), African-Americans may prefer to watch athletes from their own racial group and enjoy the feeling of affiliation. At the same time they experience eustress and release of tension, which is more relevant for black consumers than for whites, and also more important given the stress many African-Americans experience in daily life.

SPORT JOURNALISTS AND THEIR (LACK OF) POWER

There is a long and contested but symbiotic relationship between sport journalists and sport teams. They depend on each other, yet often struggle, as true journalists sometimes raise questions and address issues that shed a negative light on athletes, team management, or sport bureaucrats. The sports writers' guild votes annually on which players get selected into the various Halls of Fame or are chosen for the top awards, such as Most Valuable Player (MVP) in the major sports. Such votes provide power and the journalists can influence the outcome. The writers also rank the college teams throughout the season of play and publish and discuss the placements. This is important for the athletes and teams as press coverage brings publicity, increases attendance, sells products and merchandise (and newspapers); and ultimately can determine which teams advance to the televised, and therefore lucrative, championship tournaments. Some of the sports journalists have gained a measure of celebrity due to their numerous television appearances on the sports talk shows which are broadcast to a national audience. This gives them an influential voice, visibility, and prestige, as well as an additional income.

However, journalists and leagues/teams have, in many respects, conflicting interests. League commissioners have guaranteed the reporters access to the players and coaches before the game, during the half-time intermission of football games, and in the locker rooms after the game. The NBA has even allowed access to coaches and players during the game by placing microphones on the coaches to allow fans to hear the ongoing strategy sessions during the timeouts.

> But with teams, leagues and other sports organizations stepping ever more boldly into the media business themselves, the balance has changed. Sports entities, flush with television cash, are exerting more control over access, and reporters say their ability to provide fans with critical, unfettered analysis has been hampered along the way.
>
> (Thompson 2007)

Individual players, coaches, and schools have initiated their own internet sites as a means to communicate with fans, attract potential scholarship athletes for the universities, to augment their income or revenue, and increase their exposure (Mahan and McDaniel 2006, 416).

The pro football league also established new policies which were critically discussed in the *Wall Street Journal* (July 16, 2007):

> NFL officials say they welcome independent coverage of their 32 teams. But having made $170 million in online revenue . . . and with a young cable network to nurture, the league has plenty of incentive to limit the newspapers, TV and radio stations that cover it. And it can set its own rules: anyone not abiding by its media policies can have their credentials revoked without legal repercussions.
>
> (Thompson 2007)

The NFL decided that journalists are only allowed "45 seconds of online audio or video footage with league or team personnel per day on NFL property" (Thompson 2007). The media have to remove this material from their web pages after twenty-four hours.

The leagues, the owners, the team managers, and the athletes, however, all expect positive coverage. The Washington Redskins (NFL team) refused for a long time to talk to journalists from the *Washington Post* newspaper because it had criticized the building of a new stadium. In Chicago, two game announcers for the Chicago Cubs baseball games were dismissed from their positions for questioning the poor play and the managerial decisions. But sport journalists not only have to take the players and coaches into consideration; they also have to think about the audiences who are used to a specific style of writing, expect certain information, and are not interested in contested and critical issues and perspectives, such as political backgrounds.

While there are a multitude of African-American sports heroes to emulate, there are relatively few persons of color working in the sports media industry. A 1998 study found that television and radio announcers for professional sports were largely white: 77 percent in the NBA, 82 percent in the NFL, and 78 percent in MLB. A survey of 1,600 newspapers found that 90 percent employed no African-American sports writers (Lapchick 1999). Female sport journalists are also in a minority. They still face a patriarchal and somewhat unwelcome if not hostile work environment. In the early 1970s an estimated twenty-five brave women worked in newspaper sports departments. By 2001 they constituted about 13 percent of the sports journalists. Few women, however, have long careers, often due to the demand to integrate journalism and family work. The average career lasted ten years with few women reaching management levels. In 1998 48 percent of the women still reported sexual harassment on the job and most experienced discrimination. Nor did the increased number of female sports reporters foster greater coverage for women's sports. Many women did not see themselves as crusaders for a feminist cause and they could anticipate that the low level of priority given to women's sports, and the marginalization of journalists focusing on female athletes and women's issues, would not aid in the advancement of their careers (Hardin and Shain 2005).

However, ESPN has become a very visual transition agent by employing many minority (mostly African-American) and women journalists over the past decade. While female reporters at football games are usually consigned to inferior roles, some women are featured reporters with their own daily television shows.

MEDIA CONSUMPTION – DOES IT HAVE AN EFFECT?

It is difficult if not impossible to measure the impact of media sport on the American population. Consumers are active in selection, perception, interpretation, and evaluation of the images and messages of the media, and there are no direct, inevitable, and automatic effects of newspaper information or telecasts. However, there are several hypotheses: one assumption is that media sport encourages sport participation, among other things because the stars can function as role models. This can be doubted for the adult population (see participation in physical activities, Chapter 5), but this may be true for children who emulate their idols, dream of a college scholarship and desire to play on a professional team.

The dream of becoming a sport star is especially alluring for poor African-American children, who tend to set their goals on sporting success as a more viable and quicker route than scholarly endeavors. Basketball prowess exudes a particular cultural capital in black urban areas (and some white rural areas such as Kentucky and Indiana) where boys aspire to be the next Michael Jordan or Le Bron James. James went directly to the NBA after high school, earning millions of dollars in salary and endorsements. He maintains daily contact with his fans through a personal website (Mahan and McDaniel 2006, 417). Kevin Garnett, another African-American NBA star, earned a salary of $23,750,000 for the 2007 to 2008 season. Even the lowest paid NBA player received more than $427,000. The media report these numbers and glorify the sport stars; it is no wonder that these prospects fuel the unrealizable dreams of American youth (Tucker 2007, 16).

Media sport with its focus on competition and winning shapes an image which does not call on the adult population to participate in sport. In addition, sport consumers understand themselves as sport participants and experience some of the excitement of sport sitting in front of the TV or in the stands of a stadium. One may assume that the amount and content of mediated sport contribute to the low activity rate of the adult American population.

The empirical studies examined in this chapter and elsewhere indicate that the media and media sport have profound influence on the sociological and psychological characteristics of American culture. In addition, the media are clearly driving forces behind the economics of American sport, producing the immense profits for owners, revenues for teams, and excessive salaries of the athletes in the major professional sports.

CHAPTER FOURTEEN

SPORT AS BIG BUSINESS

Sport has merged with entertainment to become a major business in the United States and the power of the American media has spread American culture on a global scale. Sport is sold, not only as a competitive event but as a product, as merchandise to be consumed. Media sport is "produced" by a cooperation of athletes and sport organizers on the one hand, and the media, advertising agencies, and large companies on the other. However, consumers also play an active role in the sport-media-business conglomerate.

MEDIA SPORT AND THE SPORTS-INDUSTRIAL COMPLEX

Media sport and sport consumption are driving forces in the "sports-industrial complex" which developed together with globalization and became a straightforward concurrence of sport with profit-making and commercialization (Maguire 2004; Manzenreither 2007). According to Maguire (2004, 305), this complex "has several dimensions – structural, institutional, ideological, cultural, and social. It is composed of a number of key groups, including state agencies, transnational corporations (TNC's), non-governmental agencies, and sport associations." The mass media are important players and driving forces in this figuration.

Manzenreiter (2007) and other scholars characterize the leading persons and groups of the national and international sport organizations, including the professional sport leagues and the NCAA, the sportswear industry, and the sports media as a "power elite," which possesses disproportional financial resources, status and privileges, influence, power and control. Since the rise of media sports in the 1960s, the American sport power elites gained increasing influence over sport development as a whole, emphasizing performance, success, and revenues. Sport organizations and leagues own the broadcasting rights and acquired a monopoly on the market of sport events. TV networks buy these rights for their exclusive use which gives them as well a monopoly position. At the same time, the sports power elites have increasingly joined forces with big companies, especially the media conglomerates and marketing agencies. The alliance of sports and media, especially broadcast and cable TV, made it possible to target large and at the same time specific audiences which could be "sold" as potential buyers/consumers of various goods to advertisement agencies and corporations. "Sports as a mass mediated spectacle helped to sell the media to an audience and the endorsed products to consumers" (Manzenreither 2007, 11; Horne 2006). It is not the primary aim of the media to provide information and to sell information and entertainment to their viewers, but to create audiences with purchasing power in order to "rent" them to advertisers. The media companies are very successful in generating revenue in this way: in 2004, more than $135 billion have been spent on advertising (Maibach 2007, 357). Because sports programming attracts the consumption orientated group of 18- to 34-year-old men, sport is a very valuable asset. In order to place as many advertisements as possible, the TV networks have to inject commercial breaks which disrupt shows, movies, news, and sport broadcasting throughout the program. Sport events have to be enacted around the commercials: for example, during a football game television timeouts are regularly taken, such as the so-called two-minute warning. When there are two minutes left in the playing period, a referee steps on the field to stop play, allegedly to alert the teams to the limited playing time. This is an absurd action, as all coaches, players, and fans are well aware of the time, always displayed on the large scoreboard clocks in the stadium, but it provides additional time for the television networks to show advertisements.

Americans do not like the barrage of advertisements which disturb the coherence of each movie and extend each televised football game. Such interruptions also disrupt the flow of the game and any momentum established by one side or the other. Studies with TV audiences revealed that most felt "commercials were boring, insulting their intelligence, and monotonous. When asked what they did during commercials most said: leave the room, switch channels, or speak with others in the room. Only 3 percent said they frequently watch them" (Gould 1989, 9). However, those findings do not have an impact on the advertisers and the TV and radio programs. In contrast to European countries, where public TV, financed by obligatory payments of all TV users, has the obligation to inform the population, the USA has predominantly private television which depends heavily on the revenues gained via advertisements. Public television plays only a very small role. It is insufficiently supported by the government and relies on sponsorship and viewer donations.

The larger the audiences and the more attractive with regard to their ability and willingness to consume, the higher the price for advertisements and the higher the profit of the media. This means that the programs, the products, and their presentation are adjusted to the imagined taste of the audiences, who are addressed by appeals to their emotions, wishes, and dreams, which are often embodied in sport heroes. Therefore, sport broadcasting often contains commercials with famous athletes and the heroes of the predominately male audiences, such as Michael Jordan, Tiger Woods, or well-known baseball and football stars. The large endorsements contracts supplement the players' salaries, making them willing partners in the commercial marketing enterprise.

TV sports coverage is "confrontainment, the packaging of confrontation as entertainment" (Sullivan 2006, 137). Sport events are enacted as entertaining spectacles where athletes, coaches, referees, marching bands, cheerleaders, announcers, and the fans play their roles. Commentaries, often of coaches or ex-players, fill the gaps in actions and frame the contest as drama focusing on the violence, hostilities, or the rivalry. Via narration, personalization and dramatization TV sport coverage increases interest, suspense and identification of the audiences. Sport coverage presents sport as a surrogate world with actions and images which celebrate the social order, affirm dominant values, create emotional involvement, and offer role models for identification; it makes the American way of life and American sport appear as natural and inevitable.

The ability of sport to appeal not only to a national, but also an international audience increased the attractiveness of media sport and the willingness of corporations to sponsor athletes and events. Sponsorship plays a huge role in American sport, and numerous companies use events from the local to the national level to reach consumers and to deliver brand-building messages. In 2004, American companies spent $11.14 billion on sponsorship, 69 percent of which went to sport events (Kinney 2006, 296).

Another form of income for sport teams or leagues is, as described above, the affiliation with sponsorships. Visibility and image created by sport and the large interest of the audiences motivate more and more companies to sponsor sport teams, events, or facilities in order to gain a huge amount of brand contacts. Thus Comiskey Park, the stadium of the Chicago White Sox baseball team, was renamed US Cellular Field. The phone company paid $68 million to the team for this name change (*Chicago Magazine*, November 2007, 24).

COMPETITION FOR BROADCASTING RIGHTS

The US does not have a single national broadcast programming service, but a decentralized system orientated to the market. Each city has its own channel, often affiliated with one of the large networks; in addition, there are regional stations and the national networks, most importantly ABC, NBC, CBS, and Fox. Besides the broadcast "over the air" stations, there is a multitude of cable and satellite channels, among them ESPN (Entertainment and Sports Programming Network) airing twenty-four hours of programming related to sports. The US has the largest supply of TV stations in the world, which leads to fierce competition, especially among the big networks and the cable services, for audiences and for advertisers (Mondello 2006). Each channel strives to present the most attractive shows and exclusive programs. Because sports, especially ball games, are very popular, the channels compete in buying the rights for airing sport and athletic events.

In the 1960s professional sport leagues established a close alliance with TV networks which used sport programs as attractive entertainment and as an arena for advertisement. This "professional model of athletics" (Sullivan 2006) had a major impact on both sport and broadcasting. It was inaugurated by the major professional leagues and adopted by amateur sport, among others, the NCAA. The motor of this business is the broadcasting rights.

The most expensive event is the Olympic Games: in 1960, the right to cover the Games in Rome had been sold to CBS for $394, 940; for the TV rights for the Olympics in Bejing NBC paid $894 million and for the London games in 2012 $1.801 billion (Downey 2001).[1] In addition, the broadcasting rights for national events are also sold (and bought by TV networks) for astronomic sums: Thus the TV rights for professional football events from 1998 to 2005 brought in $17,600 billion (Downey 2001).

Table 14.1 shows the current TV contracts for football, basketball and baseball, but also the developments over the last years. The prices for the TV rights increased decisively, as the fees for events of the professional leagues show. When comparing these figures, one has to keep in mind that professional baseball, football, basketball, and hockey teams have additional local television contracts, as well as the national broadcasts negotiated by the league commissioners (Mondello 2006, 286). Other professional sports from NASCAR and X Games to figure skating and the NCAA could also sell their TV rights for considerable sums. The NCAA signed an eleven-year contract with CBS worth $6 billion (Mondello 2006, 292).

The selling of broadcasting rights is a very profitable business for the sport leagues and associations, but not for the networks, which spend up to 80 percent of their budget for sport production for the fees. It is debatable as to whether or not these expenses pay off, especially if one considers the TV ratings. Although the hours which Americans watch sports on TV are on the increase, the ratings for the various sport programs decreased because Americans have a growing number of channels to choose from (see Table 14.1). Why do networks pay more for a product which seems to generate less revenue? Why do they tolerate financial losses? According to Downey (2001) and Mondello (2006), sport brings prestige, the status of a major player in the network industry, and attracts loyal and predictable audiences who need the media coverage for gaining expertise and being part of the fan community (Coakley 2004). In addition, sport programming generates large sums of advertisement revenues. In 2003, sport generated $6.3 billion in advertisement revenue (Mondello 2006, 279). In 2008, ESPN signed a 15-year contract with the Southeastern Conference to televise football and basketball games for $2.25 billion (http://sports.espn.go.com/ncaa/news/story?id=3553033).

> The escalation in rights fees demonstrates the network's insistence on retaining their market power, which, combined with the monopoly control of pro sports leagues and player free agency, has generated both new leagues and new events for the networks to cover. The promise of broadcast amplification led to the creation of many more championship events, expanded play off formats, and entirely new sports.
>
> (Sullivan 2006, 135)

These new sports include women's or mixed roller derby, the X games, or pseudo sports, such as poker.

As Table 14.2 shows, pro football generates by far the most revenues, more than three times more than the second-ranked pro basketball. In the middle ranks with revenues of between

372

Table 14.1 Sport rights fees for major sports

Sports rights fees
Major League Baseball

Network	Years covered	Average cost per year in millions	Total cost in millions
ABC	1984–1989	83.3	500
NBC	1984–1989	100	600
CBS	1990–1993	265	1,060
ESPN	1990–1993	100	400
ABC/NBC	1994–1999	0-revenue sharing	0-revenue sharing
ESPN	1994–1999	42.5	255

(1994 baseball strike voided these contracts after the 1995 season)

Network	Years covered	Average cost per year in millions	Total cost in millions
FOX	1996–2000	115	575
NBC	1996–2000	80	400
ESPN	1996–2000	87	435
FOX CABLE	1997–2000	40.5	162
FOX	2001–2006	417	2,500
ESPN	2000–2005	141.8	851

Sports rights fees
NBA Basketball

Network	Years covered	Average cost per year in millions	Total cost in millions
NBC	1994/95–1997/98	187.5	750 revenue Sharing in yr. 4
TBS/TNT	1994/95–1997/98	87.5	350
NBC	1998/99–2002/03	350	1,750
TBS/TNT	1998/99–2002/03	178	890

Sports rights fees
NCAA Basketball Tournament

Network	Years covered	Average cost per year in millions	Total cost in millions
CBS	1987/88–1989/90	55.3	166
ESPN	1987/88–1989/90	2	6
CBS	1990/91–1996/97	142.9	1,000
CBS	1995/96–2001/02	215.6	1,725
CBS	2002/03–2013/14	565	6,200

Table 14.1 Continued

Sports rights fees NFL Football			
Network	Years covered	Average cost per year in millions	Total cost in millions
ABC (Mon. Night)	1998–2005	550	4,400
FOX (NFC)	1998–2005	550	4,400
CBS (AFC)	1998–2005	500	4,000
ESPN (Sun. Night)	1998–2005	600	4,800

Sports rights fees College Football			
Network	Years covered	Average cost per year in millions	Total cost in millions
ABC/Liberty (Big 8)	1996–2000	20	100
NBC (Notre Dame)	1996–2000	8	40
CBS (SEC)	1996–2000	17	85
CBS (Big East)	1996–2000	11	55
ABC (Sugar Bowl)	1996–2001	16.6	100
CBS (Fiesta Bowl)	1996–2001	19.3	116
CBS (Orange Bowl)	1996–2001	16.8	101
NBC (Notre Dame)	1998–2004	6.43	45
ABC (Rose, Sugar, Fiesta, Orange Bowl)	1999–2005	71.43	500

Sports rights fees Auto Racing			
Network	Years covered	Average cost per year in millions	Total cost in millions
NASCAR			
ABC, CBS, ESPN, NBC, TBS, TNN	2000	110	N/A
FOX/FX FOX Sports Net	2001–2008	200	1,600
NBC/TBS	2001–2006	200	1,200
IRL			
ABC	1999–2004	13	65
ABC – Indianapolis 500	2002	15+	N/A

Source: TN media analysis of Nielsen data, Mondello (2006).

$400 and $600 million are the other ball games on the professional and college level as well as golf and auto racing. In 2003, each of the national networks (with the exception of NBC) and ESPN gained more than one billion dollars from ads during sports programming, between 25 and 39 percent of the total ad revenue (ESPN 100 percent) (Table 14.1). As already mentioned, sports programming is a financial loss. In spite of these incredible revenues the networks lost 1 billion dollars (2003–2004), mostly on baseball ($370 million), but also on football ($270 million) (Mondello 2006, 282).

The money generated through the TV rights goes to the leagues and the NCAA, and is distributed to the owners/members. Right fees guarantee the sport organizations an income independent of success, fan preferences, or weather. The excessive TV coverage and the high-flying fees have not only increased the revenues of teams and leagues but also the salaries of players and coaches (see Chapter 8).

The alliance between sport and the media is not without problems. Media are aiming at advertisement revenues and are thus dependent on events and teams which results in a

Table 14.2 Sports advertising revenues

Program type	2003 ad revenue ($)
Professional football	2,000,487,690
Professional basketball	579,405,080
Golf	578,834,990
College basketball	521,737,330
Auto racing	472,624,370
College football	449,534,380
Sportscast	444,863,300
Professional baseball	438,522,490
General sports show	361,562,110
Tennis	156,562,110
Hockey	127,116,210
Sports magazine	60,916,660
Horseracing	26,295,810
Sports entertainment	24,361,330
Soccer	21,533,150
Rodeo show	11,368,350
Non-professional baseball	10,435,600
Non-professional basketball	7,110,180
Non-professional football	6,603,240
Boxing	5,308,720
Bowling	4,722,010
Track and field	3,282,040
College baseball	1,758,430
Children's sports	117,200
Total:	6,315,062,780

Source: Downey (2001).

conflict of interest for investigative journalists who aim to throw light on negative developments, such as cheating or doping. They have to bear in mind that leagues are marketing partners, and good relations with them are essential for the media. In addition, critical reporting is not always popular with the mainstream audiences. An additional problem is that some of the reporters work for newspapers or media corporations that also own the teams, making their objectivity questionable (see Chapter 13).

THE "BIG SPORTS" – REVENUES, SALARIES, AND STRATEGIES

In recent decades, the interest in sport and the amount of money involved has exploded. Whereas in 1992 the total revenue of the MLB was $1.2 billion, in 2007 the revenue figures rose 350 percent to around $5.7 billion. In the same year, the NFL had revenue of $6.3 billion (Chicago Tribune, October 7, 2007, 2). At the same time, sport business has received increasing public attention, not only the revenue but also the breathtaking salaries of top players, the incredible investments of sponsors, the high engagement of cities (e.g. in the stadia) and especially the many million-dollar sales of teams have caused discussion and concerns among the media and also the mainstream population (Oriard 2007, 140, 153–158, 173).

Although the salaries of players, coaches, and officials are discussed in the media, Americans do not seem to be annoyed about the huge differences between the players' and their own income; at least, nobody abstains from watching sports and games. Especially the big three, football, baseball, and basketball, are the "money machines" for all the groups, players, coaches, and owners involved. The largest salary in 2006 was given to Bud Selig, commissioner of MLB, with $14.5 million per year, followed by Paul Tagliabue at his peak as NFL commissioner in 2003 with $10.3 million (http://www.sportsbusinessjournal. com/index.cfm?fuseaction=article.main&articleId=55422). "In American football, the average salaries of the players rose from $47,500 in 1976 to $1.1 million, and in major league baseball athletes' earning grew from $76,000 (1977) to $2.1 million" (Seattle Post Intelligence 2002). "In order to cope with the wage burden, clubs and their owner companies are on the constant outlook for new revenue streams, markets, customers, and partnerships" (Manzenreiter 2007, 8). The revenues for teams and leagues come, to a high degree, from the TV rights described above: 60 percent of the joint representation of NFL games, and one-third of the revenues for baseball and basketball games (Jeanrenaud and Késenne 2006).

American sport is increasingly produced according to business rules. It has the main aim to enhance the revenues. The sport organizers and the media have developed numerous strategies in order to raise the number of consumers, who in the end pay all the actors in the sport industrial complex.

One opportunity to increase audiences is to reduce overlapping programs by scheduling them respectively. Today, football, basketball, and baseball are not only broadcast on weekends but the games stretch out on weekdays. Football is a good example: the games of the professional, the college, and the high school teams are broadcast on five evenings during the week and the whole of Saturday and Sunday. Thus, the maximum number of viewers can be reached.

Professional sport (see Chapter 8) follows the logic of business: not winning, but revenues are everything, at least for the owners. As already mentioned above, the highest revenues are generated if all games are exciting and attract large audiences. This means that the quality of the league as a whole has to be in the focus, and all teams have to play on a similar performance level. Thus all games generate large audiences and the tension of the audiences can be kept throughout the entire schedule. The NFL and MLB have introduced a business model which aims to create teams of equal quality. Sharing the revenues among all teams, independent of their success, is an important part of this strategy. Bud Selig explained the rise of interest and revenue with an increase in fan interest by distributing the revenues more equally to all teams which helped the weaker teams to buy better players and thus increase the interest of the audiences. The same aim had the invention of the "wild card" in the playoffs, which added one more team (the "wild card" with the next best record) to the post-season tournament that determines the national champion (Chicago Tribune, October 7, 2007, 2). Unlike European soccer, which is based on an economy of emotions, where winning at all costs is the aim, American sport is based on a market economy where winning is only a tool for generating revenues (Szymanski and Zimbalist 2005; Storm 2009). But winning is a central value of American culture and especially of the fans.

BOX 14.2 SUPER BOWL ADVERTISING

Many of the ads were filled with bizarre acts of violence, totally gross endings and perhaps the strangest collection of creepy critters to ever crawl their way onto the Super Bowl commercial stage . . . Forget those warm and fuzzy dogs, bears and monkeys of years past. This year's cast included a spider that eats a singing firefly (CareerBuilder.com); a grasshopper screaming because a car's about to squish a squirrel (Bridgestone); and carrier pigeons bigger than Bud's Clydesdales (FedEx) . . . As usual, gross human acts were tops on the bill . . . There was the burly tow-truck driver for Pepsi's Amp energy drink who connects car jumper cables to his nipples. There was E-Trade's baby who tosses his cookies. And a woman's heart literally jumped out of her chest for CareerBuilder.com, a job site partly owned by USA TODAY parent Gannett.

(Bruce Horovitz, USA Today, February 6, 2008 (http://www.usatoday.com/money/advertising/admeter/2008admeter.htm))

The rise of the Super Bowl is an excellent example of how the alliance between entertainment, business, and sports and the connection between football, media, and markets function.

Designed by two of the nation's leading entertainment industries, professional football and television, Super Bowl Sunday symbolizes the conspicuous power of consumption in contemporary American culture. The hundreds of millions who watch the Super Bowl consume not only a televised football spectacle but also a variety of other products.

(Hopsicker and Dyreson 2006, 37)

The advertisement industry, knowing the large interest of huge audiences and their orientation towards consumption, uses the Super Bowl as an arena for the presentation of various products – despite the astronomical prices for a commercial. In 2004, a thirty-second time slot cost $2.3 million (Mondello 2006, 285). Hopsicker and Dyreson (2006, S. 40) called the Super Bowl an "advertiser's goldmine."

The Super Bowl is played in alternating cities, which all aim at increasing their prestige, intensifying the identification of their inhabitants with the city, and to boost tourism. Last but not least, the Super Bowl offers a stage for stars and starlets, but also for politicians who try to partake in the charisma of the game and to present their (political) messages, especially patriotism. The Super Bowl was invented and created exclusively out of business interests and developed (as football and sport as a whole) into "big business," whereby media were and are the driving force. A full two weeks preceding the game is devoted to allowing the media to "hype" the event with analysis, speculation, player interviews, and descriptions.

OLIGOPOLIES AND MARKETS

The commercialization of sport has contributed to the establishment of large oligopolies of transnational corporations and conglomerates (large concerns with various enter-prises). The five largest and most influential global oligopolies are Time Warner, Disney, Bertelsmann, Viacom, and News Corporation. They have expanded their business activities from their traditional fields of film or newspaper production to other media, especially TV, and they own numerous channels. They hold shares in various other companies, such as publishing houses and music productions. In addition, they are involved in sport, among other things, through owning professional teams (Law *et al.* 2002).

BOX 14.3 THE GLOBAL MEDIA GIANTS

A specter now haunts the world: a global commercial media system domi-nated by a small number of super-powerful, mostly U.S.-based transnational media corporations. It is a system that works to advance the cause of the global market and promote commercial values, while denigrating journalism and culture not conducive to the immediate bottom line or long-run corporate interests. It is a disaster for anything but the most superficial notion of democracy – a democracy where . . . those who own the world ought to govern it. The global commercial system is a very recent development. Until the 1980s, media systems were generally national in scope. While there have been imports of books, films, music and TV shows for decades, the basic broadcasting systems and newspaper industries were domestically owned and regulated. Beginning in the 1980s, pressure from the IMF, World Bank

---

Conglomerates have various advantages against companies with a single focus: they spread the risk, "recycle" products (e.g. when they use the same material for print media and TV), and they gain power, not only because of their financial clout but because of their influence as global players. Since the 1960s, the media conglomerates have become involved in the sport business itself. In the form of cross-ownership, TV networks have bought stakes in professional teams or they even control ownership. News Corporation owns, for example, the Los Angeles Dodgers (baseball) and has shares of the New York Knicks (basketball) and the New York Rangers (hockey). In addition, it has a 40 percent share in the Staples Center, an arena for sport and entertainment in Los Angeles. Critique focused, among other things, on the lack of independence of journalists and the intermingling of media and sport which hinders the neutrality of sport reporting (McChesney 1998). Journalists could be enticed, or even forced, to give preferential treatment to teams owned by their employers and even to cover up cheating or doping.

At the same time, the sport leagues began to intrude into the domain of the media. Major League Baseball and its teams rely increasingly on a variety of channels (and contracts). Only forty-one of the 162 games of an average baseball team are broadcast on the major networks, and 131 games are shown via cable TV, which requires an additional subscription fee of the consumers. More and more teams negotiate TV rights with independent stations. Baseball teams like the New York Yankees established their own network and negotiate broadcast rights with various cable stations. The professional baseball team owners received more than $692 million from the local television stations in 2003 (Brown and Bryant 2006, 87). The NFL followed the example of baseball and created a new source of revenue by establishing its own cable network.

The sport industrial complex is the largest and fastest growing business in the USA. It comprises, among other things, entrance fees for sport events, TV rights fees, merchandising and sponsorship, as well as sporting goods, from clothes and shoes to equipment, facilities, and private consumption fees. In the USA, the sporting economy amounted to more than 1 percent of the value of all goods and services produced in 2001 (Schaaf 2004, 325). In 2004, its turnover was $213 billion, which is twice the size of the car and seven times the size of the movie industries. Fourteen percent of the money was spent on advertising, 13 percent on spectating, 13 percent on sporting goods, and 10 percent on gambling (Schultz-Jørgensen 2005, 2). In 2005, Americans bought nearly $24 billion-worth of sports equipment. Exercise equipment brought in $5.2 billion, golf totaled $3.5 billion; while sales of hunting gear and firearms amounted to $3.4 billion, and fishing tackle sales were $2.1 billion. Sales of camping equipment accounted for $1.4 billion (National Sporting Goods Association, cited in *Chicago Sun-Times*, August 13, 2006, 6A). The American sporting economy exceeds the national economies of smaller states like Austria, Norway, or Poland (Manzenreiter 2007, 4).

A comparison of sports markets in various regions of the world indicates that more than half of the over $100 billion-worth of goods and services are spent in the USA, and less than one-third are consumed in Europe, the Middle East, and Africa. The Asia-Pacific region, with more than one-third of the world population, spent less than 12 percent of the global sport consumption (PriceWaterhouseCoopers 2004; Manzenreiter 2007, 12).

The marketing of athletes and/or athletic bodies sold numerous products for corporate giants as capitalism extended its global reach in the twenty-first century. Models, movie stars, athletes, and assorted other celebrities hawked the spurious values of myriad products, diet plans, self-help books, and a conglomeration of remedies for a perfect body and purportedly healthier, happier, and richer life. Those wealthy enough to afford it might even forgo long-term processes and strenuous work (outs) and opt for immediate cosmetic surgery, providing the desired body and fabricated appearance, if not the reality, of eternal youth.

SPORT, MEDIA, AND BUSINESS – CONSEQUENCES

The rise of the sport-industrial complex with growing interdependencies between sport, media, and business changed the face of sport and the lives of all groups involved in sport. It brought sport into the limelight as never before and transformed it from a pastime to a central feature of American society. Media sport offers relief of tension and escape from problems, provides thrills and entertainment, represents and supports the values of the society at large, and provides "intuitively pleasing images of individual and collective identification that make such social constructions appear to be naturally occurring and inevitable" (Sullivan 2006, 143). However, as sports turned into a commodity and an object for speculative interests, it is the market that decides upon the prize, the availability, and the quality of sports. "The economism within sports clearly leaves its marks on the competitive power of single teams, national leagues and certain sports" (Manzenreiter 2007, 10). Maibach (2007) emphasizes that the commercialism and commodification, the "consumer culture" with its emphasis on buying, and "conspicuous consumption" marginalize non-commercial sport cultures and activities. The intertwinement of media, sponsors, and teams as well as the power of the huge media conglomerates impede not only the freedom of journalism, but also the diversity of opinions, tastes, and practices.

In addition, the roles of coaches and athletes have changed quite dramatically, from heroes to celebrities and to entrepreneurs: "The process of corporate sponsorship, broadcast right fees, program sponsorship, and cross-ownership have not simply transformed sport, but have transformed a principal commodity that sport sells: individual athletes themselves try to become a commodity that they can in turn sell – celebrity" (Sullivan 2006, 136). The marketing power of athletes is based on identification and the loyalty of the audiences. Their messages are focused on the importance of competition, winning, and money as the award. It may be assumed that the dominance of media sport and the globalization of a business-based sport model have a negative impact on recreational activities and sport for all.

GLOSSARY

AAU – Amateur Athletic Union, a governing body for amateur sport

Abolitionism – a social and political movement which aimed at the elimination of slave trade and the emancipation of slaves

All American Athletes – a mythical, honorary team chosen annually to honor the best players in each sport

All American team – a mythical, honorary team chosen annually to honor the best players in each sport

Alumni – graduates of a college or university

Amateur Sports Act – a law passed by Congress in 1978 which established USOC and national sport federations, removing the Amateur Athletic Union from its previous position of power

Anglican – a member of the Church of England

Antebellum area – the period between the War of 1812 and the Civil War (1814–1860)

Appropriation – an allocation of funds (money allotted for some purpose)

Athletic director – the chief athletic administrator in charge of the entire sports program at a school

Athletic trainer – a certified medical attendant to a school team who initially diagnoses and rehabilitates injuries in conjunction with a physician. This person operates independently from the coaching staff.

Athletic trainer – a certified medical attendant to a school team who initially diagnoses and rehabilitates injuries in conjunction with a physician. This person operates independently from the coaching staff.

Base – any one of the four equidistant goals in a baseball game

Batter – another term for a hitter

Batting average – the mathematical percentage of a baseball player's success as a hitter, determined by dividing the number of times he batted into the number of hits made (reached based safely)

Bear baiting, bull baiting – blood sports that involved contests or fights between two different animals, or several dogs against a bull or bear, usually fought to the death and involving gambling

Blood sport – sport that results in bloodletting, usually referring to sports involving animals, such as a bullfight

Bloomers – a short skirt and pants that gathered at the ankles or knees that provided greater mobility for women

Board of trustees – wealthy and influential people, often alumni, who have direct oversight for the school, a board of directors

booster club – an organization dedicated to providing benefits to school athletic teams. At the high school level the club usually consists of parents and local merchants who buy equipment, build facilities, pay incidental or travel expenses, etc. At the collegiate level members often include very wealthy alumni and members of the board of trustees who fund athletic scholarships, stadiums, and other expenses. They sometimes try to induce athletes to come to their school with extravagant, and illegal gifts.

Boston Tea Party – Massachusetts colonists who protested the levy on the importation of tea dressed up as Native Americans and raided three British ships in the Boston Harbor at midnight on December 16, 1773, dumping the cargo into the sea. Americans honor the occasion as one of the first rebellious acts that led to the War of Independence.

Bowl games – postseason football contests between top teams that serve as regional festivals designed to attract tourists

Caledonian games – a festival celebrating traditional Scottish folk games which evolved into commercialized track and field competitions in the U.S.

Calisthenics – exercises designed to improve strength, endurance, and flexibility

Calvinist – a Protestant follower of John Calvin. Calvinists believe in the doctrine of predestination.

Cheerleader – a male or female who tries to exhort the fans to cheer for the team, now a competitive sport in itself involving gymnastic displays

Conference – a league of teams at the interscholastic, intercollegiate, or professional level, usually organized on a regional basis

Cooper Institute – an aerobic research facility and health complex founded by Dr. Kenneth Cooper in Dallas, Texas

Dallas Cowboys are among the most popular professional football teams; their name triggers nostalgic remembrances on the glorious frontier past.

Daytona – the premier auto race of the NASCAR circuit, located in Daytona, Florida

Diamond – another term for the baseball playing field which forms a diamond shape between the four equidistant bases

Divisions – a separation of teams based on regions (professional leagues) or school size (colleges and universities)

Endowment – a gift that provides income to an institution

ESPN – Entertainment and Sports Network, the 24 hour per day television sports channel

ESPN The Magazine – a weekly periodical directed at young adult males, an offshoot of the ESPN cable television channel

Field goal – when the offensive team kicks the ball over the crossbar of the opponents' goal, worth three points

384

Fieldhouse – a building that serves as an athletic arena for various sports, and may contain meeting rooms for clubs or community groups

Fiesta Bowl – one of the major postseason football games; it is located in Arizona, a state with a largely Hispanic heritage

Flag football in which the players wear a belt with Velcro flags attached on each side. The ballcarrier is considered "tackled" when his flag is grabbed in lieu of tackling. For safety purposes this is the version of football taught in physical education classes in the public schools and played recreationally in public parks.

Football bowl games – post-season contests sponsored by large, corporate businesses and hosted by large urban sites offering large sums of money to the college teams chosen to play in the spectacle

Fox – one of the major television companies

Fraternities – a group of male students bound by initiation rituals (and national organizations) that ban together, often living communally in large houses on or off the college campuses. They are often big fans of the school athletic teams and well known for their parties.

Free agent – a professional athlete who has fulfilled the terms of his/her contract for the stipulated number of years, who may then negotiate a new contract with any other team

Freshmen – a first year student at high school or college

Frontier myth – the belief that a distinct American character was forged by the frontier experience

Fumbled ball – when a player carrying the ball drops it (a fumble) it may be recovered by either team

Gate in boxing – the amount of money collected from spectators

Gibson girl – a term popular at the turn of the twentieth century, made famous by artist **Charles Dana Gibson**, who illustrated the young, athletic, independent women of the era

Gouging – a form of wrestling practiced on the American frontier in which participants tried to remove the eye of their opponent with sharpened fingernails in order to gain a victory

Grade School – an elementary school with eight grades for children ages 6–14

Heisman trophy (Heisman memorial trophy) – the most prestigous award for most outstanding player in college football, named after the the prominent football player and coach John W. Heisman.

High School – a secondary school with four grades for children ages 14–18

Hitter – same as a batter, the player on the offensive team who tries to hit the ball and run to a safe base (the bases are run in succession, and the runner may stop at a safe base; but the team only scores a run, i.e. one point, when a runner reaches the home plate (home base from where he started as a batter).

Home run – when a batter hits the ball completely over the stadium wall in fair territory (unable to be caught by a defensive fielder) he may trot around all four bases and score a run for his team

Homecoming – one game during the fall football season chosen to honor and attract alumni to the school in a party atmosphere

Huddle – a grouping of players during the brief intermission between plays in order to call a new play (strategy and tactics) depending on the location of the ball and the distance to the goal

Indentured servant – one who sold his/her labor for a period of years in return for passage to America

Inning – an untimed period of play in which each team gets a turn to bat, each team is allowed three outs per inning. A baseball game lasts for nine innings, unless the game is tied, in which case the teams play until one team outscores the opponent.

Intramural sport – an athletic contest between teams from the same school (i.e. classes or student club teams from the same school)

Junior – a third year student at the high school or college level

Kraus Weber fitness test – a series of physical tests administered to both European and American children in the 1950s

Ku Klux Klan – a secret society dedicated to the belief in white supremacy and racial segregation, sometimes enforced by violent means. This group has historically been opposed to blacks, Jews, and Catholics.

League commissioner – the chief executive officer that governs a sports league

Little League baseball – a national organization for young boys modeled after the professional teams; but played on a smaller baseball field

March Madness – the annual post-season collegiate basketball tournament to determine the national champion

Marching band – a large contingent of uniformed musicians who perform at football games with intricate formations that accompany the musical renditions

Mennonites – a German Protestant sect that opposes infant baptisms, oaths, military service, and the acceptance of public offices. They live a simple life without modern technologies.

Minor leagues – professional teams below the top level athletes, used to develop players for the higher level

Muscular Christianity – a doctrine proposed by Protestant clergymen and adopted by the YMCA that recognized the body as a holy vessel for the soul and the necessity of physical training as a wholesome activity

NAPBBP – National Association of Professional Base Ball Players

NASCAR – National Association of Stock Car Auto Racing

Nativist – one who believes him/herself to be the true citizen of a country, usually opposed to immigrants

NCAA – National Collegiate Athletic Association, a governing body for intercollegiate sports programs

Network TV and name the networks – network television is an interlocking group of local and regional stations united within one of the major television corporations: CBS (Columbia Broadcasting System), NBC (National Broadcasting Company), ABC (American Broadcasting Company), and the Fox network.

Notre Dame – the best known college team with fans all over the USA. It is the team of a

Catholic university with long traditions and it especially has many fans among Catholics. The only team whose games are televised throughout the whole country each week during the football season.

Owners – to possess something as personal property, a person or group, such as a corporation of shareholders who possesses a professional sport team

Pedestrianism – a walking or running race over a set distance or set time, some of the first professional runners attempted to cover 10 miles (16km) in less than one hour

Pep Rally – a school assembly for the purpose of inspiring and honoring an athletic team before a big game

Play days – noncompetitive athletic events arranged by women's teams. The schools mixed teams to play friendly games and then engaged in social activities together.

Play off – a series of elimination games to determine the winner of a championship

Playground movement – a national organization to provide safe playing spaces for children in the cities

Polish Falcons – a nationalistic fraternal club devoted to promoting gymnastics and Polish Culture, similar to the German turners

Pop Warner Football – a youth football program modeled on the professional teams; but organized by age groups to better equalize the competition

Prep school – preparatory school, one which prepares students to enter a college or university. Many prep schools in the US are very expensive and cater to the children of the wealthy.

Progressive reformers – a loosely formed group of men and women, usually white, Anglo Saxon Protestants of the 1880-1920 period, who attempted to improve the American society by making widespread changes

Puritans – a Protestant sect, founders of the Massachusetts Bay Colony in 1620

Quarterback – the leader of the offense (the team with the ball) in a football game, a strategist who calls the plays and directs their development

Reserve clause – a stipulation in the contracts of professional athletes that bound them to one team for their entire career, unless the owner decided to trade them to another team or discontinue the contract (which made them a free agent able to sign a contract with another team)

Roller derby – a competitive team sport, a roller skating contest in which a team scores points by passing the opponents, defenses might employ physical contact resulting in violent collisions

Rookie – a first year player

Salary cap – a limit placed on the total salaries that an owner can pay to the players on his team, i.e. a sum figure that must be divided among the players (but not equally) based on the discretion of the owner. The best players will get more than lesser players; but the limit is meant to keep richer teams from buying all of the best players with the intent of achieving equal competition for all teams in the league.

SAT is an acronym for Scholastic Aptitude Test, a general exam given to high school students to assess their competency for college level work

Scholarship – usually means academic excellence; but relative to sports it is used to denote an athletic scholarship, which provides university students with free tuition, as well as room, board, and books in return for their athletic performance on school teams

Scrimmage line – the line on which the ball is placed in a football game to start each play, one of the features that distinguishes American football from soccer.

Senior High School – same as high school, a secondary school beyond elementaryt school for grades 9–12, ages 14–18

Senior – a fourth year student at the high school or college level, could also refer to an age group, generally 65 years old or older

Settlement house – a social agency located in immigrant neighborhoods, operated by progressive reformers for the purpose of assimilating the immigrants

Slugger – a baseball term which describes a player who gets many long hits, especially home runs

Social Darwinism – the rationalization of social inequalities based on the belief of the survival of the fittest and the consequent ranking or stereotyping of racial and ethnic groups

Socialization – to adopt or adapt to the group norms, to become friendly with a group

Sophomore – a second year student at the high school or college level

Sororities – the female version of fraternities

Sport Magazine – periodical magazine devoted to sports, first published in 1946

Sports Illustrated – weekly periodical magazine, famous for its spring swimsuit issue that features barely clad models

Stock market crash – refers to the 1929 event in which stocks abruptly lost their value, plunging the world into an economic depression

Streetball – a slang term which refers to the independent style of basketball played in urban playgrounds

Super Bowl – the National Football League's equivalent of the baseball World Series, the culminating professional championship game between the champions of the National and American Conferences

Tackle – in a football game, forcing the ballcarrier to the ground so that he can no longer run toward the goal. Some interior linemen, both on the offense and defensive team have specialized roles and are called tackles.

Tackle football – the American version of football in which a runner who is carrying the ball must be brought to the ground (tackled) by the defensive team.

Tail gating – the social practice of gathering, usually in the stadium parking lot, before a football game in order to socialize, eat grilled foods prepared on site, and drink (usually alcoholic) beverages

The Dallas Cowboys are among the most popular professional football teams; their name triggers nostalgic remembrances on the glorious frontier past.

The Sporting News (1886–) a periodical newspaper, published in St. Louis, considered to be the Bible of baseball

Title IX – a part of the Educational Amendments Act of 1972, a federal law that required

388

equal opportunities for all people in schools that receive federal funds. It is often applied in order to gain equal facilities, resources, and benefits for girls' and women's sports teams.

Touch down – the act of scoring in a football game by running with or catching a thrown football behind the opponent's goal line, worth six points.

Touch football – the recreational version of football in which a runner with the ball is simply tagged rather than tackled. Like flag football it does not require padded equipment and the chances of injury are greatly minimized.

Travelling team – a team of specially selected athletes who form a club, often managed by one or more of the players' parents, for the purpose of seeking higher levels of competition in their sport. Baseball or softball travel teams seek regional tournaments throughout the summer. Some volleyball, basketball, or soccer teams may play year round in indoor facilities in local or regional tournaments.

Tryout – an exhibition of skill by an athlete in which he or she tries to impress a coach in order to win inclusion on a school or club team

Turner – a German nationalistic movement that promoted German culture and gymnastics, transformed into athletic clubs in the U.S. after World War I

Urban sprawl – the continued growth and spread of urban areas from the core inner city to ever increasing suburbs at a greater distance from the center of the city, connected by highway systems

USOC – United States Olympic Committee

Varsity sport – the top level team in any sport at each school at the high school and collegiate level

WASP – White, Anglo-Saxon Protestant, the dominant racial and religious group in the United States

World Series – the post-season national baseball championship of the United States, played between the champions of the American League and the National League, consists of the best of seven games, i.e. the first team to win four games is the winner

YMCA – Young Men's Christian Association, an evangelical group formed in England in 1844 and established in the U.S. in 1851

Zoning – the process of determining the uses of urban and suburban space, a zoning board determines if each district will be set aside for residential, commercial, or public usage. Unlike the mixed usage of urban spaces in Europe, in the United States houses and businesses are separated, usually necessitating the use of a car or public transportation for shopping.

NOTES

INTRODUCTION: OR – WHY DO WE NEED A BOOK LIKE THIS AND WHAT IS IT ALL ABOUT?

1 The term "sport culture" refers to the structures, organizations, ideals, and values linked to sport in general or to one sport in particular, along with their discourses and practices. Sport culture is part of popular culture but also belongs to celebratory culture.

2 See, for example, Assmann and Harth 1991; Francois 1996; see also the various contributions in Francois *et al.* 1995.

3 Public history also has other meanings. Most often it refers to the employment of historians in history-related work outside academia. The second meaning of public history refers to the ways in which history is created and presented in the public arena by professional historians. The third meaning of public history involves the presentation of the past for public citizens by a host of professional and non-professional historians in ways that are especially important in shaping collective memory in America.

4 H. Hein, "Historische Mythosforschung", in: http://epub.ub.uni-muenchen.de/639/1/hein-mythosforschung-.pdf, 2005; 15 January 2008. Cf. the overview of the relevant literature given in H. Hein, "Texte zu politischen Mythen in Europa. Eine Bibliografie zur historisch-politischen Mythosforschung", *Mythos* 2 (2006), pp. 227–230.

1 AN INTRODUCTION TO THE UNITED STATES

1 While America includes Canada and Mexico geographically, the authors refer to Americans to mean the residents of the United States, as understood by common parlance.

3 A NATION OF IMMIGRANTS

1 An extensive overview about "Sports and Pastimes of the People of England" is provided in the work of Joseph Strutt (1749–1802) who published four books about activities

"From the Earliest Period, Including the Rural and Domestic Recreations, May Games, Mummeries, Pageants, Processions and Pompous Spectacles, Illustrated by Reproductions From Ancient Paintings in which are Represented most of the Popular Diversions" (New Edition, much enlarged and corrected by J. Charles Cox, LL.D., F.S.A. London, Methuen & Co. [1903] http://www.sacred-texts.com/neu/eng/spe/spe00.htm).

2 Nativists tried to prevent, among other things, immigration, naturalization, and the granting of political rights to immigrants. They used laws, threats, but also assaults and terrorism (Blum *et al.* 1977, 312–315).

3 "At the present time the people who have the all-the-year-around positions are probably receiving on the average a little more than the average teacher's salary, which is true of physical trainers the country over" (Curtis 1915, 129).

4 THE RELEVANCE OF BASEBALL

1 This web page provides an excellent access to the baseball rules: http://en.wikipedia.org/wiki/Baseball_rules.

2 See http://en.wikipedia.org/wiki/Baseball_statistics. See http://en.wikipedia.org/wiki/Baseball_statistics on how statistics are used today.

3 When one of the players sued the owner for his back pay in 1924 the "lost" confessions reappeared but have not been seen since.

4 As a US federal judge, Kenesaw Mountain Landis was a very controversial figure, presiding over labor disputes, racial affairs, anti-trust cases, and treason matters. Many of his rulings were overturned; but his 1915 decision that forced negotiation between disputing baseball leagues earned him the title of "savior of baseball" and gained him the position of the first commissioner in 1921. He mostly favored the owners, as commissioners generally do (owners pick the commissioner).

5 A player usually bats four times per game. Sometimes he gets multiple hits and sometimes no hits in one game; but nobody has been able to get a hit in every game for fifty-six consecutive times (at least one hit per game), except Joe Di Maggio.

6 Chicago has two MLB teams, one in each league. The Cubs play in the National League and the White Sox play in the American League. The loyalties of Chicago fans are bitterly divided between the two teams.

7 See the Report to the Commissioner of Baseball of an Independent Investigation into the Illegal use of Steroids and other Performance Enhancing Substances by Players in Major League Baseball (2007). The so-called "Mitchell Report" presents the results of former United States Senator George J. Mitchell's investigation of illegal drugs in Major League Baseball (MLB) (http://files.mlb.com/mitchrpt.pdf http://files.mlb.com/summary.pdf).

5 FOOTBALL GAMES

1 A millionaire heiress, Anna Jeanes, left her mineral rights to Swarthmore College upon her death, on condition that it abolished intercollegiate sports. It declined.
2 On the development of the rules see Gems (2000). The current rules may be found at http://en.wikipedia.org/wiki/American_football_rules; 24.9.2006.
3 See Introduction for political myths. The myth of the American Frontier plays an important role in different contexts; it is also addressed in Chapter 2 on the evolution of American sports and in Chapter 12 on sports heroes.
4 Athletes seem to be disproportionately often involved in cases of sexual harassment. Crosset (1999) asked for a differentiated analysis of the reasons for violence on the campus.
5 College football players are amateurs, but they may have scholarships and many get secret payments from sponsors, alumni, or booster clubs.
6 Martha Stewart, one of the richest business women in the US, Americas "best housewife," is the guru for home, garden, and lifestyle. She has earned a fortune with books, TV shows, online shops, and so on.

6 COLLEGE SPORT

1 Colleges provide four years (junior colleges provide two years) of education leading to a bachelor's degree. Some colleges may offer masters' degrees. Universities confer both undergraduate and graduate degrees; but graduate students are generally not eligible to play on the athletic teams. Exceptions to this rule, i.e. a season lost due to injury, or completing a degree ahead of schedule, may be allowed in special cases.
2 A financial endowment is money or property donated to an institution, often with the condition that it has to be invested, and only the interest is used for the intended purposes.
3 There are ongoing discussions about the graduation rates of student-athletes and about the interpretation of existing data, but there seems to be a consensus that male football and basketball players yield consistently lower graduation rates than other student-athletes and "normal" students (Rishe 2003). The graduation rates also vary considerably depending on the school. In the past year policies of the universities secured the Academic Progress Rate (APR) of the athletes, among other things by eligbility rules. See also the positive development reported by the NCAA at http://www.ncaa.org/grad_rates/.
4 An in-depth insight into college life is provided by Tom Wolfe in his novel *I am Charlotte Simmons* (New York: Pikador, 2004). Some reviewers found it engrossing and authentic, others, disturbing and full of stereotypes. However, most liked the basketball scenes. Many of his descriptions and interpretations are supported by scientific studies.

5   Students typically take three to five courses each term (usually two terms per year), which require multiple books (often at $90 per book) and additional lab and course fees.

7 PHYSICAL EDUCATION AND SPORTS IN AMERICAN SCHOOLS

1   Important sources are the Proceedings of the Conference on Physical Training, Boston, 1889 and the Proceedings of the Annual Meetings of the American Association for the Advancement of Physical Education (since 1885). In 1903 the organization changed its name to the American Physical Education Association. Today its name is the American Alliance for Health, Physical Education, Recreation, and Dance. The Proceedings have been accessed at the Library of Congress/Washington and at the National Library of Medicine, Bethesda.
2   The AAAPE changed its name several times, sometimes due to the merger with other organizations; see "The History of the Organization: 100 Years of Health, Physical Education, Sport, Gymnastic and Dance", *Journal of Physical Education, Recreation and Dance*, 56 (April 1985): 22–82.
3   For the aims and the membership of the AAAPE see Ferguson (1965, attachment).
4   Park (1987) provides extensive information about physiology and its main paradigms: a belief that the form determines function and that nerves and brain are influenced by movements.
5   In the Proceedings of this conference (*Proceedings* 1889) not only the papers, but also the discussions are published.
6   "The Shape of the Nation Report about the Status of Physical Education in the USA" is published by the National Association for Sport and Physical Education (http://www.aahperd.org/naspe/ShapeofTheNation/PDF/ShapeOfTheNation.pdf).

9 FITNESS AND RECREATIONAL SPORT

1   There are some initiatives directed largely at children's health and fitness. In 1970 the President's Council on Physical Fitness and Sports, a committee of the USA government, originally established to test the fitness of children, extended its scope. Today, it is a committee of volunteer members who advise the President through the Secretary of Health and Human Services about physical activity, fitness, and sports in America (http://www.fitness.gov/home_about.htm).
2   Workplace and Employee Survey: Better jobs in the new economy? *The Daily*, July 18, 2002 (http://www.statcan.ca/Daily/English/020718/d020718b.htm 1999).
3   Access to membership is restricted by high admission fees and high annual dues. The most expensive golf course is Liberty National, on a peninsula at the western shore of the New York Harbor. The members each paid $500,000 for admission plus another $20,000 in annual dues. See Mike Palmer, An Inside Peek at the World's Most

393

Expensive Golf Club. Daily Wealth, April 7, 2007 (http://www.dailywealth.com/archive/2007/apr/2007_apr_07.asp).

4 Park districts are administrative bodies or agencies which oversee municipal parkland (including lakeshores and beaches) and organize recreational activities.

5 Bill Pennington (2003) "As Team Sports Conflict, Some Parents Rebel", November 12 (http://query.nytimes.com/gst/fullpage.html?res=9904E7DA1638F931A25752C1A96 59C8B63&n=Top/Reference/Times%20Topics/Subjects/S/Soccer#).

6 There is a National PAL which provides its chapters "with resources and opportunities to grow their own programs and enhance the quality of individual programming. These resources include funding opportunities through various grants, general liability protection programs, programming opportunities through affiliate organizations, and goods and services provided by corporate partners and supporting organizations. In addition, National PAL provides Chapter members opportunities to bring their young athletes together to compete in a championship environment in several sports" (http://www.nationalpal.org).

7 The father of the German tennis players Thomas and Sabine Haas founded a shareholder company which financed the tennis training of the young players in Florida. Thomas Haas became a professional player but refused later to pay the money back. Spiegel online, June 26, 2001 (http://www.spiegel.de/sport/sonst/0,1518,142061,00.html).

8 Other professional associations, among them the American Alliance for Health, Physical Education, Recreation and Dance and the Cooper Institute, provide knowledge, develop programs, and educate fitness personnel.

9 The Office of the Secretary includes several assistant secretaries, one of which is the Assistant Secretary for Health, who is the primary advisor on such matters.

10 SGMA is the Sporting Goods Manufacturers Association. Frequency was counted as numbers of days per year. "Frequent" meant fifteen days per year fishing, but a hundred days per year engaging in fitness activities (Uhle 2005, 11).

11 See various information in the National Center for Health Statistics (NCDC 2007; http://www.cdc.gov/nchs/).

12 http://www.cdc.gov/mmwr/PDF/SS/SS5505.pdf. See also various information in the National Center for Health Statistics (NCDC 2007).

13 It may be assumed that "healthism," which means to make health and slimness a moral imperative, has contradictory effects and leads to resistance, which in turn means a sedentary lifestyle (Gard and Wright 2005).

14 See the information at the web page of the Centers for Disease Control and Intervention (http://www.cdc.gov/nccdphp/dnpa/obesity/).

15 On the increase of population and Urban Sprawl see NumbersUSA (http://www.numbersusa.com/interests/urbansprawl.html).

16 There are huge differences between suburbs in the "sunbelt" area and those in the northeastern states (http://goliath.ecnext.com/coms2/gi_0199-6577200/Review-roundtable-the-sprawl-debate.html).

10 SPORT AND RACE

1 The Plessy v. Ferguson case resulted when Homer Plessy, who had one black grandparent, was ordered to leave a public transport vehicle in New Orleans in 1892. He refused and sued. The case reached the US Supreme Court in 1896, which upheld the law permitting states to enact and enforce the segregation of the races as long as they were given "separate but equal" facilities. The so-called Jim Crow laws resulted in separate schools, public facilities, residential areas, and so on until the Supreme Court overturned the verdict in 1954.
2 Interracial bouts were permitted in other weight classes because only the heavyweights carried the symbolic importance of the world's toughest man.
3 Harlem is a black neighborhood in New York City.
4 Greg Toppo, "Big-City Schools Struggle with Graduation Rates", *USA Today*, 20 June, 2006 (http://www.usatoday.com/news/education/2006-06-20-dropout-rates_x.htm). Toppo refers to a study of the EPE (Editorial Projects in Education) Research Centre (http://www.edweek.org/rc/), but also mentions critique on the interpretation of the data.

11 WOMEN AND SPORT: THE LONG ROAD TO LIBERATION

1 For more information about women and sport in the USA see Guttmann (1991), and O'Reilly and Cahn (2007); see also Christensen *et al.* (2001).
2 Calisthenics are physical exercises similar to gymnastics. They consist of simple movement and usually are performed without any equipment. The aim is to gain strength and flexibility.
3 On fashion, see for example, Cunningham (2003). See also the webpage with numerous sources and links http://frank.mtsu.edu/~kmiddlet/history/women/wh-clothing.html.
4 Warner (2006) provides numerous sources and gives an excellent overview about women's struggles against sport ideologies and authorities.
5 "It is doubtful if there is a more remarkable or unconventional woman in America than Miss Eleanor Sears. . . Miss Sears is a young lady with a passion for athletic sport. She is not only a champion long-distance swimmer and an exceptionally fine lawn-tennis player, but she has also distinguished herself in numerous athletic ways" (Every Woman's Encyclopaedia; http://chestofbooks.com/food/household/Woman-Encyclopaedia-4/Miss-Eleanor-Sears.html).
6 The number of female participants varies according to the sources used; see among others Daniels and Tedder 2000; Pfister 2000.
7 In the literature the number of female participants differs between six and eight (Welch and Costa 1994, 7; Boutilier and San Giovanni 1991, 8).
8 Although Didrickson jumped the same height as Jean Shiley (USA), the judges awarded

her with the silver medal owing to her unorthodox jumping style. Didrickson could have won more medals, but women were restricted to three events.

9   The revised standards now consist of three rather unspecific parts, and compliance with any one part met adherence to the law. Schools could show that the number of female athletes comprised an equal proportion to the number of women enrolled at the institution (i.e. if 50 percent of students were women and 50 percent of athletes were women); they could demonstrate a history of increasing opportunities for female athletes (i.e. adding women's teams over the years); or show they are meeting the interests of the females in the school (survey of women's interests). Such guidelines apply to high schools as well as to colleges.

10   Division I member institutions have to sponsor at least seven sports for men and seven for women (or six for men and eight for women) with two team sports for each gender. There are contest and participant minimums for each sport, as well as scheduling criteria. Division II and Division III member institutions have to sponsor fewer sports and participate in fewer competitions.

11   See the information on the web page of the AAU: http://www.aausports.org.

12   There are five professional leagues for men's sport: basketball (National Basketball Association, NBA), football (National Football League, NFL), ice hockey (National Hockey League, NHL), baseball (Major League Baseball, MLB) and soccer (Major League Soccer, MSL), and one professional league for women's basketball (Women's National Basketball Association, WNBA) with fourteen teams; see Chapter 6.

12   THE CULTURAL IMPORTANCE OF SPORTS HEROES

1   More recent biographies, such as Faragher (1992), analyze the paradoxical nature of the man as well as the social construction of his heroism.

2   Tejanos were Mexicans who had lived in Texas for generations, and fought alongside the Americans against the Mexican government.

3   See the concept of political myths in the Introduction.

4   Roosevelt's tenure as assistant secretary enabled him to formulate war plans during the Secretary of the Navy's summer holiday absence. The enactment of such plans enabled the United States to quickly capture the Philippines (Zimmerman 2002, 237–244).

5   See the concept of "whiteness" on page 80, which excluded many immigrant groups (Jacobson 1998; Roeder 1999).

6   The American League and National League champions play in the World Series at the culmination of each season to determine the national champion.

7   When using the concept of role model, we do not refer to a functionalist approach to socialization. We understand socialization as a process with an interactive dimension and dialectical relations between individuals and the social and ecological/material environment. Socialization is appropriation of the environment and self-training in and through cultural practices (Horne *et al.* 1999).

8 Edwards, an African-American sociologist, was an athlete, a political activist, and adherent of Malcolm X. He played a considerable role in the revolt (Edwards 1969).

9 The Most Valuable Player Award was established in 1969. It is given to an outstanding player of the NBA final series.

13 SPORT, MEDIA, CONSUMPTION

1 Media sport means the construction, enactment, and presentation of sport in the media. The term indicates that the media not only cover or mirror what happens but also (have to) select, interpret, create, and package (sport) narratives.

2 A company paid $12,000,000 to sponsor the Rolling Stones' half-time appearance in 2006 (Kot 2007, 5).

3 AAF/ESPN Children and Sports Media Study April/May 2001. Online. Available at http://www.aafla.com/9arr/ResearchReports/AAF-ESPNCSMR2001.pdf. This study is based on a representative sample. It is a repetition of a survey conducted in 1999.

4 The rest of the articles did not deal with athletes. The American newspapers were *USA Today, New York Times, Nashville Tenessean, The Cleveland Plain Dealer, Atlanta Journal Constitution*; see Schultz-Jørgensen (2005). See also Duncan (2006, 235).

5 "Gender in Televised Sports" available at the AAF Website (http://www.aafla.org/Publications/Publications.htm).

6 http://www.womenssportsfoundation.org/Content/Articles/Issues/History/W/Women %20and%20Modern%20Sport.aspx.

7 We understand socialization not in a functionalist sense and do not suggest that children simply imitate their models (Horne *et al.* 1999).

8 The reason baseball draws more spectators than other games is because each of the thirty teams plays 162 games. The football teams play only sixteen games each but draw more spectators per game, and NASCAR draws more than 100,000 to its races; but it does not have as many events.

9 See the information about the sociodemographic data of the American population at the US Census Bureau: http://factfinder.census.gov/

10 Motor sports events are attended by 23 percent of men and 10 percent of women at least once a year.

11 For the various forms of sport interest and for the various groups of fans and the forms of fan culture see Horne (2006).

12 See the Introduction for the concept of Bourdieu.

13 Deutsches Sportfernsehen, Motive des Sportzuschauers (German Television, motives of the audiences), 1995. The sample consisted of 300 women and 600 men.

14 See Introduction where these terms (coined by Bourdieu) are explained.

14 SPORT AS BIG BUSINESS

1 Under the package, NBC will pay $2.001 billion in direct rights for the two Olympics: $820 million for the 2010 Winter Games and $1.181 billion for the 2012 Summer Olympics (http://www.nbc11.com/sports/2255069/detail.html).

BIBLIOGRAPHY

JOURNAL ARTICLES

——. (2007) "WIAA School to Monitor Gifts", *Athletic Management*, February/March: 10–11.

——. (2007) "Assessing the Arms Race", *Athletic Management*, February/March, 5: 7–8.

——. (2008) "Extra Bases", *Chicago Sun-Times*, April 6, 62A.

——. (2007) "High School Athletics Directors Address Participation and Funding", *JOPERD*, 78 (1): 4.

——. (2007) "High School Sports Participation Increases", *JOPERD*, 78 (1): 4.

——. (2008) "High School Sports Participation Increases", *JOPERD*, 79 (1): 53.

——. (2002) "Industry Will Continue to Prosper", *American Fitness*, May-June. Online. Available HTTP: <http://findarticles.com/p/articles/mi_m0675/is_3_20/ai_86230655> (accessed March 28, 2007).

——. (2008) "Katastrophe Schule", *Der Spiegel*, 16: 113.

——. (2007) "Richard Jefferson Donates $3.5 Million to UA Athletics", *The University of Arizona Alumnus*, 70.

——. (2007) "Where's the Love", *Chicago Sun-Times*, February 25.

PUBLICATIONS

AAF/ESPN (2001) *Children and Sports Media Study April/May*. Online. Available from: <http://www.aafla.com/9arr/ResearchReports/AAF-ESPNCSMR2001.pdf> (accessed May 10, 2007).

Aaron, C. T. and Smith, B. S. (2007) "The Travelling Fan: Understanding the Mechanisms of Sport Fan Consumption in a Sport Tourism Setting", *Journal of Sport and Tourism*, 12 (3 and 4): 155–181.

Abrams, N. D. (1995) "Inhibited But Not 'Crowded Out': The Strange Fate of Soccer in the United States", *International Journal of the History of Sport*, 12(3): 1–17.

Abu-Lughod, J.L. (1999) *New York, Los Angeles, Chicago: America's Global Cities*, Minneapolis: University of Minnesota Press.

Acosta, R.V. and Carpenter, L.J. (2008) *Women in Intercollegiate Sport: A Longitudinal, National Study, Thirty One Year Update*, New York: Brooklyn College.

Adams, D.W. (1995) *Education for Extinction: American Indians and the Boarding School Experience, 1875–1928*, Lawrence, KS: University of Kansas Press.

Adams, N.G. and Bettis, P.J. (2003) *Cheerleader! An American Icon*, Basingstoke: Palgrave/MacMillan.

Adams, T. and Tuggle, C.A. (2004) "ESPN's SportsCenter and Coverage of Women's Athletics: 'It's a Boys' Club'", *Mass Communication and Society*, 7 (2): 237–248.

Adelman, M. (1986) *A Sporting Time: New York City and the Rise of Modern Athletics, 1820–70*, Urban, IL: University of Illinois Press.

Adelman, M.L. (1989) "Baseball, Business, and the Workplace: Gelber's Thesis Reexamined", *Journal of Social History*, 23 (2): 285–301.

Allen, J. (2007) *The Culture and Sport of Skiing*, Amherst: University of Massachusetts Press.

Allen, T.W. (1998) *The Invention of the White Race: Racial Oppression and Social Control*, London: Verso.

Altherr, T.L. (ed.) (1997) *Sports in North America: A Documentary History, Vol. I:1: Sports in the Colonial Era, 1618–1783; Vol.I:2: Sports in the New Republic, 1784–1820*, Gulf Breeze, Fl: Academic International Press.

Amateur Athletic Foundation of Los Angeles (2000) *Gender in Televised Sports. News and Highlight Shows, 1989–2004*, Los Angeles, CA: Amateur Athletic Foundation of Los Angeles. Online. Available from: <http://www.la84foundation.org/9arr/Research Reports/tv2004.pdf> (accessed May 7, 2008).

Ambrose, S.E. (1996) *Undaunted Courage: Meriweather Lewis, Thomas Jefferson, and the Opening of the American West*, New York: Simon & Schuster.

Anderson, B. (1987) *Die Erfindung der Nation*, Frankfurt am Main: Campus-Verlag.

Anderson, E.D. (2006) "Using the Master's Tools: Resisting Colonization through Colonial Sports", *International Journal of the History of Sport*, 23 (2): 247–266.

Andrew, E. and Sedgwick, P. (2005) *Cultural Theory: The Key Concepts* (2nd edn), New York: Routledge.

Andrews, D. L. (1999) "Contextualizing Suburban Soccer: Consumer Culture, Lifestyle Differentiation and Suburban America", *Sport in Society*, 31–53.

Andrews, D.L. (ed.) (2001) *Michael Jordan, Inc: Corporate Sport, Media Culture, and Late Modern America*, Albany: State University of New York Press.

Andrews, D.L. (2006) *Sport-Commerce-Culture: Essays on Sport in Late Capitalist America*, New York: Peter Lang.

Andrews, D.L. and Jackson, S.J. (eds) (2001) *Sport Stars: The Cultural Politics of Sporting Celebrity*, London: Routledge.

Armstrong, K.L. (1999) "Nike's Communication with Black Audiences: A Sociological Analysis of Advertising Effectiveness via Symbolic Interactionism", *Journal of Sport & Social Issues*, 23 (3): 266–286.

Armstrong, K.L. (2002) "An Examination of the Social Psychology of Blacks' Consumption of Sport", *Journal of Sport Management*, 16 (4): 267–288.

Armstrong, K.L. (2007) "Self, Situations, and Sport Consumption: An Exploratory Study of Symbolic Interactionism", *Journal of Sport Behavior*, 30 (2): 111–129.

Ashmore, R.D., Del Boca, F.K. and Beebe, M. (2002) "'Alkie,' 'Frat Brother,' and 'Jock': Perceived Types of College Students and Stereotypes About Drinking", *Journal of Applied Social Psychology*, 32 (5): 885–907.

Ashmore, R.D., Griffo, R., Green, R. and Moreno, A.H. (2007) "Dimensions and Categories Underlying Thinking About College Student Types", *Journal of Applied Social Psychology*, 37 (12): 2922–2950.

Assmann, A. (1996) "Im Zwischenraum zwischen Geschichte und Gedächtnis", in E. Francois (ed.) *Lieux de Mémoire*, Erinnerungsorte Berlin: FU, 19–29.

Assmann, A. and Harth, D. (eds.) (1991) *Mnemosyne. Formen und Funktionen der kulturellen Erinnerung*, Frankfurt am Main: Fischer-Taschenbuch-Verlag.

Baade, R.A. (1996) "Professional Sports as Catalysts for Metropolitan Economic Development", *Journal of Urban Affairs*, 18 (1): 1–17.

Baba, A. (2003) "An Examination of the Influence of Personal Values and Ethic Identity on Black Students' Sport Consumption Behavior", Dissertation, The Ohio State University. Online. Available from: <http://www.ohiolink.edu/etd/send-pdf.cgi/Baba%20Jatong%20A.pdf?acc_num=osu1064522894> (accessed April 30, 2008).

Baker, L.D. (1998) *From Savage to Negro: Anthropology and the Construction of Race, 1896–1954*, Berkeley: University of California Press.

Baker, W. (1980) "Barbarians, Players and Gentlemen by Eric Dunning and Kenneth Sheard, New York: New York University Press 1979", *Journal of Social History*, 14 (2): 333–335.

Baldwin, D.O. (2000) *Sports in North America; A Documentary History, Vol. 8: Sports in the Depression, 1930–1940*, Gulf Breeze, FL: Academic International Press.

Barber, P. and Didinger, R. (1996) *Football America: Celebrating Our National Passion*, Atlanta: Turner Publishing.

Barber, R. and Barker, J. (1989) *Tournaments*, Woodbridge: Boydell Press.

Baroffio-Bota, D. and Banet-Weiser, S. (2006) "Women, Team Sports, and the WNBA: Playing Like a Girl", in A.A. Raney and J. Bryant (eds.) *Handbook of Sports and Media*, Mahwah, NJ: Erlbaum Associates.

Bass, A. (ed.) (2005) *In the Game: Race, Identity, and Sports in the Twentieth Century*, New York: Palgrave Macmillan.

Bennett, J. (2003) *The Perfect Woman/The Perfect Family*. Online. Available from: <http://www.bernarrmacfadden.com/macfadden4.html> (accessed April 29, 2008).

Beran, J.A. (1993) *From Six-on-six to Full Court Press: A Century of Iowa Girls' Basketball*, Ames, IA: Iowa State University Press.

Bergen, K. (2007) "Bears Winning Off the Field", *Chicago Tribune*, February 4, 5: 1,4.

Bernstein, A. (2002) "Is it Time for a Victory Lap? Changes in the Media Coverage of Women in Sport", *International Review for the Sociology of Sport*, 37 (3–4): 415–428.

Bernstein, A.B., Makuc, D.M. and Bilheimer, L.T. (2006) *Health, United States, 2006 – Chartbook on Trends in the Health of Americans*. Online. Available from: <http://www.cdc.gov/nchs/data/hus/hus06.pdf#072> (accessed November 7, 2007).

Bette, K-H. (2007) "Sporthelden", *Sport and Society*, 4 (3): 243–265.

Betts, J.R. (1984) "Mind and Body in Early American Thought", in S.A. Riess (ed.) *The American Sporting Experience: A Historical Anthology of Sport in America*, Champaign, IL: Human Kinetics, 61–79.

Billings, A.C. (2003) "Portraying Tiger Woods: Characterizations of a 'Black' Athlete in a 'White' Sport", *Howard Journal of Communications*, 14(1): 29–37.

Billings, A.C. (2004) "Depicting the Quarterback in Black and White: A Content Analysis of College and Professional Football Broadcast Commentary", *Howard Journal of Communications*, 15(4) 201–210.

Billings, A.C. and Eastman, S.T. (2002) "Selective Representation of Gender, Ethnicity, and Nationality in American Television Coverage of the 2000 Summer Olympics", *International Review for the Sociology of Sport*, 37(3/4): 351–370.

Billings, A.C., Halone, K.K. and Denham, B.E. (2002) "'Man, That was a Pretty Shot': An Analysis of Gendered Broadcast Commentary Surrounding the 2000 Men's and Women's NCAA Final Four basketball championships", *Mass Communication and Society*, 5 (3): 295–315.

Bilyeu, J.K. and Wann, D.L. (2002) "An Investigation of Racial Differences in Sport Fan Motivation", *International Sports Journal*, 6(2): 93–106.

Bishop, R. (2003) "Missing in Action: Feature Coverage", *Journal of Sport & Social Issues*, 27 (2): 184–194.

Bissel, K.L. (2004) "Sports Model/Sports Mind: The Relationship between Entertainment and Sports Media Exposure, Sports Participation, and Body Image Distortion in Division I Female Athletes", *Mass Communication and Society*, 7 (4): 453–473.

Bissinger, H.G. (2006) *Friday Night Lights: A Town, a Team. A Dream*, Cambridge, MA: Da Capo Press.

Block, D. (2005) *Baseball Before we Knew It: A Search for the Roots of the Game*, Lincoln: University of Nebraska Press.

Bloom, J. (2000) *To Show What an Indian Can Do: Sports at Native American Boarding Schools*, Minneapolis: University of Minnesota Press.

Blum, J.M., McFeely, W.S., Morgan, E.S., Schlesinger Jr., A.M. and Stamp, K.M. (1989) *The National Experience. A History of the United States* (7th edn), New York: Harcourt Brace Jovanovich.

Blum, J.M., Morgan, E.S., Rose, W.L., Schlesinger Jr., A.M., Stamp, K.M. and Woodward, C.V. (1977) *The National Experience: A History of the United States*, New York: Harcourt Brace Jovanovich.

Bogue, A.G. (1998) *Frederick Jackson Turner: Strange Roads Going Down*, Norman, OK: University of Oklahoma Press.

Borish, L.J. (1987) "The Robust Woman and the Muscular Christian: Catharine Beecher, Thomas Higginson and Their Vision of American Society, Health, and Physical Activities", *International Journal of the History of Sport*, 4: 139–154.

Borish, L. J. (1996) "Women at the Modern Olympic Games: An Interdisciplinary Look at

American Culture", *Quest*, 48(1): 43–56.

Borish, L.J. (1997) "'A Fair, Without the Fair, is No Fair at All': Women at the New England Agricultural Fair in the Mid-Nineteenth Century", *Journal of Sport History*, 24 (2): 155–176.

Borish, L.J. (2004) "'The Cradle of American Champions, Women Champions . . . Swim Champions': Charlotte Epstein, Gender and Jewish Identity, and the Physical Emancipation of Women in Aquatic Sports", *The International Journal of the History of Sport*, 21: 197–235.

Borish, L.J. (2005) "Benevolent America: Rural Women, Physical Recreation, Sport and Health Reform in Ante-Bellum New England", *International Journal of the History of Sport*, 22 (6): 946–973.

Bourdieu, P. (1984) *Distinction: A Social Critique of the Judgement of Taste*, London: Routledge & Kegan Paul.

Bourdieu, P. (1986) "Historische und soziale Voraussetzungen modernen Sports" In: Hortleder, G.and Gebauer, G. (eds) *Sport - Eros - Tod*, Frankfurt am Main: Suhrkamp, 91–112.

Bourdieu, P. (1988) "Program for a Sociology of Sport", *Sociology Sport Journal*, 5: 153–161.

Bourdieu, P. (1991) "Sport and Social Class", in C. Mukerji and M. Schudson (eds) *Rethinking Popular Culture: Contemporary Perspectives in Cultural Studies*, Berkeley/Los Angeles: University California Press, 357–373.

Boutilier, A. and San Giovanni, B. (1991) *The Sporting Woman*, Champaign, IL: Human.

Brailsford, D. (1969) *Sport and Society: Elizabeth to Anne*, London: Routledge.

Breen, T.H. (1977) "Horses and Gentlemen: The Cultural Significance of Gambling among the Gentry of Virginia", *William and Mary Quarterly*, 3 (34): 239–257.

Brettschneider, W. D. and Brandl-Bredenbeck, H. (1997) *Sportkultur und jugendliches Selbstkonzept*, Weinheim: Beltz.

Brodkin, K. (1998) *How Jews Became White Folks and What That Says about Race in America*, Brunswick, NJ: Rutgers University Press.

Brown, D. and Bryant, J. (2006) "Sport Content on U.S. Television", in A.A. Raney and J. Bryant (eds) *Handbook of Sports Media*, Mahwah, NJ: Lawrence Erlbaum Associates, 77–104.

Brown, S.F. (2005) "Exceptionalist America: American Sorts Fans' Reactions to Internationalization", *International Journal of the History of Sport*, 22:6 (November), 1106–1135.

Brownson, R.C., Boehmer, T.K. and Luke, D.A. (2005) "Declining Rates of Physical Activity in the United States", *Annual Revue of Public Health*, 26: 421–443.

Brubacher, J.S. and Rudy, W. (1997) *Higher Education in Transition: A History of American Colleges and Universities*, New Brunswick, NJ: Transaction Publishers.

Brumwell, S. (2004) *White Devil: A True Story of War, Savagery, and Vengeance in Colonial America*, Cambridge, MA: Da Capo Press.

Bryant, J. and Holt, A.M. (2006) "A Historical Overview of Sports and Media in the United

States", in A. Raney and J. Bryant (eds) *Handbook of Sports Media*, Mahwah, NJ: Lawrence Erlbaum Associates, 21–43.

Buckworth, J. and Nigg, C. (2004) "Physical Activity, Exercise, and Sedentary Behavior in College Students", *Journal of American College Health*, 53: 28–34.

Bulger, M.A. (1982) "American Sporstwomen in the 19th Century", *Journal of Popular Culture*, 16 (2): 1–16.

Bureau of Recreation (1931) *Bureau of Recreation of the Board of Education, Annual Report, 1930–31*, Chicago: City of Chicago.

Byers, W. (1997) *Unsportsmanlike Conduct: Exploiting College Athletes*, Ann Arbor: University of Michigan Press.

Cahan, A. (1896) Yekl. *A Tale of the New York Ghetto*, New York: D. Appleton & Company.

Cahn, S. (2004) "'Cinderellas' of Sport: Black Women in Track and Field", in P. Miller and D.K. Wiggins (eds) *Sport and the Color Line*, New York: Routledge, 211–232.

Carney, S. (2006) "Youth Sport Participation", *UpdatePlus*, 21.

Carpenter, L.J. and Acosta, R.V. (2005) *Title IX*, Champaign, IL: Human Kinetics.

Carpenter, L. and Acosta, V. (2008) "Women in Intercollegiate Sport – A Longitudinal, National Study. Thirty One Year Update". Online. Available from: <http://www.acosta carpenter.org/2008%20Summary%20Final.pdf>.

Carriere, M.H. (2005) "'A Diamond Is a Boy's Best Friend': The Rise of Little League Baseball, 1939–1964", *Journal of Sport History*, 32 (3): 351–378.

Carson, M. (1990) *Settlement Folk: Social Thought and the American Settlement Movement, 1885–1930*, Chicago: University of Chicago Press.

Carter, J.M. (1988) *Sports and Pastimes of the Middle Ages*, Lanham, MD: University Press of America.

Chin, E. (2007) "Consumption, African Americans", in G. Ritzer (ed.) *Blackwell Encyclopedia of Sociology*, Blackwell Publishing. Online. Available from: <http://www.blackwell reference.com.ep.fjernadgang.kb.dk/subscriber/tocnode?id=g9781405124331_ chunk_g97814051243319_ss1-104> (accessed April 30, 2008).

Christensen, K., Guttmann, A. and Pfister, G. (2001) *International Encyclopedia of Women and Sports*, New York: Macmillan.

Christopherson, N.J., McConnell, M. and Diaz, E. (2002) "Two Kicks Forward, One Kick Back: A Content Analysis of Media Discourses on the 1999 Women's World Cup Soccer Championship", *Sociology of Sport Journal*, 19 (2): 170–188.

City of Chicago (1916) *Annual Report of the Committee on Parks, Playgrounds and Beaches*, Chicago: City of Chicago.

Clark, D.A.T. (2005) "Wa a o, wa ba ski na me ska ta!: 'Indian' Mascots and the Pathology of Anti-indigenous Racism", in A. Bass (ed.) *In the Game: Race, Identity and Sports in the Twentieth Century*, New York: Palgrave Macmillan, 137–166.

Coakley, J. J. (1998) *Sport in Society* (6th edn), New York: McGraw-Hill.

Coakley, J.J. (2004) *Sports in Society: Issues and Controversies*, Boston: McGraw-Hill.

Coakley, J.J. (2007) *Sports in Society: Issues and Controversies*, New York: McGraw-Hill.

Cobb, J.C. (2005) *Way Down South: A History of Southern Identity*, New York: Oxford University Press.

Cohen, L. (1990) *Making a New Deal: Industrial Workers in Chicago, 1919–1939*, New York: Cambridge University Press, 213–368.

Cole, C.L. and Andrews, D.L. (2001) "America's New Son: Tiger Woods and America's Multiculturalism (*sic*)", in D. L. Andrews and S. J. Jackson, *Sport Stars*, London: Routledge, 70–86.

Collier, B.S. (2004) "Running", in C.R. King (ed.) *Native Americans in Sports, Vol. 2*, Armonk, NY: M.E. Sharpe, 262–266.

Connell, R.W. (2002) *Gender*, Cambridge: Polity Press.

Conzen, K.N. (1989) "Ethnicity as Festive Culture: German-America on Parade", in W. Sollors (ed.) *The Invention of Ethnicity*, Oxford: Oxford University Press, 44–76.

Cooper, J.F. (1824) *On the Proper Occupations of Women in America*. Online. Available from: <http://xroads.virginia.edu/~HYPER/DETOC/FEM/employment.htm> (accessed April 29, 2008).

Corn, J.J. (2002) *The Winged Gospel: America's Romance with Aviation*. Baltimore: JHU Press.

Countryman, E. (1996) *Americans: A Collision of Histories*, New York: Hill & Wang.

Coventry, B.T. (2004) "On the Sidelines: Sex and Racial Segregation Within Sports Broadcasting", *SSJ 21*, 3, 322–341.

Cramer, R. B. (2000) *Joe Di Maggio: The Hero's Life*, New York: Simon & Schuster.

Crawford, G. (2004) *Consuming Sport: Fans, Sport and Culture*, London: Routledge.

Creamer, R.W. (1974) *Babe: The Legend Comes to Life*, New York: Simon & Schuster.

Crepeau, R.C. (2003) *Sport and Society for H-Arete*. Online. Available from: <http://h-net.msu.edu/cgi-bin/logbrowse.pl?trx=vx&list=H-Arete&month=0302&week=d&msg=71DSAebscgE455pYXpQPRw&user=&pw=> (accessed May 5, 2008).

Crichton, K. (2000) "Indiana Madness", *Collier's* (6 February 1937), 18, 38, cited in D. O. Baldwin, *Sports in North America: A Documentary History, Vol. 8: Sports in the Depression, 1930–1940*, Gulf Breeze, FL: Academic International Press.

Crosset, B. and McDonald, M. (1995) "Male Student-athletes Reported for Sexual Assault: A Survey of Campus", *Journal of Sport and Social Issues*, 19(2): 126–140.

Crosset, T. (1999) "Male Athletes' Violence Against Women: A Critical Assessment of the Athletic Affiliation, Violence Against Women Debate", *QUEST*, 51(3): 244–257.

Crossman, J., Vincent, J. and Speed, H. (2007) "The Times They Are A-changin: Gender Comparisons in Three National Newspapers of the 2004 Wimbledon", *International Review for the Sociology of Sport*, 42 (1): 27–41.

Csikszentmihalyi, M. (1975) *Beyond Boredom and Anxiety: Experiencing Flow in Work and Play*, San Francisco: Jossey-Bass.

Csikszentmihalyi, M. (1990) *Flow: The Psychology of Optimal Experience*. New York: Harper & Row.

Cunningham, G.B. (2003) "Media Coverage of Women's Sport: A New Look at an Old Problem", *Physical Educator*, 60(2): 43–59.

Cunningham, G.B., Sagas, M., Sartore, M., Amsden, M. and Schelihase, A. (2004) "Gender Representation in the NCAA News: Is the Glass Half Full or Half Empty?", *Sex Roles*, 50(11/12): 861–870.

Curtis, H.S. (2006 [1915]) *The Practical Conduct of Play*, New York: Macmillan. Da Capo Press.

Daniels, S. and Tedder, A. (2000) *"A Proper Spectacle": Women Olympians 1900–1936*, Houghton Conquest, Bedforshire: ZeNaNA Press.

Dant, T. and Wheaton, B. (2007) "Windsurfing: An Extreme Form of Material and Embodied Interaction?", *Anthropology Today*, 23(6): 8–12.

Danzig, A. (1956) *The History of American Football*, Englewood Cliffs, NJ: Prentice-Hall.

Darby, P. (2006) "Emigrants at Play: Gaelic Games and the Irish Diaspora in Chicago, 1884–v.1900", *Sport in History*, 26: 47–63.

Darst, P.W. and Pangrazi, R.P. (2008) *Dynamic Physical Education for Secondary School Students*.

David, K. and Washington, R. (2001) "Sport and Society", *Annual Review of Sociology*, 27: 187–212.

Davidson, S. (1997) *Changing the Game: The Inside Stories of Tennis Champions Alice Marble and Althea Gibson*, Seattle, WA: Seal Press.

Davies, R. (2002) "Media Power and Responsibility in Sport and Globalisation." Online. Available from: <http://www.playthegame.org/knowledge-bank/articles/media-power-and-responsibility-in-sport-and-globalisation.html>.

Davies, R.O. (2007) *Sports in American Life: A History*, Malden, MA: Blackwell.

Davis, J.A. (1911) *"The Missing Link" and the Howard Theatre*, Washington: Murray Bros. Press.

Dawley, A. (1991) *Struggles for Justice: Social Responsibility and the Liberal State*, Cambridge, MA: The Belknap Press, 334–417.

Decker, L. (2004) *Frauen und Olympische Spiele – Vom Ausschluss zur Integration? Eine historische Betrachtung der Entwicklung*, Unpublished Master Thesis. Heidelberg University.

Degler, C.N. (1998) "National Identity and the Conditions of Tolerance", in N. Finzsch and D. Schirmer (eds) *Identity and Tolerance: Nationalism, Racism, and Xenophobia in Germany and the United States*, Cambridge: Cambridge University Press, 1–19.

Delaney, K. and Eckstein, R. (2003) *Public Dollars, Private Stadiums: The Battle Over Building Sports Stadiums*, New Brunswick, NJ: Rutgers University Press.

Demos, J. (1994) *The Unredeeemed Captive: A Family Story from Early America*, New York: Alfred A. Knopf.

Dickson, P. (2008) *Baseball's Greatest Quotations*, New York: Collins.

Dietl, H., Franck, E. and Roy, P. (2003) "Determinanten der Nachfrage nach Fussballhighlights im Free-TV. Eine empirische Analyse am Beispiel der Sendung 'ran'", *Working Paper Series*, University of Zurich.

Dietz-Uhler, B., Harrick, E. A., End, C. M. and Jacquemotte, L. (2000) "Sex Differences in Sport Fan Behavior and Reasons for Being a Sport Fan", *Journal of Sport Behavior*, 23: 219–231.

Dinerstein, J. (2005) "Backfield in Motion: The Transformation of the NFL by Black Culture", in A. Bass (ed.) *In the Game: Race, Identity, and Sports in the Twentieth*

Century, New York: Palgrave Macmillan, 169–189.

Douglas, D.D. (2002) "To be young, gifted, black and female: A meditation on the cultural politics at play in representations of Venus and Serena Williams", *Sosol* 5 (2) Online. Available from: http://physed.otago.ac.nz/sosol/v5i2/v5i2_3.html.

Douglas, D.D. (2005) "Venus, Serena, and the Women's Tennis Association: When and Where 'Race' Enters", *Sociology of Sport Journal*, 22 (3): 256–282.

Downey, K. (2001) "Sports TV Get Pricier and Pricier. Here's Why. Primer on the Economics of Jumping Jockstraps", *Media life magazine*. Online. Available from: <http://www.medialifemagazine.com/news2001/apr01/apr09/4_thurs/news1thursday.html> (accessed April 30, 2008).

Doyle, A. (1996) "Bear Bryant: Symbol of an Embattled South", *Colby Quarterly*, 32, 1 (March): 72–86.

Duany, A., Plater-Zyberk, E. and Jeff Speck, J. (2000) *Suburban Nation: The Rise of Sprawl and the Decline of the American Dream*, New York: North Point Press.

Duderstadt, J.J. (2003) *Intercollegiate Athletics and the American University: A University President's Perspective*, Ann Arbor, MI: University of Michigan Press.

Duncan, M. C. (2006) "Gender Warriors in Sport: Women and the Media", in A. A. Raney and J. Bryant (eds) *Handbook of Sports and Media*, Mahwah, NJ: Lawrence Erlbaum Associates, 231–252.

Duncan, M., Messner, M. and Willms, N. (2005) *Gender in Televised Sports: News and Highlights Shows, 1989–2004*. Online. Available from: <http://www.la84foundation.org/9arr/ResearchReports/tv2004.pdf> (accessed May 5, 2008).

Dunning, E. and Elias, N. (1986) *Quest for Excitement: Sport and Leisure in Civilizing Process*, Oxford: Blackwell.

Dyreson, M. (2002) "Reading Football History: New Vistas in the Landscape of Sport", *Journal of Sport History*, 29, 2 (summer): 203–220.

Dyreson, M. (2005) "The Paradoxes of American Insularity, Exceptionalism and Imperialism", *International Journal of the History of Sport*, 22(6): 938–945.

Dyreson, M. (2006) "Jesse Owens: Leading Man in Modern American Tales of Racial Progress and Limits", in D.K. Wiggins (ed) *Out of the Shadows*, Fayetteville, AK: University of Arkansas Press, 110–131.

Dyreson, M. (2008) "Johnny Weismuller and the Old Global Capitalism: The Origins of the Federal Blueprint for Selling American Culture to the World", *International Journal of the History of Sport*, 25, 2 (February 15): 268–283.

Dyreson, M. (2008) "Marketing Weissmuller to the World: Hollywood's Olympics and Federal Schemes for Americanization through Sport", *International Journal of the History of Sport*, 25, 2 (February 15): 284–306.

Dzikus, L. (2004) "American Football in West Germany: Cultural Transformation, Adaptation, and Resistance", in A. Hofmann (ed.) *Turnen and Sport: Transatlantic Transfers*, Münster: Waxman, S. 221–239.

Eastman, S.T. and Billings, A.C. (1999) "Gender Parity in the Olympics: Hyping Women Athletes, Favouring Men Athletes", *Journal of Sport and Social Issues*, 23: 140–170.

Eastman, S.T. and Billings, A.C. (2001) "Biased Voices of Sports: Racial and Gender

Stereotyping in College Basketball Announcing", *Howard Journal of Communications*, 12(4): 183–201.

Eastman, S.T. and Land, A.M. (1997) "The Best of Both Worlds: Sports Fans Find Good Seats at the Bar", *Journal of Sport and Social Issues*, 21: 156–178.

Edwards, H. (1969) *The Revolt of the Black Athletes*, New York: The Free Press.

Eisen, G., Kaufmann, H. and Lämmer, M. (eds) (2003) *Sport and Physical Education in Jewish History*, Israel: Wingate.

Elias, N. (1971) "The Genesis of Sport as a Sociological Problem", in E.G. Dunning (ed.) *The Sociology of Sport*, London: Frank Cass, 88–115.

Elias, N. (1978) *The Civilizing Process*, New York: Urizen Books.

Elias, N. and Dunning, E. (1982) "Freitzeit und Muße", in N. Elias and E. Dunning (eds) *Sport im Zivilisationsprozess*, Münster: Lit-Verlag o.J, 133–144.

Elias, N. and Dunning, E. (1986) *Sport im Zivilisationsprozess*, Münster: Lit-Verlag o.J.

Elliot, S. (2008, August 18) Olympics draw high percentage of women viewers, and ads intended for them, *New York Times*. Online. Available from: http://nytimes.com/ 2008/08/19/sports/olympics/19adco.html?_r=1&ref=business.

End, C.M., Kretschmar, J. and Dietz-Uhler, B. (2004) "College Students' Perceptions of Sport Fandom as a Social Status Determinant", *International Sports Journal*, 8: 114–123.

Ernst, R. (1991) *Weakness is a Crime; The Life of Bernarr Macfadden*, Syracuse: Syracuse University Press.

Eskes, T.B, Duncan, M.C. and Miller, E.M. (1998) "The Discourse of Empowerment: Foucault, Marcuse, and Women's Fitness Texts", *Journal of Sport and Social Issues*, 22: 317–344.

Everhart, R.B. and Pemberton, C.L.A. (2001) "The Institutionalization of a Gender Biased Sport Value System". Online. Available from: <http://www.advancingwomen.com/ awl/winter2001/everhart_pemberton.html> (accessed November 1, 2004).

Ewing, R., Schmid, T., Killingsworth, R., Zlot, A. and Raudenbush, S. (2003) "Relationship between Urban Sprawl and Physical Activity, Obesity, and Morbidity", *American Journal of Health Promotion*, 18(1): 47–57.

Fain, P. (2008) "Buckeyes' Leader Believes Presidents Should Help Contain Sports Spending", *Chronicle of Higher Education*, January 11, A24.

Falk, G. (2005) *Football and American Identity*, Binghamton, NY: Haworth Press.

Faragher, J. M. (1992) *Daniel Boone: The Life and Legend of an American Pioneer*, New York: Henry Holt.

Feldman, A.F. and Matjasko, J.L. (2005) "The Role of School-based Extracurricular Activities in Adolescent Development: A Comprehensive Review and Future Directions", *Review of Educational Research*, 75(2): 159–210.

Ferguson, P. (1965) *"The Evolution of the Division for Girls and Women's Sport"*. Masters Thesis, Eastern Illinois University.

Fields, S.K. (2003) "Hoover v. Meiklejohn: The Equal Protection Clause, Girls, and Soccer", *Journal of Sport History*, 30(3): 309–321.

Fields, S.K. (2005) *Female Gladiators: Gender, Law, and Contact Sport in America,*

Champaign, IL: University of Illinois Press.

Fink, J.S. and Kensicki, L.J. (2002) "An Imperceptible Difference: Visual and Textual Constructions of Femininity in Sports Illustrated and Sports Illustrated for Women", *Mass Communication & Society*, 5(3): 317–339.

Fink, J.S., Trail, G.T. and Anderson, D.F. (2002) "Environmental Factors Associated with Spectator Attendance and Sport Consumption Behavior: Gender and Team Differences", *Sport Marketing Quarterly*, 11 (1): 8–19.

Flexner, E and Fitzpatrick, E.F. (1996) *Century of struggle: The woman's rights movement in the United State,* Cambridge, MA: Harvard University Press.

Flood, C. (1996) *Political Myth: A Theoretical Introduction*, New York: Garland.

Folsom, F. (1991) *Impatient Armies of the Poor: The Story of Collective Action of the Unemployed. 1808–1942*, Niwot, CO: University Press of Colorado, 231–431.

Foner, E. (1983) *Nothing But Freedom: Emancipation and Its Legacy*, Baton Rouge, LA: Louisiana State University Press.

Foner, E. and Garraty, J.A. (eds) (1991) *The Reader's Companion to American History*, Boston: Houghton Mifflin.

Foster, M (2008, May 9) "Fans long to have their ashes scattered on sporting sites", *Seattle Times*. Online. Available from: <http://seattletimes.nwsource.com/html/sports/2004402982_apathleticashes.html>.

Fox, S. (1994) *Big Leagues: Professional Baseball, Football, and Basketball in National Memory*, New York: William Morrow & Co., 106–109.

Francois, E. (ed.) (1996) *Lieux de Mémoire*, Erinnerungsorte, Berlin: FU.

Francois, E. and Schulze, H. (1999) *Worum geht es bei den "Deutsche Erinnerungsorten"*, Berlin: Freie Universität.

Francois, E. and Schulze, H. (eds) (2001) *Deutsche Erinnerungsorte*, 2–3, München: Beck.

Francois, E., Siegrist, H. and Vogel, J. (eds) (1995) *Nation und Emotion: Deutschland und Frankreich im Vergleich*, Göttingen: Vandenhoeck & Ruprecht.

Frank, M. (2000) "Fan Interest Rebounds Sharply", *Street and Smith's Sports Business Journal*, 3(18): 41–47.

Franks, J.S. (ed.) (2004) *Sports in North America: A Documentary History, Vol. 10: Sports, Prosperity, Conformity, Cultural Stirrings, 1950–1960*, Gulf Breeze, FL: Academic International Press.

Frevert, U. (1986) *Frauen-Geschichte. Zwischen bürgerlicher Verbesserung und Neuer Weiblichkeitt*, Frankfurt am Main: Suhrkamp.

Friedman, J.E., Shade, W.G. and Capozzoli, A.J. (eds) (1984) *Our American Sisters. Women in American Life and Thought*, Lexington, MA: D.C. Heath & Co.

Fry, J. (2006) *The Story of Modern Skiing*, Lebanon: University Press of New England.

Galson, D. W. (1981) *White Servitude in Colonial America: An Economic Analysis*, Cambridge: Cambridge University Press. Online. Available from: <http://www.geo cities.com/nai_cilh/servitude.html>.

Gantz, W. (2006) "Sports Versus All Comers: Comparing TV Sports Fans with Fans of Other Programming Genres", *Journal of Broadcasting and Electronic Media*, 50 (1): 95–118.

Gantz, W., Wang, Z. and Bradley, S.D. (2006) "Televised NFL Games, the Family, and Domestic Violence", in A. A. Raney and J. Bryant (eds) *Handbook of Media and Sports*, Mahwah, NJ: Lawrence Erlbaum Associates, 365–381.

Gard, M. and Wright, J. (2005) *The Obesity Epidemic Science, Morality, and Ideology*, London: Routledge.

Garraty, J.A. (1983) *The American Nation: A History of the United States*, New York: Harper & Row.

Gelber, S.M. (1983) "Working at Playing: The Culture of the Workplace and the Rise of Baseball", *Journal of Social History*, 16 (summer): 3–21.

Gems, G.R. (1993a) "Sport, Religion, and Americanization: Bishop Sheil and the Catholic Youth Organization", *International Journal of the History of Sport*: 233–241.

Gems, G.R. (1993b) "Working Class Women and Sport: An Untold Story", *Women in Sport and Physical Activity Journal*, 2: 17–30.

Gems, G.R. (1995a) "Blocked Shot: The Development of Basketball in the African American Community of Chicago", *Journal of Sport History*, 22(2): 135–148.

Gems, G.R. (1995b) "Sport and the Forging of a Jewish-American Culture: The Chicago Hebrew Institute", *Journal of American Jewish History*, 83: 15–26.

Gems, G.R. (ed.) (1996a) *Sports in North America: A Documentary History*, Vol. 5: *Sports Organized, 1880–1900*, Gulf Breeze, FL: Academic International Press.

Gems, G.R. (1996b) "The Prep Bowl: Sport, Religion and Americanization in Chicago", *Journal of Sport History* (Fall), 284–302.

Gems, G.R. (1997) *Windy City Wars: Labor, Leisure, and Sport in the Making of Chicago*, Lanham, MD: Scarecrow Press.

Gems, G.R. (2000) *For Pride, Profit, and Patriarchy: Football and the Incorporation of American Cultural Values*, Lanham, MD: Scarecrow Press.

Gems, G.R. (2006a) "Jack Johnson and the Quest for Racial Respect", in David K. Wiggins (ed.) *Out of the Shadows: A Biographical History of African American Athletes*, Fayetteville: University of Arkansas Press.

Gems, G.R. (2006b) *The Athletic Crusade: Sport and American Cultural Imperialism*, Lincoln: University of Nebraska Press.

Gems, G.R. (2007) "Football und Feminismus", in U. Roger *et al.* (eds) *Frauen am Ball*, Hamburg: Czwalina, 19–27.

Gems, G.R. and Pfister, G. (2007) "Warum die Amerikaner Football lieben" (Why Americans Love Football), *Sportwissenschaft*, 2: 151–171.

Gerber, E. (1975) "The Controlled Development of Collegiate Sport for Women, 1923–1936", *Journal of Sport History*, 2 (1): 1–28.

Gerber, E. *et al.* (1974) *The American Woman in Sport*, New York: Addison Wesley.

Gerhard, U. (1989) *Verhältnisse und Verhinderungen* (4th edn), Frankfurt: Suhrkamp.

Gilfoyle, T.J. (2006) *A Pickpocket's Tale: the Underworld of Nineteenth-century New York*, New York: W.W. Norton.

Gleeck Jr., L.E. (1976) *American Institutions in the Philippines (1898–1941)*, Manila: Historical Conservation Society.

Goffmann, E. (1971) *Relations in Public*, New York: Basic Books.

Goldberg, D.T. (1998) "Call and Response. Sports, Talk Radio, and the Death of Democracy", *Journal of Sport and Social Issues*, 22 (2): 212–223.

Gordon, L.D. (1990) *Gender and Higher Education in the Progressive Era*, New Haven, CT: Yale University Press.

Gorn, E.J. (1985) "The Manassa Mauler and the Fighting Marine: An Interpretation of the Dempsey-Tunney Fights", *Journal of American Studies*, 19: 27–47.

Gorn, E.J. (1995) "'Gouge and Bite, Pull Hair and Scratch': The Social Significance of Gouging in the Southern Backcountry", in D.K. Wiggins (ed.) *Sport in America: From Wicked Amusements to National Obsession*, Champaign, IL: Human Kinetics, 35–50.

Gorn, E.J. and Goldstein, W. (1993) *A Brief History of American Sports*, New York: Hill and Wang.

Gould, J.S. (1989) "Television Viewers' Attitudes and Recall of 15 Second Versus 30 Second Commercials", *Mid-Atlantic Journal of Business*. Online. Available from: <http://www.allbusiness.com/marketing-advertising/advertising-television-advertising/112898–1.html> (accessed April 30, 2008).

Grainger, A., Newman, J. and Andrews, D. (2006) "Sport, the Media, and the Construction of Race", in A. Raney and J. Bryant (eds) *Handbook of Sports and Media*, Mahwah, NJ: Lawrence Erlbaum, 447–464.

Gregorich, B. (1993) *Women at Play: The Story of Women in Baseball*, New York: Harcourt, Brace, Jovanovich.

Gropman, D. (1988) *Say It Ain't So, Joe!: The True Story of Shoeless Joe Jackson and the 1919 World Series*, New York: Lynx Books.

Grossman, J.R. (1989) *Land of Hope: Chicago, Black Southerners, and the Great Migration*, Chicago: University of Chicago Press.

Grundy, P. (2004) "A Special Type of Discipline: Manhood and Community in African-American Institutions, 1923–1957", in P. Miller and D.K. Wiggins (eds) *Sport and the Color Line*, New York: Routledge, 101–122.

Grundy, P. (2006) "Ora Washington: The First Black Female Athletic Star", in D.K. Wiggins (ed.) *Out of the Shadows*, Fayetteville: University of Arkansas Press 79–92.

Guglielmo, T.A. (2003) *White on Arrival: Italians, Race, Color, and Power in Chicago, 1890–1945*, New York: Oxford University Press.

Gulick, L.H. (1906) "Athletics do not test womanliness", *American Physical Education Review*, 9: 157–158.

Guralnick, D.B. (1970) *Webster's New World Dictionary*, New York: World Publishing Co., 657.

Guterl, M.P. (2001) *The Color of Race in America, 1900–1940*, Cambridge, MA: Harvard University Press.

Guttmann, A. (1978) *From Ritual to Record*, New York: Columbia University Press.

Guttmann, A. (1986) *Sports Spectators*, New York: Columbia University Press.

Guttmann, A. (1988) *Whole New Ballgame: An Interpretation of American Sports*, Chapel Hill, NC: University of North Carolina Press.

Guttmann, A. (1991) *Women's Sports: A History*, New York: Columbia University Press.

Guttmann, A. (1994) *Games and Empires. Modern Sports and Cultural Imperialism*, New York: Columbia University Press.

Guttmann, A. (2002) *The Olympics: A History of the Modern Games* (2nd ed.), Urbana and Chicago: University of Illinois Press.

Guttmann, A. (2004) *Sports: The First Five Millennia*, Amherst: University of Massachusetts Press.

Guttmann, A. (2006) "Civilized Mayhem: Origins and Early Development of American Football", *Sport in Society*, 9: 533–541.

Hall, G.S. (1904). *Adolescence: Its Psychology and Its Relations to Physiology, Anthropology, Sociology, Sex, Crime, Religion, and Education*, New York: Appleton.

Hall, S. (1904) *Adolescence*, New York: Appleton.

Hallmark, J.L. and Armstrong, R.N. (1999) "Gender Equity in Televised Sports: A Comparative Analysis of Men's and Women's NCAA Division I Basketball Championship Broadcasts, 1991–1995", *Journal of Broadcasting and Electronic Media*, 43(2): 222–235.

Hampe, M. (1994) *Stilwandel im Eiskunstlauf*, Frankfurt: P. Lang.

Handlin, O. (1951) *The Uprooted*, New York: Grosset & Dunlap.

Hanson, M.E. (1995) *Go! Fight! Win! Cheerleading in American Culture*, Bowling Green, OH: Bowling Green University Popular Press.

Hardin, M., Dodd, J.E., Chance, J. and Walsdorff, K. (2004) "Sporting Images in Black and White: Race in Newspaper Coverage of the 2000 Olympic Games", *Howard Journal of Communications*, 15 (4): 211–227.

Hardin, M. and Shain, S. (2005) "Strength in Numbers? The Experiences and Attitudes of Women in Sports Media Careers", *Journalism and Mass Communication Quarterly*, 82 (4): 804–819.

Harris, D. (2005) "NASCAR Takes Religion to the Raceway", *ABC News*, May. Online. Available from: <http://abcnewsgo.com/WNT?Beliefs/story?id=727941&page=1> (accessed May 10, 2007).

Hart, A.B., Matteson, D.M. and Bolton, H.E. (eds.) (1930) *American History Atlas*, Chicago: Donyer – Geppert Co.

Harvey, A. (2001) "´An Epoch in the Annals of National Sport´: Football in the Sheffield and the Creation of Modern Soccer and Rugby", *The International Journal of the History of Sport*. 18, (4), 53–87.

Hein, H. (2006) "Texte zu politischen Mythen in Europa", *Mythos* 2, 227–230.

Hein, H. (2008) Historische Mythosforschung. Online. Available from: <http://epub.ub.uni-muenchen.de/639/1/hein-mythosforschung-.pdf>.

Heritage, A. (ed.) (2001) *Essential World Atlas*, New York: Dorling Kindersley.

Herman, D.J. (2003) "Hunter's Aim: The Cultural Politics of American Sport Hunters, 1880–1910 (1)", *Journal of Leisure Research*, 4: 321–339.

Herman, E.S. (2001) "The Global Media Giants: Firms that Dominate the World",

Educate Magazine. Online. Available from: <http://www.thirdworldtraveler.com /Media_control_propaganda/GlobalMediaGiants_Herman.html> (accessed April 30, 2008).

Hettinger, H.S. (1930) *A Decade of Radio Advertising*, Chicago, IL: University of Chicago Press.

Hewitt, B. (1993) "Results in Pain for Life: Equipment No Savior", *Chicago Sun-Times*, September 19, 19–20B.

Heywood, L. and Dworkin, S.L. (2003) *Built to Win: The Female Athlete as Cultural Icon*, Minneapolis: University of Minnesota Press.

Hibner, J.C. (1993) *The Rose Bowl, 1902–1929*, Jefferson, NC: McFarland.

Hickok, R. (2004) *Sports Biographies. Sears, Eleonora R.* Online. Available from: <http:// www.hickoksports.com/biograph/searseleanora.shtml> (accessed April 29, 2008).

Higginson, T.W. (1984) "Saints and Their Bodies", in S.A. Riess, *The American Sporting Experience: A Historical Anthology of Sport in America*, Champaign, IL: Human Kinetics, 80–90.

Higgs, C.T., Weiller, K.H. and Martin, S.B. (2003) "1996 Olympic Games: A Comparative Analysis", *Journal of Sport and Social Issues*, 27(1): 52–64.

Hilgers, L. (2006) "Youth Sports Drawing More than Ever", Special to CNN.com Wednesday, July 5. Online. Available from: http://www.cnn.com/2006/US/07/03/rise. kids.sports/index.html.

Hoberman, J. (1997) *Darwin's Athletes: How Sports Has Damaged Black America and Preserved the Myth of Race*, New York: Mariner.

Hoberman, J. (1998) "Fitness and National Vitality: A Comparative Study of Germany and the United States", in K.A. Volkwein (ed.) *Fitness as Cultural Phenomenon*, New York: Waxman, 231–247.

Hobsbawm, Eric (1983) Introduction: Inventing Tradition. In: E. Hobsbawm and T. Ranger (eds) *The Invention of Tradition*. Cambridge: Cambridge University Press, 1–14.

Hobsbawm, E.J. and Ranger T.O. (1983) *The Invention of Tradition*, Cambridge: Cambridge University Press.

Hofmann, A. (2001) *Aufstieg und Niedergang des deutschen Turnens in den USA*, Schorndorf: Hofmann.

Hofmann, A. and Pfister, G. (2004) "Turnen – a Forgotten Movement Culture: Its Beginnings in Germany and Diffusion in the United States", in A.R. Hofmann, *Turnen and Sport. Transatlantic Transfers*, Münster: Waxmann, 11–24.

Hofmann, A. and Preuss, A. (2005). Amazonen der Lüfte. Geschichte und Entwicklungen im Frauenskispringen. In Falkner, G. (ed.), *Internationale Skihistoriographie und Deutscher Skilauf*, München: ILDA Druck.

Hofmann, A. (2008) "German Immigrants and their Athletic Endeavors in America", *International Journal of the History of Sport*, 25: 993–1009.

Holst, D.L. (1988) "Charles G. Radbourne: The Greatest Pitcher of the Nineteenth Century", *Illinois Historical Journal*, 81(4): 255–268.

Hopsicker, P. and Dyreson, M. (2006) "Super Bowl Sunday: An American Holiday?", in

L. Travers (ed.) *Encyclopedia of American Holidays and National Days*, 1: 30–55, Westport, CT: Greenwood Press.

Horne, J. (2006) *Sport in Consumer Culture*, Basingstoke: Palgrave Macmillan.

Horne, J., Tomlinson, A. and Whannel, G. (1999) *Understanding Sport*, London: Taylor & Francis.

Horsman, R. (1981) *Race and Manifest Destiny: The Origins of American Racial Anglo-Saxonism*, Cambridge, MA: Harvard University Press.

Hoxie, F.E. (1989) *Final Promise: The Campaign to Assimilate the Indians, 1880–1920*, New York: Cambridge University Press.

Huffman, S., Tuggle, C.A. and Rosengard, D.S. (2004) "How Campus Media Cover Sports: The Gender-equity Issue, One Generation Later", *Mass Communication and Society*, 7 (4): 475–489.

Hughes, G. (2004) "Managing Black Guys: Representation, Corporate Culture, and the NBA", *Sociology of Sport Journal*, 21(2): 163–184.

Hult, J.S. (1980) "The Philosophical Conflicts in Men's and Women's Collegiate Athletics", *Quest*, 32 (1): 77–94.

Hult, J.S. and Trekell, M. (eds) (1991) *A Century of Women's Basketball: From Frailty to Final Four*, Reston, VA: American Alliance for Health, Physical Education, Recreation, and Dance.

Hums, M.A. and MacLean, J.C. (2004) *Governance and Policy in Sport Organizations*, Scottsdale, AZ: H. Hathaway Publishers.

Huntington, S.P. (1996) *The Clash of Civilizations and the Remaking of World Order*, New York: Simon & Schuster.

Ignatiev, N. (1995) *How the Irish Became White*, New York: Routledge.

International Journal of the History of Sport (2004) 21:2: 161–180.

Isenberg, M.T. (1988) *John Sullivan and his times,* London: Robson.

Jackson, K. (2006) "Transnational Borderland: Metropolitan Growth in the United States, Germany and Japan Since World War II", *GHI Bulletin*, 38: 11–32.

Jackson, S.J. and Ponic, P. (2001) "Pride and Prejudice: Reflecting on Sport Heroes, National Identity, and Crisis in Canada", in S.G. Weiting (ed.) *Sport and Memory in North America*, London: Frank Cass, 43–62.

Jacobson, M.F. (1998) *Whiteness of a Different Color: European Immigrants and the Alchemy of Race*, Cambridge, MA: Harvard University Press.

James, J.D. and Ridinger, L.L. (2002) "Female and Male Sport Fans: A Comparison of Sport Consumption Motives", *Journal of Sport Behavior*, 25 (3): 260–278.

Jeanrenaud, C. and Késenne, S. (eds) (2006) *The Economics Of Sport And The Media: an overview"*, Montpellier: Edward Elgar Publishing.

Jeffers, H.P. and Roosevelt, C. (1996) *Theodore Roosevelt goes to war, 1897 – 1898,* New York: John Wiley & Sons.

Jessen, G.N. (2002) *The Powder Puff Derby of 1929: The True Story of the First Women's Cross-Country Air race*, Naperville, IL: Sourcebooks.

Jones, R., Murrell, A.J. and Jackson, J. (1999) "Pretty Versus Powerful in the Sports Pages:

Print Media Coverage of the US Women's Olympic Gold Medal Winning Teams", *Journal of Sport and Social Issues*, 23(2): 183–192.

Jones-Palm, D.H. (2002) "United States: Sport for All as a Complex and Uncoordinated Network", in P. Lamartine, P. DaCosta and A. Miragaya (eds) *Worldwide Experiences and Trends in Sport for All*, Oxford: Meyer & Meyer.

Jordan, T. (1984) *Cowgirls: Women of the American West*, Garden City, NY: Anchor Books.

Josephy Jr., A.M. (1991) "Origins of American Indians", in E. Foner and J.A. Garraty (eds) *The Reader's Companion to American History*, Boston, MA: Houghton Mifflin, 544–545.

Kamper, E. (1972) *Enzyklopädie der Olympischen Spiele: Daten, Fakten, Namen*, Stuttgart: Römer.

Kane, M.J. and Greendorfer, S. (1994) "The Media's Role in Accommodating and Resisting Stereotyped Images of Women in Sport" in P.J. Creedon (ed.) *Women, Media and Sport*, London: Sage, 28–44.

Karnow, S., (1983) *Vietnam: A History*, New York: Viking Press.

Kasson, J.S. (2000) *Buffalo Bill's Wild West: Celebrity, Memory, and Popular History*, New York: Hill & Wang.

Kaufman, K. (2007) *Beer, Babes, and Balls: Inside the "Neanderthal" – but sometimes surprisingly liberal – world of Jim Rome and sports-talk radio*. Online. Available from: <http://www.salon.com/sports/col/kaufman/2007/12/12/wednesday/print.html> (accessed May 5, 2008).

Keeney, E.B. (1992) The Botanizers: Amateur Scientists in Nineteenth-Century America. Chapel Hill and London: University of North Carolina Press.

Kerber, L.K. and Sherron De Hart, J. (1999) *Women's America: Refocusing the Past*, New York: Oxford University Press.

Kessler-Harris, A. (1982) *Out to Work: A History of Wage Earning Women in the United States*, New York: Oxford University Press.

King, C.R. (ed.) (2004) *Native Americans in Sports*, Armonk, NY: Sharpe Reference.

Kinney, L. (2006) "Sports Sponsorship", in A. Raney and J. Bryant (eds) *Handbook of Sports and Media*, Mahwah, NJ: Lawrence Erlbaum Associates.

Kirsch, G.B. (ed.) (1992) *Sports in North America: A Documentary History, Vol. 3: The Rise of Modern Sports, 1840–1860*, Gulf Breeze, FL: Academic International Press.

Kirsch, G.B. (ed.) (1995) *Sports in North America: A Documentary History, Vol. 4: Sports in War, Revival and Expansion, 1860–1880*, Gulf Breeze, FL: Academic International Press.

Kirsch, G.B., Harris, O. and Nolte, C.E. (2000) *Encyclopedia of Ethnicity and Sports in the United States*, Westport, CT: Greenwood Press.

Klapp, O.E. (1969) *Collective Search for Identity*, New York: Holt, Rinehart, & Winston.

Kluge, V. (1997) *Olmypische Spiele. Die Chronik*, Berlin: Sportverlag Berlin.

König, T. (2002) *Fankultur: eine soziologische Studie am Beispiel des Fussballfans*, Münster: LIT Verlag.

Kot, G. (2007) "The Big Show", *Chicago Tribune*, January 28: 7:5.

Kovach, J.M. (2005) *Women's Baseball*, Charleston, SC: Arcadia Publishing.

Krzemienski, E.D. (2004) "Fulcrum of Change: Boxing and Society at a Crossroads", *International Journal of the History of Sport*, 21, 2: 161–180.

Kühnert, D. (2004) *Sportfernsehen und Fernsehsport*, München: Reinhard Fischer.

Lamster, M. (1992) *Spalding's World Tour: The Epic Adventure that Took Baseball Around the Globe and Made It America's Game*, New York: Public Affairs.

Lansbury, J.H. (2006) "Alice Coachman: Quiet Champion of the 1940s", in D.K. Wiggins (ed.) *Out of the Shadows*, Fayetteville, AK: University of Arkansas Press, 146–161.

Lapchick, R.E. (1999) *The 1998 Racial and Gender Report Card*, Boston, MA: Northeastern University: Center for the Study of Sport Sociology.

Lapchick, R. (2003) *Racial and Gender Report Card*, Orlando, FL: Institute for Diversity and Ethics in Sport.

Lapchick, R.E. (2006) *New Game Plan for College Sport*, Portsmouth: Greenwood Publishing Group.

Lapchick, R.E. (2006) *The 2005 Racial and Gender Report Card: College Sports*, Florida: University of Central Florida.

Lasch, C. (2007) "The Degradation of Sport", in A. Tomlinson (ed.) *The Sport Studies Reader*, London: Routledge, 435–440.

Law, A., Harvey, J. and Kemp, S. (2002) "The Global Sport Mass Media Oligopoly. The Three Usual Suspects and More", *International Review for the Sociology of Sport*, 37(3–4): 279–302.

Learmonth, M. (2008) *March Madness: Ratings Down, Online to Blame?* Online. Available from: <http://www.businessinsider.com/2008/4/march-madness-ratings-down-online-to-blame-> (accessed June 8, 2008).

LeCompte, M.L. (1993) *Cowgirls of the Rodeo: Pioneer Professional Athletes*, Urbana: University of Illinois Press.

Lehnert, G. (1997) *Wenn Frauen Männerkleidung tragen*, München: Verlag.

Leigh, M.H. (1974) "Pierre Coubertin: A Man of his Time", *Quest*, 22: 19–24.

Leigh, M.H. (1980) "The Enigma of Avery Brundage because of Fear of Compromising Job Security or Women Athletes", *Arena Review*, 4(2): 11–21.

Lennartz, K. and Teutenburg, W. (1995) *II. Olympische Spiele 1900 in Paris*, Agon: Kassel.

Leonard, F. (1922) *Pioneers of Modern Physical Training*, New York: Association Press.

Lester, R. (1995) *Stagg's University: The Rise, Decline, and Fall of Big-time Football at Chicago*, Urbana, IL: University of Illinois Press.

Lever, J. and Wheeler, S. (1984) "The Chicago Tribune Sports Page: 1900–1975", *Sociology of Sport Journal*, 1: 299–313.

Levine, P. (1992) *Ellis Island to Ebbets Field: Sport and the American Jewish Experience*, New York: Oxford University Press.

Levinson, D. and Christensen, K. (2005) *Berkshire Encyclopedia of World Sport*, Great Barrington: Berkshire Publishing.

Levy, D.P. (2005) "Fantasy Sports and Fanship Habitus: Understanding the Process of Sport

Consumption". Paper presented at the annual meeting of the American Sociological Association, Philadelphia.

Lewis Jr., R. (1995) "Racial Position Segregation", *Journal of Black Studies*, 25(4): 431.

Lewis, R. M. (1991) "American Croquet in the 1860s: Playing the Game and Winning", *Journal of Sport History*, 18 (3): 365–386.

Liberti, R. (2004) "'We Were Ladies, We Just Played Like Boys:' African-American Womanhood and Competitive Basketball at Bennett College, 1928–1942", in P. Miller and D.K. Wiggins (eds) *Sport and the Color Line*, New York: Routledge, 83–99.

Lieberman, J. (2006) "Peanuts and Crackerjacks versus Hair Ribbons and Short Skirts: The Story of the Blondes and Brunettes . . . A Sin on the All-American Pastime", unpublished graduate research paper.

Lieberman, S. (1991) "The Popular Culture: Sport in America – A Look at the Avid Sports Fan", *The Public Perspective: A Roper Center Review of Public Opinion and Polling*, 2 (6): 28–29.

Lipsey, R.A. (2006) *The Sporting Goods Industry*, Jefferson, NC: McFarland & Co.

Lipsyte, R. (2001) "NASCAR and Religion", *Religion and Ethics*, 426 (February 23) Online. Available from: <http://www.pbs.org/wnet/religionandethics/week426/feature.html> (accessed May 10, 2007).

Littlewood, T.B. (1990) *Arch: A Promoter, Not a Poet*, Ames, IA: Iowa State University Press.

Lomax, M.E. (2003) *Operating By Any Means Necessary: Black Baseball and Black Entrepreneurship in the National Pastime*, Syracuse, NY: Syracuse University Press.

Lorber, J. (1994) *Paradoxes of Gender*, New Haven, CT: Yale University Press.

Lorber, J. (2000) "Using Gender to Undo Gender", *Feminist Theory*, 1: 79–96.

Lowe, S.R. (2002) "Jones, Robert Tyre, Jr. 'Bobby'", in A. Markoe (ed) *Scribner's Encyclopedia of American Lives*, New York: Charles Scribner's Sons, Vol. 1, 494–496.

Lu, C-Y. and Pitts, B.G. (2004) "Culture and Other Market Demand Variables: An Exploration with Professional Baseball in the USA and Taiwan", in B.G. Pitts (ed.) *Sharing Best Practices in Sport Marketing*, Morgantown, VA: Fitness Information Technology, 141–165.

Lucas, J. and Smith, R. (1982) "Women's Sport: A Trial of Equality", in R. Howell (ed.) *Her Story in Sport*, Westpoint: Leisure Press, 239–265.

Lucas, S. (2003) "Courting Controversy: Gender and Power in Iowa Girls' Basketball", *Journal of Sport History*, 30(3): 281–308.

Lumpkin, A. (1999) *Early American Physical Education*. Online. Available from: <http://www.westga.edu/~coe/phed2602/american.html> (accessed April 29, 2008).

Maguire, J. (2004) "Challenging the Sports-industrial Complex: Human Sciences, Advocacy and Service", *European Physical Education Review*, 10 (3): 299–322.

Maguire, J. (2006) "Sport and Globalization: Key Issues, Phrases, and Trends", in A. A. Raney and J. Bryant (eds) *Handbook of Sports and Media*, Mahwah, NJ: Lawrence Erlbaum Associates, 435–446.

Mahan III, J.E. and McDaniel, S.R. (2006) "The New Online Arena: Sport, Marketing, and

Media Converge in Cyberspace", in A.A. Raney and J. Bryant (eds) *Handbook of Sports and Media*, Mahwah, NJ: Lawrence Erlbaum Associates, 409–431.

Maibach, E. (2007) *The Influence of the Media Environment on Physical Activity: Looking for the Big Picture*, Active Living Research. Online. Available from: <http://www.activelivingresearch.org/files/Maibach_AJHP_2007.pdf> (accessed May 5, 2008).

Maitland, W. (1756) *The history of London from its foundation to the present time*, London: Wilkie.

Mallon, B. (1998) *The 1900 Olympic Games*, London: McFarland, Jefferson & London.

Mandelbaum, M. (2004). *The Meaning of Sports: Why Americans Watch Baseball, Football, and Basketball, and What They See When They Do*, New York: Public Affairs.

Mangan, J.A. (1981) *Athleticism in the Victorian and Edwardian Public School. The Emergence and Consolidation of an Educational Ideology*, Cambridge/London/New York: Cambridge University Press.

Manzenreiter, W. (2007) *The Business of Sports and the Manufacturing of Global Social Inequality*. Online. Available from: <http://www.lazer.eefd.ufrj.br/espsoc/pdf/es603.pdf> (accessed April 30, 2008).

Maraniss, D. (1999) *When Pride Still Mattered: A Life of Vince Lombardi*, New York: Touchstone.

Margolick, D. (2005) *Beyond Glory: Joe Louis vs. Max Schmeling, and a World on the Brink,* New York: Knopf.

Markels, R.B. (2000) "Bloomer Basketball and Its Suspender Suppressions: Women's Intercollegiate Competition at Ohio State University, 1904–1907", *Journal of Sport History*, 27 (1): 30–49.

Markovits, A.S. and Hellerman, S.L. (2001) *Offside: Soccer and American Exceptionalism*, Princeton: Princeton University Press.

Markovits, A.S. and Hellerman, S.L. (2003) "Women's soccer in the United States: Yet another American ´Exceptionalism´", *Soccer and Society*, 4 (2-3), 14–29.

Markovits, A. and Hellerman, S. (2004) "Die Olympianisierung des Fußballs in den USA: Von der Marginalisierung in der amerikanischen Mainstream-Kultur zur Anerkennung als ein alle vier Jahre stattfindendes Ereignis", *Sport und Gesellschaft*, 1: 7–29.

Markovits, S.H. (2002) *Im Abseits – Fußball in der amerikanischen Sportkultur*, Hamburg: HIS.

Marks, P. (1990) *Bicycles, Bangs, and Bloomers: The New Woman in the Popular Press*, Lexington, KY: University Press of Kentucky.

Marples, M. (1954) *A History of Football*, London: Secker & Warburg.

Marquis, A.G. (1986) *Hopes and Ashes: The Birth of Modern Times*, New York: Free Press.

Marryat, F. (1837) *Outdoor Amusements in America*. Online. Available from: <http://xroads.virginia.edu/~HYPER/DETOC/FEM/employment.htm> (accessed April 29, 2008).

Marshall, S., Biddle, S., Gorely, T., Cameron, N. and Murdey, I. (2004) "Relationships Between TV Viewing, BMI and Physical Activity: A Meta-analysis", *International Journal of Obesity*, 28: 1238–1246.

418

Martin, C. and Reeves, J.L. (2001) "The Whole World Isn't Watching (But We Thought They Were): The Super Bowl and American Solipsism", *Culture, Sport, Society*, 4 (2): 213–236.

Martineau, H. (1883) *General Treatise on Duties of Wives; Unhealthy Habit of Young Married Couples Residing in Boarding Houses; Domestic Servants; Charity and Religious Work; Manufacturing Professions; Governesses*. Online. Available from: <http://xroads.virginia.edu/~HYPER/DETOC/FEM/employment.htm#martineau> (accessed April 29, 2008).

Mason, J.P. (1982) *The English Gentleman. The Rise and Fall of an Ideal*, New York: William Morrow.

McCarthy, M. (2006) "Media Deals Become Cash Machines", *USA Today*, November 17, 2006, 1B–2B.

McChesney, R.W. (1998) Making Media Democratic, Online. Available from: <http://bostonreview.net/BR23.3/mcchesney.html > (accessed Nov. 2, 2008).

McClellan, K. (1998) *The Sunday Game: At the Dawn of Professional Football*, Akron, OH: University of Akron Press.

McCullick, B. and Hofmann, A. (2009) "Die Rolle des amerikanischen Schulsports", in A. Hofmann and A. Krüger (eds) *Amerikanische Sportstrukturen*, Münster: Waxmann.

McGinnis, L., Chun, S. and McQuillan, J. (2003) *A Review of Gendered Consumption in Sport and Leisure*, Academy of Marketing Science Review. Online. Available from: <http://www.amsreview.org/articles/mcginnis05_2003.pdf> (accessed May 5, 2008).

McKnight, D. (2003) *Schooling, the Puritan Imperative, and the Modeling of an American National Identity*, Mahwah, NJ: Lawrence Erlbaum Associates.

McMurtry, L. (2005) *The Colonel and Little Missie: Buffalo Bill, Annie Oakley, and the Beginnings of Superstardom in America*, New York: Simon & Schuster.

Meneses, D. (2004) "Shuttlecock", in C. Richard King (ed.) *Native Americans in Sports*, Armonk, NY: M.E. Sharpe, Vol. 2, 280–281.

Menna, L. (1995) *Sports in North America: A Documentary History, Vol. 2: Origins of Modern Sports, 1820–1840*, Gulf Breeze, FL: Academic International Press.

Merington, M. (1897) "Women and the Bicycle", in *Athletic Sports*, New York: Chas. Scribner's Sons, 209–219.

Messerli, F.M. (1952) *La participation feminine aux jeux Olympique modern*, Lausanne: Comité international olympique.

Messner, M. (1988) "Sports and Male Domination", *Sociology of Sport Journal*, 5: 197–211.

Messner, M. (1999) *Boys to Men. Sports Media. Messages about Masculinity. A National Poll of Children, Focus Groups, and Content Analysis of Sports Programs and Commercials*, Oakland, CA: Children Now.

Messner, M.A. and Sabo, D. (eds) (1990) *Sport, Men, and the Gender Order: Critical Feminist Perspectives*, Champaign, IL: Human Kinetics Books.

Messner, M.A., Dunbar, M. and Hunt, D. (2000) "The Televised Sports Manhood Formula", *Journal of Sport and Social Issues*, 24: 380–394.

Messner, M.A., Duncan, M.C. and Cooky, C. (2003) "Silence, Sports Bras, and Wrestling

Porn: Women in Televised Sports News and Highlights Shows", *Journal of Sport and Social Issues*, 27: 38–51.

Mickle, T. (2007) "Bettman, Daly get $2M raises", *Sports Business Journal*. Online. Available from: <http://www.sportsbusinessjournal.com/index.cfm?fuseaction=article.main&articleId=55422> (accessed April 30, 2008).

Miller, D.S. (2000) *Adventurous Women: The Inspiring Lives of Nine Early Outdoorswomen*, Boulder, CO: Pruett Publishing.

Miller, J. and Gillentine, A. (2006) "An Analysis of Risk Management Policies for Tailgaiting Activities at Selected NCAA Division 1", *Journal of Legal Aspects of Sport*, 16(2): 197–214.

Miller, P. and Wiggins, D.K. (eds) (2004) *Sport and the Color Line: Black Athletes and Race Relations in Twentieth-century America*, New York: Routledge.

Miracle Jr., A.W. and Rees, C.R. (1994) *Lessons of the Locker Room: The Myth of School Sports*, Amherst, NY: Prometheus Books.

Mohr, R. (2000) "Tyrannei der Geschwatzigkeit", *Der Spiegel*, 40, 150.

Mondello, M. (2006) "Sport Economics and the Media", in A.A. Raney and J. Bryant (eds) *Handbook of Sports and Media*, Mahwah, NJ: Lawrence Erlbaum Associates, 277–294.

Montville, L. (2006) *The Big Bam: The Life and Times of Babe Ruth*, New York: Doubleday.

Mrozek, D.J. (1983) *Sport and American Mentality, 1880–1910*, Knoxville, TN: University of Tennessee Press.

Murswieck, A. (1998) Die Sozialpolitik der USA: Ein Weg für die Zukunft? *Aus Politik und Zeitgeschichte*, 19: 42–45.

Nader, P. (2003) "Frequency and Intensity of Activity of Third Grade Children in Physical Education", *Archives of Pediatrics and Adolescent Medicine* 157: 185–190.

Nathan, D. (2003) *Saying It's So: A Cultural History of the Black Sox Scandal*, Urbana: University of Illinois Press.

National Center for Health Statistics, http://www.cdc.gov/nchs/fastats/exercise.htm.

National Geographic Society (1991) "2A Native American Heritage", map supplement, 180(4).

National Geographic Society (2007) "A World Transformed", map supplement.

Nelson, D.M. (1994) *Anatomy of a Game: Football, the Rules and the Men Who Made the Game*, Newark: University of Delaware Press.

Nelson, M.B. (1996) *The Stronger Women Get, the More Men Love Football: Sexism and the Culture of Sport*, London: The Women's Press.

Nendel, J. (2004) "New Hawaiian Monarchy: The Media Representations of Duke Kahanamoku, 1911–1912", *Journal of Sport History*, 31 (Spring): 33–52.

Newberry, J. (1744) *A Little Pretty Pocket-Book, intended for the Amusement of Little Master Tommy and Pretty Miss Polly*, Worcester, MA: Isaiah Thomas.

Newcombe, J. (1975) *The Best of the Athletic Boys: The White Man's Impact on Jim Thorpe*, Garden City, NY: Doubleday.

Newman, J. (2007) "A Detour Through Nascar Nation: Ethnographic Articulations of a

Neoliberal Sporting Spectacle", *International Review for the Sociology of Sport*, 42(3): 289–308.

Niven, D. (2005) "Race, Quarterbacks, and the Media: Testing the Rush Limbaugh Hypothesis", *Journal of Black Studies*, 35 (5): 684–694.

Nolte, C.E. (1993) "Our Brothers Across the Ocean: The Czech Sokol in America to 1914", *Czechoslovak and Central European Journal*, 11: 15–37.

Nora, P. (ed.) (1984) *Les Lieux de mémoire*, Paris: Gallimard.

Northrop, H.D. (1902) *Home Studies in American History*, Philadelphia, PA: Home Study Circle.

Nuwer, H. (2001) *Wrongs of Passage: Fraternities, Sororities, Hazing, and Binge Drinking*, Bloomington: Indiana University Press.

Nye, S.B. (2008) "Fun Club: A Physical Activity Program for Elementary Schools", *Journal of Physical Education, Recreation, and Dance*, 79(1): 36–38, 44.

Odenkirchen, E. (1995/1996) "Die Teilnahme von Frauen an den Olympischen Spielen 1900 in Paris", *Stadion*, XXI–XXII: 147–170.

Ohl, F. and Taks, M. (2007) "Secondary Socialisation and the Consumption of Sporting Goods: Cross Cultural Dimensions", *International Journal of Sport management*, 2(1/2): 160–174.

O'Reilly, J. and Cahn, K. (2007) *Women and Sports in the United States*, Boston, MA: North-Eastern Press.

Oriard, M. (1993) *Reading Football: How the Popular Press Created an American Spectacle*, Chapel Hill, NC: University of North Carolina Press.

Oriard, M. (2007) *Brand NFL: Making and Selling America's Favorite Sport*, Chapel Hill, NC: University of North Carolina Press.

Orsega-Smith, E., Getchell, N., Neeld, K. and Mackenzie, S. (2008) "Teaming Up for Senior Fitness: A Group Based Approach", *Journal of Physical Education, Recreation, and Dance*, 79(1): 39–43.

Owens, J.W. (2006) "The Coverage of Sports on Radio", in A. A. Raney and J. Bryant (eds) *Handbook of Sports and Media*, Mahwah, NJ: Lawrence Erlbaum Associates, 117–129.

Oxendine, J. (1995) *American Indian Sport Heritage*, Lincoln, NE: University of Nebraska Press.

Palmer, D.R. (1978) *Summons of the Trumpet: U.S.-Vietnam in Perspective*, San Rafael, CA: Presidio Press.

Park, R.J. (1976) "Education or Entertainment: The Controversial Face of American Sport, 1880–1930", in R. Renson *et al.* (eds) *The History, the Evolution and Diffusion of Sports and Games in Different Cultures*, Brussels: BLOSO, 353–365.

Park, R.J. (1978) "'Embodied Selves': The Rise and Development of Concern for Physical Education, Active Games, and Recreation for American Women, 1776–1865", *Journal of Sport History*, 5 (2): 5–41.

Park, R.J. (1987) "Physiologists, Physicians, and Physical Educators: Nineteenth Century Biology and Exercise, Hygienic and Educative", *Journal of Sport History*, 14 (1): 28–60.

Park, R.J. (1991) "Physiology and Anatomy Are Destiny!?: Brains, Bodies, and Exercise in Nineteenth Century American Thought", *Journal of Sport History*, 18 (1): 31–63.

Park, R.J. (2005) "'Blending Business and Basketball:' Industrial Sports and Recreation in the United States from the Late 1800s to 1960", *Stadion*, 31 (1): 35–49.

Park, R.J. (2007) "'Boys' Clubs Are Better Than Policemen's Clubs': Endeavours by Philanthropists, Social Reformers, and Others to Prevent Juvenile Crime, Late 1880 to 1917", *International Journal of the History of Sport*, 24 (6): 749–775.

Paxson, F.L. (1917) "The Rise of Sport", *Mississippi Valley Historical Review*, 4: 143–168.

Peavy, L. and Smith, U. (2007) "Leav[ing] the White[s] . . . Far Behind Them: The Girls from Fort Shaw (Montana) Indian School, Basketball Champions of the 1904 World's Fair", *International Journal of the History of Sport*, 24 (6): 819–840.

Pedersen, P.M., Whisenant, W.A. and Schneider, R.G. (2003) "Using a Content Analysis to Examine the Gendering of Sports Newspaper Personnel and their Coverage", *Journal of Sport Management*, 17: 376–393.

Pesavento, W.J. (1982) "Sport and Recreation in the Pullman Experiment, 1880–1900", *Journal of Sport History*, 9 (2): 38–62.

Pesavento, W.J. and Raymond, L. (1985) "Men Must Play, Men Will Play: Occupations of Pullman Athletes, 1880–1900", *Journal of Sport History*, 12 (3): 233–251.

Peterson, M. (1975) *The Portable Thomas Jefferson*, New York: Penguin Books, 290.

Peterson, M.D. (ed.) (1975) *The Portable Thomas Jefferson*, New York: Penguin Books.

Pfister, G. (1989) *Fliegen – ihr Leben. Die ersten Pilotinnen*, Berlin: Orlanda.

Pfister, G. (1996) "Physical Activity in the Name of the Fatherland: Turnen and the National Movement (1810–1820)", *Sporting Heritage*, H. 1: 14–36.

Pfister, G. (2000) "Die Frauenweltspiele und die Beteiligung von Frauen an Olympischen Spielen", in M. Behrendt and G. Steins (eds) *Sport(geschichte). Berichte und Materialien. Sporthistorische Blätter*, 7/8: 157–171.

Pfister, G. (2004) "Gender, Sport und Massenmedien", in C. Kugelmann, G. Pfister and C. Zipprich (eds) *Geschlechterforschung im Sport. Differenz und/oder Gleichheit*, Hamburg: Czwalina, 59–88.

Pfister, G. (2005) "Islamic Countries' Women's Sports; Solidarity Games", in D. Levinson and K. Christensen (eds) *Berkshire Encyclopedia of World Sport*, Great Barrington: Berkshire Publishing Group, 244–246.

Pfister, G. (2006) "Watching Sport – A Universal Phenomenon?", New Aspects of Sport History, *ISHPES Studies*, 13(1): 379–393.

Pfister, G. (2007a) "Deutsches Turnen und Amerikanische Gesellschaft. Entwicklungen und Veränderungen der Turnbewegung in den USA", in L. Wieser and P. Wanner, *Adolf Cluss und die Tunrbewegung*, Heilbronn: Stadtarchiv.

Pfister, G. (2007b) "Watching Sport – A Universal Phenomenon?", in M. Lämmer, E. Mertin and T. Terret (eds) *New Aspects of Sport History*, Cologne: Academia, 379–394.

Pfister, G. (2009) "The Role of German Turners in American Physical Education", *International Journal of the History*, 26, in press.

Pfister, G. and Hofmann, A. (2004) "Female Turners in Germany and the United States until

World War: Structural Similarities – Cultural Differences", in A.R. Hofmann (ed.) *Turnen and Sport. Transatlantic Transfers*, Münster: Waxmann, 25–68.

Pfister, G. and Niewerth, T. (1999) "Jewish Women in Gymnastics and Sport in Germany", *Journal of Sport History*, 9: 287–326.

Phinizy, C. (2006) "It Was Upon This Rock", *Sports Illustrated Presents Notre Dame, special issue*, September 20: 13–18.

Pitts, B.G. (ed.) (2004) *Sharing Best Practices in Sport Marketing*, Morgantown, W. VA: Fitness Information Technology.

Plaut, D. (ed.) (1993) *Speaking of Baseball: Quotes and Notes on the National Pastime*, Philadelphia: Running Press.

Pope, S. (1997) *Patriotic Games: Sporting Traditions in the American Imagination*, New York: Oxford University Press.

PriceWaterhouseCoopers (2004) *Global Entertainment and Media Outlook: 2004–2008*. Online. Available from: <http://www.fipp.com/Default.aspx?PageIndex=2002& ItemId=11975>.

Priest, L. (2003) "The Whole IX Yards: The Impact of Title IX: the Good, the Bad, and the Ugly", *Women in Sport and Physical Activity Journal*, 12 (2): 27–43.

Proceedings of the Annual Meetings of the AAAPE.

Putnam, R.D. (2000) *Bowling Alone: The Collapse and Revival of American Community*, New York: Simon & Schuster.

Putney, C. (2001) *Muscular Christianity: Manhood and Sports in Protestant America, 1880–1920*, Cambridge, MA: Harvard University Press.

Rada, J.A. and Wulfemeyer, K.T. (2005) "Color Coded: Racial Descriptors in Television Coverage of Intercollegiate Sports", *Journal of Broadcasting and Electronic Media*, March.

Rader, B.G. (1983) *From the Age of Folk Games to the Age of Spectators*, Englewood Cliffs, NJ: Prentice Hall.

Rader, B.G. (1990) *American Sports: From the Age of Folk Games to the Age of Televised Sports*, Englewood Cliffs, NJ: Prentice Hall.

Rader, R. (1977) "The Quest for Subcommunities and the Rise of American Sport", *American Quarterly*, 29: 356–369.

Raney, A.A. (2006) "Why We Watch and Enjoy Mediated Sports", in A.A. Raney and J. Bryant (eds) *Handbook of Sports Media*, Mahwah, NJ: Lawrence Erlbaum Associates, 313–331.

Raney, A.A. and Bryant, J. (2006) *Handbook of Sports and Media*, Mahwah, NJ: Lawrence Erlbaum Associates.

Ratey, J.J. and Hagerman, E. (2008) *Spark: The Revolutionary New Science of Exercise and the Brain*, New York: Little, Brown & Co.

Reaves, J.A. (2007) "Generation Gap for Blacks in Baseball", *Arizona Republic*, April 15. Online. Available from: <http://www.azcentral.com/sports/diamondbacks/articles/ 0414jackie0415.html> (accessed May 12, 2007).

Reel, G. (2006) *The National Police Gazette and the Making of the Modern American Man, 1879–1906*, New York: Palgrave Macmillan.

Reichel, P. (1996) "Denkmal und Gegendenkmal ein kommunikativer Gedächtnisort", in E. Francois (ed.) *Lieux de Mémoire*, Erinnerungsorte, Berlin: Centre Marc Bloch, 105–119.

Riegel, R.E. (1963) "Women's Clothes and Women's Rights", *American Quarterly*, 15 (3): 390–401.

Riesman, D. and Denney, R. (1951) "Football in America: A Study in Cultural Diffusion", *American Quarterly*, 3: 309–325.

Riess, S.A. (1980) *Touching Base: Professional Baseball and American Culture in the Progressive Era*, Westport, CT: Greenwood Press.

Riess, S.A. (1984a) "The Baseball Magnates and Urban Politics in the Progressive Era, 1895–1920", in S.A. Riess (ed.) *The American Sporting Experience: A Historical Anthology of Sport in America*, Champaign, IL: Leisure Press, 271–290.

Riess, S.A. (1984b) *The American Sporting Experience: A Historical Anthology of Sport in America*, Champaign, IL: Leisure Press, 255–263.

Riess, S.A. (1995) *Sport in Industrial America, 1850–1920*, Wheeling, IL: Harlan Davidson.

Riess, S.A. (ed.) (1998) *Sports in North America: A Documentary History, Vol. 6: Sports in the Progressive Era, 1900–1920*, Gulf Breeze, FL: Academic International Press.

Rinehart, R. and Sydnor, S. (2003) *To the Extreme: Alternative Sports, Inside and Out*, New York: SUNY Press.

Rishe, P.J. (2003) "A Reexamination of How Athletic Success Impacts Graduation Rates: Comparing Student-Athletes to All Other Undergraduates", *American Journal of Economics and Sociology*. Online. Available from: <http://findarticles.com/p/articles/mi_m0254/is_2_62/ai_100202313/pg_7>.

Roberts, R. (1983) *Papa Jack: Jack Johnson and the Era of White Hopes*, New York: The Free Press.

Roe, F.M.A. (1909) *Army Letters from an Officer's Wife, 1871–1888*, New York: D. Appleton.

Roediger, David R. (1999) *The Wages of Whiteness: Race and the Making of the American Working Class*, London: Verso.

Rogers, P. (2007a) "MLB Cash Cow Breaking Away", *Chicago Tribune*, October 7, Section 3: 2.

Rogers, P. (2007b) "Path to the States?", *Chicago Tribune*, February 11, 6–7.

Ronda, J.P. (2001) *Finding the West: Explorations with Lewis and Clark*, Albuquerque, NM: University of New Mexico Press.

Ross, C.K. (ed.) (2004) *Race and Sport: The Struggle for Equality on and off the Field*, Jackson, MS: University Press of Mississippi.

Rowe, D. (2007) Media Sport Culture: An Education in the Politics of Acquisition. Play the game. Online. Available from: <http://www.playthegame.org/Knowledge%20Bank/Articles/Media_Sport_Culture_An_Education_in_the_Politics_of_Acquisition.aspx>.

Ryan, J. (1995) *Little Girls in Pretty Boxes: The Making and Breaking of Elite Gymnasts and Figure Skaters*, New York: Doubleday.

Sabo, D. (1989) *Pigskin, Patriarchy and Pain*, Champaign: Human Kinetics Books.

Sabo, D. (2007) "Psychosocial Impacts of Athletic Participation on American Women", in J. O'Reilly and S.K. Kahn (eds) *Women and Sports in the United States: A Documentary Reader*, Boston, MA: Northeastern University Press, 61–75.

Sagas, M., Cunningham, G.B., Wigley, B.J. and Ashley, F.B. (2000) "Gender Bias in the Internet Coverage of University Softball and Baseball Web Sites: The Inequity Continues", *Sociology of Sport Journal*, 17 (2): 198–205.

Sage, G.H. (1998a) "The Political Economy of Fitness in the United States", in K.A.E. Volkwein (ed.) *Fitness as Cultural Phenomenon*, New York: Waxmann, 111–130.

Sage, G.H. (1998b) *Power and Ideology in American Sport*, Champaign, IL: Human Kinetics.

Sailes, G.A. (1998) *African Americans In Sport: Contemporary Themes*, Rutgers, NJ: Transaction Publishers.

Salmon, M. (1988) *Women and the Law of Property in Early America*, Studies in Legal History, Chapel Hill: University of North Carolina Press.

Sargent, D. (1889) "The Physical Development of Women", *Scribner's Magazine*, January to June, 181–184.

Sargent, D.A. (1912) "Are Athletics Making Girls Masculine? A Practical Answer to a Question every Girl Asks", *Ladies Home Journal*, 29 (11): 71–73.

Sargent, S.L., Zillmann, D. and Weaver III, J.B. (1998) "The Gender Gap in the Enjoyment of Televised Sports", *Journal of Sport and Social Issues*, 22 (1): 46–64.

Schaaf, P. (2004) *Sports, Inc: 100 Years of Sports Business*, Amherst, NY: Prometheus.

Schellhaaβ, H. (2003) "Strategien zur Vermarktung des Sports im Fernsehen", *Betriebswirtschaftliche Forschung und Praxis (BFuP)*, 5: 513–527.

Schmidt, R. (2007) *Shaping College Football: The Transformation of an American Sport, 1919–1930*, Syracuse, NY: Syracuse University Press.

Schultz, J., Batts, C., Cohen, P., Olson, S., Chaudry, A., Ryan, J. et al (2009) American Sports, 1990 to the present. In Nelson, M. (ed) *Encyclopedia of Sports in America: A History from Foot Races to Extreme Sports*. (496–497), Westport, CT: Greenwood.

Schultz-Jørgensen, S. (2005) "The Sports Press: The World's Best Advertising Agency", *Mandag Morgen*, 37: 1–7. Online. Available from: <http://www.playthegame.org/Knowledge%20Bank/Articles/International%20_Sports_Press_Survey_2005.aspx> (accessed May 5, 2008).

Schumann, F. (2004) *"Professionalisierungstendenzen im deutschen Fuβball aus sportökonomischer Perspektive"*, PhD thesis, University of Heidelberg.

Seattle Post Intelligence (2002) "Innocence Lost. How Money Changed Sports". Online. Available from: http://seattlepi.nwsource.com/specials/moneyinsports/>.

Seymour, H. (1990) *Baseball: The People's Game*, New York: Oxford University Press.

Shattuck, D.A. (1989) "Playing a Man's Game: Women and Baseball in the United States, 1866–1954", *Baseball History*, 2: 57–77.

Shattuck, D.A. (1991) "Bats, Balls, and Books: Baseball and Higher Education for Women at Three Eastern Women's Colleges, 1866–1900", *Journal of Sport History*, 19 (2): 91–109.

Shaulis, D. (1999) "Pedestriennes: Newsworthy but Controversial Women in Sporting Entertainment", *Journal of Sport History*, 26 (1): 29–50.

Shugart, H.A. (2003) "She Shoots, She Scores: Mediated Constructions of Contemporary Female Athletes in Coverage of the 1999 U.S. Women's Soccer Team", *Western Journal of Communication*, 67(1): 1–31.

Shulman, J.L. (2001) *The Game of Life: College Sports and Educational Values*, Princeton, NJ: Princeton University Press.

Simri, U. (1977) *A Historical Analysis of the Role of Women in the Modern Olympic Games*, Netanya: The Wingate-Institute for Physiologie.

Slotkin, R. (1985) *The Fatal Environment: The Myth of the Frontier in the Age of Industrialization, 1800–1890*, Norman: University of Oklahoma Press.

Slotkin, R. (1992) *Gunfighter Nation: The Myth of the Frontier in Twentieth-century America*, New York: Atheneum.

Smith, E. and Hattery, A.J. (2006) "Hey Stud: Race, Sex and Sports", Sexuality and Culture, 10 (2): 3–32.

Smith Maguire, J. (2007) *Fit for Consumption: Sociology and the Business of Fitness*, London: Routledge.

Smith, M.M. (2006) "Billie Jean King: Portrait of a Pioneer", movie review, *Journal of Sport History*, 33 (1): 113–117.

Smith, R.A. (1988) *Sports and Freedom: The Rise of Big-time College Athletics*, New York: Oxford University Press.

Smith, R.A. (ed.) (1994) *Big-time Football at Harvard, 1905: The Diary of Coach Bill Reid*, Urbana: University of Illinois Press.

Smith, R.A. (2001) *Play-by-play: Radio, Television, and Big-Time College Sport*, Baltimore, MD: Johns Hopkins University Press.

Smith, R.A. (2007) "Football Coaching Salaries and the 1922 Hiring of 'Pop' Warner at Stanford", North American Society for Sport History Conference, Texas Tech University, Lubbock, Texas, May 26.

Smith, W.C. (1867) *Indiana miscellany: Consisting of sketches of Indian life, the early settlement, customs, and hardships of the people and the introduction of the gospel and of schools; together with biographical notices of the pioneer Methodist preachers of the state*, Cincinnati: Poe & Hitchcock.

Smith-Rosenberg, C. (1985) *Disorderly Conduct: Visions of Gender in Victorian America*, New York: A. A. Knopf.

Sollors, W. (ed.) (1989) *The Invention of Ethnicity*, New York: Oxford University Press.

Spears, B. (1986) *Leading the Way: Amy Morris Homans and the Beginnings of Professional Education for Women*, Westport, CT: Greenwood Press.

Spencer, N.E. (2000) "Reading Between the Lines: A Discursive Analysis of the Billie Jean King vs. Bobby Riggs 'Battle of the Sexes'", *Sociology of Sport Journal*, 17, 386–402.

Spencer, N.E. and McClung, L.R. (2001) "Women and Sport in the 1990s: Reflections on 'Embracing Stars, Ignoring Players'", *Journal of Sport Management*, 15: 318–349.

426

Sperber, M. (1990) *College Sports, Inc.: The Athletic Department vs. the University*, New York: Henry Holt.

Sperber, M. (1993) *Shake Down the Thunder: The Creation of Notre Dame Football*, New York: Henry Holt.

Sperber, M. (1998) *Onward to Victory: The Creation of Modern College Sports*, New York: Henry Holt.

Sperber, M. (2000) *Beer and Circus: How Big-time College Sports Is Crippling Undergraduate Education*, New York: Henry Holt.

St. John, W. (2004) *Rammer Jammer Yellow Hammer: A Trip Into the Heart of Fan Mania*, New York: Crown Publishers.

Statistical Research Inc. [SRI] (2001) *AAF/ESPN Children and Sports Media Study April–May 2001*, AAF/ESPN. Online. Available from: <http://www.aafla.com/9arr/Research Reports/AAF-ESPNCSMR2001.pdf> (accessed May 5, 2008).

Steinberg, S. (1989) *The Ethnic Myth: Race, Ethnicity, and Class in America*, Boston, MA: Beacon Press.

Sterngass. J. (1998) "Cheating, Gender Roles, and the Nineteenth-century Croquet Craze", *Journal of Sport History*, 25 (3): 398–418.

Stewart, B., Smith, A. and Nicholson, M. (2003) "Sport Consumer Typologies: A Critical Review", *Sport Marketing Quarterly*, 12 (4): 206–216.

Stewart, B., Smith, A. and Nicholson, M. (2006) "Sport Consumer Typologies: A Critical Review", in Douvis *et al.* (eds) *Readings in Sport Management*, Durham, NC: Carolina Academic Press.

Storm, R. (2009) "The Rational Emotions of F.C. Copenhagen – A Lesson on Generating Profit in Professional Soccer", in B. Carlsson and T. Andersson (eds) *Football in Scandinavia*, London: Routledge.

Strasser, S. (1982) *Never Done: A History of American Housework*, New York: Pantheon Books.

Stratton, J.L. (1981) *Pioneer Women: Voices from the Kansas Frontier*, New York: Simon & Schuster.

Strecker, L. and Young, J. (2007) "Today's Coaching Careers", *Update Plus* (September/ October): 26–27.

Struna, N. (1977) "Puritans and Sports: The Irretrievable Tide of Change", *Journal of Sport History*, 4 (Spring): 1–21.

Struna, N. (1984) "Beyond Mapping Experience: The Need for Understanding the History of American Sporting Women", *Journal of Sport History*. 11, 120–133.

Struna, N.L. (1996) *People of Prowess: Sport, Leisure, and Labor in Early Anglo-America*, Urbana: University of Illinois Press.

Struna, N.L. (1997) "Gender and Sporting Practice in Early America, 1750–1810", in S. W. Pope (ed) *The New American Sport History*, Champaign, IL: University of Illinois Press, 147–172.

Strutt, J. (1903) *From the Earliest Period, Including the Rural and Domestic Recreations, May Games, Mummeries, Pageants, Processions and Pompous Spectacles*, Illustrated by reproductions from ancient paintings in which are represented most of the popular diversions, new edition, much enlarged and corrected by J. Charles Cox, L.A. London: Methuen & Co.

Sullivan, D.B. (2006) "Broadcast Television and the Game of Packaging Sports", in A.A. Raney and J. Bryant (eds) *Handbook of Sports Media*, Mahwah, NJ: Lawrence Erlbaum Associates, 131–147.

Sullivan, R. (2002) *Rocky Marciano: The Rock of his Times*, Urbana: University of Illinois Press.

Summers, J. and Morgan, M.J. (2004) "A Cross National Analysis of Sport Consumption", in B.G. Pitts (ed.) *Sharing Best Practices in Sport Management*, Morgantown, W. VA: Fitness Information Technology, 195–206.

Svinth, J.R. (2000) "Professor Yamashita Goes to Washington", *Journal of Combative Sport*. Online. Available from: <http://ejmas.com/jcs/jcsart_svinth1_1000.htm> (accessed 2 April 2009).

Swyers, H. (2005) "Who Owns Wrigley Field? Sport in American Society – Past and Present", *International Journal of the History of Sport*, 22 (6): 1086–1105.

Szymanski, S. and Zimbalist, A.S. (2005) *National Pastime: How Americans Play Baseball and the Rest of the World Plays Soccer*, Washington, DC: Brookings Institution Press.

Tajfel, H. and Turner, J.C. (1986) "The Social Identity Theory of Inter-group Behavior", in S. Worchel and L.W. Austin (eds) *Psychology of Intergroup Relations*, Chicago, IL: Nelson-Hall.

Tamborini, R., Skalski, P., Lachlan, K., Westerman, D., Davis, J. and Smith, S.L. (2005) "The Raw Nature of Televised Professional Wrestling: Is the Violence a Cause for Concern?", *Journal of Broadcasting and Electronic Media*, 49(2): 202–220.

Telander, R. (2006) "Bo's Death Brings Back Memories of Woody, Old Days", *Chicago Sun-Times*, November 19, 101A.

Texas Tech University (2007) *Shaping America*, Special Collections Library: Southwest Collection.

"The History of the Organization: 100 Years of Health, Physical Education, Sport, Gymnastic and Dance", *Journal of Physical Education, Recreation and Dance*, 56 (April 1985): 22–82.

Thelin, J.R. (1994) *Games Colleges Play: Scandals and Reform in Intercollegiate Athletics*, Baltimore, MD: Johns Hopkins University Press.

Thompson, A. (2007) "Sports Leagues Impose More Rules on Coverage", *Wall Street Journal*, July 16. Online. Available from: <http://online.wsj.com/public/article_print/SB118454824975767224.html> (accessed May 5, 2008).

Thorpe, H. (2008) "Foucault, Techniques of Self, and the Media: Discourses of Femininity in Snowboarding Culture", *Journal of Sport and Social Issues*, May: 199–229.

Todd, J. (1987) "Bernarr Macfadden: Reformer of Feminine Form", *Journal of Sport History*, 14: 61–75.

Townson, N. (1997) *The British at Play – A Social History of British Sport from 1600 to the Present*, Bucharest: Cavallioti Publishers.

Traxel, D. (2006) *Crusader Nation: The United States in Peace and the Great War, 1898–1920*, New York: Alfred A. Knopf.

Tucker Center for Research on Girls and Women in Sport (2007) *Developing Physically Active Girls: An Evidence Based Multidisciplinary Approach*, Minneapolis: University of Minnesota Press.

Tucker, R. (2007) "Opposing Forces", *USA Weekend*, December 21–23: 16.

Tuggle, C.A. (1997) "Differences in Television Sports Reporting of Men's and Women's Athletics: ESPN SportsCenter and CNN Sports Tonight", *Journal of Broadcasting & Electronic Media*, 41 (1): 14–24.

Tuggle, C.A., Huffman, S. and Rosengard, D.S. (2002) "A Descriptive Analysis of NBC's Coverage of the 2000 Summer Olympics", *Mass Communication & Society*, 5 (3): 361–375.

Turner, F.J. (1935) *The Frontier in American History.* New York: Henry and Holt Company. Online. Available from: <http://xroads.virginia.edu/~HYPER/TURNER/>.

Uhle, F. (2005) *Recreation: Leisure in American Society*, Farmington Hills, MI: Thomas Gale.

Ulrich, L.T. (1990) *A Midwife's Tale: The Life of Martha Ballard. Based on Her Diary, 1785–1812*, New York: Vintage Books.

Underwood, R., Bond, E. and Baer, R. (2001) "Building Service Brands via Social Identity: Lessons from the Sports Marketplace", *Journal of Marketing Theory and Practice*, 9, 1–13.

Upton, J. and Wieberg, S. (2006) "Contracts for College Coaches Cover More Than Salaries", *USA Today*. Online. Available from: <http://www.usatoday.com/sports/college/football/2006-11-16-coaches-salaries-cover_x.htm> (accessed November 2, 2006).

Valgeirsson, G. and Snyder, E.E. (1986) "A Cross-cultural Comparison of Newspaper Sports Sections", *International Review for the Sociology of Sport*, 21 (2/3): 131–140.

Van Dalen, D.B. and Bennett, B.L. (1971) *A World History of Physical Education: Cultural, Philosophical, Comparative*, Englewood Cliffs, NJ: Prentice Hall.

Vennum Jr., T. (1994) *American Indian Lacrosse: Little Brother of War*, Washington, DC: Smithsonian Institution Press.

Verbrugge, M.H. (1997) "Recreating the Body: Women's Physical Education and the Science of Sex Differences in America, 1900–1940", *Bulletin of the History of Medicine*, 71 (2): 273–304.

Verney, K. (2003) *African Americans and US Popular Culture*, London: Routledge.

Vertinsky, P. (1994) "The Racial Body and the Anatomy of Difference: Anti-Semitism, Physical Culture and the Jew's Foot", *Sport Science Review*, 4(1): 1–24.

Vincent, J., Imwold, C., Masemann, V. and Johnson, J.T. (2002) "A Comparison of Selected 'Serious' and 'Popular' British, Canadian and United States Newspaper Coverage of Female and Male Athletes Competing in the Centennial Olympic Games", *International Review for the Sociology of Sport*, 37: 319–335.

Volkwein, K.A.E. and Zohner-Nassi, J.B. (1998) "Conclusion: Comparison of the Fitness Movement in Germany and the USA", in K.A.E. Volkwein (ed.) *Fitness as Cultural Phenomenon*, New York: Waxmann, 249–255.

Waddington, I. and Roderick, M. (1996) "American Exceptionalism: Soccer and American Football", *The Sports Historian*, 16: 42–63.

Walter, J.C. (1968) "The Changing Status of the Black Athlete in the Twentieth Century United States". Online. Available from: <http://www.americansc.org.uk/online/walters.htm>.

Walvin, J. (1994) *The People's Game*, London: Mainstream Publishing.

Wann, D.L. (2006) "The Causes and Consequences of Sport Team Identification", in A.A. Raney and J. Bryant (eds) *Handbook of Sports and Media*, Mahwah, NJ: Lawrence Erlbaum Associates, 331–353.

Wanta, W. (2006) "The Coverage of Sports in Print Media", in A.A. Raney and J. Bryant (eds) *Handbook of Sports and Media*, Mahwah, NJ: Lawrence Erlbaum Associates, 105–115.

Warner, P.C. (2006) *When the Girls Came Out to Play: The Birth of American Sportswear*, Amherst: University of Massachusetts Press.

Warner, P.C. (2006) *When the Girls Came Out to Play: The Birth of American Sportswear. Part One: The Influence of Fashion*. Chapter 5, *"Women Enter the Olympics: A Sleeker Swimsuit"*. Online. Available from: <http://scholarworks.umass.edu/cgi/viewcontent.cgi?article=1006&context=umpress_wtg> (accessed April 29, 2008).

Washburn Wilcomb E. (1991) "Indian-White Relations", in E. Foner and J.A. Garraty (eds), *The Reader's Companion to American History*, Boston, MA: Houghton Mifflin, 556–559.

Washington, R.E. and Karen, D. (2001) "Sport and Society", *Annual Review of Sociology*, 27: 187–212.

Wassong, S. (2005) "The Failure of US Playground Politics in Child and Youth Welfare", *Stadion*, 31(2): 259–271.

Watterson, J.S. (2000) *College Football: History, Spectacle, Controversy*, Baltimore, MD: Johns Hopkins University Press.

Weissmuller, J., Reed, W. and Reed, W.C. (2002) *Tarzan, My Father*, Toronto: ECW Press.

Weiting, S.G. (ed.) (2001) *Sport and Memory in North America*, London: Frank Cass.

Welch, P. and Costa, D.M. (1994) "A Century of Olympic Competition", in D.M Costa and S.R. Guthrie (eds) *Women and Sport: Interdisciplinary Perspectives*, Champaign: Human Kinetics.

Welch, P.D. and Lerch, H. (1996) *History of American Physical Education and Sport*, Springfield, IL: Charles C. Thomas.

Weston, A. (1962) *The Making of American Physical Education*, New York: Appleton-Century-Crofts.

Weyand, A.M. (1955) *The Saga of American Football*, New York: Macmillan.

Whannel, G. (2002) *Media Sports Stars: Masculinities and Moralities*, London: Routledge.

Whisenant, W.A. and Pedersen, P.M. (2004) "Analyzing Attitudes Regarding Quantity and Quality of Sports Page Coverage: Athletic Director Perceptions of Newspaper Coverage Given to Interscholastic Sports", *International Sports Journal*, 8 (1): 54–64.

Whitley, D. (2007) "Pure Hitter: Ted Williams". ESPN. Online. Available from: <http://espn.go.com/classic/00706tedwilliams.html> (accessed July 21, 2007).

Wiggins, D.K. (1977) "Good Times On the Old Plantation: Popular Recreations Of The Black Slave In Antebellum South, 1810–1860", *Journal of Sport History*, 4: 260–284.

Wiggins, D.K. (ed.) (2006) *Out of the Shadows: A Biographical History of African American Athletes*, Fayetteville, AK: University of Arkansas Press.

Williams, D.M. (2007) "Where's the Honor: Attitudes Toward the 'Fighting Sioux' Nickname and Logo", *Sociology of Sport Journal*, 24 (4): 437–456.

Williams, J. and Wagg, S. (eds) (1991) *British Football and Social Change: Getting into Europe*, Leicester: Leicester University Press.

Wills, C. (2005) *Destination America: The People and Cultures that Created a Nation*, New York: DK Publishing.

Wills, M. and Wills, C.A. (1984) *Manbirds: Hang Gliders and Hang Gliding*, Englewood Cliffs, NJ: Prentice-Hall.

Wilson, R. (2008) "A Texas Team Loads Up on All-American Talent, With No Americans", *Chronicle of Higher Education*, January 11: A30–31.

Wilson, R. and Wolverton, B. (2008) "The New Face of College Sports", *Chronicle of Higher Education*, January 11: A27–29.

Wilson, T.C. (2002) "The Paradox of Social Class and Sports Involvement. The Roles of Cultural and Economic Capital", *International Review for the Sociology of Sport*, 37 (1): 5–16.

Wilson, W. (1996) "The IOC and the Status of Women in the Olympic Movement: 1972–1996", *Research Quarterly for Exercise and Sport*, 67 (2): 183–192.

Wilson, W. (ed.) (2005) "Gender in Televised Sports. News and Highlight Shows, 1989–2004", AAFLA. Online. Available from: <http://www.la84.org> (accessed June 20, 2008).

Wimmer, D. (2001) *The Extreme Game*, Springfield, NJ: Burford Books.

Wolfe, T. (2005) *I am Charlotte Simmons*, London: Vintage.

Woloch, N. (1991) "Feminist Movement," in E. Foner and J.A. Garraty (eds) *The Reader's Companion to American History*, Boston, MA: Houghton Mifflin, 390–394.

Wolverton, B. (2007) "Growth in Sports Gifts May Mean Fewer Academic Donations", *The Chronicle of Higher Education*, October 5(1): 34–35.

Woodward, J.R. (2004) "Professional Football Scouts: An Investigation of Racial Stacking", *Sociology of Sport Journal*, 21 (4): 356–375.

Wrynn, A.M. (2004) "Tidye Pickett", in D.K. Wiggins (ed.) *African Americans in Sports*, Armonk, NY: Sharpe Reference, 282–283.

Wu, Y. (1999) "Early NCAA Attempts at the Governance of Women's Intercollegiate Athletics, 1968–1973", *Journal of Sport History*, 26 (3): 585–601.

Wyatt-Brown, B. (1982) *Southern Honor: Ethics and Behavior in the Old South*, New York: Oxford University Press.

Yiannakis, A. and Melnick, M. (2001) *Contemporary Issues in Sociology of Sport*, Champaign, IL: Human Kinetics.

Zang, D. (2001) *Sport Wars: Athletes in the Age of Aquarius,* Little Rock, AK: University of Arkansas Press.

Zelinsky, W. (1988) *Nation Into State: The Shifting Symbolic Foundations of American Nationalism*, Chapel Hill: University of North Carolina Press.

Zieff, S. (1994) "The Medicalization of Higher Education: Women Physicians and Physical Training", 1870–1920, Ph.D. Dissertation, San Francisco: University of California, Berkeley.

Ziemba, J. (1999) *When Football was Football: The Chicago Cardinals and the Birth of the NFL*, Chicago, IL: Triumph Books.

Zimmerman, W. (2002) *First Great Trumph: How five Americans made their country a world power*, New York: Farrar, Straus, *iGiroux.* http://www.athleticmanagement.com/2007/03/assessing_the_arms_race_1.html

Zuckerman, M. (1977) "Pilgrims in the Wilderness: Community, Modernity, and the Maypole at Merry Mount", *New England Quarterly*, 50 (June): 255–277.

WEBSITES

http://abcnews.go.com/Sports/wireStory?id=3058636 (April 23, 2007).

http://asp.usatoday.com/sports/baseball/salaries/playerdetail.aspx?lname=Rodriguez&player=53 (April 17, 2007).

http://dsc.discovery.com/convergence/greatestamerican/greatestamerican.html

http://ejmas.com/jcs/jcsart_svinth1_1000.htm

http:en.wikipedia.org/wiki/Amateur_Sports_Act_of_1978 (May 1, 2007).

http://en.wikipedia.org/wiki/American_football_rules

http://en.wikipedia.org/wiki/Athletes_in_Action (March 28, 2007).

http://en.wikipedia.org/wiki/Baseball_rules

http://en.wikipedia.org/wiki/Baseball_statistics

http://en.wikipedia.org/wiki/Category:Sports_governing_bodies_of_the_United_States (April 7, 2007).

http://en.wikipedia.org/wiki/Civil_Rights_Game (July 21, 2007).

http://en.wikipedia.org/wiki/Dale_Earnhardt (July 21, 2007).

http://en.wikipedia.org/wiki/Demographics of the United States (March 6, 2007).

http://en.wikipedia.org/wiki/Fellowship_of_Christian_Athletes (March 28, 2007).

http://en.wikipedia.org/wiki/Jim_Thorpe

http://en.wikipedia.org/wiki/Joe_DiMaggio#Military_service (May 16, 2007).

http://en.wikipedia.org/wiki/List_of_United_States_metropolitan_areas

http://en.wikipedia.org/wiki/Little_League (April 8, 2007)

http://en.wikipedia.org/wiki/National_Wheelchair_Basketball_Association (April 7, 2007).

http://en.wikipedia.org/wiki/United_States (August 13, 2007)

http://en.wikipedia.org/wiki/Women's_National_Basketball_Association#Finance (April 17, 2007).

http://en.wikipedia.org/wiki/World_Series_television_ratings

http://cyclingsisters.org/node/3242

http://factfinder.census.gov/jsp/saff/SAFFInfo.jsp?_pageId=tp5_education (August 16, 2007).

http://files.mlb.com/mitchrpt.pdf

http://files.mlb.com/summary.pdf

http://finance.myway.com/jsp/nw/nwdt_rt_top.jsp?news_id=ap-d8oer2jg0&.html (April 12, 2007).

http://goliath.ecnext.com/coms2/gi_0199-6577200/Review-roundtable-the-sprawl-debate.html

http://library.osu.edu/sites/archives/manuscripts/oralhistory/geiger.htm (August 18, 2007).

http://newsinfo.iu.edu/news/page/normal/2600.html (August 18, 2007).

http://query.nytimes.com/gst/fullpage.html?res=9904E7DA1638F931A25752C1A9659C8B63&n=Top/Reference/Times%20Topics/Subjects/S/Soccer#

http://quotationsbook.com/quote/38641

http://soccer.org/NR/exeres/9A81AF77-B9E8-4F55-815C-2130490F109A,frameless. . . . (March 28, 2007).

http://surgeongeneral.gov/sghist.htm (April 5, 2007).

http://tiss.zdv.uni-tuebingen.de/webroot/sp/spsba01_W98_1/usa1.htm)

http://web.ebscohost.com.ep.fjernadgang.kb.dk/ehost/detail?vid=3&hid=113&sid=0e94ad24-d57f-4149-ba11-4a8940a6492b%40sessionmgr102 – bib10up#bib10up

http://web.usfca.edu/~southerr/boxing/cruelest.html

http://xroads.virginia.edu/~HYPER/DETOC/FEM/education.htm to racism and slaves

http://xroads.virginia.edu/~HYPER/DETOC/FEM/entertain.htm

http://www.aafla.com/9arr/ResearchReports/AAF-ESPNCSMR2001.pdf

http://www.aafla.org/ Publications/Publications.htm

http://www.aahperd.org/aahperd/ (March 28, 2007).

http://www.aausports.org

http://www.acefitness.org/aboutace/factsheet.aspx (March 28, 2007).

http://www.acoatacarpenter.ORG (January 14, 2008).

http://www.acsm.org (April 6, 2007).

http://www.alfred.edu/sports_hazing/introduction.html

http://www.americanheart.org/presenter.jhtml?identifier=10860 (April 5, 2007).

http://www.associatedcontent.com/article/450199/alex_rodriguez_gets_275_million_give.html

http://www.athleticmanagement.com/ 2007/03/assessing_the_arms_race_1.html

http://www.bbyo.org/index.php?c=56&kat=The+History+of+BBYO (March 28, 2007).

http://www.bernarrmacfadden.com/macfadden4.html

http://www.btcavemen.de/statistik.html

http://www.boston.com/bostonglobe/editorial_opinion/oped/articles/2008/01/14/electoral_politics_as_sport/

http://www.brainyquote.com/quotes/quotes/v/vincelomba127517.html

433

http://www.bus.ucf.edu/sport/public/downloads/2006_RGRC_MLB.pdf (July 21, 2007).

http://www.cdc.gov/mmwr/PDF/SS/SS5505.pdf

http://www.cdc.gov/mmwr/preview/mmwrhtml/mm5233a1.htm (August 16, 2007).

http://www.cdc.gov/nccdphp/dnpa/obesity/

http://www.cdc.gov/nchs/

http://www.census.gov/hhes/www/ housing/ahs/ahs01/ahs01.html

http://www.collegeboard.com/student/pay/add-it-up/4494.html (August 18, 2007).

http://www.colorlines.com/article.php?ID=118

http://www.colorlines.com/article.php?ID=118&limit=0&limit2=1000&page=1

http://www.cooperinst.org/research/index.cfm (April 5, 2007).

http://www.dailyprincetonian.com/archives/2005/03/01/sports/12187.shtml (August 18, 2007).

http://www.dailywealth.com/ archive/2007/apr/2007_apr_07.asp

http://www.fitness.gov/about_history.htm (March 28, 2007).

http://www.fitness.gov/home_about.htm

http://www.gibbsmagazine.com/blacks_in_prisons.htm (August 13, 2007)

http://www.globalpolicy.org/ globaliz/cultural/2003/0804media.htm

http://www.goldsgym.com/golds/franchising/facts.php (March 28, 2007).

http://www.hickoksports.com/biograph/searseleanora.shtml

http://www. imgacademies.com/hq/default.sps?itype=7939

http://www.jbhe.com/preview/winter07preview.html (August 16, 2007).

http://www.kfc.com.about/history.asp (April 5, 2007).

http://www.mallwalker.org/index.php?option=com_content&view=frontpage

http://www.nationalpal.org

http://www.nationalpal.org/ (March 28, 2007).

http://www.nbc11.com/sports/2255069/detail.html

http://www.ncaa.org/

http://www.ncaa.org/grad_rates/

http://www.nhl.com/nhl/app?service=page&page=NewsPage&articleid=280069 (April 17, 2007).

http://www.njcaa.org (April 15, 2007).

http://www.nsga.com/history.html (March 28, 2007).

http://www.polishfalcons.org/

http://www.popwarner.com/football/pop.asp (March 28, 2007).

http://www.racejesus.com/about.htm (June 17, 2008).

http://www.rauzulusstreet.com/hockey/nhlhistory/nhlhistory.html (April 17, 2007).

http://www.realsportsmag.com/

http://www2.rgu.ac.uk/publicpolicy/introduction/wstate.htm

http://www.rockymarciano.net/about/achievements.htm (July 21, 2007).

http://scriptorium.lib.duke.edu/slavery/oldsouth.html

http://www.specialolympics.org/Special+Olympics+Public+Website/English/About_Us/History/default.htm (April 7, 2007).

http://www.spiegel.de/sport/sonst/0,1518,142061,00.html

http://www.sportsbusinessjournal.com/index.cfm?fuseaction=article.main&articleId=55422

http://www.statcan.ca/Daily/English/020718/d020718b.htm1999

http://www-tech.mit.edu/V127/N58/concussions.html

http://www.thesportjournal.org/2005Journal/Vol8-No1/michael_lovaglia.asp (August 18, 2007).

http://www.thirdworldtraveler.com/Media_control_propaganda/GlobalMediaGiants_ Herman.html

http://www.time.com/time/magazine/article/0,9171,719669,00.html

http://www.uh.edu/ednews/2005/abj/200506/20050621athleticbudget.html (August 18, 2007).

http://www.usatoday.com/money/advertising/admeter/2008admeter.htm

http://www.usdeafsports.org/about.html (April 7, 2007).

http://www.usoc.org/paralympics/paralympic_games.html (April 7, 2007).

http:www.westga.edu/~coe/phed2602/American.html (November 1, 2004).

http://www.womenssportsfoundation.org/cgi-bin/iowa/index.html (July 21, 2007).

http://www.ymca.net/about_the_ymca

www.census.gov/popest/national/asrh/NC-EST2007-sa.html

www.gpoaccess.gov/constitution/pdf2002/006-Constitution.pdf

www.sabr.org

INDEX

438

440

index

Disability and Youth Sport

Edited by *Hayley Fitzgerald*
Leeds Metropolitan University, UK

International Studies in Physical Education and Youth Sport

Edited by Hayley Fitzgerald

Disability and Youth Sport

How can or does youth sport reconcile what seems to be a fundamental contradiction between understandings of sport and disability? Has youth sport been challenged in anyway? Have alternative views of sport for disabled people been presented? Examining some of the latest research, this book considers the relationship between sport and disability by exploring a range of questions such as these.

December 2008: 180pp / HB: 978-0-415-47041-4 £75.00 / PB: 978-0-415-42353-3: £22.99

Disability and Youth Sport further challenges current thinking and therefore serves to stimulate progressive debate in this area. Drawing on a breadth of literature from sports pedagogy, sociology of sport, disability studies, inclusive education, and adapted physical activity, a socially critical dialogue is developed where the voices of young disabled people are central. Topics covered include:

- researching disability and youth sport
- inclusion policy towards physical education and youth sport
- constructions of disability through youth sport
- the voices of young disabled people
- the historical context of disability sport

With its comprehensive coverage and expert contributors from around the globe, this book is an ideal text for students at all levels with an interest in youth sport, disability studies, or sport policy.

Contents: 1. Bringing disability into youth sport *Hayley Fitzgerald* 2. Disability Sport: Historical Context *Karen DePauw* 3. Disability and Inclusion Policy Towards Physical Education and Youth Sport *Andy Smith* 4. Disability, Physical Education and sport: Some Critical Observations and Questions *Len Barton* 5. The Voices of Students with Disabilities: Are They Informing Inclusive Physical Education Practice? *Donna Goodwin* 6. 'We Want to Play Football' – Girls Experiencing Learning Disabilities and Their Footballing Experiences *Annette Stride* 7. Physical education as a normaliZing practice: Is there a space for disability sport? *Hayley Fitzgerald and David Kirk* 8. Picture this! Student co-researchers *Aspley Wood School* 9. The pedagogy of inclusive youth sport: working towards real solutions *Pam Stevenson* 10. Reflecting on Teaching, Learning and physical culture through Narrative *Catherine Morrison* 11. Are you a 'Parasite' Researcher? Researching disability and youth sport *Hayley Fitzgerald* 12. Future directions in youth sport and disability: development, aspirations and research *Hayley Fitzgerald and Anne Jobling*

Visit www.routledge.com/9780415423533 for more details.

Routledge
Taylor & Francis Group

For more information and online ordering
www.routledge.com

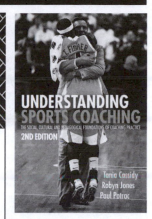